PENGUIN C

THOMAS MIDDLETON: FIVE PLAYS

THOMAS MIDDLETON was born in 1580, the son of a well-to-do London bricklayer. He went up to Oxford but seems not to have gained a degree. Thereafter he pursued the precarious career of a professional writer in London. In a quarter of a century he wrote, either on his own or in collaboration with other established playwrights, nearly fifty plays and other theatrical pieces. His modern reputation as one of the greatest of Jacobean dramatists rests on his achievements in both comedy and tragedy (examples of which form the content of this volume) but he wrote in other dramatic genres too and published some verse and prose pamphlets. His greatest contemporary success was *A Game at Chess*, an anti-Catholic satire which played to packed houses in 1624 but offended the government and was suppressed. By this time, however, he had at last achieved relative financial security in the post of City Chronologer, which entailed keeping records of important civic events and organizing public entertainments and pageants. He died in 1627.

Little is known of WILLIAM ROWLEY's life. He was a member of the Duke of York's company before joining the King's Men and acting in a number of Middleton's plays. Rowley was a prolific author who collaborated with many leading dramatists of the period. He died a year earlier than Middleton.

BRYAN LOUGHREY is Research Director and NEIL TAYLOR is Dean of Arts and Humanities at the Roehampton Institute. In addition to a number of joint publications (mainly on Renaissance drama), each has published in his sole name.

Five Plays

THOMAS MIDDLETON

EDITED BY
BRYAN LOUGHREY AND NEIL TAYLOR

PENGUIN BOOKS

PENGUIN BOOKS

Published by the Penguin Group
Penguin Books Ltd, 27 Wrights Lane, London W8 5TZ, England
Penguin Putnam Inc., 375 Hudson Street, New York, New York 10014, USA
Penguin Books Australia Ltd, Ringwood, Victoria, Australia
Penguin Books Canada Ltd, 10 Alcorn Avenue, Toronto, Ontario, Canada M4V 3B2
Penguin Books (NZ) Ltd, Private Bag 102902, NSMC, Auckland, New Zealand

Penguin Books Ltd, Registered Offices: Harmondsworth, Middlesex, England

This edition published in Penguin Classics 1988
10

Printed in England by Clays Ltd, St Ives plc
Filmset in Baskerville

For Alexis, Angus, Anna, Tess and Will

CONTENTS

INTRODUCTION

Thomas Middleton lived almost the whole of his life in London, subject to and yet frequently critical of its values. He was baptized at St Lawrence in the Old Jewry on 18 April 1580 and buried in his parish church of Newington Butts on 4 July 1627. During this period, London was experiencing an extraordinary growth in its size and importance. It was already the centre of government and, increasingly, of commerce; lawyers and merchants and shopkeepers were becoming very rich very quickly; at the same time London was drawing in the poor and the unemployed who saw in its prosperity the hope of cash and work. Middleton's father, William, was a bricklayer and in the booming conditions of the property market the building trade must have thrived; he himself became a prosperous man and a property-owner in the City. Indeed, he could boast a coat-of-arms (with a curious family crest consisting of an ape passant wearing a collar and gold chain) and this signalled the fact that capital, and the Capital, had secured for him the status of 'gentleman'.

William died in January 1586, leaving in his will one-third of his substantial estate to his children, Thomas and Avis. But the legacies were never paid over in full, for in November of the same year their mother Anne rashly married an adventurer, Thomas Harvey, and promptly fell into dispute with him over the control of the inheritance. The family feud which developed led to separation, violent assaults, and a series of bizarre legal ploys. Soon after the marriage, for example, Anne Harvey arranged for her own arrest for her non-payment of the children's share of the family estate, knowing that her husband was legally responsible for her actions. In fact, he was forced to raise ready money by auctioning off his personal possessions. The legal and family situation was further complicated when Alan Waterer, who had married Avis Middleton, entered into litigation against his in-laws.

It is difficult to judge the extent of Thomas Middleton's involvement in these disputes. From the evidence of his later plays they appear to have left him with a jaundiced view of the judicial process, although it is as well to remember that satire aimed at corrupt officers of the law was a well-established tradition. One consequence of the litigation was that London would not let him go. He went up to Queen's College, Oxford, in 1598, but was forced to return home, at least temporarily, 'to ayde his mother against his brother in lawe'. Although he later seems to have patched matters up with Waterer, and agreed to mortgage his half-share in the properties that he had been bequeathed in exchange for an allowance while at Oxford, he does not appear to have ever graduated.

It is possible that he abandoned his studies to pursue a literary career. Printing and publishing were largely confined to London, and literary patronage was best found at Court or in the City. Middleton had made a precocious début at the age of seventeen with a didactic biblical poem, *The Wisdom of Solomon Paraphrased* (1597), and followed this up with *Micro-Cynicon: Six Snarling Satires* (1599) and *The Ghost of Lucrece* (1600). Although interesting for the light they throw both on Middleton's early development and on the contemporary atmosphere of religious controversy (*Micro-Cynicon* was publicly burned at the order of the ecclesiastical censors), these poems have little intrinsic merit and are now probably read only by professional scholars.

Early in the new century Middleton married Anne Marbeck, the granddaughter of the famous Calvinist musician John Marbeck. Little is known of their life together other than that their son Edward was born in 1603 or 1604. At the same time, however, Middleton seems to have committed himself to a career in the theatre. A legal document of 1601 describes him as residing 'heare in London daylie accompanynge the players'. The career he chose was that of professional dramatist, producing nearly fifty theatrical pieces in a quarter of a century. The phrase 'theatrical pieces' includes not only the thirty or so stage plays which are currently attributed to him, but masques and pageants commissioned by the Court, by the four legal colleges known as the Inns of Court and by such civic authorities as his namesake, Sir Thomas Middleton (Lord Mayor of London in 1613). In 1620 he was also appointed Chronologer to the City of London, responsible to the City Fathers for recording public events. But the bulk of his writing career was dependent upon the production of plays to satisfy the various acting companies with which he became associated.

In some ways the theatre might seem to have been an odd career for someone whom many critics have regarded as belonging to the Puritan camp in contemporary politics. He married into a Calvinist family, his later patrons were certainly Puritans, and he himself has often been described as being Calvinist in the moral position implicit in his great tragedies. Yet Puritan preachers and pamphleteers attacked the theatre as being a centre of moral corruption. Many dramatists, including Middleton, hit back by satirizing Puritans within their plays. The contradictions operating within the politics of Puritanism and our notions of Middleton's location within those politics have been skilfully explored in Margot Heinemann's book, *Puritanism and Theatre: Thomas Middleton and*

Opposition Drama under the Early Stuarts (Cambridge, 1980). They are just one manifestation of the larger contradictions within English drama in the late sixteenth and early seventeenth centuries.

The Elizabethan and Jacobean theatre, with its professional acting companies performing in purpose-built playhouses, was a brand-new commercial enterprise. Its product sold almost exclusively in London and the industry was viable because London was now big enough and wealthy enough to maintain it. Yet London was ambivalent in its attitude. The performance and publication of plays was strictly censored lest they offend against the Church, the State or the City. Actors occupied an ambiguous position in society, obliged to enjoy the patronage of courtiers, and even of the royal family, while nevertheless being officially categorized as belonging to the class of rogues and vagabonds. And although the theatre thrived, patronized by all classes, the civic authorities, regarding it as morally and politically subversive, pretended it did not exist by relegating it to the suburbs, an area associated not, as today, with middle-class domesticity but rather with unemployment and poverty and criminality, with disease and insanity and sexual licence.

The two principal companies of actors of the last years of Elizabeth I's reign had been the Lord Chamberlain's Men and the Admiral's Men. Shakespeare was a shareholder and actor in the former and its principal dramatist. When Elizabeth died in 1603 and James I came to the throne the new king redesignated Shakespeare's company the 'King's Men' and Shakespeare's comparatively secure career continued until he retired, around 1612. Middleton's earliest recorded plays were written for the rival company, the Admiral's Men. Their manager, Philip Henslowe, kept a diary of all his financial transactions and it is in this document that we find references in 1602 to three plays by Thomas Middleton – one whose title Henslowe neglected to record, one called *The Chester Tragedy or Randal, Earl of Chester*, and one which Middleton seems to have written in collaboration with four other playwrights, *Caesar's Fall or Two Shapes*.

Middleton's brother-in-law was an actor in the Admiral's Men, and Middleton's connection with Henslowe continued until and, in a sense, even beyond Henslowe's death in 1616. Henslowe had his finger in many theatrical pies and Middleton wrote about a dozen plays for companies which were, or had been, controlled by him. Of those that have survived, the earliest is the satirical comedy, *The Family of Love* (*c.* 1602), and the latest the famous domestic tragedy, *The Changeling* (1622). Yet Middleton managed to establish himself as a principal playwright within two other companies, both major rivals to Henslowe's theatrical empire – the Children of Paul's and the King's Men themselves.

The Children of Paul's was one of the companies of boy actors which flourished towards the end of Elizabeth's reign. The plays which the boys' companies performed in the so-called 'private' indoor theatres in the City at times posed a real threat to the livelihood of the adult companies in the 'public' outdoor theatres on the south bank of the Thames. In the first years of the new century some of the most important writers of the period – including George Chapman, Ben Jonson and John Marston – were contributing to the boys' repertoires. And the majority of the plays they wrote were 'citizen' comedies.

Shakespeare's most famous comedies are usually referred to as 'romantic'. In other words, each is festive, set in a faraway place, and concerned with the developing love-relationship of a young man and a young woman. Citizen comedy is very different and Middleton's earliest attempts at this sub-genre bring out the difference. *The Family of Love* has a plot involving two young lovers, but their function is primarily to provide a framework for Middleton's real interest, the satirizing of contemporary London's manners and morals. *The Phoenix* (*c.* 1603) is the first of six comedies written for the Paul's boys. In it, romantic love is virtually eliminated as plot material. Instead, the play is organized around the exposure of legal corruption and domestic lust in the life of a city which, for all that it is somewhere in Italy, clearly represents the community in which Middleton's audience lived and worked.

Of Middleton's citizen comedies the three greatest are *A Trick to Catch the Old One*, *Michaelmas Term* and *A Mad World My Masters* (each composed at some point in the years 1604–6). All three plays work within the so-called 'New Comedy' plot-structure established by the Roman dramatists, Plautus and Terence. A young man comes into conflict with his parents: he wishes to marry one girl and they want him to marry another. He comes up with an ingenious plan to outwit his parents, puts it successfully into practice and is always reconciled with his parents by the end of the play. As George E. Rowe has argued in his book on *Thomas Middleton and the New Comedy Tradition* (Lincoln, Nebraska, 1979), Middleton's comedies observe this formula (except that the father is frequently replaced by some other representative of the older generation, such as an uncle or a grandfather) but nevertheless often move beyond it by introducing some element to challenge it.

In the case of *A Trick to Catch the Old One*, Rowe suggests that the alien element is the play's debt to quite another dramatic formula, that of those medieval Morality Plays which follow the pattern laid down by Christ's parable of the Prodigal Son. In New Comedy, the father is harsh and denying, and the story ends in celebration of the son's ingenuity in disobedience. In the Prodigal Son plays, by contrast, the father-figure is forgiving and generous, and the story ends in celebration of the son's penitence and wise humility. *A Trick to Catch the Old One* attempts a fusion of the two formulae, with the effect that our attitudes to both parties are complicated by ambivalent feeling.

The play is justly famous for the felicity and purity of its plotting. Young Witgood, the prodigal, has lost his inheritance before the play opens. He has been cheated out of his estate by his usurious uncle, Lucre. The plot revolves around the brilliant trick whereby Witgood passes off his whore as a wealthy widow whom he is courting, and dupes his uncle into returning him his lands in the expectation of future profit. Furthermore, another 'old one' is tricked in the process, for Lucre's enemy Walkadine Hoard ends up married to the whore (a conventionally harsh punishment within the world of Jacobean drama). The wit of Middleton's plot is reflected in the wit with which Witgood perceives the nature of *his* plot. Since he ends by marrying Hoard's niece, he thereby becomes Hoard's nephew. At the same time, Hoard has just married Witgood's whore. Witgood plays upon the slang usage, *aunt* = *whore*, establishing the senses in which his relationship with his ex-mistress has and has not been transformed: 'She's mine aunt now, by my faith, and there's no meddling with mine aunt, you know' (V.ii.141–2).

A theatre audience's immediate response is to identify with Witgood. He is, after all, the young victim of an avaricious relative and in love with a virtuous young woman. We delight in his quick thinking and skill in intrigue. But this apparently happy consonance between aesthetic response (a pleasure in the display of skill) and moral response (a satisfaction in the administration of justice) cannot remain unqualified. Although Lucre has swindled Witgood, Witgood's spendthrift ways have contributed to his impecuniosity, and when the play begins we find him disentangling himself from his loyal mistress in order to make what is not only a love-match but a marriage which will be financially convenient. The world of the play is one in which kinship counts for very little. Indeed, all the families are flawed – every character has lost a parent and the plot turns upon the willingness of *cousins* (relatives) to *cozen* one another (IV.ii.90–91). Witgood is forced to observe of his uncle Lucre, 'if ever I trust you . . . again, would I might be truss'd up for my labour!' (IV.ii. 63–4). In order to regain his inheritance Witgood is prepared to be as unscrupulous as ever Lucre had been, except that he will always stay 'within the compass of the law'. His creditors are presented by Middleton as grotesque caricatures, but Witgood's treatment of them is unfeeling. His public repentance in the last act is a surprise and, arguably, even ironic.

As for the villainous characters, there has to be some qualification here, too. Lucre is human and not a monster, and he shows a delight in his rival's discomfiture which is essentially childish. Hoard himself is required to draw the moral from the play (V.ii.183) and knows he could have suffered worse punishment than marrying Witgood's pretty mistress. She is perhaps the most sympathetic character in the play. Despite being labelled 'Courtesan' in the speech-prefixes and a 'Dutch widow' (i.e. whore) within the text (V.ii.90) she appears to have been a virgin until she met Witgood, and faithful to him before he cast her off. The part she plays in his machinations is prompted not by self-interest but by concern for his well-being. And she is careful to warn her future husband before they marry that she has no wealth at all. Dampit alone is irredeemably evil (his name suggests the damned pit of hell, and therefore the Old One, the Devil). He alone cannot repent. On his deathbed he drunkenly curses Audrey, his maid, the one person who has shown him any affection. And yet even Dampit holds a certain attraction for us, derived from his extravagant linguistic inventiveness and the inordinate gusto of his self-love. Thus, a play which on the surface dazzles by the cleverness of its plot also engages us in its presentation of the contradictions in human behaviour and feeling.

The Children of Paul's seem to have ceased playing in 1606, but some of their repertoire, including *A Trick to Catch the Old One*, was taken over by the Children of Blackfriars. There is some evidence that Middleton wrote at least one play specifically for this company, since a legal document of 1606 records the fact that he handed over the text of *The Viper's Brood* to the manager of the Children of Blackfriars, Robert Keysar, in payment for a debt. But no play of this name is now extant.

It is possible, however, that *The Viper's Brood* was an alternative title for *The Revenger's Tragedy*, which was entered (coupled with *A Trick to Catch the Old One*) in the Stationers' Register in 1607. On the other hand, *The Revenger's Tragedy*, according to its title page, had been acted 'sundry times' by an adult company, the King's Men.

Like *A Trick to Catch the Old One*, *The Revenger's Tragedy* satirizes city values. *A Trick to Catch the Old One* has as its twin polarities Leicestershire and London. *The Revenger's Tragedy* is set in Italy. But the fictional Italian courts of Jacobean tragedy are never far away from the perceived Court of King James. Middleton again sets off the values of the court by proposing the perspective of the country. The impoverished Vindice has come up to the city. His father has died, disappointed by the Duke whose corrupt court forms the initial focus of the play's satire. But Vindice's discontent extends beyond an antipathy between country and city, and a sensitivity to the social defeat suffered by his immediate family. At his first entry he is carrying the skull of his mistress, whom the Duke had murdered when she would not satisfy his lust. Vindice is committed to avenge this grotesque crime. But his aggressive rhetoric extends beyond the immediate sources of injustice towards a morbid fascination with corruption – a corruption he is prepared to embrace in pursuit of his revenge. Jonathan Dollimore has observed that in the play 'a vital irony and a deep pessimism exist in disjunction'. He goes on to argue that the self-stultifying ethos of *The Revenger's Tragedy* reflects contradictions within the Jacobean society in which it was conceived.[1]

But *The Revenger's Tragedy* belongs to the genre of the Revenge Play, which first came into prominence on the professional English stage in the form of Thomas Kyd's *Spanish Tragedy* (1587), and received its most original treatment in Shakespeare's *Hamlet* (*c.* 1601). And the hero of a Revenge Play is always committed to a contradictory role, caught and isolated between two societies. As the protesting victim of a corrupt court, Vindice seeks justice in an unjust society. As its enemy and, ultimately, its purifier, he belongs to an alternative society, the ideal and just society to which the audience is automatically committed. But when he takes the law into his own hands and kills the killer, he necessarily engages in the values of his enemies and seems to become corrupted by them. He is alienated from *our* society and we fail to protest when he pays the ultimate price, punished by the loss of his own life.

In *Hamlet* Shakespeare is interested in exploring sympathetically the sensibility of his hero and, thereby, raising some doubts as to the validity of his role as a revenger. Middleton characteristically ignores such a possibility. The play's characters and action lack the inwardness and specificity of Shakespeare. Vindice is not an individual in the sense that Hamlet is. And if, in *A Trick to Catch the Old One*, Middleton combined two forms which do not go easily together, so, here, Vindice's individuated role as revenge-hero is contradicted by the allegorical nature of his name, 'Revenge'. *The Revenger's Tragedy* is tragic, but it is tragedy informed by the universality of ritual, the externality of farce and the symbolic thinking of the medieval Morality Play.

However, the play is not a game with counters, each bearing a narrowly conceived significance. Lussurioso, for example, is not the only embodiment of lust. The whole of the court is consumed with greed and ambition. But the play's characteristic formulation is failure in desire, the experience of the illusory nature of all satisfaction and gratification. The lecherous Duke dies literally rather than sexually when his pimp, Vindice, secures him the services of a poisoned skeleton. Ambitioso and Supervacuo experience a similar anti-climax when they discover that they have arranged the execution of their own younger brother rather than that of the heir to the dukedom, their hated stepbrother. Lussurioso rushes into his father's bedchamber expecting to expose his stepmother's incest with

[1] *Radical Tragedy* (Brighton, 1984), p. 147.

his illegitimate half-brother: what he actually finds is the Duchess tucked up with her legal bedfellow, the Duke. Finally, the play's chief protagonist, Vindice, robs himself of his own triumph when, having murdered all his enemies, he boasts about it to the new Duke, is arrested as a criminal and himself condemned to die.

Such formulations of desire are similar to those which the influential French psychoanalyst, Jacques Lacan, has described in a seminar on *Hamlet*.[1] In Shakespeare's play Lacan found what Ernest Jones had found – an Oedipal triangle involving Hamlet and his mother and father. But he also found much more. In Lacan's reading, Hamlet's experience of constant frustration is also an allegory of the truth that we are always disappointed in our attempts to satisfy desire, be it to love another human being, to give significance to our experience of the world, or to murder a king who has popp'd in between the election and our hopes. Claudius illegally took over Hamlet's father's role, so Hamlet is trying to displace a father who displaced a father. But, in Lacan's opinion, all story-telling such as Shakespeare's and, probably, all human activity is a matter of coping with acts of displacement. Take language, for example. It attempts to substitute words for things. But language has taken over. The things are already lost beyond recall. Hamlet kills Claudius, but by the time he has killed him it is too late to have achieved anything. For everyone of any significance for Hamlet – including himself – is dead. Except Horatio, that is. But he is forced by Hamlet into a role which is subject to this whole tragic action, namely to retell the story to others, to substitute language for reality.

Middleton's play tells a not dissimilar story. Vindice's father was cheated of his desire for social advancement by the Duke, and is now dead. Vindice's own Oedipal wish to kill his father has already been satisfied, but by another party. The Duke, being 'father' of the state as well as father of the family that makes up the court, has become a kind of father-substitute. By an irony characteristic of the whole play – its dominant mode is irony – Vindice has actually engineered that Lussurioso stumble across a version of the Primal Scene, the Duke in bed with the Duchess. Meanwhile, by substituting a false nature for his own, Vindice has proved the frailty of his literal mother, Gratiana. The motif of substitution extends to the language of the play (its frequent punning) and to the larger action (one Duke succeeds another and the latest, Antonio, may or may not be an improvement on those he has displaced). At a local level of plot there is frequent disguising. Vindice disguises his mistress's corpse as a courtesan,

[1] 'Desire and the Interpretation of Desire in *Hamlet*', in *Literature and Psychoanalysis: The Question of Reading, Otherwise*, ed. Shoshana Felman (Baltimore, 1982), pp. 11–52.

himself as Piato, Piato as himself, and the dead Duke as Piato. Finally, one group of characters in disguise displaces another group in disguise, in hot pursuit of revenge. But their desire turns to disappointment as they find the Duke already stabbed and dying. They stab one another in their frustration. Addressing Vindice, the new Duke comments, 'You that would murder him would murder me' (V.iii.105).

The Revenger's Tragedy may not be the only tragedy which Middleton was writing for the King's Men at this period. Many scholars now believe that he was the author of *The Second Maiden's Tragedy* (1611); and it has even been argued recently that Middleton adapted *Macbeth* (1606) and actually collaborated with Shakespeare on *Timon of Athens* (1607).[1] Nevertheless, he continued to turn his hand to a wide range of forms and, at some point between 1611 and 1613, wrote *A Chaste Maid in Cheapside*. This play is in many ways his most sophisticated achievement in comedy, particularly in terms of tonal and formal complexity.

The sardonic wit of *The Revenger's Tragedy* arises out of the relentless irony of its action. The tone of *A Chaste Maid in Cheapside* is far trickier to apprehend. Middleton's unremitting use of *double entendre* inhibits both idealization and the brutality of the dirty laugh. In general, the handling of feeling is subtle but sometimes slippery and, on occasion, jarring. Middleton seems to dislike some of his characters intensely; others behave with a disconcertingly realistic inconsistency or ambiguity. Even the rhythms of the characters' speeches are difficult to interpret: editors are faced with the impossible task of deciding line by line whether Middleton is writing in verse or prose.

The multi-level plot of *A Chaste Maid in Cheapside* makes a notable contrast with the purer linearity of *A Trick to Catch the Old One*. For the initiating action Middleton returned to the New Comedy formula and the material of citizen comedy. A London goldsmith and his wife attempt to marry their daughter to an influential knight, Sir Walter Whorehound (plot 1), and their undergraduate son to a wealthy widow from Wales (plot 2). Their insensitive greed for material and social advancement is matched only by their gullibility. The son's marriage goes forward but the 'widow' turns out to be Sir Walter's whore. Meanwhile, the daughter outwits her parents by eloping with her own choice of husband. Through this action Middleton can satirize the manners and the motivation of both the gentry and the middle class.

But he also returns to one of his preoccupations in *The Revenger's Tragedy*: the relationship between money and sex. Plots 1 and 2 both concern the structural motif of two men competing (in radically different ways) over a

[1] See *The Complete Oxford Shakespeare*, edited by S. Wells and G. Taylor (Oxford, 1986).

woman. In plot 1, Touchwood Junior ultimately triumphs over Sir Walter, his rival for the hand of Moll Yellowhammer; in plot 2, Tim Yellowhammer 'wins' Sir Walter's penniless whore. But such triangles also form the core of each of the play's remaining plots. Plot 3, like all the others, depends upon Sir Walter: he conducts a long-standing affair with Mrs Allwit, fathering her children and lining the pocket of her complaisant husband. Meanwhile, in plot 4, Touchwood Senior obliges the erstwhile barren Lady Kix by fathering her child – and thereby disinheriting her relation, Sir Walter Whorehound.

Clearly, the motivation, procedures and resolutions of these 'Oedipal' triangles are all very different. Indeed, much of Middleton's skill has gone into devising an ingenious pattern of symmetries, complementarities and oppositions within this constellation of interdependent plots. And, at the heart of it all, is a common activity of trading sex for money. As Richard Levin has pointed out, Allwit's confidence that cuckoldom is the happiest state that ever man was born to (I.ii.21) is irrefutable if life is reduced to the economic terms of profit and loss, 'since then love itself becomes a commodity to sell, and its physical and emotional demands an expense to be avoided . . . Allwit's household is thus a *reductio ad absurdum* of the values of the Yellowhammers and their middle-class world'.[1]

Middleton sets his play in Cheapside because it is 'the heart of the City of London' (I.i.85–6), a heart which he wishes to probe and dissect. But one end of the street was known for its meat-market, and so it also provides him with a controlling metaphor. An unwanted bastard child is passed off as a joint of lamb in the season celebrating the sacrifice of the Lamb of God (II.ii). The reduction of the human to mere flesh is universal in the play, but the abuse is at its most intense in respect of women. The Welsh woman is regarded as merely Sir Walter's 'ewe mutton' (I.i.132), while Tim thinks Moll should be 'sold to fishwives' (IV.iii.36). She may be a chaste maid but chastity is valued, not as a spiritual state but as a rare commodity to be traded for profit. The competition for a woman in each plot's 'Oedipal' triangle reflects not only the operation of desire but also the social reality of male property-rights in an acquisitive society.[2]

*

[1] *The Multiple Plot in English Renaissance Drama* (Chicago, 1971), pp. 200–201.

[2] For all that Moll represents a predominantly passive virtue in a man's world, the titles of three other Middleton comedies reflect a wish to cast women in the prominent role, not only in moral terms but also in terms of the play's action. Hence *The Roaring Girl* (*c.* 1611), another Moll but this time based on a real-life underworld character (Moll Firth). Middleton and Dekker, who collaborated on this play, make her into the most energetic champion of virtue, denouncing and outmanoeuvring the male fools of the City. Later on, while there will be *More Dissemblers Besides Women* (*c.* 1619), there is nevertheless *No Wit, No Help Like a Woman's* (1611–12).

Middleton employed a double plot in four of his tragedies, *The Second Maiden's Tragedy* (1611), *Hengist, King of Kent* (*c.* 1617–20), *Women Beware Women* (*c.* 1621) and *The Changeling* (1622).[1] But the multiple plot in Elizabethan and Jacobean drama was normally the property of comedy. Middleton not only appropriated for his tragedies this element of comic structure but, in his later years, chose also to appropriate comedy's romantic action and domesticated, familial world. In the main plot of *Women Beware Women*, for example, Bianca wishes to marry a young Florentine merchant, who is not the choice of her Venetian parents. In the subplot, Isabella's father wants her to marry a rich, half-witted Ward, who is not *her* choice. Bianca defies her parents and elopes to Florence, while Isabella complies with her father's wishes and marries the Ward.

With characteristic irony, Middleton introduces challenging variants to these New Comedy triangles, revealing a common gullibility and immorality in both women. Having broken free from parental tyranny, Bianca finds herself imprisoned by her husband's conception of her as his prize possession. Indeed, he sets his mother to keep her locked up at home while he is away on business. So she breaks out again, allowing the Duke of Florence to take possession of her sexually, and ultimately becoming his wife. The setting for Bianca's seduction by the Duke is Livia's private art-gallery, where erotic pictures reflect the pervading pornographic devaluation of the human to the status of visual, physical and economic possessions. By trading her body for her freedom, Bianca recommits herself to the commercial ethos that her husband represented when he boasted that in marrying her he had made 'the most unvalued'st purchase' (I.i.12).

Livia also ensures the moral destruction of Isabella in the other plot. As her niece observes, 'Men buy their slaves but women buy their masters' (I.ii.175). But Livia persuades her that marriage to the Ward will be not only materially rewarding but effective cover for conducting a love-affair with someone else. That someone else is Livia's brother, but Livia manages to deceive Isabella into thinking that he is not, in fact, her uncle. The play explores the moral evasiveness and blindness of its characters, their treachery and duplicity, their guilt. Middleton's Calvinism is informed by a secular knowledge of how the human mind behaves under the influence of historical and institutional forces. The individuals he portrays are held to be morally responsible for their actions but are determined, nevertheless, by the nature of the society in which they live.

[1] Some critics – for example, Nicholas Brooke in *Horrid Laughter in Jacobean Tragedy* (London, 1979), p. 15 – would also regard the scenes between Vindice and his mother as constituting a secondary plot within *The Revenger's Tragedy*.

While the society of Middleton's plays is an aggressively competitive, emergent capitalist society, it has also been described as 'a society of games which have no substance, a society in which a universal pursuit of pleasure leads to a cynical disregard for all conventional moral codes'.[1] A paradox about many games is the fact that, though mere idle recreation, they have strict rules and penalties. *Women Beware Women* is much concerned with the contravention of rules (in theft, adultery, incest, murder) and the punitive consequences of such contravention. At the same time, Middleton is interested in those profounder experiential laws, both psychological and moral, which seem to hold good for all societies and all times. And games, in so far as they are rule-bound, provide Middleton with a powerful metaphor for the Calvinist conception of life as being strict, competitive and teleological. In the play's most famous scene (II.ii) Livia and Bianca's mother-in-law play chess, while Bianca is seduced by the Duke over their heads. At line 302, Livia reminds her opponent, 'Here's a duke/ Will strike a sure stroke for the game anon;/ Your pawn cannot come back to relieve itself'. When the Mother replies, 'I know that, madam,' the audience is likely to ponder the fatal moves which Bianca is making with the Duke up in the gallery.

A number of Middleton's plays, including *The Revenger's Tragedy* and *The Changeling*, involve a ritualized disguising or a performance of some kind. Apart from the sensational nature of some of the incidents in his plays, this tendency towards theatrical ceremony and emblematic representation in the final phase of the action is one of Middleton's few concessions towards a 'heightened' dramatic language. In general, in keeping with his analytic characterization, Middleton's use of words is spare and primarily denotative; any rhetorical flights are undercut by contextual irony. In Act V scene ii of *Women Beware Women*, the ducal marriage is celebrated through a masque of the kind Ben Jonson and Inigo Jones had been writing for the Court of King James. This one is informed by irony at every level. It is an easy development from playing to plays, from games of skill to works of art. Being Art, confusing the roles of author, actor and audience, featuring as one of its themes Slander, and acting as it does as a cover for murder, this masque acts as a rich emblem of deception. It teaches a general distrust, for 'In time of sports Death may steal in securely' (V.ii.22) and 'great mischiefs/ Mask in expected pleasures!' (V.ii.172–3). Right from the beginning of the play, Bianca was deceived into believing that 'there is nothing can be wanting/ To her that does enjoy all her desires' (I.i.125–6), but her career is a lesson in the fruitless nature of desire. Ironically, it is only when she finally feels death's power within her that she can say 'So, my desires are satisfied' (V.ii.202).

*

[1] G. E. Rowe, op. cit., p. 195.

Although the selection in this volume gives a different impression, many of Middleton's plays were written in collaboration with other dramatists. His most frequent collaborator was the actor and playwright William Rowley (d. 1626), and it was with Rowley that he composed *The Changeling*. Its setting is the Spanish seaport of Alicante, with the main plot located in a castle and the comic subplot (the bulk of which is usually attributed to Rowley rather than to Middleton) in a madhouse somewhere else in the city. The old polarities of London and Leicestershire or Florence and Venice have been replaced by the conceptual categories of the sane and the mad – and, ultimately, the saved and the damned. At the play's conclusion the madmen are supposed to come into the castle to perform a dance in celebration of the governor's daughter's wedding. Alicante may not be the City of London but the madhouse's role in relation to those who govern the city bears comparison with the role played in London by the theatres in the suburbs. Carnival, licence and seeming disorder work as agents of containment, social control and the celebration of order. *The Changeling*, however, is no New Comedy, the madmen are denied the opportunity to perform their dance, and the governor's daughter is discovered to be guilty of adultery and murder.

In the seventeenth century the play's fame derived from the antics of Antonio, a young gentleman who disguises himself as one of the madmen (the word 'changeling' could be used to mean a fool) in order to woo the wife of the keeper of the asylum. But the play's modern popularity (until recently, Middleton's reputation rested largely on *The Changeling*) arises from the portrait of the governor's daughter, Beatrice-Joanna. In the opinion of Una Ellis-Fermor, Middleton's supreme gift was 'his discernment of the minds of women'.[1] The play is distinguished by the psychological realism of the scenes in which Beatrice-Joanna is drawn into a fatal intimacy with the man she hires to murder her betrothed.

Beatrice-Joanna rejects not only the role provided for a young woman in real Jacobean society but also the role which New Comedy provided for the children of tyrannical parents. She seems at first to be her father's creature, marrying whom the Alicante nobleman pleases. Then, secretly and criminally, she challenges his authority, killing his choice so that she can be free to marry whom she chooses. In fact, just as in *Women Beware Women*, acts of liberation turn out to be acts of incarceration. Beatrice-Joanna merely succeeds in making herself the creature of a man again. In Roman New Comedy the child defeats the parent by employing the services of a witty slave. Beatrice-Joanna employs a servant, the ugly De Flores. He brings her, as an emblem, her dead lover's finger thrust into her ring; it is as if he thereby becomes an emblem himself, the phallus which

[1] *The Jacobean Drama* (London, 1936), p. 152.

she cannot bear to look at directly but to which she is ambiguously committed – committed through desire and committed through entrapment in the male social machine. The governor is eventually to discover them rehearsing their scene of lust and locked in a closet within his citadel. Daughter and servant both prove to be his creatures.

De Flores, as G. R. Hibbard once wrote, is 'perhaps the most convincing picture of uninhibited sexual desire in Elizabethan drama'.[1] But, as Hibbard also remarked, De Flores is Beatrice-Joanna's unconscious self of which she is instinctively afraid. The impersonal force of desire, her own and others', moves her on from man to man. Meanwhile, her maidservant is obliged to act as her mistress's substitute in the marriage-bed, prostituted to preserve the male conception of marriage, and ensuring a continuing chain of displaced desire. De Flores appears to gain sexual satisfaction but Beatrice-Joanna finds herself 'undone . . . endlessly' (IV.i.1).

The mechanism by which Beatrice-Joanna is undone is the pun, the tactical displacement of meaning as one signifier is shown to have more than one signified. Christopher Ricks has written perceptively of the 'obsessive turns of speech' which characterize De Flores's language:

> . . . the words *act* and *deed*, which for him so indispensably compact his murderous act and the sexual act which will be his reward, recur as the essence of his character, of his need for sardonic *double-entendre* and his unsentimental lucidity as to the inescapable relationships of person to person and of act to consequence. He is rebuffed but can menacingly bide his time.
>
> BEATRICE: I would not hear so much offence again
> For such another deed.
> DE FLORES: Soft, lady, soft;
> The last is not yet paid for. O this act
> Has put me into spirit;
> (III.iv.104–7)
>
> That clinching sexual pun on 'spirit' is true to De Flores the individual; and it is true to a generalized psychology of the relationship between murderous violence and lust. De Flores had been sexually excited at the prospect of murdering Alonzo, and he is sexually excited after he has committed the murder. So that the elaborate patterning of words like *blood* (murder and lust), *act* and *deed* in *The Changeling* does not ask to be valued for itself alone, but for its relationship both to an individual psychology and to a general one.[2]

[1] 'The Tragedies of Thomas Middleton and the Decadence of the Drama', *Renaissance and Modern Studies*, 1 (1957), p. 58.

[2] 'The Tragedies of Webster, Tourneur and Middleton: Symbols, Imagery and Conventions', *English Drama to 1710*, vol. 3 of *The Sphere History of Literature in the English Language* (London, 1971), p. 328.

A crucial difference between the use of *double entendre* in *The Changeling* and, say, *A Chaste Maid in Cheapside* is that the irony in the later play lies, not in the characters' conscious introduction of bawdy quibbles, but in the tragic discrepancy between different characters' interpretations of the same words. Beatrice-Joanna fails to realize until it is too late that De Flores sees a significance in her words which she has never consciously intended.

At the same time, Middleton has deliberately chosen for the title of his play a multiple pun. Beatrice-Joanna is a changeling in that she changes her sexual allegiance, first from her betrothed to an attractive stranger, and then, seemingly against her will, from him to an unattractive member of her own household. There is another sense, too, in which she might be called a 'changeling'. In 1589 George Puttenham wrote that the figure of speech which the ancient Greeks had called *hypallage* 'I had rather have him called the *Changeling*'.[1] English rhetoricians of the period tended to use the term to denote any transference of attributes from their proper subjects to others, and one can readily see the appropriateness of the idea to the beautiful Beatrice-Joanna, who commits herself to the ugly De Flores and thereby renders her soul ugly. Because of this, she is a changeling in yet another sense. A 'changeling' is a fairy child substituted for a mortal child so that the fairy can be fed on human milk. Beatrice-Joanna is just such a changeling, moving from one world to another. She is transformed from a wilful New Comedy daughter into a tragic heroine, and at the same time she transforms Alicante into Hell.

Middleton's final play, *A Game at Chess* (1624), brought him his greatest contemporary success. This anti-Catholic satire, aimed at the Court's pro-Spanish policies, caught the popular mood and played to packed houses for an unprecedented nine days, the first recorded 'run' in the history of the English stage. The play, however, did not merely pander to popular prejudice, but was a considerable imaginative achievement in its own right, translating the game of diplomacy into the stylized intrigues of allegorical chess-pieces on a theatrical chessboard.

Middleton's triumph was short-lived. The play was suppressed by the authorities and the author's son was summoned before the Privy Council to explain the behaviour of his father, who had prudently gone into hiding. He may even have been imprisoned for a time, but was probably protected from the full force of Royal fury by his Parliamentary patrons.[2] No one can be certain whether this brush with the law persuaded Middleton to abandon writing for the theatre – particularly as after his appointment as City Chronologer in 1620 he was no longer dependent on his earnings as

[1] *The Arte of English Poesie*, III.xv, p. 144.

[2] See Margot Heinemann, op. cit., pp. 131, 169.

an author. In any event, Middleton devoted the remainder of his career to his civic employments, keeping records of important events, providing occasional speeches, and organizing public entertainments and pageants. He appears to have carried out these duties conscientiously, although the City Fathers on occasion found cause to complain of his 'ill management' of certain pageants. He died in debt, but his employers thought sufficiently highly of him to award his distressed widow a grant of twenty nobles after his death.

After the Restoration his works were comprehensively ignored. Even after 1840, when the editorial labours of Alexander Dyce put his work back into print (if not on to the stage), many of his readers were wary of what they regarded as his coarse, indelicate sensibility and language. Despite the late-nineteenth-century revival of interest in the Jacobean drama, Middleton received little approving attention in the first half of the twentieth century. The main plot of *The Changeling* was admired, but otherwise the critics found him frequently clumsy, lewd, cynical and lacking in moral seriousness.

More recent critics, however, have found Middleton increasingly congenial, relishing his irony and attributing to his treatment of sexuality both realism and psychological insight. Furthermore, Nicholas Brooke has written that 'His is the subtlest moral intelligence of the Jacobeans. He was also, I think, the most controlled artist . . .'[1] His penetrating anatomies of a society whose value-systems have broken down have impressed not only the critics but also theatre and broadcasting managements. As a result, there have been productions of a number of Middleton's plays in the last ten years. Playwrights such as Peter Barnes, Edward Bond and Howard Barker have also written their own adaptations of such plays as *A Trick to Catch the Old One*, *A Mad World My Masters* and *A Chaste Maid in Cheapside*.

A challenging product of this renewal in Middleton's fortunes has been Howard Barker's adaptation of *Women Beware Women* (1986), which accepts most of Middleton's first four acts but is in radical disagreement with him over the dénouement. 'Middleton says lust leads to the grave. I say desire alters perception . . . Middleton knew the body was the source of politics. He did not know it was also the source of hope.'[2] For all that Barker is at odds with what he regards as Middleton's pessimism, he nevertheless clearly believes that Middleton's plays are in touch with momentous historical forces active in our society as much as in Jacobean London. Barker's play is a brilliant piece of theatre and Middleton's skills as a collaborator seem to have persisted even beyond the grave.

[1] *Horrid Laughter in Jacobean Tragedy*, p. 110.

[2] Programme note to William Gaskill's production at the Royal Court Theatre, London, in February 1986.

THE AUTHORSHIP OF *THE REVENGER'S TRAGEDY*

The decision to include *The Revenger's Tragedy* in an anthology of Thomas Middleton's plays needs some defending. There is only one strong reason for *not* including it, however, and that is the force of tradition. Tradition is not to be ignored. The editors of the recent *Complete Oxford Shakespeare* (Oxford, 1986) believe that the heroine of *Cymbeline* should be called Innogen (there is a lot of sense in the theory), but it may well be too late to re-educate the world over the matter. Is it too late to revise the canon of both Cyril Tourneur and Thomas Middleton, and claim *The Revenger's Tragedy* for the latter?

In the last ten years, the proposition that Middleton wrote *The Revenger's Tragedy* has ceased to be a provocatively eccentric claim and has become instead the prevailing scholarly opinion. However, the practice of publishers has largely ignored this development, and some scholars have been forced into the curious position of writing books which give *The Revenger's Tragedy* to Tourneur on the dust-jacket and yet repudiate this position within the covers.[1] It may seem rather caddish to deprive Tourneur of *The Revenger's Tragedy* and leave him with only one, though admittedly considerable, play (*The Atheist's Tragedy*), but Tourneur has been basking in its glory for over three hundred years now and maybe Middleton should be allowed his turn, too.

The play was probably written *c.* 1606. It was published as a quarto in 1607 with the following title-page: 'The Revengers Tragaedie. As it hath beene sundry times Acted, by the Kings Maiesties seruants'. The relevant entry in the Stationers' Register is for 7 October 1607, when the printer George Eld(e) submitted 'Twoo plaies th one called the revengers tragedie th other A trick to catch the old one'. Thus there is no author's name for the play. But there are three pieces of evidence for scholars to chew on, one pointing towards Middleton and two which are sometimes regarded as pointing away.

The first of these pieces of evidence is the fact that *The Revenger's Tragedy* is one of two plays within the same entry in the Register. In every other double entry throughout the Elizabethan and Jacobean period where the texts are plays, those plays prove to be *by the same author*. If *The Revenger's*

[1] E.g. Philip J. Ayres, in his *Tourneur: The Revenger's Tragedy* (London, 1977).

Tragedy were not by the author of *A Trick to Catch the Old One*, it would be the only case of its kind. And *A Trick to Catch the Old One* is by Middleton.

The other two pieces of evidence are not easy to interpret. Some scholars have argued that at this period in his career Middleton was writing comedies for the Paul's boys' company and that he would therefore be unlikely to be writing (a) tragedy or (b) for the King's Men.

Since Middleton is best known as the author of tragedies (*Women Beware Women* and *The Changeling*), there would have to come a point in his career when he turned from comedy to tragedy. Why should it not have been 1606–7? The absurdity of the argument that Middleton could only have been writing comedies in these years is reinforced when one considers that he had already written tragedies at an earlier period (1602, when he wrote *The Chester Tragedy* and collaborated in *Caesar's Fall*) and that in 1606 he seems to have written a tragedy called *The Viper and Her Brood* (which might even be another name for *The Revenger's Tragedy*).[1]

The Paul's boys appear to have stopped performing in 1606. The title-page of *The Revenger's Tragedy* refers to performances by the King's Men. The play could surely have been written for children and then, at some stage, been performed by adults. Or it could have been written for the adult company after Middleton had ceased writing for the defunct children's company. One might also bear in mind the fact that title-pages are not always to be trusted.

Nor, for that matter, is Edward Archer, who was responsible for the first attribution of *The Revenger's Tragedy* to a particular author. There is obviously something powerful in the sudden attribution of an anonymous play to Cyril Tourneur in a playlist which Archer published in 1656. This man, one imagines, must have some knowledge lost to the rest of us. But Archer is notoriously unreliable in his attributions. W. W. Greg considered that two-thirds of the original attributions in Archer's list were 'either careless blunders or irresponsible guesses'.[2] Yet all subsequent

[1] Many critics have commented on the hybrid generic nature of *The Revenger's Tragedy*. Brian Gibbons, in the New Mermaid edition, claims that 'the basic method of dramatic articulation seems to belong to comic art' (Introduction, p. xiv), and in his *Jacobean City Comedy* (1968) compares Middleton's characteristic use of 'the satiric-comic form and the tragic themes of savagery, disease and evil' with *The Revenger's Tragedy* (p. 205). If one were worried that Middleton might have been moving too violently from comedy to tragedy in 1606–7, these observations might allay one's worries.

[2] 'Authorship Attributions in the Early Play-Lists, 1656–1671', *Edinburgh Bibliographical Society Transactions* 2 (1938–45), pp. 316–17. In the same article Greg also expressed his own doubts as to whether, but for Archer, anyone would ever have suggested that, considering 'their manifest dissimilarity', *The Revenger's Tragedy* and *The Atheist's Tragedy* were by the same author (pp. 317–18).

attributions of *The Revenger's Tragedy* to Tourneur derive from Archer's brief entry: 'Revenger | T | Tournour'.

There is only one other piece of what might be regarded as external evidence – and that points in the direction of Middleton. Nathanael Richards, who claimed in some commendatory verses printed in the Octavo of *Women Beware Women* (published in 1657) to have been a 'Familiar Acquaintance' of Middleton, employs in these same verses the phrase 'Drabs of State'. In his own tragedy, *The Tragedy of Messalina, the Roman Empress* (published in 1640), Richards has the longer phrase 'a drab/ Of state, a cloth of Silver‾slut' (E2ᵛ.10–11; ll. 1778–9), which duplicates a line from *The Revenger's Tragedy*: 'A drab of State, a cloath a siluer slut' (Q:H2ᵛ.39; IV.iv.80). The appearance of what Richards must have regarded as a quotation from *The Revenger's Tragedy* in commendatory verses to *Women Beware Women* seems to imply that both plays are by the same author.

To summarize the position with regard to external evidence. The case for Tourneur is Archer's 1656 attribution. But this case is weakened by Archer's notorious unreliability. The case for Middleton is the double entry in the Stationers' Register, and the context of Richards's quotation.

F. G. Fleay cast doubt on Archer's attribution in 1891,[1] and E. K. Chambers did the same in 1923.[2] E. H. C. Oliphant began to argue for Middleton in 1911,[3] and since then many scholars have taken up the cause. What they have produced to support their reading of the external evidence has been *internal* evidence, i.e. the stylistic character of the play. Words and phrases regarded as distinctively Tourneuresque or Middletonian have been isolated and subjected to statistical analyses. Employing this approach, David J. Lake and MacDonald P. Jackson have made a powerful case for Middleton.[4] In addition, Marco Mincoff's more subjective analyses of the differences between the versification and imagery of Tourneur and of Middleton are a compelling reinforcement of that case.[5] But doubts have been voiced by substantial scholars and critics, including

[1] *A Biographical Chronicle of the English Drama, 1559–1642* (London, 1891), vol. 2, pp. 264, 272.

[2] *The Elizabethan Stage* (Oxford, 1923), vol. 4, p. 42.

[3] 'Problems of Authorship in Elizabethan Dramatic Literature', *Modern Philology* 8 (January 1911), pp. 427–8, followed up in 'The Authorship of *The Revenger's Tragedy*', *Studies in Philology* 23 (1926).

[4] D. J. Lake, *The Canon of Thomas Middleton's Plays: Internal Evidence for the Major Problems of Authorship* (Cambridge, 1975); M. P. Jackson, *Studies in Attribution: Middleton and Shakespeare* (Salzburg, 1979).

[5] 'The Authorship of *The Revenger's Tragedy*', *Studia Historico-Philologica* 2 (1940), pp. 1–87, and *The Study of Style* (1966), p. 104.

R. A. Foakes and G. R. Proudfoot,[1] and Samuel Schoenbaum has moved from enthusiastic support for Middleton (he included a chapter on *The Revenger's Tragedy* in his book, *Middleton's Tragedies*, which was published in New York in 1955) to cautious agnosticism.[2]

What this volume provides is an opportunity to read *The Revenger's Tragedy* alongside some plays uncontroversially ascribed to Middleton.[3] We are not attempting to produce evidence to prove that Middleton wrote *The Revenger's Tragedy*. It seems unlikely that a case for or against will ever, could ever, be *proven*. And it would be dishonest of us to claim that our own subjective reading convinces us in the very marrow of our bones that *The Revenger's Tragedy* could only have come from the pen of Middleton. But, on balance, the case for Tourneur is weak, while the case for Middleton is stronger than for any other dramatist of the period.[4]

[1] R. A. Foakes, Introduction to Revels edition (1966), p. 1; G. R. Proudfoot, *Notes and Queries* 212 (1967), pp. 233–7.

[2] S. Schoenbaum, *Internal Evidence and Elizabethan Dramatic Authorship* (London, 1966), p. 213.

[3] R. V. Holdsworth provides a reading of *The Revenger's Tragedy* within the context of Middleton's *oeuvre* in an essay he has included in the Macmillan Casebook he has edited on *Three Jacobean 'Revenge' Plays* (forthcoming) – '*The Revenger's Tragedy* as a Middleton Play'.

[4] See, among others, R. H. Barker, *Thomas Middleton* (New York, 1958), p. 64; Charles Barber, 'A Rare Use of the Word "Honour" as a Criterion of Middleton's Authorship', *English Studies* 38 (1957), pp. 168ff.; Peter Murray, *A Study of Cyril Tourneur* (Philadelphia, 1964); G. R. Price, 'The Authorship and the Bibliography of *The Revenger's Tragedy*', *The Library* 5th series, 15 (1960), pp. 262–70; David L. Frost, *The School of Shakespeare: the Influence of Shakespeare on English Drama 1600–42* (Cambridge, 1968), and Introduction to the *Selected Plays of Thomas Middleton* (Cambridge, 1978), p. xv; Cyrus Hoy, 'Critical and Aesthetic Problems of Collaboration in Renaissance Drama', *Research Opportunities in Renaissance Drama* 19 (1976), pp. 3–6; Philip J. Ayres, *Tourneur: 'The Revenger's Tragedy'* (London, 1977), pp. 57–62; N. Brittin, 'Middleton's Style and Other Jacobean Styles: Adjectives and Authorship', in K. Friedenreich (ed.), *'Accompaninge the players': Essays Celebrating Thomas Middleton, 1580–1980* (New York, 1983), pp. 39–66.

THE WORKS OF THOMAS MIDDLETON

1597 *The Wisdom of Solomon Paraphrased* (poem)
1599 *Micro-Cynicon: Six Snarling Satires* (poems)
1600 *The Ghost of Lucrece* (poem)
1602 Unnamed lost play
1602 *Caesar's Fall or Two Shapes* (lost play, written with Dekker, Drayton, Munday and Webster)
1602 *The Chester Tragedy or Randal, Earl of Chester* (lost play)
c. 1602 *The Family of Love* (play, written with Dekker)
[*c.* 1602 *Blurt, Master Constable or The Spaniard's Night Walk* (play, probably by Dekker, but possibly by Middleton as well or instead)]
1603 *The Phoenix* (play)
1603 *The True Narration of the Entertainment of His Royal Majesty from Edinburgh till London* (pamphlet, thought by some to be by Middleton)
1604 *The Honest Whore (Part One)* (play, written with Dekker)
1604 *The Ant and the Nightingale or Father Hubbard's Tales* (pamphlet)
1604 *The Black Book* (pamphlet)
1604 *The Meeting of Gallants at an Ordinary* (pamphlet, probably by Middleton)
c. 1604–6 *A Mad World My Masters* (play)
c. 1604–6 *A Trick to Catch the Old One* (play)
c. 1604–6 *The Puritan or The Widow of Watling Street* (play, thought by some to be by Middleton)
c. 1604–7 *Your Five Gallants* (play)
1605 *A Yorkshire Tragedy* (play, probably by Middleton, but with others (possibly including Shakespeare))
c. 1605 *Michaelmas Term* (play)
1606 *Macbeth* (play by Shakespeare, possibly adapted by Middleton)
1606 *The Viper and her Brood* (lost play)
c. 1606 *The Revenger's Tragedy* (play)
1607 *Timon of Athens* (play by Shakespeare, possibly in collaboration with Middleton)
1609 *The Two Gates of Salvation, or the Marriage of the Old and New Testament* (pamphlet)
1609 *Sir Robert Sherley's Entertainment in Cracovia* (pamphlet)
1611 *The Second Maiden's Tragedy* (play, thought by some to be by Middleton)

c. 1611 *The Roaring Girl or Moll Cutpurse* (play, written with Dekker)
1611–12 *No Wit, No Help Like a Woman's* (play)
1611–13 *A Chaste Maid in Cheapside* (play)
1613 *Entertainment at the Opening of the New River* (civic entertainment)
1613 *Wit at Several Weapons* (play, written with Rowley and, possibly, Fletcher)
1613 *The Triumphs of Truth* (civic pageant)
1614 *The Masque of Cupid* (lost masque)
c. 1615 *The Witch* (play)
c. 1615 *The Widow* (play)
c. 1615–17 *A Fair Quarrel* (play, written with Rowley)
c. 1615–17 *The Triumphs of Honour and Industry* (civic pageant)
1616 *Civitatis Amor* (civic pageant)
c. 1616 *The Nice Valour or the Passionate Woman* (play, possibly written with Fletcher)
c. 1617–20 *Hengist, King of Kent or The Mayor of Queenborough* (play)
1618 *The Peacemaker or Great Britain's Blessing* (pamphlet)
c. 1618 *The Old Law or a New Way to Please You* (play, written with Rowley and, possibly, Massinger)
1619 *The Inner Temple Masque or Masque of Heroes* (masque)
1619 *Anything for a Quiet Life* (play, written with Webster)
1619 *The Triumphs of Love and Antiquity* (civic pageant)
1619 *On the Death of Richard Burbage* (elegy)
1619 *The Sun in Aries* (civic pageant, possibly written with Munday)
c. 1619 *More Dissemblers Besides Women* (play)
1619–20 *The World Tossed at Tennis* (masque, written with Rowley)
1620–21 *Honourable Entertainments* (civic entertainments)
c. 1621 *Women Beware Women* (play)
c. 1621–7 *The Puritan Maid, The Modest Wife and The Wanton Widow* (lost play)
c. 1621–7 *The Conqueror's Custom or The Fair Prisoner* (lost play)
1622 *The Changeling* (play written with Rowley)
1622 *An Invention for the Lord Mayor* (private entertainment)
1622 *The Triumphs of Honour and Virtue* (civic pageant)
1623 *The Triumphs of Integrity* (civic pageant)
[1623 *The Spanish Gipsy* (play, probably written by Dekker and Ford, but possibly by Middleton)]
1624 *A Game at Chess* (play)
1626 *The Triumphs of Health and Prosperity* (civic pageant)
1626 Pageant for entry of the King and Queen

FURTHER READING

Middleton's plays have appeared in two collected editions, the 5-volume edition by Alexander Dyce (London, 1840) and the 8-volume edition by A. H. Bullen (London, 1885–6, reprinted New York, 1964). The plays in this volume can also be found in the following anthologies: *Three Jacobean Tragedies*, edited by Gāmini Salgādo (Harmondsworth, 1965), which includes *The Revenger's Tragedy* (attributed to Cyril Tourneur) as well as *The Changeling*; *Jacobean and Caroline Comedies*, edited by R. G. Lawrence (London, 1973), which includes *A Trick to Catch the Old One*; *Thomas Middleton: Three Plays*, edited by Kenneth Muir (London, 1975), which includes *A Chaste Maid in Cheapside*, *Women Beware Women* and *The Changeling*; *The Plays of Cyril Tourneur*, edited by George Parfitt (Cambridge, 1978), which includes *The Revenger's Tragedy*; and *Selected Plays of Thomas Middleton*, edited by David L. Frost (Cambridge, 1978), which includes those in Muir, plus *A Mad World My Masters*.

A Trick to Catch the Old One has been edited by C. Barber, for Fountainwell Drama Texts (Edinburgh, 1968), by G. J. Watson, for New Mermaids (London, 1968), and by G. R. Price (The Hague, 1976); *The Revenger's Tragedy* by R. A. Foakes, for Revels Plays (London, 1966), by L. J. Ross, for Regents Renaissance Drama Series (Nebraska, 1966), by Brian Gibbons, for New Mermaids (London, 1967) and by M. P. Jackson, for Associated University Presses (London and Toronto, 1968) [a facsimile of the 1607/8 Quarto; Jackson attributes the play to Middleton]; *A Chaste Maid in Cheapside* by A. Brissenden, for New Mermaids (London, 1968), by C. Barber, for Fountainwell Drama Texts (Edinburgh, 1969), and by R. B. Parker, for Revels Plays (London, 1969); *Women Beware Women* by Roma Gill, for New Mermaids (London, 1968), by C. Barber, for Fountainwell Drama Texts (Edinburgh, 1969), and by J. R. Mulryne, for Revels Plays (London, 1975); and *The Changeling* by N. W. Bawcutt, for Revels Plays (London, 1958), by Patricia Thomson, for New Mermaids (London, 1964), by G. W. Williams, for Regents Renaissance Drama Series (Nebraska, 1966), and by M. W. Black (Philadelphia, 1966).

The following books and articles are recommended:

M. C. Bradbrook, *Themes and Conventions of Elizabethan Tragedy* (Cambridge, 1935)

Nicholas Brooke, *Horrid Laughter in Jacobean Tragedy* (London, 1979)
Jonathan Dollimore, *Radical Tragedy: Religion, Ideology and Power in the Drama of Shakespeare and his Contemporaries* (Brighton, 1984)
William Empson, *Some Versions of Pastoral* (London, 1935)
Brian Gibbons, *Jacobean City Comedy* (London, 1968)
Margot Heinemann, *Puritanism and Theatre: Thomas Middleton and Opposition Drama under the Early Stuarts* (Cambridge, 1980)
G. R. Hibbard, 'The Tragedies of Thomas Middleton and the Decadence of the Drama', *Nottingham Renaissance and Modern Studies* 1 (1957), pp. 35–64
R. V. Holdsworth (ed.), *Three Jacobean 'Revenge' Plays*, a Macmillan Casebook of critical essays (London, forthcoming)
M. P. Jackson, *Studies in Attribution: Middleton and Shakespeare*, Salzburg Studies in English Literature: Jacobean Drama Studies 79 (1979)
L. C. Knights, *Drama and Society in the Age of Jonson* (London, 1937)
D. J. Lake, *The Canon of Thomas Middleton's Plays: Internal Evidence for the Major Problems of Authorship* (Cambridge, 1975)
Richard Levin, *The Multiple Plot in English Renaissance Drama* (Chicago, 1971)
J. R. Mulryne, *Thomas Middleton*, Writers and their Work (Harlow, 1979)
R. B. Parker, 'Middleton's Experiments with Comedy and Judgement', *Stratford-upon-Avon Studies 1: Jacobean Theatre*, ed. J. R. Brown and B. Harris (London, 1960), pp. 179–99
Christopher Ricks, 'The Moral and Poetic Structure of *The Changeling*', *Essays in Criticism* 10 (1960), pp. 290–306
Christopher Ricks, 'The Tragedies of Webster, Tourneur and Middleton: Symbols, Imagery and Conventions', in *The Sphere History of Literature in the English Language*, vol. 3: *English Drama to 1710*, ed. Christopher Ricks (London, 1971)
Christopher Ricks, 'Word Play in *Women Beware Women*', *Review of English Studies* new series 12 (1961), pp. 238–50
George E. Rowe, Jr, *Thomas Middleton and the New Comedy Tradition* (Lincoln, Nebraska, USA, 1979)
Neil Taylor and Bryan Loughrey, 'Middleton's Chess Strategies in *Women Beware Women*', *Studies in English Literature* 24 (1984), pp. 341–54

EDITORIAL PROCEDURE

We have followed accepted editorial practice in removing what we take to be obstacles to a modern reader's understanding of Middleton's text. This has meant altering certain typographical features (such as long s) and modernizing old and inconsistent spellings of words still in current use (while retaining obsolete forms of words where meaning would be affected by modernization). We have brought punctuation into line with modern practice, but kept it fairly light. Lineation is the major problem for an editor of Middleton, since his handling of verse is often metrically audacious and, either for this reason or because of shoddy practice in the printing house, there are many places where it is not clear whether a speech is intended to be verse or prose. An editor is obliged to treat each such case on its merits, but our general principle, in this as in other respects, has been to keep faith with the copy-text wherever possible. We have silently corrected what we take to be clear errors in the printing of each copy-text, adopting the best emendations by previous editors unless we felt we could better them. The most significant substantive emendations are explained in the Notes.

A Trick
to Catch the Old One

A Trick to Catch the Old One was entered in the Stationers' Register on 7 October 1607 to George Eld and published soon after. The copy-text for this edition is the 1608 Quarto (Q). In 1970 The Scolar Press published a facsimile of a copy in the Bodleian Library.

[DRAMATIS PERSONAE

THEODORUS WITGOOD
PECUNIOUS LUCRE, *his uncle, an old usurer*
WALKADINE HOARD, *another usurer*
ONESIPHORUS, *Walkadine's brother*
LIMBER }
KIX } *Hoard's friends*
LAMPREY }
SPITCHCOCK }
HARRY DAMPIT } *usurers*
GULF }
SAM FREEDOM, *Lucre's stepson*
MONEYLOVE
HOST
SIR LANCELOT
GEORGE, *Lucre's servant*
ARTHUR, *Hoard's servant*

COURTESAN, *Witgood's former mistress*
MISTRESS LUCRE
Joyce, *Walkadine's* NIECE
LADY FOXSTONE
AUDREY, *Dampit's servant*

Creditors; Gentlemen; Servants; Drawers; Vintner; Sergeants; Scrivener; Tailor; Barber; Perfumer; Huntsman; Falconer; Boy.

Scene: Leicestershire and London.]

THEODORUS WITGOOD: 'Theodorus' is derived from the Greek for 'love of God'. 'Witgood' implies he is 'witty' in the sense of sharp-witted PECUNIOUS LUCRE: an apt name for a usurer. 'Pecunious' = 'abounding in money' and 'Lucre' = profit (with a pejorative overtone) WALKADINE: Price (his edition of 1976) suggests this derives from the Greek for 'terrible strength' HOARD: another name descriptive of usury ONESIPHORUS: 'profit-bearer' (a Greek name, see II Timothy IV. 19) LIMBER: probably with overtones of limp, easily swayed KIX: a dry stalk, hence a 'sapless' person LAMPREY: eel-like fish

[ACT ONE]

[SCENE I]

Enter WITGOOD, *a gentleman, solus.*

WITGOOD: All's gone! Still thou'rt a gentleman, that's all; but a poor one, that's nothing. What milk brings thy meadows forth now? Where are thy goodly uplands and thy downlands? All sunk into that little pit, lechery. Why should a gallant pay but two shillings for his ord'nary that nourishes him, and twenty times two for his brothel that consumes him? But where's Long-acre? In my uncle's conscience, which is three years' voyage about. He that sets out upon his conscience ne'er finds the way home again; he is either swallowed in the quicksands of law-quillets or splits upon the piles of a *praemunire*; yet these old fox-brain'd and ox-brow'd uncles have still defences for their avarice and apologies for their practices and will thus greet our follies:

He that doth his youth expose
To brothel, drink, and danger,
Let him that is his nearest kin
Cheat him before a stranger.

with the ability to stick to objects with a sucker SPITCHCOCK: a dish of fried or broiled eels HARRY DAMPIT: 'old Harry' is a nick-name for the Devil to whom Dampit is continually compared. 'Dampit' also suggests 'damned pit' = hell
GULF: again an appropriate name for a usurer, meaning 'voracious appetite'
COURTESAN: in this case, not a common prostitute but a kept mistress
FOXSTONE: possibly there is a bawdy implication, since stone = testicle

1 *gentleman*: in the 17th century the term denoted considerable rank 2 *meadows*: i.e. the cows which feed in the meadows 3 *pit*: a slang term for 'hell' and 'cunt' 4 *gallant*: gentleman of fashion and pleasure *ord'nary*: 'ordinary' meals were served at fixed prices in taverns 5 *brothel*: prostitute 6 *Long-acre*: this term for a long narrow field of one acre was employed allusively for 'one's estate or patrimony' *conscience*: inmost thoughts (i.e. out of Witgood's reach) 7 *sets out upon his*: pursues (or voyages round) Lucre's 8 *law-quillets*: legal quibbles 9 *piles*: rocks *praemunire*: writ 10 *ox-brow'd*: perhaps 'cuckolded' (because horned), or else 'stupid' (bovine) *still*: always 12–15 i.e. an uncle should take advantage of such a prodigal before someone outside the family does

And that's his uncle, 'tis a principle in usury. I dare not visit the City; there I should be too soon visited by that horrible plague, my debts, and by that means I lose a virgin's love, her portion, and her virtues. Well, how should a man live now that has no living? Hum? Why, are there not a million of men in the world that only sojourn upon their brain and make their wits their mercers? And am I but one amongst that million and cannot thrive upon't? Any trick out of the compass of law now would come happily to me.

Enter COURTESAN.

COURTESAN: My love.

WITGOOD: My loathing! Hast thou been the secret consumption of my purse, and now com'st to undo my last means, my wits? Wilt leave no virtue in me, and yet thou ne'er the better?
Hence, Courtesan, round-webb'd tarantula,
That driest the roses in the cheeks of youth.

COURTESAN: I have been true unto your pleasure, and all your lands thrice rack'd was never worth the jewel which I prodigally gave you, my virginity:
Lands mortgag'd may return, and more esteem'd,
But honesty once pawn'd is ne'er redeem'd.

WITGOOD: Forgive; I do thee wrong
To make thee sin and then to chide thee for't.

COURTESAN: I know I am your loathing now; farewell.

WITGOOD: Stay, best invention, stay.

COURTESAN: I that have been the secret consumption of your purse, shall I stay now to undo your last means, your wits? Hence, Courtesan, away!

WITGOOD: I prithee make me not mad at my own weapon; stay – a thing few women can do, I know that, and therefore they had need wear stays – be not contrary. Dost love me? Fate has so cast it that all my means I must derive from thee.

COURTESAN: From me? Be happy then;
What lies within the power of my performance
Shall be commanded of thee.

17 *plague*: London was visited by the plague every year 18 *portion*: dowry 20 *sojourn*: temporarily reside 21 *mercers*: dealers in textiles; i.e. they trade off their wits 22 *out of the compass of law*: i.e. legal (but the phrase is ambiguous – Witgood could merely be aiming to avoid being caught by the law) 27 *virtue*: strength (physical and financial)/goodness 28 *round-webb'd*: probably referring to the fashion for wide-hooped farthingales *tarantula*: this poisonous spider was reputed to transform all it touched into excrement 31 *rack'd*: rented out at excessive rates 34 *honesty*: chastity 38 *invention*: i.e. the Courtesan; Witgood has suddenly conceived a plan concerning her 41 *weapon*: i.e. words 43 *stays*: corsets

WITGOOD: Spoke like an honest drab, i'faith; it may prove something. What trick is not an embryon at first, until a perfect shape come over it?

COURTESAN: Come, I must help you. Whereabouts left you?
I'll proceed.
Though you beget, 'tis I must help to breed.
Speak, what is't? I'd fain conceive it.

WITGOOD: So, so, so; thou shalt presently take the name and form upon thee of a rich country widow, four hundred a year valiant, in woods, in bullocks, in barns and in rye stacks. We'll to London and to my covetous uncle.

COURTESAN: I begin to applaud thee; our states being both desperate, they're soon resolute. But how for horses?

WITGOOD: Mass, that's true; the jest will be of some continuance. Let me see; horses now, a bots on 'em! Stay, I have acquaintance with a mad host, never yet bawd to thee; I have rins'd the whoreson's gums in mull-sack many a time and often; put but a good tale into his ear now so it come off cleanly, and there's horse and man for us, I dare warrant thee.

COURTESAN: Arm your wits then speedily; there shall want nothing in me, either in behaviour, discourse, or fashion, that shall discredit your intended purpose.
I will so artfully disguise my wants
And set so good a courage on my state
That I will be believed.

WITGOOD: Why, then, all's furnish'd; I shall go nigh to catch that old fox mine uncle. Though he make but some amends for my undoing, yet there's some comfort in't – he cannot otherwise choose, though it be but in hope to cozen me again, but supply any hasty want that I bring to town with me. The device well and cunningly carried, the name of a rich widow and four hundred a year in good earth will so conjure up a kind of usurer's love in him to me that he will not only desire my presence,

48 *drab*: prostitute (but possibly no more here than 'wench') *prove something*: yield results 49 *perfect*: fully formed 53 *conceive*: understand; but continuing the earlier childbirth metaphors 54 *presently*: immediately 55 *valiant*: worth 59 *resolute*: full of resolve 60 *Mass*: by the Mass *be . . . continuance*: i.e. need some sustaining 61 *a bots*: an expletive; literally a disease caused by parasitical worms which affected horses 61–2 *mad host*: merry inn-keeper 62 *never . . . thee*: inn-keepers had a reputation for acting as procurers. The suggestion that the Courtesan is a common whore is puzzling as Witgood elsewhere accepts that she has been 'faithful' to him 63 *mull-sack*: warmed, spiced wine 64 *cleanly*: neatly, cleverly 66 *want*: be (in the context of 'discredit') 69 *wants*: deficiencies 70 *set so good a courage on my state*: i.e. 'act my part so boldly' or 'show much pride in my estate' 72 *I shall go nigh*: i.e. I'm going to make every effort 73 *my undoing*: i.e. financial ruin 75 *cozen*: cheat

which at first shall scarce be granted him – I'll keep off a' purpose – but I shall find him so officious to deserve, so ready to supply! I know the state of an old man's affection so well: if his nephew be poor indeed, why, he lets God alone with him; but if he be once rich, then he'll be the first man that helps him.

COURTESAN: 'Tis right the world; for in these days an old man's love to his kindred is like his kindness to his wife, 'tis always done before he comes at it.

WITGOOD: I owe thee for that jest. Begone; here's all my wealth. [*Gives money.*] Prepare thyself. Away! I'll to mine host with all possible haste, and, with the best art and most profitable form, pour the sweet circumstance into his ear, which shall have the gift to turn all the wax to honey.

[*Exit* COURTESAN.]

How now? O the right worshipful seniors of our country.

[*Enter* ONESIPHORUS, LIMBER *and* KIX.]

ONESIPHORUS: Who's that?

LIMBER: O the common rioter; take no note of him.

WITGOOD [*Aside.*]: You will not see me now; the comfort is ere it be long you will scarce see yourselves.

[*Exit.*]

ONESIPHORUS: I wonder how he breathes; h'as consum'd all upon that courtesan.

LIMBER: We have heard so much.

ONESIPHORUS: You have heard all truth. His uncle and my brother have been these three years mortal adversaries. Two old tough spirits, they seldom meet but fight, or quarrel when 'tis calmest: I think their anger be the very fire that keeps their age alive.

LIMBER: What was the quarrel, sir?

ONESIPHORUS: Faith, about a purchase, fetching over a young heir. Master Hoard, my brother, having wasted much time in beating the bargain, what did me old Lucre, but as his conscience mov'd him, knowing the poor gentleman, stepp'd in between 'em and cozen'd him himself.

80 *officious to deserve*: i.e. anxious to deserve my good will 84 *'Tis right the world*: i.e. it's the same the whole world over 85 *kindness to*: having sex with 85–6 *'tis always done before he comes at it*: i.e. he fails to have an erection (or he comes too quickly) 92 s.d. Q does not name the three gentlemen who enter, but they can be identified from the content of their speeches 94 *common rioter*: notorious wastrel 96 *you will scarce see yourselves*: i.e. because you will have been hoodwinked by my plot 97 *how*: at the way 100 *His uncle and my brother*: i.e. Pecunious Lucre and Walkadine Hoard 105 *a purchase*: profit acquired by dubious means *fetching over*: getting the better of 106–7 *beating the bargain*: haggling

LIMBER: And was this all, sir?

ONESIPHORUS: This was e'en it, sir. Yet for all this, I know no reason but the match might go forward betwixt his wife's son and my niece. What though there be a dissension between the two old men, I see no reason it should put a difference between the two younger: 'tis as natural for old folks to fall out as for young to fall in! A scholar comes a-wooing to my niece: well, he's wise, but he's poor. Her son comes a-wooing to my niece: well, he's a fool, but he's rich.

LIMBER: Ay, marry, sir.

ONESIPHORUS: Pray now, is not a rich fool better than a poor philosopher?

LIMBER: One would think so, i'faith!

ONESIPHORUS: She now remains at London with my brother, her second uncle, to learn fashions, practise music; the voice between her lips, and the viol between her legs, she'll be fit for a consort very speedily. A thousand good pound is her portion; if she marry, we'll ride up and be merry.

KIX: A match, if it be a match!

Exeunt.

[SCENE 2]

Enter at one door, WITGOOD; *at the other,* HOST.

WITGOOD: Mine host?

HOST: Young Master Witgood.

WITGOOD: I have been laying all the town for thee.

HOST: Why, what's the news, Bully Had-land?

WITGOOD: What geldings are in the house, of thine own? Answer me to that first.

HOST: Why, man, why?

WITGOOD: Mark me what I say: I'll tell thee such a tale in thine ear that thou shalt trust me spite of thy teeth, furnish me with some money,

112 *his wife's son*: i.e. Sam Freedom *niece*: i.e. Hoard's niece who is secretly betrothed to Witgood 115 *fall in*: make up/have sex *scholar*: i.e. Moneylove 118 *marry*: derived from the name of the Virgin Mary
124 *consort*: concert/husband (pointing up the bawdy implications of the musical skills discussed) 127 *A match*: agreed *a match*: a marriage 3 *laying*: searching 4 *Bully Had-land*: i.e. good fellow who once had land 5 *of thine own*: inn-keepers would also keep guests' horses in their stables 9 *spite of thy teeth*: i.e. in spite of yourself

willy-nilly, and ride up with me thyself *contra voluntatem et professionem.*

HOST: How? Let me see this trick, and I'll say thou hast more art than a conjurer.

WITGOOD: Dost thou joy in my advancement?

HOST: Do I love sack and ginger?

WITGOOD: Comes my prosperity desiredly to thee?

HOST: Come forfeitures to a usurer, fees to an officer, punks to an host, and pigs to a parson desiredly? Why, then, la!

WITGOOD: Will the report of a widow of four hundred a year, boy, make thee leap and sing and dance and come to thy place again?

HOST: Wilt thou command me now? I am thy spirit; conjure me into any shape.

WITGOOD: I ha' brought her from her friends, turn'd back the horses by a sleight; not so much as one amongst her six men, goodly large, yeomanly fellows, will she trust with this her purpose; by this light, all unmann'd, regardless of her state, neglectful of vainglorious ceremony, all for my love. O 'tis a fine little voluble tongue, mine host, that wins a widow.

HOST: No, 'tis a tongue with a great T, my boy, that wins a widow.

WITGOOD: Now, sir, the case stands thus: good mine host, if thou lov'st my happiness, assist me.

HOST: Command all my beasts i'th'house.

WITGOOD: Nay, that's not all neither; prithee, take truce with thy joy and listen to me. Thou know'st I have a wealthy uncle i'th'City, somewhat the wealthier by my follies; the report of this fortune, well and cunningly carried, might be a means to draw some goodness from the usuring rascal; for I have put her in hope already of some estate that I have, either in land or money. Now if I be found true in neither, what may I expect but a sudden breach of our love, utter dissolution of the match, and confusion of my fortunes for ever?

10 *contra voluntatem et professionem*: Latin for 'against your will and profession'
11 *How?*: conventional exclamation of surprise, i.e. What? 14 *sack*: white wine 16 *punks*: whores 17 *pigs to a parson*: proverbial, referring to tithes paid in kind to parsons *la!*: an exclamation used to reinforce a conventional phrase; i.e. 'just so' 23 *sleight*: cunning trick 24–5 *all unmann'd*: completely without male attendants *regardless of*: without regard for 28 *great T*: a capital T (the sense of the phrase is obscure but the Host clearly believes that any tongue which can persuade a rich widow to remarry deserves status) 39 *confusion*: ruin

HOST: Wilt thou but trust the managing of thy business with me?

WITGOOD: With thee? Why, will I desire to thrive in my purpose? Will I hug four hundred a year? I that know the misery of nothing? Will that man wish a rich widow, that has ne'er a hole to put his head in? With thee, mine host? Why, believe it, sooner with thee than with a covey of counsellors!

HOST: Thank you for your good report, i'faith, sir, and if I stand you not in stead, why then let an host come off *hic et haec hostis*, a deadly enemy to dice, drink, and venery. Come, where's this widow?

WITGOOD: Hard at Park End.

HOST: I'll be her serving-man for once.

WITGOOD: Why, there we let off together, keep full time; my thoughts were striking then just the same number.

HOST: I knew't. Shall we then see our merry days again?

WITGOOD: Our merry nights – which ne'er shall be more seen.

Exeunt.

[SCENE 3]

Enter at several doors old LUCRE *and old* [WALKADINE] HOARD, *Gentlemen* [LAMPREY, SPITCHCOCK, SAM FREEDOM, *and* MONEYLOVE] *coming between them to pacify 'em.*

LAMPREY: Nay, good Master Lucre, and you, Master Hoard, anger is the wind which you're both too much troubled withal.

HOARD: Shall my adversary thus daily affront me, ripping up the old wound of our malice, which three summers could not close up? Into which wound the very sight of him drops scalding lead instead of balsamum?

LUCRE: Why, Hoard, Hoard, Hoard, Hoard, Hoard! May I not pass in the state of quietness to mine own house? Answer me to that, before witness, and why? I'll refer the cause to honest, even-minded gentlemen, or require the mere indifferences of the law to decide this matter. I got the purchase, true; was't not any man's case? Yes. Will a wise man stand as a bawd, whilst another wipes his nose of the bargain? No, I answer, no, in that case.

44 *covey*: set   47 *hic et haec hostis*: a nonsensical Latin phrase, punning on 'host' and 'hostis' (= enemy)   48 *venery*: lechery   49 *Hard at*: near   51 *let off*: fire off   54 The joke, presumably, is that they won't be able to see in the dark
s.d. *several*: separate   2 *withal*: with   6 *balsamum*: balsam, an aromatic medicinal preparation   10 *indifferences*: impartiality   11 *any man's case*: open to anyone   12 *wipes his nose*: i.e. cheats him

LAMPREY: Nay, sweet Master Lucre.

HOARD: Was it the part of a friend? No, rather of a Jew. Mark what I say: when I had beaten the bush to the last bird, or, as I may term it, the price to a pound, then like a cunning usurer to come in the evening of the bargain and glean all my hopes in a minute; to enter, as it were, at the back door of the purchase, for thou ne'er cam'st the right way by it!

LUCRE: Hast thou the conscience to tell me so, without any impeachment to thyself?

HOARD: Thou that canst defeat thy own nephew, Lucre, lap his lands into bonds, and take the extremity of thy kindred's forfeitures because he's a rioter, a wastethrift, a brothel-master, and so forth – what may a stranger expect from thee but *vulnera dilacerata*, as the poet says, dilacerate dealing?

LUCRE: Upbraid'st thou me with 'nephew'? Is all imputation laid upon me? What acquaintance have I with his follies? If he riot, 'tis he must want it; if he surfeit, 'tis he must feel it; if he drab it, 'tis he must lie by't. What's this to me?

HOARD: What's all to thee? Nothing, nothing; such is the gulf of thy desire and the wolf of thy conscience; but be assured, old Pecunious Lucre, if ever fortune so bless me that I may be at leisure to vex thee, or any means so favour me that I may have opportunity to mad thee, I will pursue it with that flame of hate, that spirit of malice, unrepressed wrath, that I will blast thy comforts.

LUCRE: Ha, ha, ha!

LAMPREY: Nay, Master Hoard, you're a wise gentleman.

HOARD: I will so cross thee –

LUCRE: And I thee.

HOARD: So without mercy fret thee –

LUCRE: So monstrously oppose thee –

HOARD: Dost scoff at my just anger? O that I had as much power as usury has over thee!

LUCRE: Then thou wouldst have as much power as the Devil has over thee!

HOARD: Toad!

LUCRE: Aspic!

HOARD: Serpent!

LUCRE: Viper!

16 *beaten the bush to the last bird*: i.e. done all the hard work (the allusion is to beaters at a shoot) 17 *price to a pound*: i.e. agreed on terms 20 *impeachment*: disparagement, accusation 22 *defeat*: cheat, dispose *lap*: i.e. bind 25 *vulnera dilicerata*: Latin, 'lacerated wounds' 25–6 *dilacerate*: torn 29 *drab it*: whore *lie by't*: suffer the consequences/sleep with her/be imprisoned 31 *gulf*: voracious appetite 34 *mad*: infuriate 39 *cross*: thwart 47 *Aspic*: asp; a poisonous snake

SPITCHCOCK: Nay, gentlemen, then we must divide you perforce.

LAMPREY: When the fire grows too unreasonable hot, there's no better way than to take off the wood.

Exeunt [LAMPREY, SPITCHCOCK, LUCRE *and* HOARD].

Mane[n]t SAM [FREEDOM] *and* MONEYLOVE.

SAM: A word, good signior.

MONEYLOVE: How now, what's the news?

SAM: 'Tis given me to understand that you are a rival of mine in the love of Mistress Joyce, Master Hoard's niece: say me ay, say me no.

MONEYLOVE: Yes, 'tis so.

SAM: Then look to yourself; you cannot live long. I'm practising every morning; a month hence I'll challenge you.

MONEYLOVE: Give me your hand upon't; there's my pledge I'll meet you!

Strikes him. Exit.

SAM: O! O! What reason had you for that, sir, to strike before the month? You knew I was not ready for you, and that made you so crank. I am not such a coward to strike again, I warrant you; my ear has the law of her side, for it burns horribly. I will teach him to strike a naked face, the longest day of his life. 'Slid, it shall cost me some money, but I'll bring this box into the Chancery.

Exit.

[SCENE 4]

Enter WITGOOD *and the* HOST.

HOST: Fear you nothing, sir, I have lodg'd her in a house of credit, I warrant you.

WITGOOD: Hast thou the writings?

HOST: Firm, sir.

[*Enter* DAMPIT *and* GULF, *who talk apart.*]

WITGOOD: Prithee, stay, and behold two the most prodigious rascals that ever slipp'd into the shape of men: Dampit, sirrah, and young Gulf, his fellow caterpillar.

HOST: Dampit? Sure, I have heard of that Dampit.

62 *crank*: cocky 63 *again*: back 63–4 *my . . . horribly*: i.e. since my ear is so badly injured, I have grounds for legal action 64–5 *the longest day of his life*: i.e. he'll regret it 65 *'Slid*: oath, contracted from 'God's (eye) lid' 66 *box*: blow/case *Chancery*: court of the Lord Chancellor, at the time the highest court of justice apart from the House of Lords 3 *writings*: i.e. forged evidence of the widow's wealth 7 *caterpillar*: extortioner, one who preys on society

WITGOOD: Heard of him? Why, man, he that has lost both his ears may hear of him; a famous infamous trampler of time; his own phrase. Note him well: that Dampit, sirrah, he in the uneven beard and the serge cloak, is the most notorious, usuring, blasphemous, atheistical, brothel-vomiting rascal that we have in these latter times now extant, whose first beginning was the stealing of a mastie dog from a farmer's house.

HOST: He look'd as if he would obey the commandment well, when he began first with stealing.

WITGOOD: True. The next town he came at, he set the dogs together by th'ears.

HOST: A sign he should follow the law, by my faith.

WITGOOD: So it followed, indeed; and being destitute of all fortunes, stak'd his mastie against a noble, and by great fortune his dog had the day. How he made it up ten shillings I know not, but his own boast is that he came to town with but ten shillings in his purse, and now is credibly worth ten thousand pound.

HOST: How the Devil came he by it?

WITGOOD: How the Devil came he not by it? If you put in the Devil once, riches come with a vengeance. H'as been a trampler of the law, sir, and the Devil has a care of his footmen. The rogue has spied me now; he nibbled me finely once too; a pox search you. – O Master Dampit! [*Aside.*] The very loins of thee! – Cry you mercy, Master Gulf; you walk so low I promise you I saw you not, sir.

GULF: He that walks low walks safe, the poets tell us.

WITGOOD [*Aside.*]: And nigher hell by a foot and a half than the rest of his fellows. [*To* DAMPIT.] But my old Harry!

DAMPIT: My sweet Theodorus!

WITGOOD: 'Twas a merry world when thou cam'st to town with ten shillings in thy purse.

DAMPIT: And now worth ten thousand pound, my boy. Report it: Harry Dampit, a trampler of time; say he would be up in a morning and be here with his serge gown, dash'd up to the hams in a cause, have his feet stink about Westminster Hall, and come home again; see the galleons,

9 *he that has lost both his ears*: i.e. the deaf and the criminal, who were punished by ear-cropping 10 *trampler*: cant term for attorney, but Price suggests 'one who treads down human rights' *of time*: the phrase is obscure 11 *serge*: woollen or worsted cloth 14 *mastie*: mastiff 21 *noble*: a gold coin worth one-third of £1 26 *put in*: let in 29 *nibbled*: slang for 'caught', or 'nabbed' 30 *The very loins of thee!*: continuing the curse of 'A pox search you' 31 *low*: i.e. he is short 32 *low*: humbly 34 *old Harry*: sometimes a familiar name for the devil 40 *dash'd*: spattered with mud 41 *Westminster Hall*: where the law courts met until 1882

the galleasses, the great armadas of the law; then there be hoys and petty vessels, oars and scullers of the time; there be picklocks of the time too. Then would I be here, I would trample up and down like a mule: now to the judges, 'May it please your reverend, honourable fatherhoods'; then to my counsellor, 'May it please your worshipful patience'; then to the examiner's office, 'May it please your mastership's gentleness'; then to one of the clerks, 'May it please your worshipful lousiness', for I find him scrubbing in his codpiece; then to the hall again; then to the chamber again –

WITGOOD: And when to the cellar again?

DAMPIT: E'en when thou wilt again. Tramplers of time, motions of Fleet Street, and visions of Holborn; here I have fees of one, there I have fees of another; my clients come about me, the fooliaminy and coxcombry of the country. I still trash'd and trotted for other men's causes; thus was poor Harry Dampit made rich by others' laziness, who, though they would not follow their own suits, I made 'em follow me with their purses.

WITGOOD: Didst thou so, old Harry?

DAMPIT: Ay, and I sous'd 'em with bills of charges, i'faith; twenty pound a year have I brought in for boat-hire, and I ne'er stepp'd into boat in my life.

WITGOOD: Tramplers of time!

DAMPIT: Ay, tramplers of time, rascals of time, bull-beggars.

WITGOOD: Ah, thou'rt a mad old Harry! Kind Master Gulf, I am bold to renew my acquaintance.

GULF: I embrace it, sir.

Music.

Exeunt.

42 *galleasses*: heavy, low-built vessels *hoys*: small vessels rigged as sloops
46 *counsellor*: advocate 47 *examiner's office*: where the depositions of witnesses were recorded 49 *scrubbing*: scratching (because of lice) 52 *motions*: puppet-shows 54 *fooliaminy*: fools *coxcombry*: foolishness (Middleton appears to have coined both terms – they reflect Dampit's general linguistic exuberance) 55 *trash'd*: walked or ran through mud and mire 60 *sous'd*: i.e. swindled (Q reads 'souc'st') 64 *bull-beggars*: bugbears

ACT TWO

[SCENE I]

Enter LUCRE.

LUCRE: My adversary ever more twits me with my nephew, forsooth, my nephew; why may not a virtuous uncle have a dissolute nephew? What though he be a brotheller, a wastethrift, a common surfeiter, and, to conclude, a beggar? Must sin in him call up shame in me? Since we have no part in their follies, why should we have part in their infamies? For my strict hand towards his mortgage, that I deny not; I confess I had an uncle's pen'worth. Let me see, half in half, true. I saw neither hope of his reclaiming nor comfort in his being, and was it not then better bestow'd upon his uncle than upon one of his aunts? I need not say 'bawd', for everyone knows what 'aunt' stands for in the last translation.

[*Enter* Servant.]

Now, sir?

SERVANT: There's a country serving-man, sir, attends to speak with your worship.

LUCRE: I'm at best leisure now; send him in to me.

[*Exit* Servant.]

Enter HOST, *like a serving-man.*

HOST: Bless your venerable worship.

LUCRE: Welcome, good fellow.

HOST [*Aside.*]: He calls me thief at first sight, yet he little thinks I am an host.

LUCRE: What's thy business with me?

HOST: Faith, sir, I am sent from my mistress to any sufficient gentleman indeed, to ask advice upon a doubtful point. 'Tis indifferent, sir, to whom I come, for I know none, nor did my mistress direct me to any particular man, for she's as mere a stranger here as myself; only I found your worship within, and 'tis a thing I ever lov'd, sir, to be dispatch'd as soon as I can.

1 *twits*: taunts *forsooth*: in truth (used parenthetically in an ironic or derisive context) 7 *uncle's pen'worth*: 'to uncle' was to swindle *half in half*: i.e. 50 per cent profit 8 *reclaiming*: reforming 17 *calls me thief at first sight*: 'good fellow' was also a cant term for 'thief' 20 *sufficient gentleman*: i.e. gentleman of sufficient means

LUCRE [*Aside.*]: A good blunt honesty; I like him well. – What is thy mistress?

HOST: Faith, a country gentlewoman, and a widow, sir. Yesterday was the first flight of us, but now she intends to stay until a little Term business be ended.

LUCRE: Her name, I prithee.

HOST: It runs there in the writings, sir, among her lands: Widow Medler.

LUCRE: Medler? Mass, have I ne'er heard of that widow?

HOST: Yes, I warrant you, have you, sir; not the rich widow in Staffordshire?

LUCRE: Cuds me, there 'tis indeed. Thou hast put me into memory; there's a widow indeed! Ah, that I were a bachelor again!

HOST: No doubt your worship might do much then, but she's fairly promis'd to a bachelor already.

LUCRE: Ah, what is he, I prithee?

HOST: A country gentleman too, one whom your worship knows not, I'm sure; h'as spent some few follies in his youth, but marriage, by my faith, begins to call him home; my mistress loves him, sir, and love covers faults, you know. One Master Witgood, if ever you have heard of the gentleman.

LUCRE: Ha? Witgood, say'st thou?

HOST: That's his name indeed, sir. My mistress is like to bring him to a goodly seat yonder; four hundred a year, by my faith.

LUCRE: But, I pray, take me with you.

HOST: Ay, sir.

LUCRE: What countryman might this young Witgood be?

HOST: A Leicestershire gentleman, sir.

LUCRE [*Aside.*]: My nephew, by th'mass, my nephew! I'll fetch out more of this, i'faith; a simple country fellow, I'll work't out of him. [*To* HOST.] And is that gentleman, say'st thou, presently to marry her?

HOST: Faith, he brought her up to town, sir; h'as the best card in all the bunch for't, her heart; and I know my mistress will be married ere she go down. Nay, I'll swear that, for she's none of those widows that will go down first and be married after; she hates that, I can tell you, sir.

28–9 *Yesterday was the first flight of us*: i.e. our original intentions were to leave yesterday 29 *Term business*: legal business (which had to be conducted during the periods or terms when the courts sat) 32 *Medler*: a medlar tree produces fruit which is only eaten when over-ripe. 'Medler' was slang for both 'cunt' and 'whore' 36 *Cuds me*: an oath corrupted from 'God save me' 43–4 *love covers faults*: presumably there is a bawdy innuendo here since faults are cracks, fissures 48 *seat*: estate 49 *take me with you*: i.e. let me understand you 53 *fetch out*: i.e. bring to light 57 *bunch*: pack 57–8 *go down*: return home/fuck/perform fellatio

LUCRE: By my faith, sir, she is like to have a proper gentleman and a comely; I'll give her that gift!

HOST: Why, does your worship know him, sir?

LUCRE: I know him! Does not all the world know him? Can a man of such exquisite qualities be hid under a bushel?

HOST: Then your worship may save me a labour, for I had charge given me to inquire after him.

LUCRE: Inquire of him? If I might counsel thee, thou shouldst ne'er trouble thyself further; inquire of him of no more but of me; I'll fit thee! I grant he has been youthful, but is he not now reclaim'd? Mark you that, sir; has not your mistress, think you, been wanton in her youth? If men be wags, are there no women wagtails?

HOST: No doubt, sir.

LUCRE: Does not he return wisest, that comes home whipp'd with his own follies?

HOST: Why, very true, sir.

LUCRE: The worst report you can hear of him, I can tell you, is that he has been a kind gentleman, a liberal, and a worthy; who but lusty Witgood, thrice-noble Witgood!

HOST: Since your worship has so much knowledge in him, can you resolve me, sir, what his living might be? My duty binds me, sir, to have a care of my mistress' estate; she has been ever a good mistress to me, though I say it. Many wealthy suitors has she nonsuited for his sake; yet, though her love be so fix'd, a man cannot tell whether his nonperformance may help to remove it, sir. He makes us believe he has lands and living.

LUCRE: Who, young Master Witgood? Why believe it, he has as goodly a fine living out yonder – what do you call the place?

HOST: Nay, I know not, i'faith.

LUCRE: Hum – see, like a beast, if I have not forgot the name – puh! And out yonder again, goodly grown woods and fair meadows – pax on't, I can ne'er hit of that place neither. He? Why, he's Witgood of Witgood Hall; he, an unknown thing?

HOST: Is he so, sir? To see how rumour will alter! Trust me, sir, we heard once he had no lands, but all lay mortgag'd to an uncle he has in town here.

LUCRE: Push! 'Tis a tale, 'tis a tale.

60 *proper*: handsome 64 *hid under a bushel*: proverbial; see Matthew V.15
68 *fit*: answer 71 *wags*: merry fellows *wagtails*: wantons 77 *kind*: the adjective often carried bawdy implications *liberal*: again this could bear bawdy innuendo *lusty*: i.e. in the prime of youth 79 *resolve*: inform 80 *living*: referring both to his livelihood and to his estate 82 *nonsuited*: rejected
83 *nonperformance*: failure to fulfil promises 89 *pax*: pox 90 *hit of*: remember

HOST: I can assure you, sir, 'twas credibly reported to my mistress.

LUCRE: Why, do you think, i'faith, he was ever so simple to mortgage his lands to his uncle, or his uncle so unnatural to take the extremity of such a mortgage?

HOST: That was my saying still, sir.

LUCRE: Puh! Ne'er think it.

HOST: Yet that report goes current.

LUCRE: Nay, then you urge me; cannot I tell that best that am his uncle.

HOST: How, sir? What have I done!

LUCRE: Why, how now? In a swoon, man?

HOST: Is your worship his uncle, sir?

LUCRE: Can that be any harm to you, sir?

HOST: I do beseech you, sir, do me the favour to conceal it. What a beast was I to utter so much! Pray, sir, do me the kindness to keep it in; I shall have my coat pull'd o'er my ears an't should be known; for the truth is, an't please your worship, to prevent much rumour and many suitors, they intend to be married very suddenly and privately.

LUCRE: And dost thou think it stands with my judgment to do them injury? Must I needs say the knowledge of this marriage comes from thee? Am I a fool at fifty-four? Do I lack subtlety now, that have got all my wealth by it? There's a leash of angels for thee: come, let me woo thee. Speak; where lie they?

HOST: So I might have no anger, sir, –

LUCRE: Passion of me, not a jot. Prithee, come.

HOST: I would not have it known it came by my means.

LUCRE: Why, am I a man of wisdom?

HOST: I dare trust your worship, sir, but I'm a stranger to your house, and to avoid all intelligencers I desire your worship's ear.

LUCRE [*Aside.*]: This fellow's worth a matter of trust. [*To* HOST.] Come, sir. [HOST *whispers.*] Why now, thou'rt an honest lad. [*Aside.*] Ah, sirrah nephew!

HOST: Please you, sir, now I have begun with your worship, when shall I attend for your advice upon that doubtful point? I must come warily now.

LUCRE: Tut, fear thou nothing; tomorrow's evening shall resolve the doubt.

100 *my saying still*: i.e. that was what I was commonly told 103 *urge*: provoke 105 *swoon*: Q reads 'sowne' 110 *coat pull'd o'er my ears*: i.e. lose my livery and my job (or, be whipped) 116 *a leash of*: three *angels*: gold coins, worth 50 pence each 117 *where lie they?*: i.e. where are they staying? 123 *intelligencers*: spies 125 *sirrah*: a term of address, in this case expressing contempt 128 *that doubtful point*: i.e. the extent of Witgood's estate

HOST: The time shall cause my attendance.

Exit.

LUCRE: Fare thee well. – There's more true honesty in such a country serving-man than in a hundred of our cloak companions; I may well call 'em companions, for since blue coats have been turn'd into cloaks, we can scarce know the man from the master. – George!

[*Enter* GEORGE.]

GEORGE: Anon, sir.

LUCRE: List hither. [*Whispers.*] Keep the place secret. Commend me to my nephew; I know no cause, tell him, but he might see his uncle.

GEORGE: I will, sir.

LUCRE: And, do you hear, sir, take heed you use him with respect and duty.

GEORGE [*Aside.*]: Here's a strange alteration; one day he must be turn'd out like a beggar, and now he must be call'd in like a knight.

Exit.

LUCRE: Ah, sirrah, that rich widow! Four hundred a year! Beside, I hear she lays claim to a title of a hundred more. This falls unhappily that he should bear a grudge to me now, being likely to prove so rich. What is't, trow, that he makes me a stranger for? Hum, I hope he has not so much wit to apprehend that I cozened him; he deceives me then. Good heaven, who would have thought it would ever have come to this pass! Yet he's a proper gentleman, i'faith, give him his due. Marry, that's his mortgage, but that I ne'er mean to give him. I'll make him rich enough in words, if that be good; and if it come to a piece of money, I will not greatly stick for't: there may be hope some of the widow's lands too may one day fall upon me if things be carried wisely.

[*Enter* GEORGE.]

Now, sir, where is he?

GEORGE: He desires your worship to hold him excused; he has such weighty business it commands him wholly from all men.

LUCRE: Were those my nephew's words?

GEORGE: Yes, indeed, sir.

LUCRE [*Aside.*]: When men grow rich they grow proud too, I perceive that. He would not have sent me such an answer once within this twelvemonth; see what 'tis when a man's come to his lands. [*To* GEORGE.] Return to him again, sir; tell him his uncle desires his company for an hour; I'll trouble him but an hour, say; 'tis for his own good, tell him;

134 *cloak companions*: i.e. fashionable servants who treated their masters in a casual manner 135 *blue coats*: the traditional livery of servants, which went out of fashion early in the 17th century 137 *Anon*: straight away 138 *List hither*: i.e. listen over here 148 *trow*: do you suppose? 149 *he deceives me then*: i.e. I'll have misjudged him if he does 154 *stick for't*: grudge it

and, do you hear, sir, put 'worship' upon him. Go to, do as I bid you; he's like to be a gentleman of worship very shortly.

GEORGE [*Aside.*]: This is good sport, i'faith.

Exit.

LUCRE: Troth, he uses his uncle discourteously now. Can he tell what I may do for him? Goodness may come from me in a minute that comes not in seven year again. He knows my humour; I am not so usually good; 'tis no small thing that draws kindness from me; he may know that, and he will. The chief cause that invites me to do him most good is the sudden astonishing of old Hoard, my adversary. How pale his malice will look at my nephew's advancement! With what a dejected spirit he will behold his fortunes, whom but last day he proclaimed rioter, penurious makeshift, despised brothel-master! Ha, ha! 'Twill do me more secret joy than my last purchase, more precious comfort than all these widows' revenues.

Enter [GEORGE *and*] WITGOOD.

Now, sir.

GEORGE: With much entreaty he's at length come, sir.

[*Exit.*]

LUCRE: O nephew, let me salute you, sir; you're welcome, nephew.

WITGOOD: Uncle, I thank you.

LUCRE: Y'ave a fault, nephew; you're a stranger here. Well, heaven give you joy!

WITGOOD: Of what, sir?

LUCRE: Ha, we can hear. You might have known your uncle's house, i' faith, you and your widow; go to, you were too blame, if I may tell you so without offence.

WITGOOD: How could you hear of that, sir?

LUCRE: O pardon me! It was your will to have it kept from me, I perceive now.

WITGOOD: Not for any defect of love, I protest, uncle.

LUCRE: O 'twas unkindness, nephew. Fie, fie, fie!

WITGOOD: I am sorry you take it in that sense, sir.

LUCRE: Puh! You cannot colour it, i'faith, nephew.

WITGOOD: Will you but hear what I can say in my just excuse, sir?

LUCRE: Yes, faith, will I, and welcome.

WITGOOD: You that know my danger i'th'City, sir, so well, how great my debts are, and how extreme my creditors, could not out of your pure judgment, sir, have wish'd us hither.

LUCRE: Mass, a firm reason indeed.

169 *Troth*: truly, indeed 171 *humour*: disposition 173 *and*: if
174 *astonishing*: dismaying 188 *too blame*: i.e. blameworthy. In the 17th century, blame was often treated as an adjective 194 *unkindness*: unnaturalness/ingratitude

WITGOOD: Else my uncle's house, why, 't'ad been the only make-match.

LUCRE: Nay, and thy credit.

WITGOOD: My credit? Nay, my countenance! Push! Nay, I know, uncle, you would have wrought it so; by your wit you would have made her believe in time the whole house had been mine.

LUCRE: Ay, and most of the goods too.

WITGOOD: La, you there; well, let 'em all prate what they will, there's nothing like the bringing of a widow to one's uncle's house.

LUCRE: Nay, let nephews be ruled as they list, they shall find their uncle's house the most natural place when all's done.

WITGOOD: There they may be bold.

LUCRE: Life, they may do anything there, man, and fear neither beadle nor sum'ner. An uncle's house! A very Cole Harbour! Sirrah, I'll touch thee near now: hast thou so much interest in thy widow that by a token thou couldst presently send for her?

WITGOOD: Troth, I think I can, uncle.

LUCRE: Go to, let me see that.

WITGOOD: Pray, command one of your men hither, uncle.

LUCRE: George!

[*Enter* GEORGE.]

GEORGE: Here, sir.

LUCRE: Attend my nephew.

[WITGOOD *and* GEORGE *speak apart.*]

[*Aside.*] I love a' life to prattle with a rich widow; 'tis pretty, methinks, when our tongues go together, and then to promise much and perform little. I love that sport a' life, i'faith, yet I am in the mood now to do my nephew some good, if he take me handsomely.

[*Exit* GEORGE.]

What, have you dispatch'd?

WITGOOD: I ha' sent, sir.

LUCRE: Yet I must condemn you of unkindness, nephew.

WITGOOD: Heaven forbid, uncle!

LUCRE: Yes, faith, must I; say your debts be many, your creditors importunate, yet the kindness of a thing is all, nephew; you might have sent me close word on't, without the least danger or prejudice to your fortunes.

205 *countenance*: dignity/appearance of wealth 211 *list*: please 211–12 *uncle's house*: an 'uncle's house' was particularly appropriate for sexual assignations as 'aunts' (= bawds) could be found there 214 *beadle*: parish constable

215 *sum'ner*: a summoner was a minor official responsible for summoning people to court *Cole Harbour*: a slum area above London Bridge where debtors and criminals sought sanctuary, and hasty marriages were solemnized 216 *interest in*: claim upon 227 *take me handsomely*: i.e. properly appreciates me 234 *close*: secret

WITGOOD: Troth, I confess it, uncle, I was too blame there; but indeed my intent was to have clapp'd it up suddenly, and so have broke forth like a joy to my friends and a wonder to the world. Beside, there's a trifle of a forty-pound matter towards the setting of me forth; my friends should ne'er have known on't; I meant to make shift for that myself.

LUCRE: How, nephew! Let me not hear such a word again, I beseech you. Shall I be beholding to you?

WITGOOD: To me? Alas, what do you mean, uncle?

LUCRE: I charge you, upon my love: you trouble nobody but myself.

WITGOOD: Y'ave no reason for that, uncle.

LUCRE: Troth, I'll ne'er be friends with you while you live and you do.

WITGOOD: Nay, an you say so, uncle, here's my hand; I will not do't.

LUCRE: Why, well said! There's some hope in thee when thou wilt be ruled; I'll make it up fifty, faith, because I see thee so reclaimed. Peace, here comes my wife with Sam, her tother husband's son.

[*Enter* WIFE *and* SAM FREEDOM.]

WITGOOD: Good aunt –

SAM: Cousin Witgood! I rejoice in my salute; you're most welcome to this noble City, govern'd with the sword in the scabbard.

WITGOOD [*Aside.*]: And the wit in the pommel! [*To* SAM FREEDOM.] Good Master Sam Freedom, I return the salute.

LUCRE: By the mass, she's coming; wife, let me see now how thou wilt entertain her.

WIFE: I hope I am not to learn, sir, to entertain a widow; 'tis not so long ago since I was one myself.

[*Enter* COURTESAN.]

WITGOOD: Uncle –

LUCRE: She's come indeed.

WITGOOD: My uncle was desirous to see you, widow, and I presum'd to invite you.

COURTESAN: The presumption was nothing, Master Witgood; is this your uncle, sir?

LUCRE: Marry am I, sweet widow, and his good uncle he shall find me: ay, by this smack that I give thee, thou'rt welcome. [*Kisses her.*] Wife, bid the widow welcome the same way again.

SAM [*Aside.*]: I am a gentleman now too, by my father's occupation, and I see no reason but I may kiss a widow by my father's copy; truly, I think

237 ***clapp'd it up***: i.e. fixed it up, sewn it up 239 ***forty-pound matter***: i.e. his immediate debts, which he considerably underestimates 240 ***make shift for***: handle, deal with 250 ***tother***: other 253 ***with the sword in the scabbard***: i.e. peaceably 254 ***the wit in the pommel***: i.e. with as much wit as the knob on a sword's hilt 257 ***entertain***: receive as a guest 267 ***smack***: kiss 270 ***copy***: example/right

the charter is not against it; surely these are the words: 'The son, once a gentleman, may revel it, though his father were a dauber'; 'tis about the fifteenth page. I'll to her.

[*Attempts to kiss the* COURTESAN.]

LUCRE: Y'are not very busy now; a word with thee, sweet widow –

SAM [*Aside.*]: Coad's nigs! I was never so disgrac'd since the hour my mother whipp'd me!

LUCRE: Beside, I have no child of mine own to care for; she's my second wife, old, past bearing; clap sure to him, widow; he's like to be my heir, I can tell you.

COURTESAN: Is he so, sir?

LUCRE: He knows it already, and the knave's proud on't; jolly rich widows have been offer'd him here i'th'City, great merchants' wives, and do you think he would once look upon 'em? Forsooth, he'll none. You are beholding to him i' th' country then, ere we could be; nay, I'll hold a wager, widow, if he were once known to be in town, he would be presently sought after; nay, and happy were they that could catch him first.

COURTESAN: I think so.

LUCRE: O there would be such running to and fro, widow, he should not pass the streets for 'em; he'd be took up in one great house or other presently. Fah! They know he has it and must have it. You see this house here, widow? This house and all comes to him, goodly rooms ready furnish'd, ceil'd with plaster of Paris, and all hung about with cloth of Arras. Nephew!

WITGOOD: Sir?

LUCRE: Show the widow your house; carry her into all the rooms and bid her welcome. You shall see, widow. [*Aside.*] Nephew, strike all sure above an thou be'st a good boy, ah.

WITGOOD: Alas, sir, I know not how she would take it.

LUCRE: The right way, I warrant 'ee. A pox, art an ass? Would I were in thy stead. Get you up! I am asham'd of you.

[*Exeunt* WITGOOD *and* COURTESAN.]

[*Aside.*] So, let 'em agree as they will now; many a match has been struck up in my house a' this fashion: let 'em try all manner of ways, still there's nothing like an uncle's house to strike the stroke in. I'll hold my wife in

271 *the charter*: i.e. of a guild of craftsmen 272 *dauber*: plasterer 274 *Y'are not very busy now*: i.e. can you spare a moment? (But 'busy' also has a bawdy meaning) 275 *Coad's nigs!*: an obscure exclamation (God's nails?)
284 *beholding*: beholden, i.e. obliged 291 *it*: i.e. Lucre's wealth 293 *ceil'd*: ceilinged 293–4 *cloth of Arras*: tapestries 297 *strike all sure*: seal the match (but with a suggestion that seduction might 'do the trick')

talk a little. [*To her.*] Now, Ginny, your son there goes a-wooing to a poor gentlewoman but of a thousand portion; see my nephew, a lad of less hope, strikes at four hundred a year in good rubbish.

WIFE: Well, we must do as we may, sir.

LUCRE: I'll have his money ready told for him again he come down. Let me see too – by th'mass, I must present the widow with some jewel, a good piece of plate, or such a device; 'twill hearten her on well. I have a very fair standing cup, and a good high standing cup will please a widow above all other pieces.

Exit.

WIFE: Do you mock us with your nephew? I have a plot in my head, son; i' faith, husband, to cross you.

SAM: Is it a tragedy plot or a comedy plot, good mother?

WIFE: 'Tis a plot shall vex him. I charge you, of my blessing, son Sam, that you presently withdraw the action of your love from Master Hoard's niece.

SAM: How, mother?

WIFE: Nay, I have a plot in my head, i'faith. Here, take this chain of gold and this fair diamond; dog me the widow home to her lodging, and at thy best opportunity fasten 'em both upon her. Nay, I have a reach I can tell you. Thou art known what thou art, son, among the right worshipful, all the twelve companies.

SAM: Truly, I thank 'em for it.

WIFE: He? He's a scab to thee! And so certify her thou hast two hundred a year of thyself, beside thy good parts – a proper person and a lovely. If I were a widow I could find it in my heart to have thee myself, son, ay, from 'em all.

SAM: Thank you for your good will, mother, but indeed I had rather have a stranger; and if I woo her not in that violent fashion, that I will make her be glad to take these gifts ere I leave her, let me never be called the heir of your body.

WIFE: Nay, I know there's enough in you, son, if you once come to put it forth.

SAM: I'll quickly make a bolt or a shaft on't.

Exeunt.

306 *a thousand portion*: i.e. a dowry of a thousand pounds 307 *rubbish*: land 309 *told*: counted *again*: against, in readiness for the time when 311 *plate*: gold or silver plate 312 *standing cup*: cup with base and stem. Middleton often plays on their phallic appearance 322 *dog me*: follow 323 *reach*: plot 325 *twelve companies*: the twelve merchant guilds of London 327 *He*: i.e. Witgood 332 *violent*: vehement 337 *make a bolt or a shaft on't*: proverbial: use a thick or slender arrow; i.e. risk making something or other out of it

[SCENE 2]

Enter HOARD *and* MONEYLOVE.

MONEYLOVE: Faith, Master Hoard, I have bestowed many months in the suit of your niece, such was the dear love I ever bore to her virtues, but since she hath so extremely denied me, I am to lay out for my fortunes elsewhere.

HOARD: Heaven forbid but you should, sir; I ever told you my niece stood otherwise affected.

MONEYLOVE: I must confess you did, sir; yet in regard of my great loss of time and the zeal with which I sought your niece, shall I desire one favour of your worship?

HOARD: In regard of those two, 'tis hard, but you shall, sir.

MONEYLOVE: I shall rest grateful. 'Tis not full three hours, sir, since the happy rumour of a rich country widow came to my hearing.

HOARD: How? A rich country widow?

MONEYLOVE: Four hundred a year, landed.

HOARD: Yea?

MONEYLOVE: Most firm, sir, and I have learn'd her lodging; here my suit begins, sir: if I might but entreat your worship to be a countenance for me and speak a good word – for your words will pass – I nothing doubt but I might set fair for the widow; nor shall your labour, sir, end altogether in thanks, two hundred angels –

HOARD: So, so, what suitors has she?

MONEYLOVE: There lies the comfort, sir; the report of her is yet but a whisper, and only solicited by young riotous Witgood, nephew to your mortal adversary.

HOARD: Ha! Art certain he's her suitor?

MONEYLOVE: Most certain, sir, and his uncle very industrious to beguile the widow and make up the match.

HOARD: So! Very good.

MONEYLOVE: Now, sir, you know this young Witgood is a spendthrift, dissolute fellow.

HOARD: A very rascal.

MONEYLOVE: A midnight surfeiter.

HOARD: The spume of a brothel-house.

MONEYLOVE: True, sir! Which being well told in your worship's phrase

3 *extremely*: categorically, vehemently 5 *Heaven forbid but you should*: i.e. 'yes, you should give up' 6 *affected*: disposed 10 *'tis hard, but*: if it is at all possible 17 *be a countenance for*: support 34 *phrase*: style of speech

may both heave him out of her mind, and drive a fair way for me to the widow's affections.

HOARD: Attend me about five.

MONEYLOVE: With my best care, sir.

Exit.

HOARD: Fool, thou hast left thy treasure with a thief, to trust a widower with a suit in love! Happy revenge, I hug thee! I have not only the means laid before me extremely to cross my adversary and confound the last hopes of his nephew, but thereby to enrich my state, augment my revenues, and build mine own fortunes greater, ha, ha!
I'll mar your phrase, o'erturn your flatteries,
Undo your windings, policies, and plots,
Fall like a secret and dispatchful plague
On your secured comforts. Why, I am able
To buy three of Lucre, thrice outbid him,
Let my out-monies be reckon'd and all.

Enter three Creditors.

CREDITOR 1: I am glad of this news.

CREDITOR 2: So are we, by my faith.

CREDITOR 3: Young Witgood will be a gallant again now.

HOARD [*Aside.*]: Peace!

CREDITOR 1: I promise you, Master Cockpit, she's a mighty rich widow.

CREDITOR 2: Why, have you ever heard of her?

CREDITOR 1: Who? Widow Medler? She lies open to much rumour.

CREDITOR 3: Four hundred a year, they say, in very good land.

CREDITOR 1: Nay, tak't of my word, if you believe that, you believe the least.

CREDITOR 2: And to see how close he keeps it!

CREDITOR 1: O sir, there's policy in that, to prevent better suitors.

CREDITOR 3: He owes me a hundred pound, and I protest I ne'er look'd for a penny.

CREDITOR 1: He little dreams of our coming; he'll wonder to see his creditors upon him.

Exeunt [Creditors].

HOARD: Good, his creditors; I'll follow. This makes for me: all know the widow's wealth, and 'tis well known I can estate her fairly, ay, and will.
In this one chance shines a twice-happy fate;
I both deject my foe and raise my state.

Music. Exit.

44 *phrase*: praise 46 *dispatchful*: deadly 49 *out-monies*: non-liquid assets 56 *lies open to*: is a source of (with sexual innuendo, no doubt) 66 *makes for*: favours 69 *state*: estate/rank

ACT THREE

[SCENE I]

[*Enter*] WITGOOD *with his* Creditors.

WITGOOD: Why, alas, my creditors, could you find no other time to undo me but now? Rather your malice appears in this than the justness of the debt.

CREDITOR 1: Master Witgood, I have forborne my money long.

WITGOOD: I pray, speak low, sir; what do you mean?

CREDITOR 2: We hear you are to be married suddenly to a rich country widow.

WITGOOD: What can be kept so close but you creditors hear on't? Well, 'tis a lamentable state that our chiefest afflicters should first hear of our fortunes. Why, this is no good course, i'faith, sirs; if ever you have hope to be satisfied, why do you seek to confound the means that should work it? There's neither piety, no, nor policy in that. Shine favourably now, why, I may rise and spread again, to your great comforts.

CREDITOR 1: He says true, i'faith.

WITGOOD: Remove me now, and I consume for ever.

CREDITOR 2: Sweet gentleman!

WITGOOD: How can it thrive which from the sun you sever?

CREDITOR 3: It cannot indeed.

WITGOOD: O then, show patience! I shall have enough to satisfy you all.

CREDITOR 1: Ay, if we could be content, a shame take us.

WITGOOD: For, look you, I am but newly sure yet to the widow, and what a rend might this discredit make! Within these three days will I bind you lands for your securities.

CREDITOR 1: No, good Master Witgood; would 'twere as much as we dare trust you with.

WITGOOD: I know you have been kind; however, now either by wrong report or false incitement, your gentleness is injur'd; in such a state as this a man cannot want foes. If on the sudden he begin to rise, no man that lives can count his enemies. You had some intelligence, I warrant ye, from an ill-willer.

CREDITOR 2: Faith, we heard you brought up a rich widow, sir, and were suddenly to marry her.

12 *piety*: pity 15 *consume*: wither away 20 *content*: i.e. paid *a shame take us*: i.e. shame on us for having harassed you earlier 21 *sure*: betrothed

WITGOOD: Ay, why, there it was, I knew 'twas so: but since you are so well resolv'd of my faith towards you, let me be so much favour'd of you, I beseech you all –

ALL: O it shall not need, i'faith, sir, –

WITGOOD: As to lie still awhile and bury my debts in silence, till I be fully possess'd of the widow; for the truth is, I may tell you as my friends –

ALL: O, o, o –

WITGOOD: I am to raise a little money in the City towards the setting forth of myself, for mine own credit and your comfort. Now if my former debts should be divulg'd, all hope of my proceedings were quite extinguish'd.

CREDITOR 1 [*To* WITGOOD.]: Do you hear, sir? I may deserve your custom hereafter; pray, let my money be accepted before a stranger's. Here's forty pound I receiv'd as I came to you; if that may stand you in any stead, make use on't. Nay, pray, sir, 'tis at your service.

WITGOOD [*To* CREDITOR 1.]: You do so ravish me with kindness that I'm constrain'd to play the maid and take it!

CREDITOR 1 [*To* WITGOOD.]: Let none of them see it, I beseech you.

WITGOOD [*Aside.*]: Fah!

CREDITOR 1 [*To* WITGOOD.]: I hope I shall be first in your remembrance after the marriage rites.

WITGOOD [*To* CREDITOR 1.]: Believe it firmly.

CREDITOR 1: So. [*To* CREDITORS 2 *and* 3.] What, do you walk, sirs?

CREDITOR 2: I go. [*To* WITGOOD.] Take no care, sir, for money to furnish you; within this hour I'll send you sufficient. [*To* CREDITOR 3.] Come, Master Cockpit, we both stay for you.

CREDITOR 3: I ha' lost a ring, i'faith, I'll follow you presently.

[*Exeunt* Creditors 1 *and* 2.]

But you shall find it, sir; I know your youth and expenses have disfurnish'd you of all jewels; there's a ruby of twenty pound price, sir; bestow it upon your widow. What, man! 'Twill call up her blood to you; beside, if I might so much work with you, I would not have you beholding to those blood-suckers for any money.

WITGOOD: Not I, believe it.

CREDITOR 3: Th'are a brace of cut-throats.

WITGOOD: I know 'em.

CREDITOR 3: Send a note of all your wants to my shop, and I'll supply you instantly.

WITGOOD: Say you so? Why, here's my hand then; no man living shall do't but thyself.

CREDITOR 3: Shall I carry it away from 'em both then?

34 *resolv'd*: assured 48 *play the maid and take it*: proverbial: 'say "no", but accept the offer' 57 *stay*: wait 60 *disfurnish'd*: deprived 61 *blood*: sexual appetite 71 i.e. shall I win the day?

WITGOOD: I'faith, shalt thou!

CREDITOR 3: Troth, then, I thank you, sir.

WITGOOD: Welcome, good Master Cockpit.

Exit [Creditor 3].

Ha, ha, ha! Why, is not this better now than lying abed? I perceive there's nothing conjures up wit sooner than poverty, and nothing lays it down sooner than wealth and lechery. This has some savour yet. O that I had the mortgage from mine uncle as sure in possession as these trifles, I would forswear brothel at noonday and muscadine and eggs at midnight!

Enter COURTESAN.

COURTESAN: Master Witgood, where are you?

WITGOOD: Holla!

COURTESAN: Rich news!

WITGOOD: Would 'twere all in plate!

COURTESAN: There's some in chains and jewels. I am so haunted with suitors, Master Witgood, I know not which to dispatch first.

WITGOOD: You have the better Term, by my faith!

COURTESAN: Among the number, one Master Hoard, an ancient gentleman.

WITGOOD: Upon my life, my uncle's adversary!

COURTESAN: It may well hold so, for he rails on you,
Speaks shamefully of him.

WITGOOD: As I could wish it.

COURTESAN: I first denied him, but so cunningly
It rather promis'd him assured hopes
Than any loss of labour.

WITGOOD: Excellent.

COURTESAN: I expect him every hour, with gentlemen
With whom he labours to make good his words,
To approve you riotous, your state consum'd,
Your uncle –

WITGOOD: Wench, make up thy own fortunes now; do thyself a good turn once in thy days. He's rich in money, movables, and lands. Marry him, he's an old doting fool, and that's worth all; marry him, 'twould be a great comfort to me to see thee do well, i'faith. Marry him, 'twould ease my conscience well to see thee well bestow'd; I have a care of thee, i' faith.

79 *muscadine*: a wine which, taken with eggs, was a supposed aphrodisiac
86 *dispatch*: get rid of 87 *Term*: the period when the law courts sat saw many 'suitors' visiting London and provided profitable business for the prostitutes
98 *approve*: prove 101 *movables*: personal possessions

COURTESAN: Thanks, sweet Master Witgood.

WITGOOD: I reach at farder happiness: first, I am sure it can be no harm to thee, and there may happen goodness to me by it. Prosecute it well: let's send up for our wits, now we require their best and most pregnant assistance.

COURTESAN: Step in. I think I hear 'em.

Exit [*with* WITGOOD].

Enter HOARD *and* Gentlemen, *with the* HOST [*as*] *serving-man.*

HOARD: Art thou the widow's man? By my faith, sh'as a company of proper men then.

HOST: I am the worst of six, sir, good enough for blue-coats.

HOARD: Hark hither: I hear say thou art in most credit with her.

HOST: Not so, sir.

HOARD: Come, come, thou'rt modest. There's a brace of royals; prithee, help me to th'speech of her.

HOST: I'll do what I may, sir, always saving myself harmless.

HOARD: Go to, do't, I say; thou shalt hear better from me.

HOST [*Aside.*]: Is not this a better place than five mark a year standing wages? Say a man had but three such clients in a day, methinks he might make a poor living on't; beside, I was never brought up with so little honesty to refuse any man's money: never. What gulls there are a' this side the world! Now know I the widow's mind, none but my young master comes in her clutches. Ha, ha, ha!

Exit.

HOARD: Now, my dear gentlemen, stand firmly to me. You know his follies and my worth.

GENTLEMAN 1: We do, sir.

GENTLEMAN 2: But, Master Hoard, are you sure he is not i'th'house now?

HOARD: Upon my honesty, I chose this time
A' purpose, fit; the spendthrift is abroad.
Assist me; here she comes.
[*Enter* COURTESAN.]
Now, my sweet widow.

107 *farder*: farther 108 *Prosecute*: perform 109 *pregnant*: resourceful s.d. *Gentlemen*: Lamprey and Spitchcock? 117 *a brace of royals*: a pair of gold coins, worth about 75 pence 118 *to th' speech of*: i.e. to speak with 119 *saving myself harmless*: i.e. providing I don't get into trouble 121 *mark*: a sum equivalent to two thirds of £1, although it did not exist as a coin *standing*: fixed 123 *poor*: used ironically – three clients at the rate of a brace of royals each a day would have brought in a fabulous sum of money 124 *gulls*: dupes 124–6 *What . . . clutches*: in fact the Host has been tricked by the Widow and Witgood 127 *his*: i.e. Witgood's

COURTESAN: Y'are welcome, Master Hoard.
HOARD: Dispatch, sweet gentlemen, dispatch.
I am come, widow, to prove those my words
Neither of envy sprung nor of false tongues,
But such as their deserts and actions
Do merit and bring forth; all which these gentlemen,
Well known and better reputed, will confess.
COURTESAN: I cannot tell
How my affections may dispose of me,
But surely if they find him so desertless
They'll have that reason to withdraw themselves.
And therefore, gentlemen, I do entreat you,
As you are fair in reputation
And in appearing form, so shine in truth.
I am a widow, and, alas, you know
Soon overthrown; 'tis a very small thing
That we withstand, our weakness is so great.
Be partial unto neither, but deliver,
Without affection, your opinion.
HOARD: And that will drive it home.
COURTESAN: Nay, I beseech your silence, Master Hoard;
You are a party.
HOARD: Widow, not a word!
GENTLEMAN I: The better first to work you to belief,
Know neither of us owe him flattery,
Nor tother malice, but unbribed censure,
So help us our best fortunes.
COURTESAN: It suffices.
GENTLEMAN I: That Witgood is a riotous, undone man,
Imperfect both in fame and in estate,
His debts wealthier than he, and executions
In wait for his due body, we'll maintain
With our best credit and our dearest blood.
COURTESAN: Nor land nor living, say you? Pray, take heed you do not wrong the gentleman.
GENTLEMAN I: What we speak
Our lives and means are ready to make good.

136 *Dispatch*: quick! 138 *envy*: enmity 139 *their*: i.e. Witgood and Lucre's 150–1 *'tis a very small thing That we withstand*: i.e. we can withstand only very little (with bawdy innuendo) 153 *Without affection*: impartially 156 *a party*: an interested party 158 *him*: i.e. Hoard 159 *tother*: i.e. Witgood *censure*: judgement 163 *executions*: warrants 164 *due body*: i.e. not only are his goods to be forfeit but he will be imprisoned for debt

COURTESAN: Alas, how soon are we poor souls beguil'd!
GENTLEMAN 2: And for his uncle –
HOARD: Let that come to me.
His uncle, a severe extortioner,
A tyrant at a forfeiture, greedy of others'
Miseries, one that would undo his brother,
Nay, swallow up his father if he can,
Within the fathoms of his conscience.
GENTLEMAN 1: Nay, believe it, widow,
You had not only match'd yourself to wants,
But in an evil and unnatural stock.
HOARD [*To* Gentlemen.]: Follow hard, gentlemen, follow hard!
COURTESAN: Is my love so deceiv'd? Before you all
I do renounce him; on my knees I vow
He ne'er shall marry me.
[WITGOOD *enters apart.*]
WITGOOD [*Aside.*]: Heaven knows he never meant it!
HOARD [*To* Gentlemen.]: There, take her at the bound.
GENTLEMAN 1: Then, with a new and pure affection,
Behold yon gentleman, grave, kind, and rich,
A match worthy yourself; esteeming him,
You do regard your state.
HOARD [*To* GENTLEMAN 1.]: I'll make her a jointure, say.
GENTLEMAN 1: He can join land to land and will possess you of what you can desire.
GENTLEMAN 2: Come, widow, come.
COURTESAN: The world is so deceitful.
GENTLEMAN 1: There, 'tis deceitful,
Where flattery, want, and imperfection lies.
But none of these in him. Push!
COURTESAN: Pray, sir, –
GENTLEMAN 1: Come, you widows are ever most backward when you should do yourselves most good; but were it to marry a chin not worth a hair now, then you would be forward enough. [*Joins their hands.*] Come, clap hands, a match!
HOARD: With all my heart, widow. Thanks, gentlemen;
I will deserve your labour, and thy love.

180 *Follow hard*: i.e. pursue her hotly 185 *at the bound*: at once (completing the hunting metaphor) 189 *regard*: take care of 190 *jointure*: an agreement whereby husband and wife hold property jointly and, on the death of the husband, the widow enjoys the sole estate, at least during her life 191 *possess you of*: endow you with 194 *There*: i.e. Witgood 196 *him*: i.e. Hoard 198–9 *chin not worth a hair*: i.e. youth (without wealth) 199 *forward*: eager/wanton 202 *deserve*: requite/be worthy of

COURTESAN: Alas, you love not widows but for wealth.
I promise you I ha' nothing, sir.

HOARD: Well said, widow, well said; thy love is all I seek, before these gentlemen.

COURTESAN: Now I must hope the best.

HOARD: My joys are such they want to be express'd.

COURTESAN: But, Master Hoard, one thing I must remember you of before these gentlemen, your friends: how shall I suddenly avoid the loathed soliciting of that perjur'd Witgood and his tedious, dissembling uncle, who this very, very day hath appointed a meeting for the same purpose too, where, had not truth come forth, I had been undone, utterly undone?

HOARD: What think you of that, gentlemen?

GENTLEMAN 1: 'Twas well devis'd.

HOARD: Hark thee, widow: train out young Witgood single; hasten him thither with thee, somewhat before the hour, where, at the place appointed, these gentlemen and myself will wait the opportunity, when by some sleight, removing him from thee, we'll suddenly enter and surprise thee, carry thee away by boat to Cole Harbour, have a priest ready, and there clap it up instantly. How lik'st it, widow?

COURTESAN: In that it pleaseth you, it likes me well.

HOARD: I'll kiss thee for those words. Come, gentlemen;
Still must I live a suitor to your favours,
Still to your aid beholding.

GENTLEMAN 1: We're engag'd, sir;
'Tis for our credits now to see't well ended.

HOARD: 'Tis for your honours, gentlemen; nay, look to't:
Not only in joy, but I in wealth excel.
No more sweet widow, but sweet wife, farewell.

COURTESAN: Farewell, sir.

Exeunt [HOARD *and* Gentlemen].

Enter WITGOOD.

WITGOOD: O for more scope! I could laugh eternally. Give you joy, Mistress Hoard! I promise your fortune was good, forsooth; y'ave fell upon wealth enough, and there's young gentlemen enow can help you to the rest. Now it requires our wits; carry thyself but heedfully now, and we are both –

[*Enter* HOST.]

HOST: Master Witgood, your uncle –

208 *want*: need 209 *remember you*: remind you 210 *suddenly*: shortly
212–13 *same purpose*: i.e. marriage 217 *train out*: entice, decoy *single*: alone
222 *clap it up*: i.e. get married 226 *engag'd*: in a pact together 234 *enow*: enough

WITGOOD: Cuds me! [*To* COURTESAN.] Remove thyself awhile; I'll serve for him.

[*Exeunt* COURTESAN *and* HOST.]

Enter LUCRE.

LUCRE: Nephew, good morrow, nephew.

WITGOOD: The same to you, kind uncle.

LUCRE: How fares the widow? Does the meeting hold?

WITGOOD: O no question of that, sir.

LUCRE: I'll strike the stroke, then, for thee; no more days.

WITGOOD: The sooner the better, uncle. O she's mightily followed.

LUCRE: And yet so little rumour'd.

WITGOOD: Mightily! Here comes one old gentleman, and he'll make her a jointure of three hundred a year, forsooth; another wealthy suitor will estate his son in his lifetime and make him weigh down the widow; here's a merchant's son will possess her with no less than three goodly lordships at once, which were all pawns to his father.

LUCRE: Peace, nephew, let me hear no more of 'em; it mads me. Thou shalt prevent 'em all. No words to the widow of my coming hither. Let me see, 'tis now upon nine; before twelve, nephew, we will have the bargain struck, we will, faith, boy.

WITGOOD: O, my precious uncle!

Exit [*with* LUCRE].

[SCENE 2]

Enter HOARD *and his* NIECE.

HOARD: Niece, sweet niece, prithee have a care to my house; I leave all to thy discretion. Be content to dream awhile; I'll have a husband for thee shortly; put that care upon me, wench, for in choosing wives and husbands I am only fortunate: I have that gift given me.

Exit.

NIECE: But 'tis not likely you should choose for me,
Since nephew to your chiefest enemy
Is he whom I affect; but, o forgetful,
Why dost thou flatter thy affections so,
With name of him that for a widow's bed

238–9 *serve for*: i.e. look after 244 *days*: i.e. postponements 249 *weigh down*: outweigh in wealth as in a pair of scales (but with sexual innuendo as in 'jointure' (190) and 'possess' (191)) 251 *lordships*: estates 253 *prevent*: forestall
7 *affect*: love

Neglects thy purer love? Can it be so,
Or does report dissemble?
[*Enter* GEORGE.]
How now, sir?

GEORGE: A letter, with which came a private charge.

NIECE: Therein I thank your care.
[*Exit* GEORGE.]
I know this hand.

Reads.

'Dearer than sight, what the world reports of me, yet believe not; rumour will alter shortly. Be thou constant; I am still the same that I was in love, and I hope to be the same in fortunes.
Theodorus Witgood.'

I am resolv'd; no more shall fear or doubt
Raise their pale powers to keep affection out.
Exit.

[SCENE 3]

Enter, with a Drawer, HOARD *and two* Gentlemen.

DRAWER: You're very welcome, gentlemen. Dick, show these gentlemen the Pom'granate there.

HOARD: Hist!

DRAWER: Up those stairs, gentlemen.

HOARD: Pist! Drawer –

DRAWER: Anon, sir.

HOARD: Prithee, ask at the bar if a gentlewoman came not in lately.

DRAWER: William, at the bar, did you see any gentlewoman come in lately? Speak you ay, speak you no?

WILLIAM [*Within.*]: No, none came in yet but Mistress Florence.

DRAWER: He says none came in yet, sir, but one Mistress Florence.

HOARD: What is that Florence? A widow?

DRAWER: Yes, a Dutch widow.

HOARD: How!

DRAWER: That's an English drab, sir; give your worship good morrow.
[*Exit.*]

12 *a private charge*: an injunction to deliver the letter privately 18 *resolv'd*: decided s.d. *Drawer*: a tapster at a tavern *two Gentlemen*: again, probably Spitchcock and Lamprey 2 *Pom'granate*: it was normal to assign rooms names rather than numbers 13 *Dutch widow*: slang for whore

HOARD: A merry knave, i'faith! I shall remember 'a Dutch widow' the longest day of my life.

GENTLEMAN 1: Did not I use most art to win the widow?

GENTLEMAN 2: You shall pardon me for that, sir; Master Hoard knows I took her at best 'vantage.

HOARD: What's that, sweet gentlemen, what's that?

GENTLEMAN 2: He will needs bear me down that his art only wrought with the widow most.

HOARD: O you did both well, gentlemen, you did both well, I thank you.

GENTLEMAN 1: I was the first that mov'd her.

HOARD: You were, i'faith.

GENTLEMAN 2: But it was I that took her at the bound.

HOARD: Ay, that was you; faith, gentlemen, 'tis right.

GENTLEMAN 1: I boasted least, but 'twas I join'd their hands.

HOARD: By th' mass, I think he did. You did all well, gentlemen, you did all well. Contend no more.

GENTLEMAN 1: Come, yon room's fittest.

HOARD: True, 'tis next the door.

Exit [with Gentlemen.]

Enter WITGOOD, COURTESAN, [Drawer,] *and* HOST.

DRAWER: You're very welcome; please you to walk upstairs; cloth's laid, sir.

COURTESAN: Upstairs? Troth, I am weary, Master Witgood.

WITGOOD: Rest yourself here awhile, widow; we'll have a cup of muscadine in this little room.

DRAWER: A cup of muscadine? You shall have the best, sir.

WITGOOD: But, do you hear, sirrah?

DRAWER: Do you call? Anon, sir.

WITGOOD: What is there provided for dinner?

DRAWER: I cannot readily tell you, sir; if you please, you may go into the kitchen and see yourself, sir; many gentlemen of worship do use to do it, I assure you, sir.

[*Exit.*]

HOST: A pretty familiar, priggin' rascal, he has his part without book.

WITGOOD: Against you are ready to drink to me, widow, I'll be present to pledge you.

COURTESAN: Nay, I commend your care; 'tis done well of you.

[*Exit* WITGOOD.]

'Las, what have I forgot!

31 *'tis next the door*: and therefore convenient to make their escape 44 *familiar*: over-familiar, saucy *priggin'*: crooked *without book*: by heart 45 *Against*: by the time 48 *'Las*: Alas (Q reads 'asse')

HOST: What, mistress?

COURTESAN: I slipp'd my wedding ring off when I wash'd and left it at my lodging; prithee, run, I shall be sad without it.

[*Exit* HOST.]

So, he's gone. Boy!

[*Enter* Boy.]

BOY: Anon, forsooth.

COURTESAN: Come hither, sirrah: learn secretly if one Master Hoard, an ancient gentleman, be about house.

BOY: I heard such a one nam'd.

COURTESAN: Commend me to him.

Enter HOARD *with* Gentlemen.

HOARD: I'll do thy commendations.

COURTESAN: O you come well. Away! To boat! Begone!

HOARD: Thus wise men are reveng'd, give two for one.

Exeunt.

Enter WITGOOD *and* Vintner.

WITGOOD: I must request you, sir, to show extraordinary care; my uncle comes with gentlemen, his friends, and 'tis upon a making.

VINTNER: Is it so? I'll give a special charge, good Master Witgood. May I be bold to see her?

WITGOOD: Who, the widow? With all my heart, i'faith. I'll bring you to her!

VINTNER: If she be a Staffordshire gentlewoman, 'tis much if I know her not.

WITGOOD: How now? Boy! Drawer!

VINTNER: Hie!

[*Enter* Boy.]

BOY: Do you call, sir?

WITGOOD: Went the gentlewoman up that was here?

BOY: Up, sir? She went out, sir.

WITGOOD: Out, sir?

BOY: Out, sir. One Master Hoard, with a guard of gentlemen, carried her out at back door a pretty while since, sir.

[*Exit* Boy.]

WITGOOD: Hoard? Death and darkness, Hoard?

Enter HOST.

HOST: The devil of ring I can find!

WITGOOD: How now, what news? Where's the widow?

HOST: My mistress? Is she not here, sir?

62 *making*: matchmaking 67 *'tis much if*: i.e. I'd be surprised if 78 i.e. I'll be damned if I can find a ring

WITGOOD: More madness yet!
HOST: She sent me for a ring.
WITGOOD: A plot, a plot! To boat! She's stole away!
HOST: What?
Enter LUCRE *with* Gentlemen.
WITGOOD: Follow! Enquire, old Hoard, my uncle's adversary –
[*Exit* HOST.]
LUCRE: Nephew, what's that?
WITGOOD: Thrice-miserable wretch!
LUCRE: Why, what's the matter?
VINTNER: The widow's borne away, sir.
LUCRE: Ha! Passion of me! A heavy welcome, gentlemen.
GENTLEMAN I: The widow gone?
LUCRE: Who durst attempt it?
WITGOOD: Who but old Hoard, my uncle's adversary!
LUCRE: How!
WITGOOD: With his confederates.
LUCRE: Hoard, my deadly enemy! Gentlemen, stand to me.
I will not bear it. 'Tis in hate of me;
That villain seeks my shame, nay, thirsts my blood;
He owes me mortal malice.
I'll spend my wealth on this despiteful plot,
Ere he shall cross me and my nephew thus.
WITGOOD: So maliciously!
Enter HOST.
LUCRE: How now, you treacherous rascal?
HOST: That's none of my name, sir.
WITGOOD: Poor soul, he knew not on't.
LUCRE: I'm sorry. I see then 'twas a mere plot.
HOST: I trac'd 'em nearly –
LUCRE: Well?
HOST: And hear for certain they have took Cole Harbour.
LUCRE: The devil's sanctuary!
They shall not rest. I'll pluck her from his arms.
Kind and dear gentlemen,
If ever I had seat within your breasts –
GENTLEMAN I: No more, good sir. It is a wrong to us
To see you injur'd; in a cause so just

96 *stand to me*: i.e. stand by me 100 *on*: i.e. on frustrating *despiteful*: cruel, malignant 106 *mere*: i.e. performed without the help of anyone else 107 *nearly*: closely 109 *took*: gained refuge in

We'll spend our lives, but we will right our friends.
LUCRE: Honest and kind! Come, we have delay'd too long:
Nephew, take comfort; a just cause is strong.
WITGOOD: That's all my comfort, uncle.
Exeunt [LUCRE, Gentlemen *and* HOST].
Ha, ha, ha!
Now may events fall luckily and well;
He that ne'er strives, says wit, shall ne'er excel.
Exit.

[SCENE 4]

Enter DAMPIT, *the usurer, drunk.*

DAMPIT: When did I say my prayers? In anno '88, when the great armada was coming; and in anno '99, when the great thund'ring and lightning was, I pray'd heartily then, i'faith, to overthrow Poovies' new buildings; I kneel'd by my great iron chest, I remember.

[*Enter* AUDREY.]

AUDREY: Master Dampit, one may hear you before they see you. You keep sweet hours, Master Dampit; we were all abed three hours ago.

DAMPIT: Audrey?

AUDREY: O y'are a fine gentleman.

DAMPIT: So I am, i'faith, and a fine scholar. Do you use to go to bed so early, Audrey?

AUDREY: Call you this early, Master Dampit?

DAMPIT: Why, is't not one of clock i'th'morning? Is not that early enough? Fetch me a glass of fresh beer.

AUDREY: Here, I have warm'd your nightcap for you, Master Dampit.

DAMPIT: Draw it on then. I am very weak truly; I have not eaten so much as the bulk of an egg these three days.

AUDREY: You have drunk the more, Master Dampit.

DAMPIT: What's that?

AUDREY: You mought and you would, Master Dampit.

DAMPIT: I answer you, I cannot. Hold your prating; you prate too much and understand too little. Are you answered? Give me a glass of beer.

2 *'99*: no great storms are recorded in this year but it seems unnecessary to amend the date as the point is that Dampit's prayers are at best irregular   3 *Poovies'*: probably business rivals of Dampit. The buildings cannot be identified with certainty though it is on record that in 1607 a William Povey was forced to dismantle a wooden building in St Paul's Churchyard which contravened building regulations   19 *mought*: might   *and*: if

AUDREY: May I ask you how you do, Master Dampit?

DAMPIT: How do I? I'faith, naught.

AUDREY: I ne'er knew you do otherwise.

DAMPIT: I eat not one penn'ort' of bread these two years. Give me a glass of fresh beer, I am not sick, nor I am not well.

AUDREY: Take this warm napkin about your neck, sir, whilst I help you make you unready.

DAMPIT: How now, Audrey-prater, with your scurvy devices, what say you now?

AUDREY: What say I, Master Dampit? I say nothing but that you are very weak.

DAMPIT: Faith, thou hast more cony-catching devices than all London!

AUDREY: Why, Master Dampit, I never deceiv'd you in all my life!

DAMPIT: Why was that? Because I never did trust thee.

AUDREY: I care not what you say, Master Dampit.

DAMPIT: Hold thy prating. I answer thee, thou art a beggar, a quean, and a bawd. Are you answer'd?

AUDREY: Fie, Master Dampit! A gentleman, and have such words!

DAMPIT: Why, thou base drudge of infortunity, thou kitchen-stuff drab of beggary, roguery, and coxcombry, thou cavernesed quean of foolery, knavery, and bawdreaminy, I'll tell thee what, I will not give a louse for thy fortunes.

AUDREY: No, Master Dampit? And there's a gentleman comes a-wooing to me, and he doubts nothing but that you will get me from him.

DAMPIT: I? If I would either have thee or lie with thee for two thousand pound, would I might be damn'd! Why, thou base, impudent quean of foolery, flattery, and coxcombry, are you answer'd?

AUDREY: Come, will you rise and go to bed, sir?

DAMPIT: Rise, and go to bed too, Audrey? How does Mistress Proserpine?

AUDREY: Fooh!

DAMPIT: She's as fine a philosopher of a stinkard's wife as any within the liberties. – Fah, fah, Audrey!

28 *make you unready*: i.e. undress yourself 33 *cony-catching devices*: cheating tricks 37 *quean*: whore 40 *infortunity*: misfortune *kitchen-stuff*: kitchen refuse 41 *coxcombry*: foolery *cavernesed*: a coined word presumably meaning 'cavernous' 42 *bawdreaminy*: another coinage indicating bawdry or licentiousness 45 *doubts*: fears 50 *Mistress Proserpine*: Dampit is incoherently drunk and probably referring to a prostitute whom he associates with the Greek goddess who spent half the year in the underworld as the consort of Pluto and the remainder on earth. However, Dampit may be addressing Audrey 53 *liberties*: the suburbs outside the jurisdiction of the civic authorities, where prostitution, gambling, etc. flourished

AUDREY: How now, Master Dampit?

DAMPIT: Fie upon't, what a choice of stinks here is! What hast thou done, Audrey? Fie upon't, here's a choice of stinks indeed! Give me a glass of fresh beer and then I will to bed.

AUDREY: It waits for you above, sir.

DAMPIT: Foh, I think they burn horns in Barnard's Inn; if ever I smell'd such an abominable stink, usury forsake me.

[*Exit.*]

AUDREY: They be the stinking nails of his trampling feet, and he talks of burning of horns.

Exit.

59 ***horns***: ink-horns (?) ***Barnard's Inn***: one of the Inns of Court

ACT FOUR

[SCENE I]

Enter at Cole Harbour, HOARD, *the* WIDOW, *and Gentlemen* [*including* LAMPREY *and* SPITCHCOCK], *he married now.*

GENTLEMAN I: Join hearts, join hands,
In wedlock's bands,
Never to part,
Till death cleave your heart;
[*To* HOARD.] You shall forsake all other women;
[*To* COURTESAN.] You, lords, knights, gentlemen, and yeomen.
What my tongue slips
Make up with your lips.

HOARD: Give you joy, Mistress Hoard; let the kiss come about.
[*Knocking.*]
Who knocks? Convey my little pig-eater out.

LUCRE [*Within.*]: Hoard!

HOARD: Upon my life, my adversary, gentlemen!

LUCRE [*Within.*]: Hoard, open the door or we will force it ope.
Give us the widow.

HOARD: Gentlemen, keep 'em out.

LAMPREY: He comes upon his death that enters here.

LUCRE [*Within.*]: My friends, assist me.

HOARD: He has assistants, gentlemen.

LAMPREY: Tut! Nor him nor them, we in this action fear.

LUCRE [*Within.*]: Shall I in peace speak one word with the widow?

COURTESAN: Husband and gentlemen, hear me but a word.

HOARD: Freely, sweet wife.

COURTESAN: Let him in peaceably; you know we're sure from any act of his.

HOARD: Most true.

COURTESAN: You may stand by and smile at his old weakness; let me alone to answer him.

s.d. *he*: i.e. Hoard 2 *bands*: binding promises 7 *slips*: omits 9 *come about*: circulate 10 *pig-eater*: term of endearment 23 *sure*: safe

HOARD: Content. 'Twill be good mirth, i'faith; how think you, gentlemen?

LAMPREY: Good gullery!

HOARD: Upon calm conditions, let him in.

LUCRE [*Within.*]: All spite and malice –

LAMPREY: Hear me, Master Lucre:
So you will vow a peaceful entrance
With those your friends, and only exercise
Calm conference with the widow, without fury,
The passage shall receive you.

LUCRE [*Within.*]: I do vow it.

LAMPREY: Then enter and talk freely; here she stands.

Enter LUCRE [, Gentlemen *and* HOST].

LUCRE: O Master Hoard, your spite has watch'd the hour. You're excellent at vengeance, Master Hoard.

HOARD: Ha, ha, ha!

LUCRE: I am the fool you laugh at.
You are wise, sir, and know the seasons. Well,
Come hither, widow.
[*They speak apart.*]
Why, is it thus?
O you have done me infinite disgrace
And your own credit no small injury.
Suffer mine enemy so despitefully
To bear you from my nephew! O I had
Rather half my substance had been forfeit
And begg'd by some starv'd rascal!

COURTESAN: Why, what would you wish me do, sir?
I must not overthrow my state for love,
We have too many precedents for that.
From thousands of our wealthy undone widows
One may derive some wit. I do confess
I lov'd your nephew; nay, I did affect him
Against the mind and liking of my friends,
Believ'd his promises, lay here in hope
Of flatter'd living and the boast of lands:
Coming to touch his wealth and state indeed,
It appears dross. I find him not the man;
Imperfect, mean, scarce furnish'd of his needs;
In words, fair lordships; in performance, hovels:

30 *gullery*: gulling, i.e. trickery 33 *So*: so long as 38 *watch'd the hour*: awaited its opportunity 55 *affect*: love 56 *friends*: Q reads 'friend' 58 *flatter'd*: i.e. flatteringly portrayed 59 *touch*: test

Can any woman love the thing that is not?
LUCRE: Broke you for this?
COURTESAN: Was it not cause too much?
Send to inquire his state. Most part of it
Lay two years mortgag'd in his uncle's hands.
LUCRE: Why, say it did. You might have known my mind;
I could have soon restor'd it.
COURTESAN: Ay, had I but seen any such thing perform'd, why, 'twould have tied my affection and contain'd me in my first desires: do you think, i'faith, that I could twine such a dry oak as this, had promise in your nephew took effect?
LUCRE: Why, and there's no time pass'd, and rather than
My adversary should thus thwart my hopes,
I would –
COURTESAN: Tut, y'ave been ever full of golden speech.
If words were lands, your nephew would be rich.
LUCRE: Widow, believe it, I vow by my best bliss,
Before these gentlemen, I will give in
The mortgage to my nephew instantly,
Before I sleep or eat.
GENTLEMAN 2: We'll pawn our credits, widow, what he speaks shall be perform'd in fullness.
LUCRE: Nay, more. I will estate him
In farder blessings: he shall be my heir.
I have no son.
I'll bind myself to that condition.
COURTESAN: When I shall hear this done I shall soon yield to reasonable terms.
LUCRE: In the mean season,
Will you protest, before these gentlemen,
To keep yourself as you are now at this present?
COURTESAN: I do protest, before these gentlemen,
I will be as clear then as I am now.
LUCRE: I do believe you. Here's your own honest servant;
I'll take him along with me.
COURTESAN: Ay, with all my heart.
LUCRE: He shall see all perform'd, and bring you word.
COURTESAN: That's all I wait for.
HOARD: What, have you finish'd, Master Lucre? Ha, ha, ha, ha!

82 this Gentleman is one of those accompanying Lucre 92 Lucre does not know that the wedding ceremony has already taken place and therefore wishes her to stay single, and also in the same state of mind (i.e. to marry Witgood)
94 *clear*: unencumbered

LUCRE: So, laugh, Hoard, laugh at your poor enemy, do;
The wind may turn; you may be laugh'd at too.
Yes, marry, may you, sir. Ha, ha, ha!
Exeunt [LUCRE, Gentlemen, *and* HOST].
HOARD: Ha, ha, ha! If every man that swells in malice
Could be reveng'd as happily as I,
He would choose hate and forswear amity.
What did he say, wife, prithee?
COURTESAN: Faith, spoke to ease his mind.
HOARD: O, o, o!
COURTESAN: You know now, little to any purpose.
HOARD: True, true, true.
COURTESAN: He would do mountains now.
HOARD: Ay, ay, ay, ay.
LAMPREY: Y'ave struck him dead, Master Hoard.
SPITCHCOCK: Ay, and his nephew desperate.
HOARD: I know't, sirs, ay.
Never did man so crush his enemy.
Exeunt.

[SCENE 2]

Enter LUCRE *with* Gentlemen [*and* HOST], *meeting* SAM FREEDOM.

LUCRE: My son-in-law, Sam Freedom, where's my nephew?
SAM: O man in lamentation, father!
LUCRE: How!
SAM: He thumps his breast like a gallant dicer that has lost his doublet, and stands in's shirt to do penance.
LUCRE: Alas, poor gentleman.
SAM: I warrant you may hear him sigh in a still evening to your house at Highgate.
LUCRE: I prithee, send him in.
SAM: Were it to do a greater matter, I will not stick with you, sir, in regard you married my mother.
[*Exit.*]
LUCRE: Sweet gentlemen, cheer him up; I will but fetch the mortgage and return to you instantly.
Exit.

111 *do mountains*: i.e. do anything to win back the widow 1 *son-in-law*: stepson 2 *O man in lamentation*: possibly alluding to an old ballad, 'O man in desperation' 4 *doublet*: a close-fitting body garment with or without sleeves 10 *stick*: haggle

GENTLEMAN 1: We'll do our best, sir. See where he comes,
E'en joyless and regardless of all form.
[*Enter* WITGOOD.]

GENTLEMAN 2: Why, how, Master Witgood? Fie, you a firm scholar and an understanding gentleman, and give your best parts to passion?

GENTLEMAN 1: Come, fie!

WITGOOD: O gentlemen, –

GENTLEMAN 1: Sorrow of me, what a sigh was there, sir! Nine such widows are not worth it.

WITGOOD: To be borne from me by that lecher, Hoard!

GENTLEMAN 1: That vengeance is your uncle's, being done
More in despite to him than wrong to you,
But we bring comfort now.

WITGOOD: I beseech you, gentlemen, –

GENTLEMAN 2: Cheer thyself, man; there's hope of her, i'faith.

WITGOOD: Too gladsome to be true.

Enter LUCRE.

LUCRE: Nephew, what cheer? Alas, poor gentleman, how art thou chang'd! Call thy fresh blood into thy cheeks again: she comes –

WITGOOD: Nothing afflicts me so much
But that it is your adversary, uncle,
And merely plotted in despite of you.

LUCRE: Ay, that's it mads me, spites me! I'll spend my wealth ere he shall carry her so, because I know 'tis only to spite me. Ay, this is it. Here, nephew, before these kind gentlemen, I deliver in your mortgage, my promise to the widow. [*Gives a paper.*] See, 'tis done. Be wise, you're once more master of your own; the widow shall perceive now you are not altogether such a beggar as the world reputes you: you can make shift to bring her to three hundred a year, sir.

GENTLEMAN 1: Berlady, and that's no toy, sir.

LUCRE: A word, nephew.

GENTLEMAN 1 [*To* HOST.]: Now you may certify the widow.

LUCRE: You must conceive it aright, nephew, now; to do you good, I am content to do this.

WITGOOD: I know it, sir.

LUCRE: But your own conscience can tell I had it dearly enough of you.

WITGOOD: Ay, that's most certain.

LUCRE: Much money laid out, beside many a journey to fetch the rent; I hope you'll think on't, nephew.

15 *regardless of all form*: without regard to appearance 16 *firm*: confirmed
33 *merely plotted in despite of*: i.e. plotted with no other object than to spite
35 *carry*: win 41 *Berlady*: an oath contracted from 'By Our Lady' *toy*: trifle 43 *certify*: i.e. assure her that my promise has been carried out

WITGOOD: I were worse than a beast else, i'faith.

LUCRE: Although to blind the widow and the world, I out of policy do't, yet there's a conscience, nephew.

WITGOOD: Heaven forbid else!

LUCRE: When you are full possess'd, 'tis nothing to return it.

WITGOOD: Alas, a thing quickly done, uncle.

LUCRE: Well said! You know I give it you but in trust.

WITGOOD: Pray let me understand you rightly, uncle: you give it me but in trust?

LUCRE: No.

WITGOOD: That is, you trust me with it.

LUCRE: True, true.

WITGOOD [*Aside.*]: But if ever I trust you with it again, would I might be truss'd up for my labour!

LUCRE: You can all witness, gentlemen, and you, sir yeoman?

HOST: My life for yours, sir, now; I know my mistress's mind to well towards your nephew; let things be in preparation and I'll train her hither in most excellent fashion.

Exit.

LUCRE: A good old boy. – Wife! Ginny!

Enter WIFE.

WIFE: What's the news, sir?

LUCRE: The wedding day's at hand: prithee, sweet wife, express thy housewifery; thou'rt a fine cook, I know't; thy first husband married thee out of an alderman's kitchen. [WIFE *protests.*] Go to! He rais'd thee for raising of paste. What! Here's none but friends; most of our beginnings must be wink'd at. Gentlemen, I invite you all to my nephew's wedding against Thursday morning.

GENTLEMAN 1: With all our hearts, and we shall joy to see your enemy so mock'd.

LUCRE: He laugh'd at me, gentlemen; ha, ha, ha!

Exeunt [*all but* WITGOOD].

WITGOOD: He has no conscience, faith, would laugh at them.
They laugh at one another!
Who then can be so cruel? Troth, not I;
I rather pity now than aught envy.
I do conceive such joy in mine own happiness,

60 *No*: Lucre's reply suggests that Witgood had stressed 'give' in the preceding line 64 *truss'd up*: hanged 67 *train*: conduct 71 *express*: show 73 *Go to!*: i.e. come, come! (Lucre's wife obviously reacts against the mention of her humble origins) 74 *paste*: pastry 80 *them*: i.e. Lucre and Hoard

I have no leisure yet to laugh at their follies.
[*Kisses mortgage.*]
Thou soul of my estate, I kiss thee,
I miss life's comfort when I miss thee.
O never will we part again,
Until I leave the sight of men.
We'll ne'er trust conscience of our kin,
Since cozenage brings that title in.
[*Exit.*]

[SCENE 3]

Enter Three Creditors.

CREDITOR 1: I'll wait these seven hours but I'll see him caught.

CREDITOR 2: Faith, so will I.

CREDITOR 3: Hang him, prodigal, he's stripp'd of the widow.

CREDITOR 1: A' my troth, she's the wiser; she has made the happier choice, and I wonder of what stuff those widows' hearts are made of, that will marry unfledg'd boys before comely thrum-chinn'd gentlemen.

Enter a Boy.

BOY: News, news, news!

CREDITOR 1: What, boy?

BOY: The rioter is caught.

CREDITOR 1: So, so, so, so. It warms me at the heart; I love a' life to see dogs upon men. O here he comes.

Enter WITGOOD *with* Sergeants.

WITGOOD: My last joy was so great it took away the sense of all future afflictions. What a day is here o'ercast! How soon a black tempest rises!

CREDITOR 1: O we may speak with you now, sir! What's become of your rich widow? I think you may cast your cap at the widow, may you not, sir?

CREDITOR 2: He, a rich widow? Who, a prodigal, a daily rioter, and a nightly vomiter? He, a widow of account? He, a hole i'th'Counter!

WITGOOD: You do well, my masters, to tyrannize over misery, to afflict the afflicted; 'tis a custom you have here amongst you. I would wish you never leave it, and I hope you'll do as I bid you.

86 *soul of my estate*: i.e. the mortgage deeds 91 i.e. that title (of 'kin') is introduced by cousinship/cozenage 6 *thrum-chinn'd*: bearded. 'Thrum' is the fringed end of a warp 15 *cast your cap at*: i.e. give up hope of 18 *a hole i'th' Counter*: the worst accommodation in the debtors' prison

CREDITOR 1: Come, come, sir; what say you extempore now to your bill of a hundred pound? A sweet debt for frotting your doublets.

CREDITOR 2: Here's mine of forty.

CREDITOR 3: Here's mine of fifty.

WITGOOD: Pray, sirs, you'll give me breath?

CREDITOR: No, sir, we'll keep you out of breath still; then we shall be sure you will not run away from us.

WITGOOD: Will you but hear me speak?

CREDITOR 2: You shall pardon us for that, sir; we know you have too fair a tongue of your own; you overcame us too lately, a shame take you! We are like to lose all that for want of witnesses; we dealt in policy then: always when we strive to be most politic we prove most coxcombs, *non plus ultra*. I perceive by us we're not ordain'd to thrive by wisdom, and therefore we must be content to be tradesmen.

WITGOOD: Give me but reasonable time and I protest I'll make you ample satisfaction.

CREDITOR 1: Do you talk of reasonable time to us?

WITGOOD: 'Tis true, beasts know no reasonable time.

CREDITOR 2: We must have either money or carcass.

WITGOOD: Alas, what good will my carcass do you?

CREDITOR 3: O 'tis a secret delight we have amongst us. We that are used to keep birds in cages have the heart to keep men in prison, I warrant you.

WITGOOD [*Aside*.]: I perceive I must crave a little more aid from my wits: do but make shift for me this once, and I'll forswear ever to trouble you in the like fashion hereafter; I'll have better employment for you an I live. [*To* Creditors.] You'll give me leave, my masters, to make trial of my friends, and raise all means I can?

CREDITOR 1: That's our desires, sir.

Enter HOST.

HOST: Master Witgood.

WITGOOD: O art thou come?

HOST: May I speak one word with you in private, sir?

WITGOOD: No, by my faith, canst thou. I am in hell here, and the devils will not let me come to thee.

CREDITORS: Do you call us devils? You shall find us puritans! [*To* Sergeants.] Bear him away; let 'em talk as they go; we'll not stand to hear 'em. [*To* WITGOOD.] Ah, sir, am I a devil? I shall think the better of myself as long as I live: a devil, i'faith!

Exeunt.

22 *extempore now*: i.e. right now 23 *frotting*: rubbing with perfume 32 *policy*: cunning 33–4 *non plus ultra*: no farther 40 *carcass*: i.e. imprisonment 46 *make shift*: make an effort 56 s.p. Q reads Cit., i.e. Citizens *puritans*: i.e. strict in enforcement

[SCENE 4]

Enter HOARD.

HOARD: What a sweet blessing hast thou, Master Hoard, above a multitude! Wilt thou never be thankful? How dost thou think to be blest another time? Or dost thou count this the full measure of thy happiness? By my troth, I think thou dost: not only a wife large in possessions, but spacious in content: she's rich, she's young, she's fair, she's wise. When I wake, I think of her lands; that revives me: when I go to bed, I dream of her beauty, and that's enough for me; she's worth four hundred a year in her very smock, if a man knew how to use it. But the journey will be all, in troth, into the country; to ride to her lands in state and order following my brother and other worshipful gentlemen, whose companies I ha' sent down for already, to ride along with us in their goodly decorum beards, their broad velvet cassocks, and chains of gold twice or thrice double; against which time I'll entertain some ten men of mine own into liveries, all of occupations or qualities. I will not keep an idle man about me. The sight of which will so vex my adversary Lucre, for we'll pass by his door of purpose, make a little stand for nonce, and have our horses curvet before the window – certainly he will never endure it, but run up and hang himself presently.

[*Enter* Servant.]

How now, sirrah what news? Any that offer their service to me yet?

SERVANT: Yes, sir, there are some i'th'hall that wait for your worship's liking and desire to be entertain'd.

HOARD: Are they of occupation?

SERVANT: They are men fit for your worship, sir.

HOARD: Say'st so? Send 'em all in.

[*Exit* Servant.]

To see ten men ride after me in watchet liveries with orange-tawny capes, 'twill cut his comb, i'faith.

5 *spacious in content*: able to provide me with complete contentment *wise*: Q reads 'wife' (which is a possibility) 8 *her very smock*: i.e. nothing more than her underwear 10–11 *companies*: presence 12 *decorum*: decorous; the adjectival use of the noun *cassocks*: long loose coats (but Q reads 'chashocks') 13 *entertain*: employ 14 *liveries*: servants' uniforms *occupations or qualities*: employments or abilities 16 *for nonce*: for that particular purpose 17 *curvet*: leap in such a manner that their fore-legs are raised together and equally advanced, while the hind-legs are raised with a spring before the fore-legs touch the ground 22 i.e. Are they worth employing? Do they have trades? 25 *watchet*: pale blue 26 *cut his comb*: take him down, humiliate him

Enter [Tailor, Barber, Perfumer, Falconer, *and* Huntsman].

How now? Of what occupation are you, sir?

TAILOR: A tailor, an't please your worship.

HOARD: A tailor? O very good: you shall serve to make all the liveries. – What are you, sir?

BARBER: A barber, sir.

HOARD: A barber? Very needful: you shall have all the house, and if need require, stand for a reaper i'th'summer time. – You, sir?

PERFUMER: A perfumer.

HOARD: I smell'd you before. Perfumers, of all men, had need carry themselves uprightly, for if they were once knaves they would be smelt out quickly. – To you, sir?

FALCONER: A falc'ner, an't please your worship.

HOARD: Sa ho, sa ho, sa ho! – And you, sir?

HUNTSMAN: A huntsman, sir.

HOARD: There, boy, there, boy, there, boy! I am not so old but I have pleasant days to come. I promise you, my masters, I take such a good liking to you that I entertain you all: I put you already into my countenance, and you shall be shortly in my livery! But especially you two, my jolly falc'ner and my bonny huntsman, we shall have most need of you at my wife's manor houses i'th'country; there's goodly parks and champion grounds for you; we shall have all our sports within ourselves; all the gentlemen a'th'country shall be beholding to us and our pastimes.

FALCONER: And we'll make your worship admire, sir.

HOARD: Say'st thou so? Do but make me admire, and thou shalt want for nothing. – My tailor!

TAILOR: Anon, sir.

HOARD: Go presently in hand with the liveries.

TAILOR: I will, sir.

HOARD: My barber!

BARBER: Here, sir.

HOARD: Make 'em all trim fellows, louse 'em well, especially my huntsman, and cut all their beards of the Polonian fashion. – My perfumer!

PERFUMER: Under your nose, sir.

s.d. a 'perfumer' was employed to perfume or fumigate rooms 39 *Sa ho*: a hawking call 41 *There, boy*: a hunting call 44 *countenance*: favour 47 *champion*: champaign; i.e. level, open country *ourselves*: i.e. our own lands 50 *your*: Q reads 'you' *admire*: marvel/admired 58 *louse*: i.e. remove head-lice 59 *Polonian*: Polish (close-shaved?)

HOARD: Cast a better savour upon the knaves, to take away the scent of my tailor's feet and my barber's lotium water.

PERFUMER: It shall be carefully perform'd, sir.

HOARD: But you, my falc'ner and huntsman, the welcom'st men alive, i' faith!

HUNTSMAN: And we'll show you that, sir, shall deserve your worship's favour.

HOARD: I prithee, show me that. Go, you knaves all, and wash your lungs i'th'buttery, go.

[*Exeunt* Tailor, Barber, Perfumer, Falconer, *and* Huntsman.]

By th'mass, and well rememb'red, I'll ask my wife that question. Wife! Mistress Jane Hoard!

Enter COURTESAN, *alter'd in apparel.*

COURTESAN: Sir, would you with me?

HOARD: I would but know, sweet wife, which might stand best to thy liking, to have the wedding dinner kept here or i'th'country?

COURTESAN: Hum. Faith, sir, 'twould like me better here; here you were married, here let all rites be ended.

HOARD: Could a marquess give a better answer? Hoard, bear thy head aloft, thou'st a wife will advance it.

[*Enter* HOST *with a letter.*]

What haste comes here now? Yea, a letter? Some dreg of my adversary's malice. Come hither; what the news?

HOST: A thing that concerns my mistress, sir.

[*Gives letter to* COURTESAN.]

HOARD: Why, then it concerns me, knave.

HOST: Ay, and you, knave, too – cry your worship mercy. You are both like to come into trouble, I promise you, sir: a precontract.

HOARD: How! A precontract, say'st thou?

HOST: I fear they have too much proof on't, sir. Old Lucre, he runs mad up and down, and will to law as fast as he can; young Witgood, laid hold on by his creditors, he exclaims upon you a' tother side, says you have wrought his undoing by the injurious detaining of his contract.

HOARD: Body a' me!

HOST: He will have utmost satisfaction.
The law shall give him recompense he says.

COURTESAN [*Aside.*]: Alas, his creditors so merciless! My state being yet

62 *lotium water*: stale urine used by barbers as a cosmetic 68–9 *wash your lungs i' th' buttery*: i.e. have a drink in the store-room 72 *would you with me*: i.e. do you want to speak to me? 77 *marquess*: marchioness 84 *precontract*: a legally binding agreement to marry 89 *detaining*: withholding 90 *Body a' me*: an oath ('Body of me')

uncertain, I deem it not unconscionable to further him.

HOST: True, sir, –

HOARD: Wife, what says that letter? Let me construe it.

COURTESAN: Curs'd be my rash and unadvised words!
I'll set my foot upon my tongue
And tread my inconsiderate grant to dust.
[*Stamps on the letter*.]

HOARD: Wife –

HOST [*Aside*.]: A pretty shift, i'faith. I commend a woman when she can make away a letter from her husband handsomely, and this was cleanly done, by my troth.

COURTESAN: I did, sir.
Some foolish words I must confess did pass,
Which now litigiously he fastens on me.

HOARD: Of what force? Let me examine 'em.

COURTESAN: Too strong, I fear: would I were well freed of him.

HOARD: Shall I compound?

COURTESAN: No, sir, I'd have it done some nobler way
Of your side; I'd have you come off with honour;
Let baseness keep with them. Why, have you not
The means, sir? The occasion's offer'd you.

HOARD: Where? How, dear wife?

COURTESAN: He is now caught by his creditors; the slave's needy, his debts petty; he'll rather bind himself to all inconveniences than rot in prison; by this only means you may get a release from him. 'Tis not yet come to his uncle's hearing; send speedily for the creditors; by this time he's desperate, he'll set his hand to anything. Take order for his debts or discharge 'em quite. A pax on him, let's be rid of a rascal!

HOARD: Excellent! Thou dost astonish me. [*To* HOST.] Go, run, make haste: bring both the creditors and Witgood hither.

HOST [*Aside*.]: This will be some revenge yet.
[*Exit*.]

HOARD: In the mean space I'll have a release drawn. – Within there!
[*Enter* Servant.]

SERVANT: Sir?

HOARD: Sirrah, come take directions; go to my scrivener.
[*Speaks aside with* Servant.]

94 *unconscionable*: unreasonable 96 *construe*: read 99 *inconsiderate grant*: thoughtless promise 102 *handsomely*: cleverly *cleanly*: adroitly
109 *compound*: bargain. (This is the most likely meaning in view of later comments. However, 'compound' could also mean 'settle by way of a payment')
117 *release*: document releasing someone from contractual obligations 120 *pax*: pox 121 *astonish*: i.e. by your quick-wittedness 126 *scrivener*: notary

COURTESAN [*Aside.*]: I'm yet like those whose riches lie in dreams;
If I be wak'd, they're false; such is my fate,
Who ventures deeper than the desperate state.
Though I have sinn'd, yet could I become new,
For where I once vow, I am ever true.

HOARD: Away! Dispatch! On my displeasure, quickly.
[*Exit* Servant.]
Happy occasion! Pray heaven he be in the right vein now to set his hand to't, that nothing alter him; grant that all his follies may meet in him at once, to besot him enough.
I pray for him, i'faith, and here he comes.
[*Enter* WITGOOD *with* Creditors.]

WITGOOD: What would you with me now, my uncle's spiteful adversary?

HOARD: Nay, I am friends.

WITGOOD: Ay, when your mischief's spent.

HOARD: I heard you were arrested.

WITGOOD: Well, what then? You will pay none of my debts I am sure.

HOARD: A wise man cannot tell.
There may be those conditions 'greed upon
May move me to do much.

WITGOOD: Ay, when?
'Tis thou, perjured woman! O no name
Is vild enough to match thy treachery,
That art the cause of my confusion.

COURTESAN: Out, you penurious slave!

HOARD: Nay, wife, you are too froward,
Let him alone; give losers leave to talk.

WITGOOD: Shall I remember thee of another promise far stronger than the first?

COURTESAN: I'd fain know that.

WITGOOD: 'Twould call shame to thy cheeks.

COURTESAN: Shame?

WITGOOD: Hark in your ear. [*They talk apart.*] Will he come off, think'st thou, and pay my debts roundly?

COURTESAN: Doubt nothing; there's a release a-drawing and all, to which you must set your hand.

WITGOOD: Excellent!

COURTESAN: But methinks, i'faith, you might have made some shift to discharge this yourself, having in the mortgage, and never have burden'd my conscience with it.

133 *he*: i.e. Witgood 146 *vild*: vile 147 *confusion*: ruin 149 *froward*: unreasonable 153 *fain*: gladly 157 *roundly*: in full

WITGOOD: A' my troth, I could not, for my creditors' cruelties extend to the present.

COURTESAN: No more. [*Aloud.*] Why, do your worst for that, I defy you.

WITGOOD: Y'are impudent! I'll call up witnesses.

COURTESAN: Call up thy wits, for thou hast been devoted to follies a long time.

HOARD: Wife, y'are too bitter. Master Witgood, and you, my masters, you shall hear a mild speech come from me now, and this it is: 't'as been my fortune, gentlemen, to have an extraordinary blessing pour'd upon me a' late, and here she stands; I have wedded her and bedded her, and yet she is little the worse. Some foolish words she hath pass'd to you in the country, and some peevish debts you owe here in the City; set the hare's head to the goose-giblet: release you her of her words, and I'll release you of your debts, sir.

WITGOOD: Would you so? I thank you for that, sir; I cannot blame you, i' faith.

HOARD: Why, are not debts better than words, sir?

WITGOOD: Are not words promises, and are not promises debts, sir?

HOARD [*Aside.*]: He plays at back-racket with me.

CREDITOR 1: Come hither, Master Witgood, come hither; be rul'd by fools once.

CREDITOR 2: We are citizens and know what belong to't.

CREDITOR 1: Take hold of his offer. Pax on her, let her go. If your debts were once discharg'd, I would help you to a widow myself worth ten of her.

CREDITOR 3: Mass, partner, and now you remember me on't, there's Master Mulligrub's sister newly fall'n a widow.

CREDITOR 1: Cuds me, as pat as can be! There's a widow left for you, ten thousand in money, beside plate, jewels, *et cetera*; I warrant it a match; we can do all in all with her. Prithee, dispatch; we'll carry thee to her presently.

WITGOOD: My uncle will ne'er endure me when he shall hear I set my hand to a release.

CREDITOR 2: Hark, I'll tell thee a trick for that. I have spent five hundred pound in suits in my time, I should be wise. Thou'rt now a prisoner; make a release; take't of my word, whatsoever a man makes as long as he is in durance, 'tis nothing in law, not thus much.
[*Snaps his fingers.*]

175 *peevish*: piffling 175–6 *set the hare's head to the goose-giblet*: proverbial: 'Give tit for tat' 180 *better*: more binding 182 *back-racket*: return of the ball at tennis 190 *Mulligrub's*: 'mulligrubs' = a fit of spleen or colic 193 *all in all*: everything at once 198 *suits*: law-suits 200 *in durance*: under constraint

WITGOOD: Say you so, sir?

CREDITOR 3: I have paid for't, I know't.

WITGOOD: Proceed then: I consent.

CREDITOR 3: Why, well said.

HOARD: How now, my masters, what have you done with him?

CREDITOR 1: With much ado, sir, we have got him to consent.

HOARD: Ah-a-a! And what came his debts to now?

CREDITOR 1: Some eight score odd pounds, sir.

HOARD: Naw, naw, naw, naw, naw! Tell me the second time; give me a lighter sum. They are but desperate debts, you know, ne'er call'd in but upon such an accident; a poor, needy knave, he would starve and rot in prison. Come, come, you shall have ten shillings in the pound, and the sum down roundly.

CREDITOR 1: You must make it a mark, sir.

HOARD: Go to, then; tell your money in the meantime; you shall find little less there. [*Gives them money.*] Come, Master Witgood, you are so unwilling to do yourself good now.

[*Enter* Scrivener.]

Welcome, honest scrivener. Now you shall hear the release read.

SCRIVENER: 'Be it known to all men by these presents that I, Theodorus Witgood, gentleman, sole nephew to Pecunious Lucre, having unjustly made title and claim to one Jane Medler, late widow of Anthony Medler, and now wife to Walkadine Hoard, in consideration of a competent sum of money to discharge my debts, do for ever hereafter disclaim any title, right, estate, or interest in or to the said widow, late in the occupation of the said Anthony Medler and now in the occupation of Walkadine Hoard; as also neither to lay claim by virtue of any former contract, grant, promise or demise, to any of her manor, manor houses, parks, groves, meadow-grounds, arable lands, barns, stacks, stables, dove holes, and cony burrows, together with all her cattell, money, plate, jewels, borders, chains, bracelets, furnitures, hangings, movables, or immovables. In witness whereof, I, the said Theodorus Witgood, have interchangeably set to my hand and seal before these presents, the day and date above written.'

WITGOOD: What a precious fortune hast thou slipp'd here, like a beast as thou art!

209 *Tell me*: count 210 *desperate*: i.e. irretrievable 210–11 *ne'er called in but upon such an accident*: i.e. which would never be repaid except in the current circumstances 219 *these presents*: i.e. this document 223 *competent*: sufficient 225 *occupation*: occupancy, abode ('occupation' had sexual implications) 227 *demise*: conveyance 229 *cony burrows*: rabbit warrens *cattell*: chattels 230 *borders*: ornamental borders to gowns 232 *interchangeably*: reciprocally 233 *presents*: witnesses 234 *slipp'd*: let slip

HOARD: Come, unwilling heart, come.

WITGOOD: Well, Master Hoard, give me the pen; I see
'Tis vain to quarrel with our destiny.

HOARD: O as vain a thing as can be; you cannot commit a greater absurdity, sir. So, so, give me that hand now: before all these presents, I am friends for ever with thee.

WITGOOD: Troth, and it were pity of my heart now if I should bear you any grudge, i'faith.

HOARD: Content. I'll send for thy uncle against the wedding dinner; we will be friends once again.

WITGOOD: I hope to bring it to pass myself, sir.

HOARD [*To* Creditors.]: How now? Is't right, my masters?

CREDITOR I: 'Tis something wanting, sir, yet it shall be sufficient.

HOARD: Why, well said; a good conscience makes a fine show nowadays. Come, my masters, you shall all taste of my wine ere you depart.

ALL: We follow you, sir.

[*Exeunt* HOARD, Scrivener, *and* COURTESAN.]

WITGOOD [*Aside.*]: I'll try these fellows now. [*To* Creditors.] A word, sir: what, will you carry me to that widow now?

CREDITOR I: Why, do you think we were in earnest, i'faith? Carry you to a rich widow? We should get much credit by that! A noted rioter, a contemptible prodigal! 'Twas a trick we have amongst us to get in our money. Fare you well, sir.

Exeunt [Creditors].

WITGOOD: Farewell and be hang'd, you short pig-hair'd, ram-headed rascals! He that believes in you shall ne'er be sav'd, I warrant him. By this new league I shall have some access unto my love.

She is above.

NIECE: Master Witgood!

WITGOOD: My life!

NIECE: Meet me presently; that note directs you. [*Throws a paper.*] I would not be suspected. Our happiness attends us. Farewell.

[*Exit.*]

WITGOOD: A word's enough.

[*Exit.*]

247 *Is't right*: i.e. is the sum of money correct 252 *try*: test 258 *pig-hair'd*: close-cropped *ram-headed*: i.e. cuckolded 260 *this new league*: i.e. with Hoard, the Niece's guardian

[SCENE 5]

DAMPIT *the usurer in his bed,* AUDREY *spinning by and* Boy.

THE SONG [*sung by* AUDREY].

Let the usurer cram him, in interest that excel,
There's pits enow to damn him, before he comes to hell;
In Holborn some, in Fleet Street some,
Where'er he come, there's some, there's some.

DAMPIT: *Trahe, traheto,* draw the curtain, give me a sip of sack more.

Enter Gentlemen [LAMPREY *and* SPITCHCOCK].

LAMPREY: Look you, did not I tell you he lay like the devil in chains, when he was bound for a thousand year?

SPITCHCOCK: But I think the devil had no steel bedstaffs; he goes beyond him for that.

LAMPREY: Nay, do but mark the conceit of his drinking; one must wipe his mouth for him with a muckinder, do you see, sir?

SPITCHCOCK: Is this the sick trampler? Why, he is only bed-rid with drinking.

LAMPREY: True, sir. He spies us.

DAMPIT: What, Sir Tristram? You come and see a weak man here, a very weak man.

LAMPREY: If you be weak in body, you should be strong in prayer, sir.

DAMPIT: O I have pray'd too much, poor man.

LAMPREY [*To* SPITCHCOCK.]: There's a taste of his soul for you.

SPITCHCOCK [*To* LAMPREY.]: Fah, loathsome!

LAMPREY: I come to borrow a hundred pound of you, sir.

DAMPIT: Alas, you come at an ill time. I cannot spare it, i'faith; I ha' but two thousand i'th'house.

AUDREY: Ha, ha, ha!

1–4 a song by Thomas Ravenscroft (?1592–?1635) who published the earliest collection of rounds, catches and canons printed in English. This lyric was published in *Melismata* (1611) and here lacks the opening two lines: 'My master is so wise, so wise, that he's proceeded wittol, / My mistress is a fool, a fool, and yet is the most get-all.' 2 *pits*: cunts/brothels/taverns 5 *Trahe, traheto*: Latin commands to 'draw' (both curtains and drink) 6–7 *when he was bound for a thousand year*: see Revelation XX.2 (usurers were traditionally hung in chains) 8 *steel bedstaffs*: Dampit's bed seems to have been strengthened with a frame of steel rods 10 *conceit*: morbid symptom 11 *muckinder*: handkerchief 15 *Sir Tristram*: Tristram was a 'type' of the lover and Dampit plays on Lamprey's name, for lampreys were regarded as aphrodisiacs

DAMPIT: Out, you gernative quean, the mullipood of villainy, the spinner of concupiscency!

Enter other Gentleman [SIR LANCELOT].

SIR LANCELOT: Yea, gentlemen, are you here before us? How is he now?

LAMPREY: Faith, the same man still: the tavern bitch has bit him i'th' head.

SIR LANCELOT: We shall have the better sport with him. Peace. – And how cheers Master Dampit now?

DAMPIT: O my bosom Sir Lancelot, how cheer I? Thy presence is restorative.

SIR LANCELOT: But I hear a great complaint of you, Master Dampit, among gallants.

DAMPIT: I am glad of that, i'faith; prithee, what?

SIR LANCELOT: They say you are wax'd proud a' late, and if a friend visit you in the afternoon, you'll scarce know him.

DAMPIT: Fie, fie! Proud? I cannot remember any such thing; sure, I was drunk then.

SIR LANCELOT: Think you so, sir?

DAMPIT: There 'twas, i'faith, nothing but the pride of the sack, and so certify 'em. [*To* Boy.] Fetch sack, sirrah.

BOY [*Aside.*]: A vengeance sack you once!

AUDREY: Why, Master Dampit, if you hold on as you begin and lie a little longer, you need not take care how to dispose your wealth; you'll make the vintner your heir.

DAMPIT: Out, you babliaminy, you unfeather'd cremitoried quean, you cullisance of scabiosity!

AUDREY: Good words, Master Dampit, to speak before a maid and a virgin.

DAMPIT: Hang thy virginity upon the pole of carnality!

AUDREY: Sweet terms! My mistress shall know 'em.

LAMPREY [*Aside.*]: Note but the misery of this usuring slave: here he lies, like a noisome dunghill, full of the poison of his drunken blasphemies,

25 *gernative*: given to 'gerning' or grumbling *mullipood*: another coined term, perhaps alluding to 'mulligrubs' (= attacks of spleen or colic) and 'pode' (= toad) *spinner*: spider (but Audrey is also literally spinning: see stage direction, p. 57) 28–9 *the tavern bitch has bit him i' th' head*: i.e. he is drunk 42 *sack*: white wine from Spain or the Canaries 44 *sack*: despoil 47 *vintner*: wine-merchant 48 *babliaminy*: babbler *unfeather'd*: balding (?) *cremitoried*: another coined word, possibly meaning 'burnt out' or else 'burning', i.e. syphilitic 49 *cullisance*: corruption of 'cognizance', a badge *scabiosity*: the condition of suffering from scabies 52 *pole of carnality*: i.e. the erect penis

53 *mistress*: presumably Dampit's wife, who is nowhere else mentioned

55 *noisome*: noxious, foul-smelling

and they to whom he bequeaths all grudge him the very meat that feeds him, the very pillow that eases him. Here may a usurer behold his end. What profits it to be a slave in this world and a devil i'th'next?

DAMPIT: Sir Lancelot, let me buss thee, Sir Lancelot; thou art the only friend that I honour and respect.

SIR LANCELOT: I thank you for that, Master Dampit.

DAMPIT: Farewell, my bosom Sir Lancelot.

SIR LANCELOT [*To* LAMPREY *and* SPITCHCOCK.]: Gentlemen, and you love me, let me step behind you, and one of you fall a-talking of me to him.

LAMPREY: Content. – Master Dampit.

DAMPIT: So, sir?

LAMPREY: Here came Sir Lancelot to see you e'en now.

DAMPIT: Hang him, rascal!

LAMPREY: Who, Sir Lancelot?

DAMPIT: Pythagorical rascal!

LAMPREY: Pythagorical?

DAMPIT: Ay, he changes his cloak when he meets a sergeant.

SIR LANCELOT [*Aside.*]: What a rogue's this!

LAMPREY: I wonder you can rail at him, sir; he comes in love to see you.

DAMPIT: A louse for his love! His father was a combmaker; I have no need of his crawling love. He comes to have longer day, the superlative rascal.

SIR LANCELOT [*Aside.*]: 'Sfoot, I can no longer endure the rogue. – Master Dampit, I come to take my leave once again, sir.

DAMPIT: Who? My dear and kind Sir Lancelot, the only gentleman of England? Let me hug thee; farewell, and a thousand.

LAMPREY [*Aside.*]: Compos'd of wrongs and slavish flatteries.

SIR LANCELOT [*Aside.*]: Nay, gentlemen, he shall show you more tricks yet; I'll give you another taste of him.

LAMPREY [*Aside.*]: Is't possible?

SIR LANCELOT [*Aside.*]: His memory is upon departing.

DAMPIT: Another cup of sack!

SIR LANCELOT [*Aside.*]: Mass, then 'twill be quite gone! Before he drink that, tell him there's a country client come up and here attends for his learned advice.

LAMPREY [*Aside.*]: Enough.

59 *buss*: kiss 71 *Pythagorical*: the Greek philosopher Pythagoras believed in the transmigration of the soul. Dampit charges Lancelot with changing shape (i.e. disguising himself) whenever he meets a law-officer 77 *longer day*: i.e. more time to repay a debt 78 *'Sfoot*: an oath, corrupted from 'God's foot' 81 *a thousand*: i.e. a thousand farewells

DAMPIT: One cup more, and then let the bell toll; I hope I shall be weak enough by that time.

LAMPREY: Master Dampit.

DAMPIT: Is the sack spouting?

LAMPREY: 'Tis coming forward, sir. Here's a countryman, a client of yours, waits for your deep and profound advice, sir.

DAMPIT: A coxcombry? Where is he? Let him approach: set me up a peg higher.

LAMPREY: You must draw near, sir.

DAMPIT: Now, goodman fooliaminy, what say you to me now?

SIR LANCELOT [*Disguising his voice.*]: Please your good worship, I am a poor man, sir –

DAMPIT: What make you in my chamber then?

SIR LANCELOT: I would entreat your worship's device in a just and honest cause, sir.

DAMPIT: I meddle with no such matters; I refer 'em to Master No-man's office.

SIR LANCELOT: I had but one house left me in all the world, sir, which was my father's, my grandfather's, my great-grandfather's, and now a villain has unjustly wrung me out and took possession on't.

DAMPIT: Has he such feats? Thy best course is to bring thy *ejectione firmae*, and in seven year thou mayst shove him out by the law.

SIR LANCELOT: Alas, an't please your worship, I have small friends and less money.

DAMPIT: Hoyday! This gear will fadge well! Hast no money? Why, then, my advice is thou must set fire a'th'house and so get him out.

LAMPREY: That will break strife indeed.

SIR LANCELOT: I thank your worship for your hot counsel, sir. [*Aside.*] Altering but my voice a little, you see he knew me not; you may observe by this that a drunkard's memory holds longer in the voice than in the person. But, gentlemen, shall I show you a sight? Behold the little dive-dapper of damnation, Gulf the usurer, for his time worse than tother.

Enter HOARD *with* GULF.

LAMPREY: What's he comes with him?

SIR LANCELOT: Why, Hoard, that married lately the widow Medler.

LAMPREY: O I cry you mercy, sir.

92 *let the bell toll*: i.e. for his funeral   101 *fooliaminy*: foolishness   104 *What make you*: what are you doing   105 *device*: advice   112 *feats*: crimes   *ejectione firmae*: writ of ejection to recover possession of property   114 *small*: uninfluential/few   116 *Hoyday!*: obsolete form of 'hey-day', here used ironically   *gear*: business (a favourite word of the Vice character in medieval morality plays)   *fadge*: come off   118 *break*: cause   123 *dive-dapper*: dabchick

HOARD: Now, gentlemen visitants, how does Master Dampit?

SIR LANCELOT: Faith, here he lies, e'en drawing in, sir, good canary as fast as he can, sir; a very weak creature, truly, he is almost past memory.

HOARD: Fie, Master Dampit, you lie lazing abed here and I come to invite you to my wedding dinner: up, up, up!

DAMPIT: Who's this? Master Hoard? Who hast thou married, in the name of foolery?

HOARD: A rich widow.

DAMPIT: A Dutch widow!

HOARD: A rich widow, one widow Medler.

DAMPIT: Medler? She keeps open house.

HOARD: She did, I can tell you, in her tother husband's days, open house for all comers: horse and man was welcome, and room enough for 'em all.

DAMPIT: There's too much for thee then; thou mayst let out some to thy neighbours.

GULF: What, hung alive in chains? O spectacle! Bedstaffs of steel? *O monstrum horrendum, informe, ingens cui lumen ademptum!* O Dampit, Dampit, here's a just judgment shown upon usury, extortion, and trampling villainy!

SIR LANCELOT [*Aside.*]: 'Tis ex'llent, thief rails upon the thief!

GULF: Is this the end of cut-throat usury, brothel, and blasphemy? Now mayst thou see what race a usurer runs.

DAMPIT: Why, thou rogue of universality, do not I know thee? Thy sound is like the cuckoo, the Welsh ambassador; thou cowardly slave, that offers to fight with a sick man when his weapon's down! Rail upon me in my naked bed? Why, thou great Lucifer's little vicar, I am not so weak but I know a knave at first sight. Thou inconscionable rascal! Thou that goest upon Middlesex juries and will make haste to give up thy verdict because thou wilt not lose thy dinner, are you answered?

GULF: An't were not for shame –

Draws his dagger.

DAMPIT: Thou wouldst be hang'd then.

SIR LANCELOT: Nay, you must exercise patience, Master Gulf, always in a sick man's chamber.

129 *canary*: a sweet wine from the Canaries 138 *keeps open house*: is a generous hostess/is a whore. 'Openarse' was another name for the medlar fruit 145 *O monstrum horrendum, informe, ingens cui lumen ademptum*: Latin, 'O horrible monster, deformed, huge, deprived of sight' (Virgil's *Aeneid* III 658, alluding to Polyphemus) 152 *the cuckoo, the Welsh ambassador*: possibly an allusion to the Welsh raiders who pillaged the Border counties in 'cuckoo-time', i.e. Spring 153–4 *in my naked bed*: when I am naked in bed 156 *Middlesex juries*: these were notoriously unreliable

SIR LANCELOT [*To* DAMPIT.]: He'll quarrel with none, I warrant you, but those that are bed-rid.

DAMPIT: Let him come, gentlemen, I am arm'd: reach my close-stool hither.

SIR LANCELOT: Here will be a sweet fray anon. I'll leave you, gentlemen.

LAMPREY: Nay, we'll along with you. Master Gulf –

GULF: Hang him, usuring rascal!

SIR LANCELOT: Push! Set your strength to his, your wit to his.

AUDREY: Pray, gentlemen, depart, his hour's come upon him. [*Embracing* DAMPIT.] Sleep in my bosom, sleep.

SIR LANCELOT: Nay, we have enough of him, i'faith;
Keep him for the house. Now make your best;
For thrice his wealth, I would not have his breast.

GULF: A little thing would make me beat him, now he's asleep.

SIR LANCELOT: Mass, then 'twill be a pitiful day when he wakes. I would be loath to see that day.

GULF: You overrule me, gentlemen, i'faith.

Exeunt.

164 *close-stool*: piss-pot enclosed in a stool

ACT FIVE

[SCENE 1]

Enter LUCRE *and* WITGOOD.

WITGOOD: Nay, uncle, let me prevail with you so much. I'faith, go, now he has invited you.

LUCRE: I shall have great joy there when he has borne away the widow.

WITGOOD: Why, la, I thought where I should find you presently; uncle, a' my troth, 'tis nothing so.

LUCRE: What's nothing so, sir? Is not he married to the widow?

WITGOOD: No, by my troth, is he not, uncle.

LUCRE: How?

WITGOOD: Will you have the truth on't? He is married to a whore, i'faith.

LUCRE: I should laugh at that.

WITGOOD: Uncle, let me perish in your favour if you find it not so, and that 'tis I that have married the honest woman.

LUCRE: Ha! I'd walk ten mile afoot to see that, i'faith.

WITGOOD: And see't you shall, or I'll ne'er see you again.

LUCRE: A quean, i'faith? Ha, ha, ha!

Exeunt.

[SCENE 2]

Enter HOARD, *tasting wine, the* HOST *following in a livery cloak.*

HOARD: Pup, pup, pup, pup! I like not this wine; is there never a better tierce in the house?

HOST: Yes, sir, there are as good tierce in the house as any are in England.

HOARD: Desire your mistress, you knave, to taste 'em all over; she has better skill.

HOST [*Aside.*]: Has she so? The better for her and the worse for you.

Exit.

HOARD: Arthur!

[*Enter* Servant.]

Is the cupboard of plate set out?

2 *tierce*: cask 5 *skill*: discrimination (but the Host picks up on the sense 'skill' = cunning)

ARTHUR: All's in order, sir.

[*Exit.*]

HOARD: I am in love with my liveries every time I think on 'em. They make a gallant show, by my troth. – Niece!

[*Enter* NIECE.]

NIECE: Do you call, sir?

HOARD: Prithee, show a little diligence and overlook the knaves a little; they'll filch and steal today and send whole pasties home to their wives; and thou be'st a good niece, do not see me purloin'd.

NIECE: Fear it not, sir. [*Aside.*] I have cause: though the feast be prepared for you, yet it serves fit for my wedding dinner too.

[*Exit.*]

Enter two Gentlemen [LAMPREY *and* SPITCHCOCK].

HOARD: Master Lamprey, and Master Spitchcock, two the most welcome gentlemen alive! Your fathers and mine were all free o'th'fishmongers.

LAMPREY: They were indeed, sir. You see bold guests, sir, soon entreated.

HOARD: And that's best, sir.

[*Enter* Servant.]

How now, sirrah?

SERVANT: There's a coach come to th'door, sir.

[*Exit.*]

HOARD: My Lady Foxstone, a' my life! – Mistress Jane Hoard! Wife! – Mass, 'tis her ladyship indeed.

[*Enter* LADY FOXSTONE.]

Madam, you are welcome to an unfurnish'd house, dearth of cheer, scarcity of attendance.

LADY FOXSTONE: You are pleas'd to make the worst, sir.

HOARD: Wife!

[*Enter* COURTESAN.]

LADY FOXSTONE: Is this your bride?

HOARD: Yes, madam. [*To* COURTESAN.] Salute my Lady Foxstone.

COURTESAN: Please you, madam, a while to taste the air in the garden?

LADY FOXSTONE: 'Twill please us well.

Exeunt [LADY FOXSTONE *and* COURTESAN].

HOARD: Who would not wed? The most delicious life!
No joys are like the comforts of a wife.

LAMPREY [*Aside.*]: So we bachelors think, that are not troubled with them.

[*Enter* Servant.]

14 *pasties*: pies 19 *free o'th'fishmongers*: members of the Guild of Fishmongers (with a jocular allusion to their surnames) 20 *bold*: presumptuous
26 *unfurnish'd*: unprepared

SERVANT: Your worship's brother with another ancient gentleman are newly alighted, sir.

[*Exit.*]

HOARD: Master Onesiphorus Hoard! Why, now our company begins to come in.

[*Enter* ONESIPHORUS HOARD, LIMBER, *and* KIX.]

My dear and kind brother, welcome, i'faith.

ONESIPHORUS: You see we are men at an hour, brother.

HOARD: Ay, I'll say that for you, brother; you keep as good an hour to come to a feast as any gentleman in the shire. What, old Master Limber and Master Kix! Do we meet, i'faith, jolly gentlemen?

LIMBER: We hope you lack guests, sir.

HOARD: O welcome, welcome! We lack still such guests as your worships.

ONESIPHORUS: Ah, sirrah brother, have you catch'd up widow Medler?

HOARD: From 'em all, brother; and, I may tell you, I had mighty enemies, those that stuck sore: old Lucre is a sore fox, I can tell you, brother.

ONESIPHORUS: Where is she? I'll go seek her out; I long to have a smack at her lips.

HOARD: And most wishfully, brother. See where she comes.

[*Enter* COURTESAN.]

Give her a smack now we may hear it all the house over.

COURTESAN: O heaven, I am betray'd! I know that face.

Both [COURTESAN *and* ONESIPHORUS] *turn back.*

HOARD: Ha, ha, ha! Why, how now? Are you both asham'd? Come, gentlemen, we'll look another way.

ONESIPHORUS: Nay, brother, hark you; come, y'are dispos'd to be merry.

HOARD: Why do we meet else, man?

ONESIPHORUS: That's another matter. I was ne'er so 'fraid in my life but that you had been in earnest.

HOARD: How mean you, brother?

ONESIPHORUS: You said she was your wife.

HOARD: Did I so? By my troth, and so she is.

ONESIPHORUS: By your troth, brother?

HOARD: What reason have I to dissemble with my friends, brother? If marriage can make her mine, she is mine. Why?

ONESIPHORUS: Troth, I am not well of a sudden. I must crave pardon, brother; I came to see you but I cannot stay dinner, i'faith.

HOARD: I hope you will not serve me so, brother.

LIMBER: By your leave, Master Hoard –

HOARD: What now? What now? Pray, gentlemen, you were wont to show yourselves wise men.

42 *men at an hour*: punctual 55 *I know that face*: the two knew each other in Leicestershire 70 *serve*: treat (punning on 'serve' with dinner)

LIMBER: But you have shown your folly too much here.

HOARD: How?

KIX: Fie, fie! A man of your repute and name!
You'll feast your friends, but cloy 'em first with shame.

HOARD: This grows too deep; pray, let us reach the sense.

LIMBER: In your old age dote on a courtesan!

HOARD: Ha!

KIX: Marry a strumpet!

HOARD: Gentlemen!

ONESIPHORUS: And Witgood's quean!

HOARD: O! Nor lands nor living?

ONESIPHORUS: Living?

HOARD [*To* COURTESAN.]: Speak!

COURTESAN: Alas, you know, at first, sir. I told you I had nothing.

HOARD: Out, out! I am cheated, infinitely cozen'd!

LIMBER: Nay, Master Hoard –

HOARD: A Dutch widow, a Dutch widow, a Dutch widow!

Enter WITGOOD *and* LUCRE.

LUCRE: Why, nephew, shall I trace thee still a liar? Wilt make me mad? Is not yon thing the widow?

WITGOOD: Why, la, you are so hard a' belief, uncle! By my troth, she's a whore.

LUCRE: Then thou'rt a knave.

WITGOOD: *Negatur argumentum*, uncle.

LUCRE: *Probo tibi*, nephew: he that knows a woman to be a quean must needs be a knave; thou say'st thou know'st her to be one; *ergo*, if she be a quean, thou'rt a knave.

WITGOOD: *Negatur sequela maioris*, uncle: he that knows a woman to be a quean must needs be a knave, I deny that.

HOARD: Lucre and Witgood, y'are both villains; get you out of my house!

LUCRE: Why, didst not invite me to thy wedding dinner?

WITGOOD: And are not you and I sworn perpetual friends, before witness, sir, and were both drunk upon't?

HOARD: Daintily abused! Y'ave put a junt upon me.

LUCRE: Ha, ha, ha!

HOARD: A common strumpet!

WITGOOD: Nay, now you wrong her, sir. If I were she, I'd have the law on

87 *I told you I had nothing*: see III.i.204 91 *trace*: find 96 *Negatur argumentum*: Latin scholastic tag: 'The argument is denied' 97 *Probo tibi*: 'I will prove it to you' *knows*: punning on knows = fucks 98 *ergo*: therefore 100 *Negatur sequela maioris*: 'Your conclusion does not follow from your major premise' 106 *junt*: trick

you for that; I durst depose for her she ne'er had common use nor common thought.

COURTESAN: Despise me, publish me, I am your wife;
What shame can I have now but you'll have part?
If in disgrace you share, I sought not you;
You pursued me, nay, forc'd me;
Had I friends would follow it,
Less than your action has been prov'd a rape.

ONESIPHORUS: Brother?

COURTESAN: Nor did I ever boast of lands unto you,
Money, or goods; I took a plainer course,
And told you true I'd nothing.
If error were committed, 'twas by you;
Thank your own folly. Nor has my sin been
So odious but worse has been forgiven;
Nor am I so deform'd but I may challenge
The utmost power of any old man's love.
She that tastes not sin before, twenty to one but she'll taste it after; most of you old men are content to marry young virgins and take that which follows; where, marrying one of us, you both save a sinner and are quit from a cuckold for ever.
And more, in brief, let this your best thoughts win,
She that knows sin, knows best how to hate sin.

HOARD: Curs'd be all malice! Black are the fruits of spite
And poison first their owners. O my friends,
I must embrace shame to be rid of shame.
Conceal'd disgrace prevents a public name.
Ah, Witgood, ah, Theodorus!

WITGOOD: Alas, sir, I was prick'd in conscience to see her well bestow'd, and where could I bestow her better than upon your pitiful worship? Excepting but myself, I dare swear she's a virgin; and now by marrying your niece I have banish'd myself for ever from her. She's mine aunt now, by my faith, and there's no meddling with mine aunt, you know, a sin against my nuncle.

COURTESAN: Lo, gentlemen, before you all
In true reclaimed form I fall.
[*Kneels.*]

110 *depose*: give evidence upon oath 112 *publish*: publicly denounce
116 *follow it*: i.e. prosecute the case 125 *challenge*: lay claim to
129 *where*: whereas 129–30 *quit from a cuckold*: i.e. saved from cuckoldry
139 *pitiful*: compassionate 142 *meddling with mine aunt*: continuing the puns on meddler and aunt 143 *nuncle*: uncle 146 *defy*: renounce

Henceforth for ever I defy
The glances of a sinful eye,
Waving of fans, which some suppose
Tricks of fancy, treading of toes,
Wringing of fingers, biting the lip,
The wanton gait, th'alluring trip,
All secret friends and private meetings,
Close-borne letters and bawds' greetings,
Feigning excuse to women's labours
When we are sent for to th' next neighbours,
Taking false physic and ne'er start
To be let blood, though sign be at heart,
Removing chambers, shifting beds,
To welcome friends in husbands' steads,
Them to enjoy and you to marry,
They first serv'd while you must tarry,
They to spend and you to gather,
They to get and you to father.
These and thousand thousand more,
New reclaim'd, I now abhor.

LUCRE: Ah, here's a lesson, rioter, for you!

WITGOOD: I must confess my follies; I'll down too.
[*Kneels.*]
And here for ever I disclaim
The cause of youth's undoing: game,
Chiefly dice, those true outlanders
That shake out beggars, thieves, and panders,
Soul-wasting surfeits, sinful riots,
Queans' evils, doctors' diets,
'Pothecaries' drugs, surgeons' glisters,
Stabbing of arms for a common mistress,
Riband favours, ribald speeches,

149 *fancy*: love 151 *trip*: light, quick movements of the feet 152 *secret friends*: lovers 153 *Close-borne*: secretly conveyed 154 *women's labours*: childbirth or pregnancy 157 *though sign be at heart*: even though the astrological signs were favourable for such treatment 158 *Removing chambers, shifting beds*: i.e. moving to different bedrooms 162 *spend*: ejaculate 169 *game*: gambling 170 *outlanders*: foreigners 173 *Queans' evils*: i.e. venereal diseases (in antithesis to the King's evil = scrofula) 174 *surgeons' glisters*: enemas 175 *Stabbing of arms*: i.e. to toast a mistress in wine mixed with blood 176 *Riband favours*: knots of ribbons given as favours to lovers

Dear perfum'd jackets, penniless breeches,
Dutch flapdragons, healths in urine,
Drabs that keep a man too sure in –
I do defy you all.
Lend me each honest hand, for here I rise
A reclaim'd man, loathing the general vice.

HOARD: So, so, all friends. The wedding dinner cools.
Who seem most crafty prove oft-times most fools.
[*Exeunt.*]

FINIS

178 *Dutch flapdragons*: raisins set on fire and drunk in wine while still alight
179 *Drabs*: prostitutes 182 *general vice*: i.e. all vices

The Revenger's Tragedy

The Revenger's Tragedy was entered in the Stationers' Register on 7 October 1607 to George Eld and published soon after. The copy-text for this edition is the Quarto (Q), which appeared in three different states, Qa dated 1607 on the title-page, Qb and Qc both dated 1608 on the title-page. We have adopted some readings from Qb and Qc.

[DRAMATIS PERSONAE

The DUKE
LUSSURIOSO, *the Duke's son*
SPURIO, *the Duke's bastard*
AMBITIOSO, *the Duchess's eldest son*
SUPERVACUO, *the Duchess's second son*
JUNIOR, *the Duchess's youngest son*
ANTONIO } *nobles*
PIERO }
VINDICE } *Gratiana's sons*
HIPPOLITO }
DONDOLO, *Gratiana's servant*
NENCIO } *Lussurioso's followers*
SORDIDO }

The DUCHESS
GRATIANA
CASTIZA, *Gratiana's daughter*

Nobles; Judges; Gentlemen; Guards; Prison-Keeper; Officers; Servants.

Scene: An Italian Court.]

LUSSURIOSO: luxurious (i.e. lecherous). Like all the other characters' names this is derived from Italian SPURIO: spurious, bastard AMBITIOSO: ambitious SUPERVACUO: superfluous, vain VINDICE: revenger DONDOLO: a type-name for a foolish servant NENCIO: idiot SORDIDO: sordid, wretched GRATIANA: grace CASTIZA: chastity

ACT ONE

SCENE I

Enter VINDICE [*holding a skull*]. *The* DUKE, DUCHESS, LUSSURIOSO *his son*, SPURIO *the Bastard, with a train, pass over the stage with torch-light.*

VINDICE: Duke: royal lecher; go, grey-hair'd Adultery;
And thou his son, as impious steep'd as he;
And thou his bastard, true-begot in evil;
And thou his Duchess, that will do with Devil.
Four ex'lent characters – o that marrowless age
Would stuff the hollow bones with damn'd desires
And 'stead of heat kindle infernal fires
Within the spendthrift veins of a dry Duke,
A parch'd and juiceless luxur. O God! One
That has scarce blood enough to live upon,
And he to riot it like a son and heir?
O the thought of that
Turns my abused heart-strings into fret.
[*To the skull.*] Thou sallow picture of my poison'd love,
My study's ornament, thou shell of death,
Once the bright face of my betrothed lady,
When life and beauty naturally fill'd out
These ragged imperfections,
When two heaven-pointed diamonds were set
In those unsightly rings – then 'twas a face
So far beyond the artificial shine
Of any woman's bought complexion

s.d. *train*: retinue 1 *Adultery*: Q reads 'adultery'. We have capitalized here and at other places to emphasize the personification 4 *do*: fuck 8 *dry*: withered, sterile 9 *luxur*: lecher 13 *heart-strings*: the tendons or nerves supposed to brace the heart. The term often gave rise to allusions to stringed musical instruments *fret*: vexation/decay. Also takes up the notion of a musical instrument as 'fret' = bar of gut, wood, or metal on the fingerboard of a string instrument used to regulate the fingering 15 *study's ornament*: i.e. the object of meditation (but it is possible that there is a pun involved, and the skull has been an ornament in his study or office) 20 *unsightly*: ugly/non-seeing 22 *bought complexion*: i.e. make-up (but with an allusion to 'the condition of being bought', i.e. prostitution)

That the uprightest man (if such there be,
That sin but seven times a day) broke custom,
And made up eight with looking after her.
O she was able to ha' made a usurer's son
Melt all his patrimony in a kiss,
And what his father fifty years told,
To have consum'd, and yet his suit been cold.
But o accursed palace!
Thee when thou wert apparel'd in thy flesh
The old Duke poison'd,
Because thy purer part would not consent
Unto his palsy-lust; for old men lustful
Do show like young men angry, eager-violent,
Outbid like their limited performances.
O 'ware an old man hot and vicious:
Age, as in gold, in lust is covetous.
Vengeance, thou Murder's quit-rent, and whereby
Thou show'st thyself tenant to Tragedy,
O keep thy day, hour, minute, I beseech,
For those thou hast determin'd. Hum, who e'er knew
Murder unpaid? Faith, give Revenge her due,
Sh'as kept touch hitherto. Be merry, merry,
Advance thee, o thou terror to fat folks,
To have their costly three-pil'd flesh worn off
As bare as this – for banquets, ease and laughter
Can make great men, as greatness goes by clay,
But wise men little are more great than they.
Enter his brother HIPPOLITO.
HIPPOLITO: Still sighing o'er Death's vizard?
VINDICE: Brother, welcome,
What comfort bring'st thou? How go things at Court?
HIPPOLITO: In silk and silver, brother: never braver.

27 *Melt*: squander 28 *told*: counted, i.e. accumulated 29 *his suit been cold*: i.e. his advances would be rejected 34 *palsy-lust*: 'palsy' is a disease of the nervous system which impairs muscular activity and can provoke involuntary tremors of the limbs. The sense here seems to be that the Duke's lust is similar to an uncontrolled tremor, automatic and undiscriminating 36 *Outbid*: over-rated 37 *vicious*: prone to vice 39 *quit-rent*: i.e. due ('quit-rent' was a money payment by a freeholder to a feudal lord in lieu of services) 40 *tenant*: continuing the metaphor of 'quit-rent'. 'Tragedy' is the Lord which 'Revenge' serves 42 *determin'd*: decided on 44 *touch*: faith 45 *thee*: i.e. the skull 46 *three-pil'd*: alluding to costly 'three-piled' velvet 48 *great*: important/fat *clay*: i.e. the earthly or material part of man 49 *little*: i.e. lowly 50 *vizard*: mask or face suggestive of a mask 52 *braver*: more showy

VINDICE: Puh,
Thou play'st upon my meaning. Prithee say,
Has that bald madam, Opportunity,
Yet thought upon's? Speak, are we happy yet?
Thy wrongs and mine are for one scabbard fit.
HIPPOLITO: It may prove happiness.
VINDICE: What is't may prove?
Give me to taste.
HIPPOLITO: Give me your hearing then.
You know my place at Court.
VINDICE: Ay, the Duke's chamber,
But 'tis a marvel thou'rt not turn'd out yet!
HIPPOLITO: Faith, I have been shov'd at but 'twas still my hap
To hold by th'Duchess' skirt; you guess at that;
Whom such a coat keeps up can ne'er fall flat.
But to the purpose.
Last evening, predecessor unto this,
The Duke's son warily inquir'd for me,
Whose pleasure I attended. He began
By policy to open and unhusk me
About the time and common rumour;
But I had so much wit to keep my thoughts
Up in their built houses, yet afforded him
An idle satisfaction without danger.
But the whole aim and scope of his intent
Ended in this, conjuring me in private
To seek some strange-digested fellow forth
Of ill-contented nature, either disgrac'd
In former times, or by new grooms displac'd
Since his stepmother's nuptials; such a blood,
A man that were for evil only good;
To give you the true word, some base-coin'd pander.
VINDICE: I reach you for I know his heat is such,

55 *that bald madam, Opportunity*: in Renaissance emblem books Opportunity or Occasion was commonly depicted as a bald woman with a long forelock (which had to be seized if she were not to escape) 62 *hap*: fortune 62–4 may imply that Hippolito is the Duchess's lover 64 *coat*: petticoat 69 *policy*: stratagem *unhusk me*: i.e. seek my views 71 *so much*: sufficient 72 *in their built houses*: i.e. secure 73 *idle satisfaction*: worthless answer 76 *strange-digested fellow*: strangely-concocted fellow, i.e. malcontent 78 *grooms*: servants or attendants 79 *blood*: a hot spark, 'man of fire' 81 *base-coin'd*: bastard/low-born *pander*: procurer 82 *reach*: understand

Were there as many concubines as ladies,
He would not be contain'd, he must fly out.
I wonder how ill-featur'd, vile-proportion'd
That one should be, if she were made for woman,
Whom at the insurrection of his lust
He would refuse for once; heart, I think none;
Next to a skull, though more unsound than one,
Each face he meets he strongly dotes upon.

HIPPOLITO: Brother, y'ave truly spoke him.
He knows not you but I'll swear you know him.

VINDICE: And therefore I'll put on that knave for once,
And be a right man then, a man o'th'time,
For to be honest is not to be i'th'world.
Brother, I'll be that strange-composed fellow.

HIPPOLITO: And I'll prefer you, brother.

VINDICE: Go to then,
The small'st advantage fattens wronged men.
It may point out Occasion; if I meet her
I'll hold her by the foretop fast enough,
Or like the French mole heave up hair and all.
I have a habit that will fit it quaintly.
[*Enter* GRATIANA *and* CASTIZA.]
Here comes our mother.

HIPPOLITO: And sister.

VINDICE: We must coin.
Women are apt, you know, to take false money;
But I dare stake my soul for these two creatures,
Only excuse excepted – that they'll swallow
Because their sex is easy in belief.

GRATIANA: What news from court, son Carlo?

HIPPOLITO: Faith, mother,
'Tis whisper'd there, the Duchess' youngest son
Has play'd a rape on Lord Antonio's wife.

GRATIANA: On that religious lady!

CASTIZA: Royal blood! Monster, he deserves to die,

87 *insurrection*: outbreak 91 *spoke*: described 93 *put on*: disguise myself as 94 *right*: conventional 95 *i'th'world*: of this (courtly) world 97 *prefer*: recommend 100 *foretop*: forelock 101 *French mole*: i.e. syphilis, which causes the hair to fall out 102 *habit*: costume *fit it quaintly*: i.e. be cunningly appropriate 103 *coin*: dissemble (with a pun on 'counterfeit', which is played on in 'take false money') 104 *take false money*: accept counterfeit money (i.e. be gullible)/accept bribes 106 i.e. except that they will swallow a good excuse 108 *Carlo*: the only instance of Hippolito being called by this name

If Italy had no more hopes but he.
VINDICE: Sister, y'ave sentenc'd most direct and true,
The Law's a woman and would she were you.
Mother, I must take leave of you.
GRATIANA: Leave for what?
VINDICE: I intend speedy travel.
HIPPOLITO: That he does, madam.
GRATIANA: Speedy indeed!
VINDICE: For since my worthy father's funeral,
My life's unnatural to me, e'en compell'd
As if I liv'd now when I should be dead.
GRATIANA: Indeed he was a worthy gentleman.
Had his estate been fellow to his mind.
VINDICE: The Duke did much deject him.
GRATIANA: Much!
VINDICE: Too much.
And through disgrace, oft smother'd in his spirit
When it would mount, surely I think he died
Of discontent, the nobleman's consumption.
GRATIANA: Most sure he did!
VINDICE: Did he? 'Lack, you know all,
You were his midnight secretary.
GRATIANA: No.
He was too wise to trust me with his thoughts.
VINDICE [*Aside.*]: I'faith then, father, thou wast wise indeed,
Wives are but made to go to bed and feed. –
Come mother, sister; you'll bring me onward, brother?
HIPPOLITO: I will.
VINDICE: I'll quickly turn into another.
Exeunt.

[SCENE 2]

Enter the old DUKE, LUSSURIOSO *his son, the* DUCHESS, [SPURIO] *the Bastard, the Duchess's two sons* AMBITIOSO *and* SUPERVACUO, *the third her*

113 *hopes*: heirs 115 *The Law's a woman*: iconographically, Justice was depicted as a woman holding a sword or pair of scales 117 *speedy*: immediate *travel*: Q reads 'travail', a common spelling of 'travel' which also introduces a pun on travail = labour 120 *unnatural*: Q reads 'unnaturally' 122 *worthy*: honourable (but punning on 'worthy' = rich) 124 *deject*: depress/impoverish 128 *'Lack*: alack, an exclamation of pity 129 *secretary*: confidant

youngest [JUNIOR] *brought out with* Officers *for the rape; two* Judges.

DUKE: Duchess, it is your youngest son; we're sorry
His violent act has e'en drawn blood of honour
And stain'd our honours,
Thrown ink upon the forehead of our state
Which envious spirits will dip their pens into
After our death, and blot us in our tombs.
For that which would seem treason in our lives
Is laughter when we're dead. Who dares now whisper
That dares not then speak out, and e'en proclaim
With loud words and broad pens our closest shame?

JUDGE 1: Your Grace hath spoke like to your silver years
Full of confirmed gravity; for what is it to have
A flattering false insculption on a tomb,
And in men's hearts reproach? The bowell'd corpse
May be cer'd in, but, with free tongue I speak,
The faults of great men through their cerecloths break.

DUKE: They do, we're sorry for't, it is our fate
To live in fear and die to live in hate.
I leave him to your sentence – doom him, lords,
The fact is great – whilst I sit by and sigh.

DUCHESS [*Kneeling.*]: My gracious lord, I pray be merciful;
Although his trespass far exceed his years,
Think him to be your own, as I am yours,
Call him not son-in-law: the Law I fear
Will fall too soon upon his name and him.
Temper his fault with pity!

LUSSURIOSO: Good my lord,
Then 'twill not taste so bitter and unpleasant
Upon the judges' palate, for offences
Gilt o'er with mercy show like fairest women,
Good only for their beauties, which wash'd off,
No sin is uglier.

AMBITIOSO: I beseech your grace,
Be soft and mild, let not relentless Law
Look with an iron forehead on our brother.

SPURIO [*Aside.*]: He yields small comfort yet, hope he shall die,
And if a bastard's wish might stand in force,

10 *closest*: most secret 11 *like to*: in a manner appropriate to 13 *insculption*: inscription 14 *bowell'd*: disembowelled 15 *cer'd*: wrapped in cerecloth or winding-sheet 19 *doom*: sentence 20 *fact*: crime 24 *son-in-law*: i.e. step-son 26–31 Lussurioso is either being publicly sarcastic or ll. 30–31 are an aside

Would all the court were turn'd into a corse.
DUCHESS: No pity yet? Must I rise fruitless then?
A wonder in a woman! Are my knees
Of such low metal that without respect –
JUDGE 1: Let the offender stand forth.
'Tis the Duke's pleasure that impartial doom
Shall take fast hold of his unclean attempt.
A rape! Why 'tis the very core of lust,
Double adultery.
JUNIOR: So, sir.
JUDGE 2: And which was worse,
Committed on the Lord Antonio's wife,
That general honest lady. Confess, my lord.
What mov'd you to't?
JUNIOR: Why flesh and blood, my lord;
What should move men unto a woman else?
LUSSURIOSO: O do not jest thy doom, trust not an axe
Or sword too far; the Law is a wise serpent
And quickly can beguile thee of thy life.
Though marriage only has made thee my brother,
I love thee so far, play not with thy death.
JUNIOR: I thank you, troth; good admonitions, faith,
If I'd the grace now to make use of them.
JUDGE 1: That lady's name has spread such a fair wing
Over all Italy that, if our tongues
Were sparing toward the fact, judgment itself
Would be condemn'd and suffer in men's thoughts.
JUNIOR: Well then 'tis done, and it would please me well
Were it to do again: sure she's a goddess,
For I'd no power to see her and to live;
It falls out true in this, for I must die.
Her beauty was ordain'd to be my scaffold,
And yet methinks I might be easier ceas'd;
My fault being sport, let me but die in jest.
JUDGE 1: This be the sentence –
DUCHESS: O keep't upon your tongue, let it not slip;

36 *corse*: corpse 38 *A wonder in a woman*: i.e. there is a pun on 'rise' = swell 39 *low metal*: base metal; i.e. little value 42 *fast*: Q reads 'first' 44 *Double adultery*: i.e. twice as bad as adultery 46 *general*: completely 53 *so far*: so much/sufficiently to advise you 55 *grace*: virtue/chance 65 *ceas'd*: brought to rest. Q reads 'ceast' and possibly puns on 'to cess' ('sess) = to judge

Death too soon steals out of a lawyer's lip.
Be not so cruel-wise!
JUDGE I: Your Grace must pardon us,
'Tis but the justice of the Law.
DUCHESS: The Law
Is grown more subtle than a woman should be.
SPURIO [*Aside*.]: Now, now he dies, rid 'em away!
DUCHESS [*Aside*.]: O what it is to have an old-cool Duke,
To be as slack in tongue as in performance.
JUDGE I: Confirm'd, this be the doom irrevocable.
DUCHESS: O!
JUDGE I: Tomorrow early –
DUCHESS: Pray be abed, my lord.
JUDGE I: Your Grace much wrongs yourself.
AMBITIOSO: No, 'tis that tongue,
Your too much right, does do us too much wrong.
JUDGE I: Let that offender –
DUCHESS: Live, and be in health.
JUDGE I: Be on a scaffold –
DUKE: Hold, hold, my lord.
SPURIO [*Aside*.]: Pax on't,
What makes my dad speak now?
DUKE: We will defer the judgment till next sitting.
In the meantime let him be kept close prisoner:
Guard, bear him hence.
AMBITIOSO [*To* JUNIOR.]: Brother, this makes for thee;
Fear not, we'll have a trick to set thee free.
JUNIOR: Brother, I will expect it from you both,
And in that hope I rest.
SUPERVACUO: Farewell, be merry.
Exit [JUNIOR] *with a* Guard.
SPURIO [*Aside*.]: Delay'd, deferr'd – nay then if Judgment have
Cold blood, flattery and bribes will kill it.
DUKE: About it then, my lords, with your best powers,
More serious business calls upon our hours.
Exeunt [*all but the*] DUCHESS.

69 *lawyer's*: judge's 72 *subtle*: cunning 75 *performance*: i.e. sexual performance 79 *wrongs*: disgraces 80 *too much right*: i.e. inordinate authority and right to speak 82 *Pax*: pox 85 *close prisoner*: i.e. strictly guarded 86 *makes for thee*: is to your advantage 92 *About it then*: i.e. away!

DUCHESS: Was't ever known step-Duchess was so mild
And calm as I? Some now would plot his death
With easy doctors, those loose-living men,
And make his wither'd Grace fall to his grave
And keep church better.
Some second wife would do this, and dispatch
Her double-loathed lord at meat and sleep.
Indeed 'tis true an old man's twice a child;
Mine cannot speak; one of his single words
Would quite have freed my youngest dearest son
From death or durance, and have made him walk
With a bold foot upon the thorny law,
Whose prickles should bow under him; but 'tis not,
And therefore wedlock faith shall be forgot.
I'll kill him in his forehead, hate there feed;
That wound is deepest though it never bleed.
[*Enter* SPURIO.]
And here comes he whom my heart points unto,
His bastard son, but my love's true-begot.
Many a wealthy letter have I sent him,
Swell'd up with jewels, and the timorous man
Is yet but coldly kind;
That jewel's mine that quivers in his ear,
Mocking his master's chillness and vain fear.
H'as spied me now.
SPURIO: Madam? Your Grace so private?
My duty on your hand.
DUCHESS: Upon my hand, sir? Troth, I think you'd fear
To kiss my hand too if my lip stood there.
SPURIO: Witness I would not, madam.
[*Kisses her.*]
DUCHESS: 'Tis a wonder,
For ceremony has made many fools;
It is as easy way unto a Duchess
As to a hatted dame (if her love answer)
But that by timorous honours, pale respects,
Idle degrees of fear, men make their ways
Hard of themselves – what, have you thought of me?

96 *easy*: compliant 98 *keep church better*: i.e. the Duke will be in permanent attendance at church, once in the graveyard 100 *and*: i.e. and then
104 *durance*: imprisonment 108 *kill him in his forehead*: i.e. from the growth of cuckold's horns through her adultery 116 *his master's*: i.e. Spurio's
117 *private*: solitary 124 *hatted dame*: i.e. woman of lower class

SPURIO: Madam, I ever think of you in duty,
Regard and –
DUCHESS: Puh, upon my love, I mean.
SPURIO: I would 'twere love, but 't'as a fouler name
Than lust; you are my father's wife;
Your Grace may guess now what I could call it.
DUCHESS: Why th'art his son but falsely;
'Tis a hard question whether he begot thee.

SPURIO: I'faith 'tis true too; I'm an uncertain man, of more uncertain woman. Maybe his groom o'th'stable begot me, you know I know not; he could ride a horse well, a shrewd suspicion, marry; he was wondrous tall, he had his length, i'faith, for peeping over half-shut holiday windows; men would desire him 'light. When he was afoot, he made a goodly show under a penthouse, and when he rid, his hat would check the signs, and clatter barbers' basins.

DUCHESS: Nay, set you a-horseback once, you'll ne'er 'light off.
SPURIO: Indeed, I am a beggar.
DUCHESS: That's more the sign th'art great – but to our love.
Let it stand firm both in thy thought and mind
That the Duke was thy father, as no doubt then
He bid fair for't. Thy injury is the more;
For had he cut thee a right diamond,
Thou hadst been next set in the Dukedom's ring,
When his worn self, like Age's easy slave,
Had dropp'd out of the collet into th'grave.
What wrong can equal this? Canst thou be tame
And think upon't?
SPURIO: No, mad and think upon't.
DUCHESS: Who would not be reveng'd of such a father,
E'en in the worst way? I would thank that sin

130 *'t'as*: Q reads ''tus' 130–1 *fouler name Than lust*: i.e. incest 137–8 *he could . . . length*: there is sexual innuendo in some of this (e.g. 'ride', 'length') which the Duchess picks up in her reply 138–9 *half-shut holiday windows*: i.e. he was tall enough to peer into the living quarters of supposedly 'private' dwellings when he was on horseback 139 *'light*: alight, dismount 140 *penthouse*: subsidiary building with low, sloping roof *check*: strike 141 *signs*: shop-signs *barbers' basins*: their distinctive shape, with a cut-out for the neck which allowed the chin to protrude over the shaving dish, meant that they were easily recognizable shop signs for barbers 143 *beggar*: alluding to the proverb 'Set a beggar on horseback he will ride a gallop' 147 *bid fair for't*: i.e. made a fair attempt at it 148 *cut thee a right diamond*: i.e. fathered you legitimately (starting a chain of images dependent on diamonds) 151 *collet*: the setting for a jewel

That could most injury him, and be in league with it.
O what a grief 'tis that a man should live
But once i'th'world, and then to live a bastard,
The curse o'the womb, the thief of Nature,
Begot against the seventh commandment,
Half-damn'd in the conception, by the justice
Of that unbribed everlasting Law.

SPURIO: O I'd a hot-back'd devil to my father.

DUCHESS: Would not this mad e'en Patience, make blood rough?
Who but an eunuch would not sin, his bed
By one false minute disinherited?

SPURIO [*Aside.*]: Ay, there's the vengeance that my birth was wrapp'd in
I'll be reveng'd for all; now hate begin,
I'll call foul incest but a venial sin.

DUCHESS: Cold still: in vain then must a Duchess woo?

SPURIO: Madam, I blush to say what I will do.

DUCHESS: Thence flew sweet comfort. Earnest, and farewell.
[*Kisses him.*]

SPURIO: O one incestuous kiss picks open hell.

DUCHESS: Faith now, old Duke, my vengeance shall reach high,
I'll arm thy brow with woman's heraldry.
Exit.

SPURIO: Duke, thou didst do me wrong, and by thy act
Adultery is my nature.
Faith, if the truth were known, I was begot
After some gluttonous dinner, some stirring dish
Was my first father, when deep healths went round,
And ladies' cheeks were painted red with wine,
Their tongues as short and nimble as their heels,
Uttering words sweet and thick; and when they rose
Were merrily dispos'd to fall again.
In such a whisp'ring and withdrawing hour,
When base male-bawds kept sentinel at stair-head,
Was I stol'n softly; o Damnation met
The sin of feasts, drunken Adultery.

156 *injury*: injure 160 *seventh commandment*: which forbade adultery 169 *venial*: pardonable 172 *Earnest*: i.e. the kiss is an 'earnest' or foretaste of what is to come 175 *woman's heraldry*: i.e. cuckold's horns 179 *stirring*: stimulating 180 *healths went round*: toasts circulated 182 *short and nimble as their heels*: short cork heels were associated with loose morals 183–4 *when they rose Were merrily dispos'd to fall again*: i.e. because they were drunkenly unable to stand and wantonly disposed for sex 187 *stol'n softly*: i.e. conceived

I feel it swell me, my revenge is just,
I was begot in impudent wine and lust.
Step-mother, I consent to thy desires,
I love thy mischief well, but I hate thee,
And those three cubs thy sons, wishing confusion,
Death and disgrace may be their epitaphs.
As for my brother, the Duke's only son,
Whose birth is more beholding to report
Than mine, and yet perhaps as falsely sown
(Women must not be trusted with their own),
I'll loose my days upon him, hate all I;
Duke, on thy brow I'll draw my bastardy.
For indeed a bastard by nature should make cuckolds
Because he is the son of a cuckold-maker.
Exit.

[SCENE 3]

Enter VINDICE *and* HIPPOLITO, *Vindice in disguise to attend Lord* LUSSURIOSO, *the Duke's son.*

VINDICE: What, brother? Am I far enough from myself?
HIPPOLITO: As if another man had been sent whole
Into the world, and none wist how he came.
VINDICE: It will confirm me bold; the child o'th'Court.
Let blushes dwell i'th'country. Impudence!
Thou goddess of the palace, mistress of mistresses,
To whom the costly-perfum'd people pray,
Strike thou my forehead into dauntless marble,
Mine eyes to steady sapphires; turn my visage,
And if I must needs glow, let me blush inward
That this immodest season may not spy
That scholar in my cheeks, fool-bashfulness,

190 *impudent*: shameless, immodest 193 *confusion*: ruin 196 *beholding to report*: i.e. Lussurioso being legitimate is more acceptable to public opinion 199 *loose my days upon him*: i.e. devote my time to seeking his downfall 1 *far enough from myself*: sufficiently disguised 3 *wist*: knew 5 *Impudence*: Vindice addresses himself to the 'goddess' of immodesty and shameless effrontery 6 *mistress of mistresses*: punning on 'mistress' = woman of authority and 'mistress' = kept woman 8 *dauntless*: fearless 13–14 i.e. modesty will never prostitute itself for worldly gain (good clothes). Vindice may also be alluding to the iconographical tradition which depicted Truth as a naked maiden, having nothing to conceal

That maid in the old time, whose flush of grace
Would never suffer her to get good clothes.
Our maids are wiser, and are less asham'd;
Save Grace the bawd, I seldom hear grace nam'd!
HIPPOLITO: Nay, brother, you reach out o'th'verge now –
[*Enter* LUSSURIOSO *attended.*]
'Sfoot, the Duke's son! Settle your looks.
VINDICE: Pray let me not be doubted.
HIPPOLITO: My lord –
LUSSURIOSO: Hippolito? – [*To* Servants.] Be absent; leave us.
[*Exeunt* Servants.]
HIPPOLITO: My lord, after long search, wary inquiries,
And politic siftings, I made choice of yon fellow,
Whom I guess rare for many deep employments;
This our age swims within him, and if Time
Had so much hair, I should take him for Time,
He is so near kin to this present minute.
LUSSURIOSO: 'Tis enough,
We thank thee; yet words are but great men's blanks,
Gold, though it be dumb, does utter the best thanks.
[*Gives him money.*]
HIPPOLITO: Your plenteous honour – an ex'lent fellow, my lord.
LUSSURIOSO: So, give us leave. [*Exit* HIPPOLITO.] Welcome, be not far off, we must be better acquainted. Push, be bold with us: thy hand.
VINDICE: With all my heart, i'faith. How dost, sweet musk-cat?
When shall we lie together?
LUSSURIOSO [*Aside.*]: Wondrous knave!
Gather him into boldness? 'Sfoot, the slave's
Already as familiar as an ague,
And shakes me at his pleasure. – Friend, I can

16 *Save*: i.e. except for *Grace the bawd*: ironically prefiguring the role of Vindice's mother Gratiana (= Grace) 17 *reach out o'th' verge*: i.e. you're going too far 18 *'Sfoot*: oath contracted from 'God's foot' *Settle*: compose 19 *doubted*: suspected 22 *politic siftings*: cunning interrogations 23 *rare*: excellent 24 *This our age swims within him*: i.e. his character reflects the climate of the times 24–5 *and if Time Had so much hair*: alluding to the iconographical tradition of Time as an old, balding man 28 *blanks*: probably a form of cheque with a space left blank for the signature 32 *Push*: i.e. Pish! This exclamation is a hallmark of Middleton's writing 33 *musk-cat*: the animal from which the perfume is obtained, but the term came to mean both 'prostitute' and 'fop' by extension 35 *Gather him into boldness?*: i.e. encourage him to be familiar? 36 *ague*: a fever producing symptoms of shivering or shaking (presumably Vindice is shaking him by the hand)

Forget myself in private, but elsewhere
I pray do you remember me.
VINDICE: O very well, sir – I conster myself saucy.
LUSSURIOSO: What hast been, of what profession?
VINDICE: A bone-setter.
LUSSURIOSO: A bone-setter?
VINDICE: A bawd, my lord, one that sets bones together.
LUSSURIOSO [*Aside.*]: Notable bluntness!
Fit, fit for me, e'en train'd up to my hand. –
Thou hast been scrivener to much knavery then?
VINDICE: Fool to abundance, sir; I have been witness
To the surrenders of a thousand virgins,
And not so little;
I have seen patrimonies wash'd a-pieces,
Fruit-fields turn'd into bastards,
And in a world of acres
Not so much dust due to the heir 'twas left to
As would well gravel a petition.
LUSSURIOSO [*Aside.*] : Fine villain! Troth, I like him wondrously,
He's e'en shap'd for my purpose. – Then thou know'st
I'th'world strange lust?
VINDICE: O Dutch lust! Fulsome lust!
Drunken procreation, which begets so many drunkards.
Some father dreads not (gone to bed in wine)
To slide from the mother, and cling the daughter-in-law;
Some uncles are adulterous with their nieces,
Brothers with brothers' wives. O hour of incest!
Any kin now next to the rim o'th'sister
Is man's meat in these days, and in the morning,
When they are up and dress'd, and their mask on,
Who can perceive this, save that eternal eye
That sees through flesh and all? Well, if anything

39 *remember me*: i.e. remember my rank 40 *conster*: construe, interpret 46 *train'd up to my hand*: i.e. exactly suited for what I had in mind (the image derives from falconry) 47 *scrivener to*: secretary to, recorder of 48 *Fool to abundance*: i.e. an accessory to an abundance of knavery 50 *not so little*: i.e. a good deal worse 51 *patrimonies*: inherited estates *wash'd a-pieces*: i.e. destroyed (as though by the actions of the sea) 52 i.e. the estate squandered in the process of fathering illegitimate children 55 *gravel*: sprinkle sand on newly written documents to dry the ink 57 *shap'd*: naturally formed 58 *Dutch*: The Dutch were thought of as heavy drinkers, so the phrase means either 'drunken' or 'excessive'. (In *A Trick*, a 'Dutch widow' is a prostitute.) 64 *next to the rim o'*: i.e. short of (with 'rim' = limit, but also probably alluding to the vagina)

Be damn'd, it will be twelve o'clock at night,
That twelve will never 'scape;
It is the Judas of the hours, wherein
Honest salvation is betray'd to sin.

LUSSURIOSO: In troth it is, too; but let this talk glide.
It is our blood to err, though hell gap'd loud;
Ladies know Lucifer fell, yet still are proud.
Now, sir; wert thou as secret as thou'rt subtle
And deeply fathom'd into all estates
I would embrace thee for a near employment,
And thou shouldst swell in money, and be able
To make lame beggars crouch to thee.

VINDICE: My lord!
Secret? I ne'er had that disease o'th'mother,
I praise my father. Why are men made close
But to keep thoughts in best? I grant you this,
Tell but some woman a secret overnight,
Your doctor may find it in the urinal i'th'morning.
But my lord –

LUSSURIOSO: So, thou'rt confirm'd in me,
And thus I enter thee.
[*Gives him money.*]

VINDICE: This Indian devil
Will quickly enter any man – but a usurer;
He prevents that, by ent'ring the devil first.

LUSSURIOSO: Attend me, I am past my depth in lust.
And I must swim or drown. All my desires
Are levell'd at a virgin not far from Court,
To whom I have convey'd by messenger
Many wax'd lines, full of my neatest spirit,
And jewels that were able to ravish her
Without the help of man; all which and more
She, foolish-chaste, sent back, the messengers
Receiving frowns for answers.

73 *glide*: i.e. pass smoothly on to another topic 74 *blood*: i.e. the fleshly nature of man *gap'd*: yawned 75 *Lucifer*: Lucifer fell through pride 77 *estates*: classes of society 78 *near*: private 81 *disease o'th'mother*: i.e. gossiping (with an allusion to a disease which induced hysteria known as 'the mother')
85 Doctors were expected to inspect urine as part of the diagnosis of illness
86 *confirm'd in me*: i.e. confirmed in my confidence 87 *enter*: admit/bind
Indian devil: silver and gold were mined in the West Indies 89 *prevents* = forestalls 90 *Attend*: listen to 94 *wax'd lines*: letters sealed with wax *neatest*: purest

VINDICE: Possible?
'Tis a rare phoenix, whoe'er she be.
If your desires be such, she so repugnant,
In troth, my lord, I'd be reveng'd and marry her.
LUSSURIOSO: Push!
The dowry of her blood and of her fortunes
Are both too mean – good enough to be bad withal.
I am one of that number can defend
Marriage is good; yet rather keep a friend.
Give me my bed by stealth, there's true delight;
What breeds a loathing in't, but night by night?
VINDICE: A very fine religion!
LUSSURIOSO: Therefore thus:
I'll trust thee in the business of my heart
Because I see thee well experienc'd
In this luxurious day wherein we breathe.
Go thou, and with a smooth enchanting tongue
Bewitch her ears, and cozen her of all grace;
Enter upon the portion of her soul,
Her honour, which she calls her chastity,
And bring it into expense, for honesty
Is like a stock of money laid to sleep
Which, ne'er so little broke, does never keep.
VINDICE: You have gi'n't the tang, i'faith, my lord.
Make known the lady to me, and my brain
Shall swell with strange invention: I will move it
Till I expire with speaking, and drop down
Without a word to save me; but I'll word –
LUSSURIOSO: We thank thee, and will raise thee. Receive her name, it is the only daughter to Madam Gratiana, the late widow.
VINDICE [*Aside.*]: O my sister, my sister!
LUSSURIOSO: Why dost walk aside?

99 *phoenix*: i.e. wonder. The phoenix was a unique mythical bird which lived for a cycle of 500 or 600 years before cremating itself on a funeral pyre; from the ashes it would re-emerge with renewed youth 100 *repugnant*: hostile 103 *blood*: i.e. family rank 105 *defend*: maintain 106 *friend*: mistress 112 *luxurious*: lecherous 114 *cozen*: cheat 115 *portion*: dowry 117 *expense*: use 119 *ne'er*: i.e. 'be it ever' *broke*: this suggests all of (i) broken sleep, (ii) a stock of money broken into, (iii) the hymen broken 120 *gi'n't the tang*: given (i.e. 'caught') its flavour, described it exactly 122 *move it*: i.e. plead your case 125 *raise*: punning on 'raise' = advance, and 'raise' = lift up (after Vindice has 'dropped down') 126 *late*: recent

VINDICE: My lord, I was thinking how I might begin,
As thus, 'O lady' – or twenty hundred devices;
Her very bodkin will put a man in.
LUSSURIOSO: Ay, or the wagging of her hair.
VINDICE: No, that shall put you in, my lord.
LUSSURIOSO: Shall't? Why, content. Dost know the daughter then?
VINDICE: O ex'lent well by sight.
LUSSURIOSO: That was her brother
That did prefer thee to us.
VINDICE: My lord, I think so,
I knew I had seen him somewhere.
LUSSURIOSO: And therefore prithee let thy heart to him
Be as a virgin, close.
VINDICE: O my good lord.
LUSSURIOSO: We may laugh at that simple age within him.
VINDICE: Ha, ha, ha.
LUSSURIOSO: Himself being made the subtle instrument
To wind up a good fellow –
VINDICE: That's I, my lord.
LUSSURIOSO: That's thou.
To entice and work his sister.
VINDICE: A pure novice!
LUSSURIOSO: 'Twas finely manag'd.
VINDICE: Gallantly carried;
A pretty perfum'd villain.
LUSSURIOSO: I've bethought me,
If she prove chaste still and immovable,
Venture upon the mother, and with gifts
As I will furnish thee, begin with her.
VINDICE: O fie, fie, that's the wrong end, my lord. 'Tis mere impossible that a mother by any gifts should become a bawd to her own daughter.
LUSSURIOSO: Nay then, I see thou'rt but a puny in the subtle mystery of a woman. Why 'tis held now no dainty dish: the name
Is so in league with age that nowadays
It does eclipse three quarters of a mother.
VINDICE: Does't so, my lord?

130 *bodkin*: pin or needle *put a man in*: suggest a topic of conversation
132 *that shall put you in*: i.e. her pubic hair will move to allow penetration
139 *that simple age within him*: i.e. his innocence 142 *wind up*: incite 144 *work*: persuade 152 *puny*: novice 153 *'tis held now no dainty dish*: i.e. it's not considered anything special these days *name*: i.e. of 'bawd' 154 *age*: i.e. the middle or old age of the mother

Let me alone then to eclipse the fourth.
LUSSURIOSO: Why well said, come I'll furnish thee, but first
Swear to be true in all.
VINDICE: True?
LUSSURIOSO: Nay, but swear!
VINDICE: Swear? I hope your honour little doubts my faith.
LUSSURIOSO: Yet for my humour's sake, 'cause I love swearing.
VINDICE: 'Cause you love swearing, 'slud, I will.
LUSSURIOSO: Why, enough.
Ere long look to be made of better stuff.
VINDICE: That will do well indeed, my lord.
LUSSURIOSO: Attend me.
[*Exit.*]
VINDICE: O,
Now let me burst, I've eaten noble poison.
We are made strange fellows, brother, innocent villains;
Wilt not be angry when thou hear'st on't, think'st thou?
I'faith, thou shalt. Swear me to foul my sister!
Sword, I durst make a promise of him to thee,
Thou shall dis-heir him, it shall be thine honour;
And yet, now angry froth is down in me,
It would not prove the meanest policy
In this disguise to try the faith of both;
Another might have had the self same office,
Some slave, that would have wrought effectually,
Ay, and perhaps o'erwrought 'em; therefore I,
Being thought travell'd, will apply myself
Unto the self same form, forget my nature,
As if no part about me were kin to 'em,
So touch 'em – though I durst almost for good
Venture my lands in heaven upon their good.
Exit.

158 *furnish*: provide for 161 *humour's*: fancy's 162 *'slud*: oath contracted from 'God's blood' 164 *Attend me*: i.e. wait on me as an attendant 167 *fellows*: partners 171 *dis-heir*: i.e. prevent him from inheriting the Dukedom by his death 176 *wrought*: i.e. worked on them 177 *o'erwrought*: i.e. won over 179 *the self same form*: i.e. that of the 'slave' of l. 176 181 *touch*: test 181–2 *I . . . their good*: I'd stake almost all my chances of salvation on their virtue. (Most editors, disliking the repetition of 'good', amend the second to 'blood', i.e. character.)

[SCENE 4]

Enter the discontented Lord ANTONIO, *whose wife the Duchess's youngest son ravished; he discovering the body of her dead to certain lords,* PIERO *and* HIPPOLITO.

ANTONIO: Draw nearer, lords, and be sad witnesses
Of a fair comely building newly fall'n,
Being falsely undermined. Violent rape
Has play'd a glorious act; behold, my lords,
A sight that strikes man out of me.
PIERO: That virtuous lady!
ANTONIO: Precedent for wives!
HIPPOLITO: The blush of many women, whose chaste presence
Would e'en call shame up to their cheeks, and make
Pale wanton sinners have good colours.
ANTONIO: Dead!
Her honour first drunk poison, and her life,
Being fellows in one house, did pledge her honour.
PIERO: O grief of many!
ANTONIO: I mark'd not this before –
A prayer-book the pillow to her cheek,
This was her rich confection, and another
Plac'd in her right hand, with a leaf tuck'd up,
Pointing to these words:
Melius virtute mori, quam per dedecus vivere.
True and effectual it is indeed.
HIPPOLITO: My lord, since you invite us to your sorrows,
Let's truly taste 'em, that with equal comfort
As to ourselves we may relieve your wrongs;
We have grief too, that yet walks without tongue:
Curae leves loquuntur, maiores stupent.

s.d. *discovering*: revealing   6 *Precedent*: exemplar   7 *blush of*: i.e. cause of blushes in   9 *good colours*: both 'more attractive' and 'more virtuous' (because blushing indicated they were aware of past sins)   10 *drunk poison*: i.e. referring to the rape   11 *pledge*: toast (the lady now literally 'drinks poison')   14 *confection*: compound of drugs used as preservative   17 *Melius virtute mori, quam per dedecus vivere*: Latin for 'Better to die virtuous than to live dishonoured'   18 *effectual*: pertinent   20–21 i.e. let us experience your grief fully, so that relieving your wrongs will be an equal comfort to ourselves   23 *Curae leves loquuntur, maiores stupent*: 'Small cares speak out, greater ones are dumb.' This misquotes Seneca's play, *Hippolytus*, l. 607, which speaks of 'huge', rather than 'greater', ones

ANTONIO: You deal with truth, my lord.
Lend me but your attentions, and I'll cut
Long grief into short words. Last revelling night,
When torchlight made an artificial noon
About the Court, some courtiers in the masque,
Putting on better faces than their own,
Being full of fraud and flattery, amongst whom
The Duchess' youngest son (that moth to honour)
Fill'd up a room; and with long lust to eat
Into my wearing, amongst all the ladies
Singled out that dear form, who ever liv'd
As cold in lust as she is now in death
(Which that step-Duchess' monster knew too well);
And therefore in the height of all the revels,
When music was heard loudest, courtiers busiest,
And ladies great with laughter – o vicious minute!
Unfit but for relation to be spoke of –
Then with a face more impudent than his vizard
He harried her amidst a throng of panders
That live upon damnation of both kinds
And fed the ravenous vulture of his lust.
O death to think on't! She, her honour forc'd,
Deem'd it a nobler dowry for her name
To die with poison than to live with shame.
HIPPOLITO: A wondrous lady, of rare fire compact,
Sh'as made her name an empress by that act.
PIERO: My lord, what judgment follows the offender?
ANTONIO: Faith, none, my lord, it cools and is deferr'd.
PIERO: Delay the doom for rape?
ANTONIO: O you must note who 'tis should die:
The Duchess' son; she'll look to be a saver,
Judgment in this age is near kin to favour.
HIPPOLITO: Nay then, step forth, thou bribeless officer.
[*Draws his sword.*]
I bind you all in steel to bind you surely,
Here let your oaths meet, to be kept and paid,
Which else will stick like rust and shame the blade.

24 *deal with*: deliver 28 *in the masque*: taking part in the masque (but with a pun on 'wearing a mask') 31 *moth to honour*: i.e. capable of eating honour away 33 *wearing*: clothing (continuing the moth image) 40 *for relation*: i.e. the need to inform you 42 *harried*: raped 43 *kinds*: sexes 48 *compact*: composed 54 *a saver*: i.e. his saviour

Strengthen my vow, that if at the next sitting
Judgment speak all in gold, and spare the blood
Of such a serpent, e'en before their seats
To let his soul out, which long since was found
Guilty in heaven.

ALL: We swear it and will act it.

ANTONIO: Kind gentlemen, I thank you in mine ire.

HIPPOLITO: 'Twere pity
The ruins of so fair a monument
Should not be dipp'd in the defacer's blood.

PIERO: Her funeral shall be wealthy, for her name
Merits a tomb of pearl. My lord Antonio,
For this time wipe your lady from your eyes;
No doubt our grief and yours may one day court it
When we are more familiar with revenge.

ANTONIO: That is my comfort, gentlemen, and I joy
In this one happiness above the rest,
Which will be call'd a miracle at last,
That, being an old man, I'd a wife so chaste.

Exeunt.

60 *Strengthen my vow*: i.e. vow with me 62 *their*: i.e. the Judges' 72 *court it*: i.e. show itself openly at Court

ACT TWO

SCENE I

Enter CASTIZA *the sister.*

CASTIZA: How hardly shall that maiden be beset,
Whose only fortunes are her constant thoughts,
That has no other child's-part but her honour
That keeps her low and empty in estate.
Maids and their honours are like poor beginners;
Were not sin rich there would be fewer sinners.
Why had not virtue a revenue? Well,
I know the cause, 'twould have impoverish'd hell.
[*Enter* DONDOLO.]
How now, Dondolo?

DONDOLO: Madonna, there is one, as they say, a thing of flesh and blood, a man I take him by his beard, that would very desirously mouth to mouth with you.

CASTIZA: What's that?

DONDOLO: Show his teeth in your company.

CASTIZA: I understand thee not.

DONDOLO: Why, speak with you, Madonna.

CASTIZA: Why, say so, madman, and cut off a great deal of dirty way; had it not been better spoke in ordinary words, that one would speak with me?

DONDOLO: Ha, ha, that's as ordinary as two shillings. I would strive a little to show myself in my place; a gentleman-usher scorns to use the phrase and fancy of a serving-man.

CASTIZA: Yours be your own, sir. Go, direct him hither;
[*Exit* DONDOLO.]
I hope some happy tidings from my brother
That lately travell'd, whom my soul affects.
Here he comes.

Enter VINDICE *her brother, disguised.*

1 *hardly*: severely *beset*: assailed 3 *child's-part*: inheritance 17 *dirty way*: i.e. tedious circumlocution/'smut' 21 *place*: office *gentleman-usher*: an attendant, rather than servant, who introduces guests 23 *own*: Q reads 'one' 25 *affects*: loves

VINDICE: Lady, the best of wishes to your sex,
Fair skins and new gowns.
[*Gives her a letter.*]
CASTIZA: O they shall thank you, sir.
Whence this?
VINDICE: O from a dear and worthy friend,
Mighty!
CASTIZA: From whom?
VINDICE: The Duke's son.
CASTIZA: Receive that!
[s.d.] *A box o'th'ear to her brother.*
I swore I'd put anger in my hand,
And pass the virgin limits of myself
To him that next appear'd in that base office,
To be his sin's attorney. Bear to him
That figure of my hate upon thy cheek
Whilst 'tis yet hot, and I'll reward thee for't;
Tell him my honour shall have a rich name
When several harlots shall share his with shame.
Farewell, commend me to him in my hate!
Exit.
VINDICE: It is the sweetest box that e'er my nose came nigh,
The finest drawn-work cuff that e'er was worn;
I'll love this blow for ever, and this cheek
Shall still henceforward take the wall of this.
O I'm above my tongue! Most constant sister,
In this thou has right honourable shown;
Many are call'd by their honour that have none,
Thou art approv'd for ever in my thoughts.
It is not in the power of words to taint thee,
And yet for the salvation of my oath,
As my resolve in that point, I will lay

34 *attorney*: i.e. one who pleads on sin's behalf 40 *sweetest box*: punning on 'box' = blow and 'box' = container for perfumed ointments 41 *drawn-work cuff*: a decorated shirt-sleeve cuff (but 'cuff' also means 'blow') 43 *take the wall of*: i.e. take precedence over (walking on the inside of the pavement, where one was less likely to be splashed or struck, was a privilege) 46 *call'd by their honour*: i.e. addressed by hereditary titles 47 *approv'd*: esteemed 49 *for the salvation of my oath*: oaths extracted through trickery or threats are often considered binding in Middleton's plays 50 *As . . . point*: i.e. seeing that I was resolved to do so

Hard siege unto my mother, though I know
A siren's tongue could not bewitch her so.
[*Enter* GRATIANA.]
Mass, fitly here she comes; thanks, my disguise. –
Madam, good afternoon.

GRATIANA: Y'are welcome, sir.

VINDICE: The next of Italy commends him to you,
Our mighty expectation, the Duke's son.

GRATIANA: I think myself much honour'd that he pleases
To rank me in his thoughts.

VINDICE: So may you, lady.
One that is like to be our sudden Duke –
The crown gapes for him every tide – and then
Commander o'er us all; do but think on him,
How blest were they now that could pleasure him
E'en with anything almost.

GRATIANA: Ay, save their honour.

VINDICE: Tut, one would let a little of that go too
And ne'er be seen in't – ne'er be seen in't, mark you,
I'd wink, and let it go.

GRATIANA: Marry, but I would not.

VINDICE: Marry, but I would, I hope; I know you would too
If you'd that blood now which you gave your daughter.
To her indeed 'tis, this wheel comes about;
That man that must be all this, perhaps e'er morning
(For his white father does but mould away),
Has long desir'd your daughter.

GRATIANA: Desir'd?

VINDICE: Nay but hear me,
He desires now that will command hereafter,
Therefore be wise, I speak as more a friend
To you than him; madam, I know y'are poor
And, 'lack the day,
There are too many poor ladies already;
Why should you vex the number? 'Tis despis'd.

52 *siren's tongue*: in Greek mythology the sirens were mermaids who lured sailors to destruction by their beautiful singing 55 *next of Italy*: i.e. next in line of succession 59 *to be our sudden Duke*: i.e. to become Duke at any moment 60 *tide*: hour 65 *ne'er be seen in't*: i.e. keep it secret (Q reads 'ne'er be seen it') 66 *Marry*: interjection derived from the name of the Virgin Mary 68 *blood*: spirit/sexual appetite 69 *wheel*: opportunity, alluding to the Wheel of Fortune 77 *'lack the day*: unfortunately 79 *vex the number*: i.e. aggravate the situation by adding to the numbers of poor ladies

Live wealthy, rightly understand the world,
And chide away that foolish country-girl
Keeps company with your daughter, Chastity.

GRATIANA: O fie, fie, the riches of the world cannot hire
A mother to such a most unnatural task.

VINDICE: No, but a thousand angels can,
Men have no power, angels must work you to't.
The world descends into such base-born evils
That forty angels can make fourscore devils.
There will be fools still I perceive, still fools;
Would I be poor, dejected, scorn'd of greatness,
Swept from the palace, and see other daughters
Spring with the dew o'th'Court, having mine own
So much desir'd and lov'd – by the Duke's son?
No, I would raise my state upon her breast
And call her eyes my tenants; I would count
My yearly maintenance upon her cheeks,
Take coach upon her lip, and all her parts
Should keep men after men and I would ride
In pleasure upon pleasure.
You took great pains for her, once when it was,
Let her requite it now, though it be but some.
You brought her forth, she well may bring you home.

GRATIANA: O heavens! This overcomes me!

VINDICE [*Aside.*]: Not, I hope, already?

GRATIANA [*Aside.*]: It is too strong for me, men know that know us,
We are so weak their words can overthrow us.
He touch'd me nearly, made my virtues bate
When his tongue struck upon my poor estate.

VINDICE [*Aside.*]: I e'en quake to proceed, my spirit turns edge,
I fear me she's unmother'd, yet I'll venture:
That woman is all male, whom none can enter. –
What think you now, lady, speak, are you wiser?
What said Advancement to you? Thus it said:
The daughter's fall lifts up the mother's head.

85 *angels*: punning on angels = gold coins (which were engraved with the figure of the Archangel Michael) worth 50 pence 89 *fools*: Q reads 'foole' 90 *dejected*: humbled, lowly 94 *state*: rank/estate 98 *keep men after men*: i.e. maintain servants (but with an allusion to prostitution) 100 *once when it was*: i.e. during childbirth 102 *bring you home*: i.e. make you rich 107 *touch'd me nearly*: i.e. made a deep impression on me *bate*: abate, decline 109 *turns edge*: i.e. is blunted 110 *unmother'd*: i.e. lost her maternal affections

Did it not, madam? But I'll swear it does
In many places; tut, this age fears no man,
'Tis no shame to be bad, because 'tis common.
GRATIANA: Ay, that's the comfort on't.
VINDICE [*Aside.*]: The comfort on't! –
I keep the best for last; can these persuade you
To forget heaven – and –
[*Gives her money.*]
GRATIANA: Ay, these are they –
VINDICE [*Aside.*]: O!
GRATIANA: – that enchant our sex, these are the means
That govern our affections; that woman
Will not be troubled with the mother long,
That sees the comfortable shine of you;
I blush to think what for your sakes I'll do.
VINDICE [*Aside.*]: O suff'ring heaven, with thy invisible finger
E'en at this instant turn the precious side
Of both mine eyeballs inward, not to see myself!
GRATIANA: Look you, sir.
VINDICE: Holla.
GRATIANA: Let this thank your pains.
[*Gives him money.*]
VINDICE: O you're a kind madam.
GRATIANA: I'll see how I can move.
VINDICE [*Aside.*]: Your words will sting.
GRATIANA: If she be still chaste I'll ne'er call her mine.
VINDICE [*Aside.*]: Spoke truer than you meant it.
GRATIANA: Daughter Castiza.
[*Enter* CASTIZA.]
CASTIZA: Madam.
VINDICE: O she's yonder. Meet her.
[*Aside.*] Troops of celestial soldiers guard her heart.
Yon dam has devils enough to take her part.

124 *the mother*: maternal affections/hysteria 130 *kind*: generous, but ironically punning on 'kind' = natural 131 *move*: i.e. persuade Castiza 136 *dam*: contemptuous term for 'mother'

CASTIZA: Madam, what makes yon evil-offic'd man
In presence of you?
GRATIANA: Why?
CASTIZA: He lately brought
Immodest writing sent from the Duke's son
To tempt me to dishonourable act.
GRATIANA: Dishonourable act? – Good honourable fool,
That wouldst be honest 'cause thou wouldst be so,
Producing no one reason but thy will.
And 't'as a good report, prettily commended,
But pray, by whom? Mean people, ignorant people,
The better sort I'm sure cannot abide it,
And by what rule shouldst we square out our lives
But by our betters' actions? O if thou knew'st
What 'twere to lose it, thou would never keep it;
But there's a cold curse laid upon all maids,
Whilst others clip the sun, they clasp the shades.
Virginity is paradise lock'd up.
You cannot come by your selves without fee,
And 'twas decreed that man should keep the key.
Deny advancement, treasure, the Duke's son?
CASTIZA: I cry you mercy, lady, I mistook you.
Pray, did you see my mother? Which way went she?
Pray God I have not lost her.
VINDICE [*Aside.*]: Prettily put by.
GRATIANA: Are you as proud to me as coy to him?
Do you not know me now?
CASTIZA: Why are you she?
The world's so chang'd, one shape into another,
It is a wise child now that knows her mother!
VINDICE [*Aside.*]: Most right, i'faith.
GRATIANA: I owe your cheek my hand
For that presumption now, but I'll forget it;
Come, you shall leave those childish haviours,
And understand your time. Fortunes flow to you,

142 *honest*: chaste 144 *'t'as*: it (i.e. 'honesty') has 147 *square out*: plan 151 *clip*: embrace 153 *come*: i.e. arrive at paradise/achieve orgasm 154 *key*: i.e. penis 158 *put by*: evaded 159 *coy*: modest/disdainful 165 *haviours*: manners

What, will you be a girl?
If all fear'd drowning that spy waves ashore
Gold would grow rich and all the merchants poor.
CASTIZA: It is a pretty saying of a wicked one,
But methinks now
It does not show so well out of your mouth,
Better in his.
VINDICE [*Aside.*]: Faith, bad enough in both,
Were I in earnest, as I'll seem no less –
[*To* CASTIZA.] I wonder, lady, your own mother's words
Cannot be taken, nor stand in full force.
'Tis honesty you urge; what's honesty?
'Tis but heaven's beggar, and what woman
So foolish to keep honesty
And be not able to keep herself? No,
Times are grown wiser and will keep less charge;
A maid that has small portion now intends
To break up house and live upon her friends.
How blest are you, you have happiness alone,
Others must fall to thousands, you to one,
Sufficient in himself to make your forehead
Dazzle the world with jewels, and petitionary people
Start at your presence.
GRATIANA: O if I were young
I should be ravish'd.
CASTIZA: Ay, to lose your honour.
VINDICE: 'Slid, how can you lose your honour
To deal with my Lord's Grace?
He'll add more honour to it by his title,
Your mother will tell you how.
GRATIANA: That I will.
VINDICE: O think upon the pleasure of the palace:
Secured ease and state, the stirring meats
Ready to move out of the dishes

168 *ashore*: i.e. from the shore 169 *Gold*: i.e. goldsmiths (who acted as bankers) 181 *keep less charge*: i.e. take less care (of virtue); but punning on 'charge' = expense 183 *friends*: lovers 184 *have happiness alone*: i.e. have only happiness/need pleasure only one man 187 *petitionary people*: commoners presenting petitions at court 188 *Start*: rush forward 189 *ravish'd*: filled with delight (but Castiza plays on the meaning 'raped') 190 *'Slid*: oath contracted from 'God's lid' (i.e. eyelid)

That e'en now quicken when they're eaten,
Banquets abroad by torch-light, musics, sports,
Bare-headed vassals that had ne'er the fortune
To keep on their own hats but let horns wear 'em,
Nine coaches waiting – hurry, hurry, hurry.

CASTIZA: Ay, to the Devil.

VINDICE [*Aside.*]: Ay, to the Devil. [*Aloud.*] To th'Duke, by my faith.

GRATIANA: Ay, to the Duke. Daughter, you'd scorn to think
O'th'Devil and you were there once.

VINDICE [*Aside.*]: True, for most
There are as proud as he for his heart, i'faith. –
Who'd sit at home in a neglected room,
Dealing her short-liv'd beauty to the pictures
That are as useless as old men, when those
Poorer in face and fortune than herself
Walk with a hundred acres on their backs,
Fair meadows cut into green foreparts? O
It was the greatest blessing ever happen'd to women
When farmers' sons agreed and met again
To wash their hands and come up gentlemen.
The commonwealth has flourish'd ever since:
Lands that were mete by the rod, that labour's spar'd,
Tailors ride down and measure 'em by the yard;
Fair trees, those comely foretops of the field,
Are cut to maintain head-tires; much untold,
All thrives but chastity, she lies a-cold.
Nay, shall I come nearer to you? Mark but this:
why are there so few honest women, but because 'tis the poorer profession? That's accounted best that's best followed, least in trade,

197 *quicken*: stimulate (with a pun on 'quicken' = make pregnant) 198 *abroad*: out of doors *musics*: i.e. pieces of music 199 *vassals*: servants (in the 17th century it was the custom to remove your hat in the presence of a social superior) 200 *let horns wear 'em*: i.e. were cuckolded 205 *and*: if 206 *There*: i.e. in the Court *he*: i.e. the Devil *for his heart*: an emphatic expression, normally equivalent of 'to save his life' or 'for the life of him', but here suggesting his commitment to pride 208 *Dealing*: giving out 212 *foreparts*: front parts/ornamental stomachers 215 *come up gentlemen*: i.e. rise to the status of gentlemen/come up to Court 217 *mete*: measured *rod*: a measure of length equal to 16½ feet or of area equal to 1/160th of an acre 218 *yard*: 3 feet/ tailor's yard stick 220 *head-tires*: head-dresses *untold*: unreckoned. This could apply to the previous clause, i.e. 'there is much more to say on the topic of extravagance'; or it could qualify 'chastity' which is ignored 222 *come nearer to you*: i.e. make my remarks even more pertinent to your situation

least in fashion, and that's not honesty, believe it. And do but note the low and dejected price of it:
Lose but a pearl, we search and cannot brook it.
But that once gone, who is so mad to look it?

GRATIANA: Troth, he says true.

CASTIZA: False, I defy you both.
I have endur'd you with an ear of fire,
Your tongues have struck hot irons on my face.
Mother, come from that poisonous woman there!

GRATIANA: Where?

CASTIZA: Do you not see her? She's too inward then.
[*To him.*] Slave, perish in thy office. You heavens, please
Henceforth to make the mother a disease –
Which first begins with me, yet I've outgone you.
Exit.

VINDICE [*Aside.*]: O angels, clap your wings upon the skies
And give this virgin crystal plaudities!

GRATIANA: Peevish, coy, foolish! But return this answer:
My lord shall be most welcome when his pleasure
Conducts him this way. I will sway mine own,
Women with women can work best alone.
Exit.

VINDICE: Indeed I'll tell him so.
O more uncivil, more unnatural
Than those base-titled creatures that look downward,
Why does not heaven turn black, or with a frown
Undo the world? Why does not earth start up
And strike the sins that tread upon't? O,
Were't not for gold and women, there would be no damnation,
Hell would look like a lord's great kitchen without fire in't;
But 'twas decreed before the world began
That they should be the hooks to catch at man.
Exit.

227 *brook it*: endure the loss 228 *that*: i.e. virginity *look it*: look for it, worry over it 236 *make the mother a disease*: see note I.iii.81, above 237 *outgone*: the exact meaning is uncertain. Perhaps 'outgrown' (the influence of her mother). Foakes suggests 'circumvented' (both Vindice and Gratiana) 239 *crystal plaudities*: i.e. heavenly applause. The crystal sphere in Ptolemaic astronomy was the last sphere before the *Primum Mobile* 245 *uncivil*: uncivilized
246 *base-titled creatures that look downward*: i.e. animals. Walking upright was considered one of the distinctively human attributes

[SCENE 2]

Enter LUSSURIOSO *with* HIPPOLITO, *Vindice's brother.*

LUSSURIOSO: I much applaud thy judgment, thou art well-read in a fellow,
And 'tis the deepest art to study man.
I know this, which I never learn'd in schools,
The world's divided into knaves and fools.

HIPPOLITO [*Aside.*]: Knave in your face, my lord – behind your back!

LUSSURIOSO: And I much thank thee that thou hast preferr'd
A fellow of discourse, well-mingled,
And whose brain time hath season'd.

HIPPOLITO: True, my lord.
[*Aside.*] We shall find season once, I hope. O villain,
To make such an unnatural slave of me, but –

LUSSURIOSO: Mass, here he comes.
[*Enter* VINDICE *disguised.*]

HIPPOLITO [*Aside.*]: And now shall I have free leave to depart.

LUSSURIOSO: Your absence, leave us.

HIPPOLITO [*Aside.*]: Are not my thoughts true?
I must remove, but brother, you may stay;
Heart, we are both made bawds a new-found way!
Exit.

LUSSURIOSO: Now we're an even number. A third man's dangerous,
Especially her brother. Say, be free,
Have I a pleasure toward?

VINDICE: O my lord.

LUSSURIOSO: Ravish me in thine answer; art thou rare?
Hast thou beguil'd her of salvation
And rubb'd hell o'er with honey? Is she a woman?

VINDICE: In all but in desire.

LUSSURIOSO: Then she's in nothing –
I bate in courage now.

1 *well-read in a fellow*: i.e. a good judge of character 7 *discourse*: fluent conversation *well-mingled*: well put together 8 *season'd*: matured, brought to a state of perfection 9 *season*: i.e. a fit season for revenge 18 *toward*: coming my way 19 *rare*: of great value (having succeeded) 23 *bate in courage*: lose my ardour

VINDICE: The words I brought
Might well have made indifferent honest naught;
A right good woman in these days is chang'd
Into white money with less labour far;
Many a maid has turned to Mahomet
With easier working; I durst undertake
Upon the pawn and forfeit of my life
With half those words to flat a puritan's wife.
But she is close and good – yet 'tis a doubt
By this time. O the mother, the mother!
LUSSURIOSO: I never thought their sex had been a wonder
Until this minute. What fruit from the mother?
VINDICE [*Aside.*]: Now must I blister my soul, be forsworn,
Or shame the woman that receiv'd me first;
I will be true, thou liv'st not to proclaim;
Spoke to a dying man, shame has no shame. –
My lord.
LUSSURIOSO: Who's that?
VINDICE: Here's none but I, my lord.
LUSSURIOSO: What would thy haste utter?
VINDICE: Comfort.
LUSSURIOSO: Welcome.
VINDICE: The maid being dull, having no mind to travel
Into unknown lands, what did me I straight
But set spurs to the mother? Golden spurs
Will put her to a false gallop in a trice.
LUSSURIOSO: Is't possible that in this
The mother should be damn'd before the daughter?
VINDICE: O that's good manners, my lord; the mother for her age must go foremost, you know.
LUSSURIOSO: Thou'st spoke that true, but where comes in this comfort?
VINDICE: In a fine place, my lord – the unnatural mother
Did with her tongue so hard beset her honour
That the poor fool was struck to silent wonder,
Yet still the maid, like an unlighted taper,

24 *indifferent*: reasonably *naught*: bad, worthless 25–6 *chang'd Into white money*: i.e. persuaded to prostitution ('white money' = silver) 27 *turned to Mahomet*: converted to the Muslim faith 30 *flat*: overthrow/lay down ready for intercourse 31 *close*: reserved 35 *be forsworn*: see I.iii.169 36 *receiv'd*: greeted (i.e. his mother at his birth) 44 *false gallop*: canter (but punning on the effects of 'Golden spurs' on the mother's morality) 49 *this comfort*: i.e. that promised in l. 40 51 *beset*: besiege

Was cold and chaste, save that her mother's breath
Did blow fire on her cheeks. The girl departed
But the good ancient madam, half mad, threw me
These promising words which I took deeply note of:
'My lord shall be most welcome –'
LUSSURIOSO: Faith, I thank her.
VINDICE: 'When his pleasure conducts him this way –'
LUSSURIOSO: That shall be soon, i'faith.
VINDICE: 'I will sway mine own –'
LUSSURIOSO: She does the wiser; I commend her for't.
VINDICE: 'Women with women can work best alone.'

LUSSURIOSO: By this light, and so they can; give 'em their due, men are not comparable to 'em.

VINDICE: No, that's true, for you shall have one woman knit more in an hour than any man can ravel again in seven and twenty year.

LUSSURIOSO: Now my desires are happy, I'll make 'em freemen now;
Thou art a precious fellow, faith, I love thee,
Be wise, and make it thy revenue: beg, leg,
What office couldst thou be ambitious for?

VINDICE: Office, my lord? Marry, if I might have my wish, I would have one that was never begg'd yet.

LUSSURIOSO: Nay then, thou canst have none.

VINDICE: Yes, my lord, I could pick out another office yet, nay, and keep a horse and drab upon't.

LUSSURIOSO: Prithee, good bluntness, tell me.

VINDICE: Why I would desire but this, my lord: to have all the fees behind the arras, and all the farthingales that fall plump about twelve o'clock at night upon the rushes.

LUSSURIOSO: Thou 'rt a mad apprehensive knave; dost think to make any great purchase of that?

VINDICE: O 'tis an unknown thing, my lord; I wonder 't'as been missed so long!

LUSSURIOSO: Well, this night I'll visit her, and 'tis till then
A year in my desires – farewell, attend,
Trust me with thy preferment.
Exit.

55 *cheeks*: Q reads 'checkes' 66 *ravel*: unravel 67 *make 'em freemen*: set them free (like freed slaves) 69 *leg*: bow 75 *drab*: whore 77–8 *fees behind the arras*: i.e. fees for arranging sexual assignations behind the arras or tapestries hung on the walls of rooms 78 *farthingales*: women's hooped petticoats *plump*: an onomatopoeic phrase like 'plop!' 79 *rushes*: these were used as floor coverings 80 *apprehensive*: quick-witted 81 *purchase*: profit

VINDICE: My lov'd lord. –
[*Draws his sword.*] O shall I kill him o'th'wrong side now? No!
Sword, thou wast never a back-biter yet,
I'll pierce him to his face, he shall die looking upon me;
Thy veins are swell'd with lust, this shall unfill 'em;
Great men were gods if beggars could not kill 'em.
Forgive me, heaven, to call my mother wicked,
O lessen not my days upon the earth.
I cannot honour her; by this I fear me
Her tongue has turn'd my sister into use.
I was a villain not to be forsworn
To this our lecherous hope, the Duke's son,
For lawyers, merchants, some divines and all
Count beneficial perjury a sin small.
It shall go hard yet, but I'll guard her honour
And keep the ports sure.

Enter HIPPOLITO.

HIPPOLITO: Brother, how goes the world? I would know news
Of you, but I have news to tell you.
VINDICE: What, in the name of knavery?
HIPPOLITO: Knavery, faith,
This vicious old Duke's worthily abus'd,
The pen of his bastard writes him cuckold!
VINDICE: His bastard?
HIPPOLITO: Pray believe it, he and the Duchess
By night meet in their linen; they have been seen
By stair-foot panders.
VINDICE: O sin foul and deep,
Great faults are wink'd at when the Duke's asleep.
See, see, here comes the Spurio.
HIPPOLITO: Monstrous luxur!

[*Enter* SPURIO *with two* Servants.]

VINDICE: Unbrac'd; two of his valiant bawds with him.
O there's a wicked whisper; hell is in his ear.
Stay, let's observe his passage –

[*They retire.*]

SPURIO: O but are you sure on't?

87 *o'th'wrong side*: i.e. stab him in the back 95 *use*: prostitution/profit 97 *hope*: i.e. heir to the Dukedom 99 *beneficial perjury*: i.e. equivocation; lying or swearing a false oath for good reasons 100 *go hard*: prove difficult 101 *ports*: gates 106 *pen*: slang for 'penis' 111 *luxur*: lecher 112 *Unbrac'd*: with clothes unfastened or loosened (or without his doublet)

SERVANT 1: My lord, most sure on't, for 'twas spoke by one
That is most inward with the Duke's son's lust:
That he intends within this hour to steal
Unto Hippolito's sister, whose chaste life
The mother has corrupted for his use.
SPURIO: Sweet word, sweet occasion! Faith then, brother,
I'll disinherit you in as short time
As I was when I was begot in haste,
I'll damn you at your pleasure: precious deed!
After your lust, o 'twill be fine to bleed. –
Come, let our passing out be soft and wary.
Exeunt [SPURIO *and* Servants].
VINDICE: Mark, there, there, that step, now to the Duchess;
This their second meeting writes the Duke cuckold
With new additions, his horns newly reviv'd.
Night! Thou that look'st like funeral heralds' fees
Torn down betimes i'th'morning, thou hang'st fitly
To grace those sins that have no grace at all.
Now 'tis full sea abed over the world,
There's juggling of all sides; some that were maids
E'en at sunset are now perhaps i'th'toll-book;
This woman in immodest thin apparel
Lets in her friend by water; here a dame
Cunning nails leather hinges to a door
To avoid proclamation; now cuckolds are
A-coining, apace, apace, apace, apace!
And careful sisters spin that thread i'th'night
That does maintain them and their bawds i'th'day.
HIPPOLITO: You flow well, brother.
VINDICE: Puh, I'm shallow yet,
Too sparing and too modest. Shall I tell thee?
If every trick were told that's dealt by night,
There are few here that would not blush outright.

127 *now to the Duchess*: clearly Vindice and Hippolito do not overhear Spurio's conversation 129 *additions*: titles 130 *fees*: i.e. 'phease', black hangings put up on the occasion of a funeral 133 *full sea*: high tide (of sexual activity) 134 *juggling*: trickery 135 *i'th'toll-book*: i.e. prostitutes. The 'toll-book' recorded the sale of animals at market 137 *friend by water*: lover who arrives by boat 139 *proclamation*: i.e. detection from squeaking hinges 140 *A-coining*: being coined 141 *sisters*: i.e. prostitutes 143 *flow*: continuing the metaphor of 'full sea abed' from l. 133, above 144 *modest*: moderate 145 *trick*: act of intercourse/card hand/stratagem *told*: counted/described *dealt*: play of cards/playing sexual games/bestowed

HIPPOLITO: I am of that belief too.
VINDICE: Who's this comes?
[*Enter* LUSSURIOSO.]
The Duke's son up so late? Brother, fall back
And you shall learn some mischief. – My good lord.
[HIPPOLITO *withdraws.*]
LUSSURIOSO: Piato! Why, the man I wish'd for; come,
I do embrace this season for the fittest
To taste of that young lady.
VINDICE [*Aside.*]: Heart and hell!
HIPPOLITO [*Aside.*]: Damned villain!
VINDICE [*Aside.*]: I ha' no way now to cross it, but to kill him.
LUSSURIOSO: Come, only thou and I.
VINDICE: My lord, my lord!
LUSSURIOSO: Why dost thou start us?
VINDICE: I'd almost forgot –
The Bastard!
LUSSURIOSO: What of him?
VINDICE: This night, this hour,
This minute, now –
LUSSURIOSO: What? What?
VINDICE: Shadows the Duchess –
LUSSURIOSO: Horrible word.
VINDICE: And like strong poison eats
Into the Duke your father's forehead.
LUSSURIOSO: O!
VINDICE: He makes horn royal.
LUSSURIOSO: Most ignoble slave!
VINDICE: This is the fruit of two beds.
LUSSURIOSO: I am mad.
VINDICE: That passage he trod warily.
LUSSURIOSO: He did!
VINDICE: And hush'd his villains every step he took.
LUSSURIOSO: His villains? I'll confound them.
VINDICE: Take 'em finely, finely now.
LUSSURIOSO: The Duchess' chamber door shall not control me.
Exeunt [LUSSURIOSO *and* VINDICE].

150 *Piato*: Vindice's assumed name, which means 'hidden' in Italian 156 *start*: startle 158 *Shadows*: sexually covers 160 *forehead*: another allusion to cuckold's horns 162 *fruit of two beds*: i.e. Spurio's and the Duchess's, but also the adulterous liaison between the Duke and Spurio's mother

HIPPOLITO: Good, happy, swift, there's gunpowder i'th'Court,
Wildfire at midnight. In this heedless fury
He may show violence to cross himself;
I'll follow the event.
Exit.

[SCENE 3]

[DUKE *and* DUCHESS *discovered in bed.*]
Enter again [LUSSURIOSO *and* VINDICE].
LUSSURIOSO: Where is that villain?
VINDICE: Softly, my lord, and you may take 'em twisted.
LUSSURIOSO: I care not how.
VINDICE: O 'twill be glorious
To kill 'em doubled, when they're heap'd. Be soft, my lord.
LUSSURIOSO: Away, my spleen is not so lazy; thus and thus
I'll shake their eyelids ope, and with my sword
Shut 'em again for ever. – Villain! Strumpet!
DUKE: You upper guard defend us!
DUCHESS: Treason, treason!
DUKE: O take me not in sleep,
I have great sins, I must have days,
Nay months, dear son, with penitential heaves
To lift 'em out and not to die unclear.
O thou wilt kill me both in heaven and here.
LUSSURIOSO: I am amaz'd to death.
DUKE: Nay, villain traitor,
Worse than the foulest epithet, now I'll gripe thee
E'en with the nerves of wrath, and throw thy head
Amongst the lawyers. Guard!
Enter [Guards, HIPPOLITO,] Nobles, *and* [AMBITIOSO *and* SUPERVACUO, the Duke's] *sons.*
NOBLE 1: How comes the quiet of your grace disturb'd?
DUKE: This boy that should be myself after me
Would be myself before me, and in heat

169 *Wildfire*: highly inflammable substance used in war/furious or destructive fire/lightning 170 *cross*: thwart 2 *twisted*: i.e. having sex 5 *spleen*: violent temper 8 *upper*: i.e. innermost, nearest the bedchamber 11 *heaves*: sighs or groans 12 *unclear*: not clear of sin 15 *gripe*: seize 16 *nerves*: sinews

Of that ambition bloodily rush'd in
Intending to depose me in my bed.
NOBLE 2: Duty and natural loyalty forfend!
DUCHESS: He call'd his father villain, and me strumpet,
A word that I abhor to file my lips with.
AMBITIOSO: That was not so well done, brother.
LUSSURIOSO: I am abus'd –
I know there's no excuse can do me good.
VINDICE [*Aside.*]: 'Tis now good policy to be from sight;
His vicious purpose to our sister's honour
Is cross'd beyond our thought.
HIPPOLITO [*Aside.*]: You little dreamt
His father slept here.
VINDICE [*Aside.*]: O 'twas far beyond me.
But since it fell so, without frightful word,
Would he had kill'd him, 'twould have eas'd our swords.
[VINDICE *and* HIPPOLITO] *dissemble a flight.*
DUKE: Be comforted, our Duchess, he shall die.
LUSSURIOSO: Where's this slave-pander now? Out of mine eye,
Guilty of this abuse.
Enter SPURIO *with* [*two* Servants,] *his villains.*
SPURIO: You're villains, fablers,
You have knaves' chins and harlots' tongues, you lie,
And I will damn you with one meal a day!
SERVANT 1: O good my lord!
SPURIO: 'Sblood, you shall never sup.
SERVANT 2: O I beseech you, sir!
SPURIO: To let my sword
Catch cold so long and miss him.
SERVANT 1: Troth, my lord,
'Twas his intent to meet there.

23 *forfend*: prevent 25 *file*: defile 26 *abus'd*: imposed upon, deceived
32 *frightful*: causing alarm, i.e. he wishes he had killed the Duke without giving him any warning s.d. *dissemble a flight*: either 'slink away secretly' ('dissemble' suggesting disguise), or 'go out separately in haste' (if the intransitive verb 'dissemble', meaning 'to dispose', has been fused with the phrase 'to take a flight' = 'to flee'). Q fails to make clear whether Vindice and Hippolito, or the Duchess, are so described, but the former seems more likely 35 *slave-pander*: i.e. Piato *Out of mine eye*: i.e. nowhere to be seen 37 *harlots'*: harlot was a general term of abuse, similar to villain, that could be applied to men

SPURIO: Heart, he's yonder.
Ha? What news here? Is the day out o'th'socket
That it is noon at midnight? The Court up?
How comes the guard so saucy with his elbows?
LUSSURIOSO [*Aside.*] : The bastard here?
Nay then, the truth of my intent shall out.
[*To the Duke.*] My lord and father, hear me.
DUKE: Bear him hence.
LUSSURIOSO: I can with loyalty excuse –
DUKE: Excuse? To prison with the villain!
Death shall not long lag after him.
SPURIO [*Aside.*] : Good i'faith, then 'tis not much amiss.
LUSSURIOSO: Brothers, my best release lies on your tongues,
I pray persuade for me.
AMBITIOSO: It is our duties:
Make yourself sure of us.
SUPERVACUO: We'll sweat in pleading.
LUSSURIOSO: And I may live to thank you.
[*Exeunt* LUSSURIOSO *and* Guards.]
AMBITIOSO [*Aside.*]: No, thy death
Shall thank me better.
SPURIO [*Aside.*]: He's gone; I'll after him,
And know his trespass, seem to bear a part
In all his ills, but with a puritan heart.
Exit [SPURIO *and* Servants].
AMBITIOSO: Now brother, let our hate and love be woven
So subtly together that in speaking
One word for his life we may make three for his death;
The craftiest pleader gets most gold for breath.
SUPERVACUO: Set on, I'll not be far behind you, brother.
DUKE: Is't possible a son should be disobedient as far as the sword?
It is the highest, he can go no farther.
AMBITIOSO: My gracious lord, take pity –
DUKE: Pity, boys?
AMBITIOSO: Nay, we'd be loth to move your Grace too much,
We know the trespass is unpardonable,
Black, wicked, and unnatural –
SUPERVACUO: In a son, o monstrous!

43 *out o'th'socket*: out of joint, not running its normal course 45 *his elbows*: i.e. Lussurioso's, which are gripped by the guards 55 *Make yourself sure of us*: have confidence in us 59 *puritan*: i.e. hypocritical

AMBITIOSO: Yet, my lord,
A Duke's soft hand strokes the rough head of Law
And makes it lie smooth.
DUKE: But my hand shall ne'er do't.
AMBITIOSO: That as you please, my lord.
SUPERVACUO: We must needs confess
Some father would have enter'd into hate
So deadly-pointed that before his eyes
He would ha' seen the execution sound
Without corrupted favour.
AMBITIOSO: But my lord,
Your grace may live the wonder of all times
In pard'ning that offence which never yet
Had face to beg a pardon.
DUKE [*Aside.*]: Honey? How's this?
AMBITIOSO: Forgive him, good my lord, he's your own son,
And I must needs say 'twas the vildlier done.
SUPERVACUO: He's the next heir, yet this true reason gathers:
None can possess that dispossess their fathers.
Be merciful –
DUKE [*Aside.*]: Here's no stepmother's wit,
I'll try them both upon their love and hate.
AMBITIOSO: Be merciful – although –
DUKE: You have prevail'd,
My wrath like flaming wax hath spent itself.
I know 'twas but some peevish moon in him;
Go, let him be releas'd.
SUPERVACUO [*Aside.*]: 'Sfoot, how now, brother?
AMBITIOSO: Your Grace doth please to speak beside your spleen;
I would it were so happy.
DUKE: Why go, release him.
SUPERVACUO: O my good lord, I know the fault's too weighty
And full of general loathing, too inhuman,
Rather by all men's voices worthy death.
DUKE: 'Tis true too.
Here then, receive this signet, doom shall pass;
Direct it to the judges, he shall die
E'er many days. Make haste.

77 *sound*: fully carried out 81 *Honey*: i.e. sweet words 83 *vildlier*: vilelier 84 *gathers*: concludes 86 *no stepmother's wit*: i.e. the Duke is saying, 'these two are acting maliciously (stepmotherly) but without common sense or sufficient intelligence (mother wit)' 90 *peevish moon*: lunatic frenzy 91 *'Sfoot*: an oath deriving from 'God's foot' 92 *beside your spleen*: with your anger put aside

AMBITIOSO: All speed that may be.
We could have wish'd his burden not so sore,
We knew your Grace did but delay before.
Exeunt [AMBITIOSO *and* SUPERVACUO].
DUKE: Here's Envy with a poor thin cover o'er't,
Like scarlet hid in lawn, easily spied through.
This their ambition by the mother's side
Is dangerous and for safety must be purg'd.
I will prevent their envies; sure it was
But some mistaken fury in our son
Which these aspiring boys would climb upon:
He shall be releas'd suddenly.
Enter [*two*] Nobles.
NOBLE I: Good morning to your Grace.
DUKE: Welcome, my lords.
NOBLE 2: Our knees shall take away the office of our feet for ever,
Unless your Grace bestow a father's eye
Upon the clouded fortunes of your son,
And in compassionate virtue grant him that
Which makes e'en mean men happy – liberty.
DUKE [*Aside.*]: How seriously their loves and honours woo
For that which I am about to pray them do
Which – [*To them.*] rise, my lords, your knees sign his release:
We freely pardon him.
NOBLE I: We owe your Grace much thanks, and he much duty.
Exeunt [Nobles].
DUKE: It well becomes that judge to nod at crimes
That does commit greater himself and lives;
I may forgive a disobedient error
That expect pardon for adultery
And in my old days am a youth in lust.
Many a beauty have I turn'd to poison
In the denial, covetous of all.
Age hot is like a monster to be seen;
My hairs are white and yet my sins are green.
[*Exit.*]

101 *burden*: sentence 104 *scarlet*: rich, bright red cloth *lawn*: fine linen 107 *prevent*: forestall 110 *suddenly*: immediately 127–8 *turn'd to poison In the denial*: i.e. poisoned when they refused to be seduced 128 *all*: i.e. all beautiful women 129 *hot*: lecherous 130 *green*: i.e. youthful. Green was also emblematic of lust

ACT THREE

[SCENE I]

Enter AMBITIOSO *and* SUPERVACUO.

SUPERVACUO: Brother, let my opinion sway you once;
I speak it for the best, to have him die,
Surest and soonest. If the signet come
Unto the judges' hands, why then his doom
Will be deferr'd till sittings and court-days,
Juries and further; faiths are bought and sold,
Oaths in these days are but the skin of gold.

AMBITIOSO: In troth, 'tis true too.

SUPERVACUO: Then let's set by the judges
And fall to the officers; 'tis but mistaking
The Duke our father's meaning, and where he nam'd
'E'er many days' 'tis but forgetting that
And have him die i'th'morning.

AMBITIOSO: Excellent,
Then am I heir – Duke in a minute!

SUPERVACUO [*Aside.*]: Nay,
And he were once puff'd out, here is a pin
Should quickly prick your bladder.

AMBITIOSO: Blest occasion!
He being pack'd, we'll have some trick and wile
To wind our younger brother out of prison
That lies in for the rape; the lady's dead
And people's thoughts will soon be buried.

SUPERVACUO: We may with safety do't, and live and feed;
The Duchess' sons are too proud to bleed.

7 *skin of gold*: i.e. oaths merely cover the real process of justice, which depends on bribes 8 *set by*: by-pass 9 *fall to*: apply to 14 *puff'd out*: extinguished (applying to Lussurioso)/puffed up with honours (applying to Ambitioso) *pin*: i.e. sword or dagger 16 *pack'd*: i.e. pack'd out of the way 17 *wind*: extricate

AMBITIOSO: We are, i'faith, to say true. Come, let's not linger,
I'll to the officers, go you before
And set an edge upon the executioner.
SUPERVACUO: Let me alone to grind him.
Exit.
AMBITIOSO: Meet! Farewell,
I am next now, I rise just in that place
Where thou'rt cut off – upon thy neck, kind brother:
The falling of one head lifts up another.
Exit.

[SCENE 2]

Enter with the Nobles, LUSSURIOSO *from prison.*
LUSSURIOSO: My lords, I am so much indebted to your loves
For this, o this delivery.
NOBLE I: But our duties,
My lord, unto the hopes that grow in you.
LUSSURIOSO: If e'er I live to be myself I'll thank you.
O Liberty, thou sweet and heavenly dame!
But hell for prison is too mild a name.
Exeunt.

[SCENE 3]

Enter AMBITIOSO *and* SUPERVACUO *with* Officers.
AMBITIOSO: Officers, here's the Duke's signet, your firm warrant, brings
The command of present death along with it
Unto our brother, the Duke's son; we are sorry
That we are so unnaturally employ'd
In such an unkind office, fitter far
For enemies than brothers.
SUPERVACUO: But you know
The Duke's command must be obey'd.

24 *set an edge*: exhort/(playing on 'executioner' = axe) 25 *Meet*: perfect
26 *next*: next in succession to the Dukedom 2 *But*: only 4 *myself*: i.e. Duke 2 *present*: immediate 5 *unkind*: unnatural

OFFICER 1: It must and shall, my lord. This morning then;
So suddenly?
AMBITIOSO: Ay, alas, poor good soul,
He must break fast betimes; the executioner
Stands ready to put forth his cowardly valour.
OFFICER 2: Already?
SUPERVACUO: Already, i'faith. O sir, destruction hies,
And that is least impudent soonest dies.
OFFICER 1: Troth, you say true, my lord, we take our leaves;
Our office shall be sound, we'll not delay
The third part of a minute.
AMBITIOSO: Therein you show
Yourselves good men and upright officers.
Pray let him die as private as he may;
Do him that favour, for the gaping people
Will but trouble him at his prayers
And make him curse and swear, and so die black.
Will you be so far kind?
OFFICER 1: It shall be done, my lord.
AMBITIOSO: Why we do thank you; if we live to be
You shall have a better office.
OFFICER 2: Your good lordship.
SUPERVACUO: Commend us to the scaffold in our tears.
OFFICER 1: We'll weep and do your commendations.
Exeunt [Officers].
AMBITIOSO: Fine fools in office!
SUPERVACUO: Things fall out so fit.
AMBITIOSO: So happily, come brother, ere next clock
His head will be made serve a bigger block.
Exeunt.

[SCENE 4]

Enter in prison JUNIOR.
JUNIOR: Keeper.
[*Enter* Keeper.]

10 *betimes*: early in the morning 11 *put forth*: display 13 *hies*: draws near 14 *that*: i.e. he that *impudent*: lacking in shame or modesty 16 *sound*: i.e. soundly performed 22 *black*: damned 24 *to be*: i.e. to be Duke (presumably the 'we' is the royal we) 29 *clock*: hour 30 *block*: punning on 'block' = executioner's block (the bigger) and 'block' = hat size (smaller)

KEEPER: My lord.

JUNIOR: No news lately from our brothers? Are they unmindful of us?

KEEPER: My lord, a messenger came newly in and brought this from 'em.
[*Gives him a letter.*]

JUNIOR: Nothing but paper comforts? I look'd for my delivery before this, had they been worth their oaths. Prithee be from us.
[*Exit* Keeper.]
Now what say you, forsooth? Speak out, I pray.
[*Reads*] *letter.*
'Brother, be of good cheer.' – 'Slud, it begins like a whore, with good cheer! 'Thou shalt not be long a prisoner.' – Not five and thirty year like a bankrupt, I think so! 'We have thought upon a device to get thee out by a trick.' – By a trick? Pox o' your trick, and it be so long a-playing! 'And so rest comforted, be merry and expect it suddenly.' – Be merry? Hang merry, draw and quarter merry; I'll be mad! Is 't not strange that a man should lie in a whole month for a woman? Well, we shall see how sudden our brothers will be in their promise. I must expect still a trick. I shall not be long a prisoner.
[*Enter* Keeper.]
How now, what news?

KEEPER: Bad news, my lord, I am discharg'd of you.

JUNIOR: Slave, call'st thou that bad news? I thank you, brothers.

KEEPER: My lord, 'twill prove so; here come the officers
Into whose hands I must commit you.

JUNIOR: Ha,
Officers? What, why?
[*Enter four* Officers.]

OFFICER 1: You must pardon us, my lord,
Our office must be sound. Here is our warrant,
The signet from the Duke: you must straight suffer.

JUNIOR: Suffer? I'll suffer you to be gone, I'll suffer you
To come no more; what would you have me suffer?

OFFICER 2: My lord, those words were better chang'd to prayers,
The time's but brief with you, prepare to die.

JUNIOR: Sure 'tis not so.

OFFICER 3: It is too true, my lord.

10 *bankrupt*: bankrupts could be imprisoned until they repaid their debts. They were also in no position to bribe their way out of prison 12–13 *Hang . . . draw and quarter*: hanging, drawing and quartering was the traditional punishment for treason ('draw' = disembowel, 'quarter' = dismember) 14 *lie in*: i.e. be imprisoned. This is 'strange' because normally it is women who 'lie in' (i.e. are confined to the child-bed) for the sake of men after they have been made pregnant

JUNIOR: I tell you 'tis not, for the Duke my father
Deferr'd me till next sitting, and I look
E'en every minute threescore times an hour
For a release, a trick wrought by my brothers.
OFFICER 1: A trick, my lord? If you expect such comfort
Your hope's as fruitless as a barren woman.
Your brothers were the unhappy messengers
That brought this powerful token for your death.
JUNIOR: My brothers? No, no.
OFFICER 2: 'Tis most true, my lord.
JUNIOR: My brothers to bring a warrant for my death?
How strange this shows!
OFFICER 3: There's no delaying time.
JUNIOR: Desire 'em hither, call 'em up, my brothers!
They shall deny it to your faces.
OFFICER 1: My lord,
They're far enough by this, at least at Court,
And this most strict command they left behind 'em.
When grief swum in their eyes they show'd like brothers
Brimfull of heavy sorrow; but the Duke
Must have his pleasure.
JUNIOR: His pleasure?
OFFICER 1: These were their last words which my memory bears:
'Commend us to the scaffold in our tears'.
JUNIOR: Pox dry their tears, what should I do with tears?
I hate 'em worse than any citizen's son
Can hate salt water. Here came a letter now,
New-bleeding from their pens, scarce stinted yet –
Would I'd been torn in pieces when I tore it –
Look, you officious whoresons, words of comfort:
'Not long a prisoner'.
OFFICER 1: It says true in that, sir, for you must suffer presently.
JUNIOR: A villainous Duns upon the letter, knavish exposition. Look you then here, sir: 'We'll get thee out by a trick,' says he.
OFFICER 2: That may hold too, sir, for you know a trick is commonly four cards, which was meant by us four officers.

31 *sitting*: court session 43 *by this*: i.e. by this time 51 *citizen's son*: townsman's or burgess's son 52 *hate salt water*: because of the dangers involved in sea-travel and the practice of 'pressing' men to serve at sea 53 *stinted*: dried. 'Stinted', a term applied to the staunching of a flow of blood, takes up the image of 'new-bleeding' 54 *tore*: i.e. tore open 58 *Duns*: alluding to the scholar and theologian Duns Scotus (*c.* 1265–1308), famous for the sophistry of his arguments 60 *trick*: at the time 'trick' could refer to the cards held as well as the cards played

JUNIOR: Worse and worse dealing.
OFFICER 1: The hour beckons us,
The headsman waits, lift up your eyes to heaven.
JUNIOR: I thank you, faith; good, pretty, wholesome counsel:
I should look up to heaven as you said
Whilst he behind cozens me of my head.
Ay, that's the trick.
OFFICER 3: You delay too long, my lord.
JUNIOR: Stay, good Authority's bastards; since I must
Through brothers' perjury die, o let me venom
Their souls with curses.
OFFICER 1: Come, 'tis no time to curse.
JUNIOR: Must I bleed then, without respect of sign? Well –
My fault was sweet sport which the world approves,
I die for that which every woman loves.
Exeunt.

[SCENE 5]

Enter VINDICE [*disguised*] *with* HIPPOLITO *his brother.*
VINDICE: O sweet, delectable, rare, happy, ravishing!
HIPPOLITO: Why what's the matter, brother?
VINDICE: O 'tis able
To make a man spring up and knock his forehead
Against yon silver ceiling.
HIPPOLITO: Prithee tell me,
Why may not I partake with you? You vow'd once
To give me share to every tragic thought.
VINDICE: By th'mass I think I did too.
Then I'll divide it to thee: the old Duke,
Thinking my outward shape and inward heart
Are cut out of one piece (for he that prates
His secrets, his heart stands o'th'outside),
Hires me by price to greet him with a lady

69 *perjury*: i.e. they broke their oaths to have him released 71 *without respect of sign*: i.e. having no regard to the prevailing astrological sign. It was customary for medical 'bleeding' or blood-letting to be carried out under favourable astrological signs 4 *yon silver ceiling*: i.e. the sky, with a possible allusion to the painted canopy over the stage of the Globe, known as 'the heavens' 5 *partake*: share your thoughts 8 *divide it to*: share it with 10 *prates*: blabs

In some fit place veil'd from the eyes o'th'Court,
Some darken'd blushless angle, that is guilty
Of his forefathers' lusts and great folks' riots;
To which I easily (to maintain my shape)
Consented and did wish his impudent grace
To meet her here in this unsunned lodge
Wherein 'tis night at noon; and here the rather
Because unto the torturing of his soul
The Bastard and the Duchess have appointed
Their meeting too in this luxurious circle,
Which most afflicting sight will kill his eyes
Before we kill the rest of him.

HIPPOLITO: 'Twill, i'faith, most dreadfully digested.
I see not how you could have miss'd me, brother.

VINDICE: True, but the violence of my job forgot it.

HIPPOLITO: Ay, but where's that lady now?

VINDICE: O at that word
I'm lost again, you cannot find me yet;
I'm in a throng of happy apprehensions.
He's suited for a lady, I have took care
For a delicious lip, a sparkling eye.
You shall be witness, brother;
Be ready, stand with your hat off.
Exit.

HIPPOLITO: Troth, I wonder what lady it should be?
Yet 'tis no wonder, now I think again,
To have a lady stoop to a Duke that stoops unto his men.
'Tis common to be common through the world,
And there's more private common shadowing vices
Than those who are known both by their names and prices.
'Tis part of my allegiance to stand bare

14 *angle*: corner 16 *shape*: disguise 22 *luxurious circle*: lecherous place (with a possible allusion to the 'circle' of the Globe Theatre itself and the world) 25 *dreadfully*: so as to occasion dread *digested*: concocted 26 *miss'd me*: left me out of your plans 29 *find*: understand 30 *apprehensions*: conceptions (the notion of 'fears for the future' may also be appropriate. Vindice in his thirst for revenge looks forward to catastrophes) 31 *suited for*: provided with 34 *hat off*: as a mark of respect to a high-born lady 37 *stoop*: i.e. sexually *stoops*: degrades himself (by asking Piato to find him a woman) 38 *to be common*: i.e. a 'common-woman' or harlot 39 *private common*: i.e. vices practised in private are common (private and common are being played on as antithetical terms) *shadowing*: secret/sexual 40 *those*: both vices and whores 41 *stand bare*: i.e. bare-headed as a mark of respect

To the Duke's concubine – and here she comes.
Enter VINDICE *with the skull of his love dressed up in tires.*
VINDICE: Madam, his grace will not be absent long.
Secret? Ne'er doubt us, madam; 'twill be worth
Three velvet gowns to your ladyship. Known?
Few ladies respect that! Disgrace? A poor thin shell,
'Tis the best grace you have to do it well.
I'll save your hand that labour, I'll unmask you.
[*Reveals the skull.*]
HIPPOLITO: Why brother, brother!
VINDICE: Art thou beguil'd now? Tut, a lady can
At such all hid beguile a wiser man.
Have I not fitted the old surfeiter
With a quaint piece of beauty? Age and bare bone
Are e'er allied in action: here's an eye
Able to tempt a great man – to serve God;
A pretty hanging lip, that has forgot now to dissemble,
Methinks this mouth should make a swearer tremble,
A drunkard clasp his teeth, and not undo 'em
To suffer wet damnation to run through 'em.
Here's a cheek keeps her colour, let the wind go whistle;
Spout rain, we fear thee not; be hot or cold,
All's one with us; and is not she absurd,
Whose fortunes are upon their faces set
That fear no other god but wind and wet?
HIPPOLITO: Brother, y'ave spoke that right,
Is this the form that living shone so bright?
VINDICE: The very same.
And now methinks I could e'en chide myself
For doting on her beauty, though her death
Shall be reveng'd after no common action.
Does the silk-worm expend her yellow labours
For thee? For thee does she undo herself?
Are lordships sold to maintain ladyships

s.d. *tires*: head-dress or wig 46 *shell*: i.e. hollow notion 50 *beguil'd*: attracted to her (having drawn back the tires) 51 *At such*: i.e. at such a game (of hide and seek) *all hid*: alluding to hide and seek 53 *quaint*: dainty/ingenious 63 *set*: staked/placed as cosmetics 70 *after . . . action*: in an extraordinary way 71 *yellow labours*: i.e. the yellowish cocoon of the silk-worm from which silk is manufactured 72 *undo herself*: unwind the thread from her body/wear herself out 73 *lordships*: estates *ladyships*: i.e. the extravagance of lovers

For the poor benefit of a bewitching minute?
Why does yon fellow falsify high ways
And put his life between the judge's lips
To refine such a thing, keeps horse and men
To beat their valours for her?
Surely we are all mad people and they,
Whom we think are, are not; we mistake those,
'Tis we are mad in sense, they but in clothes.

HIPPOLITO: Faith, and in clothes too we, give us our due.

VINDICE: Does every proud and self-affecting dame
Camphor her face for this? And grieve her maker
In sinful baths of milk when many an infant starves
For her superfluous outside, all for this?
Who now bids twenty pound a night, prepares
Music, perfumes and sweetmeats, all are hush'd;
Thou mayst lie chaste now. It were fine methinks
To have thee seen at revels, forgetful feasts
And unclean brothels; sure, 'twould fright the sinner
And make him a good coward, put a reveller
Out of his antic amble
And cloy an epicure with empty dishes!
Here might a scornful and ambitious woman
Look through and through herself; see, ladies, with false forms
You deceive men but cannot deceive worms.
Now to my tragic business: look you, brother,
I have not fashion'd this only for show
And useless property, no, it shall bear a part
E'en in it own revenge. This very skull
Whose mistress the Duke poison'd with this drug,
The mortal curse of the earth, shall be reveng'd

75 *falsify high ways*: impersonate the aristocracy (although many editors have interpreted the phrase as alluding to highway robbers misleading travellers by altering signposts) 77 *refine such a thing*: i.e. improve by adding refinements to such a woman (this skull) 78 *beat their valours*: Foakes suggests 'wear out their strengths' 83 *self-affecting*: self-loving, vain 84 *Camphor*: apply or wash with camphor, a white, aromatic oil, used as a cosmetic. It was also thought to counter the effects of venereal disease *for this*: i.e. eventually to become a skull 86 *superfluous outside*: i.e. immoderate concern for her looks 87 *bids*: offers (a woman) 90 *forgetful*: i.e. forgetful of (i) virtue, (ii) cares, (iii) the fact that they will all eventually come to resemble the skull he holds 93 *antic*: grotesque *amble*: leisurely stroll/a dance movement 96 *forms*: appearances 100 *property*: i.e. as a stage-property 101 *it*: its

In the like strain and kiss his lips to death.
As much as the dumb thing can, he shall feel:
What fails in poison we'll supply in steel.

HIPPOLITO: Brother, I do applaud thy constant vengeance,
The quaintness of thy malice, above thought.
[VINDICE *poisons the skull's mouth.*]

VINDICE: So, 'tis laid on. Now come and welcome, Duke,
I have her for thee. I protest it, brother,
Methinks she makes almost as fair a sign
As some old gentlewoman in a periwig.
[*To the skull.*] Hide thy face now for shame, thou hadst need have a mask now.
[*Covers the skull with a mask.*]
'Tis vain when beauty flows, but when it fleets
This would become graves better than the streets.

HIPPOLITO: You have my voice in that. Hark, the Duke's come.

VINDICE: Peace, let's observe what company he brings
And how he does absent 'em, for you know
He'll wish all private. Brother, fall you back a little
With the bony lady.

HIPPOLITO: That I will.

VINDICE: So, so –
Now nine years' vengeance crowd into a minute!
[*Enter* DUKE *and* Gentlemen.]

DUKE: You shall have leave to leave us with this charge
Upon your lives, if we be miss'd by th'Duchess
Or any of the nobles to give out
We're privately rid forth.

VINDICE [*Aside.*]: O happiness!

DUKE: With some few honourable gentlemen, you may say;
You may name those that are away from Court.

GENTLEMEN: Your will and pleasure shall be done, my lord.
[*Exeunt* Gentlemen.]

VINDICE [*Aside.*]: 'Privately rid forth' –
He strives to make sure work on't! [*To* DUKE.] Your good Grace.

DUKE: Piato, well done, hast brought her? What lady is't?

VINDICE: Faith, my lord, a country lady, a little bashful at first as most of them are, but after the first kiss, my lord, the worst is past with them. Your Grace knows now what you have to do; sh'as somewhat a grave look with her, but –

104 *strain*: manner 108 *quaintness*: ingenuity 111 *sign*: show 114 *fleets*: passes away 115 i.e. a skull befits a grave better than the street (and therefore should wear a mask) 116 *voice*: agreement 118 *absent*: dismiss

DUKE: I love that best, conduct her.
VINDICE [*Aside.*]: Have at all!
DUKE: In gravest looks the greatest faults seem less.
Give me that sin that's rob'd in holiness.
VINDICE [*Aside.*]: Back with the torch, brother, raise the perfumes.
DUKE: How sweet can a Duke breathe? Age has no fault,
Pleasure should meet in a perfumed mist.
Lady, sweetly encounter'd, I came from Court,
I must be bold with you. [*Kisses the skull.*] O what's this? O!
VINDICE: Royal villain, white devil!
DUKE: O!
VINDICE: Brother,
Place the torch here that his affrighted eyeballs
May start into those hollows. – Duke, dost know
Yon dreadful vizard? View it well, 'tis the skull
Of Gloriana, whom thou poisonedst last.
DUKE: O 't'as poisoned me.
VINDICE: Didst not know that till now?
DUKE: What are you two?
VINDICE: Villains all three! The very ragged bone
Has been sufficiently reveng'd.
DUKE: O Hippolito! Call treason.
HIPPOLITO: Yes, my good lord, treason, treason, treason!
Stamping on him.
DUKE: Then I'm betray'd.
VINDICE: Alas, poor lecher, in the hands of knaves,
A slavish Duke is baser than his slaves.
DUKE: My teeth are eaten out.
VINDICE: Hadst any left?
HIPPOLITO: I think but few.
VINDICE: Then those that did eat are eaten.
DUKE: O my tongue!
VINDICE: Your tongue? 'Twill teach you to kiss closer,
Not like a slobbering Dutchman. You have eyes still:

136 *conduct her*: escort her in *Have at all*: i.e. let's begin! The phrase was used to commence a fight 140 *Age has no fault*: i.e. the physical inadequacies of age can be disguised (there is a shift in the Duke's meaning of 'fault' since l. 137) 144 *white devil*: hypocrite 146 *start into those hollows*: i.e. stare wildly into the skull's eye-sockets 147 *vizard*: face/mask 151 *The very ragged bone*: i.e. even these rough bones 157 *slavish*: vile (but also 'enslaved' to his passions and now to his servants) 161 *closer*: i.e. with mouth closed 162 *slobbering*: Q reads 'flobbering'

Look, monster, what a lady hast thou made me
My once betrothed wife.
[*Throwing off his disguise.*]

DUKE: Is it thou, villain?
Nay then –

VINDICE: Tis I, 'tis Vindice, 'tis I.

HIPPOLITO: And let this comfort thee: our lord and father
Fell sick upon the infection of thy frowns
And died in sadness; be that thy hope of life.

DUKE: O!

VINDICE: He had his tongue, yet grief made him die speechless.
Puh, 'tis but early yet, now I'll begin
To stick thy soul with ulcers; I will make
Thy spirit grievous sore, it shall not rest
But like some pestilent man toss in thy breast.
Mark me, Duke,
Thou'rt a renowned, high and mighty cuckold.

DUKE: O!

VINDICE: Thy bastard, thy bastard rides a-hunting in thy brow.

DUKE: Millions of deaths!

VINDICE: Nay, to afflict thee more,
Here in this lodge they meet for damned clips;
Those eyes shall see the incest of their lips.

DUKE: Is there a hell besides this, villains?

VINDICE: Villain!
Nay, heaven is just, scorns are the hire of scorns,
I ne'er knew yet adulterer without horns.

HIPPOLITO: Once e'er they die 'tis quitted.

VINDICE: Hark, the music,
Their banquet is prepar'd, they're coming –

DUKE: O kill me not with that sight!

VINDICE: Thou shalt not lose that sight for all thy Dukedom.

DUKE: Traitors, murderers!

VINDICE: What? Is not thy tongue eaten out yet? Then we'll invent a silence. Brother, stifle the torch.

DUKE: Treason, murder!

VINDICE: Nay, faith, we'll have you hush'd; now with thy dagger
Nail down his tongue and mine shall keep possession
About his heart. If he but gasp he dies.

163 *made me*: made for me 178 *rides a-hunting in thy brow*: another reference to the cuckold's horns 180 *clips*: embraces 183 *scorns*: insults *hire*: reward
185 *Once*: sooner or later *they*: i.e. 'adulterers' *quitted*: requited

We dread not death to quittance injuries, brother;
If he but wink, not brooking the foul object,
Let our two other hands tear up his lids
And make his eyes like comets shine through blood;
When the bad bleeds, then is the tragedy good.
HIPPOLITO: Whist, brother, music's at our ear, they come.
Enter the Bastard [SPURIO] *meeting the* DUCHESS.
SPURIO: Had not that kiss a taste of sin 'twere sweet.
DUCHESS: Why there's no pleasure sweet but it is sinful.
SPURIO: True, such a bitter sweetness fate hath given,
Best side to us is the worst side to heaven.
DUCHESS: Push, come; 'tis the old Duke thy doubtful father,
The thought of him rubs heaven in thy way.
But I protest by yonder waxen fire,
Forget him or I'll poison him.
SPURIO: Madam, you urge a thought which ne'er had life.
So deadly do I loathe him for my birth
That if he took me hasp'd within his bed
I would add murder to adultery
And with my sword give up his years to death.
DUCHESS: Why now thou'rt sociable, let's in and feast.
Loud'st music sound, Pleasure is Banquet's guest.
Exeunt [DUCHESS *and* SPURIO].
DUKE: I cannot brook –
[*Dies.*]
VINDICE: The brook is turn'd to blood.
HIPPOLITO: Thanks to loud music.
VINDICE: 'Twas our friend indeed,
'Tis state in music for a Duke to bleed:
The Dukedom wants a head, though yet unknown;
As fast as they peep up let's cut 'em down.
Exeunt.

196 *quittance*: repay 197 *object*: i.e. the sight of Spurio and the Duchess 201 *Whist*: a command for silence 207 *rubs*: stirs memories of 208 *waxen fire*: candle-light 210 *ne'er had life*: i.e. I have never had (any thought for heaven) 212 *hasp'd*: embraced (presumably having sex with the Duchess) 217 *cannot brook*: cannot stand (Vindice puns on 'brook' = stream) 219 It is appropriately stately for a Duke to die to the accompaniment of music 220 *wants a head*: lacks a head of state

[SCENE 6]

Enter the Duchess's two sons, AMBITIOSO *and* SUPERVACUO.

AMBITIOSO: Was not his execution rarely plotted?
We are the Duke's sons now.
SUPERVACUO: Ay, you may thank my policy for that.
AMBITIOSO: Your policy? For what?
SUPERVACUO: Why, was't not my invention, brother,
To slip the judges? And, in lesser compass,
Did I not draw the model of his death,
Advising you to sudden officers
And e'en extemporal execution?
AMBITIOSO: Heart, 'twas a thing I thought on too.
SUPERVACUO: You thought on't too? 'Sfoot, slander not your thoughts
With glorious untruth, I know 'twas from you.
AMBITIOSO: Sir, I say 'twas in my head.
SUPERVACUO: Ay, like your brains then,
Ne'er to come out as long as you liv'd.
AMBITIOSO: You'd have the honour on't, forsooth, that your wit
Led him to the scaffold.
SUPERVACUO: Since it is my due
I'll publish't, but I'll ha't in spite of you.
AMBITIOSO: Methinks y'are much too bold, you should a little
Remember us, brother, next to be honest Duke.
SUPERVACUO [*Aside.*]: Ay, it shall be as easy for you to be Duke
As to be honest, and that's never, i'faith.
AMBITIOSO: Well, cold he is by this time, and because
We're both ambitious be it our amity
And let the glory be shar'd equally.
SUPERVACUO: I am content to that.
AMBITIOSO: This night our younger brother shall out of prison;
I have a trick.
SUPERVACUO: A trick, prithee what is't?
AMBITIOSO: We'll get him out by a wile.
SUPERVACUO: Prithee what wile?

3 *policy*: cunning 6 *slip*: by-pass *in lesser compass*: at a more elementary level 8 *sudden*: i.e. prompt in performance 9 *extemporal*: immediate 12 *from you*: far from your thoughts 19 *Remember us*: respect me 21 *honest*: held in honour/virtuous 22 *he*: mistakenly assuming Lussurioso is dead

AMBITIOSO: No, sir, you shall not know it till't be done,
For then you'd swear 'twere yours.
[*Enter an* Officer *with a head.*]
SUPERVACUO: How now, what's he?
AMBITIOSO: One of the officers.
SUPERVACUO: Desired news.
AMBITIOSO: How now, my friend?
OFFICER: My lords,
Under your pardon I am allotted
To that desertless office to present you
With the yet bleeding head –
SUPERVACUO [*Aside.*]: Ha, ha, excellent.
AMBITIOSO [*Aside.*]: All's sure our own. Brother, canst weep, think'st thou?
'Twould grace our flattery much; think of some dame,
'Twill teach thee to dissemble.
SUPERVACUO [*Aside.*]: I have thought;
Now for yourself.
AMBITIOSO: Our sorrows are so fluent
Our eyes o'erflow our tongues. Words spoke in tears
Are like the murmurs of the waters, the sound
Is loudly heard but cannot be distinguish'd.
SUPERVACUO: How died he, pray?
OFFICER: O full of rage and spleen.
SUPERVACUO: He died most valiantly then, we're glad
To hear it.
OFFICER: We could not woo him once to pray.
AMBITIOSO: He show'd himself a gentleman in that,
Give him his due.
OFFICER: But in the stead of prayer
He drew forth oaths.
SUPERVACUO: Then did he pray, dear heart,
Although you understood him not.
OFFICER: My lords,
E'en at his last, with pardon be it spoke,
He curs'd you both.
SUPERVACUO: He curs'd us? 'Las, good soul.
AMBITIOSO: It was not in our powers, but the Duke's pleasure.
[*Aside.*] Finely dissembled o' both sides, sweet fate,
O happy opportunity!
Enter LUSSURIOSO.

34 *desertless*: thankless 43 *spleen*: indignation, violent passion

LUSSURIOSO: Now, my lords.
BOTH: O!
LUSSURIOSO: Why do you shun me, brothers?
You may come nearer now,
The savour of the prison has forsook me.
I thank such kind lords as yourselves, I'm free.
AMBITIOSO: Alive!
SUPERVACUO: In health!
AMBITIOSO: Releas'd!
We were both e'en amaz'd with joy to see it.
LUSSURIOSO: I am much to thank you.
SUPERVACUO: Faith, we spar'd no tongue unto my lord the Duke.
AMBITIOSO: I know your delivery, brother,
Had not been half so sudden but for us.
SUPERVACUO: O how we pleaded!
LUSSURIOSO: Most deserving brothers,
In my best studies I will think of it.
Exit.
AMBITIOSO: O death and vengeance!
SUPERVACUO: Hell and torments!
AMBITIOSO: Slave, cam'st thou to delude us?
OFFICER: Delude you, my lords?
SUPERVACUO: Ay, villain, where's this head now?
OFFICER: Why here, my lord;
Just after his delivery you both came
With warrant from the Duke to behead your brother.
AMBITIOSO: Ay, our brother, the Duke's son.
OFFICER: The Duke's son,
My lord, had his release before you came.
AMBITIOSO: Whose head's that, then?
OFFICER: His whom you left command for,
Your own brother's.
AMBITIOSO: Our brother's? O furies!
SUPERVACUO: Plagues!
AMBITIOSO: Confusions!
SUPERVACUO: Darkness!
AMBITIOSO: Devils!
SUPERVACUO: Fell it out so accursedly?
AMBITIOSO: So damnedly?
SUPERVACUO: Villain, I'll brain thee with it.

57 *savour*: smell

OFFICER: O my good lord.

[*Exit.*]

SUPERVACUO: The Devil overtake thee!

AMBITIOSO: O fatal!

SUPERVACUO: O prodigious to our bloods!

AMBITIOSO: Did we dissemble?

SUPERVACUO: Did we make our tears women for thee?

AMBITIOSO: Laugh and rejoice for thee?

SUPERVACUO: Bring warrant for thy death?

AMBITIOSO: Mock off thy head?

SUPERVACUO: You had a trick, you had a wile, forsooth.

AMBITIOSO: A murrain meet 'em, there's none of these wiles that ever come to good. I see now there is nothing sure in mortality but mortality. Well, no more words, 'shalt be reveng'd i'faith.
Come throw off clouds now, brother, think of vengeance
And deeper settled hate; sirrah, sit fast,
We'll pull down all, but thou shalt down at last.

Exeunt.

82 *prodigious*: ominous 83 *make our tears women*: i.e. dissemble grief
87 *murrain*: plague 91 *sirrah*: contemptuous form of address aimed at the absent Lussurioso

ACT FOUR

SCENE I

Enter LUSSURIOSO *with* HIPPOLITO.

LUSSURIOSO: Hippolito.
HIPPOLITO: My lord, has your good lordship
Aught to command me in?
LUSSURIOSO: I prithee leave us.
HIPPOLITO [*Aside.*]: How's this, come, and leave us?
LUSSURIOSO: Hippolito.
HIPPOLITO: Your honour, I stand ready for any duteous employment.
LUSSURIOSO: Heart, what mak'st thou here?
HIPPOLITO [*Aside.*]: A pretty lordly humour:
He bids me to be present, to depart.
Something has stung his honour.
LUSSURIOSO: Be nearer, draw nearer;
Y'are not so good, methinks, I'm angry with you.
HIPPOLITO: With me, my lord? I'm angry with myself for't.
LUSSURIOSO: You did prefer a goodly fellow to me,
'Twas wittily elected, 'twas. I thought
H'ad been a villain and he proves a knave,
To me a knave!
HIPPOLITO: I chose him for the best, my lord,
'Tis much my sorrow if neglect in him
Breed discontent in you.
LUSSURIOSO: Neglect? 'Twas will!
Judge of it:
Firmly to tell of an incredible act,
Not to be thought, less to be spoken of,
'Twixt my stepmother and the bastard, o
Incestuous sweets between 'em.

11 *wittily*: wisely *elected*: selected 12 *villain . . . knave*: the terms cannot really be distinguished except in so far as Lussurioso had expected Piato to behave villainously towards others rather than knavishly to himself 13 *chose him for the best*: i.e. I believed he was the best available (with an irony hidden from Lussurioso; Piato was the 'best' for the brothers' purposes) 15 *will*: intentional behaviour 17 *Firmly*: confidently

HIPPOLITO: Fie, my lord.
LUSSURIOSO: I in kind loyalty to my father's forehead
Made this a desperate arm, and in that fury
Committed treason on the lawful bed
And with my sword e'en ras'd my father's bosom,
For which I was within a stroke of death.
HIPPOLITO: Alack, I'm sorry. [*Aside.*] 'Sfoot, just upon the stroke
Jars in my brother, 'twill be villainous music.
Enter VINDICE.
VINDICE: My honoured lord.
LUSSURIOSO: Away, prithee forsake us, hereafter we'll not know thee.
VINDICE: Not know me, my lord? Your lordship cannot choose.
LUSSURIOSO: Be gone, I say, thou art a false knave.
VINDICE: Why, the easier to be known, my lord.
LUSSURIOSO: Push, I shall prove too bitter with a word,
Make thee a perpetual prisoner
And lay this iron-age upon thee.
VINDICE [*Aside.*]: Mum,
For there's a doom would make a woman dumb.
Missing the Bastard, next him, the wind's come about;
Now 'tis my brother's turn to stay, mine to go out.
Exit.
LUSSURIOSO: H'as greatly mov'd me.
HIPPOLITO: Much to blame, i'faith.
LUSSURIOSO: But I'll recover, to his ruin. 'Twas told me lately, I know not whether falsely, that you'd a brother.
HIPPOLITO: Who, I? Yes, my good lord, I have a brother.
LUSSURIOSO: How chance the Court ne'er saw him? Of what nature?
How does he apply his hours?
HIPPOLITO: Faith, to curse fates
Who, as he thinks, ordain'd him to be poor,
Keeps at home, full of want and discontent.
LUSSURIOSO: There's hope in him, for discontent and want
Is the best clay to mould a villain of.
Hippolito, wish him repair to us.

21 *forehead*: again the allusion is to cuckold's horns 24 *ras'd*: grazed 26 *stroke*: possibly the idea of a touch upon a musical instrument 27 *Jars in*: i.e. enters on a discordant note 35 *this iron-age*: referring to the prisoner's irons. (See IV.ii.121.) There is probably also an allusion to the Iron Age of classical mythology, the last and worst of the four stages of world history *Mum*: silence! 37 *Missing the Bastard, next him*: i.e. Now I've missed killing first Spurio, and then Lussurioso 39 *mov'd*: angered 44 *apply*: spend 49 *repair*: report

If there be aught in him to please our blood,
For thy sake we'll advance him and build fair
His meanest fortunes; for it is in us
To rear up towers from cottages.

HIPPOLITO: It is so, my lord. He will attend your honour,
But he's a man in whom much melancholy dwells.

LUSSURIOSO: Why the better: bring him to Court.

HIPPOLITO: With willingness and speed.
[*Aside.*] Whom he cast off e'en now, must now succeed.
Brother, disguise must off,
In thine own shape now I'll prefer thee to him:
How strangely does himself work to undo him.
Exit.

LUSSURIOSO: This fellow will come fitly, he shall kill
That other slave that did abuse my spleen
And made it swell to treason. I have put
Much of my heart into him, he must die.
He that knows great men's secrets and proves slight,
That man ne'er lives to see his beard turn white.
Ay, he shall speed him, I'll employ the brother,
Slaves are but nails to drive out one another.
He being of black condition, suitable
To want and ill content, hope of preferment
Will grind him to an edge.
[*Two* Nobles *enter.*]

NOBLE 1: Good days unto your honour.

LUSSURIOSO: My kind lords, I do return the like.

NOBLE 2: Saw you my lord the Duke?

LUSSURIOSO: My lord and father? Is he from Court?

NOBLE 1: He's sure from Court, but where, which way pleasure took, we know not, nor can we hear on't.

LUSSURIOSO: Here come those should tell.
[*Enter more* Nobles.]
Saw you my lord and father?

NOBLE 3: Not since two hours before noon, my lord,
And then he privately rid forth.

LUSSURIOSO: O he's rode forth.

50 *blood*: mood 52 *in us*: i.e. within my power 58 *succeed*: come next/successfully deal with Lussurioso 62 *fitly*: at an apt time 63 *spleen*: the organ believed to be the seat of violent passions 65 *Much of my heart*: i.e. confidential information 66 *slight*: untrustworthy 68 *speed*: kill 70 *black condition*: melancholic. Melancholy was thought to be induced by an excess of black bile *suitable*: prone

NOBLE 1: 'Twas wondrous privately.
NOBLE 2: There's none i'th'Court had any knowledge on't.
LUSSURIOSO: His Grace is old and sudden, 'tis no treason
To say the Duke my father has a humour
Or such a toy about him; what in us
Would appear light, in him seems virtuous.
NOBLE 3: 'Tis oracle, my lord.
Exeunt.

[SCENE 2]

Enter VINDICE *and* HIPPOLITO, VINDICE *out of his disguise.*
HIPPOLITO: So, so, all's as it should be, y'are yourself.
VINDICE: How that great villain puts me to my shifts.
HIPPOLITO: He that did lately in disguise reject thee
Shall, now thou art thyself, as much respect thee.
VINDICE: 'Twill be the quainter fallacy. But, brother,
'Sfoot, what use will he put me to now, think'st thou?
HIPPOLITO: Nay you must pardon me in that, I know not.
H'as some employment for you, but what 'tis
He and his secretary the Devil knows best.
VINDICE: Well, I must suit my tongue to his desires,
What colour soe'er they be, hoping at last
To pile up all my wishes on his breast.
HIPPOLITO: Faith, brother, he himself shows the way.
VINDICE: Now the Duke is dead the realm is clad in clay;
His death being not yet known, under his name
The people still are govern'd. Well, thou his son
Art not long-liv'd, thou shalt not joy his death.
To kill thee, then, I should most honour thee,
For 'twould stand firm in every man's belief
Thou'st a kind child and only died'st with grief.
HIPPOLITO: You fetch about well, but let's talk in present;
How will you appear in fashion different,

85 *sudden*: impetuous 86 *humour*: whim 87 *toy*: caprice 88 *light*: frivolous 89 *oracle*: the truth 2 *puts me to my shifts*: makes me change roles/forces me to devise new stratagems 5 *quainter*: wittier *fallacy*: deception 9 *secretary*: confidant 13 *shows the way*: is an example for hypocritical dissembling 14 *the realm is clad in clay*: the old regime is buried 17 *joy*: enjoy (by succeeding to the Dukedom) 20 *Thou'st*: thou wast 21 *fetch about*: digress *in present*: of what must be done at the moment 22 *fashion*: manner, personality

As well as in apparel, to make all things possible?
If you be but once tripp'd we fall for ever.
It is not the least policy to be doubtful,
You must change tongue – familiar was your first.
VINDICE: Why, I'll bear me in some strain of melancholy
And string myself with heavy-sounding wire
Like such an instrument that speaks
Merry things sadly.
HIPPOLITO: Then 'tis as I meant,
I gave you out at first in discontent.
VINDICE: I'll turn myself, and then –
HIPPOLITO: 'Sfoot, here he comes,
Hast thought upon't?
VINDICE: Salute him, fear not me.
[*Enter* LUSSURIOSO.]
LUSSURIOSO: Hippolito.
HIPPOLITO: Your lordship.
LUSSURIOSO: What's he yonder?
HIPPOLITO: 'Tis Vindice my discontented brother
Whom, 'cording to your will, I've brought to Court.
LUSSURIOSO: Is that thy brother? Beshrew me, a good presence,
I wonder h'as been from the Court so long.
Come nearer.
HIPPOLITO: Brother, Lord Lussurioso, the Duke's son.
LUSSURIOSO: Be more near to us, welcome, nearer yet.
[VINDICE] *snatches off his hat and makes legs to him.*
VINDICE: How don you? God you god den.
LUSSURIOSO: We thank thee.
[*Aside.*] How strangely such a coarse, homely salute
Shows in the palace, where we greet in fire
Nimble and desperate tongues; should we name
God in a salutation 'twould ne'er be stood on't – heaven!
Tell me, what has made thee so melancholy?
VINDICE: Why, going to Law.
LUSSURIOSO: Why, will that make a man melancholy?

25 *not the least policy*: i.e. a good policy *doubtful*: cautious 32 *turn*: transform 37 *Beshrew me*: a common imprecation meaning approximately 'the devil take me!' s.d. *makes legs*: bows low 41 *don*: do *God you god den*: God give you good evening (a deliberately rustic term of address) 44 *desperate*: reckless *tongues*: expressions 45 *'twould ne'er be stood on't*: it would never be called in question/it would never be endured

VINDICE: Yes, to look long upon ink and black buckram. I went me to Law in *anno quadragesimo secundo*, and I waded out of it in *anno sextagesimo tertio*.

LUSSURIOSO: What, three and twenty years in Law?

VINDICE: I have known those that have been five and fifty, and all about pullen and pigs.

LUSSURIOSO: May it be possible such men should breathe
To vex the Terms so much?

VINDICE: 'Tis food to some, my lord.
There are old men at the present that are so poison'd with the affectation of Law words (having had many suits canvassed) that their common talk is nothing but Barbary Latin. They cannot so much as pray but in Law, that their sins may be removed with a writ of error and their souls fetched up to heaven with a sasarara.

LUSSURIOSO: It seems most strange to me,
Yet all the world meets round in the same bent;
Where the heart's set, there goes the tongue's consent.
How dost apply thy studies, fellow?

VINDICE: Study? Why, to think how a great rich man lies a-dying and a poor cobbler tolls the bell for him; how he cannot depart the world and see the great chest stand before him when he lies speechless; how he will point you readily to all the boxes, and when he is past all memory, as the gossips guess, then thinks he of forfeitures and obligations; nay, when to all men's hearings he whurls and rattles in the throat, he's busy threatening his poor tenants: and this would last me now some seven years' thinking or thereabouts. But I have a conceit a-coming in picture upon this, I draw it myself; which, i'faith la, I'll present to your honour. You shall not choose but like it for your lordship shall give me nothing for it.

49 *black buckram*: i.e. lawyers' bags made from black linen cloth 50 *anno quadragesimo secundo*: the 42nd year (of a reign) 50–51 *anno sextagesimo tertio*: the 63rd year 52 *three and twenty*: either Lussurioso's Latin or his arithmetic is in error! 54 *pullen*: poultry 56 *Terms*: the periods when the Law Courts were in session 59 *Barbary Latin*: barbarous, or bad, Latin 60 *writ of error*: a writ obtained to reverse the ruling of an inferior court 61 *sasarara*: a writ of *certiorari*, issued by a superior court on the grounds that a complainant has not found justice in an inferior court 63 *meets round in the same bent*: i.e. follows the same tendency 68 *see*: Foakes emends to 'sees' (avoiding the idea of *not* seeing) *great chest*: treasure chest 70 *gossips*: friends and acquaintances at the bedside *forfeitures*: loss of estates and goods *obligations*: promissory notes for the payment of monies 71 *whurls*: makes a roaring or rumbling noise 73 *conceit . . . in picture*: a witty emblematic picture

LUSSURIOSO: Nay, you mistake me then,
For I am publish'd bountiful enough.
Let's taste of your conceit.
VINDICE: In picture, my lord?
LUSSURIOSO: Ay, in picture.
VINDICE: Marry, this it is –
A usuring father to be boiling in hell, and his son and heir with a whore dancing over him.
HIPPOLITO [*Aside.*]: H'as pared him to the quick.
LUSSURIOSO: The conceit's pretty, i'faith,
But take't upon my life 'twill ne'er be lik'd.
VINDICE: No? Why, I'm sure the whore will be lik'd well enough.
HIPPOLITO [*Aside.*]: Ay, if she were out o'th'picture he'd like her then himself.
VINDICE: And as for the son and heir he shall be an eyesore to no young revellers for he shall be drawn in cloth of gold breeches.
LUSSURIOSO: And thou hast put my meaning in the pockets
And canst not draw that out! My thought was this:
To see the picture of a usuring father
Boiling in hell, our rich men would ne'er like it.
VINDICE: O true, I cry you heartily mercy; I know the reason, for some of 'em had rather be damn'd indeed than damn'd in colours.
LUSSURIOSO [*Aside.*]: A parlous melancholy! H'as wit enough
To murder any man, and I'll give him means. –
I think thou art ill-monied.
VINDICE: Money? Ho, ho,
'T'as been my want so long 'tis now my scoff.
I've e'en forgot what colour silver's of.
LUSSURIOSO [*Aside.*]: It hits as I could wish.
VINDICE: I get good clothes
Of those that dread my humour, and for table-room
I feed on those that cannot be rid of me.
LUSSURIOSO: Somewhat to set thee up withal.
[*Gives him money.*]
VINDICE: O mine eyes!
LUSSURIOSO: How now, man?
VINDICE: Almost struck blind;
This bright unusual shine to me seems proud,

78 *publish'd*: i.e. have a reputation as 79 *taste of your conceit*: hear your device
83 *pared him to the quick*: i.e. hurt Lussurioso by peeling his pretensions away and describing his own position 91 *put my meaning in the pockets*: misinterpreted me 96 *colours*: a painting/appearances 97 *parlous*: perilous, cunning
102 *hits*: transpires

I dare not look till the sun be in a cloud.
LUSSURIOSO [*Aside.*]: I think I shall affect his melancholy. –
How are they now?
VINDICE: The better for your asking.
LUSSURIOSO: You shall be better yet if you but fasten
Truly on my intent. Now y'are both present
I will unbrace such a close, private villain
Unto your vengeful swords, the like ne'er heard of,
Who hath disgrac'd you much and injur'd us.
HIPPOLITO: Disgrac'd us, my lord?
LUSSURIOSO: Ay, Hippolito.
I kept it here till now that both your angers
Might meet him at once.
VINDICE: I'm covetous
To know the villain.
LUSSURIOSO: You know him, that slave-pander
Piato, whom we threatened last
With irons in perpetual prisonment.
VINDICE [*Aside.*]: All this is I.
HIPPOLITO: Is't he, my lord?
LUSSURIOSO: I'll tell you,
You first preferr'd him to me.
VINDICE: Did you, brother?
HIPPOLITO: I did indeed.
LUSSURIOSO: And the ingrateful villain
To quit that kindness strongly wrought with me,
Being as you see a likely man for pleasure,
With jewels to corrupt your virgin sister.
HIPPOLITO: O villain!
VINDICE: He shall surely die that did it.
LUSSURIOSO: I, far from thinking any virgin harm,
Especially knowing her to be as chaste
As that part which scarce suffers to be touch'd,
Th' eye, would not endure him.
VINDICE: Would you not,
My lord? 'Twas wondrous honourably done.
LUSSURIOSO: But with some fine frowns kept him out.
VINDICE [*Aside.*]: Out, slave!

109 *affect*: like 113 *unbrace*: reveal 117 *here*: perhaps pointing to his forehead 125 *wrought with me*: attempted to persuade me 128 *He shall surely die that did it*: doubly ironic, since Vindice is presumably hinting at his intentions towards Lussurioso, but unwittingly looks forward to his own fate 134 *Out*: an exclamation of anger and abhorrence

LUSSURIOSO: What did me he but in revenge of that
Went of his own free will to make infirm
Your sister's honour, whom I honour with my soul
For chaste respect, and not prevailing there
(As 'twas but desperate folly to attempt it)
In mere spleen, by the way, waylays your mother,
Whose honour being a coward, as it seems,
Yielded by little force.
VINDICE: Coward indeed.
LUSSURIOSO: He, proud of this advantage (as he thought),
Brought me these news for happy, but I, heaven
Forgive me for't –
VINDICE: What did your honour?
LUSSURIOSO: In rage push'd him from me,
Trampled beneath his throat, spurn'd him, and bruis'd;
Indeed I was too cruel, to say troth.
HIPPOLITO: Most nobly manag'd.
VINDICE [*Aside.*]: Has not heaven an ear? Is all the lightning wasted?
LUSSURIOSO: If I now were so impatient in a modest cause,
What should you be?
VINDICE: Full mad, he shall not live
To see the moon change.
LUSSURIOSO: He's about the palace,
Hippolito, entice him this way that thy brother
May take full mark of him.
HIPPOLITO: Heart, that shall not need, my lord.
I can direct him so far.
LUSSURIOSO: Yet, for my hate's sake,
Go wind him this way; I'll see him bleed myself.
HIPPOLITO [*Aside.*]: What now, brother?
VINDICE [*Aside.*]: Nay, e'en what you will; y'are put to't, brother.
HIPPOLITO [*Aside.*]: An impossible task, I'll swear,
To bring him hither that's already here.
Exit.
LUSSURIOSO: Thy name, I have forgot it.
VINDICE: Vindice, my lord.
LUSSURIOSO: 'Tis a good name that.

138 *For chaste respect*: out of regard for her chastity 140 *spleen*: spite 143 *this*: Q reads 'their', which makes some sense 151 *modest*: involving chastity/slight, not being directly involved 155 *full mark*: a close look 158 *wind*: entice

VINDICE: Ay, a revenger.
LUSSURIOSO: It does betoken courage; thou shouldst be valiant
And kill thine enemies.
VINDICE: That's my hope, my lord.
LUSSURIOSO: This slave is one.
VINDICE: I'll doom him.
LUSSURIOSO: Then I'll praise thee!
Do thou observe me best and I'll best raise thee.
Enter HIPPOLITO.
VINDICE: Indeed I thank you.
LUSSURIOSO: Now, Hippolito, where's the slave pander?
HIPPOLITO: Your good lordship
Would have a loathsome sight of him, much offensive.
He's not in case now to be seen, my lord;
The worst of all the deadly sins is in him,
That beggarly damnation, drunkenness.
LUSSURIOSO: Then he's a double slave.
VINDICE [*Aside.*]: 'Twas well convey'd,
Upon a sudden wit.
LUSSURIOSO: What, are you both
Firmly resolv'd? I'll see him dead myself.
VINDICE: Or else let not us live.
LUSSURIOSO: You may direct
Your brother to take note of him.
VINDICE: I shall.
LUSSURIOSO: Rise but in this, and you shall never fall.
VINDICE: Your honour's vassals.
LUSSURIOSO [*Aside.*]: This was wisely carried,
Deep policy in us makes fools of such:
Then must a slave die, when he knows too much.
Exit.
VINDICE: O thou almighty Patience! 'Tis my wonder
That such a fellow, impudent and wicked,
Should not be cloven as he stood,
Or with a secret wind burst open!
Is there no thunder left, or is't kept up
In stock for heavier vengeance? There it goes!
HIPPOLITO: Brother, we lose ourselves.

168 *observe*: serve, treat with reverence 173 *in case*: in a condition
176 *convey'd*: handled 190 *There it goes!*: That's it! (i.e. Vindice has formed his plan) 191 *we lose ourselves*: we are losing control of the situation

VINDICE: But I have found it,
'Twill hold, 'tis sure; thanks, thanks to any spirit
That mingled it 'mongst my inventions.
HIPPOLITO: What is't?
VINDICE: 'Tis sound and good, thou shalt partake it.
I'm hired to kill myself.
HIPPOLITO: True.
VINDICE: Prithee mark it:
And the old Duke being dead, but not convey'd,
For he's already miss'd too, and you know
Murder will peep out of the closest husk –
HIPPOLITO: Most true.
VINDICE: What say you then to this device:
If we dress'd up the body of the Duke?
HIPPOLITO: In that disguise of yours?
VINDICE: Y'are quick, y'have reach'd it.
HIPPOLITO: I like it wondrously.
VINDICE: And being in drink, as you have publish'd him,
To lean him on his elbow, as if sleep had caught him,
Which claims most interest in such sluggy men.
HIPPOLITO: Good yet, but here's a doubt:
We, thought by th'Duke's son to kill that pander,
Shall, when he is known, be thought to kill the Duke.
VINDICE: Neither, o thanks, it is substantial;
For that disguise being on him which I wore,
It will be thought I, which he calls the pander, did kill the Duke and fled away in his apparel, leaving him so disguis'd to avoid swift pursuit.
HIPPOLITO: Firmer and firmer.
VINDICE: Nay, doubt not 'tis in grain;
I warrant it hold colour.
HIPPOLITO: Let's about it.
VINDICE: But by the way too, now I think on't, brother,
Let's conjure that base devil out of our mother.
Exeunt.

191 *it*: i.e. a plan 192 *'Twill hold*: it will work 195 *mark it*: keep that fact in mind 196 *convey'd*: disposed of 201 *reach'd*: understood 205 *sluggy*: sluggish 206 *doubt*: difficulty 209 *it is substantial*: the plan is sound 213 *in grain*: dyed in grain (= nothing can go wrong with it) 216 *conjure*: exorcize

[SCENE 3]

Enter the DUCHESS *arm in arm with the Bastard* [SPURIO]; *he seemeth lasciviously to her. After them, enter* SUPERVACUO, *running with a rapier; his brother* [AMBITIOSO] *stops him.*

SPURIO: Madam, unlock yourself, should it be seen
Your arm would be suspected.
DUCHESS: Who is't that dares suspect or this or these?
May not we deal our favours where we please?
SPURIO: I'm confident you may.
Exeunt [DUCHESS *and* SPURIO].
AMBITIOSO: 'Sfoot, brother, hold.
SUPERVACUO: Wouldst let the bastard shame us?
AMBITIOSO: Hold, hold, brother!
There's fitter time than now.
SUPERVACUO: Now, when I see it?
AMBITIOSO: 'Tis too much seen already.
SUPERVACUO: Seen and known,
The nobler she's the baser is she grown.
AMBITIOSO: If she were bent lasciviously, the fault
Of mighty women that sleep soft – o death!
Must she needs choose such an unequal sinner
To make all worse?
SUPERVACUO: A bastard, the Duke's bastard!
Shame heap'd on shame!
AMBITIOSO: O our disgrace!
Most women have small waist the world throughout,
But their desires are thousand miles about.
SUPERVACUO: Come, stay not here, let's after and prevent,
Or else they'll sin faster than we'll repent.
Exeunt.

s.d. *lasciviously*: an error for 'lascivious'? Or is something missing in the sentence? 1 *unlock yourself*: release my arm 3 *or this or these*: i.e. either this arm or these other tokens (perhaps kisses) 10 *bent lasciviously*: inclined to lasciviousness 12 *unequal*: i.e. inferior in rank 17–18 Qb. These lines are transposed in Qa

[SCENE 4]

Enter VINDICE *and* HIPPOLITO, *bringing out their mother* [GRATIANA], *one by one shoulder, and the other by the other, with daggers in their hands.*

VINDICE: O thou, for whom no name is bad enough!
GRATIANA: What means my sons? What, will you murder me?
VINDICE: Wicked, unnatural parent!
HIPPOLITO: Fiend of women!
GRATIANA: O are sons turn'd monsters? Help!
VINDICE: In vain!
GRATIANA: Are you so barbarous to set iron nipples
Upon the breast that gave you suck?
VINDICE: That breast
Is turn'd to quarled poison.
GRATIANA: Cut not your days for't, am not I your mother?
VINDICE: Thou dost usurp that title now by fraud
For in that shell of mother breeds a bawd.
GRATIANA: A bawd? O name far loathsomer than hell.
HIPPOLITO: It should be so, knew'st thou thy office well.
GRATIANA: I hate it.
VINDICE: Ah, is't possible? Thou only? You powers on high,
That women should dissemble when they die!
GRATIANA: Dissemble?
VINDICE: Did not the Duke's son direct
A fellow of the world's condition hither
That did corrupt all that was good in thee?
Made thee uncivilly forget thyself
And work our sister to his lust?
GRATIANA: Who, I?
That had been monstrous! I defy that man
For any such intent. None lives so pure
But shall be soil'd with slander – good son, believe it not.
VINDICE: O I'm in doubt whether I'm myself or no.
Stay, let me look again upon this face.
Who shall be sav'd when mothers have no grace?
HIPPOLITO: 'Twould make one half despair.

5 *iron nipples*: i.e. their daggers 7 *quarled*: curdled 8 *Cut not your days*: i.e. do not cut short your days (by being executed for murder) 12 *knew'st*: Qb. Qa has 'knowst' *office*: duty 17 *A fellow of the world's condition*: i.e. a worldly fellow 19 *uncivilly*: barbarously 20 *work*: manipulate

VINDICE: I was the man,
Defy me now! Let's see, do't modestly.
GRATIANA: O hell unto my soul.
VINDICE: In that disguise I, sent from the Duke's son,
Tried you and found you base metal
As any villain might have done.
GRATIANA: O no,
No tongue but yours could have bewitch'd me so.
VINDICE: O nimble in damnation, quick in tune,
There is no devil could strike fire so soon.
I am confuted in a word.
GRATIANA: O sons,
Forgive me, to myself I'll prove more true,
You that should honour me, I kneel to you.
[*Kneels and weeps.*]
VINDICE: A mother to give aim to her own daughter!
HIPPOLITO: True, brother; how far beyond nature 'tis,
Though many mothers do't.
VINDICE: Nay, and you draw tears once, go you to bed,
Wet will make iron blush and change to red.
Brother, it rains, 'twill spoil your dagger, house it.
HIPPOLITO: 'Tis done.
VINDICE: I'faith, 'tis a sweet shower, it does much good.
The fruitful grounds and meadows of her soul
Has been long dry. Pour down thou blessed dew,
Rise mother; troth, this shower has made you higher.
GRATIANA: O you heavens,
Take this infectious spot out of my soul,
I'll rinse it in seven waters of mine eyes!
Make my tears salt enough to taste of grace!
To weep is to our sex naturally given,
But to weep truly, that's a gift from heaven.
VINDICE: Nay, I'll kiss you now; kiss her, brother.
Let's marry her to our souls, wherein's no lust,
And honourably love her.
HIPPOLITO: Let it be.
VINDICE: For honest women are so seld and rare
'Tis good to cherish those poor few that are. –

34 *quick in tune*: i.e. quick to harmonize with the prevailing situation 39 *to give aim to*: a term from archery meaning 'to direct someone's aim', here Lussurioso's 40 *'tis*: Qb. Qa has 'to't' 42 *and*: if *you*: i.e. the dagger 43 Qc. Qa has 'Wee' for 'wet' and 'you' for 'iron'; Qb emends 'Wee' to 'Wet' 49 *troth*: in troth, truly 51 *infectious*: infected 59 *seld*: seldom found

O you of easy wax, do but imagine
Now the disease has left you, how leprously
That office would have cling'd unto your forehead;
All mothers that had any graceful hue
Would have worn masks to hide their face at you.
It would have grown to this: at your foul name
Green-colour'd maids would have turn'd red with shame.

HIPPOLITO: And then our sister, full of hire and baseness.

VINDICE: There had been boiling lead again.
The Duke's son's great concubine,
A drab of state, a cloth o'silver slut;
To have her train borne up and her soul
Trail i'th'dirt; great –

HIPPOLITO: To be miserably great;
Rich, to be eternally wretched.

VINDICE: O common madness!
Ask but the thriving'st harlot in cold blood,
She'd give the world to make her honour good.
Perhaps you'll say, 'But only to the Duke's son
In private'. Why, she first begins with one
Who afterward to thousand proves a whore:
Break ice in one place, it will crack in more.

GRATIANA: Most certainly applied.

HIPPOLITO: O brother, you forget our business.

VINDICE: And well remember'd. Joy's a subtle elf,
I think man's happiest when he forgets himself.
Farewell, once dried, now holy-water'd mead,
Our hearts wear feathers that before wore lead.

GRATIANA: I'll give you this, that one I never knew
Plead better for and 'gainst the Devil than you.

VINDICE: You make me proud on 't.

HIPPOLITO: Commend us in all virtue to our sister.

VINDICE: Ay, for the love of heaven, to that true maid.

GRATIANA: With my best words.

VINDICE: Why, that was motherly said.

61 *of easy wax*: impressionable 64 *hue*: appearance 67 *Green-colour'd maids*: i.e. young and inexperienced girls 68 *hire*: prostitution and its payment 70 *The*: Qb 71 *drab*: whore 72 *train*: trailing skirt worn by women of rank 73 *To be*: Qb. Qa has 'Too' 76 *in cold blood*: while her passions are not excited 82 *certainly*: appropriately 84 *subtle elf*: spirit not easily grasped or perceived 86 *mead*: meadow 88 *one I never*: i.e. no one I ever

Exeunt [VINDICE *and* HIPPOLITO].

GRATIANA: I wonder now what fury did transport me.
I feel good thoughts begin to settle in me.
O with what forehead can I look on her
Whose honour I've so impiously beset?
And here she comes.

[*Enter* CASTIZA.]

CASTIZA: Now mother, you have wrought with me so strongly
That what for my advancement, as to calm
The trouble of your tongue, I am content.

GRATIANA: Content to what?

CASTIZA: To do as you have wish'd me,
To prostitute my breast to the Duke's son
And put myself to common usury.

GRATIANA: I hope you will not so.

CASTIZA: Hope you I will not?
That's not the hope you look to be sav'd in.

GRATIANA: Truth, but it is.

CASTIZA: Do not deceive yourself;
I am as you e'en out of marble wrought.
What would you now? Are ye not pleas'd yet with me?
You shall not wish me to be more lascivious
Than I intend to be.

GRATIANA: Strike not me cold.

CASTIZA: How often have you charg'd me on your blessing
To be a cursed woman? When you knew
Your blessing had no force to make me lewd
You laid your curse upon me. That did more,
The mother's curse is heavy: where that fights
Suns set in storm and daughters lose their lights.

GRATIANA: Good child, dear maid, if there be any spark
Of heavenly intellectual fire within thee
O let my breath revive it to a flame;
Put not all out with woman's wilful follies.
I am recover'd of that foul disease

96 *forehead*: shameful countenance 100 *what for*: on account of, as much for 104 *usury*: OED gives this as a rare instance of the noun meaning 'The use or employment of anything'. The main idea is that the money she will earn from prostitution is a kind of interest 106 i.e. yours is not the kind of hope associated with Divine Salvation 108 i.e. now that you have worked me out of my former marble state I am pliable to your wishes 117 *lose their lights*: lose their sense of moral direction 119 *intellectual*: spiritual

That haunts too many mothers; kind, forgive me,
Make me not sick in health. If then
My words prevail'd when they were wickedness,
How much more now when they are just and good!
CASTIZA: I wonder what you mean; are not you she
For whose infect persuasions I could scarce
Kneel out my prayers, and had much ado
In three hours' reading to untwist so much
Of the black serpent as you wound about me?
GRATIANA: 'Tis unfruitful, held tedious to repeat what's past,
I'm now your present mother.
CASTIZA: Push, now 'tis too late.
GRATIANA: Bethink again, thou know'st not what thou say'st.
CASTIZA: No? Deny advancement, treasure, the Duke's son?
GRATIANA: O see, I spoke those words, and now they poison me.
What will the deed do then?
Advancement: true, as high as shame can pitch!
For treasure: who e'er knew a harlot rich,
Or could build by the purchase of her sin
An hospital to keep their bastards in?
The Duke's son! O when women are young courtiers
They are sure to be old beggars;
To know the miseries most harlots taste
Thou'dst wish thyself unborn when thou art unchaste.
CASTIZA: O mother, let me twine about your neck
And kiss you till my soul melt on your lips;
I did but this to try you.
GRATIANA: O speak truth!
CASTIZA: Indeed I did not,
For no tongue has force to alter me from honest.
If maidens would, men's words could have no power,
A virgin honour is a crystal tower
Which, being weak, is guarded with good spirits;
Until she basely yields no ill inherits.
GRATIANA: O happy child! Faith and thy birth hath sav'd me.
'Mongst thousand daughters happiest of all others,
Be thou a glass for maids and I for mothers.
Exeunt.

123 *kind*: kind one/child (one of my kin) 128 *infect*: infected 133 *present*: true 134 *Bethink*: consider 140 *purchase*: profit 141 *hospital*: orphanage 149 *did not*: i.e. did not previously speak truth 151 *would*: i.e. remain chaste 154 *inherits*: resides there 155 *happy*: blessed 157 *glass*: mirror (and, by extension, exemplar)

[ACT FIVE]

[SCENE I]

Enter VINDICE *and* HIPPOLITO [*carrying the corpse of the* DUKE *dressed as 'Piato'; they arrange it in a seated position*].

VINDICE: So, so he leans well, take heed you wake him not, brother.

HIPPOLITO: I warrant you, my life for yours.

VINDICE: That's a good lay, for I must kill myself. Brother, that's I, that sits for me, do you mark it? And I must stand ready here to make away myself yonder – I must sit to be killed, and stand to kill myself. I could vary it not so little as thrice over again; 't'as some eight returns like Michaelmas Term.

HIPPOLITO: That's enow, o'conscience.

VINDICE: But sirrah, does the Duke's son come single?

HIPPOLITO: No, there's the hell on't, his faith's too feeble to go alone. He brings flesh-flies after him that will buzz against supper-time and hum for his coming out.

VINDICE: Ah, the fly-flop of vengeance beat 'em to pieces! Here was the sweetest occasion, the fittest hour to have made my revenge familiar with him, shown him the body of the Duke his father and how quaintly he died, like a politician in hugger-mugger, made no man acquainted with it, and in catastrophe slain him over his father's breast; and o I'm mad to lose such a sweet opportunity.

HIPPOLITO: Nay, push, prithee be content, there's no remedy present. May not hereafter times open in as fair faces as this?

VINDICE: They may if they can paint so well.

HIPPOLITO: Come now, to avoid all suspicion let's forsake this room and be going to meet the Duke's son.

VINDICE: Content, I'm for any weather. Heart, step close, here he comes.

3 *good lay*: 'appropriate bet' (since I have already 'exchanged lives') 6 *eight returns*: literally the eight days on which 'returns' or sheriff's reports could be submitted to the court during Michaelmas Term. Hence the phrase here means 'eight possible descriptions of the situation' 8 *That's enow, o'conscience*: that's enough (possible descriptions), upon my word 10 *faith's*: Qb. Qa has 'faith' 11 *flesh-flies*: blowflies, bluebottles *against*: in readiness for 13 *fly-flop*: an instrument to drive away flies 16 *hugger-mugger*: secret 17 *catastrophe*: conclusion (the final act of a tragedy) 20 *open*: present themselves 21 *paint*: use make-up 24 *I'm for any weather*: proverbial: 'I'm game for anything'

Enter LUSSURIOSO.

HIPPOLITO: My honour'd lord!

LUSSURIOSO: O me, you both present?

VINDICE: E'en newly, my lord, just as your lordship entered now. About this place we had notice given he should be, but in some loathsome plight or other.

HIPPOLITO: Came your honour private?

LUSSURIOSO: Private enough for this, only a few
Attend my coming out.

HIPPOLITO [*Aside.*]: Death rot those few.

LUSSURIOSO: Stay, yonder's the slave.

VINDICE: Mass, there's the slave indeed, my lord.
[*Aside.*] 'Tis a good child, he calls his father slave.

LUSSURIOSO: Ay, that's the villain, the damn'd villain. Softly,
Tread easy.

VINDICE: Puh, I warrant you, my lord,
We'll stifle in our breaths.

LUSSURIOSO: That will do well.
Base rogue, thou sleep'st thy last. [*Aside.*] 'Tis policy
To have him kill'd in's sleep, for if he wak'd
He would betray all to them.

VINDICE: But my lord!

LUSSURIOSO: Ha, what say'st?

VINDICE: Shall we kill him now he's drunk?

LUSSURIOSO: Ay, best of all.

VINDICE: Why, then he will ne'er live to be sober.

LUSSURIOSO: No matter, let him reel to hell.

VINDICE: But being so full of liquor, I fear he will put out all the fire.

LUSSURIOSO: Thou art a mad beast.

VINDICE [*Aside.*]: And leave none to warm your lordship's golls withal, for he that dies drunk falls into hellfire like a bucket o'water, qush, qush.

LUSSURIOSO: Come, be ready, nake your swords, think of your wrongs.
This slave has injur'd you.

VINDICE: Troth, so he has. [*Aside.*] And he has paid well for't.

LUSSURIOSO: Meet with him now.

VINDICE: You'll bear us out, my lord?

30 *private*: alone 34 *Mass*: oath contracted from 'By the Mass' 47 *mad*: merry 48 *golls*: hands *withal*: with 50 *nake*: make naked, i.e. unsheathe ('nake' is Qb's reading; Qa has 'make') 53 *Meet with him*: deal with him *bear us out*: support us

LUSSURIOSO: Puh, am I a lord for nothing, think you?
Quickly now.
VINDICE: Sa, sa, sa, thump! [*Stabs the corpse.*] There he lies.
LUSSURIOSO: Nimbly done. Ha! O villains, murderers,
'Tis the old Duke my father!
VINDICE [*Aside.*]: That's a jest.
LUSSURIOSO: What, stiff and cold already?
O pardon me to call you from your names,
'Tis none of your deed: that villain Piato,
Whom you thought now to kill, has murder'd him
And left him thus disguis'd.
HIPPOLITO: And not unlikely.
VINDICE: O rascal! Was he not asham'd
To put the Duke into a greasy doublet?
LUSSURIOSO: He has been cold and stiff, who knows how long?
VINDICE [*Aside.*]: Marry, that do I.
LUSSURIOSO: No words, I pray, of anything intended.
VINDICE: O my lord.
HIPPOLITO: I would fain have your lordship think that we have small reason to prate.
LUSSURIOSO: Faith, thou say'st true. I'll forthwith send to Court
For all the nobles, Bastard, Duchess, all,
How here by miracle we found him dead
And in his raiment that foul villain fled.
VINDICE: That will be the best way, my lord, to clear us all; let's cast about to be clear.
LUSSURIOSO: Ho, Nencio, Sordido, and the rest.
Enter [SORDIDO, NENCIO *and* Attendants].
SORDIDO: My lord.
NENCIO: My lord.
LUSSURIOSO: Be witnesses of a strange spectacle:
Choosing for private conference that sad room
We found the Duke my father geal'd in blood.
SORDIDO: My lord the Duke? – Run, hie thee, Nencio,
Startle the Court by signifying so much.
[*Exit* NENCIO.]
VINDICE [*Aside.*]: Thus much by wit a deep revenger can,

55 *Sa, sa, sa*: exclamation announcing a thrust at sword-fighting derived from the French, 'ça, ça, ça' 59 *call you from your names*: address you by the wrong names (i.e. those of 'villains' and 'murderers') 64 *doublet*: close-fitting body garment, with or without sleeves 70 *prate*: gossip 75–6 *cast about*: contrive means 76 *clear*: free from suspicion 82 *geal'd*: congealed 85 *can*: i.e. can perform

When murder's known to be the clearest man.
We're furthest off and with as bold an eye
Survey his body as the standers-by.
LUSSURIOSO: My royal father, too basely let blood
By a malevolent slave!
HIPPOLITO [*Aside.*]: Hark,
He calls thee slave again.
VINDICE [*Aside.*]: H'as lost, he may.
LUSSURIOSO: O sight! Look hither, see, his lips are gnawn
With poison.
VINDICE: How, his lips? By th'mass, they be.
LUSSURIOSO: O villain! O rogue! O slave! O rascal!
HIPPOLITO [*Aside.*]: O good deceit, he quits him with like terms!
[*Enter* Nobles, AMBITIOSO *and* SUPERVACUO.]
NOBLE 1: Where?
NOBLE 2: Which way?
AMBITIOSO: Over what roof hangs this prodigious comet
In deadly fire?
LUSSURIOSO: Behold, behold, my lords,
The Duke my father's murder'd by a vassal
That owes this habit and here left disguis'd.
[*Enter* DUCHESS *and* SPURIO.]
DUCHESS: My lord and husband!
NOBLE 2: Reverend majesty.
NOBLE 1: I have seen these clothes often attending on him.
VINDICE [*Aside.*]: That nobleman has been i'th'country, for he does not lie!
SUPERVACUO [*To* AMBITIOSO.]: Learn of our mother, let's dissemble too;
I am glad he's vanish'd – so, I hope, are you.
AMBITIOSO [*To* SUPERVACUO.]: Ay, you may take my word for't.
SPURIO [*Aside.*]: Old dad dead?
I, one of his cast sins, will send the fates
Most hearty commendations by his own son;

86 i.e. when the murderer is the man most free from suspicion 95 *quits him*: repays him (the Duke) *like*: befitting, appropriate. Foakes suggests 'like' = similar, referring back to II.iii.14 98 *prodigious*: ill-omened *comet*: often thought to herald disasters. Here the term is used metaphorically for 'catastrophe' 101 *owes*: owns 103 *these clothes*: i.e. the man who wore these clothes (Piato, who had been engaged by the Duke to procure women for him) 104 *has been i'th'country*: i.e. and therefore had some acquaintance with country simplicity and truth, as opposed to Court deceits 107 *vanish'd*: i.e. dead 109 *cast*: cast off, rejected

I'll tug in the new stream till strength be done.
LUSSURIOSO: Where be those two that did affirm to us
My lord the Duke was privately rid forth?
NOBLE 1: O pardon us, my lords, he gave that charge
Upon our lives, if he were miss'd at Court,
To answer so. He rode not anywhere,
We left him private with that fellow here.
VINDICE [*Aside.*]: Confirm'd.
LUSSURIOSO: O heavens, that false charge was his death!
Impudent beggars! Durst you to our face
Maintain such a false answer? Bear him straight
To execution.
NOBLE 1: My lord!
LUSSURIOSO: Urge me no more.
In this, the excuse may be call'd half the murder.
VINDICE [*Aside.*]: You've sentenc'd well.
LUSSURIOSO: Away, see it be done.
[*Exit* First Noble *under guard.*]
VINDICE [*Aside.*]: Could you not stick? See what confession doth!
Who would not lie, when men are hang'd for truth?
HIPPOLITO [*Aside.*]: Brother, how happy is our vengeance!
VINDICE [*Aside.*]: Why, it hits
Past the apprehension of indifferent wits.
LUSSURIOSO: My lord, let post-horse be sent
Into all places to entrap the villain.
VINDICE [*Aside.*]: Post-horse, ha, ha!
NOBLE 2: My lord, we're something bold to know our duty.
Your father's accidentally departed,
The titles that were due to him meet you.
LUSSURIOSO: Meet me? I'm not at leisure, my good lord.
I've many griefs to dispatch out o'th'way.
[*Aside.*] Welcome, sweet titles! – Talk to me, my lords,
Of sepulchres and mighty emperors' bones;
That's thought for me.
VINDICE [*Aside.*]: So one may see by this

111 *tug*: i.e. tug on my oar (the sense seems to be 'I'll continue to work for my ends just as energetically in this new situation') 114 *charge*: order 122 *excuse*: i.e. the excuse the Noble provided for the Duke's absence 124 *stick*: keep silent 126 *hits*: succeeds 127 *indifferent*: moderate, ordinary *wits*: intellects 128 *post-horse*: i.e. swift messengers (literally, horses used by post-riders) 132 *accidentally*: unexpectedly 133 *meet you*: succeed to you

How foreign markets go:
Courtiers have feet o'th'nines and tongues o'th'twelves,
They flatter dukes and dukes flatter themselves.
NOBLE 2: My lord, it is your shine must comfort us.
LUSSURIOSO: Alas, I shine in tears like the sun in April.
SORDIDO: You're now my lord's Grace.
LUSSURIOSO: My lord's Grace? I perceive you'll have it so.
SORDIDO: 'Tis but your own.
LUSSURIOSO: Then heavens give me grace to be so.
VINDICE [*Aside.*]: He prays well for himself.
NOBLE 3 [*To the* DUCHESS.]: Madam, all sorrows
Must run their circles into joys. No doubt but time
Will make the murderer bring forth himself.
VINDICE [*Aside.*]: He were an ass then, i'faith.
NOBLE 2: In the mean season
Let us bethink the latest funeral honours
Due to the Duke's cold body – and, withal,
Calling to memory our new happiness
Spread in his royal son. Lords, gentlemen,
Prepare for revels.
VINDICE [*Aside.*]: Revels!
NOBLE 3: Time hath several falls,
Griefs lift up joys, feasts put down funerals.
LUSSURIOSO: Come then, my lords, my favours to you all.
[*Aside.*] The Duchess is suspected foully bent,
I'll begin Dukedom with her banishment!
Exeunt LUSSURIOSO, SORDIDO, Nobles *and* DUCHESS.
HIPPOLITO [*To* VINDICE.]: Revels!
VINDICE [*To* HIPPOLITO.]: Ay, that's the word, we are firm yet.
Strike one strain more and then we crown our wit.
Exeunt VINDICE *and* HIPPOLITO.
SPURIO [*Aside.*]: Well, have at the fairest mark! – So said the Duke when he begot me –

139 An obscure phrase, perhaps equivalent to the modern 'You can see how the wind's blowing'. (Salgādo glosses 'foreign markets' as 'abandoned titles')
140 i.e. the flattering tongues of courtiers are three sizes larger than their feet
144 *my lord's Grace*: a courtesy title afforded to Dukes 151 *mean season*: meantime 152 *bethink*: plan 153 *withal*: moreover 156–7 *Time . . . funerals*: i.e. we have to endure many shifts in fortune, but the experience of joy and festivities counteracts the effects of funerals 159 *foully bent*: lecherously inclined
161 *firm*: safe, secure 162 *Strike one strain more*: play one tune more, i.e. make one last effort 163 *have at*: see note III.v.136, above *mark*: target (i.e. Lussurioso, the new Duke)

And if I miss his heart or near about
Then have at any, a bastard scorns to be out.
[*Exit.*]

SUPERVACUO: Notest thou that Spurio, brother?

AMBITIOSO: Yes, I note him to our shame.

SUPERVACUO: He shall not live, his hair shall not grow much longer; in this time of revels tricks may be set afoot. Seest thou yon new moon? It shall outlive the new Duke by much, this hand shall dispossess him, then we're mighty.
A masque is treason's licence – that build upon;
'Tis murder's best face when a vizard's on.
Exit.

AMBITIOSO: Is't so? 'Tis very good.
And do you think to be Duke then, kind brother?
I'll see fair play: drop one and there lies tother.
Exit.

[SCENE 2]

Enter VINDICE *and* HIPPOLITO *with* PIERO *and other* Nobles.

VINDICE: My lords, be all of music,
Strike old griefs into other countries
That flow in too much milk and have faint livers,
Not daring to stab home their discontents.
Let our hid flames break out as fire, as lightning,
To blast this villainous Dukedom vex'd with sin;
Wind up your souls to their full height again.

PIERO: How?

NOBLE 1: Which way?

NOBLE 2: Any way: our wrongs are such,
We cannot justly be reveng'd too much.

VINDICE: You shall have all enough. Revels are toward,
And those few nobles that have long suppress'd you
Are busied to the furnishing of a masque
And do affect to make a pleasant tale on't;
The masquing suits are fashioning; now comes in

166 *out*: i.e. left out of influence 1 Continues the imagery of music from the previous scene 2 *Strike*: banish/play (a tune) 10 *toward*: imminent 13 *affect*: aspire (but it is possible that Vindice has learned of Ambitioso's plot and is punning on 'affect' = pretend) *tale*: i.e. narrative or allegory of the masque 14 *fashioning*: being made

That which must glad us all – we to take pattern
Of all those suits, the colour, trimming, fashion,
E'en to an undistinguish'd hair almost;
Then, ent'ring first, observing the true form,
Within a strain or two we shall find leisure
To steal our swords out handsomely
And, when they think their pleasure sweet and good,
In midst of all their joys they shall sigh blood.

PIERO: Weightily, effectually.

NOBLE 3: Before the t'other maskers come –

VINDICE: We're gone, all done and past.

PIERO: But how for the Duke's guard?

VINDICE: Let that alone,
By one and one their strengths shall be drunk down.

HIPPOLITO: There are five hundred gentlemen in the action
That will apply themselves and not stand idle.

PIERO: O let us hug your bosoms!

VINDICE: Come, my lords,
Prepare for deeds, let other times have words.
Exeunt.

[SCENE 3]

In a dumb show, the possessing of the young Duke [LUSSURIOSO] *with all his* Nobles*; then sounding music. A furnished table is brought forth; then enters the Duke and his* Nobles *to the banquet. A blazing star appeareth.*

NOBLE 1: Many harmonious hours and choicest pleasures
Fill up the royal numbers of your years.

LUSSURIOSO: My lords, we're pleas'd to thank you – though we know
'Tis but your duty now to wish it so.

NOBLE 2: That shine makes us all happy.

NOBLE 3 [*Aside.*]: His grace frowns.

NOBLE 2 [*Aside.*]: Yet we must say he smiles.

15 *take pattern*: make a copy 17 *undistinguish'd hair almost*: scarcely distinguishable hair (i.e. the minutest detail) 18 *true form*: correct order 19 *strain*: i.e. of music 20 *handsomely*: conveniently 23 *Weightily*: i.e. the victims will sigh heavily *effectually*: to good effect (i.e. they will die) 27 *By one and one*: one by one *drunk down*: overcome by drink s.d. *possessing*: i.e. installation as Duke s.d. *sounding*: loud, sonorous *blazing star*: the comet is not remarked on until l. 14 5 *shine*: smile

NOBLE 1 [*Aside.*]: I think we must.
LUSSURIOSO [*Aside.*]: That foul, incontinent Duchess we have banish'd,
The Bastard shall not live. After these revels
I'll begin strange ones; he and the stepsons
Shall pay their lives for the first subsidies.
We must not frown so soon, else 't'ad been now.
NOBLE 1: My gracious lord, please you prepare for pleasure,
The masque is not far off.
LUSSURIOSO: We are for pleasure.
[*Aside.*] Beshrew thee, what art thou? Mad'st me start!
Thou hast committed treason! – A blazing star!
NOBLE 1: A blazing star? O where, my lord?
LUSSURIOSO: Spy out.
NOBLE 2: See, see, my lords, a wondrous dreadful one.
LUSSURIOSO: I am not pleas'd at that ill-knotted fire,
That bushing, flaring star. Am not I Duke?
It should not quake me now. Had it appear'd
Before it, I might then have justly fear'd,
But yet they say, whom Art and Learning weds,
When stars wear locks they threaten great men's heads.
Is it so? You are read, my lords.
NOBLE 1: May it please your Grace,
It shows great anger.
LUSSURIOSO: That does not please our Grace.
NOBLE 2: Yet here's the comfort, my lord: many times,
When it seems most it threatens farthest off.
LUSSURIOSO: Faith, and I think so, too.
NOBLE 1: Beside, my lord,
You're gracefully establish'd with the loves
Of all your subjects; and for natural death,
I hope it will be threescore years a-coming.
LUSSURIOSO: True. No more but threescore years?
NOBLE 1: Fourscore I hope, my lord.
NOBLE 2: And fivescore, I.
NOBLE 3: But 'tis my hope, my lord, you shall ne'er die.
LUSSURIOSO: Give me thy hand, these others I rebuke;

10 *subsidies*: instalments 14 *Beshrew thee*: i.e. the Devil take thee (Lussurioso addresses the comet) 15 *committed treason*: i.e. by threatening the Duke, since comets were held to foretell the deaths of princes 17 *dreadful*: frightening 18 *ill-knotted*: looking ahead to the image of hair at l. 23? 19 *bushing*: spreading like a bush (referring to the comet's trail) 21 *it*: i.e. my installation as Duke 22 *Art*: skill 23 *locks*: i.e. locks of hair, referring to the comet's trail 24 *read*: well read 27 *most*: most threatening

He that hopes so is fittest for a Duke,
Thou shalt sit next me. Take your places, lords,
We're ready now for sports, let 'em set on.
You thing, we shall forget you quite anon!

NOBLE 3: I hear 'em coming, my lord.

Enter the masque of revengers, the two brothers [VINDICE *and* HIPPOLITO] *and two Lords more.*

LUSSURIOSO [*Aside.*]: Ah, 'tis well,
Brothers and Bastard, you dance next in hell.

The revengers dance. At the end, steal out their swords, and these four kill the four at the table in their chairs. It thunders.

VINDICE [*Aside.*]: Mark, thunder! Dost know thy cue, thou big-voic'd crier?
Dukes' groans are thunder's watchwords.

HIPPOLITO [*Aside.*]: So, my lords,
You have enough.

VINDICE [*Aside.*]: Come, let's away, no ling'ring.

HIPPOLITO [*Aside.*]: Follow, go!

Exeunt [*all the masquers but* VINDICE].

VINDICE: No power is angry when the lustful die,
When thunder claps heaven likes the tragedy.
Exit.

LUSSURIOSO: O! O!

Enter the other masque of intended murderers, stepsons [AMBITIOSO *and* SUPERVACUO], *Bastard* [SPURIO], *and a* Fourth Man, *coming in dancing. The Duke* [LUSSURIOSO] *recovers a little in voice, and groans – calls,* 'A guard! Treason!' *At which they all start out of their measure and, turning towards the table, they find them all to be murdered.*

SPURIO: Whose groan was that?

LUSSURIOSO: Treason, a guard!

AMBITIOSO: How now? All murder'd!

SUPERVACUO: Murder'd!

NOBLE 4: And those his nobles!

AMBITIOSO [*Aside.*]: Here's a labour sav'd,
I thought to have sped him. – 'Sblood, how came this?

SUPERVACUO: Then I proclaim myself. Now I am Duke.

39 *thing*: i.e. the comet 44 *enough*: i.e. enough revenge 47 *heaven likes*: in fact the thunder, like the other portents in the play, is morally ambiguous

s.d. *measure*: dance step 52 *sped*: i.e. sent him on his way 53 Q gives this speech to Spurio. This makes it difficult to affix enough stage directions in which the brothers can stab one another. We have followed earlier editors in reassigning it to Supervacuo, but problems remain: Spurio, as the Duke's bastard, might well claim to be his heir, and Ambitioso, who seems to be the Duchess's eldest son, would have a better claim than Supervacuo

AMBITIOSO: Thou Duke? Brother, thou liest.
[*Stabs* SUPERVACUO.]
SPURIO: Slave, so dost thou.
[*Stabs* AMBITIOSO.]
NOBLE 4: Base villain, hast thou slain my lord and master?
[*Stabs* SPURIO.]
Enter [VINDICE, HIPPOLITO, *and the other*] *first masquers.*
VINDICE: Pistols! Treason! Murder! Help! Guard my lord
The Duke!
[*Enter* ANTONIO *with a Guard.*]
HIPPOLITO: Lay hold upon this traitor.
[*The Guard seizes the* Fourth Noble.]
LUSSURIOSO: O!
VINDICE: Alas, the Duke is murder'd.
HIPPOLITO: And the nobles.
VINDICE: Surgeons, surgeons! [*Aside.*] Heart, does he breathe so long?
ANTONIO: A piteous tragedy, able to make
An old man's eyes bloodshot.
LUSSURIOSO: O!
VINDICE: Look to my lord the Duke. [*Aside.*] A vengeance throttle him! –
Confess, thou murderous and unhallow'd man,
Didst thou kill all these?
NOBLE 4: None but the Bastard, I.
VINDICE: How came the Duke slain, then?
NOBLE 4: We found him so.
LUSSURIOSO: O villain!
VINDICE: Hark!
LUSSURIOSO: Those in the masque did murder us.
VINDICE: Law you now, sir,
O marble impudence! Will you confess now?
NOBLE 4: 'Sblood, 'tis all false.
ANTONIO: Away with that foul monster,
Dipp'd in a prince's blood.
NOBLE 4: Heart, 'tis a lie!
ANTONIO: Let him have bitter execution.
[*Exit the* Fourth Noble *under guard.*]
VINDICE [*Aside.*]: New marrow! No, I cannot be express'd. –
How fares my lord the Duke?

59 *Heart*: exclamation (from 'God's heart') 68 *Law you now*: an expression of surprise 73 *New marrow*: i.e. new food for revenge *be express'd*: express myself

LUSSURIOSO: Farewell to all,
He that climbs highest has the greatest fall.
My tongue is out of office.
VINDICE: Air, gentlemen, air!
[*Whispers to* LUSSURIOSO.] Now thou'lt not prate on't, 'twas Vindice murder'd thee –
LUSSURIOSO: O!
VINDICE: – murder'd thy father –
LUSSURIOSO: O!
[*Dies.*]
VINDICE: – and I am he.
Tell nobody. So, so, the Duke's departed.
ANTONIO: It was a deadly hand that wounded him;
The rest, ambitious who should rule and sway,
After his death were so made all away.
VINDICE: My lord was unlikely.
HIPPOLITO: Now the hope
Of Italy lies in your reverend years.
VINDICE: Your hair will make the silver age again
When there was fewer but more honest men.
ANTONIO: The burden's weighty and will press age down;
May I so rule that heaven may keep the crown.
VINDICE: The rape of your good lady has been 'quited
With death on death.
ANTONIO: Just is the Law above!
But of all things it puts me most to wonder
How the old Duke came murder'd.
VINDICE: O my lord.
ANTONIO: It was the strangeliest carried, I not heard of the like.
HIPPOLITO: 'Twas all done for the best, my lord.
VINDICE: All for your Grace's good. We may be bold to speak it now; 'twas somewhat witty carried, though we say it. 'Twas we two murdered him.
ANTONIO: You two?
VINDICE: None else, i'faith, my lord; nay, 'twas well manag'd.
ANTONIO: Lay hands upon those villains.
[VINDICE *and* HIPPOLITO *are seized.*]
VINDICE: How? On us?

84 *unlikely*: unsuited (to rule) 86 *silver age*: in classical mythology, an age of peace and prosperity 88 *press age down*: i.e. weary my old age 89 *keep*: protect/perform the duties of 97 *witty carried*: cleverly executed

ANTONIO: Bear 'em to speedy execution.
VINDICE: Heart, was't not for your good, my lord?
ANTONIO: My good?
Away with 'em! Such an old man as he,
You that would murder him would murder me.
VINDICE: Is't come about?
HIPPOLITO: 'Sfoot, brother, you begun.
VINDICE: May not we set as well as the Duke's son?
Thou hast no conscience; are we not reveng'd?
Is there one enemy left alive amongst those?
'Tis time to die when we are ourselves our foes.
When murd'rers shut deeds close this curse does seal 'em:
If none disclose 'em they themselves reveal'em.
This murder might have slept in tongueless brass,
But for ourselves, and the world died an ass.
Now I remember too, here was Piato
Brought forth a knavish sentence once.
No doubt, said he, but time
Will make the murderer bring forth himself.
'Tis well he died; he was a witch.
And now, my lord, since we are in for ever
This work was ours, which else might have been slipp'd,
And if we list we could have nobles clipp'd
And go for less than beggars; but we hate
To bleed so cowardly. We have enough, i'faith:
We're well, our mother turn'd, our sister true;
We die after a nest of dukes. Adieu.
Exeunt [VINDICE *and* HIPPOLITO *under guard*].
ANTONIO: How subtly was that murder clos'd! Bear up
Those tragic bodies; 'tis a heavy season.
Pray heaven their blood may wash away all treason!
Exeunt.

FINIS

106 *about*: to this 107 *set*: die (punning on sun/son) 108 *conscience*: either 'moral understanding' or 'self-assurance' 111 *seal 'em*: i.e. seal their fate 113 *brass*: i.e. the brass memorial tablets of the murdered victims 119 *witch*: fortune-teller 120 *in for ever*: either 'in this thing up to our necks' or 'sentenced to death' 122 *list*: chose *nobles clipp'd*: nobles beheaded (i.e. those who joined in their plot); but punning on 'clipping' or paring the edges of 'nobles' or gold coins. Hence they could be 'less than beggars' 125 *turn'd*: converted 127 *clos'd*: concealed

A Chaste Maid in Cheapside

A Chaste Maid in Cheapside was entered in the Stationers' Register on 8 April 1630 to Francis Constable and published soon after. The copy-text for this edition is the 1630 Quarto (Q). In 1969 the Scolar Press published a facsimile of a copy in the British Library.

[DRAMATIS PERSONAE]

The Names of the Principal Persons

MR YELLOWHAMMER, *a goldsmith*
MAUDLINE, *his wife*
TIM, *their son*
MOLL, *their daughter*
TUTOR *to Tim*
SIR WALTER WHOREHOUND, *a suitor to Moll*
SIR OLIVER KIX, *and his* WIFE, *kin to Sir Walter*
MR ALLWIT, *and his* WIFE, *whom Sir Walter keeps*
WELSH GENTLEWOMAN, *Sir Walter's whore*
WAT *and* NICK, *his bastards*
DAVY DAHUMMA, *his man*
TOUCHWOOD SENIOR, *and his* WIFE, *a decayed gentleman*
TOUCHWOOD JUNIOR, *another suitor to Moll*
[JUGG, *Lady Kix's maid*
SUSAN, *Moll's maid*]
Two Promoters; Servants; Watermen; [Wench; Dry Nurse; Wet Nurse; Porter; Gentleman; Men with baskets; Puritans; Gossips; Midwife; Parson

Scene: Cheapside.]

ACT ONE

[SCENE I]

Enter MAUDLINE *and* MOLL, *a shop being discovered.*

MAUDLINE: Have you play'd over all your old lessons o' the virginals?

MOLL: Yes.

MAUDLINE: Yes, you are a dull maid a' late, methinks you had need have somewhat to quicken your green sickness; do you weep? A husband! Had not such a piece of flesh been ordained, what had us wives been

s.d. it is not clear how this shop setting would have been 'discovered', i.e. revealed. Some theatres may have had an inner stage at the back of the stage, with a curtain in front of it

1 *virginals*: a keyboard instrument, similar to a spinet but without legs; its name allowed plenty of opportunity for sexual innuendo 4 *quicken*: restore to vigour (with a pun on 'make pregnant') *green sickness*: chlorosis, a disease affecting young women giving rise to anaemia and thus a greenish complexion. Often identified as a form of 'love-sickness'

MR: contracted form of Master rather than the more modern form of Mister YELLOWHAMMER: his name indicates his profession, but is also slang for both 'a fool' and 'a gold coin' MAUDLINE: anglicized version of Magdalene; the early career of Mary Magdalene, a reformed prostitute, is probably relevant MOLL: diminutive of 'Mary', which she is sometimes called. Also a cant term for prostitute KIX: a dry, hollow, plant stalk and thus figuratively a sterile person ALLWIT: punning on 'wittol', a complaisant cuckold, but also indicating his cold rationality DAHUMMA: phonetic rendering of 'dewch yma', Welsh for 'Come here' TOUCHWOOD: tinder, and thus prone to set fire in an emotional or sexual sense *decayed*: reduced in prosperity *Promoters*: informers. Two were required for their evidence to be accepted by the court *Watermen*: the Thames provided the main mode of transport in London, and these boatmen were the equivalent of modern taxi-drivers *Gossips*: female friends present at a birth or christening

Cheapside: Cheapside, or Westcheap, was the City's commercial centre, running from St Paul's to Poultry. Prostitutes were 'chac'd', or whipped, along its length

good for? To make sallets, or else cried up and down for sampier. To see the difference of these seasons! When I was of your youth, I was lightsome and quick two years before I was married. You fit for a knight's bed! Drowsy-brow'd, dull-eyed, drossy-sprited – I hold my life you have forgot your dancing: when was the dancer with you?

MOLL: The last week.

MAUDLINE: Last week? When I was of your bord, he miss'd me not a night, I was kept at it; I took delight to learn, and he to teach me, pretty brown gentleman, he took pleasure in my company; but you are dull, nothing comes nimbly from you, you dance like a plumber's daughter and deserve two thousand pounds in lead to your marriage and not in goldsmith's ware.

Enter YELLOWHAMMER.

YELLOWHAMMER: Now what's the din betwixt mother and daughter, ha?

MAUDLINE: Faith, small, telling your daughter Mary of her errors.

YELLOWHAMMER: Errors? Nay, the City cannot hold you, wife, but you must needs fetch words from Westminster; I ha' done, i'faith. Has no attorney's clerk been here a' late and changed his half-crown-piece his mother sent him, or rather cozen'd you with a gilded twopence, to bring the word in fashion for her faults or cracks in duty and obedience? Term 'em e'en so, sweet wife. As there is no woman made without a flaw, your purest lawns have frays, and cambrics bracks.

MAUDLINE: But 'tis a husband sowders up all cracks.

MOLL: What, is he come, sir?

YELLOWHAMMER: Sir Walter's come.
He was met at Holborn Bridge, and in his company

6 *To make sallets*: to become salads (continuing the metaphor of 'green sickness') *cried up and down for sampier*: sold in the street as samphire (marsh-sampier, the 'herbe de Saint Pierre', a plant used in salads) 6–7 *To see the difference of these seasons*: i.e. how times have changed 8 *quick*: spirited/pregnant 10 *dancing*: like playing on the spinet, another lady-like accomplishment capable of suggesting bawdy innuendo 12 *bord*: bore, calibre, i.e. age (and, continuing the bawdy, size) 15 *plumber's daughter*: i.e. presumably leaden-footed 19 *Mary*: perhaps the use of this name for Moll indicates an unrevised first intention on the part of Middleton. But it is also possible that the two names hint at ambivalent attitudes towards the subplot on the part of the author, Mary having associations with purity and Moll with wantonness
21 *fetch words from Westminster*: i.e. borrow terms from the Law French employed in the courts at Westminster 22 *half-crown-piece*: difficult terms were known as 'half-crown-words' 23 *cozen'd*: cheated *gilded twopence*: i.e. counterfeit money; the twopence could be 'gilded' to resemble the similar-sized gold half-crown
26 *lawns/cambrics*: both are kinds of fine white linen *bracks*: flaws 27 *sowders*: solders *cracks*: imperfections/cunts 30 *Holborn Bridge*: which carried the main road from Wales over the Fleet Ditch

A proper fair young gentlewoman, which I guess
By her red hair and other rank descriptions
To be his landed niece brought out of Wales,
Which Tim our son (the Cambridge boy) must marry.
'Tis a match of Sir Walter's own making
To bind us to him, and our heirs for ever.

MAUDLINE: We are honour'd then, if this baggage would be humble,
And kiss him with devotion when he enters.
I cannot get her for my life
To instruct her hand thus, before and after,
Which a knight will look for, before and after.
I have told her still, 'tis the waving of a woman
Does often move a man and prevails strongly.
But sweet, ha' you sent to Cambridge,
Has Tim word on't?

YELLOWHAMMER: Had word just the day after when you sent him the silver spoon to eat his broth in the hall amongst the gentlemen commoners.

MAUDLINE: O 'twas timely.

Enter Porter.

YELLOWHAMMER: How now?

PORTER: A letter from a gentleman in Cambridge.

YELLOWHAMMER: O one of Hobson's porters, thou art welcome. I told thee, Maud, we should hear from Tim. [*Reads.*] '*Amantissimis carissimisque ambobus parentibus patri et matri.*'

MAUDLINE: What's the matter?

YELLOWHAMMER: Nay, by my troth, I know not, ask not me, he's grown too verbal; this learning is a great witch.

32 *rank*: indicative of status/lascivious 41 *before and after*: i.e. the 'waving' of the hands in front of and behind the body (with bawdy innuendo) 42 *waving*: movement 47–8 *gentlemen commoners*: wealthy students who paid for special privileges, and dined separately from the poorer undergraduates 52 *Hobson*: the Cambridge carrier who insisted that customers take the first available horse for hire, a practice which may have given rise to the phrase 'Hobson's choice' 53–4 Latin, 'To my father and mother, both my most loving parents'. The Latin throughout the play is riddled with errors and it is tempting to leave these uncorrected as they may serve to indicate the foolish pretentiousness of the speakers. However, in other plays of the period corrupt Latin is given even to cultivated speakers (e.g. several of Hieronimo's speeches in *The Spanish Tragedy* are badly garbled), probably as a result of faulty transcription. We have therefore followed the corrected Latin of Dyce, the indefatigable 19th-century editor and distinguished classical scholar. The translations have been provided by Dr Roland Mayer of Birkbeck College, London University 55 *matter*: content

MAUDLINE: Pray let me see it, I was wont to understand him. [*Reads.*] '*Amantissimis carissimis*', he has sent the carrier's man, he says; '*ambobus parentibus*', for a pair of boots; '*patri et matri*', pay the porter, or it makes no matter.

PORTER: Yes by my faith! Mistress, there's no true construction in that, I have took a great deal of pains and come from the Bell sweating. Let me come to't, for I was a scholar forty years ago. 'Tis thus, I warrant you: *matri*, it makes no matter; *ambobus parentibus*, for a pair of boots; *patri*, pay the porter; *amantissimis carissimis*, he's the carrier's man, and his name is Sims – and there he says true, forsooth, my name is Sims indeed. I have not forgot all my learning. A money matter, I thought I should hit on't.

YELLOWHAMMER: Go, thou art an old fox, there's a tester for thee. [*Gives money.*]

PORTER: If I see your worship at Goose Fair, I have a dish of birds for you.

YELLOWHAMMER: Why, dost dwell at Bow?

PORTER: All my lifetime, sir, I could ever say Bo, to a goose. Farewell to your worship.

Exit Porter.

YELLOWHAMMER: A merry porter.

MAUDLINE: How can he choose but be so, coming with Cambridge letters from our son Tim?

YELLOWHAMMER: What's here? [*Reads.*] '*Maxime diligo*'. Faith, I must to my learned counsel with this gear, 'twill ne'er be discern'd else.

MAUDLINE: Go to my cousin then, at Inns of Court.

YELLOWHAMMER: Fie, they are all for French, they speak no Latin.

MAUDLINE: The parson then will do it.

Enter a Gentleman *with a chain.*

YELLOWHAMMER: Nay, he disclaims it, calls Latin 'Papistry', he will not deal with it. What is't you lack, gentleman?

GENTLEMAN: Pray weigh this chain.

[YELLOWHAMMER *weighs it.*]

62 *no true construction*: i.e. you have misconstrued the Latin 63 *the Bell*: clearly an inn (but whether it is the Bell in Coleman Street, or a misprint for the Black Bull in Bishopsgate Street, is not clear) 69 *tester*: sixpence 70 *Goose Fair*: a fair where young geese were roasted and sold during Whitsun week at Stratford-le-Bow. The porter's offer of a 'dish of birds' is probably indecent as the term 'green goose' at the time meant both 'gosling' and 'harlot' (in *Michaelmas Term* II.i.111–16, 'bow' = cunt, so this points a further possible joke at line 72) 77 *Maxime diligo*: Latin, 'I love most highly' 78 *gear*: stuff *discern'd*: understood 79 *Inns of Court*: colleges where students trained to enter the legal profession 80 *French*: Law French was much used in the Inns of Court 82 *Papistry*: the Roman Catholic mass was still celebrated in Latin

Enter SIR WALTER WHOREHOUND, WELSH GENTLEWOMAN *and* DAVY DAHUMMA. [*They talk apart.*]

SIR WALTER: Now, wench, thou art welcome to the heart of the City of London.

WELSH GENTLEWOMAN: *Dugat a whee.*

SIR WALTER: You can thank me in English if you list.

WELSH GENTLEWOMAN: I can, sir, simply.

SIR WALTER: 'Twill serve to pass, wench; 'twas strange that I should lie with thee so often, to leave thee without English – that were unnatural. I bring thee up to turn thee into gold, wench, and make thy fortune shine like your bright trade; a goldsmith's shop sets out a City maid. Davy Dahumma, not a word!

DAVY: Mum, mum, sir.

SIR WALTER: Here you must pass for a pure virgin.

DAVY [*Aside.*]: Pure Welsh virgin! She lost her maidenhead in Brecknockshire.

SIR WALTER: I hear you mumble, Davy.

DAVY: I have teeth, sir, I need not mumble yet this forty years.

SIR WALTER [*Aside.*]: The knave bites plaguily.

YELLOWHAMMER [*To* Gentleman.]: What's your price, sir?

GENTLEMAN: A hundred pound, sir.

YELLOWHAMMER: A hundred marks the utmost, 'tis not for me else.

[*Exit* Gentleman.]

– What, Sir Walter Whorehound!

MOLL [*Aside.*]: O death!

Exit MOLL.

MAUDLINE: Why, daughter! Faith, the baggage!
A bashful girl, sir; these young things are shamefast,
Besides you have a presence, sweet Sir Walter,
Able to daunt a maid brought up i'the City:
Enter [MOLL].
A brave Court spirit makes our virgins quiver
And kiss with trembling thighs. Yet see, she comes, sir.

SIR WALTER: Why, how now, pretty mistress, now I have caught you. What, can you injure so your time to stray thus from your faithful servant?

87 *Dugat a whee*: probably a phonetic rendering of the Welsh for 'God preserve you' 90 *'twas strange that*: it would be strange if 93 *your*: one's *sets out*: displays to advantage 97–8 *Brecknockshire*: a county in S.E. Wales; with a punning reference to 'nock', another cant term for cunt 101 *plaguily*: confoundedly; presumably Sir Walter lacks his own teeth 104 *marks*: a mark was a sum equivalent to two-thirds of £1 108 *shamefast*: bashful
112 *trembling thighs*: sexual intercourse in a standing position was known as a 'knee-trembler'

YELLOWHAMMER: Pish, stop your words, good knight, 'twill make her blush else, which wound too high for the daughters of the Freedom. 'Honour', and 'faithful servant', they are compliments for the worthies of Whitehall or Greenwich. E'en plain, sufficient, subsidy words serves us, sir. And is this gentlewoman your worthy niece?

SIR WALTER: You may be bold with her on these terms, 'tis she, sir, heir to some nineteen mountains.

YELLOWHAMMER: Bless us all! You overwhelm me, sir, with love and riches.

SIR WALTER: And all as high as Paul's.

DAVY [*Aside.*]: Here's work, i'faith.

SIR WALTER: How sayest thou, Davy?

DAVY: Higher, sir, by far; you cannot see the top of 'em.

YELLOWHAMMER: What, man? Maudline, salute this gentlewoman – [*Aside.*] our daughter, if things hit right.

Enter TOUCHWOOD JUNIOR.

TOUCHWOOD JUNIOR [*Aside.*]: My knight with a brace of footmen
Is come and brought up his ewe mutton
To find a ram at London; I must hasten it,
Or else pick a famine; her blood's mine,
And that's the surest. Well, knight, that choice spoil
Is only kept for me.
[*Draws* MOLL *aside.*]

MOLL: Sir?

TOUCHWOOD JUNIOR: Turn not to me till thou may'st lawfully, it but whets my stomach, which is too sharp set already. [*Gives letter.*] Read that note carefully, keep me from suspicion still, nor know my zeal but in thy heart; read and send but thy liking in three words, I'll be at hand to take it.

YELLOWHAMMER: O turn, sir, turn.
A poor plain boy, an university man,

117 *wound*: past tense of 'wind' in the sense of 'go' *the Freedom*: i.e. the City of London 119 *Whitehall or Greenwich*: both were royal palaces at the time *subsidy*: bourgeois, commercial (i.e. not courtly) 125 *as high as Paul's*: proverbial, the steeple of the Old Cathedral rose to 450 feet, but was burnt down in 1561 129 *salute*: greet/kiss 132 *ewe mutton*: cant term for prostitute 133 *ram*: i.e. husband *hasten it*: work fast 134 *pick a famine*: choose to starve *her blood's mine*: she's sexually attracted towards me ('blood' may be an allusion to hunting, and this could be taken up in 'spoil' in l. 135) 135 *surest*: strongest assurance of success *choice spoil*: i.e. Moll (Q reads 'spoy' rather than 'spoil') 139 *stomach*: sexual appetite 140 *keep me from suspicion still*: don't draw attention to me/don't be suspicious of my actions 141 *liking*: content 143 *O turn, sir, turn*: presumably beckoning Sir Walter further into his premises. Some editors emend to 'O Tim. . . .'

Proceeds next Lent to a Bachelor of Art;
He will be call'd Sir Yellowhammer then
Over all Cambridge, and that's half a knight.

MAUDLINE: Please you draw near, and taste the welcome of the City, sir?

YELLOWHAMMER: Come, good Sir Walter, and your virtuous niece here.

SIR WALTER: 'Tis manners to take kindness.

YELLOWHAMMER: Lead 'em in, wife.

SIR WALTER: Your company, sir.

YELLOWHAMMER: I'll give't you instantly.

[*Exeunt* MAUDLINE, SIR WALTER, DAVY *and* WELSH GENTLEWOMAN.]

TOUCHWOOD JUNIOR [*Aside.*]: How strangely busy is the Devil and riches;
Poor soul kept in too hard, her mother's eye
Is cruel toward her, being to him.
'Twere a good mirth now to set him a-work
To make her wedding ring. I must about it.
Rather than the gain should fall to a stranger,
'Twas honesty in me to enrich my father.

YELLOWHAMMER [*Aside.*]: The girl is wondrous peevish; I fear nothing
But that she's taken with some other love,
Then all's quite dash'd. That must be narrowly look'd to;
We cannot be too wary in our children.
[*To* TOUCHWOOD JUNIOR.] What is't you lack?

TOUCHWOOD JUNIOR [*Aside.*]: O nothing now, all that I wish is present.
[*To* YELLOWHAMMER.] I would have a wedding ring made for a gentlewoman
With all speed that may be.

YELLOWHAMMER: Of what weight, sir?

TOUCHWOOD JUNIOR: Of some half ounce,
Stand fair and comely, with the spark of a diamond.
Sir, 'twere pity to lose the least grace.

YELLOWHAMMER [*Taking the stone.*]: Pray let's see it; indeed, sir, 'tis a pure one.

TOUCHWOOD: So is the mistress.

146 *Sir*: a rendering of the title 'Dominus' accorded to graduates from Oxford and Cambridge. It constituted only 'half a knight' because it preceded the surname only, unlike the distinctive title of a knight or baronet which was placed before the Christian name 156 *being to him*: i.e. favouring Sir Walter 160 *'Twas*: It would be 170 *Stand*: i.e. it should stand *spark*: small stone

YELLOWHAMMER: Have you the wideness of her finger, sir?
TOUCHWOOD JUNIOR: Yes, sure, I think I have her measure about me –
Good faith, 'tis down; I cannot show't you,
I must pull too many things out to be certain.
Let me see: long, and slender, and neatly jointed;
Just such another gentlewoman that's your daughter, sir.
YELLOWHAMMER: And therefore, sir, no gentlewoman.
TOUCHWOOD JUNIOR: I protest I never saw two maids handed more alike;
I'll ne'er seek farther, if you'll give me leave, sir.
YELLOWHAMMER: If you dare venture by her finger, sir.
TOUCHWOOD JUNIOR: Ay, and I'll bide all loss, sir.
YELLOWHAMMER: Say you so, sir? Let's see hither, girl.
TOUCHWOOD JUNIOR: Shall I make bold with your finger, gentlewoman?
MOLL: Your pleasure, sir.
[*Tries the ring on* MOLL*'s finger.*]
TOUCHWOOD JUNIOR: That fits her to a hair, sir.
YELLOWHAMMER: What's your posy now, sir?
TOUCHWOOD: Mass, that's true, posy, i'faith. E'en thus, sir:
'Love that's wise, blinds parents' eyes.'
YELLOWHAMMER: How, how? If I may speak without offence, sir,
I hold my life –
TOUCHWOOD JUNIOR: What, sir?
YELLOWHAMMER: Go to, you'll pardon me?
TOUCHWOOD JUNIOR: Pardon you? Ay, sir.
YELLOWHAMMER: Will you, i'faith?
TOUCHWOOD JUNIOR: Yes, faith I will.
YELLOWHAMMER: You'll steal away some man's daughter, am I near you?
Do you turn aside? You gentlemen are mad wags!
I wonder things can be so warily carried
And parents blinded so; but they're served right
That have two eyes and wear so dull a sight.
TOUCHWOOD JUNIOR [*Aside.*]: Thy doom take hold of thee.

175 *measure*: measurement, with a bawdy pun on penis. The sexual symbolism of wedding rings is a common theme in Middleton 176 *down*: at the bottom of my pocket/detumescent 179 *that's*: as is 180 *no gentlewoman*: Yellowhammer again insists on the family's bourgeois status 184 *bide*: stand 188 *to a hair*: perfectly, but with a pun on 'pubic hair' 189 *posy*: a motto, normally a line of verse, inscribed inside a ring 199 *am I near you*: have I found you out (with irony in the 'near') 203 *wear*: Q reads 'were' but this is probably merely an alternative spelling

YELLOWHAMMER: Tomorrow noon shall show your ring well done.
TOUCHWOOD JUNIOR: Being so, 'tis soon; thanks, and your leave, sweet gentlewoman.
Exit.
MOLL: Sir, you are welcome.
[*Aside.*] O were I made of wishes, I went with thee.
YELLOWHAMMER: Come now, we'll see how the rules go within.
MOLL [*Aside.*]: That robs my joy, there I lose all I win.
Ex[*eunt*].

[SCENE 2]

Enter DAVY *and* ALLWIT *severally.*
DAVY [*Aside.*]: Honesty wash my eyes, I have spied a wittol.
ALLWIT: What, Davy Dahumma? Welcome from North Wales
I'faith, and is Sir Walter come?
DAVY: New come to town, sir.

ALLWIT: In to the maids, sweet Davy, and give order his chamber be made ready instantly; my wife's as great as she can wallow, Davy, and longs for nothing but pickled cucumbers and his coming, and now she shall ha't, boy.

DAVY: She's sure of them, sir.
ALLWIT: Thy very sight will hold my wife in pleasure,
Till the knight come himself. Go in, in, in, Davy.
Exit [DAVY].
The founder's come to town; I am like a man
Finding a table furnish'd to his hand,
As mine is still to me, prays for the founder:
'Bless the right worshipful, the good founder's life.'
I thank him, h'as maintain'd my house this ten years,
Not only keeps my wife, but a keeps me
And all my family; I am at his table,
He gets me all my children, and pays the nurse,
Monthly, or weekly, puts me to nothing,
Rent, nor church duties, not so much as the scavenger:

210 *rules*: revels   s.d. *severally*: separately   1 *wittol*: complaisant cuckold   11 *founder*: one who endows an institution   12 *furnish'd to his hand*: with provisions to hand (blasphemously echoing Psalm 23: 'Thou preparest a table before me . . .')   16 *a*: he   20 *church duties*: church dues   *scavenger*: an official responsible for the maintenance of streets and pavements

The happiest state that ever man was born to.
I walk out in a morning, come to breakfast,
Find excellent cheer, a good fire in winter;
Look in my coal house about midsummer eve,
That's full, five or six chaldron, new laid up;
Look in my back yard, I shall find a steeple
Made up with Kentish faggots, which o'erlooks
The waterhouse and the windmills; I say nothing,
But smile and pin the door. When she lies in,
And now she's even upon the point of grunting,
A lady lies not in like her; there's her embossings,
Embroid'rings, spanglings, and I know not what,
As if she lay with all the gaudy shops
In Gresham's Burse about her; then her restoratives,
Able to set up a young 'pothecary
And richly stock the foreman of a drug shop;
Her sugar by whole loaves, her wines by rundlets.
I see these things, but like a happy man,
I pay for none at all, yet fools think's mine;
I have the name, and in his gold I shine;
And where some merchants would in soul kiss hell
To buy a paradise for their wives, and dye
Their conscience in the bloods of prodigal heirs
To deck their night-piece, yet all this being done,
Eaten with jealousy to the inmost bone –
As what affliction nature more constrains
Than feed the wife plump for another's veins? –
These torments stand I freed of, I am as clear
From jealousy of a wife as from the charge:
O two miraculous blessings! 'Tis the knight
Hath took that labour all out of my hands:
I may sit still and play, he's jealous for me,
Watches her steps, sets spies. I live at ease,

25 *chaldron*: a measure of 32 bushels 27 *Kentish faggots*: bundles of brushwood, approximately 8 feet long *o'erlooks*: stands higher than 29 *pin*: bolt 31 *embossings*: ornamental reliefs 32 *spanglings*: cloth decorated with spangles 33 *gaudy shops*: shops selling trinkets, etc. 34 *Gresham's Burse*: the Royal Exchange, founded by Thomas Gresham in 1566 as a centre of commercial activity *restoratives*: medicines or cordials 37 *sugar by whole loaves*: loaf-sugar was a moulded conical mass of refined sugar *rundlets*: casks 39 *think's*: think it is 42–3 i.e. gull prodigal heirs, a favourite theme of Jacobean dramatists 44 *night-piece*: mistress 46 *nature more constrains*: more violates nature 47 *another's veins*: i.e. another's sexual pleasure 49 *charge*: cost

He has both the cost and torment; when the strings
Of his heart frets, I feed, laugh, or sing,
La dildo, dildo la dildo, la dildo diido de dildo.
Enter two Servants.
SERVANT 1: What has he got a-singing in his head now?
SERVANT 2: Now's out of work he falls to making dildoes.
ALLWIT: Now, sirs, Sir Walter's come.
SERVANT 1: Is our master come?
ALLWIT: Your master? What am I?
SERVANT 1: Do not you know, sir?
ALLWIT: Pray am not I your master?
SERVANT 1: O you are but our mistress's husband.
Enter SIR WALTER *and* DAVY.
ALLWIT: *Ergo* knave, your master.
SERVANT 1: *Negatur argumentum.* Here comes Sir Walter. [*Aside to* Servant 2.] Now a stands bare as well as we; make the most of him, he's but one peep above a servingman, and so much his horns make him.
SIR WALTER: How dost, Jack?
ALLWIT: Proud of your worship's health, sir.
SIR WALTER: How does your wife?
ALLWIT: E'en after your own making, sir,
She's a tumbler, a' faith, the nose and belly meets.
SIR WALTER: They'll part in time again.
ALLWIT: At the good hour, they will, and please your worship.
SIR WALTER [*To* Servant.]: Here, sirrah, pull off my boots. [*To* ALLWIT.]
Put on, put on, Jack.
ALLWIT: I thank your kind worship, sir.
SIR WALTER: Slippers! [Servant *brings slippers.*] Heart, you are sleepy.
ALLWIT [*Aside.*]: The game begins already.
SIR WALTER: Pish, put on, Jack.
ALLWIT [*Aside.*]: Now I must do it, or he'll be as angry now as if I had put it on at first bidding; 'tis but observing, [*Puts on his hat.*] 'tis but

54 *strings*: the heart was thought to be braced with string 55 *frets*: are corroded away (by emotional stress) 56 *dildo*: common nonsense refrain in ballads/artificial penis 58 *out of work*: unemployed/sexually deprived
65 *Ergo*: Latin, 'therefore' 66 *Negatur argumentum*: Latin, 'the argument is denied', a standard scholastic tag 67 *a*: he *bare*: bare-headed 68 *peep*: pip, as in the pips of playing cards, i.e. degree *horns*: i.e. cuckold's horns
73 *tumbler*: acrobat/copulator *nose and belly meets*: i.e. her pregnancy is far advanced 77 *Put on*: i.e. put your hat on (which Allwit has removed as a mark of deference) 79 *Heart*: exclamation derived from 'God's heart'

observing a man's humour once, and he may ha' him by the nose all his life.

SIR WALTER: What entertainment has lain open here?
No strangers in my absence?
SERVANT 1: Sure, sir, not any.
ALLWIT [*Aside.*]: His jealousy begins. Am not I happy now
That can laugh inward whilst his marrow melts?
SIR WALTER: How do you satisfy me?
SERVANT 1: Good sir, be patient.
SIR WALTER: For two months' absence I'll be satisfied.
SERVANT 1: No living creature ent'red –
SIR WALTER: Ent'red? Come, swear –
SERVANT 1: You will not hear me out, sir –
SIR WALTER: Yes, I'll hear't out, sir.
SERVANT 1: Sir, he can tell himself.
SIR WALTER: Heart, he can tell!
Do you think I'll trust him? As a usurer
With forfeited lordships! Him? O monstrous injury!
Believe him? Can the Devil speak ill of darkness?
What can you say, sir?

ALLWIT: Of my soul and conscience, sir, she's a wife as honest of her body to me as any lord's proud lady can be.

SIR WALTER: Yet, by your leave, I heard you were once off'ring to go to bed to her.

ALLWIT: No, I protest, sir.
SIR WALTER: Heart if you do, you shall take all. I'll marry!
ALLWIT: O I beseech you, sir –
SIR WALTER [*Aside.*]: That wakes the slave, and keeps his flesh in awe.
ALLWIT [*Aside.*]: I'll stop that gap
Where e'er I find it open; I have poisoned
His hopes in marriage already –
Some old rich widows, and some landed virgins,
Enter two children [WAT *and* NICK].
And I'll fall to work still before I'll lose him;
He's yet too sweet to part from.
WAT [*To* ALLWIT.]: God-den, father.
ALLWIT: Ha, villain, peace!
NICK: God-den, father.

84 *humour*: temperament 89 *marrow melts*: i.e. with the heat of jealousy 90 *satisfy*: furnish with sufficient proof 97–8 *usurer With forfeited lordships*: i.e. not at all. The Jacobean stage regularly depicted dishonest usurers obtaining possession of 'lordships' or estates 'forfeited' through the non-repayment of loans 115 *God-den*: good evening; contracted from 'God give ye good even', but also used to mean 'good afternoon'

ALLWIT: Peace, bastard! [*Aside.*] Should he hear 'em! –
These are two foolish children, they do not know the gentleman that sits there.

SIR WALTER: O Wat! How dost, Nick? Go to school, ply your books, boys, ha?

ALLWIT [*To the children.*]: Where's your legs, whoresons! [*Aside.*] They should kneel indeed if they could say their prayers.

SIR WALTER [*Aside.*]: Let me see, stay;
How shall I dispose of these two brats now
When I am married? For they must not mingle
Amongst my children that I get in wedlock,
'Twill make foul work that, and raise many storms.
I'll bind Wat prentice to a goldsmith – my father Yellowhammer,
As fit as can be! Nick with some vintner; good, goldsmith
And vintner; there will be wine in bowls, i'faith.

Enter ALLWIT'S WIFE.

MISTRESS ALLWIT: Sweet knight,
Welcome; I have all my longings now in town,
Now well-come the good hour.

SIR WALTER: How cheers my mistress?

MISTRESS ALLWIT: Made lightsome e'en by him that made me heavy.

SIR WALTER: Methinks she shows gallantly, like a moon at full, sir.

ALLWIT: True, and if she bear a male child, there's the man in the moon, sir.

SIR WALTER: 'Tis but the boy in the moon yet, goodman calf.

ALLWIT: There was a man, the boy had never been there else.

SIR WALTER: It shall be yours, sir.

ALLWIT: No, by my troth, I'll swear it's not of mine, let him that got it keep it! [*Aside.*] Thus do I rid myself of fear,
Lie soft, sleep hard, drink wine, and eat good cheer.

[*Exeunt.*]

123 *Where's your legs*: children were expected to kneel before their parents
136 *heavy*: pregnant/sad 140 *calf*: fool

ACT TWO

[SCENE I]

Enter TOUCHWOOD SENIOR *and his* WIFE.

MISTRESS TOUCHWOOD: 'Twill be so tedious, sir, to live from you,
But that necessity must be obeyed.

TOUCHWOOD SENIOR: I would it might not, wife, the tediousness
Will be the most part mine, that understand
The blessings I have in thee; so to part,
That drives the torment to a knowing heart.
But as thou say'st, we must give way to need
And live awhile asunder; our desires
Are both too fruitful for our barren fortunes.
How adverse runs the destiny of some creatures:
Some only can get riches and no children,
We only can get children and no riches!
Then 'tis the prudent'st part to check our wills
And till our state rise make our bloods lie still.
[*Aside.*] Life, every year a child, and some years two,
Besides drinkings abroad, that's never reckon'd;
This gear will not hold out.

MISTRESS TOUCHWOOD: Sir, for a time, I'll take the courtesy of my uncle's house,
If you be pleas'd to like on't, till prosperity
Look with a friendly eye upon our states.

TOUCHWOOD SENIOR: Honest wife, I thank thee; I ne'er knew
The perfect treasure thou brought'st with thee more
Than at this instant minute. A man's happy
When he's at poorest that has match'd his soul
As rightly as his body. Had I married
A sensual fool now, as 'tis hard to 'scape it
'Mongst gentlewomen of our time, she would ha' hang'd

6 *knowing*: understanding 13 *wills*: sexual drives 14 *bloods*: sexual passions 15 *Life*: mild oath constructed from 'By God's Life' 16 *drinkings abroad*: fornication away from home *reckon'd*: counted; i.e. he has fathered an unknown number of children by other women 17 *gear*: business/genitals

About my neck, and never left her hold
Till she had kiss'd me into wanton businesses,
Which at the waking of my better judgement
I should have curs'd most bitterly
And laid a thicker vengeance on my act
Than misery of the birth, which were enough
If it were born to greatness, whereas mine
Is sure of beggary, though it were got in wine.
Fulness of joy showeth the goodness in thee.
Thou art a matchless wife; farewell, my joy.

MISTRESS TOUCHWOOD: I shall not want your sight?

TOUCHWOOD SENIOR: I'll see thee often,
Talk in mirth, and play at kisses with thee,
Anything, wench, but what may beget beggars;
There I give o'er the set, throw down the cards,
And dare not take them up.

MISTRESS TOUCHWOOD: Your will be mine, sir.

Exit.

TOUCHWOOD SENIOR: This does not only make her honesty perfect,
But her discretion, and approves her judgement.
Had her desires been wanton, they'd been blameless
In being lawful ever, but of all creatures
I hold that wife a most unmatched treasure
That can unto her fortunes fix her pleasure,
And not unto her blood: this is like wedlock;
The feast of marriage is not lust but love,
And care of the estate. When I please blood,
Merely I sing, and suck out others'; then,
'Tis many a wise man's fault, but of all men
I am the most unfortunate in that game
That ever pleas'd both genders, I ne'er play'd yet
Under a bastard; the poor wenches curse me

32 *thicker vengeance*: i.e. by cursing it 33–5 i.e. it is misery enough to be born to rich parents, but even worse to be born to poor ones 38 *want*: lack 41 *give o'er the set*: abandon the game 44 *approves*: confirms 46 *lawful*: i.e. marriage legitimizes sexual desire 52 *sing*: have sexual intercourse. It has been suggested that this may be a misreading of 'sting', emblematizing lust as a flesh-fly, which would make excellent sense of the following phrase *suck out others'*: i.e. fire the 'blood' of another with lust; but see preceding note 55–6 *I ne'er play'd yet Under a bastard*: i.e. 'I'm always left with a bastard at the very least'. The metaphor derives from card games where a 'bastard' is a card left in the hand which scores against the player. Being left with a bastard therefore is not as expensive as being left with a legitimate child to maintain

To the pit where e'er I come; they were ne'er served so,
But us'd to have more words than one to a bargain.
I have such a fatal finger in such business
I must forth with't, chiefly for country wenches,
For every harvest I shall hinder hay-making;
Enter a Wench *with a child.*
I had no less than seven lay in last Progress,
Within three weeks of one another's time.

WENCH: O snaphance, have I found you?

TOUCHWOOD SENIOR: How 'snaphance'?

WENCH [*Shows her child.*]: Do you see your workmanship?
Nay turn not from it, nor offer to escape, for if you do,
I'll cry it through the streets and follow you.
Your name may well be called Touchwood, a pox on you,
You do but touch and take; thou hast undone me;
I was a maid before, I can bring a certificate for it,
From both the churchwardens.

TOUCHWOOD SENIOR: I'll have the parson's hand too, or I'll not yield to't.

WENCH: Thou shalt have more, thou villain! Nothing grieves me but Ellen, my poor cousin in Derbyshire, thou hast crack'd her marriage quite; she'll have a bout with thee.

TOUCHWOOD SENIOR: Faith, when she will, I'll have a bout with her.

WENCH: A law bout, sir, I mean.

TOUCHWOOD SENIOR: True, lawyers use such bouts as other men do,
And if that be all thy grief, I'll tender her a husband;
I keep of purpose two or three gulls in pickle
To eat such mutton with, and she shall choose one.
Do but in courtesy, faith, wench, excuse me
Of this half yard of flesh, in which I think it wants

57 *pit*: hell/cunt *serv'd*: treated/fucked 58 i.e. are not used to becoming pregnant after one sexual encounter 59 *fatal finger*: penis 61 the 'harvest' of his pregnancies prevents the girls from helping with the hay-making 62 *lay in*: confined *last Progress*: i.e. last summer. The Court toured the estates of the nobility during the summer months 64 *snaphance*: highwayman/flintlock (which ignites the 'touchwood' in the touch-hole (i.e. cunt) of a musket) 70 *touch and take*: i.e. he works like tinder, quick to ignite (and impregnate) 71 *certificate*: i.e. to establish her chastity. Certificates of good character, which were required by those travelling outside their home parish, were notoriously unreliable, particularly when signed by such petty officials as churchwardens 73 *hand*: signature 76 *bout*: quarrel/sexual encounter/law suit 81 *gulls*: dupes *in pickle*: in reserve/poxed (syphilis was treated by 'pickling' the victim by mercurial fumigation in a 'sweating' tub) 82 *mutton*: whore 84 *half yard of flesh*: i.e. the child

A nail or two.
WENCH: No, thou shalt find, villain,
It hath right shape, and all the nails it should have.
TOUCHWOOD SENIOR: Faith, I am poor; do a charitable deed, wench;
I am a younger brother, and have nothing.
WENCH: Nothing! Thou hast too much, thou lying villain,
Unless thou wert more thankful.
TOUCHWOOD SENIOR: I have no dwelling,
I brake up house but this morning. Pray thee pity me;
I am a good fellow, faith, have been too kind
To people of your gender: if I ha't
Without my belly, none of your sex shall want it.
[*Aside.*] That word has been of force to move a woman. –
There's tricks enough to rid thy hand on't, wench:
Some rich man's porch, tomorrow before day,
Or else anon i'th'evening; twenty devices.
Here's all I have, i'faith, take purse and all.
[*Aside.*] And would I were rid of all the ware i'the shop so.
WENCH: Where I find manly dealings, I am pitiful:
This shall not trouble you.
TOUCHWOOD SENIOR: And I protest, wench, the next I'll keep myself.
WENCH: Soft, let it be got first.
[*Aside.*] This is the fifth; if e'er I venture more,
Where I now go for a maid, may I ride for a whore.
Exit.
TOUCHWOOD SENIOR: What shift she'll make now with this piece of flesh
In this strict time of Lent, I cannot imagine;
Flesh dare not peep abroad now; I have known
This city now above this seven years,
But I protest in better state of government
I never knew it yet, nor ever heard of;

85 *A nail or two*: a 'nail' was a measure of 2¼ inches, so the primary meaning of the phrase is that the child is 'not even a half yard long yet'. The mother indignantly rejects the comment, however, for the children of syphilitics were supposed to lack nails and be stunted at birth 88 *younger brother*: primogeniture, the custom by which all property was inherited by the eldest son, ensured that younger brothers were proverbially poor 94 *without my belly*: an obscure phrase possibly meaning 'if I have unconsumed food' or 'if I have money in my purse' ('without' means 'outside' here and there is certainly a sexual quibble) 98 *anon*: immediately 100 *ware*: bastards/whores 106 *ride*: i.e. punished by public exhibition in a cart, punning on the sexual implication 107 *shift*: expedient *flesh*: i.e. the child. It was illegal to eat, sell, or slaughter meat during Lent

There has been more religious, wholesome laws
In the half circle of a year erected
For common good, than memory ever knew of,
Enter SIR OLIVER KIX *and his* LADY.
Setting apart corruption of promoters
And other poisonous officers that infect
And with a venomous breath taint every goodness.

LADY KIX: O that e'er I was begot, or bred, or born!

SIR OLIVER: Be content, sweet wife.

TOUCHWOOD SENIOR [*Aside.*]: What's here to do, now?
I hold my life she's in deep passion
For the imprisonment of veal and mutton
Now kept in garrets, weeps for some calf's head now;
Methinks her husband's head might serve, with bacon.
Enter TOUCHWOOD JUNIOR.

LADY KIX: Hist!

SIR OLIVER: Patience, sweet wife.
[*They walk aside.*]

TOUCHWOOD JUNIOR: Brother, I have sought you strangely.

TOUCHWOOD SENIOR: Why, what's the business?

TOUCHWOOD JUNIOR: With all speed thou canst, procure a licence for me.

TOUCHWOOD SENIOR: How, a licence?

TOUCHWOOD JUNIOR: Cud's foot, she's lost else, I shall miss her ever.

TOUCHWOOD SENIOR: Nay, sure, thou shalt not miss so fair a mark
For thirteen shillings fourpence.

TOUCHWOOD JUNIOR: Thanks by hundreds.
Exit [TOUCHWOOD JUNIOR].

SIR OLIVER: Nay, pray thee cease, I'll be at more cost yet,
Thou know'st we are rich enough.

LADY KIX: All but in blessings,
And there the beggar goes beyond us. O! O! O!
To be seven years a wife and not a child! O not a child!

SIR OLIVER: Sweet wife, have patience.

LADY KIX: Can any woman have a greater cut?

116 *setting apart*: except for 122 *For the imprisonment*: i.e. because of the ban on 123 *garrets*: attics 127 *strangely*: extremely, i.e. I've searched everywhere for you 129 *licence*: a special licence was required before a marriage could take place without the calling of banns, or somewhere other than in church
131 *Cud's foot*: mild oath, contracted from 'By God's foot' 132 *mark*: target/the price of the special licence/cunt 139 *cut*: disaster/gelding (i.e. Sir Oliver)/cunt

SIR OLIVER: I know 'tis great, but what of that, wife?
I cannot do withal; there's things making
By thine own doctor's advice at 'pothecary's;
I spare for nothing, wife, no, if the price
Were forty marks a spoonful,
I'd give a thousand pound to purchase fruitfulness;
'Tis but bating so many good works
In the erecting of Bridewells and spital-houses,
And so fetch it up again, for, having none,
I mean to make good deeds my children.
LADY KIX: Give me but those good deeds, and I'll find children.
[*Exit* TOUCHWOOD SENIOR.]
SIR OLIVER: Hang thee, thou hast had too many!
LADY KIX: Thou liest, brevity!
SIR OLIVER: O horrible! Dar'st thou call me 'brevity'?
Dar'st thou be so short with me?
LADY KIX: Thou deservest worse.
Think but upon the goodly lands and livings
That's kept back through want on't.
SIR OLIVER: Talk not on't, pray thee;
Thou'lt make me play the woman and weep too.
LADY KIX: 'Tis our dry barrenness puffs up Sir Walter;
None gets by your not-getting, but that knight;
He's made by th'means, and fats his fortune shortly
In a great dowry with a goldsmith's daughter.
SIR OLIVER: They may all be deceived,
Be but you patient, wife.
LADY KIX: I have suff'red a long time.
SIR OLIVER: Suffer thy heart out, a pox suffer thee!
LADY KIX: Nay thee, thou desertless slave!
SIR OLIVER: Come, come, I ha' done.
You'll to the gossiping of Master Allwit's child?
LADY KIX: Yes, to my much joy!
Everyone gets before me: there's my sister

141 *do withal*: help it/copulate 146 *bating*: reducing 147 *Bridewells*: Bridewell was a house of correction for prostitutes *spital-houses*: hospitals for venereal diseases 148 *fetch it up again*: recover expenses/recover virility/produce children to make up for the reduction in charity 152 *brevity*: shortness/sexually inadequate 154 *short*: rude 160 *'Tis our dry barrenness puffs up Sir Walter*: the exact relationship between the Kixes and Sir Walter is unclear, but there is entailed property which will pass to Sir Walter if the Kixes bear no children to inherit it 162 *th'means*: i.e. lack of children 170 *gossiping*: christening

Was married but at Barthol'mew eve last,
And she can have two children at a birth.
O one of them, one of them would ha' serv'd my turn.
SIR OLIVER: Sorrow consume thee, thou art still crossing me,
And know'st my nature –
Enter a maid [JUGG]
JUGG: O mistress! [*Aside.*] Weeping or railing,
That's our house harmony.
LADY KIX: What say'st, Jugg?
JUGG: The sweetest news.
LADY KIX: What is't, wench?
JUGG: Throw down your doctor's drugs,
They're all but heretics; I bring certain remedy
That has been taught, and proved, and never fail'd.
SIR OLIVER: O that, that, that or nothing.
JUGG: There's a gentleman,
I haply have his name, too, that has got
Nine children by one water that he useth:
It never misses; they come so fast upon him,
He was fain to give it over.
LADY KIX: His name, sweet Jugg?
JUGG: One Master Touchwood, a fine gentleman,
But run behind hand much with getting children.
SIR OLIVER: Is't possible?
JUGG: Why, sir, he'll undertake,
Using that water, within fifteen year,
For all your wealth, to make you a poor man,
You shall so swarm with children.
SIR OLIVER: I'll venture that, i'faith.
LADY KIX: That shall you, husband.
JUGG: But I must tell you first, he's very dear.
SIR OLIVER: No matter, what serves wealth for?
LADY KIX: True, sweet husband.
[SIR OLIVER]: There's land to come. Put case his water stands me

173 *Barthol'mew eve*: 23 August. As it is not yet mid-Lent Sunday, the twins must have been conceived out of wedlock 180 *Jugg*: a pet-name for 'Joan', often applied as a common noun to a maid-servant 184 *all but heretics*: doctors were often believed to indulge in magical practices 188 *haply*: by chance (but possibly a contraction of 'happily') 189 *water*: medicine/semen 193 *run behind hand*: run into debt 201–4 The text in Q is corrupt at this point. The entire passage is given to 'Lady [Kix]' 201 *Put case*: suppose

In some five hundred pound a pint,
'Twill fetch a thousand, and a kersten soul.
I'll about it.
[LADY KIX]: And that's worth all, sweet husband.
Ex[eunt].

[SCENE 2]

Enter ALLWIT.
ALLWIT: I'll go bid gossips presently myself,
That's all the work I'll do; nor need I stir,
But that it is my pleasure to walk forth
And air myself a little; I am tied to nothing
In this business, what I do is merely recreation,
Not constraint.
Here's running to and fro, nurse upon nurse,
Three charwomen, besides maids and neighbours' children.
Fie, what a trouble have I rid my hands on!
It makes me sweat to think on't.
Enter SIR WALTER WHOREHOUND.
SIR WALTER: How now, Jack?
ALLWIT: I am going to bid gossips for your worship's child, sir.
A goodly girl, i'faith, give you joy on her,
She looks as if she had two thousand pound to her portion
And run away with a tailor; a fine, plump, black-eyed slut;
Under correction, sir,
I take delight to see her. – Nurse!
Enter Dry Nurse.
DRY NURSE: Do you call, sir?
ALLWIT: I call not you, I call the wet nurse hither.
Give me the wet nurse.
Exit [Dry Nurse].
Enter Wet Nurse [*carrying baby*].
Ay, 'tis thou.
Come hither, come hither,
Let's see her once again; I cannot choose
But buss her thrice an hour.

203 *kersten*: christened 1 *presently*: immediately 14 *run away with a tailor*: i.e. she is finely dressed s.d. *Dry Nurse*: had general responsibility for the child 17 *wet nurse*: employed to breastfeed the child 21 *buss*: kiss

WET NURSE: You may be proud on't, sir,
'Tis the bes. piece of work that e'er you did.
ALLWIT: Think'st thou so, nurse? What sayest to Wat and Nick?
WET NURSE: They're pretty children both, but here's a wench
Will be a knocker.
ALLWIT: Pup! Say'st thou me so? Pup, little countess.
Faith, sir, I thank your worship for this girl,
Ten thousand times, and upward.
SIR WALTER: I am glad I have her for you, sir.
ALLWIT: Here, take her in, nurse; wipe her, and give her spoon-meat.
WET NURSE [*Aside.*]: Wipe your mouth, sir.
Exit [*with child*].
ALLWIT: And now about these gossips.
SIR WALTER: Get but two, I'll stand for one myself.
ALLWIT: To your own child, sir?
SIR WALTER: The better policy, it prevents suspicion;
'Tis good to play with rumour at all weapons.
ALLWIT: Troth, I commend your care, sir; 'tis a thing
That I should ne'er have thought on.
SIR WALTER [*Aside.*]: The more slave!
When man turns base, out goes his soul's pure flame,
The fat of ease o'erthrows the eyes of shame.
ALLWIT: I am studying who to get for godmother
Suitable to your worship. Now I ha' thought on't.
SIR WALTER: I'll ease you of that care, and please myself in't.
[*Aside.*] My love, the goldsmith's daughter, if I send,
Her father will command her. – Davy Dahumma!
Enter DAVY.
ALLWIT: I'll fit your worship then with a male partner.
SIR WALTER: What is he?
ALLWIT: A kind, proper gentleman, brother to Master Touchwood.
SIR WALTER: I know Touchwood: has he a brother living?
ALLWIT: A neat bachelor.
SIR WALTER: Now we know him, we'll make shift with him.
Dispatch, the time draws near. – Come hither, Davy.
Exit [*with* DAVY].
ALLWIT: In troth, I pity him, he ne'er stands still.
Poor knight, what pains he takes: sends this way one,

26 *a knocker*: a good looker/good in bed 27 *Pup*: meaningless exclamation 31 *spoon-meat*: i.e. baby food 32 *Wipe your mouth, sir*: i.e. you idiot! 34 *stand for one*: i.e. be a godparent myself 37 *play with rumour at all weapons*: i.e. fight rumour with any weapon available 51 *neat*: elegant 52 *make shift*: be content

That way another, has not an hour's leisure.
I would not have thy toil for all thy pleasure.
Enter two Promoters.
[*Aside.*] Ha, how now? What are these that stand so close
At the street corner, pricking up their ears
And snuffing up their noses, like rich men's dogs
When the first course goes in? By the mass, promoters!
'Tis so, I hold my life, and planted there
To arrest the dead corpse of poor calves and sheep,
Like ravenous creditors that will not suffer
The bodies of their poor departed debtors
To go to th'grave, but e'en in death to vex
And stay the corps, with bills of Middlesex.
This Lent will fat the whoresons up with sweetbreads
And lard their whores with lamb-stones; what their golls
Can clutch goes presently to their Molls and Dolls:
The bawds will be so fat with what they earn
Their chins will hang like udders by Easter eve
And, being strok'd, will give the milk of witches.
How did the mongrels hear my wife lies in?
Well, I may baffle 'em gallantly. – By your favour, gentlemen,
I am a stranger both unto the City
And to her carnal strictness.

PROMOTER 1: Good; your will, sir?

ALLWIT: Pray tell me where one dwells that kills this Lent.

PROMOTER 1: How, kills? [*Aside.*] Come hither, Dick; a bird, a bird!

PROMOTER 2: What is't that you would have?

ALLWIT: Faith, any flesh,
But I long especially for veal and green sauce.

PROMOTER 1 [*Aside.*]: Green goose, you shall be sauc'd.

ALLWIT: I have half a scornful stomach, no fish will be admitted.

67 *corps*: plural form of 'corpse' *bills of Middlesex*: writs involving bogus charges concerning offences committed in Middlesex; once arrested, the plaintiff was faced with the real charge 68 *sweetbreads*: pancreas or thymus glands of animals, commonly regarded as aphrodisiacs 69 *lamb-stones*: lambs' testicles, again often thought of as aphrodisiacs *golls*: hands 70 *Molls and Dolls*: cant names for whores 72 *chins will hang like udders*: double chins were considered to be the distinguishing feature of a bawd 73 *milk of witches*: witches were accused of feeding their familiar spirits from teats variously located 75 *baffle*: hoodwink, disgrace 81 *veal and green sauce*: green sauce was a strong, spicy sauce used to mask the fact that meat was undercooked (to 'eat veal and green sauce' meant to be cheated) 82 *Green goose*: gosling/naïve fool 83 *I have half a scornful stomach*: i.e. I'm selectively fasting

PROMOTER 1: Not this Lent, sir?

ALLWIT: Lent! What cares colon here for Lent?
[*Slaps his belly*.]

PROMOTER 1: You say well, sir;
Good reason that the colon of a gentleman,
As you were lately pleas'd to term your worship, sir,
Should be fulfill'd with answerable food,
To sharpen blood, delight health, and tickle nature.
Were you directed hither to this street, sir?

ALLWIT: That I was, ay, marry.

PROMOTER 2: And the butcher, belike,
Should kill and sell close in some upper room?

ALLWIT: Some apple loft, as I take it, or a coal house,
I know not which, i'faith.

PROMOTER 2: Either will serve.
[*Aside*.] This butcher shall kiss Newgate, 'less he turn up
The bottom of the pocket of his apron. –
You go to seek him?

ALLWIT: Where you shall not find him;
I'll buy, walk by your noses with my flesh,
Sheep-biting mongrels, hand-basket freebooters!
My wife lies in; a foutra for promoters!
Exit.

PROMOTER 1: That shall not serve your turn. What a rogue's this! How cunningly he came over us!

Enter a Man *with meat in a basket*.

PROMOTER 2: Hush't, stand close.

MAN: I have 'scap'd well thus far; they say the knaves are wondrous hot and busy.

PROMOTER 1: By your leave, sir,
We must see what you have under your cloak there.

MAN: Have? I have nothing.

PROMOTER 1: No, do you tell us that? What makes this lump stick out then? We must see, sir.

MAN: What will you see, sir? A pair of sheets, and two of my wife's foul smocks going to the washers?

85 *colon*: the belly 89 *fulfill'd*: filled up *answerable*: suitable 90 *tickle*: agreeably excite 93 *close*: secretly 96 *kiss Newgate*: go to prison 96–7 *'less he turn up The bottom of the pocket of his apron*: i.e. unless he bribes them
100 *hand-basket freebooters*: i.e. plunderers of baskets (with a pun on basket = whore) 101 *My wife lies in*: women recovering from childbirth were exempt from the Lent prohibitions *foutra*: term of contempt derived from French *foutre* = fuck

PROMOTER 2: O we love that sight well, you cannot please us better!
[*Searches the basket.*]
What, do you gull us? Call you these shirts and smocks?
MAN: Now a pox choke you!
You have cozen'd me and five of my wife's kin'red
Of a good dinner; we must make it up now
With herrings and milk-pottage.
Exit.
PROMOTER 1: 'Tis all veal.
PROMOTER 2: All veal? Pox, the worse luck! I promis'd faithfully to send this morning a fat quarter of lamb to a kind gentlewoman in Turnbull Street that longs, and how I'm cross'd.
PROMOTER 1: Let's share this, and see what hap comes next then.
Enter another with a basket.
PROMOTER 2: Agreed. Stand close again; another booty.
What's he?
PROMOTER 1: Sir, by your favour.
MAN: Meaning me, sir?
PROMOTER 1: Good Master Oliver? Cry thee mercy, i'faith!
What hast thou there?
MAN: A rack of mutton, sir, and half a lamb;
You know my mistress' diet.
PROMOTER 1: Go, go, we see thee not; away, keep close.
[*Aside.*] Heart, let him pass! Thou'lt never have the wit
To know our benefactors.
[*Exit* Man.]
PROMOTER 2: I have forgot him.
PROMOTER 1: 'Tis Master Beggarland's man, the wealthy merchant
That is in fee with us.
PROMOTER 2: Now I have a feeling of him.
PROMOTER 1: You know he purchas'd the whole Lent together,
Gave us ten groats a-piece on Ash Wednesday.
PROMOTER 2: True, true.
Enter a Wench *with a basket, and a child in it under a loin of mutton.*
PROMOTER 1: A wench.
PROMOTER 2: Why then, stand close indeed.
WENCH [*Aside.*]: Women had need of wit, if they'll shift here,

119 *pottage*: soup 121–2 *Turnbull Street*: Turnmill Street near Clerkenwell Green was notorious for its brothels 122 *longs*: i.e. has yearning desires of pregnancy *cross'd*: thwarted 123 *hap*: chance 128 *rack*: neck 134 *in fee*: in league (having paid a bribe) 136 *the whole Lent together*: immunity for the whole of Lent 137 *groats*: coins of low value 139 *shift*: succeed in a stratagem/palm off something on someone

And she that hath wit may shift anywhere.
PROMOTER 1: Look, look! Poor fool,
She has left the rump uncover'd too,
More to betray her; this is like a murd'rer
That will outface the deed with a bloody band.
PROMOTER 2: What time of the year is't, sister?
WENCH: O sweet gentlemen, I am a poor servant,
Let me go.
PROMOTER 1: You shall, wench, but this must stay with us.
WENCH: O you undo me, sir!
'Tis for a wealthy gentlewoman that takes physic, sir;
The doctor does allow my mistress mutton.
O as you tender the dear life of a gentlewoman,
I'll bring my master to you; he shall show you
A true authority from the higher powers,
And I'll run every foot.
PROMOTER 2: Well, leave your basket then,
And run and spare not.
WENCH: Will you swear then to me
To keep it till I come.
PROMOTER 1: Now by this light, I will.
WENCH: What say you, gentleman?
PROMOTER 2: What a strange wench 'tis!
Would we might perish else.
WENCH: Nay then I run, sir.
Exit.
PROMOTER 1: And ne'er return, I hope.
PROMOTER 2: A politic baggage,
She makes us swear to keep it;
I prithee, look what market she hath made.
PROMOTER 1 [*Emptying the basket.*]: *Imprimis*, sir, a good fat loin of mutton;
What comes next under this cloth?
Now for a quarter of lamb.
PROMOTER 2: Now for a shoulder of mutton.
PROMOTER 1: Done.

144 *band*: collar 154 *authority*: certificate of exemption 160 *politic*: cunning 162 *market*: purchase 163 *Imprimis*: Latin for 'first' (of a series)
166 *Now*: Q reads 'not'. The two promoters are betting as to what they will discover next in the basket and the first promoter thinks that a lamb's head would win the bet, so Q's 'not' seems unlikely to be correct

PROMOTER 2: Why, done, sir!
PROMOTER 1 [*Feeling in the basket.*]: By the mass, I feel I have lost:
'Tis of more weight, i'faith.
PROMOTER 2: Some loin of veal?
PROMOTER 1: No, faith, here's a lamb's head,
I feel that plainly. Why yet [I'll] win my wager.
[*Discovers child.*]
PROMOTER 2: Ha?
PROMOTER 1: Swounds, what's here?
PROMOTER 2: A child!
PROMOTER 1: A pox of all dissembling cunning whores!
PROMOTER 2: Here's an unlucky breakfast!
PROMOTER 1: What shall's do?
PROMOTER 2: The quean made us swear to keep it too.
PROMOTER 1: We might leave it else.
PROMOTER 2: Villainous strange!
Life, had she none to gull but poor promoters
That watch hard for a living?
PROMOTER 1: Half our gettings must run in sugar-sops
And nurses' wages now, besides many a pound of soap
And tallow; we have need to get loins of mutton still,
To save suet to change for candles.
PROMOTER 2: Nothing mads me but this was a lamb's head with you,
you felt it. She has made calves' heads of us.
PROMOTER 1: Prithee, no more on't.
There's time to get it up; it is not come
To mid-Lent Sunday yet.
PROMOTER 2: I am so angry, I'll watch no more today.
PROMOTER 1: Faith, nor I neither.
PROMOTER 2: Why then I'll make a motion.
PROMOTER 1: Well, what is't?
PROMOTER 2: Let's e'en go to the Checker at Queenhive and roast the loin of mutton, till young flood; then send the child to Brainford.
[*Exeunt.*]

174 *Swounds*: an oath, contracted from 'God's wounds' 179 *quean*: whore 184 *sugar-sops*: dishes of slices of bread, soaked in sugar water and sometimes spiced 186 *tallow*: animal fat normally made into candles, but the promoters will need it to grease the baby's bottom 187 *suet*: impure form of tallow *change for*: change into/exchange for (they will need these to care for the baby during the night) 189 *calves' heads*: fools 191 *get it up*: recover the loss 192 *mid-Lent Sunday*: fourth Sunday in Lent 195 *motion*: proposal 197 *Queenhive*: Queenhithe was a large quay near Southwark Bridge where most Lenten fish was landed 198 *young flood*: i.e. when the tide begins to rise *Brainford*: Brentford, a suburb where children were frequently put out to nurse

A CHASTE MAID IN CHEAPSIDE

[SCENE 3]

Enter ALLWIT *in one of Sir Walter's suits, and* DAVY *trussing him.*

ALLWIT: 'Tis a busy day at our house, Davy.
DAVY: Always the kurs'ning day, sir.
ALLWIT: Truss, truss me, Davy.
DAVY [*Aside.*]: No matter and you were hang'd, sir.
ALLWIT: How does this suit fit me, Davy?
DAVY: Excellent neatly; my master's things were ever fit for you, sir, e'en to a hair, you know.
ALLWIT: Thou hast hit it right, Davy,
We ever jump'd in one, this ten years, Davy.
Enter a Servant *with a box.*
So, well said. What art thou?
SERVANT: Your comfit-maker's man, sir.
ALLWIT: O sweet youth, into the nurse quick,
Quick, 'tis time, i'faith;
Your mistress will be here?
SERVANT: She was setting forth, sir.
Enter two Puritans.
ALLWIT: Here comes our gossips now. O I shall have such kissing work today. Sweet Mistress Underman, welcome, i'faith.
PURITAN 1: Give you joy of your fine girl, sir,
Grant that her education may be pure,
And become one of the faithful.
ALLWIT: Thanks to your sisterly wishes, Mistress Underman.
PURITAN 2: Are any of the brethren's wives yet come?
ALLWIT: There are some wives within, and some at home.
PURITAN 1: Verily, thanks, sir.
Ex[*eunt* Puritans].
ALLWIT: Verily, you are an ass, forsooth;
I must fit all these times, or there's no music.
Enter two Gossips.

s.d. *trussing*: doing up the laces which joined the hose to the doublet 2 *kurs'ning*: christening 4 *No matter and*: it would not matter if . . . *hang'd*: punning on the secondary sense of truss = hang 6–7 *e'en to a hair*: exactly/even your wife's (pubic) hair (perhaps there is a humorous suggestion that Allwit is 'cuckolding' Sir Walter!) 8 *hit it*: guessed 9 *jump'd in one*: totally agreed/fucked the same women 11 *comfit*: sweetmeat made from fruit preserved in sugar 20 *become*: befit 26 *I must fit all these times, or there's no music*: I must put up with these occasions or my easy way of life will come to an end

Here comes a friendly and familiar pair;
Now I like these wenches well.

GOSSIP 1: How dost, sirrah?

ALLWIT: Faith, well, I thank you, neighbour, and how dost thou?

GOSSIP 2: Want nothing, but such getting, sir, as thine.

ALLWIT: My gettings, wench? They are poor.

GOSSIP 1: Fie that thou'lt say so!
Th'ast as fine children as a man can get.

DAVY [*Aside.*]: Ay, as a man can get,
And that's my master.

ALLWIT: They are pretty, foolish things.
Put to making in minutes;
I ne'er stand long about 'em.
Will you walk in, wenches?

[*Exeunt* Gossips.]

Enter TOUCHWOOD JUNIOR *and* MOLL.

TOUCHWOOD JUNIOR: The happiest meeting that our souls could wish for. Here's the ring ready; I am beholding unto your father's haste, h'as kept his hour.

MOLL: He never kept it better.

Enter SIR WALTER WHOREHOUND.

TOUCHWOOD JUNIOR: Back, be silent.

SIR WALTER: Mistress and partner, I will put you both into one cup.

[*Drinks their health.*]

DAVY [*Aside.*]: Into one cup! Most proper:
A fitting compliment for a goldsmith's daughter.

ALLWIT: Yes, sir, that's he must be your worship's partner
In this day's business, Master Touchwood's brother.

SIR WALTER: I embrace your acquaintance, sir.

TOUCHWOOD JUNIOR: It vows your service, sir.

SIR WALTER: It's near high time. Come, Master Allwit.

ALLWIT: Ready, sir.

SIR WALTER: Will't please you walk?

TOUCHWOOD JUNIOR: Sir, I obey your time.

Ex[*eunt*].

31 *getting*: children/earnings 38 *stand*: stay/maintain an erection 45 *I will put you both into one cup*: I'll drink one toast to you both 52 *high time*: the appropriate time

[SCENE 4]

Enter Midwife *with the child*, [MAUDLINE, *two* Puritans] *and the* Gossips *to the kurs'ning*.

[*Exit* Midwife *with child*.]

GOSSIP 1 [*Offering precedence*.]: Good Mistress Yellowhammer.

MAUDLINE: In faith, I will not.

GOSSIP 1: Indeed it shall be yours.

MAUDLINE: I have sworn, i'faith.

GOSSIP 1: I'll stand still then.

MAUDLINE: So will you let the child go without company
And make me forsworn.

GOSSIP 1: You are such another creature.

[*Exeunt* Gossip 1 *and* MAUDLINE.]

GOSSIP 2: Before me? I pray come down a little.

GOSSIP 3: Not a whit; I hope I know my place.

GOSSIP 2: Your place? Great wonder, sure! Are you any better than a comfit-maker's wife?

GOSSIP 3: And that's as good at all times as a 'pothecary's.

GOSSIP 2: Ye lie! Yet I forbear you too.

[*Exeunt* Gossips 2 *and* 3.]

PURITAN 1: Come, sweet sister, we go in unity and show the fruits of peace like children of the spirit.

PURITAN 2: I love lowliness.

[*Exeunt* Puritans.]

GOSSIP 4: True, so say I: though they strive more,
There comes as proud behind as goes before.

GOSSIP 5: Every inch, i'faith.

Ex[*eunt*].

19 proverbial, with a pun on 'proud' = erect (perhaps with a suggestion of buggery)

ACT THREE

[SCENE I]

Enter TOUCHWOOD JUNIOR *and a* Parson.

TOUCHWOOD JUNIOR: O sir, if ever you felt the force of love, pity it in me!

PARSON: Yes, though I ne'er was married, sir,
I have felt the force of love from good men's daughters,
And some that will be maids yet three years hence.
Have you got a licence?

TOUCHWOOD JUNIOR: Here, 'tis ready, sir.

PARSON: That's well.

TOUCHWOOD JUNIOR: The ring and all things perfect, she'll steal hither.

PARSON: She shall be welcome, sir; I'll not be long
A-clapping you together.

Enter MOLL *and* TOUCHWOOD SENIOR.

TOUCHWOOD JUNIOR: O here she's come, sir.

PARSON: What's he?

TOUCHWOOD JUNIOR: My honest brother.

TOUCHWOOD SENIOR: Quick, make haste, sirs!

MOLL: You must dispatch with all the speed you can,
For I shall be miss'd straight; I made hard shift
For this small time I have.

PARSON: Then I'll not linger;
Place that ring upon her finger:
[TOUCHWOOD JUNIOR *places the ring on* MOLL*'s finger.*]
This the finger plays the part,
Whose master-vein shoots from the heart.
Now join hands –

Enter YELLOWHAMMER *and* SIR WALTER.

YELLOWHAMMER: Which I will sever,
And so ne'er again meet never!

MOLL: O we are betray'd.

3–5 the parson here hints at his past sexual exploits   11 *dispatch*: complete the business   16 *master-vein*: a blood vessel which in popular belief ran directly from the third finger to the heart   17 *join hands*: the joining of hands, or handfasting, was the legally binding part of the contract. Yellowhammer disrupts the ceremony just before this critical point is reached

TOUCHWOOD JUNIOR: Hard fate!
SIR WALTER: I am struck with wonder.
YELLOWHAMMER: Was this the politic fetch, thou mystical baggage,
Thou disobedient strumpet?
[*To* SIR WALTER.] And were so wise to send for her to such an end?
SIR WALTER: Now I disclaim the end; you'll make me mad.
YELLOWHAMMER [*To* TOUCHWOOD JUNIOR.]: And what are you, sir?
TOUCHWOOD JUNIOR: And you cannot see with those two glasses, put on a pair more.
YELLOWHAMMER: I dreamt of anger still. Here, take your ring, sir.
[*Removes the ring from* MOLL'*s finger*.]
Ha, this? Life, 'tis the same: abominable!
Did not I sell this ring?
TOUCHWOOD JUNIOR: I think you did, you received money for't.
YELLOWHAMMER: Heart, hark you, knight,
Here's no inconscionable villainy!
Set me a-work to make the wedding ring,
And come with an intent to steal my daughter:
Did ever runaway match it?
SIR WALTER [*To* TOUCHWOOD SENIOR.]: This your brother, sir?
TOUCHWOOD SENIOR: He can tell that as well as I.
YELLOWHAMMER: The very posy mocks me to my face:
'*Love that's wise, blinds parents' eyes*.'
I thank your wisdom, sir, for blinding of us;
We have good hope to recover our sight shortly;
In the meantime, I will lock up this baggage
As carefully as my gold: she shall see as little sun,
If a close room or so can keep her from the light on't.
MOLL: O sweet father, for love's sake pity me.
YELLOWHAMMER: Away!
MOLL [*To* TOUCHWOOD JUNIOR.]: Farewell, sir, all content bless thee,
And take this for comfort:
Though violence keep me, thou canst lose me never;
I am ever thine although we part for ever.
YELLOWHAMMER: Ay, we shall part you, minx.
Exit [*with* MOLL].
SIR WALTER [*To* TOUCHWOOD JUNIOR]: Your acquaintance, sir, came very lately,
Yet it came too soon;

20 *politic fetch*: cunning trick *mystical*: concealed 25 *And*: if 32 *no inconscionable*: having no regard to conscience. The 'no' is a double negative employed for emphasis 44 *close*: confined 51 *minx*: hussy, wanton woman

I must hereafter know you for no friend,
But one that I must shun like pestilence,
Or the disease of lust.

TOUCHWOOD JUNIOR: Like enough, sir; you h' ta'en me at the worst time for words that e'er ye pick'd out; faith, do not wrong me, sir.
Exit [*with* Parson].

TOUCHWOOD SENIOR: Look after him and spare not: there he walks
That never yet received baffling; you're bless'd
More than e'er I knew. Go take your rest.
Exit.

SIR WALTER: I pardon you, you are both losers.
Exit.

[SCENE 2]

A bed thrust out upon the stage, ALLWIT'S WIFE *in it. Enter all the* Gossips [*with* MAUDLINE, LADY KIX, *the* Puritans, *and* Dry Nurse *with the child*].

GOSSIP 1: How is't, woman? We have brought you home a kursen soul.

MISTRESS ALLWIT: Ay, I thank your pains.

PURITAN 1: And verily well kursen'd, i'the right way,
Without idolatry or superstition,
After the pure manner of Amsterdam.

MISTRESS ALLWIT: Sit down, good neighbours. – Nurse!

NURSE: At hand, forsooth.

MISTRESS ALLWIT: Look they have all low stools.

NURSE: They have, forsooth.

GOSSIP 2: Bring the child hither, nurse. How say you now,
Gossip, is't not a chopping girl, so like the father?

GOSSIP 3: As if it had been spit out of his mouth,
Eyed, nos'd and brow'd as like a girl can be,
Only, indeed, it has the mother's mouth.

GOSSIP 2: The mother's mouth up and down, up and down!

GOSSIP 3: 'Tis a large child; she's but a little woman.

59 *Look after him*: watch out for him (i.e. Touchwood Jr) 60 *baffling*: public disgrace *bless'd*: lucky 61 *e'er I knew*: any I've ever known 1 *kursen*: christened (with a possible pun on 'cursed' since the child was baptized 'After the pure manner of Amsterdam' which was a centre of Puritan dissent) 9 *chopping*: strapping 13 *up and down*: in all respects

PURITAN 1: No believe me, a very spiny creature, but all heart,
Well mettl'd, like the faithful, to endure
Her tribulation here, and raise up seed.
GOSSIP 2: She had a sore labour on't, I warrant you, you can tell, neighbour.
GOSSIP 3: O she had great speed;
We were afraid once,
But she made us all have joyful hearts again;
'Tis a good soul, i'faith;
The midwife found her a most cheerful daughter.
PURITAN 1: 'Tis the spirit; the sisters are all like her.

Enter SIR WALTER *with two spoons and plate* [, MOLL] *and* ALLWIT.

GOSSIP 2: O here comes the chief gossip, neighbours.

[*Exit* Nurse *with child.*]

SIR WALTER: The fatness of your wishes to you all, ladies.
GOSSIP 3: O dear sweet gentleman, what fine words he has:
'The fatness of our wishes'.
GOSSIP 2: Calls us all 'ladies'!
GOSSIP 4: I promise you, a fine gentleman, and a courteous.
GOSSIP 2: Methinks her husband shows like a clown to him.
GOSSIP 3: I would not care what clown my husband were too, so I had such fine children.
GOSSIP 2: She's all fine children, gossip.
GOSSIP 3: Ay, and see how fast they come.
PURITAN 1: Children are blessings, if they be got with zeal,
By the brethren, as I have five at home.
SIR WALTER [*To* MISTRESS ALLWIT.]: The worst is past, I hope now, gossip.
MISTRESS ALLWIT: So I hope too, good sir.
ALLWIT [*Aside.*]: Why then so hope I too for company!
I have nothing to do else.
SIR WALTER [*Giving cup and spoons.*]: A poor remembrance, lady,
To the love of the babe; I pray accept of it.
MISTRESS ALLWIT: O you are at too much charge, sir.
GOSSIP 2: Look, look, what has he given her! What is't, gossip?

15 *spiny*: spindly 16 *Well mettl'd*: full of spirit 20 *speed*: good fortune 25 *spirit*: Holy Spirit/alcohol 26 *chief gossip*: referring to Sir Walter, the child's godfather; but it is clear from II.ii.45 and III.ii.222 that Moll is also present as godmother s.d. *plate*: silver or gold utensils 27 *fatness*: richest part 31 *clown*: peasant 34 *She's*: she has 36 *zeal*: spiritual enthusiasm/sexual fervour 44 *charge*: expense

GOSSIP 3: Now, by my faith, a fair high standing cup and two great 'postle spoons, one of them gilt.

PURITAN 1: Sure that was Judas then with the red beard.

PURITAN 2: I would not feed my daughter with that spoon for all the world, for fear of colouring her hair; red hair the brethren like not, it consumes them much; 'tis not the sisters' colour.

Enter Nurse *with comfits and wine.*

ALLWIT: Well said, nurse;
About, about with them amongst the gossips.
[*Aside.*] Now out comes all the tassell'd handkerchers,
They are spread abroad between their knees already;
Now in goes the long fingers that are wash'd
Some thrice a day in urine – my wife uses it.
Now we shall have such pocketing;
See how they lurch at the lower end.

PURITAN 1: Come hither, nurse.

ALLWIT [*Aside.*]: Again! She has taken twice already.

PURITAN 1: I had forgot a sister's child that's sick.
[*Takes more comfits.*]

ALLWIT [*Aside.*]: A pox! It seems your purity loves sweet things well that puts in thrice together. Had this been all my cost now I had been beggar'd. These women have no consciences at sweetmeats, where e'er they come; see and they have not cull'd out all the long plums too, they have left nothing here but short wriggle-tail comfits, not worth mouthing; no mar'l I heard a citizen complain once that his wife's belly only broke his back: mine had been all in fitters seven years since, but for this worthy knight that with a prop upholds my wife and me, and all my estate buried in Bucklersberrie.
[*Wine is served.*]

MISTRESS ALLWIT: Here, Mistress Yellowhammer, and neighbours,
To you all that have taken pains with me,
All the good wives at once.
[*Drinks to their health.*]

46 *high standing cup*: cup with base or legs 46–7 *'postle spoons*: spoons with handles depicting figures of the apostles, and thus idolatrous in the view of the Puritan 48 *red beard*: Judas was traditionally depicted with a red beard 50 *red hair*: held to be a sign of lasciviousness 51 *consumes*: angers them/eats them up (i.e. with lust) 52 *said*: done 57 *urine*: used as cleansing agent and cosmetic 58 *pocketing*: i.e. in order to take the comfits home with them 59 *lurch*: filch/sway (from drunkenness) *lower end*: farther end of the room/arse 66 *cull'd out*: picked out 68 *mar'l*: marvel 69 *broke his back*: i.e. through work, having to provide for children/through her sexual demands *fitters*: fragments 71 *Bucklersberrie*: street running from Cheapside to Walbrook

PURITAN 1: I'll answer for them.
They wish all health and strength,
And that you may courageously go forward,
To perform the like and many such,
Like a true sister with motherly bearing.
[*Drinks.*]
ALLWIT [*Aside.*]: Now the cups troll about to wet the gossips' whistles;
It pours down, i'faith; they never think of payment.
PURITAN 1: Fill again, nurse.
[*Drinks again.*]
ALLWIT [*Aside.*]: Now bless thee, two at once! I'll stay no longer;
It would kill me and if I paid for't.
[*To* SIR WALTER.] Will it please you to walk down and leave the women?
SIR WALTER: With all my heart, Jack.
ALLWIT: Troth, I cannot blame you.
SIR WALTER: Sit you all, merry ladies.
ALL GOSSIPS: Thank your worship, sir.
PURITAN 1: Thank your worship, sir.
ALLWIT [*Aside.*]: A pox twice tipple ye, you are last and lowest!
Exit [ALLWIT *with* SIR WALTER].
PURITAN 1: Bring hither that same cup, nurse, I would fain drive away this (hup!) antichristian grief.
[Nurse *refills the glass, then exits.*]
GOSSIP 3: See, gossip, and she lies not in like a countess;
Would I had such a husband for my daughter!
GOSSIP 4: Is not she toward marriage?
GOSSIP 3: O no, sweet gossip!
GOSSIP 4: Why, she's nineteen!
GOSSIP 3: Ay, that she was last Lammas;
But she has a fault, gossip, a secret fault.
GOSSIP 4: A fault, what is't?
GOSSIP 3: I'll tell you when I have drunk.
[*Drinks.*]
GOSSIP 4 [*Aside.*]: Wine can do that, I see, that friendship cannot.
GOSSIP 3: And now I'll tell you, gossip: she's too free.
GOSSIP 4: Too free?
GOSSIP 3: O ay, she cannot lie dry in her bed.
GOSSIP 4: What, and nineteen?

79 *troll about*: circulate 90 *tipple*: topple 95 *toward*: approaching the age for 96 *Lammas*: 1 August, Harvest Festival 100 *free*: incontinent

GOSSIP 3: 'Tis as I tell you, gossip.
[*Enter* Nurse *who speaks aside to* MAUDLINE.]
MAUDLINE: Speak with me, nurse? Who is't?
NURSE: A gentleman from Cambridge;
I think it be your son, forsooth.
MAUDLINE: 'Tis my son Tim, i'faith.
Prithee call him up among the women;
[*Exit* Nurse.]
'Twill embolden him well,
For he wants nothing but audacity.
Would the Welsh gentlewoman at home were here now.
LADY KIX: Is your son come, forsooth?
MAUDLINE: Yes, from the university, forsooth.
LADY KIX: 'Tis great joy on ye.
MAUDLINE: There's a great marriage towards for him.
LADY KIX: A marriage?
MAUDLINE: Yes, sure, a huge heir in Wales,
At lease to nineteen mountains,
Besides her goods and cattell.
Enter [Nurse *with*] TIM.
TIM: O I'm betray'd!
Exit.
MAUDLINE: What, gone again? Run after him, good nurse;
[*Exit* Nurse.]
He's so bashful, that's the spoil of youth;
In the university they're kept still to men,
And ne'er train'd up to women's company.
LADY KIX: 'Tis a great spoil of youth, indeed.
Enter Nurse *and* TIM.
NURSE: Your mother will have it so.
MAUDLINE: Why son, why Tim!
What, must I rise and fetch you? For shame, son!
TIM: Mother, you do intreat like a freshwoman;
'Tis against the laws of the university
For any that has answered under Bachelor
To thrust 'mongst married wives.
MAUDLINE: Come, we'll excuse you here.
TIM: Call up my tutor, mother, and I care not.

114 *towards*: in prospect 118 *cattell*: an obsolete form of 'cattle', meaning chattel property (which will include cattle) 120 *spoil*: destruction
127 *freshwoman*: first-year female undergraduate (although at this period none existed!) 129 *answered under Bachelor*: satisfied the requirements of a Bachelor of Arts degree

MAUDLINE: What is your tutor come? Have you brought him up?
TIM: I ha' not brought him up, he stands at door:
Negatur. There's logic to begin with you, mother.
MAUDLINE: Run, call the gentleman, nurse, he's my son's tutor.
[*Exit* Nurse.]
Here, eat some plums.
TIM: Come I from Cambridge, and offer me six plums?
MAUDLINE: Why, how now, Tim,
Will not your old tricks yet be left?
TIM: Serv'd like a child,
When I have answer'd under Bachelor?
MAUDLINE: You'll never lin till I make your tutor whip you; you know how I serv'd you once at the free school in Paul's churchyard?
TIM: O monstrous absurdity!
Ne'er was the like in Cambridge since my time;
Life, whip a Bachelor? You'd be laugh'd at soundly;
Let not my tutor hear you!
'Twould be a jest through the whole university;
No more words, mother.
Enter Tutor.
MAUDLINE: Is this your tutor, Tim?
TUTOR: Yes surely, lady, I am the man that brought him in league with logic, and read the Dunces to him.
TIM: That did he, mother, but now I have 'em all in my own pate, and can as well read 'em to others.
TUTOR: That can he, mistress, for they flow naturally from him.
MAUDLINE: I'm the more beholding to your pains, sir.
TUTOR: *Non ideo sane*.
MAUDLINE: True, he was an idiot indeed
When he went out of London, but now he's well mended.
Did you receive the two goose pies I sent you?
TUTOR: And eat them heartily, thanks to your worship.
MAUDLINE: 'Tis my son Tim: I pray bid him welcome, gentlewomen.
TIM: 'Tim'? Hark you, 'Timothius', mother, 'Timothius'.
MAUDLINE: How? Shall I deny your name? 'Timothius', quoth he?
Faith, there's a name! 'Tis my son Tim, forsooth.

133 *brought him up*: from Cambridge to London/up the stairs 135 *Negatur*: Latin, 'it is denied' 143 *lin*: cease 144 *free school*: St Paul's school for poor scholars, founded by John Colet in 1512 153 *Dunces*: adherents of the scholastic theologian Duns Scotus (*c.* 1265–*c.* 1308). The term had, however, already come to mean a dullard 156 *naturally*: spontaneously/foolishly 158 *Non ideo sane*: Latin, 'not on that account indeed'

LADY KIX: You're welcome, Master Tim.
Kiss.

TIM [*Aside to* Tutor.]: O this is horrible, she wets as she kisses!
Your handkercher, sweet tutor, to wipe them off as fast as they come on.

GOSSIP 2: Welcome from Cambridge.
Kiss.

TIM [*Aside to* Tutor.]: This is intolerable! This woman has a villainous sweet breath, did she not stink of comfits. Help me, sweet tutor, or I shall rub my lips off.

TUTOR: I'll go kiss the lower end the whilst.

TIM: Perhaps that's the sweeter, and we shall dispatch the sooner.

PURITAN 1: Let me come next. Welcome from the well-spring of discipline, that waters all the brethren.
Reels and falls.

TIM: Hoist, I beseech thee.

GOSSIP 3: O bless the woman! – Mistress Underman!
[Puritan 1 *is helped to her feet.*]

PURITAN 1: 'Tis but the common affliction of the faithful,
We must embrace our falls.

TIM [*Aside to* Tutor.]: I'm glad I 'scap'd it, it was some rotten kiss, sure:
It dropp'd down before it came at me.
Enter ALLWIT *and* DAVY.

ALLWIT [*Aside.*]: Here's a noise! Not parted yet?
Hyda, a looking glass! They have drunk so hard in plate
That some of them had need of other vessels.
[*Aloud.*] Yonder's the bravest show.

ALL GOSSIPS: Where? Where, sir?

ALLWIT: Come along presently by the Pissing-conduit,
With two brave drums and a standard bearer.

ALL GOSSIPS: O brave!

TIM: Come, tutor.
Ex[*eunt* TIM *and* Tutor].

172 *stink of comfits*: 'kissing-comfits' were taken to sweeten the breath 174 *lower end*: i.e. those at the lower end of the table (with a bawdy innuendo)
176–7 *wellspring of discipline*: i.e. Cambridge, which was a centre of Puritan learning 178 *Hoist*: lift yourself up (to the woman)/lift her up (to the tutor)
179 *Mistress Underman*: her name has a bawdy significance 181 *falls*: tumbles/sins; travestying Puritan beliefs concerning the need to accept the fallen state of Man 185 *Hyda*: meaningless exclamation *a looking glass*: a piss-pot *in plate*: i.e. from the silver christening cups 189 *Pissing-conduit*: popular name of the conduit near the Royal Exchange

ALL GOSSIPS: Farewell, sweet gossip.
Ex[*eunt* Gossips].
MISTRESS ALLWIT: I thank you all for your pains.
PURITAN 1: Feed and grow strong.
[*Exeunt all except* ALLWIT *and* DAVY.]
ALLWIT: You had more need to sleep than eat;
Go take a nap with some of the brethren, go,
And rise up a well-edified, boldified sister!
O here's a day of toil well pass'd o'er,
Able to make a citizen hare mad!
How hot they have made the room with their thick bums;
Dost not feel it, Davy?
DAVY: Monstrous strong, sir.
ALLWIT: What's here under the stools?
DAVY: Nothing but wet, sir; some wine spilt here, belike.
ALLWIT: Is't no worse, think'st thou?
Fair needlework stools cost nothing with them, Davy.
DAVY [*Aside.*]: Nor you neither, i'faith.
ALLWIT: Look how they have laid them,
E'en as they lie themselves, with their heels up;
How they have shuffled up the rushes too, Davy,
With their short, figging, little shittle-cork heels!
These women can let nothing stand as they find it.
But what's the secret thou'st about to tell me,
My honest Davy?
DAVY: If you should disclose it, sir –
ALLWIT: Life, rip my belly up to the throat then, Davy.
DAVY: My master's upon marriage.
ALLWIT: Marriage, Davy? Send me to hanging rather.
DAVY [*Aside.*]: I have stung him.
ALLWIT: When, where? What is she, Davy?
DAVY: E'en the same was gossip, and gave the spoon.
ALLWIT: I have no time to stay, nor scarce can speak;
I'll stop those wheels, or all the work will break.
Exit.

197–8 alluding to the Anabaptist doctrine that it was permissible for any man or woman to lie together if they were asleep   200 *hare mad*: i.e. mad as a hare in the breeding season/sex-mad   201 *bums*: padding under the skirt/arses   206 *no worse*: i.e. urine   207 *needlework stools*: stools with embroidered seats   211 *rushes*: rushes were strewn on floors as a covering   212 *short*: i.e. short-heeled; but also slang for 'tart'   *figging*: fidgeting; also slang for fucking   *shittle-cork*: old form of 'shuttle-cock'; but also slang for 'whore'   *heels*: wedge heels were fashionable

DAVY: I knew t'would prick. Thus do I fashion still
All mine own ends by him and his rank toil:
'Tis my desire to keep him still from marriage;
Being his poor nearest kinsman, I may fare
The better at his death; there my hopes build
Since my Lady Kix is dry, and hath no child.
Exit.

[SCENE 3]

Enter both the TOUCHWOODS.

TOUCHWOOD JUNIOR: Y'are in the happiest way to enrich yourself
And pleasure me, brother, as man's feet can tread in,
For though she be lock'd up, her vow is fix'd only to me;
Then time shall never grieve me, for by that vow,
E'en absent I enjoy her, assuredly confirm'd that none
Else shall, which will make tedious years seem gameful
To me. In the mean space, lose you no time, sweet brother;
You have the means to strike at this knight's fortunes
And lay him level with his bankrout merit;
Get but his wife with child, perch at tree top,
And shake the golden fruit into her lap.
About it before she weep herself to a dry ground,
And whine out all her goodness.

TOUCHWOOD SENIOR: Prithee, cease;
I find a too much aptness in my blood
For such a business without provocation;
You might' well spar'd this banquet of eryngoes,
Artichokes, potatoes, and your butter'd crab;
They were fitter kept for your own wedding dinner.

TOUCHWOOD JUNIOR: Nay and you'll follow my suit, and save my purse too,

226 *rank*: excessive/sinful/sweaty 230 *dry*: barren 5 *I*: not in Q 6 *gameful*: joyful/full of sexual pleasure 9 *bankrout*: bankrupt 10 *his*: i.e. Sir Oliver's 10–11 *perch at tree top And shake the golden fruit into her lap*: the 'golden fruit' are the apples of the Hesperides, symbolic of illicit pleasure. The image is therefore of the harvester shaking down the apples to fall into the woman's 'lap of pleasure' 12 *weep herself to a dry ground*: cries herself dry/barren 16 *might'*: might have *eryngoes*: sea-hollies; like the other items in the list, considered to be an aphrodisiac 17 *potatoes*: probably sweet potatoes or yams 19 *suit*: courtship/cause

Fortune dotes on me: he's in happy case
Finds such an honest friend i'the common place.

TOUCHWOOD SENIOR: Life, what makes thee so merry? Thou hast no cause
That I could hear of lately since thy crosses,
Unless there be news come, with new additions.

TOUCHWOOD JUNIOR: Why there thou hast it right,
I look for her this evening, brother.

TOUCHWOOD SENIOR: How's that, 'look for her'?

TOUCHWOOD JUNIOR: I will deliver you of the wonder straight, brother:
By the firm secrecy and kind assistance
Of a good wench i'the house, who, made of pity,
Weighing the case her own, she's led through gutters,
Strange hidden ways, which none but love could find,
Or ha' the heart to venture; I expect her
Where you would little think.

TOUCHWOOD SENIOR: I care not where,
So she be safe, and yours.

TOUCHWOOD JUNIOR: Hope tells me so;
But from your love and time my peace must grow.
Exit.

TOUCHWOOD SENIOR: You know the worst then, brother. Now to my Kix,
The barren he and she; they're i'the next room;
But to say which of their two humours hold them
Now at this instant, I cannot say truly.

SIR OLIVER *to his* LADY *within*: Thou liest, barrenness!

TOUCHWOOD SENIOR: O is't that time of day? Give you joy of your tongue,
There's nothing else good in you: this their life
The whole day, from eyes open to eyes shut,
Kissing or scolding, and then must be made friends,
Then rail the second part of the first fit out,
And then be pleas'd again, no man knows which way;
Fall out like giants, and fall in like children;

21 *i'the common place*: Court of Common Pleas at Westminster/the world; i.e. 'you're lucky to have a friend when in need' or 'you're lucky to find a friend in this world' 23 *crosses*: set-backs (and, in contrast to 'additions' in l. 24, deletions) 31 *gutters*: i.e. over roof tops 37 *You . . . brother*: i.e. things are going to get better now for you 39 *humours*: moods 46 *fit*: section of long poem/seizure/struggle 48 *fall in like children*: i.e. make up. 'Fall in' often indicated sexual intercourse

showing the strife that comes of barrenness

Their fruit can witness as much.
Enter SIR OLIVER KIX *and his* LADY.
SIR OLIVER: 'Tis thy fault.
LADY KIX: Mine, drouth and coldness?
SIR OLIVER: Thine, 'tis thou art barren.
LADY KIX: I barren! O life, that I durst but speak now,
In mine own justice, in mine own right! I barren!
'Twas otherways with me when I was at Court;
I was ne'er call'd so till I was married.
SIR OLIVER: I'll be divorc'd.
LADY KIX: Be hang'd! I need not wish it,
That will come too soon to thee: I may say
'Marriage and hanging goes by destiny',
For all the goodness I can find in't yet.
SIR OLIVER: I'll give up house, and keep some fruitful whore,
Like an old bachelor, in a tradesman's chamber;
She and her children shall have all.
LADY KIX: Where be they?
TOUCHWOOD SENIOR: Pray cease;
When there are friendlier courses took for you
To get and multiply within your house,
At your own proper costs in spite of censure,
Methinks an honest peace might be establish'd.
SIR OLIVER: What, with her? Never.
TOUCHWOOD SENIOR: Sweet sir!
SIR OLIVER: You work all in vain.
LADY KIX: Then he doth all like thee.
TOUCHWOOD SENIOR: Let me intreat, sir.
SIR OLIVER: Singleness confound her!
I took her with one smock.
LADY KIX: But indeed you came not so single,
When you came from shipboard.
SIR OLIVER [*Aside.*]: Heart, she bit sore there!
[*To* TOUCHWOOD SENIOR.] Prithee, make's friends.
TOUCHWOOD SENIOR [*Aside.*]: Is't come to that? The peal begins to cease.

51 *drouth*: drought 57 *divorc'd*: divorces were difficult to obtain and barrenness was not a ground. Perhaps Sir Oliver is thinking of seeking a decree on the grounds of non-consummation 59 proverbial 67 *own proper costs*: own expense *censure*: your mutual recrimination (or, possibly, 'others' unfavourable opinion') 71 *Singleness*: i.e. divorce 73 *single*: i.e. ill-equipped/celibate (conceivably, Lady Kix is accusing him of being lousy) 76 *make's*: make us 77 *peal*: discharge of cannons, i.e. the quarrel

SIR OLIVER: I'll sell all at an outcry.
LADY KIX: Do thy worst, slave!
[*To* TOUCHWOOD SENIOR.] Good sweet sir, bring us into love again.
TOUCHWOOD SENIOR [*Aside*.]: Some would think this impossible to compass. –
Pray let this storm fly over.
SIR OLIVER: Good sir, pardon me: I'm master of this house,
Which I'll sell presently, I'll clap up bills this evening.
TOUCHWOOD SENIOR: Lady, friends – come!
LADY KIX: If e'er ye lov'd woman, talk not on't, sir.
What, friends with him? Good faith, do you think I'm mad?
With one that's scarce the hinder quarter of a man?
SIR OLIVER: Thou art nothing of a woman.
LADY KIX: Would I were less than nothing.
Weeps.
SIR OLIVER: Nay, prithee, what dost mean?
LADY KIX: I cannot please you.
SIR OLIVER: I'faith, thou art a good soul, he lies that says it;
Buss, buss, pretty rogue.
[*Kisses her*.]
LADY KIX: You care not for me.
TOUCHWOOD SENIOR [*Aside*.]: Can any man tell now which way they came in?
By this light, I'll be hang'd then!
SIR OLIVER: Is the drink come?
TOUCHWOOD SENIOR [*Aside*.]: Here's a little vial of almond-milk
That stood me in some three pence.
SIR OLIVER: I hope to see thee, wench, within these few years,
Circled with children, pranking up a girl,
And putting jewels in their little ears;
Fine sport, i'faith!
LADY KIX: Ay, had you been aught, husband,
It had been done ere this time.
SIR OLIVER: 'Had I been aught'! Hang thee, hadst thou been aught!
But a cross thing I ever found thee.
LADY KIX: Thou art a grub to say so.
SIR OLIVER: A pox on thee!

78 *outcry*: auction 80 *compass*: accomplish 83 *clap up bills*: post advertisements for the auction 91 *it*: i.e. that you cannot please me 92 *Buss*: kiss 96 *almond-milk*: sweetened drink made from almonds and barley water 97 *stood me in*: cost 99 *pranking up*: dressing in fine clothes 105 *a grub*: bad mannered/dwarfish/sexually inadequate

TOUCHWOOD SENIOR [*Aside.*]: By this light they are out again at the same door,
And no man can tell which way. –
Come, here's your drink, sir.
SIR OLIVER: I will not take it now, sir,
And I were sure to get three boys ere midnight.
LADY KIX: Why there thou show'st now of what breed thou com'st,
To hinder generation! O thou villain,
That knows how crookedly the world goes with us
For want of heirs, yet put by all good fortune.
SIR OLIVER: Hang, strumpet, I will take it now in spite!
TOUCHWOOD SENIOR: Then you must ride upon't five hours.
SIR OLIVER: I mean so. – Within there!
Enter a SERVANT.
SERVANT: Sir?
SIR OLIVER: Saddle the white mare;
I'll take a whore along, and ride to Ware.
LADY KIX: Ride to the Devil!
SIR OLIVER: I'll plague you every way.
Look ye, do you see, 'tis gone.
Drinks.
LADY KIX: A pox go with it!
SIR OLIVER: Ay, curse and spare not now.
TOUCHWOOD SENIOR: Stir up and down, sir, you must not stand.
SIR OLIVER: Nay, I'm not given to standing.
TOUCHWOOD SENIOR: So much the better, sir, for the –
SIR OLIVER: I never could stand long in one place yet,
I learnt it of my father, ever figient.
How if I cross'd this, sir?
Capers.

TOUCHWOOD SENIOR: O passing good, sir, and would show well a-horseback; when you come to your inn, if you leap'd over a joint-stool or two 'twere not amiss. [*Aside.*] Although you brake your neck, sir.

SIR OLIVER: What say you to a table thus high, sir?

TOUCHWOOD SENIOR: Nothing better, sir. [*Aside.*] If it be furnished with good victuals. – You remember how the bargain runs about this business?

SIR OLIVER: Or else I had a bad head; you must receive, sir, four hundred

114 *put by*: reject 120 *Ware*: a town in Hertfordshire, 20 miles north of London, with a reputation as a meeting place for lovers 125 *standing*: remaining still/maintaining an erection 126 –: the dash in Q probably represents a passage censored by the Master of the Revels 128 *figient*: restless 129 *cross'd*: he probably jumps over a stool here 135 *victuals*: provisions

pounds of me at four several payments: one hundred pound now in hand.

TOUCHWOOD SENIOR: Right, that I have, sir.

SIR OLIVER: Another hundred when my wife is quick; the third when she's brought a-bed; and the last hundred when the child cries, for if it should be stillborn, it doth no good, sir.

TOUCHWOOD SENIOR: All this is even still; a little faster, sir.

SIR OLIVER: Not a whit, sir,
I'm in an excellent pace for any physic.

Enter a SERVANT.

SERVANT: Your white mare's ready.

SIR OLIVER: I shall up presently.

[*Exit* SERVANT.]

One kiss, and farewell.

LADY KIX: Thou shalt have two, love.

SIR OLIVER: Expect me about three.

Exit.

LADY KIX: With all my heart, sweet.

TOUCHWOOD SENIOR [*Aside.*]: By this light they have forgot their anger since,
And are as far in again as e'er they were.
Which way the Devil came they? Heart, I saw 'em not,
Their ways are beyond finding out. – Come, sweet lady.

LADY KIX: How must I take mine, sir?

TOUCHWOOD SENIOR: Clean contrary, yours must be taken lying.

LADY KIX: Abed, sir?

TOUCHWOOD SENIOR: Abed, or where you will for your own ease;
Your coach will serve.

LADY KIX: The physic must needs please.

Ex[*eunt*].

141 *quick*: pregnant 144 *even*: i.e. our accounts are squared *a little faster*: i.e. dance faster 150 *anger since*: previous anger 152 *Which way the Devil came they?*: how the hell did they get into this mood?

ACT FOUR

[SCENE I]

Enter TIM *and* Tutor.

TIM: *Negatur argumentum*, tutor.

TUTOR: *Probo tibi*, pupil, *stultus non est animal rationale.*

TIM: *Falleris sane.*

TUTOR: *Quaeso ut taceas: probo tibi –*

TIM: *Quomodo probas, domine?*

TUTOR: *Stultus non habet rationem, ergo non est animal rationale.*

TIM: *Sic argumentaris, domine: stultus non habet rationem, ergo non est animal rationale. Negatur argumentum* again, tutor.

TUTOR: *Argumentum iterum probo tibi, domine: qui non participat de ratione, nullo modo potest vocari rationalis*; but *stultus non participat de ratione, ergo stultus nullo modo potest dici rationalis.*

TIM: *Participat.*

TUTOR: *Sic disputas: qui participat, quomodo participat?*

TIM: *Ut homo, probabo tibi in syllogismo.*

TUTOR: *Hunc proba.*

1–20:

Tim: Your proof is denied, tutor.

Tutor: I demonstrate, pupil, that a fool is not a rational creature.

Tim: You are surely wrong.

Tutor: I beg you be silent: I prove it to you –

Tim: How do you prove it, sir?

Tutor: A fool does not have the power of reason, therefore he is not a rational creature.

Tim: Thus you argue, sir: a fool does not have the power of reason, therefore he is not a rational creature. Your argument is denied again, tutor.

Tutor: Again I demonstrate the proof, sir: he who does not share the power of reason, can in no way be said to be rational; but a fool does not share the power of reason, therefore a fool can in no way be said to be rational.

Tim: He does share it.

Tutor: Thus you argue: who shares it, how does he share it?

Tim: As a man, I will prove it to you by a syllogism.

Tutor: Prove this.

TIM: *Sic probo, domine: stultus est homo sicut tu et ego sumus, homo est animal rationale, sicut stultus est animal rationale.*

Enter MAUDLINE.

MAUDLINE: Here's nothing but disputing all the day long with 'em.

TUTOR: *Sic disputas: stultus est homo sicut tu et ego sumus, homo est animal rationale, sicut stultus est animal rationale.*

MAUDLINE: Your reasons are both good what e'er they be;
Pray, give them o'er; faith, you'll tire yourselves.
What's the matter between you?

TIM: Nothing but reasoning about a fool, mother.

MAUDLINE: About a fool, son? Alas, what need you trouble your heads about that? None of us all but knows what a fool is.

TIM: Why, what's a fool, mother?
I come to you now.

MAUDLINE: Why, one that's married before he has wit.

TIM: 'Tis pretty, i'faith, and well guess'd of a woman never brought up at the university; but bring forth what fool you will, mother, I'll prove him to be as reasonable a creature as myself or my tutor here.

MAUDLINE: Fie, 'tis impossible.

TUTOR: Nay, he shall do't, forsooth.

TIM: 'Tis the easiest thing to prove a fool by logic;
By logic I'll prove anything.

MAUDLINE: What, thou wilt not!

TIM: I'll prove a whore to be an honest woman.

MAUDLINE: Nay, by my faith, she must prove that herself, or logic will never do't.

TIM: 'Twill do't I tell you.

MAUDLINE: Some in this street would give a thousand pounds that you could prove their wives so.

TIM: Faith, I can, and all their daughters too, though they had three bastards. When comes your tailor hither?

MAUDLINE: Why what of him?

TIM: By logic I'll prove him to be a man,
Let him come when he will.

Tim: Thus I prove it, sir: a fool is a man just as you and I are; a man is a rational creature, so that a fool is a rational creature.
Maudline: . . .
Tutor: Thus you argue . . .

23 *matter*: issue 28 *I come to you*: I pose the question to you 31 *bring forth*: produce (with an ironic pun, since Maudline brought forth Tim from the womb) 47 *prove him to be a man*: tailors were often thought effeminate

MAUDLINE: How hard at first was learning to him! Truly, sir, I thought he would never a took the Latin tongue. How many Accidences do you think he wore out ere he came to his Grammar?

TUTOR: Some three or four?

MAUDLINE: Believe me, sir, some four and thirty.

TIM: Pish, I made haberdines of 'em in church porches.

MAUDLINE: He was eight years in his Grammar and stuck horribly at a foolish place there call'd *as in presenti*.

TIM: Pox, I have it here now.

[*Taps his forehead.*]

MAUDLINE: He so sham'd me once before an honest gentleman that knew me when I was a maid.

TIM: These women must have all out.

MAUDLINE: *'Quid est grammatica?'* says the gentleman to him (I shall remember by a sweet, sweet token), but nothing could he answer.

TUTOR: How now, pupil, ha? *Quid est grammatica?*

TIM: *Grammatica?* Ha, ha, ha!

MAUDLINE: Nay, do not laugh, son, but let me hear you say it now: there was one word went so prettily off the gentleman's tongue, I shall remember it the longest day of my life.

TUTOR: Come, *quid est grammatica?*

TIM: Are you not asham'd, tutor? *Grammatica?* Why, *recte scribendi atque loquendi ars*, sir-reverence of my mother.

MAUDLINE: That was it, i'faith! Why now, son, I see you are a deep scholar; and, master tutor, a word I pray. [*Aside to* Tutor.] Let us withdraw a little into my husband's chamber; I'll send in the North Wales gentlewoman to him, she looks for wooing. I'll put together both and lock the door.

TUTOR: I give great approbation to your conclusion.

Exit [*with* MAUDLINE].

TIM: I mar'l what this gentlewoman should be
That I should have in marriage: she's a stranger to me;

50 *Accidences*: text books on Latin inflexions, as opposed to grammar, or syntax 54 *haberdines*: salt or sun-dried cod. In this context it seems to be the name of a children's game which cannot now be traced. 56 *as in presenti*: Latin (quoting from Lily's *Brevissima Institutio*), referring to the *-as* endings of some Latin verbs in the present tense. Middleton puns on ass/arse 58 *knew*: another bawdy quibble, which is continued in Tim's comment in the following line 60 *have all out*: reveal all 61 *Quid est grammatica?*: Latin, 'What is grammar?' 62 *a sweet, sweet token*: this turns out to be 'ars' (the Latin for art, *ars*, would have been pronounced 'arse' at the time, thus making the pun obvious) 69–70 *recte scribendi atque loquendi ars*: Latin, 'the art of writing and speaking correctly' 70 *sir-reverence of*: with apologies to/human excrement of 77 *mar'l*: marvel

I wonder what my parents mean, i'faith,
To match me with a stranger so:
A maid that's neither kiff nor kin to me.
Life, do they think I have no more care of my body
Than to lie with one that I ne'er knew,
A mere stranger,
One that ne'er went to school with me neither,
Nor ever playfellows together?
They're mightily o'erseen in't, methinks.
They say she has mountains to her marriage;
She's full of cattell, some two thousand runts;
Now what the meaning of these runts should be,
My tutor cannot tell me;
I have look'd in *Rider's Dictionary* for the letter R
And there I can hear no tidings of these runts neither;
Unless they should be Rumford hogs,
I know them not.

Enter WELSH GENTLEWOMAN.

And here she comes.
If I know what to say to her now
In the way of marriage, I'm no graduate!
Methinks, i'faith, 'tis boldly done of her
To come into my chamber, being but a stranger;
She shall not say I'm so proud yet, but I'll speak to her:
Marry, as I will order it,
She shall take no hold of my words, I'll warrant her.
[*She curtsys.*]
She looks and makes a cur'sey! –
Salve tu quoque, puella pulcherrima,
Quid vis nescio nec sane curo, –
Tully's own phrase to a heart!

WELSH GENTLEWOMAN [*Aside.*]: I know not what he means;
A suitor, quotha?
I hold my life he understands no English.

81 *kiff*: kith, neighbours and friends 87 *o'erseen*: rash/deluded 88 *to her marriage*: as a dowry 89 *runts*: small breed of Welsh cow 92 *Rider's Dictionary*: a Latin and English dictionary compiled by John Rider, Bishop of Killaloe, and published in 1589 94 *Rumford hogs*: Romford in Essex, 12 miles N.E. of London, held weekly hog markets 102 *Marry*: mild exclamation originally derived from the name of the Virgin Mary 105–6 Latin, 'Save you also, most beautiful girl; I do not know what you want, nor truly do I care' 107 *Tully*: the Roman orator Cicero *to a heart*: exactly 109 *quotha*: literally 'said he', but used in a sarcastic sense; i.e. 'indeed!' or 'forsooth!'

TIM: *Fertur, mehercule tu virgo,*
Wallia ut opibus abundas maximis.
WELSH GENTLEWOMAN [*Aside.*]: What's this *fertur* and *abundundis?*
He mocks me sure, and calls me a bundle of farts.

TIM [*Aside.*]: I have no Latin word now for their runts; I'll make some shift or other. – *Iterum dico, opibus abundas maximis montibus et fontibus et, ut ita dicam, rontibus; attamen vero homunculus ego sum natura simul et arte baccalaureus, lecto profecto non paratus.*

WELSH GENTLEWOMAN [*Aside.*]: This is most strange. May be he can speak Welsh. – *Avedera whee comrage, derdue cog foginis?*

TIM [*Aside.*]: *Cog foggin?* I scorn to cog with her; I'll tell her so too, in a word near her own language. – *Ego non cogo.*

WELSH GENTLEWOMAN: *Rhegosin a whiggin harle ron corid ambre.*

TIM: By my faith, she's a good scholar, I see that already:
She has the tongues plain; I hold my life she has travell'd.
What will folks say? 'There goes the learned couple!'
Faith, if the truth were known, she hath proceeded.
Enter MAUDLINE.
MAUDLINE: How now, how speeds your business?
TIM [*Aside.*]: I'm glad my mother's come to part us.
MAUDLINE: How do you agree, forsooth?
WELSH GENTLEWOMAN: As well as e'er we did before we met.
MAUDLINE: How's that?
WELSH GENTLEWOMAN: You put me to a man I understand not;
Your son's no English man methinks.
MAUDLINE: No English man? Bless my boy,
And born i'the heart of London!
WELSH GENTLEWOMAN: I ha' been long enough in the chamber with him
And I find neither Welsh nor English in him.
MAUDLINE: Why, Tim, how have you us'd the gentlewoman?
TIM: As well as a man might do, mother, in modest Latin.
MAUDLINE: Latin, fool!

111–12 Latin, 'It is said, by Hercules, young lady, that you abound in great wealth in Wales' ('Fertur' would have been pronounced 'Fartur', on the analogy of 'Clerk') 116–18 Latin, 'Again I say, you abound in great riches, in mountains and fountains and, to coin a phrase, runts; but, truly, I am a little man by nature and a bachelor by art, really not prepared for bed' 120 *Avedera whee comrage*: probably a phonetic rendering of the Welsh *A fedrwch chwi Gymraeg* (can you speak Welsh?). The rest of this phrase and the other Welsh line [123] are so garbled as to render translation impossible 121 *Cog foggin*: Tim may well interpret this in a bawdy sense *cog*: cheat/quibble 122 *Ego non cogo*: Latin, 'I do not compel [you]' 127 *proceeded*: passed her degree/passed beyond virginity

TIM: And she recoil'd in Hebrew.

MAUDLINE: In Hebrew, fool? 'Tis Welsh.

TIM: All comes to one, mother.

MAUDLINE: She can speak English too.

TIM: Who told me so much?
Heart, and she can speak English, I'll clap to her;
I thought you'd marry me to a stranger.

MAUDLINE: You must forgive him, he's so inur'd to Latin,
He and his tutor, that he hath quite forgot
To use the Protestant tongue.

WELSH GENTLEWOMAN: 'Tis quickly pardon'd, forsooth.

MAUDLINE: Tim, make amends and kiss her.
[*To her.*] He makes towards you, forsooth.

[TIM *kisses* WELSH GENTLEWOMAN.]

TIM: O delicious! One may discover her country by her kissing. 'Tis a true saying, 'There's nothing tastes so sweet as your Welsh mutton.' – It was reported you could sing.

MAUDLINE: O rarely, Tim, the sweetest British songs.

TIM: And 'tis my mind, I swear, before I marry
I would see all my wife's good parts at once,
To view how rich I were.

MAUDLINE: Thou shalt hear sweet music, Tim.
[*To* WELSH GENTLEWOMAN.] Pray, forsooth.

Music and Welsh Song.

THE SONG [*sung by* WELSH GENTLEWOMAN].

Cupid is Venus' only joy,
But he is a wanton boy,
A very, very wanton boy;
He shoots at ladies' naked breasts,
He is the cause of most men's crests,
I mean upon the forehead,
Invisible but horrid;

142 *recoil'd*: replied 147 *clap*: stick, seize, with an unconscious allusion to catching gonorrhoea 148 *stranger*: foreigner 151 *the Protestant tongue*: i.e. English 155 *country*: punning on 'cunt' 156 *Welsh mutton*: with an unconscious pun on the slang for whore 157 *sing*: quibbling on the common euphemism for 'fuck' 158 *British*: i.e. Welsh 160 *good parts*: acquirements/physical attributes 168 *crests*: the cuckold's horns/erections

'Twas he first taught upon the way
To keep a lady's lips in play.

Why should not Venus chide her son
For the pranks that he hath done,
The wanton pranks that he hath done?
He shoots his fiery darts so thick,
They hurt poor ladies to the quick,
Ah me, with cruel wounding!
His darts are so confounding
That life and sense would soon decay,
But that he keeps their lips in play.

Can there be any part of bliss
In a quickly fleeting kiss,
A quickly fleeting kiss?
To one's pleasure, leisures are but waste,
The slowest kiss makes too much haste,
We lose it ere we find it;
The pleasing sport they only know
That close above and close below.

TIM: I would not change my wife for a kingdom;
I can do somewhat too in my own lodging.
Enter YELLOWHAMMER *and* ALLWIT [*who is disguised*].
YELLOWHAMMER: Why well said, Tim! The bells go merrily;
I love such peals a' life; wife, lead them in a while;
Here's a strange gentleman desires private conference.
[*Exeunt* MAUDLINE, TIM *and* WELSH GENTLEWOMAN.]
You're welcome, sir, the more for your name's sake:
Good Master Yellowhammer, I love my name well,
And which a' the Yellowhammers take you descent from,
If I may be so bold with you? Which, I pray?
ALLWIT: The Yellowhammers in Oxfordshire,
Near Abbington.
YELLOWHAMMER: And those are the best Yellowhammers and truest

172 *lips*: i.e. of the mouth and cunt 177 *quick*: tenderest part/and to the extent of making them pregnant 179 *darts*: arrows/penis *confounding*: destructive 180 alluding to the belief that each fuck shortened one's life by a day 185 *leisures*: unoccupied time 187 *We*: Q reads 'And'. It is possible that a line has been lost at this point 189 *close above and close below*: embrace in heaven and on earth/embrace above and below the waist 191 *do*: sing/fuck 193 *a'life*: dearly (contracted from 'as my life') 194 *strange*: unfamiliar, from a different locality 200 *Abbington*: Abingdon in Berkshire

bred: I came from thence myself, though now a Citizen. I'll be bold with you; you are most welcome.

ALLWIT: I hope the zeal I bring with me shall deserve it.
YELLOWHAMMER: I hope no less; what is your will, sir?
ALLWIT: I understand by rumours, you have a daughter,
Which my bold love shall henceforth title 'cousin'.
YELLOWHAMMER: I thank you for her, sir.
ALLWIT: I heard of her virtues and other confirm'd graces.
YELLOWHAMMER: A plaguey girl, sir.
ALLWIT: Fame sets her out with richer ornaments
Than you are pleas'd to boast of; 'tis done modestly.
I hear she's towards marriage.
YELLOWHAMMER: You hear truth, sir.
ALLWIT: And with a knight in town, Sir Walter Whorehound.
YELLOWHAMMER: The very same, sir.
ALLWIT: I am the sorrier for't.
YELLOWHAMMER: The sorrier? Why, cousin?
ALLWIT: 'Tis not too far past, is't? It may be yet recall'd?
YELLOWHAMMER: Recall'd? Why, good sir?
ALLWIT: Resolve me in that point, ye shall hear from me.
YELLOWHAMMER: There's no contract pass'd.
ALLWIT: I am very joyful, sir.
YELLOWHAMMER: But he's the man must bed her.
ALLWIT: By no means, cuz; she's quite undone then
And you'll curse the time that e'er you made the match;
He's an arrant whoremaster, consumes his time and state, –
[*Whispers.*] – whom in my knowledge he hath kept this seven years;
Nay, cuz, another man's wife too.
YELLOWHAMMER: O abominable!
ALLWIT: Maintains the whole house, apparels the husband,
Pays servants' wages, not so much but – [*Whispers.*]
YELLOWHAMMER: Worse and worse! And doth the husband know this?
ALLWIT: Knows? Ay, and glad he may too, 'tis his living:
As other trades thrive, butchers by selling flesh,
Poulters by venting conies, or the like, cuz.

202 *Citizen*: i.e. of the City of London 209 *confirm'd*: firmly established 210 *plaguey*: troublesome, confounded 221 *Resolve me in that point*: if you can, give me a clear understanding as to whether or not the marriage can be cancelled 222 *contract*: a *de praesenti* contract of marriage before witnesses was binding even in the absence of a church service 225 *cuz*: familiar term for 'cousin' 228 here and in l. 232 the dashes represent a lacuna, probably resulting from censorship 236 *Poulters*: i.e. poulterers (who normally dealt in game as well as poultry)/pimps *venting conies*: selling rabbits/procuring prostitutes

YELLOWHAMMER: What an incomparable wittol's this!
ALLWIT: Tush, what cares he for that?
Believe me, cuz, no more than I do.
YELLOWHAMMER: What a base slave is that!
ALLWIT: All's one to him: he feeds and takes his ease,
Was ne'er the man that ever broke his sleep
To get a child yet, by his own confession,
And yet his wife has seven.
YELLOWHAMMER: What, by Sir Walter?
ALLWIT: Sir Walter's like to keep 'em, and maintain 'em,
In excellent fashion; he dares do no less, sir.
YELLOWHAMMER: Life, has he children too?
ALLWIT: Children? Boys thus high,
In their Cato and Cordelius.
YELLOWHAMMER: What, you jest, sir!
ALLWIT: Why, one can make a verse
And is now at Eton College.
YELLOWHAMMER: O this news has cut into my heart, cuz!
ALLWIT: It had eaten nearer if it had not been prevented.
One Allwit's wife.
YELLOWHAMMER: Allwit? Foot, I have heard of him;
He had a girl kurs'ned lately?
ALLWIT: Ay, that work did cost the knight above a hundred mark.
YELLOWHAMMER: I'll mark him for a knave and villain for't;
A thousand thanks and blessings! I have done with him.
ALLWIT [*Aside.*]: Ha, ha, ha! This knight will stick by my ribs still;
I shall not lose him yet, no wife will come;
Where'er he woos, I find him still at home. Ha, ha!
Exit.
YELLOWHAMMER: Well grant all this, say now his deeds are black,
Pray what serves marriage, but to call him back;
I have kept a whore myself, and had a bastard,
By Mistress Anne, in *Anno* –

246 *Walter's like*: either 'Walter's pleasure is' or 'Walter is likely' 250 *Cato and Cordelius*: i.e. Dionysius Cato's *Disticha de Moribus* (*c.* A.D. 300) and Mathurin Cordier's *Colloquia Scholastica* (1564), both commonly set school texts 253 *Eton College*: the school founded in 1440 255 *nearer*: deeper 262 *stick by my ribs*: stick to me like my skin (perhaps 'ribs' = wife) 263 *no wife will come*: i.e. he'll not marry 266 *call him back*: i.e. to the path of virtue, and so reform him 268 *Anno*: the year (with a bawdy pun on the mother's name). The gap was probably left so that the actor could provide a suitable date, but may indicate censorship

I care not who knows it; he's now a jolly fellow,
H'as been twice warden; so may his fruit be:
They were but base begot, and so was he.
The knight is rich, he shall be my son-in-law,
No matter, so the whore he keeps be wholesome;
My daughter takes no hurt then, so let them wed,
I'll have him sweat well e'er they go to bed.

Enter MAUDLINE.

MAUDLINE: O husband, husband!

YELLOWHAMMER: How now, Maudline?

MAUDLINE: We are all undone! She's gone, she's gone!

YELLOWHAMMER: Again? Death! Which way?

MAUDLINE: Over the houses.
Lay the waterside, she's gone forever, else.

YELLOWHAMMER: O vent'rous baggage!

Exit [*with* MAUDLINE].

Enter TIM *and* Tutor.

TIM: Thieves, thieves! My sister's stol'n!
Some thief hath got her.
O how miraculously did my father's plate 'scape!
'Twas all left out, tutor.

TUTOR: Is't possible?

TIM: Besides three chains of pearl and a box of coral.
My sister's gone, let's look at Trig stairs for her;
My mother's gone to lay the Common stairs
At Puddle wharf, and at the dock below
Stands my poor silly father. Run, sweet tutor, run.

Exit [*with* Tutor].

[SCENE 2]

Enter both the TOUCHWOODS.

TOUCHWOOD SENIOR: I had been taken, brother, by eight sergeants,

270 *warden*: churchwarden or member of the governing body of a guild/a kind of pear *his fruit*: i.e. Sir Walter's bastards (continuing the pun on warden)
275 *sweat*: victims of venereal diseases were treated by mercurial fumigation in sweating-tubs 281 *Lay*: search 282 *vent'rous*: bold, daring 289 *Trig stairs*: wharf at the bottom of Trig Lane 290 *Common stairs*: another point of embarkation some 300 yards up river 291 *Puddle wharf*: where the Mermaid Theatre now stands *dock below*: i.e. Dung wharf, where the City refuse was loaded 292 *silly*: helpless, pitiful 1 *sergeants*: sheriff's officers

But for the honest watermen; I am bound to them,
They are the most requiteful'st people living:
For as they get their means by gentlemen,
They are still the forwardest to help gentlemen.
You heard how one 'scap'd out of the Blackfriars
But a while since from two or three varlets
Came into the house with all their rapiers drawn,
As if they'd dance the sword-dance on the stage,
With candles in their hands like chandlers' ghosts,
Whilst the poor gentleman so pursued and bandied
Was by an honest pair of oars safely landed.

TOUCHWOOD JUNIOR: I love them with my heart for't.

Enter three or four Watermen.

WATERMAN 1: Your first man, sir.

WATERMAN 2: Shall I carry you gentlemen with a pair of oars?

TOUCHWOOD SENIOR: These be the honest fellows:
Take one pair, and leave the rest for her.

TOUCHWOOD JUNIOR: Barn Elms.

TOUCHWOOD SENIOR: No more, brother.

WATERMAN 1: Your first man.

[*Exit* TOUCHWOOD SENIOR *with* Waterman 1.]

WATERMAN 2: Shall I carry your worship?

TOUCHWOOD JUNIOR: Go. –
And you honest watermen that stay,
Here's a French crown for you;
[*Gives money.*]
There comes a maid with all speed to take water,
Row her lustily to Barn Elms after me.

WATERMAN 3: To Barn Elms, good sir. Make ready the boat, Sam.
We'll wait below.

[*Exeunt* Watermen.]

Enter MOLL.

TOUCHWOOD JUNIOR: What made you stay so long?

MOLL: I found the way more dangerous than I look'd for.

TOUCHWOOD JUNIOR: Away, quick! There's a boat waits for you;
And I'll take water at Paul's wharf and overtake you.

3 *requiteful'st*: eager to requite, or pay back, a favour 4 *get their means*: earn their livings 6 *the Blackfriars*: private indoor theatre, lit by candles 10 *chandlers*: candle-makers 11 *bandied*: buffeted 14 *Your first man, sir*: a trade-cry to attract the customer's attention 18 *Barn Elms*: a lovers' resort on the south bank of the Thames opposite Hammersmith 24 *French crown*: an *écu*, a French silver coin with an accepted value of 5 shillings 25 *to take water*: to embark 32 *Paul's wharf*: opposite the Cathedral, between Trig stairs and Puddle wharf

MOLL: Good sir, do; we cannot be too safe.

[*Exeunt.*]

[SCENE 3]

Enter SIR WALTER, YELLOWHAMMER, TIM *and* Tutor.

SIR WALTER: Life, call you this close keeping?

YELLOWHAMMER: She was kept under a double lock.

SIR WALTER: A double devil!

TIM: That's a buff sergeant, tutor, he'll ne'er wear out.

YELLOWHAMMER: How would you have women lock'd?

TIM: With padlocks, father; the Venetian uses it, my tutor reads it.

SIR WALTER: Heart, if she were so lock'd up, how got she out?

YELLOWHAMMER: There was a little hole look'd into the gutter;
But who would have dreamt of that?

SIR WALTER: A wiser man would.

TIM: He says true, father, a wise man for love will seek every hole; my tutor knows it.

TUTOR: *Verum poeta dicit.*

TIM: *Dicit Virgilius*, father.

YELLOWHAMMER: Prithee, talk of thy gills somewhere else, she's play'd the gill with me. Where's your wise mother now?

TIM: Run mad, I think; I thought she would have drown'd herself, she would not stay for oars, but took a smelt boat: sure, I think she be gone a-fishing for her!

YELLOWHAMMER: She'll catch a goodly dish of gudgeons now,
Will serve us all to supper.

Enter MAUDLINE *drawing* MOLL *by the hair, and* Watermen.

MAUDLINE: I'll tug thee home by the hair.

WATERMEN: Good mistress, spare her.

MAUDLINE: Tend your own business.

WATERMEN: You are a cruel mother.

Ex[*eunt* Watermen].

MOLL: O my heart dies!

4 *buff sergeant*: a sergeant's uniform included a 'buff', i.e. ox-hide leather jerkin. By extension the term came to denote the proverbial dogged determination of such men 6 *padlocks*: chastity belts *reads*: has read 13 *Verum poeta dicit*: Latin, 'The poet speaks the truth' 14 *Dicit Virgilius*: Latin, 'Virgil says it.' Tim wrongly attributes his smutty comment to Virgil 15 *gills*: wenches 18 *smelt*: small fish, whose name was slang for 'fool' 20 *gudgeons*: small fresh-water fish whose name was again slang for 'fool'

MAUDLINE: I'll make thee an example for all the neighbours' daughters.
MOLL: Farewell, life!
MAUDLINE: You that have tricks can counterfeit.
YELLOWHAMMER: Hold, hold, Maudline!
MAUDLINE: I have brought your jewel by the hair.
YELLOWHAMMER: She's here, knight.
SIR WALTER: Forbear or I'll grow worse.
TIM: Look on her, tutor, she hath brought her from the water like a mermaid: she's but half my sister now, as far as the flesh goes, the rest may be sold to fishwives.
MAUDLINE: Dissembling, cunning baggage!
YELLOWHAMMER: Impudent strumpet!
SIR WALTER: Either give over both, or I'll give over!
[*To* MOLL.] Why have you us'd me thus, unkind mistress?
Wherein have I deserved?
YELLOWHAMMER: You talk too fondly, sir. We'll take another course and prevent all; we might have done't long since; we'll lose no time now, nor trust to't any longer: tomorrow morn as early as sunrise we'll have you join'd.
MOLL: O bring me death tonight, love-pitying Fates,
Let me not see tomorrow up upon the world.
YELLOWHAMMER: Are you content, sir, till then she shall be watch'd?
MAUDLINE: Baggage, you shall!
Exit [*with* MOLL *and* YELLOWHAMMER].
TIM: Why, father, my tutor and I will both watch in armour.
TUTOR: How shall we do for weapons?
TIM: Take you no care for that, if need be I can send for conquering metal, tutor, ne'er lost day yet; 'tis but at Westminster; I am acquainted with him that keeps the monuments; I can borrow Harry the Fifth's sword, 'twill serve us both to watch with.
Exit [*with* Tutor].
SIR WALTER: I never was so near my wish, as this chance
Makes me; ere tomorrow noon,
I shall receive two thousand pound in gold
And a sweet maidenhead
Worth forty.

33 *worse*: more angry 35 *mermaid*: slang for 'whore' 36 *fishwives*: slang for 'bawds' 50 *in armour*: slang for 'Dutch courage' from alcohol 54 *him that keeps the monuments*: i.e. the custodian of those at Westminster Abbey *Harry the Fifth's sword*: as Henry V's armour had been stolen, Tim is probably making a mistaken reference to Edward III's 7-foot double-handed sword 60 *forty*: £40 was the price a virgin-prostitute could command

Enter TOUCHWOOD JUNIOR *with a* Waterman.

TOUCHWOOD JUNIOR: O thy news splits me!

WATERMAN: Half drown'd, she cruelly tugg'd her by the hair,
Forc'd her disgracefully, not like a mother.

TOUCHWOOD JUNIOR: Enough, leave me, like my joys.

Exit Waterman.

[*To* SIR WALTER.] Sir, saw you not a wretched maid pass this way? –
Heart, villain, is that thou?

SIR WALTER: Yes, slave, 'tis I!

Both draw and fight.

TOUCHWOOD JUNIOR: I must break through thee then: there is no stop
That checks my tongue and all my hopeful fortunes,
That breast excepted, and I must have way.

SIR WALTER: Sir, I believe 'twill hold your life in play.

[*Wounds* TOUCHWOOD JUNIOR.]

TOUCHWOOD JUNIOR: Sir, you'll gain the heart in my breast at first!

SIR WALTER: There is no dealing then? Think on the dowry for two thousand pounds.

TOUCHWOOD JUNIOR [*Wounding* SIR WALTER.]: O now 'tis quit, sir.

SIR WALTER: And being of even hand, I'll play no longer.

TOUCHWOOD JUNIOR: No longer, slave?

SIR WALTER: I have certain things to think on
Before I dare go further.

TOUCHWOOD JUNIOR: But one bout?
I'll follow thee to death, but ha't out.

Ex[*eunt*].

68 ***checks my tongue***: prevents me wooing 70 ***in play***: at risk (initiating a series of gaming metaphors, such as 'dealing' at l. 72) 71 ***at first***: first 72 ***dealing***: compromising; i.e. Sir Walter wishes to buy off Touchwood with a promise of part of the dowry 74 ***quit***: requited 77 ***certain things to think on***: almost certainly the religious qualms of the next scene

ACT FIVE

[SCENE I]

Enter ALLWIT, *his* WIFE, *and* DAVY DAHUMMA.

MISTRESS ALLWIT: A misery of a house!

ALLWIT: What shall become of us?

DAVY: I think his wound be mortal.

ALLWIT: Think'st thou so, Davy?
Then am I mortal too, but a dead man, Davy;
This is no world for me, when e'er he goes,
I must e'en truss up all, and after him, Davy;
A sheet with two knots, and away!

Enter SIR WALTER, *led in hurt* [*by two* Servants].

DAVY: O see, sir,
How faint he goes! Two of my fellows lead him.

MISTRESS ALLWIT: O me!
[*Faints.*]

ALLWIT: Hyday, my wife's laid down too! Here's like to be
A good house kept, when we are altogether down.
Take pains with her, good Davy, cheer her up there.
Let me come to his worship, let me come.
[*Exeunt* Servants.]

SIR WALTER: Touch me not, villain! My wound aches at thee,
Thou poison to my heart!

ALLWIT: He raves already,
His senses are quite gone, he knows me not. –
Look up, an't like your worship; heave those eyes;
Call me to mind; is your remembrance left?
Look in my face: who am I, an't like your worship?

SIR WALTER: If any thing be worse than slave or villain,
Thou art the man.

ALLWIT: Alas, his poor worship's weakness!
He will begin to know me by little and little.

SIR WALTER: No devil can be like thee!

7 *truss up all*: pack up everything 8 *sheet with two knots*: i.e. a shroud
11 *Hyday*: a form of the exclamation 'Hey-day!' 18 *an't*: if it

ALLWIT: Ah, poor gentleman,
Methinks the pain that thou endurest.
SIR WALTER: Thou know'st me to be wicked, for thy baseness
Kept the eyes open still on all my sins;
None knew the dear account my soul stood charg'd with
So well as thou, yet like hell's flattering angel
Would'st never tell me on't, let'st me go on
And join with death in sleep: that if I had not wak'd
Now by chance, even by a stranger's pity,
I had everlastingly slept out all hope
Of grace and mercy.
ALLWIT: Now he is worse and worse.
Wife, to him, wife, thou wast wont to do good on him.
MISTRESS ALLWIT: How is't with you, sir?
SIR WALTER: Not as with you,
Thou loathsome strumpet! Some good pitying man
Remove my sins out of my sight a little;
I tremble to behold her, she keeps back
All comfort while she stays. Is this a time,
Unconscionable woman, to see thee?
Art thou so cruel to the peace of man,
Not to give liberty now? The Devil himself
Shows a far fairer reverence and respect
To goodness than thyself: he dares not do this,
But part[s] in time of penitence, hides his face;
When man withdraws from him, he leaves the place.
Hast thou less manners, and more impudence,
Than thy instructor? Prithee, show thy modesty,
If the least grain be left, and get thee from me.
Thou should'st be rather lock'd many rooms hence
From the poor miserable sight of me,
If either love or grace had part in thee.
MISTRESS ALLWIT: He is lost for ever.
ALLWIT: Run, sweet Davy, quickly,
And fetch the children hither; sight of them
Will make him cheerful straight.
[*Exit* DAVY.]
SIR WALTER [*To* MISTRESS ALLWIT.]: O death! Is this
A place for you to weep? What tears are those?
Get you away with them, I shall fare the worse

25 *Methinks*: I understand 28 *dear*: costly 35 *do good on*: cheer/fuck
41 *Unconscionable*: having no conscience/unscrupulous

As long as they are a-weeping; they work against me;
There's nothing but thy appetite in that sorrow,
Thou weep'st for lust; I feel it in the slackness
Of comforts coming towards me.
I was well till thou began'st to undo me:
This shows like the fruitless sorrow of a careless mother
That brings her son with dalliance to the gallows,
And then stands by, and weeps to see him suffer.

Enter DAVY *with the children* [WAT, NICK *and baby*].

DAVY: There are the children, sir, an't like your worship;
Your last fine girl; in troth she smiles!
Look, look, in faith, sir.

SIR WALTER: O my vengeance!
Let me for ever hide my cursed face
From sight of those that darkens all my hopes
And stands between me and the sight of heaven.
Who sees me now, he too and those so near me,
May rightly say, I am o'er-grown with sin.
O how my offences wrestle with my repentance!
It hath scarce breath;
Still my adulterous guilt hovers aloft
And with her black wings beats down all my prayers
Ere they be half way up. What's he knows now
How long I have to live? O what comes then?
My taste grows bitter; the round world, all gall now;
Her pleasing pleasures now hath poison'd me,
Which I exchang'd my soul for:
Make way a hundred sighs at once for me.

ALLWIT: Speak to him, Nick.

NICK: I dare not, I am afraid.

ALLWIT: Tell him he hurts his wounds, Wat, with making moan.

SIR WALTER: Wretched, death of seven.

ALLWIT: Come, let's be talking somewhat to keep him alive. –
Ah, sirrah Wat, and did my lord bestow that jewel on thee,
For an epistle thou mad'st in Latin?
Thou art a good forward boy, there's great joy on thee.

65 *dalliance*: overindulgence 69 *my vengeance*: i.e. the children are a part of God's vengeance on him 73 *he too*: i.e. God. Q reads 'Ho too' and editors have put forward a variety of emendations ('O too', 'O, O', 'her too') none of which seems entirely satisfactory 81 *gall*: bitter-tasting substance/bitterness of spirit 84 i.e. may my hundred sighs clear me a way to heaven 87 *death of seven*: i.e. he is responsible for the spiritual death of his seven bastards, and they are a sign of his own spiritual death

SIR WALTER: O sorrow!
ALLWIT [*Aside.*]: Heart, will nothing comfort him?
If he be so far gone, 'tis time to moan.
[*To* SIR WALTER.] Here's pen, and ink, and paper, and all things ready;
Will't please your worship for to make your will?
SIR WALTER: My will? Yes, yes, what else? Who writes apace now?
ALLWIT: That can your man Davy, an't like your worship,
A fair, fast, legible hand.
SIR WALTER: Set it down then:
[DAVY *writes.*]
Imprimis, I bequeath to yonder wittol
Three times his weight in curses –
ALLWIT: How?
SIR WALTER: All plagues of body and of mind –
ALLWIT: Write them not down, Davy.
DAVY: It is his will; I must.
SIR WALTER: Together also
With such a sickness, ten days ere his death.
ALLWIT [*Aside.*]: There's a sweet legacy,
I am almost chok'd with't.
SIR WALTER: Next I bequeath to that foul whore his wife
All barrenness of joy, a drouth of virtue,
And dearth of all repentance; for her end,
The common misery of an English strumpet,
In French and Dutch beholding ere she dies
Confusion of her brats before her eyes
And never shed a tear for it.
Enter a Servant.
SERVANT: Where's the knight?
O sir, the gentleman you wounded is newly departed.
SIR WALTER: Dead? Lift, lift! Who helps me?
ALLWIT: Let the law lift you now, that must have all;
I have done lifting on you, and my wife too.
SERVANT: You were best lock yourself close.
ALLWIT: Not in my house, sir,
I'll harbour no such persons as men-slayers.
Lock yourself where you will.

96 *apace*: with speed 113 *French and Dutch*: venereal disease. The 'French disease' was syphilis and 'Dutch widow' was slang for a whore 114 *confusion*: ruin/incest 117 *Lift*: help me up 119 *lifting*: assisting/pillaging/copulating

SIR WALTER: What's this?
MISTRESS ALLWIT: Why husband!
ALLWIT: I know what I do, wife.
MISTRESS ALLWIT: You cannot tell yet;
For having kill'd the man in his defence,
Neither his life nor estate will be touch'd, husband.
ALLWIT: Away, wife! Hear a fool! His lands will hang him.
SIR WALTER: Am I denied a chamber?
What say you, forsooth?
MISTRESS ALLWIT: Alas, sir, I am one that would have all well,
But must obey my husband. [*To* ALLWIT.] Prithee, love,
Let the poor gentleman stay, being so sore wounded;
There's a close chamber at one end of the garret
We never use, let him have that, I prithee.
ALLWIT: We never use? You forget sickness then,
And physic times: is't not a place for easement?
Enter a [*second*] Servant.
SIR WALTER: O death! Do I hear this with part
Of former life in me? [*To* Servant 2.] What's the news now?
SERVANT 2: Troth, worse and worse; you're like to lose your land
If the law save your life, sir, or the surgeon.
ALLWIT [*Aside.*]: Hark you there, wife.
SIR WALTER: Why how, sir?
SERVANT 2: Sir Oliver Kix's wife is new quick'ned;
That child undoes you, sir.
SIR WALTER: All ill at once.
ALLWIT: I wonder what he makes here with his consorts?
Cannot our house be private to ourselves,
But we must have such guests? I pray depart, sirs,
And take your murtherer along with you;
Good he were apprehended ere he go,
H'as kill'd some honest gentleman. Send for officers.
SIR WALTER: I'll soon save you that labour.
ALLWIT: I must tell you, sir,
You have been somewhat bolder in my house
Than I could well like of; I suff'red you
Till it stuck here at my heart; I tell you truly
I thought you had been familiar with my wife once.

124–5 convicted murderers faced the death penalty and their goods were confiscated, but self-defence was an adequate defence to the charge 126 *His lands will hang him*: i.e. those wishing to seize his land will ensure that he is found guilty 135 *place for easement*: privy 142 *quick'ned*: impregnated 144 *makes*: does *consorts*: companions (in this case, servants)

MISTRESS ALLWIT: With me? I'll see him hang'd first: I defy him
And all such gentlemen in the like extremity.
SIR WALTER: If ever eyes were open, these are they;
Gamesters, farewell, I have nothing left to play.
Exit.
ALLWIT: And therefore get you gone, sir.
DAVY: Of all wittols
Be thou the head! [*To* MISTRESS ALLWIT.] Thou, the grand whore of spitals!
Exit [*with* Servants].
ALLWIT: So, since he's like now to be rid of all,
I am right glad I am so well rid of him.
MISTRESS ALLWIT: I knew he durst not stay when you nam'd officers.
ALLWIT: That stopp'd his spirits straight.
What shall we do now, wife?
MISTRESS ALLWIT: As we were wont to do.
ALLWIT: We are richly furnish'd, wife, with household stuff.
MISTRESS ALLWIT: Let's let out lodgings then,
And take a house in the Strand.
ALLWIT: In troth, a match, wench:
We are simply stock'd with cloth-of-tissue cushions,
To furnish out bay windows; push, what not that's quaint
And costly, from the top to the bottom.
Life, for furniture, we may lodge a countess!
There's a close-stool of tawny velvet too,
Now I think on't wife.
MISTRESS ALLWIT: There's that should be, sir;
Your nose must be in every thing!
ALLWIT: I have done, wench;
And let this stand in every gallant's chamber:
'There's no gamester like a politic sinner,
For who e'er games, the box is sure a winner.'
Exit [*with* MISTRESS ALLWIT].

159 *Gamesters*: gamblers/fornicators 161 *the head*: i.e. exemplar *spitals*: hospitals for sufferers from venereal disease 170 *the Strand*: was then a fashionable residential area, but notorious for high-class prostitution *a match*: i.e. it's a deal 171 *cloth-of-tissue*: cloth interwoven with gold and silver thread 172 *what not*: whatever 175 *close-stool*: piss-pot enclosed in a stool 180 *box*: i.e. the gambling-house, since all gamblers had to place a fee in the 'box' provided. There is also a pun on 'box' = coffin

[SCENE 2]

Enter YELLOWHAMMER *and his* WIFE.

MAUDLINE: O husband, husband, she will die, she will die!
There is no sign but death.
YELLOWHAMMER: 'Twill be our shame then.
MAUDLINE: O how she's chang'd in compass of an hour!
YELLOWHAMMER: Ah, my poor girl! Good faith, thou wert too cruel
To drag her by the hair.
MAUDLINE: You would have done as much, sir,
To curb her of her humour.
YELLOWHAMMER: 'Tis curb'd sweetly, she catch'd her bane o'th' water.

Enter TIM.

MAUDLINE: How now, Tim?
TIM: Faith, busy, mother, about an epitaph
Upon my sister's death.
MAUDLINE: Death! She is not dead, I hope?
TIM: No, but she means to be, and that's as good,
And when a thing's done, 'tis done;
You taught me that, mother.
YELLOWHAMMER: What is your tutor doing?
TIM: Making one too, in principal pure Latin,
Cull'd out of *Ovid de Tristibus*.
YELLOWHAMMER: How does your sister look? Is she not chang'd?
TIM: Chang'd? Gold into white money was never so chang'd
As is my sister's colour into paleness.

Enter MOLL [*carried in by* Servants].

YELLOWHAMMER: O here she's brought; see how she looks like death!
TIM: Looks she like death, and ne'er a word made yet?
I must go beat my brains against a bed post
And get before my tutor.

[*Exit.*]

YELLOWHAMMER: Speak, how dost thou?
MOLL: I hope I shall be well, for I am as sick at heart
As I can be.
YELLOWHAMMER: 'Las, my poor girl!

17 *principal*: choice 18 *Ovid de Tristibus*: Ovid on 'Dismal Surroundings' (his *Tristia* was a Latin text book used in schools) 20 *white money*: silver 23 *ne'er a word made yet*: i.e. I haven't even begun my elegy 25 *get*: beget (the poem)

The doctor's making a most sovereign drink for thee,
The worst ingredience, dissolv'd pearl and amber;
We spare no cost, girl.

MOLL: Your love comes too late;
Yet timely thanks reward it. What is comfort,
When the poor patient's heart is past relief?
It is no doctor's art can cure my grief.

YELLOWHAMMER: All is cast away then;
Prithee, look upon me cheerfully.

MAUDLINE: Sing but a strain or two, thou wilt not think
How 'twill revive thy spirits: strive with thy fit,
Prithee, sweet Moll.

MOLL: You shall have my good will, mother.

MAUDLINE: Why, well said, wench.

THE SONG
[*sung by* MOLL].

Weep eyes, break heart,
My love and I must part;
Cruel fates true love do soonest sever,
O I shall see thee never, never, never!
O happy is the maid whose life takes end,
Ere it knows parent's frown, or loss of friend.
Weep eyes, break heart,
My love and I must part.

Enter TOUCHWOOD SENIOR *with a letter.*

MAUDLINE: O I could die with music: well sung, girl.

MOLL: If you call it so, it was.

YELLOWHAMMER: She plays the swan, and sings herself to death.

TOUCHWOOD SENIOR: By your leave, sir.

YELLOWHAMMER: What are you, sir? Or what's your business, pray?

TOUCHWOOD SENIOR: I may be now admitted, though the brother
Of him your hate pursu'd; it spreads no further,
Your malice sets in death, does it not, sir?

YELLOWHAMMER: In death?

TOUCHWOOD SENIOR: He's dead: 'twas a dear love to him,

29 *ingredience*: either 'ingredient' or a common misspelling of 'ingredients' *pearl and amber*: these were renowned for their medicinal properties 37 *fit*: mortal crisis/capricious impulse/stave of music 51 *plays the swan*: alluding to the belief that mute swans sang only on the point of death 56 *sets*: abates 57 *dear*: expensive/sweet

It cost him but his life, that was all, sir:
He paid enough, poor gentleman, for his love.
YELLOWHAMMER [*Aside.*]: There's all our ill remov'd, if she were well now.
[*To* TOUCHWOOD SENIOR.] Impute not, sir, his end to any hate
That sprung from us; he had a fair wound brought that.
TOUCHWOOD SENIOR: That help'd him forward, I must needs confess;
But the restraint of love, and your unkindness,
Those were the wounds that from his heart drew blood;
But being past help, let words forget it too.
Scarcely three minutes ere his eyelids clos'd
And took eternal leave of this world's light,
He wrote this letter, which by oath he bound me
To give to her own hands: that's all my business.
YELLOWHAMMER: You may perform it then; there she sits.
TOUCHWOOD SENIOR: O with a following look.
YELLOWHAMMER: Ay, trust me, sir, I think she'll follow him quickly.
TOUCHWOOD SENIOR: Here's some gold
He will'd me to distribute faithfully amongst your servants.
[*Distributes the gold.*]
YELLOWHAMMER: 'Las, what doth he mean, sir?
TOUCHWOOD SENIOR [*To* MOLL]: How cheer you, mistress?
MOLL: I must learn of you, sir.
TOUCHWOOD SENIOR: Here's a letter from a friend of yours,
[*Gives letter.*]
And where that fails in satisfaction
I have a sad tongue ready to supply.
MOLL: How does he, ere I look on't?
TOUCHWOOD SENIOR: Seldom better, h'as a contented health now.
MOLL: I am most glad on't.
[*Reads letter.*]
MAUDLINE [*To* TOUCHWOOD SENIOR]: Dead, sir?
YELLOWHAMMER: He is. [*Aside.*] Now, wife, let's but get the girl
Upon her legs again, and to church roundly with her.
MOLL: O sick to death he tells me:
How does he after this?
TOUCHWOOD SENIOR: Faith, feels no pain at all; he's dead, sweet mistress.
MOLL: Peace close mine eyes!
[*Faints.*]

72 *following*: about to follow (i.e. die)/similar (to Touchwood Jr) 77 *cheer you*: are you feeling 87 *roundly*: immediately

YELLOWHAMMER: The girl, look to the girl, wife!
MAUDLINE: Moll, daughter, sweet girl, speak!
Look but once up, thou shalt have all the wishes of thy heart
That wealth can purchase.
YELLOWHAMMER: O she's gone for ever! That letter broke her heart.
TOUCHWOOD SENIOR: As good now, then, as let her lie in torment
And then break it.
Enter SUSAN.
MAUDLINE: O Susan, she thou lovedst so dear is gone!
SUSAN: O sweet maid!
TOUCHWOOD SENIOR: This is she that help'd her still.
I've a reward here for thee.
[*Passes* SUSAN *a note.*]
YELLOWHAMMER: Take her in,
Remove her from our sight, our shame, and sorrow.
TOUCHWOOD SENIOR: Stay, let me help thee; 'tis the last cold kindness
I can perform for my sweet brother's sake.
[*Exeunt* TOUCHWOOD SENIOR, SUSAN *and* Servants, *carrying* MOLL.]
YELLOWHAMMER: All the whole street will hate us and the world
Point me out cruel. It is our best course, wife,
After we have given order for the funeral,
To absent ourselves, till she be laid in ground.
MAUDLINE: Where shall we spend that time?
YELLOWHAMMER: I'll tell thee where, wench: go to some private church
And marry Tim to the rich Brecknock gentlewoman.
MAUDLINE: Mass, a match!
We'll not lose all at once, somewhat we'll catch.
Exit [*with* YELLOWHAMMER].

[SCENE 3]

Enter SIR OLIVER *and* Servants.
SIR OLIVER: Ho, my wife's quick'ned; I am a man for ever!
I think I have bestirr'd my stumps, i'faith.
Run, get your fellows all together instantly,
Then to the parish church and ring the bells.
SERVANT 1: It shall be done, sir.
[*Exit.*]

114 *a match*: agreed/a wedding 2 *bestirr'd my stumps*: been busy/been sexually active

SIR OLIVER: Upon my love I charge you, villain, that you make a bonfire before the door at night.

SERVANT 2: A bonfire, sir?

SIR OLIVER: A thwacking one I charge you.

SERVANT 2 [*Aside.*]: This is monstrous.
[*Exit.*]

SIR OLIVER: Run, tell a hundred pound out for the gentleman
That gave my wife the drink, the first thing you do.

SERVANT 3: A hundred pounds, sir?

SIR OLIVER: A bargain! As our joys grows,
We must remember still from whence it flows,
Or else we prove ungrateful multipliers;
The child is coming and the land comes after;
The news of this will make a poor Sir Walter.
I have strook it home, i'faith.

SERVANT 3: That you have, marry, sir.
But will not your worship go to the funeral
Of both these lovers?

SIR OLIVER: Both? Go both together?

SERVANT 3: Ay, sir, the gentleman's brother will have it so;
'Twill be the pitifullest sight; there's such running,
Such rumours, and such throngs, a pair of lovers
Had never more spectators, more men's pities,
Or women's wet eyes.

SIR OLIVER: My wife helps the number then?

SERVANT 3: There's such a drawing out of handkerchers,
And those that have no handkerchers, lift up aprons.

SIR OLIVER: Her parents may have joyful hearts at this.
I would not have my cruelty so talk'd on,
To any child of mine, for a monopoly.

SERVANT 3: I believe you, sir.
'Tis cast so too, that both their coffins meet,
Which will be lamentable.

SIR OLIVER: Come, we'll see't.
Ex[*eunt*].

11 *tell*: count 19 *strook it home*: delivered a decisive blow, with a pun on 'strike' = copulate 28 *helps the number*: i.e. is one of the mourners 33 *monopoly*: James I's grants of exclusive commercial rights were notoriously profitable for the holders 35 *cast*: arranged

[SCENE 4]

Recorders dolefully playing. Enter at one door the coffin of the gentleman [TOUCHWOOD JUNIOR], *solemnly deck'd, his sword upon it, attended by many in black, his brother* [TOUCHWOOD SENIOR] *being the chief mourner. At the other door, the coffin of the virgin* [MOLL], *with a garland of flowers, with epitaphs pinn'd on it, attended by maids and women. Then set them down one right over against the other, while all the company* [*including* SIR OLIVER *and* LADY KIX, MASTER *and* MISTRESS ALLWIT, SUSAN *and the* Parson] *seem to weep and mourn; there is a sad song in the music room.*

TOUCHWOOD SENIOR: Never could death boast of a richer prize
From the first parent, let the world bring forth
A pair of truer hearts. To speak but truth
Of this departed gentleman, in a brother
Might, by hard censure, be call'd flattery,
Which makes me rather silent in his right
Than so to be deliver'd to the thoughts
Of any envious hearer starv'd in virtue
And therefore pining to hear others thrive.
But for this maid, whom envy cannot hurt
With all her poisons, having left to ages
The true, chaste monument of her living name,
Which no time can deface, I say of her
The full truth freely, without fear of censure:
What nature could there shine, that might redeem
Perfection home to woman, but in her
Was fully glorious; beauty set in goodness
Speaks what she was, that jewel so infix'd;
There was no want of any thing of life
To make these virtuous precedents man and wife.

ALLWIT: Great pity of their deaths!

ALL: Ne'er more pity!

LADY KIX: It makes a hundred weeping eyes, sweet gossip.

TOUCHWOOD SENIOR: I cannot think there's any one amongst you
In this full fair assembly, maid, man, or wife,
Whose heart would not have sprung with joy and gladness
To have seen their marriage day!

2 *first parent*: Adam 5 *censure*: judgement 15–16 *that might redeem Perfection home to woman*: undo the harm caused by Eve's first disobedience 18 *Speaks*: expresses 20 *precedents*: exemplars

ALL: It would have made a thousand joyful hearts!
TOUCHWOOD SENIOR [*To* MOLL *and* TOUCHWOOD JUNIOR.]: Up then apace, and take your fortunes!
Make these joyful hearts, here's none but friends.
[MOLL *and* TOUCHWOOD JUNIOR *rise from their coffins.*]
ALL: Alive, sir? O sweet, dear couple!
TOUCHWOOD SENIOR: Nay, do not hinder 'em now, stand from about 'em;
If she be caught again, and have this time,
I'll ne'er plot further for 'em, nor this honest chambermaid
That help'd all at a push.
TOUCHWOOD JUNIOR [*To* Parson.]: Good sir, apace!
PARSON: Hands join now, but hearts for ever,
Which no parent's mood shall sever.
[*To* TOUCHWOOD JUNIOR.] You shall forsake all widows, wives, and maids;
[*To* MOLL.] You, lords, knights, gentlemen, and men of trades;
[*To both.*] And if, in haste, any article misses
Go interline it with a brace of kisses.
[*They kiss.*]
TOUCHWOOD SENIOR: Here's a thing troll'd nimbly.
Give you joy, brother!
Were't not better thou should'st have her,
Than the maid should die?
MISTRESS ALLWIT: To you, sweet mistress bride.
ALL: Joy, joy to you both.
TOUCHWOOD SENIOR: Here be your wedding sheets you brought along with you; you may both go to bed when you please to.
TOUCHWOOD JUNIOR: My joy wants utterance.
TOUCHWOOD SENIOR: Utter all at night then, brother.
MOLL: I am silent with delight.
TOUCHWOOD SENIOR: Sister, delight will silence any woman;
But you'll find your tongue again, among maidservants,
Now you keep house, sister.
ALL: Never was hour so fill'd with joy and wonder.
TOUCHWOOD SENIOR: To tell you the full story of this chambermaid
And of her kindness in this business to us,

32 *have this time*: lose this opportunity 34 *at a push*: in a crisis; but punning on 'push' = copulate s.p. Q has 'Touchwood Senior' 35 *Hands join now, but hearts for ever*: the parson simply continues the ceremony from the point where it was broken off at III.i.17 40 *interline*: i.e. insert additional clauses into a document 41 *troll'd*: uttered rapidly, i.e. over and done with quickly 46 *wedding sheets*: i.e. the shrouds they were carried in 49 *utter*: speak/ejaculate

'Twould ask an hour's discourse. In brief, 'twas she
That wrought it to this purpose cunningly.
ALL: We shall all love her for't.
Enter YELLOWHAMMER *and his wife.*
ALLWIT: See who comes here now.
TOUCHWOOD SENIOR: A storm, a storm, but we are shelt'red for it.
YELLOWHAMMER: I will prevent you all and mock you thus,
You, and your expectations: I stand happy,
Both in your lives and your hearts' combination.
TOUCHWOOD SENIOR: Here's a strange day again!
YELLOWHAMMER: The knight's prov'd villain,
All's come out now, his niece an arrant baggage;
My poor boy Tim is cast away this morning,
Even before breakfast: married a whore
Next to his heart.
ALL: A whore?
YELLOWHAMMER: His 'niece', forsooth!
ALLWIT [*Aside.*]: I think we rid our hands in good time of him.
MISTRESS ALLWIT [*Aside.*]: I knew he was past the best, when I gave him over.
[*To* YELLOWHAMMER.] What is become of him pray, sir?
YELLOWHAMMER: Who, the knight? He lies i'th'knight's ward now.
[*To* LADY KIX.] Your belly, lady, begins to blossom, there's no peace for him,
His creditors are so greedy.
SIR OLIVER: Master Touchwood, hear'st thou this news?
I am so endear'd to thee for my wife's fruitfulness
That I charge you both, your wife and thee,
To live no more asunder for the world's frowns:
I have purse, and bed, and board for you;
Be not afraid to go to your business roundly;
Get children, and I'll keep them.
TOUCHWOOD SENIOR: Say you so, sir?
SIR OLIVER: Prove me, with three at a birth, and thou dar'st now.
TOUCHWOOD SENIOR: Take heed how you dare a man, while you live, sir,
That has good skill at his weapon.
Enter TIM *and* WELSH GENTLEWOMAN [*with* Tutor].

73 *knight's ward*: i.e. debtor's prison. Such prisons offered four grades of accommodation, depending on payment: the master's side; the knight's ward; the twopenny ward; and, for the destitute, the hole 81 *roundly*: with gusto, but punning on 'round' = pregnant 83 *Prove me*: test me 85 *weapon*: i.e. penis

SIR OLIVER: Foot, I dare you, sir!
YELLOWHAMMER: Look, gentlemen, if ever you saw the picture
Of the unfortunate marriage, yonder 'tis.
WELSH GENTLEWOMAN: Nay, good sweet Tim –
TIM: Come from the university,
To marry a whore in London, with my tutor too?
O tempora! O mors!
TUTOR: Prithee, Tim, be patient.
TIM: I bought a jade at Cambridge;
I'll let her out to execution, tutor,
For eighteen pence a day, or Brainford horse races;
She'll serve to carry seven miles out of town well.
Where be these mountains? I was promis'd mountains,
But there's such a mist, I can see none of 'em.
What are become of those two thousand runts?
Let's have a bout with them in the meantime.
A vengeance runt thee!
MAUDLINE: Good sweet Tim, have patience.
TIM: *Flectere si nequeo superos, Acheronta movebo*, mother.
MAUDLINE: I think you have married her in logic, Tim.
You told me once, by logic you would prove
A whore an honest woman; prove her so, Tim,
And take her for thy labour.
TIM: Troth, I thank you.
I grant you I may prove another man's wife so,
But not mine own.
MAUDLINE: There's no remedy now, Tim,
You must prove her so as well as you may.
TIM: Why then, my tutor and I will about her
As well as we can.

87 *saw*: Q reads 'say', which may either be an error or the obsolete form of the past tense of 'to see' 92 *O tempora! O mors!*: Latin, 'O time! O death!' The ignorant Tim may have intended the commonplace 'O tempora! O mores!' (O times! O manners!). However, Tim quotes the Virgil below correctly 94 *jade*: horse of inferior quality/whore 95 *to execution*: for hire 96 *Brainford*: Brentford in Middlesex, notorious as a place of resort for lovers, provided a variety of entertainments including horse (= whores) racing 101 *have a bout with them*: the sense is obscure (Q reads 'about' rather than 'a bout') 102 *runt*: reprove 103 *Flectere . . . movebo*: Latin, 'Since I cannot move the powers above, I shall work on the lower regions' (Virgil *Aeneid*, VII, 312) 107 *for thy labour*: for your trouble/for your sexual efforts 111 *will about*: direct our attentions to (with sexual implications)

Uxor non est meretrix, ergo fallacis.

WELSH GENTLEWOMAN: Sir, if your logic cannot prove me honest,
There's a thing call'd marriage, and that makes me honest.

MAUDLINE: O there's a trick beyond your logic, Tim.

TIM: I perceive then a woman may be honest according to the English print, when she is a whore in the Latin. So much for marriage and logic! I'll love her for her wit, I'll pick out my runts there; and for my mountains, I'll mount upon –

YELLOWHAMMER: So fortune seldom deals two marriages
With one hand, and both lucky; the best is,
One feast will serve them both! Marry, for room
I'll have the dinner kept in Goldsmiths' Hall.
To which, kind gallants, I invite you all.
[*Exeunt.*]

FINIS

113 Latin, 'A wife is not a whore, therefore you are wrong' 117–18 *I . . . Latin*: punning on 'merry trick' = 'meretrix', the Latin for 'whore' 118 *print*: spelling 120 *mount*: in the sexual sense. The dash probably indicates intervention by the Master of the Revels 124 *Goldsmiths' Hall*: hall of the Goldsmiths' Company, in Foster Lane, off Cheapside

Women Beware Women

Women Beware Women was entered in the Stationers' Register on 9 September 1653 to Humphrey Moseley. The only surviving early text of the play is that of the 1657 Octavo (O), a volume of '*Two New Playes. viz. More Dissemblers besides Women. Women beware Women.* Written By *Tho. Middleton*, Gent.', which has served as the copy-text of this edition.

Upon
The Tragedy of
My Familiar Acquaintance,

THO[MAS] MIDDLETON

Women Beware Women, 'tis a true text
Never to be forgot. Drabs of state vex'd
Have plots, poisons, mischiefs that seldom miss
To murther Virtue with a venom kiss.
Witness this worthy tragedy, express'd
By him that well deserv'd among the best
Of poets in his time. He knew the rage,
Madness of women cross'd, and for the stage
Fitted their humours – hell-bred malice, strife –
Acted in state, presented to the life.
I that have seen't can say, having just cause,
Never came tragedy off with more applause.

Nath[anael] Richards

Upon The Tragedy . . .: This poem is by Nathanael Richards (fl. 1630–54), whose most famous play, *The Tragedy of Messalina, the Roman Empress*, was published in 1640. The poem appears after a publisher's address 'To the Reader' which runs

'When these amongst others of Mr. *Thomas Middleton*'s Excellent Poems, came to my hands, I was not a little confident but that his name would prove as great an Inducement for thee to Read, as me to Print them: Since those issues of his Brain that have already seen the Sun, have by their worth gained themselves a free entertainment amongst all that are ingenious: And I am most certain, that these will no way lessen his Reputation, nor hinder his Admission to any Noble and Recreative Spirits. All that I require at thy hands, is to continue the Author in his deserved Esteem, and to accept of my Endeavors which have ever been to please thee. *Farewel.*'

Drabs: whores

[DRAMATIS PERSONAE]

DUKE *of Florence*
LORD CARDINAL, *brother to the Duke*
Two Cardinals more
A Lord
FABRITIO, *father to Isabella*
HIPPOLITO, *brother to Fabritio*
GUARDIANO, *uncle to the foolish Ward*
WARD, *a rich young heir*
LEANTIO, *a factor, husband to Bianca*
SORDIDO, *the Ward's man*

LIVIA, *sister to Fabritio*
ISABELLA, *niece to Livia*
BIANCA, *Leantio's wife*
Widow, his MOTHER

States of Florence; Citizens; A 'Prentice; Boys; Messenger; Servants; [Lords; Ladies; Knights; Nymphs; Hymen; Ganymede; Hebe; Pages; Guard; Attendants].

The Scene: Florence.

factor: agent BIANCA: in O the name is 'Brancha' throughout, but this is probably a misreading of 'Beancha'. The character derives from Bianca Capello, who was born in Venice in 1548, eloped with a Florentine, became the mistress of Francesco de' Medici (whom John Webster used in his play *The White Devil* in 1612) and died in 1587 States: nobles

ACT ONE

SCENE I

Enter LEANTIO *with* BIANCA *and* MOTHER.

MOTHER: Thy sight was never yet more precious to me;
Welcome with all the affection of a mother
That comfort can express from natural love:
Since thy birth-joy, a mother's chiefest gladness
After sh'as undergone her curse of sorrows,
Thou wast not more dear to me than this hour
Presents thee to my heart. Welcome again.

LEANTIO [*Aside.*]: 'Las, poor affectionate soul, how her joys speak to me!
I have observ'd it often, and I know it is
The fortune commonly of knavish children
To have the loving'st mothers.

MOTHER: What's this gentlewoman?

LEANTIO: O you have nam'd the most unvalued'st purchase
That youth of man had ever knowledge of.
As often as I look upon that treasure
And know it to be mine – there lies the blessing –
It joys me that I ever was ordain'd
To have a being, and to live 'mongst men;
Which is a fearful living, and a poor one,
Let a man truly think on't.
To have the toil and griefs of fourscore years
Put up in a white sheet, tied with two knots.
Methinks it should strike earthquakes in adulterers
When ev'n the very sheets they commit sin in
May prove, for aught they know, all their last garments.
O what a mark were there for women then!
But beauty able to content a conqueror,

3 *comfort*: i.e. the pleasure of your arrival *express*: elicit 5 *curse of sorrows*: i.e. labour 8 *speak to*: move 11 *What's*: who is 12 *unvalued'st*: priceless *purchase*: acquisition/capture (the prevailing commercial imagery applied to personal relations is discussed in the Introduction) 21 *white sheet, tied with two knots*: i.e. a shroud 25 *mark*: sign

Whom earth could scarce content, keeps me in compass;
I find no wish in me bent sinfully
To this man's sister, or to that man's wife:
In Love's name let 'em keep their honesties
And cleave to their own husbands, 'tis their duties.
Now when I go to church, I can pray handsomely;
Not come like gallants only to see faces,
As if Lust went to market still on Sundays.
I must confess I am guilty of one sin, mother,
More than I brought into the world with me;
But that I glory in: 'tis theft, but noble
As ever greatness yet shot up withal.

MOTHER: How's that?

LEANTIO: Never to be repented, mother,
Though sin be death. I had died if I had not sinn'd.
And here's my masterpiece. Do you now behold her!
Look on her well, she's mine, look on her better:
Now say, if't be not the best piece of theft
That ever was committed. And I have my pardon for't:
'Tis seal'd from heaven by marriage.

MOTHER: Married to her!

LEANTIO: You must keep counsel, mother, I am undone else;
If it be known, I have lost her; do but think now
What that loss is, life's but a trifle to't.
From Venice her consent and I have brought her
From parents great in wealth, more now in rage.
But let storms spend their furies; now we have got
A shelter o'er our quiet innocent loves
We are contented. Little money sh'as brought me.
View but her face, you may see all her dowry,
Save that which lies lock'd up in hidden virtues,
Like jewels kept in cabinets.

MOTHER: Y'are too blame,

27 *Whom earth could scarce content*: probably alluding to Alexander the Great who was reputed to have wept because there were too few countries to conquer *in compass*: within due limits 28 *bent*: inclined 30 *honesties*: chastities 32 *handsomely*: genuinely (unlike the 'gallants' whose main aim in attending church is to 'pick up' women) 37–8 *noble As ever greatness yet shot up withal*: as noble a theft as ever helped the rise of a great man 40 *Though sin be death*: alluding to Romans 6. 23: 'the wages of sin is death' 45 *seal'd*: ratified 46 *keep counsel*: observe secrecy 56 *too blame*: in the 17th century 'blame' was often incorrectly thought to be an adjective (i.e. blameworthy), hence the use of 'too' rather than 'to'

If your obedience will give way to a check,
To wrong such a perfection.

LEANTIO: How?

MOTHER: Such a creature,
To draw her from her fortune which, no doubt,
At the full time might have prov'd rich and noble:
You know not what you have done. My life can give you
But little helps, and my death lesser hopes;
And hitherto your own means has but made shift
To keep you single, and that hardly too.
What ableness have you to do her right, then,
In maintenance fitting her birth and virtues,
Which ev'ry woman of necessity looks for,
And most to go above it, not confin'd
By their conditions, virtues, bloods, or births,
But flowing to affections, wills, and humours?

LEANTIO: Speak low, sweet mother; you are able to spoil as many
As come within the hearing. If it be not
Your fortune to mar all, I have much marvel.
I pray do not you teach her to rebel,
When she's in a good way to obedience;
To rise with other women in commotion
Against their husbands, for six gowns a year,
And so maintain their cause, when they're once up,
In all things else that require cost enough.
They are all of 'em a kind of spirits soon rais'd,
But not so soon laid, mother. As for example,
A woman's belly is got up in a trice,
A simple charge ere it be laid down again;
So ever in all their quarrels, and their courses.
And I'm a proud man, I hear nothing of 'em;
They're very still, I thank my happiness,
And sound asleep; pray let not your tongue wake 'em.
If you can but rest quiet, she's contented
With all conditions that my fortunes bring her to:

57 *give way to a check*: allow a rebuke 63 *but made shift*: only just managed 64 *keep you single*: maintain you as a bachelor *hardly*: with difficulty/barely 65 *ableness*: ability 68 *above it*: i.e. to improve on the condition of life to which they were born 69 *conditions*: circumstances *virtues*: abilities *bloods*: family ties *births*: social rank at birth 70 *affections*: desires *humours*: whims 76 *commotion*: insurrection 78 *they're once up*: i.e. when they have gained the upper hand 80 *kind of spirits soon rais'd*: demon easily summoned/personality easily inflamed 83 *A simple charge*: nothing but expense 84 *So ever*: so it is always (they always end up costing a lot) *courses*: bad ways

To keep close as a wife that loves her husband;
To go after the rate of my ability,
Not the licentious swindge of her own will,
Like some of her old school-fellows. She intends
To take out other works in a new sampler
And frame the fashion of an honest love,
Which knows no wants but, mocking poverty,
Brings forth more children, to make rich men wonder
At divine Providence, that feeds mouths of infants
And sends them none to feed, but stuffs their rooms
With fruitful bags, their beds with barren wombs.
Good mother, make not you things worse than they are
Out of your too much openness (pray take heed on't)
Nor imitate the envy of old people,
That strive to mar good sport, because they are perfect.
I would have you more pitiful to youth,
Especially to your own flesh and blood.
I'll prove an excellent husband, here's my hand,
Lay in provision, follow my business roundly,
And make you a grandmother in forty weeks.
Go, pray salute her, bid her welcome cheerfully.

MOTHER: Gentlewoman, thus much is a debt of courtesy
[*Kisses her.*]
Which fashionable strangers pay each other
At a kind meeting; then there's more than one,
Due to the knowledge I have of your nearness.
[*Kisses her again.*]
I am bold to come again, and now salute you
By th'name of daughter, which may challenge more
Than ordinary respect.
[*Kisses her again.*]

LEANTIO [*Aside.*]: Why, this is well now,
And I think few mothers of threescore will mend it.

90 *keep close*: live secluded 91 to live at a rate I can afford 92 *licentious*: unrestrained *swindge*: sway, rule 94 *take out*: copy *sampler*: a piece of embroidery which acts as a pattern which could be copied 95 *frame*: the finished embroidered cloth would be 'framed' in the way that pictures are *frame the fashion of*: establish a fashion for 100 *bags*: money-bags 104 *perfect*: in grammar the perfect tense refers to completed actions, and this probably therefore means 'past it' rather than 'faultless' 108 *business*: punning on 'business' = sexual intercourse *roundly*: wholeheartedly, energetically 110 *salute*: kiss 116 *challenge*: lay claim to 118 *mend it*: do better

MOTHER: What I can bid you welcome to, is mean;
But make it all your own; we are full of wants
And cannot welcome worth.
LEANTIO [*Aside.*]: Now this is scurvy
And spake as if a woman lack'd her teeth.
These old folks talk of nothing but defects
Because they grow so full of 'em themselves.
BIANCA: Kind mother, there is nothing can be wanting
To her that does enjoy all her desires.
Heaven send a quiet peace with this man's love,
And I am as rich as Virtue can be poor;
Which were enough after the rate of mind
To erect temples for content plac'd here.
I have forsook friends, fortunes, and my country,
And hourly I rejoice in't. Here's my friends,
And few is the good number. Thy successes,
Howe'er they look, I will still name my fortunes;
Hopeful or spiteful, they shall all be welcome.
Who invites many guests has of all sorts,
As he that trafficks much drinks of all fortunes,
Yet they must all be welcome, and us'd well.
I'll call this place the place of my birth now,
And rightly too; for here my love was born,
And that's the birthday of a woman's joys.
[*To* LEANTIO.] You have not bid me welcome since I came.
LEANTIO: That I did questionless.
BIANCA: No sure, how was't?
I have quite forgot it.
LEANTIO: Thus.
[*Kisses her.*]
BIANCA: O sir, 'tis true,
Now I remember well. I have done thee wrong,
Pray take't again, sir.
[*Kisses him.*]
LEANTIO: How many of these wrongs
Could I put up in an hour, and turn up the glass
For twice as many more!

120 *wants*: material deficiencies, shortcomings 122 *lack'd her teeth*: one of the symptoms of scurvy was loss of teeth 128 *Virtue*: virtuous people 129 *after the rate of mind*: when valued in terms of spiritual contentment 130 *here*: probably indicating both the widow's home and Bianca's heart 133 *successes*: fortunes (good or bad) 136 *has of all sorts*: receives all sorts of people 137 *trafficks*: trades 147 *turn up*: reverse *glass*: hour-glass

MOTHER: Will't please you to walk in, daughter?
BIANCA: Thanks, sweet mother;
The voice of her that bare me is not more pleasing.
Exeunt [BIANCA *and* MOTHER].
LEANTIO: Though my own care and my rich master's trust
Lay their commands both on my factorship,
This day and night I'll know no other business
But her and her dear welcome. 'Tis a bitterness
To think upon tomorrow, that I must leave her
Still to the sweet hopes of the week's end.
That pleasure should be so restrain'd and curb'd,
After the course of a rich work-master
That never pays till Saturday night!
Marry, it comes together in a round sum then,
And does more good, you'll say. O fair-eyed Florence!
Didst thou but know what a most matchless jewel
Thou now art mistress of, a pride would take thee
Able to shoot destruction through the bloods
Of all thy youthful sons! But 'tis great policy
To keep choice treasures in obscurest places:
Should we show thieves our wealth, 'twould make 'em bolder.
Temptation is a devil will not stick
To fasten upon a saint; take heed of that,
The jewel is cas'd up from all men's eyes;
Who could imagine now a gem were kept
Of that great value under this plain roof?
But how in times of absence? What assurance
Of this restraint then? Yes, yes, there's one with her.
Old mothers know the world, and such as these,
When sons lock chests, are good to look to keys.
[*Exit.*]

151 *my own care*: my sense of responsibility/care for my own advancement
152 *factorship*: the position of a factor (a mercantile agent or steward of an estate) 158 *After the course*: following the practice 163 *a pride*: pride/sexual desire (a meaning reinforced by the 'bloods' of the following line) 165 *policy*: prudence 168 *stick*: scruple

SCENE 2

Enter GUARDIANO, FABRITIO, *and* LIVIA [*with* Servant].

GUARDIANO: What, has your daughter seen him yet? Know you that?
FABRITIO: No matter, she shall love him.
GUARDIANO: Nay, let's have fair play,
He has been now my ward some fifteen year,
And 'tis my purpose, as time calls upon me,
By custom seconded and such moral virtues,
To tender him a wife. Now sir, this wife
I'd fain elect out of a daughter of yours –
You see my meaning's fair. If now this daughter
So tendered (let me come to your own phrase, sir)
Should offer to refuse him, I were hansell'd.
[*Aside.*] Thus am I fain to calculate all my words
For the meridian of a foolish old man,
To take his understanding. – What do you answer, sir?
FABRITIO: I say still she shall love him.
GUARDIANO [*Aside.*]: Yet again? –
And shall she have no reason for this love?
FABRITIO: Why, do you think that women love with reason?
GUARDIANO [*Aside.*]: I perceive fools are not at all hours foolish,
No more than wise men wise.
FABRITIO: I had a wife,
She ran mad for me; she had no reason for't
For aught I could perceive. What think you, lady sister?
GUARDIANO [*Aside.*]: 'Twas a fit match that,
Being both out of their wits! – A loving wife, it seem'd
She strove to come as near you as she could.

2–10 in Jacobean England the child of any noble became a ward of the King on the death of the father, but in practice this right was farmed out, often with a view to speculative advantage. The guardians appointed by the King controlled the estates of the ward until the child reached the age of majority, 21. Up to that time the guardian was empowered to propose a suitable marriage to the ward and levy a fine if the match was refused. However, if the prospective bride, rather than the ward, refused, no payment could be extracted 2 *fair play*: not out of regard to the girl's sensibilities, but because if she should refuse after the match was formally proposed the guardian could lose financially (see previous note) 4 *as time calls upon me*: as the ward has almost reached the age of majority 5 *moral*: righteous/customary 8 *fair*: clear/pleasing 10 *I were hansell'd*: a 'hansell' was a gift given at New Year or other auspicious occasion. Here the sense is ironic: 'I'd be left a fine gift indeed!' 12 *For the meridian*: to the limits (of the understanding) 13 *take*: catch

FABRITIO: And if her daughter prove not mad for love too,
She takes not after her; nor after me,
If she prefer reason before my pleasure.
You're an experienc'd widow, lady sister,
I pray let your opinion come amongst us.
LIVIA: I must offend you then, if truth will do't,
And take my niece's part, and call't injustice
To force her love to one she never saw.
Maids should both see and like; all little enough;
If they love truly after that, 'tis well.
Counting the time, she takes one man till death,
That's a hard task, I tell you. But one may
Enquire at three years' end amongst young wives
And mark how the game goes.
FABRITIO: Why, is not man
Tied to the same observance, lady sister,
And in one woman?
LIVIA: 'Tis enough for him;
Besides, he tastes of many sundry dishes
That we poor wretches never lay our lips to:
As obedience, forsooth, subjection, duty, and such kickshaws,
All of our making, but serv'd in to them;
And if we lick a finger then sometimes
We are not too blame: your best cooks use it.
FABRITIO: Th'art a sweet lady, sister, and a witty.
LIVIA: A witty! O the bud of commendation
Fit for a girl of sixteen! I am blown, man,
I should be wise by this time; and, for instance,
I have buried my two husbands in good fashion
And never mean more to marry.
GUARDIANO: No, why so, lady?
LIVIA: Because the third shall never bury me.
I think I am more than witty; how think you, sir?
FABRITIO: I have paid often fees to a counsellor
Has had a weaker brain.
LIVIA: Then I must tell you
Your money was soon parted.

34 *Counting the time*: considering the length of the commitment 37 *the game goes*: matters have turned out (but punning on 'game' = sex) 38 *observance*: obligation, duty 42 *kickshaws*: trifles ('kickshaws' were fancy, insubstantial dishes in cookery) 45 *use it*: commonly do so 48 *am blown*: have seen better days ('blown' = fully blossomed) 54 *counsellor*: lawyer

GUARDIANO: Light her now, brother.
LIVIA: Where is my niece? Let her be sent for straight.
[*Exit* Servant.]
If you have any hope 'twill prove a wedding
'Tis fit, i'faith, she should have one sight of him,
And stop upon't, and not be join'd in haste
As if they went to stock a new-found land.
FABRITIO: Look out her uncle and y'are sure of her.
Those two are nev'r asunder: they've been heard
In argument at midnight, moonshine nights
Are noondays with them; they walk out their sleeps –
Or rather at those hours appear like those
That walk in 'em, for so they did to me.
Look you, I told you truth; they're like a chain,
Draw but one link, all follows.
Enter HIPPOLITO, *and* ISABELLA *the niece.*
GUARDIANO: O affinity,
What piece of excellent workmanship art thou!
'Tis work clean wrought; for there's no lust, but love in't,
And that abundantly. When in stranger things
There is no love at all, but what lust brings.
FABRITIO [*To* ISABELLA.]: On with your mask, for 'tis your part to see now
And not be seen. Go to, make use of your time;
See what you mean to like; nay, and I charge you,
Like what you see. Do you hear me? There's no dallying,
The gentleman's almost twenty and 'tis time
He were getting lawful heirs, and you a-breeding on 'em.
ISABELLA: Good father!
FABRITIO: Tell not me of tongues and rumours.
You'll say the gentleman is somewhat simple:
The better for a husband, were you wise,
For those that marry fools, live ladies' lives.

56 *Light her now, brother*: the meaning of this phrase is obscure but no plausible emendations have been proposed. (Frost suggests that Guardiano's comment indicates he is Fabritio's brother-in-law, but the term 'brother' could be being used loosely between prospective relations – Isabella is going to marry the Ward – or fellow men) 60 *stop upon't*: consider the matter 61 *stock a new-found land*: alluding to the fact that many of the marriages between settlers in the American colonies were hastily arranged 69 *affinity*: blood-relationship 71 *clean wrought*: perfectly fashioned 72 *stranger things*: things not related through kinship 80 *tongues*: gossip

On with the mask, I'll hear no more, he's rich;
The fool's hid under bushels.

LIVIA: Not so hid neither,
But here's a foul great piece of him, methinks;
What will he be when he comes altogether?

Enter the WARD *with a trap-stick, and* SORDIDO *his man.*

WARD: Beat him?
I beat him out o'th'field with his own cat-stick,
Yet gave him the first hand.

SORDIDO: O strange!

WARD: I did it,
Then he set jacks on me.

SORDIDO: What, my lady's tailor?

WARD: Ay, and I beat him too.

SORDIDO: Nay, that's no wonder,
He's us'd to beating.

WARD: Nay, I tickl'd him
When I came once to my tippings.

SORDIDO: Now you talk on 'em, there was a poulterer's wife made a great complaint of you last night to your guardianer, that you struck a bump in her child's head as big as an egg.

WARD: An egg may prove a chicken then in time; the poulterer's wife will get by't. When I am in game I am furious; came my mother's eyes in my way, I would not lose a fair end. No, were she alive, but with one tooth in her head, I should venture the striking out of that. I think of nobody when I am in play, I am so earnest. Coads me, my guardianer!
Prithee lay up my cat and cat-stick safe.

SORDIDO: Where, sir, i'th'chimney-corner?

85 *bushels*: a measure of capacity used for grain, etc. containing 8 gallons; but here used in the looser sense of 'a large quantity' (of money) and alluding ironically to Matthew 5. 15: 'A wise man does not light a candle and set it under a bushel' 86 presumably some portion of the Ward's anatomy, probably his arse, protrudes on to the stage at this point s.d. *trap-stick*: a cudgel, used in the country game Cat and Trap to strike the 'cat', a piece of wood approximately 6 inches long and 2 inches wide shaped into a double cone 90 *first hand*: first strike 91 *jacks*: ruffians *tailor*: possibly Sordido pretends that the Ward was referring to a tailor called Jacques 93 *us'd to beating*: tailors were proverbial cowards (but also punning on 'beaten' = embroidered) *tickl'd*: i.e. hit violently 94 *tippings*: the action of knocking up the 'cat' preparatory to striking it away 95 *'em*: i.e. the tippings (the Ward's 'cat' evidently struck the child's head) *poulterer*: dealer in poultry 96 *of*: about 99 *get*: gain (i.e. by selling the chickens) *in game*: i.e. playing Cat and Trap (but punning on 'in game' = having sex, a sense taken up in 'fair end') *furious*: passionate 100 *a fair end*: a win 102 *Coads me*: obsolete expression of surprise (God save me [?]) 104 *chimney-corner*: punning on 'chimney' = cunt and 'chimney-corner' = brothel

WARD: Chimney-corner!
SORDIDO: Yes, sir, your cats are always safe i'th'chimney-corner,
Unless they burn their coats.
WARD: Marry, that I am afraid on.
SORDIDO: Why, then I will bestow your cat i'th'gutter,
And there she's safe I am sure.
WARD: If I but live
To keep a house, I'll make thee a great man,
If meat and drink can do't. I can stoop gallantly
And pitch out when I list; I'm dog at a hole.
I mar'l my guardianer does not seek a wife for me;
I protest I'll have a bout with the maids else,
Or contract myself at midnight to the larder-woman
In presence of a fool or a sack-posset.
GUARDIANO: Ward.
WARD: I feel myself after any exercise
Horribly prone: let me but ride, I'm lusty;
A cockhorse straight, i'faith.
GUARDIANO: Why, Ward, I say!
WARD: I'll forswear eating eggs in moonshine nights;
There's nev'r a one I eat but turns into a cock
In four-and-twenty hours; if my hot blood
Be not took down in time, sure 'twill crow shortly.
GUARDIANO: Do you hear, sir? Follow me, I must new school you.
WARD: School me? I scorn that now, I am past schooling.
I am not so base to learn to write and read;

105 *cats*: punning on the term for the wooden cones of Cat and Trap and the slang term for 'whores' 106 *burn*: a slang term for the experience of venereal disease 109 *great*: important/fat 110–11 *I can . . . at a hole*: the literal sense of this passage is obscure. Probably 'stoop', 'pitch out' and 'hole' were part of the technical vocabulary of Cat and Trap and the Ward is bragging of his prowess. However, each of these terms also has a bawdy meaning: 'stoop' = fuck; 'pitch out' = ejaculate; and 'hole' = cunt. 111 *dog at*: i.e. old dog at, or experienced in 112 *mar'l*: marvel 113 *have a bout*: fornicate 114 *contract myself*: i.e. go through the forms of a marriage pre-contract, which was binding when a witness was present 115 *fool*: a dish made from fruit and cream *sack-posset*: spiced drink made from hot milk curdled with the dry white wine known as sack 117 *prone*: lecherous *ride*: ride/mount a woman 118 *cockhorse*: child's hobby horse/stallion/a whore 119 eggs were thought to be an aphrodisiac. The phrase could mean either 'I will give up eggs on nights when the moon shines' (and there is a danger of madness); or 'I will give up "eggs in moonshine" (the name of a dish resembling poached eggs) at night' 120 *cock*: cockerel/erection 122 *crow*: punning on 'crow' = ejaculate

I was born to better fortunes in my cradle.
Exit [WARD, *with* GUARDIANO *and* SORDIDO].

FABRITIO: How do you like him, girl? This is your husband.
Like him or like him not, wench, you shall have him
And you shall love him.

LIVIA: O soft there, brother! Though you be a Justice,
Your warrant cannot be serv'd out of your liberty;
You may compel out of the power of father
Things merely harsh to a maid's flesh and blood;
But when you come to love, there the soil alters;
Y'are in another country, where your laws
Are no more set by than the cacklings
Of geese in Rome's great Capitol.

FABRITIO: Marry him she shall then,
Let her agree upon love afterwards.
Exit.

LIVIA: You speak now, brother, like an honest mortal
That walks upon th'earth with a staff;
You were up i'th'clouds before. You'd command love,
And so do most old folks that go without it.
[*To* HIPPOLITO.] My best and dearest brother, I could dwell here;
There is not such another seat on earth
Where all good parts better express themselves.

HIPPOLITO: You'll make me blush anon.

LIVIA: 'Tis but like saying grace before a feast, then,
And that's most comely; thou art all a feast,
And she that has thee, a most happy guest.
Prithee cheer up that niece with special counsel.
[*Exit*.]

HIPPOLITO [*Aside*.]: I would 'twere fit to speak to her what I would, but
'Twas not a thing ordain'd, heaven has forbid it;
And 'tis most meet that I should rather perish
Than the decree divine receive least blemish.
Feed inward you my sorrows, make no noise,
Consume me silent, let me be stark dead

130 *Justice*: a Justice of the Peace 131 *out of your liberty*: outside the limits of your jurisdiction 136 *set by*: set store by, taken notice of 136–7 *cacklings . . . Capitol*: the Romans kept sacred geese on the Capitoline Hill, so presumably the inhabitants became inured to their cackling. The famous legend of the geese alerting the Romans to a surprise attack by the invading Gauls seems inappropriate in context 139–40 *an . . . staff*: i.e. a pilgrim 143 *here*: in this place/in your presence 144 *seat*: estate/person 145 *parts*: features 149 *thee*: O reads 'that'

Ere the world know I'm sick. You see my honesty;
If you befriend me, so.
ISABELLA [*Aside.*]: Marry a fool!
Can there be greater misery to a woman,
That means to keep her days true to her husband
And know no other man, so virtue wills it!
Why, how can I obey and honour him
But I must needs commit idolatry?
A fool is but the image of a man,
And that but ill made neither. O the heart-breakings
Of miserable maids, where love's enforc'd!
The best condition is but bad enough:
When women have their choices, commonly
They do but buy their thraldoms and bring great portions
To men to keep 'em in subjection;
As if a fearful prisoner should bribe
The keeper to be good to him, yet lies in still,
And glad of a good usage, a good look
Sometimes, by'r Lady; no misery surmounts a woman's.
Men buy their slaves but women buy their masters.
Yet honesty and love makes all this happy
And, next to angels', the most blest estate.
That Providence, that has made ev'ry poison
Good for some use, and sets four warring elements
At peace in man, can make a harmony
In things that are most strange to human reason.
O but this marriage! – What, are you sad too, uncle?
Faith then there's a whole household down together!
Where shall I go to seek my comfort now
When my best friend's distress'd? What is't afflicts you, sir?
HIPPOLITO: Faith, nothing but one grief that will not leave me,
And now 'tis welcome; ev'ry man has something
To bring him to his end, and this will serve
Join'd with your father's cruelty to you.
That helps it forward.
ISABELLA: O be cheer'd, sweet uncle!

157 *You*: i.e. his sorrows *honesty*: i.e. his silence 158 *so*: i.e. kill me
163 *idolatry*: i.e. by worshipping a counterfeit image or idol of a 'man', who ought to be created in God's image 165 *neither*: as well 169 *portions*: dowries
170 *'em*: women 177 *estate*: condition 179 *four warring elements*: matter was held to be composed of four basic elements: earth, air, fire and water. Ideally, in man, the properties of each were fused in a harmonious balance

How long has't been upon you? I nev'r spied it,
What a dull sight have I! How long, I pray, sir?

HIPPOLITO: Since I first saw you, niece, and left Bologna.

ISABELLA: And could you deal so unkindly with my heart
To keep it up so long hid from my pity?
Alas, how shall I trust your love hereafter?
Have we pass'd through so many arguments
And miss'd of that still, the most needful one?
Walk'd out whole nights together in discourses
And the main point forgot? We are too blame both;
This is an obstinate wilful forgetfulness
And faulty on both parts. Let's lose no time now.
Begin, good uncle, you that feel't. What is it?

HIPPOLITO: You of all creatures, niece, must never hear on't,
'Tis not a thing ordain'd for you to know.

ISABELLA: Not I, sir! All my joys that word cuts off.
You made profession once you lov'd me best;
'Twas but profession!

HIPPOLITO: Yes, I do't too truly,
And fear I shall be chid for't. Know the worst then:
I love thee dearlier than an uncle can.

ISABELLA: Why so you ever said, and I believ'd it.

HIPPOLITO [*Aside.*]: So simple is the goodness of her thoughts,
They understand not yet th'unhallow'd language
Of a near sinner. I must yet be forc'd
(Though blushes be my venture) to come nearer.
– As a man loves his wife, so love I thee.

ISABELLA: What's that?
Methought I heard ill news come toward me,
Which commonly we understand too soon,
Than over-quick at hearing. I'll prevent it,
Though my joys fare the harder; welcome it,
It shall nev'r come so near mine ear again.
Farewell all friendly solaces and discourses;
I'll learn to live without ye, for your dangers
Are greater than your comforts. What's become

197 *arguments*: discussions 207 *made profession*: declared, vowed 208 *but profession*: words only *do't*: love 215 *Though blushes be my venture*: though I risk blushing *come nearer*: be more explicit 218–21 i.e. which we frequently understand intuitively and then bring to life a second time ('over-quick(en)') when we hear it. I'll anticipate it and, though it will be painful, welcome it; that way I'll never have to endure that second pain of having to hear it

Of truth in love, if such we cannot trust,
When blood that should be love is mix'd with lust?
Exit.

HIPPOLITO: The worst can be but death, and let it come;
He that lives joyless, ev'ry day's his doom.
Exit.

SCENE 3

Enter LEANTIO *alone.*

LEANTIO: Methinks I'm ev'n as dull now at departure
As men observe great gallants the next day
After a revels; you shall see 'em look
Much of my fashion, if you mark 'em well.
'Tis ev'n a second hell to part from pleasure
When man has got a smack on't. As many holidays
Coming together makes your poor heads idle
A great while after, and are said to stick
Fast in their fingers' ends, ev'n so does game
In a new married couple for the time;
It spoils all thrift, and indeed lies a-bed
To invent all the new ways for great expenses.
[*Enter*] BIANCA *and* MOTHER *above.*
See, and she be not got on purpose now
Into the window to look after me!
I have no power to go now, and I should be hang'd.
Farewell all business, I desire no more
Than I see yonder; let the goods at quay
Look to themselves; why should I toil my youth out?
It is but begging two or three year sooner,
And stay with her continually. Is't a match?
O fie, what a religion have I leap'd into!
Get out again for shame, the man loves best
When his care's most; that shows his zeal to love.
Fondness is but the idiot to affection,

225 *such*: i.e. Hippolito 6 *smack on't*: taste of it (but punning on 'smack' = kiss) 7 *poor heads*: i.e. workmen 8–9 *stick Fast in their fingers' ends*: i.e. hamper their work 9 *game*: love-making 12 *expenses*: costs/ejaculations 13 *and*: if 15 *and*: if 20 *a match*: agreed 24 *Fondness*: infatuation *the idiot to affection*: the caricature of reasonable love

That plays at hot-cockles with rich merchants' wives –
Good to make sport withal when the chest's full
And the long warehouse cracks. 'Tis time of day
For us to be more wise; 'tis early with us,
And if they lose the morning of their affairs
They commonly lose the best part of the day.
Those that are wealthy and have got enough,
'Tis after sunset with 'em, they may rest,
Grow fat with ease, banquet, and toy and play,
When such as I enter the heat o'th'day;
And I'll do't cheerfully.

BIANCA: I perceive, sir,
Y'are not gone yet. I have good hope you'll stay now.

LEANTIO: Farewell, I must not.

BIANCA: Come, come, pray return.
Tomorrow, adding but a little care more,
Will dispatch all as well; believe me 'twill, sir.

LEANTIO: I could well wish myself where you would have me;
But love that's wanton must be rul'd a while
By that that's careful, or all goes to ruin.
As fitting is a government in love
As in a kingdom; where 'tis all mere lust
'Tis like an insurrection in the people
That, rais'd in self-will, wars against all reason.
But love that is respective for increase
Is like a good king that keeps all in peace.
Once more, farewell.

BIANCA: But this one night, I prithee.

LEANTIO: Alas, I'm in for twenty, if I stay,
And then for forty more, I have such luck to flesh.
I never bought a horse but he bore double.
If I stay any longer, I shall turn
An everlasting spendthrift. As you love
To be maintain'd well, do not call me again,

25 *hot-cockles*: a rustic game in which one player lay face downward, and, being struck by the others in turn, guessed who had struck him. The full phrase 'plays at hot-cockles with' also clearly means 'interferes with (touches up)' 26 *withal*: with 27 *cracks*: bursts (because full of goods) 38 *care*: trouble, effort 47 *is respective for increase*: has regard for future prosperity ('increase' may also allude to 'children') 51–2 *I . . . double*: Leantio seems to be saying that he encourages fertility (hence his horses are doubly fertile). But, possibly, 'flesh' is a verb = excite sexually (an intransitive use of OED 2.c, perhaps?). 'Bore double' might be ironically prophetic, meaning Bianca will carry two riders

For then I shall not care which end goes forward.
Again farewell to thee.
Exit.
BIANCA: Since it must, farewell too.
MOTHER: Faith daughter, y'are too blame; you take the course
To make him an ill husband, troth you do,
And that disease is catching, I can tell you
Ay, and soon taken by a young man's blood,
And that with little urging. Nay, fie, see now,
What cause have you to weep? Would I had no more,
That have liv'd threescore years; there were a cause
And 'twere well thought on. Trust me, y'are too blame,
His absence cannot last five days at utmost.
Why should those tears be fetch'd forth? Cannot love
Be ev'n as well express'd in a good look
But it must see her face still in a fountain?
It shows like a country maid dressing her head
By a dish of water. Come, 'tis an old custom
To weep for love.
Enter two or three Boys, *and a* Citizen *or two, with an* Apprentice.
BOYS: Now they come, now they come!
SECOND BOY: The Duke!
THIRD BOY: The State!
CITIZEN: How near, boy?
FIRST BOY: I'th'next street, sir, hard at hand.
CITIZEN: You, sirrah, get a standing for your mistress,
The best in all the city.
APPRENTICE: I have't for her, sir.
'Twas a thing I provided for her overnight,
'Tis ready at her pleasure.
CITIZEN: Fetch her to't then; away, sir!
[*Exit* Apprentice.]
BIANCA: What's the meaning of this hurry?
Can you tell, mother?
MOTHER: What a memory
Have I! I see by that years come upon me.
Why 'tis a yearly custom and solemnity,

56 *I shall not care which end goes forward*: proverbial phrase meaning 'I won't care what happens' 60 *that disease*: i.e. abandoning work for pleasure 69 *in a fountain*: reflected in a fountain/in tears 71 *By a dish of water*: by means of a dish of water (acting as a mirror) 73 *The State*: the nobles and great men of the realm 75 *standing*: vantage point 83 *yearly custom and solemnity*: the festival of St Mark (which is actually celebrated on 25 April)

Religiously observ'd by th'Duke and State,
To St Mark's temple, the fifteenth of April.
See if my dull brains had not quite forgot it!
'Twas happily question'd of thee, I had gone down else,
Sat like a drone below, and never thought on't.
I would not to be ten years younger again
That you had lost the sight. Now you shall see
Our Duke, a goodly gentleman of his years.

BIANCA: Is he old then?

MOTHER: About some fifty-five.

BIANCA: That's no great age in man, he's then at best
For wisdom and for judgment.

MOTHER: The Lord Cardinal
His noble brother, there's a comely gentleman,
And greater in devotion than in blood.

BIANCA: He's worthy to be mark'd.

MOTHER: You shall behold
All our chief States of Florence; you came fortunately
Against this solemn day.

BIANCA: I hope so always.

Music.

MOTHER: I hear 'em near us now; do you stand easily?

BIANCA: Exceeding well, good mother.

MOTHER: Take this stool.

BIANCA: I need it not, I thank you.

MOTHER: Use your will, then.

Enter in great solemnity six Knights *bare-headed, then two* Cardinals, *and then the* LORD CARDINAL, *then the* DUKE; *after him the* States of Florence *by two and two, with variety of Music and Song.*

Exit [procession].

MOTHER: How like you, daughter?

BIANCA: 'Tis a noble State.
Methinks my soul could dwell upon the reverence
Of such a solemn and most worthy custom.
Did not the Duke look up? Methought he saw us.

MOTHER: That's ev'ryone's conceit that sees a duke.

87 *down*: downstairs (the Mother and Bianca are on the balcony having entered above at I.iii.12) 88 *drone*: idler 89–90 *I . . . sight*: I'd rather have lost the chance to be ten years younger, than for you to have missed this sight
95 *comely*: handsome, proper 99 *Against*: in time for 100 *easily*: comfortably
107 *conceit*: idea/fanciful notion

If he look steadfastly, he looks straight at them –
When he perhaps, good careful gentleman,
Never minds any, but the look he casts
Is at his own intentions, and his object
Only the public good.

BIANCA: Most likely so.

MOTHER: Come, come, we'll end this argument below.

Exeunt.

109 *careful*: full of concern 110 *minds*: notices

ACT TWO

SCENE I

Enter HIPPOLITO, *and Lady* LIVIA *the widow.*

LIVIA: A strange affection, brother, when I think on't!
I wonder how thou cam'st by't.
HIPPOLITO: Ev'n as easily
As man comes by destruction, which oft-times
He wears in his own bosom.
LIVIA: Is the world
So populous in women, and creation
So prodigal in beauty and so various?
Yet does love turn thy point to thine own blood?
'Tis somewhat too unkindly. Must thy eye
Dwell evilly on the fairness of thy kindred,
And seek not where it should? It is confin'd
Now in a narrower prison than was made for't.
It is allow'd a stranger; and where bounty
Is made the great man's honour, 'tis ill husbandry
To spare, and servants shall have small thanks for't.
So he heaven's bounty seems to scorn and mock
That spares free means and spends of his own stock.
HIPPOLITO: Never was man's misery so soon sew'd up,
Counting how truly.
LIVIA: Nay, I love you so,
That I shall venture much to keep a change from you
So fearful as this grief will bring upon you.
Faith, it even kills me, when I see you faint
Under a reprehension, and I'll leave it,

7 *turn thy point*: the image is that of a compass needle, but there is a bawdy pun on 'point' = penis 8 *unkindly*: cruel/incestuous 12 *stranger*: i.e. anyone outside the family 12–14 *where . . . spare*: 'since liberality is a mark of honour and esteem, it is a false economy to be sparing'. The implication is that Hippolito should go and sow his wild oats freely, in order to forget Isabella 16 *spares free means*: neglects free offers (i.e. all women not debarred by ties of kinship) *spends*: consumes/ejaculates *stock*: goods/family 17 *sew'd up*: O reads 'sow'd up' 22 *reprehension*: reprimand

Though I know nothing can be better for you.
Prithee, sweet brother, let not passion waste
The goodness of thy time, and of thy fortune;
Thou keep'st the treasure of that life I love
As dearly as mine own; and if you think
My former words too bitter, which were minist'red
By truth and zeal, 'tis but a hazarding
Of grace and virtue, and I can bring forth
As pleasant fruits as Sensuality wishes
In all her teeming longings. This I can do.
HIPPOLITO: O nothing that can make my wishes perfect!
LIVIA: I would that love of yours were pawn'd to't, brother,
And as soon lost that way as I could win.
Sir, I could give as shrewd a lift to Chastity
As any she that wears a tongue in Florence.
Sh'ad need be a good horsewoman and sit fast
Whom my strong argument could not fling at last.
Prithee take courage, man; though I should counsel
Another to despair, yet I am pitiful
To thy afflictions, and will venture hard –
I will not name for what, 'tis not handsome.
Find you the proof, and praise me.
HIPPOLITO: Then I fear me
I shall not praise you in haste.
LIVIA: This is the comfort,
You are not the first, brother, has attempted
Things more forbidden than this seems to be.
I'll minister all cordials now to you
Because I'll cheer you up, sir.
HIPPOLITO: I am past hope.
LIVIA: Love, thou shalt see me do a strange cure then,
As e'er was wrought on a disease so mortal
And near akin to shame. When shall you see her?
HIPPOLITO: Never in comfort more.
LIVIA: Y'are so impatient too.

24 *passion*: suffering 29 *hazarding*: putting at risk (through gambling) 30 *grace and virtue*: perhaps referring to her own integrity, but more likely to Isabella 33 *perfect*: completed, satisfied/ideal 34 *pawn'd to't*: bet on the issue (taking up the gaming metaphor of 'hazard') 35 i.e. and you would lose your love for her as easily as I can win hers for you 36 *shrewd*: depraved/cunning *lift to*: assault on 42 *hard*: strenuously 43 *handsome*: decent 44 *Find you*: once you have tested 48 *cordials*: restoratives, medicines stimulating to the heart 51 *mortal*: deadly

HIPPOLITO: Will you believe? Death, sh'as forsworn my company
And seal'd it with a blush.

LIVIA: So, I perceive
All lies upon my hands then; well, the more glory
When the work's finish'd.

Enter Servant.

How now, sir, the news!

SERVANT: Madam, your niece, the virtuous Isabella,
Is 'lighted now to see you.

LIVIA [*To* HIPPOLITO.]: That's great fortune.
Sir, your stars bless. – You simple, lead her in.

Exit Servant.

HIPPOLITO: What's this to me?

LIVIA: Your absence, gentle brother;
I must bestir my wits for you.

HIPPOLITO: Ay, to great purpose.

Exit HIPPOLITO.

LIVIA: Beshrew you, would I lov'd you not so well!
I'll go to bed and leave this deed undone.
I am the fondest where I once affect,
The carefull'st of their healths, and of their ease, forsooth,
That I look still but slenderly to mine own.
I take a course to pity him so much now
That I have none left for modesty and myself.
This 'tis to grow so liberal: y'have few sisters
That love their brothers' ease 'bove their own honesties,
But if you question my affections
That will be found my fault.

Enter ISABELLA *the niece.*

Niece, your love's welcome.
Alas, what draws that paleness to thy cheeks?
This enforc'd marriage towards?

ISABELLA: It helps, good aunt,
Amongst some other griefs; but those I'll keep
Lock'd up in modest silence, for they're sorrows
Would shame the tongue more than they grieve the thought.

LIVIA: Indeed the Ward is simple.

ISABELLA: Simple! that were well:

55 *seal'd*: confirmed 59 *'lighted*: arrived 60 *simple*: fool 63 *Beshrew you*: shame on you 65 *the fondest*: most infatuated *affect*: love 66 *forsooth*: in truth 70 *liberal*: generous/licentious 71 *ease*: comfort, pleasure 75 *towards*: in the offing

Why, one might make good shift with such a husband.
But he's a fool entail'd, he halts downright in't.

LIVIA: And knowing this, I hope 'tis at your choice
To take or refuse, niece.

ISABELLA: You see it is not.
I loathe him more than beauty can hate death
Or age, her spiteful neighbour.

LIVIA: Let't appear, then.

ISABELLA: How can I, being born with that obedience
That must submit unto a father's will?
If he command, I must of force consent.

LIVIA: Alas, poor soul! Be not offended, prithee,
If I set by the name of niece awhile,
And bring in pity in a stranger fashion.
It lies here in this breast would cross this match.

ISABELLA: How, cross it, aunt?

LIVIA: Ay, and give thee more liberty
Than thou hast reason yet to apprehend.

ISABELLA: Sweet aunt, in goodness keep not hid from me
What may befriend my life.

LIVIA: Yes, yes, I must,
When I return to reputation,
And think upon the solemn vow I made
To your dead mother, my most loving sister –
As long as I have her memory 'twixt mine eyelids,
Look for no pity now.

ISABELLA: Kind, sweet, dear aunt.

LIVIA: No, 'twas a secret I have took special care of,
Deliver'd by your mother on her deathbed;
That's nine years now, and I'll not part from't yet,
Though nev'r was fitter time nor greater cause for't.

ISABELLA: As you desire the praises of a virgin –

LIVIA: Good sorrow! I would do thee any kindness
Not wronging secrecy or reputation.

ISABELLA: Neither of which, as I have hope of fruitfulness,
Shall receive wrong from me.

LIVIA: Nay 'twould be your own wrong,
As much as any's, should it come to that once.

80 *make good shift*: succeed 81 *fool entail'd*: congenital idiot *halts downright in't*: i.e. he'll never progress past the stage of an idiot 91 *stranger fashion*: i.e. as though coming from one not of the family 92 *It*: i.e. information *cross*: thwart 93 *liberty*: freedom/sexual licence 100 *'twixt mine eyelids*: in my mind's eye 109 *fruitfulness*: O reads 'fruit-/ness'

ISABELLA: I need no better means to work persuasion then.
LIVIA: Let it suffice, you may refuse this fool
Or you may take him, as you see occasion
For your advantage; the best wits will do't.
Y'have liberty enough in your own will,
You cannot be enforc'd; there grows the flower,
If you could pick it out, makes whole life sweet to you.
That which you call your father's command's nothing;
Then your obedience must needs be as little.
If you can make shift here to taste your happiness,
Or pick out aught that likes you, much good do you.
You see your cheer, I'll make you no set dinner.
ISABELLA: And trust me, I may starve for all the good
I can find yet in this. Sweet aunt, deal plainlier.
LIVIA: Say I should trust you now upon an oath
And give you in a secret that would start you,
How am I sure of you, in faith and silence?
ISABELLA: Equal assurance may I find in mercy
As you for that in me.
LIVIA: It shall suffice.
Then know, however custom has made good,
For reputation's sake, the names of niece
And aunt 'twixt you and I, w'are nothing less.
ISABELLA: How's that?
LIVIA: I told you I should start your blood.
You are no more allied to any of us,
Save what the courtesy of opinion casts
Upon your mother's memory and your name,
Than the mer'st stranger is, or one begot
At Naples, when the husband lies at Rome:
There's so much odds betwixt us. Since your knowledge
Wish'd more instruction, and I have your oath
In pledge for silence, it makes me talk the freelier.
Did never the report of that fam'd Spaniard,
Marquis of Coria, since your time was ripe
For understanding, fill your ear with wonder?
ISABELLA: Yes, what of him? I have heard his deeds of honour
Often related when we liv'd in Naples.

121 *make shift*: contrive 122 *that likes you*: that you like 123 *cheer*: gladness/food, provisions *I'll make you no set dinner*: i.e. I won't have to explain everything 'course by course' 125 *deal plainlier*: explain yourself more clearly 129 *mercy*: i.e. God's mercy 133 *nothing less*: not related at all 134 *start your blood*: startle you/arouse your passion 140 *odds*: difference

LIVIA: You heard the praises of your father then.
ISABELLA: My father!
LIVIA: That was he. But all the business
So carefully and so discreetly carried,
That fame receiv'd no spot by't, not a blemish.
Your mother was so wary to her end
None knew it but her conscience and her friend,
Till penitent confession made it mine,
And now my pity, yours. It had been long else,
And I hope care and love alike in you,
Made good by oath, will see it take no wrong now.
How weak his commands now, whom you call father!
How vain all his enforcements, your obedience!
And what a largeness in your will and liberty
To take or to reject, or to do both!
For fools will serve to father wise men's children.
All this y'have time to think on. O my wench,
Nothing o'erthrows our sex but indiscretion!
We might do well else of a brittle people
As any under the great canopy.
I pray forget not but to call me aunt still;
Take heed of that, it may be mark'd in time else.
But keep your thoughts to yourself, from all the world,
Kindred or dearest friend, nay, I entreat you,
From him that all this while you have call'd uncle;
And though you love him dearly, as I know
His deserts claim as much ev'n from a stranger,
Yet let not him know this, I prithee do not;
As ever thou hast hope of second pity
If thou shouldst stand in need on't, do not do't.
ISABELLA: Believe my oath, I will not.
LIVIA: Why, well said:
[*Aside.*] Who shows more craft t'undo a maidenhead,
I'll resign my part to her.
Enter HIPPOLITO.
[*Aside to him.*] She's thine own, go.
Exit.
HIPPOLITO [*Aside.*]: Alas, fair flattery cannot cure my sorrows!

149 *business*: affair 151 *fame*: reputation 152 *to her end*: until her death 153 *friend*: lover 160 *largeness*: scope, opportunity 162 *father*: i.e. 'pay the upkeep for', rather than 'beget' 165–6 i.e. but for our indiscretion we might prosper as well as any other frail mortals under the sky 175 *second pity*: i.e. Livia's help again

ISABELLA [*Aside.*]: Have I pass'd so much time in ignorance
And never had the means to know myself
Till this blest hour? Thanks to her virtuous pity
That brought it now to light; would I had known it
But one day sooner! He had then receiv'd
In favours what, poor gentleman, he took
In bitter words: a slight and harsh reward
For one of his deserts.

HIPPOLITO [*Aside.*]: There seems to me now
More anger and distraction in her looks.
I'm gone, I'll not endure a second storm;
The memory of the first is not past yet.

ISABELLA: Are you return'd, you comforts of my life,
In this man's presence? I will keep you fast now,
And sooner part eternally from the world
Than my good joys in you. Prithee, forgive me,
I did but chide in jest; the best loves use it
Sometimes, it sets an edge upon affection.
When we invite our best friends to a feast
'Tis not all sweetmeats that we set before them,
There's somewhat sharp and salt, both to whet appetite
And make 'em taste their wine well. So, methinks,
After a friendly, sharp and savoury chiding,
A kiss tastes wondrous well and full o'th'grape.
[*Kisses him.*]
How think'st thou, does't not?

HIPPOLITO: 'Tis so excellent,
I know not how to praise it, what to say to't.

ISABELLA: This marriage shall go forward.

HIPPOLITO: With the Ward!
Are you in earnest?

ISABELLA: 'Twould be ill for us else.

HIPPOLITO [*Aside.*]: For us? How means she that?

ISABELLA [*Aside.*]: Troth, I begin
To be so well, methinks, within this hour;
For all this match able to kill one's heart,
Nothing can pull me down now. Should my father
Provide a worse fool yet (which I should think
Were a hard thing to compass) I'd have him either:
The worse the better, none can come amiss now

186 *favours*: love tokens 200 *somewhat*: something 210 *match*: i.e. marriage to the Ward 213 *compass*: accomplish *either*: as an alternative 214 *none*: i.e. no fool

If he want wit enough. So discretion love me,
Desert and judgment, I have content sufficient.
– She that comes once to be a housekeeper
Must not look every day to fare well, sir,
Like a young waiting gentlewoman in service;
For she feeds commonly as her lady does,
No good bit passes her but she gets a taste on't;
But when she comes to keep house for herself
She's glad of some choice cates then once a week,
Or twice at most, and glad if she can get 'em.
So must affection learn to fare with thankfulness.
Pray make your love no stranger, sir, that's all.
[*Aside.*] Though you be one yourself, and know not on't,
And I have sworn you must not.
Exit.

HIPPOLITO: This is beyond me!
Never came joys so unexpectedly
To meet desires in man. How came she thus?
What has she done to her, can any tell?
'Tis beyond sorcery, this, drugs or love-powders;
Some art that has no name, sure, strange to me
Of all the wonders I ere met withal
Throughout my ten years' travels; but I'm thankful for't.
This marriage now must of necessity forward.
It is the only veil wit can devise
To keep our acts hid from sin-piercing eyes.
Exit.

SCENE 2

Enter GUARDIANO *and* LIVIA.

LIVIA: How, sir, a gentlewoman so young, so fair
As you set forth, spied from the widow's window!
GUARDIANO: She!
LIVIA: Our Sunday-dinner woman?

215 *want*: lack 215–16 *discretion . . . Desert . . . judgment*: i.e. Hippolito
218 *fare*: eat 220 *she*: i.e. the waiting gentlewoman 223 *cates*: delicacies
230 *she*: i.e. Livia 1 *How*: interjection equivalent to 'What' 2 *set forth*: described 4 *Sunday-dinner woman*: probably the widow, as a poor neighbour, was entertained as an act of charity

GUARDIANO: And Thursday-supper woman, the same still.
I know not how she came by her, but I'll swear
She's the prime gallant for a face in Florence;
And no doubt other parts follow their leader.
The Duke himself first spied her at the window,
Then in a rapture, as if admiration
Were poor when it were single, beck'ned me
And pointed to the wonder warily,
As one that fear'd she would draw in her splendour
Too soon, if too much gaz'd at. I nev'r knew him
So infinitely taken with a woman,
Nor can I blame his appetite, or tax
His raptures of slight folly; she's a creature
Able to draw a State from serious business,
And make it their best piece to do her service.
What course shall we devise? H'as spoke twice now.
LIVIA: Twice?
GUARDIANO: 'Tis beyond your apprehension.
How strangely that one look has catch'd his heart!
'Twould prove but too much worth in wealth and favour
To those should work his peace.
LIVIA: And if I do't not,
Or at least come as near it (if your art
Will take a little pains and second me)
As any wench in Florence of my standing,
I'll quite give o'er, and shut up shop in cunning.
GUARDIANO: 'Tis for the Duke, and if I fail your purpose
All means to come, by riches or advancement,
Miss me and skip me over.
LIVIA: Let the old woman then
Be sent for with all speed, then I'll begin.
GUARDIANO: A good conclusion follow, and a sweet one,
After this stale beginning with old ware. –
Within there!
Enter Servant.
SERVANT: Sir, do you call?
GUARDIANO: Come near, list hither.

7 *prime gallant*: outstanding beauty (presumably only Bianca's face could be seen from the street below her window) 16–17 *tax His raptures of slight folly*: accuse his passions of seizing on a trivial fancy 19 *best piece*: serious concern 22 *strangely*: extremely/strongly (O reads 'strangly') 23 *but too much*: considerable 24 *work his peace*: satisfy his desires 34 *old ware*: i.e. the widow 35 *list*: listen

[*Talks to him apart.*]

LIVIA: I long myself to see this absolute creature
That wins the heart of love and praise so much.

GUARDIANO: Go, sir, make haste.

LIVIA: Say I entreat her company;
Do you hear, sir?

SERVANT: Yes, madam.

Exit.

LIVIA: That brings her quickly.

GUARDIANO: I would 'twere done, the Duke waits the good hour
And I wait the good fortune that may spring from't.
I have had a lucky hand these fifteen year
At such court-passage with three dice in a dish.

Enter FABRITIO.

Signor Fabritio!

FABRITIO: O sir, I bring an alteration in my mouth now.

GUARDIANO [*Aside.*]: An alteration! No wise speech, I hope;
He means not to talk wisely, does he, trow? –
Good! what's the change, I pray, sir?

FABRITIO: A new change.

GUARDIANO [*Aside.*]: Another yet! Faith, there's enough already.

FABRITIO: My daughter loves him now.

GUARDIANO: What, does she, sir?

FABRITIO: Affects him beyond thought, who but the Ward, forsooth!
No talk but of the Ward; she would have him
To choose 'bove all the men she ever saw.
My will goes not so fast as her consent now;
Her duty gets before my command still.

GUARDIANO: Why then, sir, if you'll have me speak my thoughts
I smell 'twill be a match.

FABRITIO: Ay, and a sweet young couple,
If I have any judgment.

GUARDIANO [*Aside.*]: Faith, that's little. –
Let her be sent tomorrow before noon
And handsomely trick'd up, for 'bout that time
I mean to bring her in and tender her to him.

36 *absolute*: perfect 43 *court-passage*: a dice game (involving 2 players and 3 dice)/amorous encounter (the 3 dice suggest the 3 parties to such an affair) 49 *Another yet*: Guardiano mocks Fabritio's tautologous 'new change' and may also glance at the building of the New Change in 1609, a meeting place for merchants in the Strand, which was felt by some to be redundant, given the existence of the Royal Exchange 55 *gets before*: anticipates 57 *smell*: predict (Guardiano picks up his metaphor in the 'sweet' of the next line) 60 *trick'd up*: dressed, adorned

FABRITIO: I warrant you for handsome. I will see
Her things laid ready, every one in order,
And have some part of her trick'd up tonight.
GUARDIANO: Why, well said.
FABRITIO: 'Twas a use her mother had
When she was invited to an early wedding;
She'ld dress her head o'ernight, sponge up herself,
And give her neck three lathers.
GUARDIANO [*Aside.*]: Ne'er a halter?
FABRITIO: On with her chain of pearl, her ruby bracelets,
Lay ready all her tricks and jiggambobs.
GUARDIANO: So must your daughter.
FABRITIO: I'll about it straight, sir.
Exit FABRITIO.
LIVIA: How he sweats in the foolish zeal of fatherhood
After six ounces an hour, and seems
To toil as much as if his cares were wise ones!
GUARDIANO: Y'have let his folly blood in the right vein, lady.
LIVIA: And here comes his sweet son-in-law that shall be.
They're both allied in wit before the marriage;
What will they be hereafter, when they are nearer?
Yet they can go no further than the fool:
There's the world's end in both of 'em.
Enter WARD *and* SORDIDO, *one with a shittlecock, the other a battledore.*
GUARDIANO: Now, young heir!
WARD: What's the next business after shittlecock, now?
GUARDIANO: Tomorrow you shall see the gentlewoman
Must be your wife.
WARD: There's ev'n another thing too
Must be kept up with a pair of battledores.
My wife! what can she do?
GUARDIANO: Nay, that's a question you should ask yourself, Ward,
When y'are alone together.
WARD: That's as I list!

62 *I warrant you for handsome*: I guarantee she will look beautiful 65 *use*: custom 68 *halter*: an anagram of lather and perhaps also referring to the fact that 'lather' is a variant form of 'leather' (from which halters are made) 70 *tricks and jiggambobs*: trinkets and knick-knacks 73 *After six ounces an hour*: i.e. he will sweat at a rate to lose six ounces in weight every hour 75 *let his folly blood in the right vein*: i.e. described his disease accurately (employing the terminology of blood-letting, which was supposed to relieve the symptom of over-emotional behaviour) 80 *world's end*: i.e. the limit to their attainments s.d. *shittlecock*: shuttlecock *battledore*: a small racquet 84 *thing*: i.e. the penis 88 *list*: please

A wife's to be ask'd anywhere, I hope;
I'll ask her in a congregation, if I have a mind to't, and so save a licence. [*To* SORDIDO.] My guardiner has no more wit than an herb-woman, that sells away all her sweet herbs and nosegays, and keeps a stinking breath for her own pottage.

SORDIDO: Let me be at the choosing of your beloved
If you desire a woman of good parts.

WARD: Thou shalt, sweet Sordido.

SORDIDO: I have a plaguey guess. Let me alone to see what she is; if I but look upon her, 'way, I know all the faults to a hair that you may refuse her for.

WARD: Dost thou? I prithee let me hear 'em, Sordido.

SORDIDO: Well, mark 'em then; I have 'em all in rhyme.
The wife your guardiner ought to tender
Should be pretty, straight and slender;
Her hair not short, her foot not long,
Her hand not huge, nor too too loud her tongue;
No pearl in eye, nor ruby in her nose,
No burn or cut, but what the catalogue shows.
She must have teeth, and that no black ones,
And kiss most sweet when she does smack once;
Her skin must be both white and plump,
Her body straight, not hopper-rump'd,
Or wriggle sideways like a crab;
She must be neither slut nor drab,
Nor go too splay-foot with her shoes,
To make her smock lick up the dews.
And two things more, which I forgot to tell ye:
She neither must have bump in back, nor belly.
These are the faults that will not make her pass.

WARD: And if I spy not these, I am a rank ass!

89 *ask'd*: proposed to (O reads 'ask') 90 *I'll . . . licence*: the Ward will have the wedding banns 'asked' in church and so save the cost of a special licence 92 *nosegays*: bunches of sweet-smelling flowers or herbs 93 *pottage*: either a thick soup or porridge. Probably the entire phrase alludes to the proverb 'Save your breath to cool your porridge' 97 *I have a plaguey guess*: i.e. I'm good at working things out 98 *'way*: this may mean either 'straightway' or 'anyway' or 'away!' 106 *pearl*: cataract *ruby*: pimple 107 venereal disease caused 'burning'; Sordido will allow one kind of 'cut', since 'cut' = cunt 109 *smack*: kiss 110 *plump*: many editors emend to 'plump'd' for the sake of a rhyme 111 *hopper-rump'd*: i.e. large buttocks which wobble, thus resembling the motion of a 'hopper' into which grain was poured prior to grinding 117 *bump in back, nor belly*: i.e. hunch-backed or pregnant

SORDIDO: Nay, more; by right, sir, you should see her naked,
For that's the ancient order.
WARD: See her naked?
That were good sport, i'faith. I'll have the books turn'd over,
And if I find her naked on record
She shall not have a rag on. But stay, stay,
How if she should desire to see me so too?
I were in sweet case then, such a foul skin!
SORDIDO: But y'have a clean shirt, and that makes amends, sir.
WARD: I will not see her naked for that trick, though.
Exit.
SORDIDO: Then take her with all faults with her clothes on!
And they may hide a number with a bum-roll.
Faith, choosing of a wench in a huge farthingale
Is like the buying of ware under a great penthouse:
What with the deceit of one
And the false light of th'other, mark my speeches,
He may have a diseas'd wench in's bed
And rotten stuff in's breeches.
Exit.
GUARDIANO: It may take handsomely.
LIVIA: I see small hindrance.
How now, so soon return'd?
Enter [Servant *with*] MOTHER.
GUARDIANO: She's come.
[*Exit* Servant.]
LIVIA: That's well.
Widow, come, come, I have a great quarrel to you,
Faith, I must chide you, that you must be sent for!
You make yourself so strange, never come at us;
And yet so near a neighbour, and so unkind!
Troth, y'are too blame, you cannot be more welcome
To any house in Florence, that I'll tell you.

121 *ancient order*: probably alluding to More's *Utopia* (1516). Before marriage both the male and female were exhibited naked to the prospective partner 123 *naked on record*: i.e. records of this custom 126 *case*: situation/garment 128 *for that trick*: i.e. in case she asks to see him naked 130 *bum-roll*: a cushion worn round the hips to support the skirt 131 *farthingale*: a hooped petticoat
132 *penthouse*: a building with a sloping roof (which would have been dark and therefore would have created difficulty in judging the quality of goods)
134 *false light*: i.e. the poor light of the shop with a penthouse 136 *rotten stuff*: rotting cloth/venereal disease 137 *take*: succeed 141 *so strange*: so like a stranger *come at us*: visit us

MOTHER: My thanks must needs acknowledge so much, madam.
LIVIA: How can you be so strange then? I sit here
Sometime whole days together without company,
When business draws this gentleman from home,
And should be happy in society
Which I so well affect as that of yours.
I know y'are alone too; why should not we,
Like two kind neighbours, then, supply the wants
Of one another, having tongue-discourse,
Experience in the world, and such kind helps
To laugh down time and meet age merrily?
MOTHER: Age, madam! You speak mirth! 'Tis at my door,
But a long journey from your ladyship yet.
LIVIA: My faith, I'm nine-and-thirty, ev'ry stroke, wench,
And 'tis a general observation
'Mongst knights' wives or widows, we accompt
Ourselves then old when young men's eyes leave looking at's.
'Tis a true rule amongst us, and ne'er fail'd yet
In any but in one, that I remember.
Indeed, she had a friend at nine-and-forty;
Marry, she paid well for him, and in th'end
He kept a quean or two with her own money,
That robb'd her of her plate and cut her throat.
MOTHER: She had her punishment in this world, madam,
And a fair warning to all other women
That they live chaste at fifty.
LIVIA: Ay or never, wench.
Come, now I have thy company I'll not part with't
Till after supper.
MOTHER: Yes, I must crave pardon, madam.
LIVIA: I swear you shall stay supper. We have no strangers, woman,
None but my sojourners and I; this gentleman
And the young heir, his ward; you know our company.
MOTHER: Some other time I will make bold with you, madam.
GUARDIANO: Nay, pray stay, widow.

149 *society*: company 153 *tongue-discourse*: i.e. conversational ability
155 *merrily*: O reads 'meerly', but this almost certainly represents an error in transcription from the copy, Middleton's undotted 'i' being easily confused with 'e'. Thus 'merilie' could be mis-read as 'merelie' and the spelling then standardized to 'meerly' 160 *accompt*: account 166 *quean*: prostitute
167 *plate*: i.e. gold or silver plate 174 *sojourners*: guests

LIVIA: Faith, she shall not go.
Do you think I'll be forsworn?
[*Prepares*] *table and chess.*
MOTHER: 'Tis a great while
Till supper-time; I'll take my leave then now, madam,
And come again i'th'evening, since your ladyship
Will have it so.
LIVIA: I'th'evening! By my troth, wench,
I'll keep you while I have you; you have great business, sure,
To sit alone at home; I wonder strangely
What pleasure you take in't! Were't to me now,
I should be ever at one neighbour's house
Or other all day long. Having no charge,
Or none to chide you if you go or stay,
Who may live merrier, ay or more at heart's ease?
Come, we'll to chess, or draughts; there are an hundred tricks
To drive out time till supper, never fear't, wench.
MOTHER: I'll but make one step home and return straight, madam.
LIVIA: Come, I'll not trust you; you use more excuses
To your kind friends than ever I knew any.
What business can you have, if you be sure
Y'have lock'd the doors? And that being all you have,
I know y'are careful on't. One afternoon
So much to spend here! Say I should entreat you now
To lie a night or two, or a week, with me,
Or leave your own house for a month together,
It were a kindness that long neighbourhood
And friendship might well hope to prevail in.
Would you deny such a request? I'faith,
Speak truth, and freely.
MOTHER: I were then uncivil, madam.
LIVIA: Go to then, set your men; we'll have whole nights
Of mirth together ere we be much older, wench.
MOTHER [*Aside.*]: As good now tell her, then, for she will know't;
I have always found her a most friendly lady.
LIVIA: Why, widow, where's your mind?
MOTHER: Troth, ev'n at home, madam.
To tell you truth, I left a gentlewoman

178 *forsworn*: i.e. because Livia had sworn the Widow would stay to supper
186 *charge*: responsibilities 195 *all you have*: i.e. all the responsibilities you have 204 *men*: chessmen

Ev'n sitting all alone, which is uncomfortable,
Especially to young bloods.

LIVIA: Another excuse!

MOTHER: No, as I hope for health, madam, that's a truth;
Please you to send and see.

LIVIA: What gentlewoman? Pish!

MOTHER: Wife to my son, indeed, but not known, madam,
To any but yourself.

LIVIA: Now I beshrew you,
Could you be so unkind to her and me
To come and not bring her? Faith, 'tis not friendly.

MOTHER: I fear'd to be too bold.

LIVIA: Too bold? O what's become
Of the true hearty love was wont to be
'Mongst neighbours in old time?

MOTHER: And she's a stranger, madam.

LIVIA: The more should be her welcome. When is courtesy
In better practice than when 'tis employ'd
In entertaining strangers? I could chide, i'faith.
Leave her behind, poor gentlewoman, alone too!
Make some amends and send for her betimes, go.

MOTHER: Please you command one of your servants, madam.

LIVIA: Within there!

Enter Servant.

SERVANT: Madam.

LIVIA: Attend the gentlewoman.

MOTHER: It must be carried wondrous privately
From my son's knowledge; he'll break out in storms else. –
Hark you, sir.

[*Speaks aside to* Servant, *who goes out.*]

LIVIA [*Aside.*]: Now comes in the heat of your part.

GUARDIANO [*Aside.*]: True, I know it, lady, and if I be out
May the Duke banish me from all employments,
Wanton or serious.

LIVIA: So, have you sent, widow?

MOTHER: Yes, madam, he's almost at home by this.

LIVIA: And, faith, let me entreat you that henceforward
All such unkind faults may be swept from friendship,

215 *beshrew*: blame 220 *stranger*: foreigner 225 *betimes*: immediately
228 *carried wondrous privately*: managed with total secrecy 230 *the heat*: the critical moment 231 *be out*: forget my lines (taking up the theatrical metaphor of 'part') 234 *by this*: by this time

Which does but dim the lustre. And think thus much,
It is a wrong to me, that have ability
To bid friends welcome, when you keep 'em from me;
You cannot set greater dishonour near me,
For bounty is the credit and the glory
Of those that have enough. I see y'are sorry,
And the good 'mends is made by't.

MOTHER: Here she's, madam.

Enter BIANCA, *and* Servant.

BIANCA [*Aside.*]: I wonder how she comes to send for me now?

[*Exit* Servant.]

LIVIA: Gentlewoman, y'are most welcome, trust me y'are,
As courtesy can make one, or respect
Due to the presence of you.

BIANCA: I give you thanks, lady.

LIVIA: I heard you were alone, and't had appear'd
An ill condition in me, though I knew you not
Nor ever saw you (yet humanity
Thinks ev'ry case her own), to have kept your company
Here from you and left you all solitary:
I rather ventur'd upon boldness then
As the least fault, and wish'd your presence here:
A thing most happily motion'd of that gentleman,
Whom I request you, for his care and pity,
To honour and reward with your acquaintance;
A gentleman that ladies' rights stands for,
That's his profession.

BIANCA: 'Tis a noble one,
And honours my acquaintance.

GUARDIANO: All my intentions
Are servants to such mistresses.

BIANCA: 'Tis your modesty,
It seems, that makes your deserts speak so low, sir.

LIVIA: Come, widow. [*To* BIANCA.] Look you lady, here's our business;
Are we not well employ'd, think you? An old quarrel
Between us, that will never be at an end.

243 *'mends*: amends 247 *the presence of you*: your noble appearance 249 *An ill condition*: bad manners 250 *humanity*: a humane sensibility 251 *your company*: i.e. the Widow 255 *motion'd*: proposed by 259 *profession*: boast (but probably punning on 'profession' = livelihood since Guardiano is a professional guardian who manages the 'rights' of his wards) 262 *deserts*: good qualities 264 *An old quarrel*: i.e. between the black and white chess pieces (the symbolic significance of the colours is important throughout the chess scene)

BIANCA: No, and methinks there's men enough to part you, lady.
LIVIA: Ho! But they set us on, let us come off
As well as we can, poor souls, men care no farther.
I pray sit down, forsooth, if you have the patience
To look upon two weak and tedious gamesters.
GUARDIANO: Faith, madam, set these by till evening.
You'll have enough on't then; the gentlewoman,
Being a stranger, would take more delight
To see your rooms and pictures.
LIVIA: Marry, good sir,
And well rememb'red! I beseech you show 'em her;
That will beguile time well; pray heartily do, sir,
I'll do as much for you; here, take these keys,
Show her the Monument too, and that's a thing
Everyone sees not; you can witness that, widow.
MOTHER: And that's worth sight indeed, madam.
BIANCA: Kind lady,
I fear I came to be a trouble to you.
LIVIA: O nothing less, forsooth.
BIANCA: And to this courteous gentleman,
That wears a kindness in his breast so noble
And bounteous to the welcome of a stranger.
GUARDIANO: If you but give acceptance to my service,
You do the greatest grace and honour to me
That courtesy can merit.
BIANCA: I were too blame else,
And out of fashion much. I pray you lead, sir.
LIVIA: After a game or two w'are for you, gentlefolks.
GUARDIANO: We wish no better seconds in society
Than your discourses, madam, and your partner's there.
MOTHER: I thank your praise. I listen'd to you, sir,
Though when you spoke there came a paltry rook
Full in my way and chokes up all my game.
Exit GUARDIANO *and* BIANCA.
LIVIA: Alas, poor widow, I shall be too hard for thee.
MOTHER: Y'are cunning at the game, I'll be sworn, madam.

266 *No*: i.e. no, the quarrel never will end *there's men enough to part you*: i.e. the chessmen separate the two protagonists 267 *set us on*: stir up antagonisms between us/sexually excite us *come off*: get out of the situation/achieve orgasm 278 *Monument*: probably here a statue 291 *seconds*: assistants 297 *cunning at the game*: skilful in chess (but also unconsciously alluding to Livia's role as a procuress)

LIVIA: It will be found so, ere I give you over.
She that can place her man well –
MOTHER: As you do, madam.
LIVIA: As I shall, wench, can never lose her game.
Nay, nay, the black king's mine.
MOTHER: Cry you mercy, madam.
LIVIA: And this my queen.
MOTHER: I see't, now.
LIVIA: Here's a duke
Will strike a sure stroke for the game anon;
Your pawn cannot come back to relieve itself.
MOTHER: I know that, madam.
LIVIA: You play well the whilst;
How she belies her skill! I hold two ducats
I give you check and mate to your white king,
Simplicity itself, your saintish king there.
MOTHER: Well, ere now, lady,
I have seen the fall of subtlety. Jest on.
LIVIA: Ay, but simplicity receives two for one.
MOTHER: What remedy but patience!
Enter above GUARDIANO *and* BIANCA.
BIANCA: Trust me, sir,
Mine eye nev'r met with fairer ornaments.
GUARDIANO: Nay, livelier, I'm persuaded, neither Florence
Nor Venice can produce.
BIANCA: Sir, my opinion
Takes your part highly.
GUARDIANO: There's a better piece
Yet than all these.
[*Enter*] DUKE *above*.
BIANCA: Not possible, sir!

301 *the black king's mine*: the Widow's mistake in picking up the wrong king allows Livia to declare her true allegiance 302 *a duke*: in the 17th century the rook or castle was also known as a 'duke'. Livia's employment of this term highlights the ironic relationship between the action on the chess board and that being played out on the upper stage 303 This line continues the ironic sexual innuendo *anon*: soon 304 *pawn . . . itself*: the pawn is the only chess piece which cannot retreat. Bianca is presumably a pawn in the hands of the Duke 306 *she belies her skill*: i.e. the Widow disguises her skill (but probably also ironically alluding to the fact that Livia is deceiving the Widow through the chess game) *hold*: bet 311 *two*: perhaps this means two *blows* (loses two pieces as a result of an exchange?) but the meaning is obscure 314 *livelier*: more lifelike 315 *Venice*: Bianca was born in Venice

GUARDIANO: Believe it,
You'll say so when you see't. Turn but your eye now,
Y'are upon't presently.
Exit.
BIANCA: O sir!
DUKE: He's gone, beauty!
Pish, look not after him. He's but a vapour
That when the sun appears is seen no more.
BIANCA: O treachery to honour!
DUKE: Prithee tremble not,
I feel thy breast shake like a turtle panting
Under a loving hand that makes much on't.
Why art so fearful? As I'm friend to brightness,
There's nothing but respect and honour near thee.
You know me, you have seen me; here's a heart
Can witness I have seen thee.
BIANCA: The more's my danger.
DUKE: The more's thy happiness. Pish, strive not, sweet!
This strength were excellent employ'd in love, now,
But here 'tis spent amiss. Strive not to seek
Thy liberty and keep me still in prison.
I'faith, you shall not out till I'm releas'd now;
We'll be both freed together, or stay still by't;
So is captivity pleasant.
BIANCA: O my lord!
DUKE: I am not here in vain; have but the leisure
To think on that, and thou'lt be soon resolv'd.
The lifting of thy voice is but like one
That does exalt his enemy who, proving high,
Lays all the plots to confound him that rais'd him.
Take warning, I beseech thee; thou seem'st to me
A creature so compos'd of gentleness
And delicate meekness, such as bless the faces
Of figures that are drawn for goddesses
And makes Art proud to look upon her work;
I should be sorry the least force should lay
An unkind touch upon thee.
BIANCA: O my extremity!
My lord, what seek you?

319 *presently*: immediately 323 *turtle*: turtle-dove 325 *brightness*: beauty
334 *by't*: i.e. imprisoned 339 *exalt*: raise up in rank or power/'lift up' the voice in song/extol/sexually stimulate

DUKE: Love.
BIANCA: 'Tis gone already,
I have a husband.
DUKE: That's a single comfort;
Take a friend to him.
BIANCA: That's a double mischief,
Or else there's no religion.
DUKE: Do not tremble
At fears of thine own making.
BIANCA: Nor, great Lord,
Make me not bold with death and deeds of ruin
Because they fear not you; me they must fright;
Then am I best in health. Should thunder speak
And none regard it, it had lost the name
And were as good be still. I'm not like those
That take their soundest sleeps in greatest tempests;
Then wake I most, the weather fearfullest,
And call for strength to virtue.
DUKE: Sure I think
Thou know'st the way to please me. I affect
A passionate pleading 'bove an easy yielding,
But never pitied any; they deserve none
That will not pity me. I can command:
Think upon that. Yet if thou truly knewest
The infinite pleasure my affection takes
In gentle, fair entreatings, when love's businesses
Are carried courteously 'twixt heart and heart,
You'd make more haste to please me.
BIANCA: Why should you seek, sir,
To take away that you can never give?
DUKE: But I give better in exchange: wealth, honour.
She that is fortunate in a duke's favour
Lights on a tree that bears all women's wishes;
If your own mother saw you pluck fruit there,
She would commend your wit and praise the time
Of your nativity. Take hold of glory.
Do not I know y'have cast away your life
Upon necessities, means merely doubtful
To keep you in indifferent health and fashion

350 *friend to him*: lover in addition 353 *Make me not bold with*: do not make me take liberties with *death*: i.e. spiritual death 354 *fear*: frighten 355 *health*: i.e. spiritual health 361 *affect*: prefer 373 *Lights*: alights 378 *necessities*: i.e. Leantio (who can only provide bare necessities) *merely*: extremely

(A thing I heard too lately and soon pitied).
And can you be so much your beauty's enemy
To kiss away a month or two in wedlock,
And weep whole years in wants for ever after?
Come play the wise wench, and provide for ever;
Let storms come when they list, they find thee shelter'd.
Should any doubt arise let nothing trouble thee,
Put trust in our love for the managing
Of all to thy heart's peace. We'll walk together
And show a thankful joy for both our fortunes.
Exit [DUKE *and* BIANCA] *above*.

LIVIA: Did not I say my duke would fetch you over, widow?
MOTHER: I think you spoke in earnest when you said it, madam.
LIVIA: And my black king makes all the haste he can, too.
MOTHER: Well, madam, we may meet with him in time yet.
LIVIA: I have given thee blind mate twice.
MOTHER: You may see, madam,
My eyes begin to fail.
LIVIA: I'll swear they do, wench.
Enter GUARDIANO.

GUARDIANO [*Aside*.]: I can but smile as often as I think on't,
How prettily the poor fool was beguil'd,
How unexpectedly; it's a witty age,
Never were finer snares for women's honesties
Than are devis'd in these days; no spider's web
Made of a daintier thread than are now practis'd
To catch love's flesh-fly by the silver wing.
Yet to prepare her stomach by degrees
To Cupid's feast, because I saw 'twas queasy,
I show'd her naked pictures by the way:
A bit to stay the appetite. Well, Advancement!
I venture hard to find thee; if thou com'st
With a greater title set upon thy crest,

384 *wise*: O reads 'wife' 385 *list*: choose 390 *fetch you over*: get the better of you 394 *blind mate*: a technical term indicating that a player has placed the opponent in checkmate but not noticed this and failed to claim the win. Here the sense is ironic: Livia did notice the positions but chose to prolong the game as a cover for the sexual intrigue going on above. It is the Widow who has been 'blind', as the following conversation makes clear 398 *witty*: skilful in contriving evil 399 *honesties*: chastities 402 *flesh-fly*: blow-fly or blue-bottle 403 *stomach*: sexual appetite 406 *A bit to stay the appetite*: since this image seems to be describing the reining in of the appetite, Guardiano must also be punning on another meaning of 'stay' = strengthen

I'll take that first cross patiently, and wait
Until some other comes greater than that.
I'll endure all.

LIVIA: The game's ev'n at the best now; you may see, widow,
How all things draw to an end.

MOTHER: Ev'n so do I, madam.

LIVIA: I pray take some of your neighbours along with you.

MOTHER: They must be those are almost twice your years, then,
If they be chose fit matches for my time, madam.

LIVIA: Has not my duke bestirr'd himself?

MOTHER: Yes, faith, madam,
H'as done me all the mischief in this game.

LIVIA: H'as show'd himself in's kind.

MOTHER: In's kind, call you it?
I may swear that.

LIVIA: Yes, faith, and keep your oath.

GUARDIANO [*Aside.*]: Hark, list, there's somebody coming down; 'tis she.

Enter BIANCA.

BIANCA [*Aside.*]: Now bless me from a blasting! I saw that now
Fearful for any woman's eye to look on.
Infectious mists and mildews hang at's eyes,
The weather of a doomsday dwells upon him.
Yet since mine honour's leprous, why should I
Preserve that fair that caus'd the leprosy?
Come, poison all at once! [*To him.*] Thou in whose baseness
The bane of virtue broods, I'm bound in soul
Eternally to curse thy smooth-brow'd treachery
That wore the fair veil of a friendly welcome,
And I a stranger; think upon't, 'tis worth it.
Murders pil'd up upon a guilty spirit
At his last breath will not lie heavier
Than this betraying act upon thy conscience.

409 *take . . . cross*: to take the cross = to accept the sign or badge of a cross in ratification of a vow, to engage on a crusade (OED cross *sb.* B 4. c). Guardiano will accept the first title as a mark of allegiance to Ambition (Advancement) rather than Christ, and wait patiently for further honours 413 *Ev'n so do I*: the Mother applies Livia's remark concerning the chess game (and seduction) to her own approaching death 414 *neighbours*: i.e. Livia herself 419 *kind*: true nature 421 *list*: listen 422 *bless me*: save me *blasting*: withering up/scandal 424 *at's*: at his 426 *why*: O reads 'who' 427 *that fair*: i.e. her beauty 429 *bane*: poison *broods*: breeds, hatches 430 *smooth-brow'd*: hypocritically calm

Beware of off'ring the first-fruits to sin:
His weight is deadly who commits with strumpets
After they have been abas'd and made for use;
If they offend to th'death, as wise men know,
How much more they, then, that first make 'em so?
I give thee that to feed on. I'm made bold now,
I thank thy treachery; sin and I'm acquainted,
No couple greater; and I'm like that great one
Who, making politic use of a base villain,
He likes the treason well, but hates the traitor;
So I hate thee, slave.

GUARDIANO: Well, so the Duke love me,
I fare not much amiss then; two great feasts
Do seldom come together in one day;
We must not look for 'em.

BIANCA: What, at it still, mother?

MOTHER: You see we sit by't. Are you so soon return'd?

LIVIA [*Aside.*]: So lively and so cheerful? A good sign that.

MOTHER: You have not seen all since, sure?

BIANCA: That have I, mother,
The Monument and all. I'm so beholding
To this kind, honest, courteous gentleman,
(You'd little think it, mother) show'd me all,
Had me from place to place, so fashionably;
The kindness of some people, how't exceeds!
Faith, I have seen that I little thought to see
I'th'morning when I rose.

MOTHER: Nay, so I told you
Before you saw't, it would prove worth your sight.
I give you great thanks for my daughter, sir,
And all your kindness towards her.

GUARDIANO: O good widow!
Much good may't do her – [*Aside.*] forty weeks hence, i'faith.
Enter Servant.

LIVIA: Now, sir?

SERVANT: May't please you, madam, to walk in?
Supper's upon the table.

436 *first-fruits*: normally an offering to God from the first harvest gathered in a season 437–8 i.e. he who fornicates with prostitutes commits a mortal sin even though they have already been corrupted 440 *more*: more guilty are
444 *politic*: expedient 445 proverbial 463 *may't*: O reads 'may' *forty weeks hence*: i.e. when she would expect to give birth if she were pregnant by the Duke

LIVIA: Yes, we come;
Will't please you gentlewoman?
BIANCA: Thanks, virtuous lady,
[*Aside to* LIVIA.] Y'are a damn'd bawd. – I'll follow you forsooth.
Pray take my mother in. [*Aside.*] An old ass go with you –
This gentleman and I vow not to part.
LIVIA: Then get you both before.
BIANCA [*Aside.*]: There lies his art.
LIVIA: Widow, I'll follow you.
Exeunt [*all except* LIVIA].
Is't so, 'damn'd bawd'!
Are you so bitter? 'Tis but want of use;
Her tender modesty is sea-sick a little,
Being not accustom'd to the breaking billow
Of woman's wavering faith, blown with temptations.
'Tis but a qualm of honour, 'twill away;
A little bitter for the time, but lasts not.
Sin tastes at the first draught like wormwood water,
But, drunk again, 'tis nectar ever after.
Exit.

467 *bawd*; procuress, brothel-keeper 468 *An old ass*: insulting the Mother for her stupidity 470 *There lies his art*: i.e. Guardiano is skilful in 'getting before' in the sense of preparing the ground for seductions 478 *wormwood water*: a drink flavoured with the bitter taste of the herb wormwood

ACT THREE

SCENE I

Enter MOTHER.

MOTHER: I would my son would either keep at home
Or I were in my grave!
She was but one day abroad, but ever since
She's grown so cutted, there's no speaking to her.
Whether the sight of great cheer at my lady's,
And such mean fare at home, work discontent in her,
I know not; but I'm sure she's strangely alter'd.
I'll nev'r keep daughter-in-law i'th'house with me
Again, if I had an hundred. When read I of any
That agreed long together, but she and her mother
Fell out in the first quarter? (Nay, sometime
A grudging of a scolding the first week, by'r Lady!)
So takes the new disease, methinks, in my house.
I'm weary of my part, there's nothing likes her;
I know not how to please her here a'late;
And here she comes.

Enter BIANCA.

BIANCA: This is the strangest house
For all defects, as ever gentlewoman
Made shift withal, to pass away her love in!
Why is there not a cushion-cloth of drawn work,
Or some fair cut-work pinn'd up in my bed-chamber,
A silver-and-gilt casting-bottle hung by't?
Nay, since I am content to be so kind to you
To spare you for a silver basin and ewer,
Which one of my fashion looks for of duty;
She's never offer'd under, where she sleeps –

3 *abroad*: away from home 4 *cutted*: curt 12 *A grudging of a scolding*: a slight scolding (a grudging of an illness was the first signs of it) 13 *the new disease*: i.e. the insubordination of the young. The phrase 'the new disease' was used around the turn of the century to describe certain mysterious fevers 14 *likes*: pleases 18 *Made shift withal*: put up with 19 *cushion-cloth of drawn work*: decorated cushion cover 20 *cut-work*: open-work embroidery 21 *casting-bottle*: bottle for sprinkling perfumed waters 23 *ewer*: a jug for carrying water 25 *under*: less

MOTHER [*Aside.*]: She talks of things here my whole state's not worth.
BIANCA: Never a green silk quilt is there i'th'house, mother,
To cast upon my bed?
MOTHER: No, by troth, is there,
Nor orange-tawny neither!
BIANCA: Here's a house
For a young gentlewoman to be got with child in!
MOTHER: Yes, simple though you make it, there has been three
Got in a year in't, since you move me to't;
And all as sweet-fac'd children and as lovely
As you'll be mother of; I will not spare you.
What, cannot children be begot, think you,
Without gilt casting-bottles? Yes, and as sweet ones.
The miller's daughter brings forth as white boys
As she that bathes herself with milk and bean-flower.
'Tis an old saying, 'One may keep good cheer
In a mean house'. So may true love affect
After the rate of princes, in a cottage.
BIANCA: Troth, you speak wondrous well for your old house here;
'Twill shortly fall down at your feet to thank you,
Or stoop when you go to bed, like a good child
To ask you blessing. Must I live in want,
Because my fortune match'd me with your son?
Wives do not give away themselves to husbands
To the end to be quite cast away; they look
To be the better us'd and tender'd rather,
Highlier respected, and maintain'd the richer;
They're well rewarded else for the free gift
Of their whole life to a husband. I ask less now
Than what I had at home when I was a maid
And at my father's house; kept short of that
Which a wife knows she must have, nay, and will –
Will, mother, if she be not a fool born;
And report went of me that I could wrangle
For what I wanted when I was two hours old,
And by the copy, this land still I hold.
You hear me, mother.
Exit.

26 *state*: estate 29 *orange-tawny*: a colour associated with the Court
32 *move me to't*: either 'provoke me' or 'mention it' 37 *white boys*: darlings/boys with white complexions (because of the flour) 49 *tender'd*: cherished
59 *copy*: copyhold – a form of feudal land tenure. Bianca claims the 'land' (her freedom to 'wrangle') by the right conferred by her childhood behaviour

MOTHER: Ay, too plain, methinks;
And were I somewhat deafer when you spake
'Twere nev'r a whit the worse for my quietness.
'Tis the most sudden'st, strangest alteration,
And the most subtlest that ev'r wit at threescore
Was puzzled to find out. I know no cause for't; but
She's no more like the gentlewoman at first
Than I am like her that nev'r lay with man yet
(And she's a very young thing, where'er she be).
When she first lighted here, I told her then
How mean she should find all things; she was pleas'd, forsooth,
None better. I laid open all defects to her,
She was contented still. But the Devil's in her,
Nothing contents her now. Tonight my son
Promis'd to be at home; would he were come once,
For I'm weary of my charge, and life too.
She'd be serv'd all in silver by her good will,
By night and day; she hates the name of pewterer,
More than sick men the noise, or diseas'd bones
That quake at fall o'th'hammer, seeming to have
A fellow-feeling with't at every blow.
What course shall I think on? She frets me so.
Exit.
Enter LEANTIO.
LEANTIO: How near am I now to a happiness
That earth exceeds not! Not another like it.
The treasures of the deep are not so precious
As are the conceal'd comforts of a man
Lock'd up in woman's love. I scent the air
Of blessings when I come but near the house,
What a delicious breath marriage sends forth!
The violet-bed's not sweeter. Honest Wedlock
Is like a banqueting-house built in a garden,
On which the spring's chaste flowers take delight
To cast their modest odours; when base Lust,
With all her powders, paintings and best pride,
Is but a fair house built by a ditch side.
When I behold a glorious dangerous strumpet,
Sparkling in beauty and destruction too,

62 *quietness*: tranquillity 64 *subtlest*: least comprehensible 69 *lighted*: arrived 74 *once*: at once 77 *pewterer*: a manufacturer of inferior pewter products (alluding to the noise of the pewterer's hammer, which is less hateful than his name) 93 *pride*: splendour

Both at a twinkling, I do liken straight
Her beautifi'd body to a goodly temple
That's built on vaults where carcasses lie rotting;
And so by little and little I shrink back again,
And quench desire with a cool meditation;
And I'm as well, methinks. Now for a welcome
Able to draw men's envies upon man:
A kiss now that will hang upon my lip
As sweet as morning dew upon a rose,
And full as long. After a five days' fast
She'll be so greedy now and cling about me,
I take care how I shall be rid of her;
And here't begins.

Enter BIANCA *and* MOTHER.

BIANCA: O sir, y'are welcome home.
MOTHER: O is he come? I am glad on't.
LEANTIO [*Aside.*]: Is that all?
Why this? As dreadful now as sudden death
To some rich man, that flatters all his sins
With promise of repentance when he's old,
And dies in the midway before he comes to't. –
Sure, y'are not well, Bianca! How dost, prithee?
BIANCA: I have been better than I am at this time.
LEANTIO: Alas, I thought so.
BIANCA: Nay, I have been worse too
Than now you see me, sir.
LEANTIO: I'm glad thou mend'st yet,
I feel my heart mend too. How came it to thee?
Has any thing dislik'd thee in my absence?
BIANCA: No, certain, I have had the best content
That Florence can afford.
LEANTIO: Thou makest the best on't.
Speak, mother, what's the cause? You must needs know.
MOTHER: Troth, I know none, son, let her speak herself;
[*Aside.*] Unless it be the same gave Lucifer
A tumbling cast: that's pride.
BIANCA: Methinks this house stands nothing to my mind;

100 *shrink back*: withdraw my thought/lose my erection 102 *I'm as well*: either 'I'm wise to do so' or 'I'm myself again' (well again) 103 *man*: a man 108 *take care*: worry 111 *this? As*: i.e. this lack of affection? It is as 118 *yet*: still 120 *dislik'd*: displeased 121 *best content*: alluding to the Duke 126 *tumbling cast*: a throw which sent him tumbling 127 *stands nothing to my mind*: has no attractions in its setting for me

I'd have some pleasant lodging i'th'high street, sir,
Or if 'twere near the Court, sir, that were much better;
'Tis a sweet recreation for a gentlewoman
To stand in a bay-window and see gallants.

LEANTIO: Now I have another temper, a mere stranger
To that of yours, it seems: I should delight
To see none but yourself.

BIANCA: I praise not that;
Too fond is as unseemly as too churlish;
I would not have a husband of that proneness
To kiss me before company for a world.
Beside, 'tis tedious to see one thing still, sir,
Be it the best that ever heart affected;
Nay, were't yourself whose love had power, you know,
To bring me from my friends, I would not stand thus
And gaze upon you always. Troth, I could not, sir.
As good be blind and have no use of sight
As look on one thing still. What's the eye's treasure
But change of objects? You are learned, sir,
And know I speak not ill. 'Tis full as virtuous
For woman's eye to look on several men
As for her heart, sir, to be fix'd on one.

LEANTIO: Now thou com'st home to me; a kiss for that word.

BIANCA: No matter for a kiss, sir, let it pass;
'Tis but a toy, we'll not so much as mind it;
Let's talk of other business and forget it.
What news now of the pirates; any stirring?
Prithee discourse a little.

MOTHER [*Aside.*] I am glad he's here yet
To see her tricks himself; I had lied monstrously
If I had told 'em first.

LEANTIO: Speak, what's the humour, sweet,
You make your lip so strange? This was not wont.

BIANCA: Is there no kindness betwixt man and wife
Unless they make a pigeon-house of friendship

132 *temper*: attitude *mere*: total 135 *fond*: foolishly infatuated
136 *proneness*: disposition/sexual eagerness 144 *still*: always 150 *matter*: occasion 151 *toy*: trifle *mind it*: pay it any attention 153 *pirates*: the Duke of Florence guarded the coast against African pirates 154 *yet*: now 155 *I had lied*: he would have believed that I was lying 156 *humour*: mood 157 *wont*: customary 159 *pigeon-house*: dove-cote. The affection between turtle-doves was proverbial

And be still billing; 'tis the idlest fondness
That ever was invented, and 'tis pity
It's grown a fashion for poor gentlewomen;
There's many a disease kiss'd in a year by't,
And a French cur'sey made to't. Alas, sir,
Think of the world, how we shall live; grow serious;
We have been married a whole fortnight now.

LEANTIO: How? A whole fortnight! Why, is that so long?

BIANCA: 'Tis time to leave off dalliance; 'tis a doctrine
Of your own teaching, if you be remember'd,
And I was bound to obey it.

MOTHER [*Aside.*]: Here's one fits him! –
This was well catch'd, i'faith, son – like a fellow
That rids another country of a plague
And brings it home with him to his own house.

Knock within.

Who knocks?

LEANTIO: Who's there now? Withdraw you, Bianca,
Thou art a gem no stranger's eye must see,
Howev'r thou please now to look dull on me.

Exit [BIANCA].

Enter Messenger.

Y'are welcome, sir; to whom your business, pray?

MESSENGER: To one I see not here now.

LEANTIO: Who should that be, sir?

MESSENGER: A young gentlewoman I was sent to.

LEANTIO: A young gentlewoman?

MESSENGER: Ay, sir, about sixteen. Why look you wildly, sir?

LEANTIO: At your strange error. Y'have mistook the house, sir.
There's none such here, I assure you.

MESSENGER: I assure you too,
The man that sent me cannot be mistook.

LEANTIO: Why, who is't sent you, sir?

MESSENGER: The Duke.

LEANTIO: The Duke?

MESSENGER: Yes, he entreats her company at a banquet
At Lady Livia's house.

164 *French cur'sey*: syphilis (the French disease) follows from sexual 'stooping' and leads to an affliction of stooping too 170 *fits him*: punishes him appropriately 171 *catch'd*: incurred, contracted (as in 'to catch a cold') 176 *thou please now*: you were pleased just now

LEANTIO: Troth shall I tell you, sir,
It is the most erroneous business
That ere your honest pains was abus'd with.
I pray forgive me, if I smile a little
(I cannot choose, i'faith, sir) at an error
So comical as this (I mean no harm though).
His grace has been most wondrous ill inform'd:
Pray so return it, sir. What should her name be?
MESSENGER: That I shall tell you straight too: Bianca Capella.
LEANTIO: How, sir, Bianca? What do you call th'other?
MESSENGER: Capella, sir. It seems you know no such then?
LEANTIO: Who should this be? I never heard o'th'name.
MESSENGER: Then 'tis a sure mistake.
LEANTIO: What if you enquir'd
In the next street, sir? I saw gallants there
In the new houses that are built of late.
Ten to one, there you find her.
MESSENGER: Nay, no matter,
I will return the mistake and seek no further.
LEANTIO: Use your own will and pleasure, sir, y'are welcome.
Exit Messenger.
What shall I think of first? Come forth, Bianca,
Thou art betray'd, I fear me.
Enter BIANCA.
BIANCA: Betray'd? How, sir?
LEANTIO: The Duke knows thee.
BIANCA: Knows me! How know you that, sir?
LEANTIO: H'as got thy name.
BIANCA [*Aside.*]: Ay, and my good name too,
That's worse o'th'twain.
LEANTIO: How comes this work about?
BIANCA: How should the Duke know me? Can you guess, mother?
MOTHER: Not I with all my wits; sure, we kept house close.
LEANTIO: Kept close! Not all the locks in Italy
Can keep you women so. You have been gadding.
And ventur'd out at twilight to th'court-green yonder
And met the gallant bowlers coming home;
Without your masks too, both of you, I'll be hang'd else!

193 *return it*: i.e. return my message 206 *Knows*: is acquainted with/has had sex with 210 *house close*: i.e. we confined ourselves to the house 214 *bowlers*: bowls was a popular Court game; presumably it was played on the 'court-green' 215 *Without your masks*: a sign of immodesty since Italian women were expected to shield their faces from public gaze with veils or masks when out of doors

Thou hast been seen, Bianca, by some stranger,
Never excuse it.
BIANCA: I'll not seek the way, sir.
Do you think y'have married me to mew me up
Not to be seen? What would you make of me?
LEANTIO: A good wife, nothing else.
BIANCA: Why, so are some
That are seen ev'ry day, else the Devil take 'em.
LEANTIO: No more then, I believe all virtuous in thee
Without an argument; 'twas but thy hard chance
To be seen somewhere, there lies all the mischief.
But I have devis'd a riddance.
MOTHER: Now I can tell you, son,
The time and place.
LEANTIO: When, where?
MOTHER: What wits have I?
When you last took your leave, if you remember,
You left us both at window.
LEANTIO: Right, I know that.
MOTHER: And not the third part of an hour after,
The Duke pass'd by in a great solemnity
To St Mark's temple, and to my apprehension
He look'd up twice to th'window.
LEANTIO: O there quick'ned
The mischief of this hour!
BIANCA [*Aside.*]: If you call't mischief,
It is a thing I fear I am conceiv'd with.
LEANTIO: Look'd he up twice, and could you take no warning!
MOTHER: Why, once may do as much harm, son, as a thousand.
Do not you know one spark has fir'd an house,
As well as a whole furnace?
LEANTIO: My heart flames for't!
Yet let's be wise and keep all smother'd closely;
I have bethought a means. Is the door fast?
MOTHER: I lock'd it myself after him.
LEANTIO: You know, mother,
At the end of the dark parlour there's a place
So artificially contriv'd for a conveyance,
No search could ever find it. When my father

218 *mew*: coop, shut 231 *apprehension*: knowledge 232 *quick'ned*: was born
243 *artificially*: ingeniously *conveyance*: secret passage

Kept in for manslaughter, it was his sanctuary;
There will I lock my life's best treasure up.
Bianca!

BIANCA: Would you keep me closer yet?
Have you the conscience? Y'are best ev'n choke me up, sir!
You make me fearful of your health and wits,
You cleave to such wild courses. What's the matter?

LEANTIO: Why, are you so insensible of your danger
To ask that now? The Duke himself has sent for you
To Lady Livia's, to a banquet, forsooth.

BIANCA: Now I beshrew you heartily, has he so!
And you the man would never yet vouchsafe
To tell me on't till now! You show your loyalty
And honesty at once; and so farewell, sir.

LEANTIO: Bianca, whither now?

BIANCA: Why, to the Duke, sir.
You say he sent for me.

LEANTIO: But thou dost not mean
To go, I hope.

BIANCA: No? I shall prove unmannerly,
Rude and uncivil, mad – and imitate you.
Come, mother, come, follow his humour no longer.
We shall be all executed for treason shortly.

MOTHER: Not I, i'faith. I'll first obey the Duke
And taste of a good banquet; I'm of thy mind.
I'll step but up and fetch two handkerchiefs
To pocket up some sweetmeats, and o'ertake thee.
Exit.

BIANCA [*Aside.*]: Why, here's an old wench would trot into a bawd now
For some dry sucket or a colt in marchpane.
Exit.

LEANTIO: O thou the ripe time of man's misery, Wedlock,
When all his thoughts, like over-laden trees,
Crack with the fruits they bear, in cares, in jealousies!
O that's a fruit that ripens hastily
After 'tis knit to marriage. It begins
As soon as the sun shines upon the bride

245 *Kept in for manslaughter*: i.e. hid at home when charged with manslaughter
248 *choke me up*: suffocate me/totally imprison 254 *beshrew*: curse
267 *sweetmeats*: confectionery, sugared pastries, fruits, nuts, etc. 268 *trot into*: readily become 269 *dry sucket*: candied fruit *colt in marchpane*: marzipan sweet shaped into the figure of a young horse

A little to show colour. Blessed Powers!
Whence comes this alteration? The distractions,
The fears and doubts it brings are numberless,
And yet the cause I know not. What a peace
Has he that never marries! If he knew
The benefit he enjoy'd, or had the fortune
To come and speak with me, he should know then
The infinite wealth he had, and discern rightly
The greatness of his treasure by my loss.
Nay, what a quietness has he 'bove mine
That wears his youth out in a strumpet's arms
And never spends more care upon a woman
Than at the time of lust; but walks away,
And if he find her dead at his return
His pity is soon done: he breaks a sigh
In many parts and gives her but a piece on't!
But all the fears, shames, jealousies, costs and troubles,
And still renew'd cares of a marriage bed
Live in the issue when the wife is dead.
Enter Messenger.

MESSENGER: A good perfection to your thoughts.

LEANTIO: The news, sir?

MESSENGER: Though you were pleas'd of late to pin an error on me,
You must not shift another in your stead too:
The Duke has sent me for you.

LEANTIO: How, for me, sir?
[*Aside.*] I see then 'tis my theft; w'are both betray'd.
Well, I'm not the first has stol'n away a maid;
My countrymen have us'd it. – I'll along with you, sir.
Exeunt.

SCENE 2

A banquet prepared. Enter GUARDIANO *and* WARD.

GUARDIANO: Take you especial note of such a gentlewoman,
She's here on purpose. I have invited her,

276 *to show colour*: i.e. to ripen (alluding to the 'fruit' of jealousy – and perhaps to the women walking out of doors without veils or masks) 287 *spends*: punning on 'spends' = ejaculates 294 *issue*: children 295 *perfection*: conclusion 297 *shift another in your stead*: substitute another on your own account 299 *my theft*: i.e. stealing Bianca away from her parents 301 *us'd*: practised

Her father and her uncle, to this banquet.
Mark her behaviour well, it does concern you;
And what her good parts are, as far as time
And place can modestly require a knowledge of,
Shall be laid open to your understanding.
You know I'm both your guardian and your uncle;
My care of you is double, ward and nephew,
And I'll express it here.

WARD: Faith, I should know her
Now, by her mark, among a thousand women:
A little, pretty, deft and tidy thing, you say?

GUARDIANO: Right.

WARD: With a lusty sprouting sprig in her hair?

GUARDIANO: Thou goest the right way still. Take one mark more:
Thou shalt nev'r find her hand out of her uncle's,
Or else his out of hers, if she be near him.
The love of kin'red never yet stuck closer
Than theirs to one another; he that weds her
Marries her uncle's heart too.

Cornets.

WARD: Say you so, sir;
Then I'll be ask'd i'th'church to both of them.

GUARDIANO: Fall back, here comes the Duke.

WARD: He brings a gentlewoman,
I should fall forward rather.

Enter DUKE, BIANCA, FABRITIO, HIPPOLITO, LIVIA, MOTHER, ISABELLA, *and* Attendants.

DUKE: Come, Bianca,
Of purpose sent into the world to show
Perfection once in woman; I'll believe
Henceforward they have ev'ry one a soul too,
'Gainst all the uncourteous opinions
That man's uncivil rudeness ever held of 'em.
Glory of Florence, light into mine arms!

Enter LEANTIO.

BIANCA: Yon comes a grudging man will chide you, sir;
The storm is now in's heart, and would get nearer
And fall here if it durst; it pours down yonder.

10 *express*: demonstrate 11 *mark*: distinctive features 12 *deft*: petite 13 *lusty sprouting sprig*: probably a large decorative spray of flowers 20 *ask'd i'th'church*: i.e. have both their names read out in the banns 22 *fall forward*: i.e. fuck 25 *they have ev'ry one a soul*: the question of whether women possessed souls was hotly debated in the early 17th century 28 *light*: arrive

DUKE: If that be he, the weather shall soon clear.
List, and I'll tell thee how.
[*Whispers to her.*]
LEANTIO [*Aside.*]: A-kissing too?
I see 'tis plain lust now, adultery bold'ned;
What will it prove anon, when 'tis stuff'd full
Of wine and sweetmeats, being so impudent fasting?
DUKE [*To* LEANTIO.]: We have heard of your good parts, sir, which we honour
With our embrace and love. – Is not the captainship
Of Rouans citadel, since the late deceas'd,
Suppli'd by any yet?
GENTLEMAN: By none, my lord.
DUKE [*To* LEANTIO.]: Take it, the place is yours then, and as faithfulness
And desert grows, our favour shall grow with't:
Rise now the Captain of our Fort at Rouans.
LEANTIO: The service of whole life give your Grace thanks.
DUKE: Come, sit, Bianca.
LEANTIO [*Aside.*]: This is some good yet,
And more then ev'r I look'd for; a fine bit
To stay a cuckold's stomach. All preferment
That springs from sin and lust, it shoots up quickly,
As gardeners' crops do in the rotten'st grounds;
So is all means rais'd from base prostitution,
Ev'n like a sallet growing upon a dunghill.
I'm like a thing that never was yet heard of,
Half merry and half mad, much like a fellow
That eats his meat with a good appetite
And wears a plague-sore that would fright a country;
Or rather like the barren, hard'ned ass
That feeds on thistles till he bleeds again;
And such is the condition of my misery.
LIVIA: Is that your son, widow?
MOTHER: Yes, did your ladyship
Never know that till now?
LIVIA: No, trust me, did I.
[*Aside.*] Nor ever truly felt the power of love

33 *A-kissing*: perhaps Leantio mistakes the whispered conversation between the Duke and Bianca, but it is just as possible that the Duke intersperses advice with kisses 36 *impudent*: shameless 37 *parts*: qualities 39 *Rouans*: cannot be reliably identified but perhaps the fort described by Moryson in his *Itinerary* (1617) as *Le Ruinate*. 'Rouens' is unlikely, as Leantio expects to remain near Florence 46–7 *a fine bit To stay a cuckold's stomach*: see note II.ii.406 50 *means*: wealth 51 *sallet*: salad plant 56 *barren*: slow-witted

And pity to a man, till now I knew him.
I have enough to buy me my desires,
And yet to spare, that's one good comfort. [*To* LEANTIO.] Hark you?
Pray let me speak with you, sir, before you go.

LEANTIO: With me, Lady? You shall, I am at your service.
[*Aside.*] What will she say now, trow? More goodness yet?

WARD: I see her now, I'm sure; the ape's so little,
I shall scarce feel her; I have seen almost
As tall as she sold in the fair for ten pence.
See how she simpers it, as if marmalade
Would not melt in her mouth! She might have the kindness, i'faith,
To send me a gilded bull from her own trencher,
A ram, a goat, or somewhat to be nibbling.
These women, when they come to sweet things once,
They forget all their friends, they grow so greedy –
Nay, oftentimes their husbands.

DUKE: Here's a health now, gallants,
To the best beauty at this day in Florence.

BIANCA: Whoe'er she be, she shall not go unpledg'd, sir.

DUKE: Nay, you're excus'd for this.

BIANCA: Who I, my lord?

DUKE: Yes, by the law of Bacchus; plead your benefit,
You are not bound to pledge your own health, lady.

BIANCA: That's a good way, my lord, to keep me dry.

DUKE: Nay, then I will not offend Venus so much;
Let Bacchus seek his 'mends in another court.
Here's to thyself, Bianca.

BIANCA: Nothing comes
More welcome to that name than your Grace.

LEANTIO [*Aside.*]: So, so;
Here stands the poor thief now that stole the treasure,

67 *trow?*: do you think? 68 *ape*: colloquial term of endearment 70 *sold in the fair for ten pence*: presumably toy dolls (perhaps, as Frost suggests, the 'Bartholomew babies' sold at Bartholomew Fair); the price expresses derision 71 *marmalade*: at the time this preserve could be made from any fruit 73 *gilded bull*: another marzipan figure coloured to resemble gold. Bulls, rams and goats were all emblematic of lechery (and since all are horned beasts he may unconsciously be anticipating his cuckoldry) *trencher*: plate or platter 77 *health*: toast 81 *Bacchus*: Greek god of wine *plead your benefit*: i.e. claim an exemption (alluding to Benefit of Clergy which allowed clergy and, in practice, any literate claimants to evade the secular law) 83 *dry*: sober/thirsty/lacking vaginal lubrication 84 *offend Venus*: by encouraging dryness as opposed to the warm and moist qualities with which she was associated 85 *'mends*: reparation

And he's not thought on. Ours is near kin now
To a twin misery born into the world:
First the hard-conscienc'd worldling, he hoards wealth up;
Then comes the next, and he feasts all upon't;
One's damn'd for getting, th'other for spending on't.
O equal Justice, thou hast met my sin
With a full weight; I'm rightly now oppress'd,
All her friends' heavy hearts lie in my breast.
DUKE: Methinks there is no spirit amongst us, gallants,
But what divinely sparkles from the eyes
Of bright Bianca; we sat all in darkness
But for that splendour. Who was't told us lately
Of a match-making right, a marriage-tender?
GUARDIANO: 'Twas I, my lord.
DUKE: 'Twas you indeed. Where is she?
GUARDIANO: This is the gentlewoman.
FABRITIO: My lord, my daughter.
DUKE: Why, here's some stirring yet.
FABRITIO: She's a dear child to me.
DUKE: That must needs be, you say she is your daughter.
FABRITIO: Nay, my good lord, dear to my purse I mean,
Beside my person, I nev'r reckon'd that.
She has the full qualities of a gentlewoman:
I have brought her up to music, dancing, what not,
That may commend her sex and stir her husband.
DUKE: And which is he now?
GUARDIANO: This young heir, my lord.
DUKE: What is he brought up to?
HIPPOLITO [*Aside.*]: To cat and trap.
GUARDIANO: My lord, he's a great ward, wealthy but simple;
His parts consist in acres.
DUKE: O wise-acres!
GUARDIANO: Y'have spoke him in a word, sir.
BIANCA: 'Las, poor gentlewoman,
She's ill bestead, unless sh'as dealt the wiselier
And laid in more provision for her youth:
Fools will not keep in summer.

89 *Ours*: i.e. mine and those in similar positions 96 *her friends*: i.e. Bianca's friends left behind in Venice 101 *right*: either 'rite' or 'privilege' *marriage-tender*: betrothal 104 *stirring*: excitement (including, presumably, sexual excitement) 110 *stir*: sexually excite 115 *spoke*: described 116 *bestead*: situated, circumstanced 118 *Fools*: punning on 'fools' = dishes made from fruit and cream *keep*: keep fresh/stay indoors

LEANTIO [*Aside.*]: No, nor such wives
From whores in winter.
DUKE: Yea, the voice too, sir?
FABRITIO: Ay, and a sweet breast too, my lord, I hope,
Or I have cast away my money wisely;
She took her pricksong earlier, my lord,
Than any of her kindred ever did.
A rare child, though I say't, but I'd not have
The baggage hear so much; 'twould make her swell straight,
And maids of all things must not be puff'd up.
DUKE: Let's turn us to a better banquet, then,
For music bids the soul of a man to a feast,
And that's indeed a noble entertainment
Worthy Bianca's self. You shall perceive, beauty,
Our Florentine damsels are not brought up idly.
BIANCA: They are wiser of themselves, it seems, my lord,
And can take gifts when goodness offers 'em.
Music.
LEANTIO [*Aside.*]: True, and damnation has taught you that wisdom,
You can take gifts too. O that music mocks me!
LIVIA [*Aside.*]: I am as dumb to any language now
But love's, as one that never learn'd to speak.
I am not yet so old, but he may think of me.
My own fault, I have been idle a long time;
But I'll begin the week and paint tomorrow,
So follow my true labour day by day.
I never thriv'd so well as when I us'd it.

THE SONG [*sung by* ISABELLA].

What harder chance can fall to woman,
Who was born to cleave to some man,
Than to bestow her time, youth, beauty,
Life's observance, honour, duty,

119 *whores*: i.e. from becoming whores (with a possible pun on 'hoars' = 'hoar' frosts) 120 *breast*: voice 121 *wisely*: i.e. foolishly (it is not clear whether this is deliberate irony or muddled error on Fabritio's part) 122 *took her pricksong*: learned to read music (in pricksong the harmony was written or pricked down, rather than left to the singer's invention) 124 *rare*: talented 126 *puff'd up*: proud/pregnant (continuing the probably unconscious bawdy innuendo of 'pricksong' and 'swell') 132 *of themselves*: either 'left to themselves' or 'innately' 140 *paint*: put on make-up 146 *observance*: dutiful service

On a thing for no use good,
But to make physic work, or blood
Force fresh in an old lady's cheek?
She that would be
Mother of fools, let her compound with me.

WARD [*While she sings.*]: Here's a tune indeed! Pish, I had rather hear one ballad sung i'th'nose now, of the lamentable drowning of fat sheep and oxen, than all these simpering tunes play'd upon cats' guts and sung by little kitlings.

FABRITIO: How like you her breast now, my lord?

BIANCA [*To* DUKE.]: Her breast?
He talks as if his daughter had given suck
Before she were married, as her betters have;
The next he praises sure will be her nipples.

DUKE [*To* BIANCA.]: Methinks now, such a voice to such a husband
Is like a jewel of unvalued worth
Hung at a fool's ear.

FABRITIO: May it please your Grace
To give her leave to show another quality?

DUKE: Marry, as many good ones as you will, sir,
The more the better welcome.

LEANTIO [*Aside.*]: But the less
The better practis'd. That soul's black indeed
That cannot commend virtue. But who keeps it?
The extortioner will say to a sick beggar
'Heaven comfort thee', though he give none himself.
This good is common.

FABRITIO: Will it please you now, sir,
To entreat your ward to take her by the hand
And lead her in a dance before the Duke?

GUARDIANO: That will I, sir, 'tis needful. Hark you, nephew.
[*Speaks aside to the* WARD.]

148 *physic*: laxative (made more effective by slight physical exertions – an allusion to the Ward's sexual inadequacy) 148–9 *blood . . . cheek*: i.e. the erotic excitement such a man can provide is scarcely enough to make an old woman blush 151 *compound*: come to an agreement 152–5 in O this speech and the song are printed side by side 155 *kitlings*: kittens (but punning on 'young cat' = whore, and 'kit' = small fiddle) 156 *breast*: voice (Bianca understands only the modern meaning) 160 *to*: with 161 *unvalued*: priceless 165–6 *the less The better practis'd*: i.e. the fewer a woman possesses, the more likely she is to practise the essential ones 170 *This good is common*: i.e. there is plenty of this (merely professed) kind of virtue around

FABRITIO: Nay, you shall see, young heir, what y'have for your money,
Without fraud or imposture.
WARD: Dance with her!
Not I, sweet guardiner, do not urge my heart to't,
'Tis clean against my blood. Dance with a stranger!
Let whos' will do't, I'll not begin first with her.
HIPPOLITO [*Aside.*]: No, fear't not, fool, sh'as took a better order.
GUARDIANO: Why, who shall take her, then?
WARD: Some other gentleman.
Look, there's her uncle, a fine-timber'd reveller.
Perhaps he knows the manner of her dancing too;
I'll have him do't before me. I have sworn, guardiner;
Then may I learn the better.
GUARDIANO: Thou'lt be an ass still.
WARD: Ay, all that, uncle, shall not fool me out.
Pish, I stick closer to myself than so.
GUARDIANO: I must entreat you, sir, to take your niece
And dance with her; my ward's a little wilful,
He would have you show him the way.
HIPPOLITO: Me, sir?
He shall command it at all hours, pray tell him so.
GUARDIANO: I thank you for him, he has not wit himself, sir.
HIPPOLITO [*Aside to* ISABELLA.]: Come, my life's peace, I have a strange office on't here.
'Tis some man's luck to keep the joys he likes
Conceal'd for his own bosom, but my fortune
To set 'em out now for another's liking –
Like the mad misery of necessitous man,
That parts from his good horse with many praises
And goes on foot himself. Need must be obey'd
In ev'ry action, it mars man and maid.
Music.
A dance [*by* HIPPOLITO *and* ISABELLA], *making honours to the* DUKE *and cur'sey to themselves, both before and after.*

177 ***blood***: desire 178 ***whos'***: whoso (Q reads who's) ***begin first***: i.e. dance first, but initiating a chain of unconscious bawdy puns 179 ***took a better order***: planned matters better 180 ***take***: dance/have sex 181 ***fine-timber'd***: well-built 185 ***Ay, all that, uncle, shall not fool me out***: O reads 'I, all that Uncle shall not fool me out'. The most likely interpretation is 'all that you have to say, uncle (i.e. Guardiano), will not foolishly persuade me out of my decision'. But it is possible 'uncle' refers to the mention of Isabella's uncle, Hippolito 186 ***I stick closer to myself***: i.e. I stick more closely to my decisions 196 ***mad***: furious 198 ***Need***: necessity s.d. ***honours***: bows

DUKE: Signor Fabritio, y'are a happy father,
Your cares and pains are fortunate, you see,
Your cost bears noble fruits. Hippolito, thanks.
FABRITIO: Here's some amends for all my charges yet:
She wins both prick and praise where'er she comes.
DUKE: How lik'st, Bianca?
BIANCA: All things well, my lord,
But this poor gentlewoman's fortune, that's the worst.
DUKE: There is no doubt, Bianca, she'll find leisure
To make that good enough; he's rich and simple.
BIANCA: She has the better hope o'th'upper hand, indeed,
Which women strive for most.
GUARDIANO [*To* WARD.]: Do't when I bid you, sir.
WARD: I'll venture but a hornpipe with her guardiner,
Or some such married man's dance.
GUARDIANO: Well, venture something, sir.
WARD: I have rhyme for what I do.
GUARDIANO: But little reason, I think.
WARD: Plain men dance the measures, the cinquepace the gay;
Cuckolds dance the hornpipe, and farmers dance the hay;
Your soldiers dance the round, and maidens that grow big;
Your drunkards the canaries, your whore and bawd, the jig.
Here's your eight kind of dancers, he that finds the ninth let him pay the minstrels.
DUKE: O here he appears once in his own person!
I thought he would have married her by attorney,
And lain with her so too.
BIANCA: Nay, my kind lord,

203 *charges*: expenses, troubles, responsibilities 204 *prick and praise*: success and its acknowledgement. The phrase derives from the term 'prick' meaning the centre of an archery target, and Fabritio is probably unconscious of the obscene innuendo 211 *hornpipe*: a lively solo dance. It is a married man's dance since its name suggests the cuckold's horns 214 *measures*: a slow, formal dance in five movements *cinquepace*: a kind of lively dance related to the 'galliard'; its five steps consisted of four hops and a jump 215 *the hay*: a country dance having a winding or serpentine movement 216 *round*: a dance in which the performers move in a circle or ring, or around a room. Associated with soldiers since the term also describes a military inspection patrol *maidens that grow big*: the verb 'to round' was used to describe the swelling of pregnancy 217 *Your, your*: O reads 'you' in each case *canaries*: a lively Spanish dance, the idea of which was thought to have derived from the natives of the Canary Islands, associated with drunkards, since the Islands were famous for their sweet wine *jig*: lively, rapid, springy kind of dance with bawdy associations 221 *attorney*: proxy

There's very seldom any found so foolish
To give away his part there.
LEANTIO [*Aside.*]: Bitter scoff!
Yet I must do't; with what a cruel pride
The glory of her sin strikes by my afflictions!
Music.
WARD *and* ISABELLA *dance; he ridiculously imitates* HIPPOLITO.
DUKE: This thing will make shift, sirs, to make a husband,
For aught I see in him. How think'st, Bianca?
BIANCA: Faith, an ill-favoured shift, my lord. Methinks
If he would take some voyage when he's married,
Dangerous, or long enough, and scarce be seen
Once in nine year together, a wife then
Might make indifferent shift to be content with him.
DUKE: A kiss! [*Kisses* BIANCA.] That wit deserves to be made much on.
Come, our caroch!
GUARDIANO: Stands ready for your Grace.
DUKE: My thanks to all your loves. Come, fair Bianca,
We have took special care of you and provided
Your lodging near us now.
BIANCA: Your love is great, my lord.
DUKE: Once more, our thanks to all.
OMNES: All blest honours guard you.
Cornets flourish. Exeunt all but LEANTIO *and* LIVIA.
LEANTIO [*To himself.*]: O hast thou left me then, Bianca, utterly!
Bianca! Now I miss thee. O return
And save the faith of woman! I nev'r felt
The loss of thee till now; 'tis an affliction
Of greater weight than youth was made to bear,
As if a punishment of after-life
Were fall'n upon man here; so new it is
To flesh and blood, so strange, so insupportable,
A torment ev'n mistook, as if a body
Whose death were drowning must needs therefore suffer it
In scalding oil.
LIVIA: Sweet sir!
LEANTIO [*To himself.*]: As long as mine eye saw thee
I half enjoy'd thee.

226 *glory*: boast *strikes by*: disregards 227 *make shift*: struggle
229 *ill-favoured shift*: offensive change of clothing/offensive substitute for a husband/offensive expedient or necessity 233 *make indifferent shift*: make some effort/just about manage 235 *caroch*: coach 245 *after-life*: i.e. hell
248 *mistook*: suffered in error 249 *were*: i.e. were meant (fated) to be

LIVIA: Sir?
LEANTIO [*To himself.*]: Canst thou forget
The dear pains my love took: how it has watch'd
Whole nights together in all weathers for thee,
Yet stood in heart more merry than the tempests
That sung about mine ears (like dangerous flatterers
That can set all their mischief to sweet tunes);
And then receiv'd thee from thy father's window
Into these arms at midnight; when we embrac'd
As if we had been statues only made for't,
To show art's life, so silent were our comforts,
And kiss'd as if our lips had grown together!
LIVIA [*Aside.*]: This makes me madder to enjoy him now.
LEANTIO [*To himself.*]: Canst thou forget all this? And better joys
That we met after this, which then new kisses
Took pride to praise?
LIVIA [*Aside.*]: I shall grow madder yet! – Sir!
LEANTIO [*To himself.*]: This cannot be but of some close bawd's working. –
Cry mercy, lady. What would you say to me?
My sorrow makes me so unmannerly,
So comfort bless me, I had quite forgot you.
LIVIA: Nothing but, ev'n in pity to that passion,
Would give your grief good counsel.
LEANTIO: Marry, and welcome, lady;
It never could come better.
LIVIA: Then first, sir,
To make away all your good thoughts at once of her,
Know most assuredly she is a strumpet.
LEANTIO: Ha! 'Most assuredly'! Speak not a thing
So vild so certainly, leave it more doubtful.
LIVIA: Then I must leave all truth, and spare my knowledge
A sin which I too lately found and wept for.
LEANTIO: Found you it?
LIVIA: Ay, with wet eyes.
LEANTIO: O perjurious friendship!
LIVIA: You miss'd your fortunes when you met with her, sir.
Young gentlemen that only love for beauty,
They love not wisely; such a marriage rather
Proves the destruction of affection:

252 *watch'd*: kept vigil 259–60 *only . . . life*: specifically designed to show off the naturalism of art 266 *close*: furtive 276 *vild*: vile

It brings on want, and want's the key of whoredom.
I think y'had small means with her.

LEANTIO: O not any, lady.

LIVIA: Alas, poor gentleman, what meant'st thou, sir,
Quite to undo thyself with thine own kind heart?
Thou art too good and pitiful to woman.
Marry, sir, thank thy stars for this blest fortune
That rids the summer of thy youth so well
From many beggars that had lain a-sunning
In thy beams only else, till thou hadst wasted
The whole days of thy life in heat and labour.
What would you say now to a creature found
As pitiful to you, and as it were
Ev'n sent on purpose from the whole sex general
To requite all that kindness you have shown to't?

LEANTIO: What's that, madam?

LIVIA: Nay, a gentlewoman,
And one able to reward good things, ay, and bears
A conscience to't. Couldst thou love such a one
That, blow all fortunes, would never see thee want?
Nay more, maintain thee to thine enemy's envy?
And shalt not spend a care for't, stir a thought,
Nor break a sleep, unless love's music wak'd thee;
No storm of fortune should; look upon me,
And know that woman.

LEANTIO: O my life's wealth, Bianca!

LIVIA: Still with her name? Will nothing wear it out?
That deep sigh went but for a strumpet, sir.

LEANTIO: It can go for no other that loves me.

LIVIA [*Aside.*]: He's vex'd in mind; I came too soon to him:
Where's my discretion now, my skill, my judgment?
I'm cunning in all arts but my own love.
'Tis as unseasonable to tempt him now
So soon, as a widow to be courted
Following her husband's corse, or to make bargain
By the grave-side and take a young man there:

285 ***had small means with her***: received only a small dowry 291 ***beggars***: i.e. Bianca and her progeny 293 ***whole***: entire/wholesome ***heat***: sexual infatuation/toil 296 ***whole sex general***: i.e. all women 299–300 ***bears A conscience to't***: considers it a duty 301 ***blow all fortunes***: despite everything 303 ***And shalt***: and you shall 305 ***should***: i.e. should wake thee 315 ***corse***: corpse

Her strange departure stands like a hearse yet
Before his eyes; which time will take down shortly.
Exit.

LEANTIO: Is she my wife till death, yet no more mine?
That's a hard measure. Then what's marriage good for?
Methinks by right I should not now be living,
And then 'twere all well. What a happiness
Had I been made of, had I never seen her;
For nothing makes man's loss grievous to him
But knowledge of the worth of what he loses;
For what he never had, he never misses.
She's gone for ever, utterly; there is
As much redemption of a soul from hell
As a fair woman's body from his palace.
Why should my love last longer than her truth?
What is there good in woman to be lov'd
When only that which makes her so, has left her?
I cannot love her now, but I must like
Her sin, and my own shame too, and be guilty
Of Law's breach with her, and mine own abusing;
All which were monstrous. Then my safest course,
For health of mind and body, is to turn
My heart, and hate her, most extremely hate her;
I have no other way. Those virtuous powers
Which were chaste witnesses of both our troths
Can witness she breaks first, and I'm rewarded
With Captainship o'th'Fort; a place of credit
I must confess, but poor; my factorship
Shall not exchange means with't; he that died last in't,
He was no drunkard, yet he died a beggar
For all his thrift. Besides the place not fits me:
It suits my resolution, not my breeding.
Enter LIVIA.

LIVIA [*Aside.*]: I have tried all ways I can and have not power
To keep from sight of him. – How are you now, sir?

317 *strange*: recent (and thus not yet familiar) *hearse*: a temporary memorial structure of wood decorated with epitaphs, etc., which covered the coffin of a dead person 320 *hard measure*: harsh punishment 329 *his*: i.e. the Duke's 330 *truth*: faithfulness 334–5 *be guilty Of Law's breach*: i.e. by condoning Bianca's adultery 340 *troths*: marriage vows 342–4 *a place . . . with't*: an honourable post, indeed, but poorly paid; I earn at least as much as a merchant's agent 347 *resolution*: determination *breeding*: social rank (probably with the suggestion that professional soldiers are born to the trade)

LEANTIO: I feel a better ease, madam.
LIVIA: Thanks to blessedness!
You will do well I warrant you, fear it not, sir.
Join but your own good will to't; he's not wise
That loves his pain or sickness, or grows fond
Of a disease whose property is to vex him
And spitefully drink his blood up. Out upon't, sir,
Youth knows no greater loss. I pray let's walk, sir.
You never saw the beauty of my house yet,
Nor how abundantly fortune has bless'd me
In worldly treasure; trust me, I have enough, sir,
To make my friend a rich man in my life,
A great man at my death; yourself will say so.
If you want anything and spare to speak,
Troth, I'll condemn you for a wilful man, sir.
LEANTIO: Why, sure, this can be but the flattery of some dream.
LIVIA: Now by this kiss, my love, my soul and riches,
'Tis all true substance.
[*Kisses him.*]
Come, you shall see my wealth, take what you list;
The gallanter you go, the more you please me.
I will allow you, too, your page and footman,
Your race-horses, or any various pleasure
Exercis'd youth delights in. But to me
Only, sir, wear your heart of constant stuff;
Do but you love enough, I'll give enough.
LEANTIO: Troth then, I'll love enough and take enough.
LIVIA: Then we are both pleas'd enough.
Exeunt.

SCENE 3

Enter GUARDIANO *and* ISABELLA *at one door, and the* WARD *and* SORDIDO *at another.*

GUARDIANO: Now, nephew, here's the gentlewoman again.
WARD: Mass, here she's come again; mark her now, Sordido.
GUARDIANO: This is the maid my love and care has chose
Out for your wife, and so I tender her to you;

355 *drink his blood up*: unrequited love was thought to dry up the life-blood *Out upon't*: an indignant exclamation of reproach 369 *allow*: assign 372 *constant stuff*: material which is of a constant colour (taffeta, by contrast, changes colour when moved)

Yourself has been eye-witness of some qualities
That speak a courtly breeding, and are costly.
I bring you both to talk together now,
'Tis time you grew familiar in your tongues;
Tomorrow you join hands, and one ring ties you,
And one bed holds you (if you like the choice).
Her father and her friends are i'th'next room,
And stay to see the contract ere they part;
Therefore dispatch, good Ward, be sweet and short.
Like her or like her not, there's but two ways;
And one your body, th'other your purse pays.

WARD: I warrant you, guardiner, I'll not stand all day thrumming
But quickly shoot my bolt at your next coming.

GUARDIANO: Well said! Good fortune to your birding then.
[*Exit.*]

WARD: I never miss'd mark yet.

SORDIDO: Troth, I think, master, if the truth were known,
You never shot at any but the kitchen-wench,
And that was a she-woodcock, a mere innocent
That was oft lost and cried at eight and twenty.

WARD: No more of that meat, Sordido, here's eggs o'th'spit now;
We must turn gingerly. Draw out the catalogue
Of all the faults of women.

SORDIDO: How, all the faults! Have you so little reason to think so much paper will lie in my breeches? Why, ten carts will not carry it, if you set down but the bawds. All the faults? Pray let's be content with a few of 'em; and, if they were less, you would find 'em enough, I warrant you. Look you, sir.

ISABELLA [*Aside.*]: But that I have th'advantage of the fool
As much as woman's heart can wish and joy at,
What an infernal torment 'twere to be
Thus bought and sold and turn'd and pried into; when, alas,

13 *dispatch*: settle promptly   15 *your purse pays*: see note I.ii.2–10
16 *thrumming*: i.e. making my mind up ('thrumming' a hat, fidgeting with it in one's hands, was proverbially indicative of indecision)   17 *shoot my bolt*: announce my decision. The metaphor derives from the missile or bolt fired from a cross-bow. The Ward unconsciously alludes to the proverb 'a fool's bolt is soon shot' with its bawdy suggestion of premature ejaculation   18 *birding*: wenching/bird-catching (playing on the cross-bow imagery of the Ward's phrase, since a bird-bolt was a blunt-headed arrow used in birding)   19 *mark*: target/cunt   22 *she-woodcock*: game bird proverbially easy to snare   *innocent*: simpleton   23 *cried*: children that were lost were handed in to the town crier who announced their whereabouts   24 *eggs o'th'spit*: a dish requiring constant attention and thus by extension 'a delicate business'

The worst bit is too good for him! And the comfort is,
H'as but a cater's place on't, and provides
All for another's table; yet how curious
The ass is, like some nice professor on't,
That buys up all the daintiest food i'th'markets.
And seldom licks his lips after a taste on't!

SORDIDO: Now to her, now y'have scann'd all her parts over.

WARD: But at which end shall I begin now, Sordido?

SORDIDO: O ever at a woman's lip, while you live, sir; do you ask that question?

WARD: Methinks, Sordido, sh'as but a crabbed face to begin with.

SORDIDO: A crabbed face? That will save money.

WARD: How! Save money, Sordido?

SORDIDO: Ay, sir; for having a crabbed face of her own, she'll eat the less verjuice with her mutton; 'twill save verjuice at year's end, sir.

WARD: Nay, and your jests begin to be saucy once, I'll make you eat your meat without mustard.

SORDIDO: And that in some kind is a punishment.

WARD: Gentlewoman, they say 'tis your pleasure to be my wife; and you shall know shortly whether it be mine or no to be your husband; and thereupon thus I first enter upon you.
[*Kisses her.*]
O most delicious scent! Methinks it tasted as if a man had stepped into a comfit-maker's shop to let a cart go by, all the while I kiss'd her. It is reported, gentlewoman, you'll run mad for me, if you have me not.

ISABELLA: I should be in great danger of my wits, sir,
For being so forward, [*Aside.*] should this ass kick backward now!

WARD: Alas, poor soul! And is that hair your own?

ISABELLA: Mine own? Yes, sure, sir; I owe nothing for't.

37 *cater's place*: the position of one responsible for the buying of cates, or provisions, for a household – who may thus buy delicacies he will never eat
38 *curious*: fastidious 39 *nice*: refined *professor*: expert 43 *at which end*: O reads 'at end' 50 *verjuice*: an acidic juice which could be obtained from crab apples and other fruit, used as a sauce with meats 51 *and*: if *once*: now
53 Sordido seems to be unimpressed by the severity of the punishment 56 *enter upon*: claim possession of 58 *comfit-maker's shop*: a shop selling comfits and other confectionery. Its fragrant smells would have contrasted strongly with the stink of the street outside 60–1 Isabella pretends she's in danger of going mad for love of the Ward, to whom she is making her feelings indecorously clear. Then, in an aside, she switches to another meaning of 'forward': she is too near the ass and in danger of having her head kicked

WARD: 'Tis a good hearing; I shall have the less to pay when I have married you. [*To* SORDIDO.]
Look, does her eyes stand well?

SORDIDO: They cannot stand better
Than in her head, I think; where would you have them?
And for her nose, 'tis of a very good last.

WARD: I have known as good as that has not lasted a year, though.

SORDIDO: That's in the using of a thing; will not any strong bridge fall down in time, if we do nothing but beat at the bottom? A nose of buff would not last always, sir, especially if it came in to th'camp once.

WARD: But Sordido, how shall we do to make her laugh, that I may see what teeth she has? For I'll not bate her a tooth, nor take a black one into th'bargain.

SORDIDO: Why, do but you fall in talk with her, you cannot choose but one time or other make her laugh, sir.

WARD: It shall go hard but I will. [*To her.*] Pray what qualities have you beside singing and dancing? Can you play at shittlecock, forsooth?

ISABELLA: Ay, and at stool-ball too, sir; I have great luck at it.

WARD: Why, can you catch a ball well?

ISABELLA: I have catch'd two in my lap at one game.

WARD: What have you, woman? I must have you learn
To play at trap too, then y'are full and whole.

ISABELLA: Anything that you please to bring me up to
I shall take pains to practise.

WARD [*Aside to* SORDIDO.]: 'Twill not do, Sordido, we shall never get her mouth open'd wide enough.

SORDIDO: No, sir? That's strange! Then here's a trick for your learning.
He yawns [*and* ISABELLA *yawns too but covers her mouth with a handkerchief*].
Look now, look now; quick, quick there.

WARD: Pox of that scurvy, mannerly trick with handkerchief;
It hind'red me a little but I am satisfied.
When a fair woman gapes and stops her mouth so
It shows like a cloth stopple in a cream-pot.
I have fair hope of her teeth now, Sordido.

64 *'Tis a good hearing*: it's good to hear that 66 *eyes*: punning on 'eye' = cunt 68 *last*: shape. A shoemaker's 'last' is used to shape shoes 70 *bridge*: syphilis brings about the collapse of the 'bridge' of the nose 71 *buff*: tough leather, used for soldiers' jerkins 72 *camp*: military camp. Camp followers were prone to contract syphilis 74 *bate her a tooth*: accept her with a tooth deficient 80 *stool-ball*: a form of indoor cricket normally played by women 82 *catch'd two in my lap*: the 'balls' Isabella refers to are Hippolito's 91 *mannerly*: polite 94 *cloth stopple*: a cloth plug for a jar

SORDIDO: Why, then y'have all well, sir, for aught I see.
She's right and straight enough, now as she stands;
They'll commonly lie crooked, that's no matter. Wise gamesters
Never find fault with that, let 'em lie still so.

WARD: I'd fain mark how she goes, and then I have all. For of all creatures I cannot abide a splay-footed woman. She's an unlucky thing to meet in a morning. Her heels keep together so, as if she were beginning an Irish dance still, and the wriggling of her bum, playing the tune to't. But I have bethought a cleanly shift to find it: dab down as you see me, and peep of one side when her back's toward you; I'll show you the way.

SORDIDO: And you shall find me apt enough to peeping;
I have been one of them has seen mad sights
Under your scaffolds.

WARD: Will it please you walk, forsooth,
A turn or two by yourself? You are so pleasing to me,
I take delight to view you on both sides.

ISABELLA: I shall be glad to fetch a walk to your love, sir;
'Twill get affection a good stomach, sir.
[*Aside.*] Which I had need have, to fall to such coarse victuals.
[*She walks, while* WARD *and* SORDIDO *peer up her skirt.*]

WARD: Now go thy ways for a clean-treading wench,
As ever man in modesty peep'd under.

SORDIDO: I see the sweetest sight to please my master:
Never went Frenchman righter upon ropes
Than she on Florentine rushes.

WARD: 'Tis enough, forsooth.

ISABELLA: And how do you like me now, sir?

WARD: Faith, so well.
I never mean to part with thee, sweetheart,
Under some sixteen children, and all boys.

ISABELLA: You'll be at simple pains, if you prove kind,
And breed 'em all in your teeth.

98 *gamesters*: sexual athletes 101 *splay-footed*: i.e. having feet pointing outwards *unlucky*: because witches were believed to have splay-feet 102–3 *Irish dance*: many traditional Irish dances begin with the participants tucking the heel of the right foot against the instep of the left 104 *cleanly shift*: clever trick *dab*: duck 108 *scaffolds*: platforms which provided views for spectators of processions, etc. 112 *get affection a good stomach*: set an edge to sexual appetite 117 *Frenchman*: the French seem to have specialized in tightrope displays 118 *rushes*: the normal floor-covering of the period 122 *simple*: great *kind*: affectionate/amorously disposed 122–3 alluding to the belief that husbands suffered sympathetic toothaches during the wife's pregnancy

WARD: Nay, by my faith,
What serves your belly for? 'Twould make my cheeks
Look like blown bagpipes.
Enter GUARDIANO.
GUARDIANO: How now, ward and nephew,
Gentlewoman and niece! Speak, is it so or not?
WARD: 'Tis so, we are both agreed, sir.
GUARDIANO: In to your kindred, then;
There's friends, and wine, and music, waits to welcome you.
WARD: Then I'll be drunk for joy.
SORDIDO: And I for company,
I cannot break my nose in a better action.
Exeunt.

130 *break my nose in a better action*: suffer in a better cause. The 'broken nose' will be inflamed by alcohol

ACT FOUR

SCENE I

Enter BIANCA *attended by two* Ladies.
BIANCA: How goes your watches, ladies? What's a'clock now?
FIRST LADY: By mine, full nine.
SECOND LADY: By mine, a quarter past.
FIRST LADY: I set mine by St Marks.
SECOND LADY: St Anthony's they say
Goes truer.
FIRST LADY: That's but your opinion, madam,
Because you love a gentleman o'th'name.
SECOND LADY: He's a true gentleman, then.
FIRST LADY: So may he be
That comes to me tonight, for aught you know.
BIANCA: I'll end this strife straight. I set mine by the sun.
I love to set by th'best, one shall not then
Be troubled to set often.
SECOND LADY: You do wisely in't.
BIANCA: If I should set my watch as some girls do
By ev'ry clock i'th'town, 'twould nev'r go true;
And too much turning of the dial's point,
Or tamp'ring with the spring, might in small time
Spoil the whole work too. Here it wants of nine now.
FIRST LADY: It does indeed, forsooth; mine's nearest truth yet.
SECOND LADY: Yet I have found her lying with an advocate, which show'd
Like two false clocks together in one parish.

1 *watches*: these were a relatively new invention and extremely unreliable. They were thus often compared to the sexual behaviour of women; in particular, to 'set a watch' was slang for having sex 3 *St Anthony's*: Mulryne believes the name was perhaps suggested by the famous church of St Anthony in Padua which, along with St Mark's in Venice, was one of the two most famous churches in Italy 8 *sun*: in this context almost certainly implies the Duke 9–10 *one . . . often*: the Duke's sexual stamina is here probably called in question 13 *dial's point*: i.e. penis 14 *spring*: i.e. cunt 15 *wants of nine*: is a little before nine 17–18 i.e. The lady was lying (sleeping) with the advocate, a professional liar – so they are both false

BIANCA: So now I thank you, ladies. I desire
A while to be alone.
FIRST LADY: And I am nobody,
Methinks, unless I have one or other with me.
Faith, my desire and hers will nev'r be sisters.
Exeunt Ladies.
BIANCA: How strangely woman's fortune comes about!
This was the farthest way to come to me,
All would have judg'd, that knew me born in Venice
And there with many jealous eyes brought up,
That never thought they had me sure enough
But when they were upon me; yet my hap
To meet it here, so far off from my birthplace,
My friends or kindred. 'Tis not good, in sadness,
To keep a maid so strict in her young days;
Restraint breeds wand'ring thoughts, as many fasting days
A great desire to see flesh stirring again.
I'll nev'r use any girl of mine so strictly;
Howev'r they're kept, their fortunes find 'em out;
I see't in me. If they be got in Court
I'll never forbid 'em the country, nor the Court
Though they be born i'th'country. They will come to't
And fetch their falls a thousand mile about,
Where one would little think on't.
Enter LEANTIO.
LEANTIO [*Aside.*]: I long to see how my despiser looks,
Now she's come here to Court. These are her lodgings,
She's simply now advanc'd; I took her out
Of no such window, I remember, first;
That was a great deal lower and less carv'd.
BIANCA [*Aside.*]: How now? What silkworm's this, i'th'name of pride?
What, is it he?
LEANTIO: A bow i'th'ham to your greatness;
You must have now three legs, I take it, must you not?

21 *one or other*: somebody 24 i.e. this was the least likely fate for me 28 *hap*: fortune 30 *in sadness*: in earnest, seriously 32 *fasting days*: the prohibition on eating meat during Lent was strictly enforced from 1608 onwards 33 *flesh stirring*: the reappearance of meat/an erect penis 36 *got*: begotten 39 *fetch*: go in search of and bring back *falls*: i.e. into sin *a thousand mile about*: i.e. via a thousand-mile detour 43 *simply*: absolutely 44 *first*: i.e. when we first met 46 *silkworm*: contemptuous term for a dandy dressed in silk 48 *three legs*: three bows

BIANCA: Then I must take another, I shall want else
The service I should have; you have but two there.
LEANTIO: Y'are richly plac'd.
BIANCA: Methinks y'are wond'rous brave, sir.
LEANTIO: A sumptuous lodging.
BIANCA: Y'ave an excellent suit there.
LEANTIO: A chair of velvet.
BIANCA: Is your cloak lin'd through, sir?
LEANTIO: Y'are very stately here.
BIANCA: Faith, something proud, sir.
LEANTIO: Stay, stay, let's see your cloth-of-silver slippers.
BIANCA: Who's your shoemaker? H'as made you a neat boot.
LEANTIO: Will you have a pair? The Duke will lend you spurs.
BIANCA: Yes, when I ride.
LEANTIO: 'Tis a brave life you lead.
BIANCA: I could nev'r see you in such good clothes
In my time.
LEANTIO: In your time?
BIANCA: Sure, I think, sir,
We both thrive best asunder.
LEANTIO: Y'are a whore!
BIANCA: Fear nothing, sir.
LEANTIO: An impudent, spiteful strumpet!
BIANCA: O sir, you give me thanks for your captainship;
I thought you had forgot all your good manners.
LEANTIO: And to spite thee as much, look there, there read!
[*Gives her a letter.*]
Vex! Gnaw! Thou shalt find there I am not love-starv'd.
The world was never yet so cold or pitiless
But there was ever still more charity found out
Than at one proud fool's door; and 'twere hard, faith,
If I could not pass that. Read to thy shame, there –
A cheerful and a beauteous benefactor too,
As ev'r erected the good works of love.

49 *another*: i.e. 'leg' = penis *want*: lack 50 *service*: deference/sexual satisfaction (continuing the bawdy quibble on 'legs') 51 *brave*: splendidly dressed 54 *proud*: magnificent 57 *spurs*: money (coins worth £3–4)/encouragement (in your social progress)/his testicles 58 *ride*: taking up the bawdy innuendo of 'spurs' *brave*: grand 62 *impudent*: shameless 70 *pass that*: pass by that door/surpass that charity 72 *erected the good works of love*: built charitable institutions/aroused erections

BIANCA [*Aside.*]: Lady Livia!
Is't possible? Her worship was my pand'ress,
She dote and send and give, and all to him!
Why, here's a bawd plagu'd home! – Y'are simply happy, sir,
Yet I'll not envy you.
LEANTIO: No, court-saint, not thou!
You keep some friend of a new fashion.
There's no harm in your devil, he's a suckling,
But he will breed teeth shortly, will he not?
BIANCA: Take heed you play not then too long with him.
LEANTIO: Yes, and the great one too. I shall find time
To play a hot religious bout with some of you,
And perhaps drive you and your course of sins
To their eternal kennels. I speak softly now
('Tis manners in a noblewoman's lodgings,
And I well know all my degrees of duty)
But, come I to your everlasting parting once,
Thunder shall seem soft music to that tempest.
BIANCA: 'Twas said last week there would be change of weather
When the moon hung so, and belike you heard it.
LEANTIO: Why, here's sin made, and nev'r a conscience put to't;
A monster with all forehead, and no eyes!
Why do I talk to thee of sense or virtue,
That art as dark as death? And as much madness
To set light before thee, as to lead blind folks
To see the monuments, which they may smell as soon
As they behold; marry, oft-times their heads
For want of light may feel the hardness of 'em.
So shall thy blind pride my revenge and anger,
That canst not see it now; and it may fall
At such an hour when thou least seest of all.
So to an ignorance darker than thy womb
I leave thy perjur'd soul. A plague will come.
Exit.

75 *plagu'd home*: punished with the very disease (lust) with which she has injected others *simply*: greatly 78 *your devil*: i.e the Duke *a suckling*: alluding to the belief that witches suckled their familiar spirits 79 *breed teeth*: cut teeth/grow dangerous (to Leantio) 81 *the great one*: i.e. the real Lucifer 83 *course*: flow/coursing greyhounds 86 *know*: O reads 'knew' (which could be correct if 'and' = if) 90 *hung so*: Bianca probably mocks Leantio at this point by making a pair of horns with her fingers, indicating the crescent moon and Leantio's cuckoldry 91 *put to't*: troubled 92 *all forehead and no eyes*: i.e. all effrontery and no moral discrimination 96 *monuments*: unconsciously alluding back to the 'Monument' which the 'blind' Bianca was led to see in II.ii

BIANCA: Get you gone first, and then I fear no greater!
Nor thee will I fear long; I'll have this sauciness
Soon banish'd from these lodgings and the rooms
Perfum'd well after the corrupt air it leaves.
His breath has made me almost sick, in troth.
A poor, base start-up! Life! Because h'as got
Fair clothes by foul means, comes to rail, and show 'em.
Enter the DUKE.
DUKE: Who's that?
BIANCA: Cry you mercy, sir.
DUKE: Prithee, who's that?
BIANCA: The former thing, my lord, to whom you gave
The captainship; he eats his meat with grudging still.
DUKE: Still!
BIANCA: He comes vaunting here of his new love
And the new clothes she gave him: Lady Livia!
Who but she now his mistress?
DUKE: Lady Livia?
Be sure of what you say.
BIANCA: He show'd me her name, sir,
In perfum'd paper, her vows, her letter,
With an intent to spite me; so his heart said,
And his threats made it good; they were as spiteful
As ever malice utter'd, and as dangerous,
Should his hand follow the copy.
DUKE: But that must not.
Do not you vex your mind. Prithee, to bed, go.
All shall be well and quiet.
BIANCA: I love peace, sir.
DUKE: And so do all that love; take you no care for't,
It shall be still provided to your hand.
Exit [BIANCA].
Who's near us there?
Enter Messenger.
MESSENGER: My lord.
DUKE: Seek out Hippolito,
Brother to Lady Livia, with all speed.
MESSENGER: He was the last man I saw, my lord.
Exit.

114 *vaunting*: boasting 122 *his hand follow the copy*: his actions follow his threats

DUKE: Make haste.
He is a blood soon stirr'd, and as he's quick
To apprehend a wrong, he's bold and sudden
In bringing forth a ruin. I know likewise
The reputation of his sister's honour's
As dear to him as life-blood to his heart;
Beside, I'll flatter him with a goodness to her
Which I now thought on, but nev'r meant to practise
(Because I know her base), and that wind drives him.
The ulcerous reputation feels the poise
Of lightest wrongs, as sores are vex'd with flies.
[*Enter* HIPPOLITO.]
He comes. Hippolito, welcome.

HIPPOLITO: My lov'd lord.

DUKE: How does that lusty widow, thy kind sister?
Is she not sped yet of a second husband?
A bed-fellow she has, I ask not that;
I know she's sped of him.

HIPPOLITO: Of him, my lord?

DUKE: Yes, of a bed-fellow. Is the news so strange to you?

HIPPOLITO: I hope 'tis so to all.

DUKE: I wish it were, sir,
But 'tis confess'd too fast. Her ignorant pleasures,
Only by Lust instructed, have receiv'd
Into their services an impudent boaster,
One that does raise his glory from her shame,
And tells the midday sun what's done in darkness;
Yet blinded with her appetite, wastes her wealth,
Buys her disgraces at a dearer rate
Than bounteous housekeepers purchase their honour.
Nothing sads me so much as that, in love
To thee and to thy blood, I had pick'd out
A worthy match for her, the great Vincentio,
High in our favour and in all men's thoughts.

HIPPOLITO: O thou destruction of all happy fortunes,
Unsated blood! Know you the name, my lord,
Of her abuser?

130 *blood soon stirred*: fiery-tempered gallant 136 *practise*: put into practice 137 *that wind drives him*: that prospect will spur him into action 138 *poise*: weight 141 *lusty*: vigorous/lecherous 142 *sped*: got rid 144 *sped of*: acquired 147 *But 'tis confess'd too fast*: i.e. it is only too clear 149 *services*: with a pun on 'sexual satisfactions' 152 *wastes*: i.e. she wastes 154 *bounteous housekeepers*: i.e. householders who entertain freely 156 *blood*: family 160 *blood*: sexual desire

DUKE: One Leantio.
HIPPOLITO: He's a factor!
DUKE: He nev'r made so brave a voyage
By his own talk.
HIPPOLITO: The poor old widow's son!
I humbly take my leave.
DUKE [*Aside.*]: I see 'tis done: –
Give her good counsel, make her see her error.
I know she'll hearken to you.
HIPPOLITO: Yes, my lord,
[*Aside.*] I make no doubt, as I shall take the course
Which she shall never know till it be acted;
And when she wakes to honour, then she'll thank me for't.
I'll imitate the pities of old surgeons
To this lost limb, who, ere they show their art,
Cast one asleep, then cut the diseas'd part.
So out of love to her I pity most,
She shall not feel him going till he's lost;
Then she'll commend the cure.
Exit.
DUKE: The great cure's past.
I count this done already; his wrath's sure
And speaks an injury deep. Farewell, Leantio,
This place will never hear thee murmur more.
Enter LORD CARDINAL *attended.*
Our noble brother, welcome!
LORD CARDINAL: Set those lights down.
Depart till you be called.
[*Exeunt Attendants.*]
DUKE [*Aside.*]: There's serious business
Fix'd in his look; nay, it inclines a little
To the dark colour of a discontentment. –
Brother, what is't commands your eye so powerfully?
Speak, you seem lost.
LORD CARDINAL: The thing I look on seems so
To my eyes, lost for ever.
DUKE: You look on me.
LORD CARDINAL: What a grief 'tis to a religious feeling
To think a man should have a friend so goodly,

162 *voyage*: business trip/sexual adventure 170 *pities of old surgeons*: i.e. in using anaesthetics 175 *cure's*: care (concern) is 184 *lost*: lost in thought

So wise, so noble, nay, a duke, a brother,
And all this certainly damn'd.

DUKE: How!

LORD CARDINAL: 'Tis no wonder,
If your great sin can do't. Dare you look up
For thinking of a vengeance? Dare you sleep,
For fear of never waking, but to death?
And dedicate unto a strumpet's love
The strength of your affections, zeal and health?
Here you stand now; can you assure your pleasures
You shall once more enjoy her, but once more?
Alas, you cannot; what a misery 'tis, then,
To be more certain of eternal death
Than of a next embrace? Nay, shall I show you
How more unfortunate you stand in sin
Than the low private man? All his offences,
Like enclos'd grounds, keep but about himself
And seldom stretch beyond his own soul's bounds;
And when a man grows miserable 'tis some comfort
When he's no further charg'd than with himself.
'Tis a sweet ease to wretchedness. But, great man,
Ev'ry sin thou commit'st shows like a flame
Upon a mountain. 'Tis seen far about
And, with a big wind made of popular breath,
The sparkles fly through cities. Here one takes,
Another catches there, and in short time
Waste all to cinders. But remember still,
What burnt the valleys first came from the hill.
Ev'ry offence draws his particular pain,
But 'tis example proves the great man's bane.
The sins of mean men lie like scatter'd parcels
Of an unperfect bill; but when such fall
Then comes example, and that sums up all.
And this your reason grants: if men of good lives,
Who by their virtuous actions stir up others
To noble and religious imitation,
Receive the greater glory after death

201 *low*: O reads 'love' 202 *enclos'd grounds*: fenced-off lands 205 *charg'd*: accused/burdened/responsible 209 *popular breath*: i.e. the gossip of the people 215 *example*: i.e. the fact that great men are held up as examples 216 *parcels*: items 217 *unperfect*: uncompleted *such*: i.e. great men 218 *sums up all*: continuing the metaphor of a 'bill' of sins, which are not totalled for private men but are for public figures

(As sin must needs confess), what may they feel
In height of torments and in weight of vengeance,
Not only they themselves not doing well,
But sets a light up to show men to hell?

DUKE: If you have done, I have; no more, sweet brother.

LORD CARDINAL: I know time spent in goodness is too tedious;
This had not been a moment's space in lust, now.
How dare you venture on eternal pain
That cannot bear a minute's reprehension?
Methinks you should endure to hear that talk'd of
Which you so strive to suffer. O my brother!
What were you, if you were taken now?
My heart weeps blood to think on't; 'tis a work
Of infinite mercy you can never merit,
That yet you are not death-struck, no, not yet.
I dare not stay you long, for fear you should not
Have time enough allow'd you to repent in.
There's but this wall betwixt you and destruction
When y'are at strongest; and but poor thin clay.
Think upon't, brother. Can you come so near it
For a fair strumpet's love, and fall into
A torment that knows neither end nor bottom
For beauty but the deepness of a skin,
And that not of their own neither? Is she a thing
Whom sickness dare not visit, or age look on,
Or death resist? Does the worm shun her grave?
If not (as your soul knows it) why should lust
Bring man to lasting pain, for rotten dust?

DUKE: Brother of spotless honour, let me weep
The first of my repentance in thy bosom,
And show the blest fruits of a thankful spirit;
And if I e'er keep woman more, unlawfully,
May I want penitence at my greatest need,
And wise men know there is no barren place
Threatens more famine than a dearth in grace.

LORD CARDINAL: Why, here's a conversion is at this time, brother,
Sung for a hymn in heaven; and, at this instant,
The powers of darkness groan, makes all hell sorry.
First, I praise heaven, then in my work I glory. –
Who's there attends without?

231 *reprehension*: rebuke 238 *stay*: detain 240 *this wall*: i.e. the body
246 *not of their own*: women's cosmetics were a constant source of complaint for the moralists of the period 255 *want*: lack

Enter Servants.

SERVANTS: My lord.

LORD CARDINAL: Take up those lights; there was a thicker darkness
When they came first. The peace of a fair soul
Keep with my noble brother.

DUKE: Joys be with you, sir!

Exit LORD CARDINAL, *etc.*

She lies alone tonight for't; and must still
Though it be hard to conquer. But I have vow'd
Never to know her as a strumpet more,
And I must save my oath. If fury fail not
Her husband dies tonight, or, at the most,
Lives not to see the morning spent tomorrow;
Then will I make her lawfully mine own
Without this sin and horror. Now I'm chidden
For what I shall enjoy then unforbidden,
And I'll not freeze in stoves; 'tis but a while,
Live like a hopeful bridegroom, chaste from flesh,
And pleasure then will seem new, fair and fresh.

Exit.

SCENE 2

Enter HIPPOLITO.

HIPPOLITO: The morning so far wasted, yet his baseness
So impudent? See if the very sun do not blush at him!
Dare he do thus much and know me alive!
Put case one must be vicious (as I know myself
Monstrously guilty), there's a blind time made for't;
He might use only that, 'twere conscionable.
Art, silence, closeness, subtlety and darkness,
Are fit for such a business. But there's no pity
To be bestow'd on an apparent sinner,
An impudent daylight lecher! The great zeal
I bear to her advancement in this match
With Lord Vincentio, as the Duke has wrought it,
To the perpetual honour of our house,

269 *save my oath*: keep my word 271 *spent*: finished 275 *stoves*: rooms heated by stoves 4 *Put case*: let us suppose for the sake of argument *vicious*: depraved 5 *a blind time*: i.e. the night 6 *conscionable*: scrupulous 7 *Art*: cunning *closeness*: secrecy 9 *apparent*: open, manifest

Puts fire into my blood, to purge the air
Of this corruption, fear it spread too far
And poison the whole hopes of this fair fortune.
I love her good so dearly, that no brother
Shall venture farther for a sister's glory
Than I for her preferment.

Enter LEANTIO *and a* Page.

LEANTIO [*Aside.*]: Once again
I'll see that glist'ring whore shines like a serpent,
Now the Court sun's upon her. – Page!

PAGE: Anon, sir!

LEANTIO: I'll go in state too; see the coach be ready.
I'll hurry away presently.

[*Exit* Page.]

HIPPOLITO: Yes, you shall hurry,
And the Devil after you; take that at setting forth!

[*Wounds him.*]

Now, and you'll draw, we are upon equal terms, sir.
Thou took'st advantage of my name in honour
Upon my sister; I nev'r saw the stroke
Come, till I found my reputation bleeding;
And therefore count it I no sin to valour
To serve thy lust so. Now we are of even hand,
Take your best course against me. You must die.

LEANTIO: How close sticks envy to man's happiness!
When I was poor and little car'd for life
I had no such means offer'd me to die,
No man's wrath minded me. Slave, I turn this to thee,

[*Draws.*]

To call thee to account for a wound lately
Of a base stamp upon me.

HIPPOLITO: 'Twas most fit
For a base metal. Come and fetch one now
More noble, then, for I will use thee fairer
Than thou hast done thine own soul or our honour.

[*They fight.*]

And there, I think, 'tis for thee.

[LEANTIO *falls.*]

VOICES [*Within*]: Help, help, o part 'em!

15 *fear*: i.e. for fear 21 *Anon*: at once 25 *and*: if 35 *minded*: noticed
37 *base stamp*: base nature (because struck from behind)/counterfeit coin
38 *metal*: with a pun on 'mettle' = nature 40 *thine own*: O reads 'thine'

LEANTIO: False wife! I feel now th'hast pray'd heartily for me;
Rise, strumpet, by my fall, thy lust may reign now;
My heart-string and the marriage-knot that tied thee
Breaks both together.
[*Dies.*]
HIPPOLITO: There I heard the sound on't,
And never liked string better.
Enter GUARDIANO, LIVIA, ISABELLA, WARD, *and* SORDIDO.
LIVIA: 'Tis my brother!
Are you hurt, sir?
HIPPOLITO: Not anything.
LIVIA: Blessed fortune!
Shift for thyself. What is he thou hast kill'd?
HIPPOLITO: Our honour's enemy.
GUARDIANO: Know you this man, lady?
LIVIA: Leantio? My love's joy? [*To* HIPPOLITO.] Wounds stick upon thee
As deadly as thy sins! Art thou not hurt?
The Devil take that fortune. And he dead!
Drop plagues into thy bowels without voice,
Secret and fearful. – Run for officers,
Let him be apprehended with all speed
For fear he 'scape away; lay hands on him.
We cannot be too sure; 'tis wilful murder.
You do heaven's vengeance and the Law just service.
You know him not as I do: he's a villain,
As monstrous as a prodigy, and as dreadful.
HIPPOLITO: Will you but entertain a noble patience
Till you but hear the reason, worthy sister!
LIVIA: The reason! That's a jest hell falls a-laughing at!
Is there a reason found for the destruction
Of our more lawful loves? And was there none
To kill the black lust 'twixt thy niece and thee
That has kept close so long?
GUARDIANO: How's that, good madam?
LIVIA: Too true, sir, there she stands, let her deny't;
The deed cries shortly in the midwife's arms,
Unless the parents' sins strike it still-born;

45 *sound on't*: i.e. that of Leantio's heart-string (a tendon supposed to brace the heart) breaking 48 *Shift for thyself*: watch out for yourself (in case you are arrested) 53 *without voice*: silently 60 *prodigy*: omen/monster (often in the sense of a child deformed at birth) 65 *more lawful*: i.e. more lawful than Hippolito's incestuous relationship 67 *close*: secret

And if you be not deaf and ignorant,
You'll hear strange notes ere long. [*To* ISABELLA.] Look upon me, wench!
'Twas I betray'd thy honour subtly to him
Under a false tale; it lights upon me now;
His arm has paid me home upon thy breast,
My sweet belov'd Leantio!

GUARDIANO: Was my judgment
And care in choice so dev'lishly abus'd,
So beyond shamefully? All the world will grin at me.

WARD: O Sordido, Sordido, I'm damn'd, I'm damn'd!

SORDIDO: Damn'd! Why, sir?

WARD: One of the wicked; dost not see't?
A cuckold, a plain reprobate cuckold!

SORDIDO: Nay, and you be damn'd for that, be of good cheer, sir; y'have gallant company of all professions; I'll have a wife next Sunday too, because I'll along with you myself.

WARD: That will be some comfort yet.

LIVIA [*To* GUARDIANO.]: You, sir, that bear your load of injuries
As I of sorrows, lend me your griev'd strength
To this sad burthen who, in life, wore actions
Flames were not nimbler. We will talk of things
May have the luck to break our hearts together.

GUARDIANO: I'll list to nothing but revenge and anger,
Whose counsels I will follow.

Exeunt LIVIA *and* GUARDIANO [*carrying* LEANTIO's *body*].

SORDIDO: A wife quoth'a!
Here's a sweet plum-tree of your guardiner's graffing!

WARD: Nay, there's a worse name belongs to this fruit yet, and you could hit on't, a more open one. For he that marries a whore looks like a fellow bound all his lifetime to a medlar tree; and that's good stuff, 'tis no sooner ripe but it looks rotten; and so do some queans at nineteen. A pox on't, I thought there was some knavery abroach, for something stirr'd in her belly the first night I lay with her.

SORDIDO: What, what, sir!

71 *ignorant*: wilfully disregarding 74–5 *it . . . home*: i.e. my treachery has turned back on me now; Hippolito's arm has thoroughly paid me back 88 *burthen*: burden 89 *Flames . . . nimbler*: than which fire was not more spirited 90 *May*: which may 91 *list*: listen 92 *quoth'a!*: sarcastic form for 'said he' 93 *sweet plum-tree*: slang for loose woman, and cunt *graffing*: grafting (into the family) 95 *more open one*: i.e. 'open-arse', a term for the fruit of the medlar tree which, because of its appearance and the fact that it was eaten when decaying, became a name for both the cunt and whores 97 *rotten*: decaying/suffering from venereal disease 98 *abroach*: astir

WARD: This is she brought up so courtly! Can sing and dance, and tumble too, methinks. I'll never marry wife again that has so many qualities.

SORDIDO: Indeed, they are seldom good, master. For likely when they are taught so many, they will have one trick more of their own finding out. Well, give me a wench but with one good quality, to lie with none but her husband, and that's bringing-up enough for any woman breathing.

WARD: This was the fault when she was tend'red to me; you never look'd to this.

SORDIDO: Alas, how would you have me see through a great farthingale, sir! I cannot peep through a mill-stone, or in the going, to see what's done i'th'bottom.

WARD: Her father prais'd her breast, sh'ad the voice, forsooth! I marvell'd she sung so small, indeed, being no maid. Now I perceive there's a young querister in her belly. This breeds a singing in my head, I'm sure.

SORDIDO: 'Tis but the tune of your wives' cinquepace, danc'd in a featherbed. Faith, go lie down, master, but take heed your horns do not make holes in the pillowberes! [*Aside.*] I would not batter brows with him for a hogshead of angels; he would prick my skull as full of holes as a scrivener's sandbox.

Exeunt WARD *and* SORDIDO.

ISABELLA [*Aside.*]: Was ever maid so cruelly beguil'd
To the confusion of life, soul, and honour,
All of one woman's murd'ring! I'd fain bring
Her name no nearer to my blood than woman,
And 'tis too much of that. O shame and horror!
In that small distance from yon man to me
Lies sin enough to make a whole world perish.
[*To* HIPPOLITO.] 'Tis time we parted, sir, and left the sight
Of one another; nothing can be worse
To hurt repentance, for our very eyes
Are far more poisonous to religion
Than basilisks to them. If any goodness

101 *tumble*: perform acrobatics/fuck 109 *farthingale*: hooped skirt 110 *peep through a mill-stone*: i.e. see through the situation totally *in the going*: Frost suggests 'in the mill-mechanism/into the woman as she walks' 111 *i'th' bottom*: at the bottom of the mill/at the bottom of the matter/within the womb
113 *small*: high *no maid*: presumably in the sense 'not a very young girl'. He had thus expected a deeper voice 114 *querister*: chorister *singing in my head*: thought to be one of the symptoms of cuckoldry 117 *pillowberes*: pillowcases
118 *hogshead of angels*: barrel of gold coins stamped with the figure of St Michael
119 *scrivener's sandbox*: perforated box containing fine sand used to blot the wet ink on manuscripts 121 *confusion*: ruin 124 *And 'tis too much of that*: and that's too near 131 *basilisks*: mythical creatures that could kill at a glance

Rest in you, hope of comforts, fear of judgments,
My request is I nev'r may see you more;
And so I turn me from you everlastingly,
So is my hope to miss you. But for her,
That durst so dally with a sin so dangerous,
And lay a snare so spitefully for my youth,
If the least means but favour my revenge,
That I may practise the like cruel cunning
Upon her life as she has on mine honour,
I'll act it without pity.

HIPPOLITO: Here's a care
Of reputation and a sister's fortune
Sweetly rewarded by her. Would a silence,
As great as that which keeps among the graves,
Had everlastingly chain'd up her tongue;
My love to her has made mine miserable.

Enter GUARDIANO *and* LIVIA [*who talk apart*].

GUARDIANO: If you can but dissemble your heart's griefs now,
Be but a woman so far.

LIVIA: Peace! I'll strive, sir.

GUARDIANO: As I can wear my injuries in a smile,
Here's an occasion offer'd, that gives anger
Both liberty and safety to perform
Things worth the fire it holds, without the fear
Of danger or of law; for mischiefs acted
Under the privilege of a marriage-triumph
At the Duke's hasty nuptials will be thought
Things merely accidental; all's by chance,
Not got of their own natures.

LIVIA: I conceive you, sir,
Even to a longing for performance on't;
And here behold some fruits. –
[*Kneels before* HIPPOLITO *and* ISABELLA.]
Forgive me both.
What I am now, return'd to sense and judgment,
Is not the same rage and distraction
Presented lately to you; that rude form
Is gone for ever. I am now myself,
That speaks all peace and friendship; and these tears

135 *So is my hope to miss you*: i.e. so I may hope to miss meeting you in hell by refraining from conscious incest 148 *Be but a woman so far*: be true to your sex in this respect (women are dissemblers) 149 *As*: in so far as 157 *Not got of their own natures*: not deliberately conceived

Are the true springs of hearty penitent sorrow
For those foul wrongs which my forgetful fury
Sland'red your virtues with. This gentleman
Is well resolv'd now.

GUARDIANO: I was never otherways.
I knew, alas, 'twas but your anger spake it,
And I nev'r thought on't more.

HIPPOLITO: Pray rise, good sister.

ISABELLA [*Aside.*]: Here's ev'n as sweet amends made for a wrong now
As one that gives a wound, and pays the surgeon;
All the smart's nothing, the great loss of blood,
Or time of hind'rance! Well, I had a mother,
I can dissemble too. [*To* LIVIA.] What wrongs have slipp'd
Through anger's ignorance, aunt, my heart forgives.

GUARDIANO: Why, thus tuneful now!

HIPPOLITO: And what I did, sister,
Was all for honour's cause, which time to come
Will approve to you.

LIVIA: Being awak'd to goodness,
I understand so much, sir, and praise now
The fortune of your arm, and of your safety;
For by his death y'have rid me of a sin
As costly as ev'r woman doted on.
'T has pleas'd the Duke so well too, that (behold, sir)
H'as sent you here your pardon, which I kiss'd
With most affectionate comfort. When 'twas brought,
Then was my fit just past; it came so well, methought,
To glad my heart.

HIPPOLITO: I see his Grace thinks on me.

LIVIA: There's no talk now but of the preparation
For the great marriage.

HIPPOLITO: Does he marry her, then?

LIVIA: With all speed, suddenly, as fast as cost
Can be laid on with many thousand hands.
This gentleman and I had once a purpose
To have honour'd the first marriage of the Duke
With an invention of his own. 'Twas ready,

168 *resolv'd*: satisfied/resolute 174 *hind'rance*: incapacity 177 *thus*: so O, but some editors emend to 'this is' 179 *approve*: show 193 *This gentleman*: i.e. Guardiano 195 *invention*: literary composition *of his own*: although grammatically this could refer to the Duke, he later denies knowledge of the plot of the masque; so Guardiano seems intended

The pains well past, most of the charge bestow'd on't;
Then came the death of your good mother, niece,
And turn'd the glory of it all to black.
'Tis a device would fit these times so well, too,
Art's treasury not better. If you'll join,
It shall be done, the cost shall all be mine.

HIPPOLITO: Y'have my voice first; 'twill well approve my thankfulness
For the Duke's love and favour.

LIVIA: What say you, niece?

ISABELLA: I am content to make one.

GUARDIANO: The plot's full, then;
Your pages, madam, will make shift for cupids.

LIVIA: That will they, sir.

GUARDIANO: You'll play your old part still.

LIVIA: What, is't good? Troth, I have ev'n forgot it!

GUARDIANO: Why, Juno Pronuba, the marriage-goddess.

LIVIA: 'Tis right, indeed.

GUARDIANO [*To* ISABELLA.]: And you shall play the nymph
That offers sacrifice to appease her wrath.

ISABELLA: Sacrifice, good sir?

LIVIA: Must I be appeased, then?

GUARDIANO: That's as you list yourself, as you see cause.

LIVIA: Methinks 'twould show the more state in her deity
To be incens'd.

ISABELLA: 'Twould, but my sacrifice
Shall take a course to appease you, or I'll fail in't,
[*Aside.*] And teach a sinful bawd to play a goddess.

GUARDIANO: For our parts, we'll not be ambitious, sir;
Please you walk in and see the project drawn,
Then take your choice.

HIPPOLITO: I weigh not, so I have one.

[*Exeunt all but* LIVIA.]

LIVIA: How much ado have I to restrain fury
From breaking into curses! O how painful 'tis

196 *charge bestow'd*: expenses incurred 199 *device*: allegory/stratagem/masque 204 *The plot's full*: the cast is complete/the scheme is ready 205 *make shift*: substitute, play the part of 208 *Juno Pronuba*: one of Juno's roles. Ironically, Livia is more of a marriage breaker than a marriage broker 212 *list*: choose 213 *state*: dignity 214 *incens'd*: angry/perfumed with incense 218 *project drawn*: masque written down 219 *I . . . one*: i.e. I don't care which part I get as long as I'm included

To keep great sorrow smother'd! Sure, I think
'Tis harder to dissemble grief than love.
Leantio, here the weight of thy loss lies,
Which nothing but destruction can suffice.
Exit.

SCENE 3

Hoboys.

Enter in great state the DUKE *and* BIANCA, *richly attir'd, with* Lords, Cardinals, Ladies, *and other* Attendants. *They pass solemnly over. Enter* LORD CARDINAL *in a rage, seeming to break off the ceremony.*

LORD CARDINAL: Cease, cease! Religious honours done to sin
Disparage Virtue's reverence, and will pull
Heaven's thunder upon Florence; holy ceremonies
Were made for sacred uses, not for sinful.
Are these the fruits of your repentance, brother?
Better it had been you had never sorrow'd
Than to abuse the benefit, and return
To worse than where sin left you.
Vow'd you then never to keep strumpet more,
And are you now so swift in your desires
To knit your honour and your life fast to her?
Is not sin sure enough to wretched man
But he must bind himself in chains to't? Worse!
Must Marriage, that immaculate robe of Honour
That renders Virtue glorious, fair, and fruitful
To her great Master, be now made the garment
Of Leprosy and Foulness? Is this penitence
To sanctify hot Lust? What is it otherways
Than worship done to devils? Is this the best
Amends that Sin can make after her riots?
As if a drunkard, to appease Heaven's wrath,
Should offer up his surfeit for a sacrifice!
If that be comely, then Lust's offerings are
On Wedlock's sacred altar.

DUKE: Here y'are bitter
Without cause, brother. What I vow'd, I keep
As safe as you your conscience, and this needs not;

s.d. *Hoboys*: oboes s.d. *over*: i.e. over the stage 23 *comely*: decent 26 *this needs not*: this outburst is unnecessary

I taste more wrath in't, than I do religion,
And envy more than goodness. The path now
I tread is honest, leads to lawful love,
Which Virtue in her strictness would not check.
I vow'd no more to keep a sensual woman:
'Tis done, I mean to make a lawful wife of her.

LORD CARDINAL: He that taught you that craft,
Call him not master long, he will undo you.
Grow not too cunning for your soul, good brother.
Is it enough to use adulterous thefts
And then take sanctuary in marriage?
I grant, so long as an offender keeps
Close in a privileged temple, his life's safe;
But if he ever venture to come out,
And so be taken, then he surely dies for't.
So now y'are safe; but when you leave this body,
Man's only privileg'd temple upon earth,
In which the guilty soul takes sanctuary,
Then you'll perceive what wrongs chaste vows endure,
When Lust usurps the bed that should be pure.

BIANCA: Sir, I have read you over all this while
In silence, and I find great knowledge in you,
And severe learning; yet 'mongst all your virtues
I see not Charity written, which some call
The first-born of Religion, and I wonder
I cannot see't in yours. Believe it, sir,
There is no virtue can be sooner miss'd
Or later welcom'd; it begins the rest
And sets 'em all in order. Heaven and angels
Take great delight in a converted sinner:
Why should you, then, a servant and professor,
Differ so much from them? If ev'ry woman
That commits evil should be therefore kept
Back in desires of goodness, how should Virtue
Be known and honour'd? From a man that's blind
To take a burning taper, 'tis no wrong,
He never misses it. But to take light
From one that sees, that's injury and spite.

33 *He*: i.e. the Devil 39 *privileged temple*: i.e. churches claiming right of sanctuary 47 *read you over*: observed you closely 49 *severe*: austere, unsparing in censure 54 *later welcom'd*: welcomed even when belated 57 *professor*: i.e. one professing Christianity

Pray, whether is religion better serv'd,
When lives that are licentious are made honest,
Than when they still run through a sinful blood?
'Tis nothing Virtue's temples to deface;
But build the ruins, there's a work of grace.

DUKE: I kiss thee for that spirit; thou hast prais'd thy wit
A modest way. – On, on there!

Hoboys.

LORD CARDINAL: Lust is bold,
And will have Vengeance speak, ere't be controll'd.

Exeunt.

65 *whether is*: is 68–9 it is easy to debauch virtuous women, but to reclaim them to virtue is an act of grace (punning on 'Grace' = duke)

ACT FIVE

SCENE I

Enter GUARDIANO *and* WARD.

GUARDIANO: Speak, hast thou any sense of thy abuse?
Dost thou know what wrong's done thee?

WARD: I were an ass else.
I cannot wash my face, but I am feeling on't.

GUARDIANO: Here, take this galtrop, then; convey it secretly
Into the place I show'd you. Look you, sir,
This is the trap-door to't.

WARD: I know't of old, uncle, since the last triumph; here rose up a devil with one eye, I remember, with a company of fireworks at's tail.

GUARDIANO: Prithee leave squibbing now, mark me and fail not. But when thou hear'st me give a stamp, down with't. The villain's caught then.

WARD: If I miss you, hang me; I love to catch a villain, and your stamp shall go current, I warrant you. But how shall I rise up and let him down too, all at one hole? That will be a horrible puzzle. You know I have a part in't, I play Slander.

GUARDIANO: True, but never make you ready for't.

WARD: No? My clothes are bought and all, and a foul fiend's head with a long contumelious tongue i'th'chaps on't, a very fit shape for Slander i'th'out-parishes.

GUARDIANO: It shall not come so far; thou understand'st it not.

WARD: O! O!

GUARDIANO: He shall lie deep enough ere that time, and stick first upon those.

3 *feeling on't*: feeling the cuckold's horn 4 *galtrop*: an anti-cavalry device consisting of an iron ball armed with four sharp spikes placed so that when thrown on the ground it has always one spike projecting upwards 7 *triumph*: pageant 9 *squibbing*: letting off fireworks/making smart or sarcastic comments 12 *If I miss you*: i.e. if I miss your signal (but again a clear example of dramatic irony) 12–13 *your stamp shall go current*: your stamp will be accepted as valid (punning on the 'stamp' imprinted on coins) 14 *one hole*: i.e. the one trap-door 18 *contumelious*: insolent *chaps*: cheeks 19 *out-parishes*: areas, exempt from the jurisdiction of the City, where 'slanderous' entertainments flourished 23 *those*: i.e. the spikes of the galtrop

WARD: Now I conceive you, guardiner.
GUARDIANO: Away, list to the privy stamp, that's all thy part.
WARD: Stamp my horns in a mortar if I miss you, and give the powder in white wine to sick cuckolds; a very present remedy for the headache.
Exit WARD.
GUARDIANO: If this should any way miscarry now
(As, if the fool be nimble enough, 'tis certain)
The pages that present the swift-wing'd cupids
Are taught to hit him with their shafts of love
(Fitting his part) which I have cunningly poison'd.
He cannot 'scape my fury; and those ills
Will be laid all on fortune, not our wills.
That's all the sport on't! For who will imagine
That at the celebration of this night
Any mischance that haps can flow from spite?
Exit.

SCENE 2

Flourish.
Enter above DUKE, BIANCA, LORD CARDINAL, FABRITIO, *and other* Cardinals, Lords *and* Ladies *in state.*
DUKE: Now our fair Duchess, your delight shall witness
How y'are belov'd and honour'd; all the glories
Bestow'd upon the gladness of this night
Are done for your bright sake.
BIANCA: I am the more
In debt, my lord, to loves and courtesies
That offer up themselves so bounteously
To do me honour'd grace, without my merit.
DUKE: A goodness set in greatness! How it sparkles
Afar off, like pure diamonds set in gold!
How perfect my desires were, might I witness
But a fair noble peace, 'twixt your two spirits!
The reconcilement would be more sweet to me,
Than longer life to him that fears to die.
[*To the* CARDINAL.] Good sir?

25 *privy*: secret 26 *Stamp*: pound 27 *present*: immediate *headache*: i.e. the irritation caused by the sprouting horns 29 *certain*: i.e. certain to succeed 30 *present*: act the parts of 32 *(Fitting his part)*: i.e. Hippolito's part as a lovelorn shepherd s.d. *Flourish*: i.e. flourish of trumpets *above*: the upper stage where the seduction of Bianca took place

LORD CARDINAL: I profess peace, and am content.
DUKE: I'll see the seal upon't, and then 'tis firm.
LORD CARDINAL: You shall have all you wish.
[*Kisses* BIANCA.]
DUKE: I have all indeed now.
BIANCA [*Aside.*]: But I have made surer work; this shall not blind me.
He that begins so early to reprove,
Quickly rid him, or look for little love.
Beware a brother's envy; he's next heir too.
Cardinal, you die this night, the plot's laid surely:
In time of sports Death may steal in securely.
Then 'tis least thought on,
For he that's most religious, holy friend,
Does not at all hours think upon his end;
He has his times of frailty, and his thoughts
Their transportations too, through flesh and blood
(For all his zeal, his learning, and his light),
As well as we, poor soul, that sin by night.
[FABRITIO *gives a paper to the* DUKE.]
DUKE: What's this, Fabritio?
FABRITIO: Marry, my lord, the model
Of what's presented.
DUKE: O we thank their loves.
Sweet Duchess, take your seat, list to the Argument.
Reads.

There is a nymph that haunts the woods and springs,
In love with two at once, and they with her.
Equal it runs; but to decide these things
The cause to mighty Juno they refer,
She being the marriage-goddess. The two lovers,
They offer sighs; the nymph, a sacrifice;
All to please Juno, who by signs discovers
How the event shall be; so that strife dies.
Then springs a second; for the man refus'd
Grows discontent, and out of love abus'd
He raises Slander up, like a black fiend,
To disgrace th'other, which pays him i'th'end.

24 *holy friend*: a mock address to the Cardinal 27 *transportations*: raptures
30 *model*: synopsis 32 *Argument*: subject-matter 39 *discovers*: reveals
40 *event*: outcome 42 *abus'd*: frustrated 44 *which*: it is not clear whether this refers to the man's action or to 'th'other' *pays him i'th'end*: finally brings retribution on his own head

BIANCA: In troth, my lord, a pretty, pleasing Argument,
And fits th'occasion well. Envy and Slander
Are things soon rais'd against two faithful lovers;
But comfort is, they are not long unrewarded.
Music.
DUKE: This music shows they're upon entrance now.
BIANCA [*Aside.*]: Then enter all my wishes!
Enter Hymen *in yellow,* Ganymede *in a blue robe powdered with stars, and* Hebe *in a white robe with golden stars, with covered cups in their hands. They dance a short dance, then bowing to the* DUKE, *etc.,* Hymen *speaks.*
HYMEN [*Giving* BIANCA *a cup.*]: To thee, fair bride, Hymen offers up
Of nuptial joys this the celestial cup.
Taste it, and thou shalt ever find
Love in thy bed, peace in thy mind.
BIANCA: We'll taste you, sure; 'twere pity to disgrace
So pretty a beginning.
DUKE: 'Twas spoke nobly.
GANYMEDE: Two cups of nectar have we begg'd from Jove;
Hebe give that to Innocence, I this to Love.
[Hebe *gives a cup to the* CARDINAL, *and* Ganymede *a cup to the* DUKE; *they drink.*]
Take heed of stumbling more, look to your way;
Remember still the Via Lactea.
HEBE: Well, Gȧnymede, you have more faults, though not so known;
I spill'd one cup, but you have filch'd many a one.
HYMEN: No more, forbear for Hymen's sake;
In love we met, and so let's part.
Exeunt [Hymen, Ganymede *and* Hebe].
DUKE: But soft! Here's no such persons in the Argument
As these three, Hymen, Hebe, Ganymede.
The actors that this model here discovers
Are only four – Juno, a nymph, two lovers.

50 s.d. *Hymen*: the goddess of marriage who wears her traditional saffron robe *Ganymede*: the beautiful youth Zeus employed as page and cupbearer. His star-sprinkled robe alludes to the fact Zeus made him into the constellation of Aquarius *Hebe*: Zeus's daughter and cupbearer 58 s.d. the cups are wrongly distributed and this could be because the pages are drunk (see ll. 59 and 62) 60 *Via Lactea*: the Milky Way. In one myth this was created when Hebe stumbled and spilt Jove's milk, thus staining the heavens 64 *part*: So O. For the sake of rhyme and metrical consistency, some editors emend to 'parting take'

BIANCA: This is some antemasque belike, my lord,
To entertain time. [*Aside.*] Now my peace is perfect. –
Let sports come on apace; now is their time, my lord.
Music.
Hark you, you hear from 'em.

DUKE: The nymph indeed!

Enter two dress'd like Nymphs, *bearing two tapers lighted; then* ISABELLA *dress'd with flowers and garlands, bearing a censer with fire in it. They set the censer and tapers on Juno's altar with much reverence, this ditty being sung in parts.*

Ditty.

Juno, nuptial-goddess,
Thou that rul'st o'er coupled bodies,
Ti'st man to woman, never to forsake her;
Thou only powerful marriage-maker,
Pity this amaz'd affection;
I love both, and both love me;
Nor know I where to give rejection,
My heart likes so equally,
Till thou set'st right my peace of life,
And with thy power conclude this strife.

ISABELLA: Now with my thanks depart you to the springs,
I to these wells of love.
[*Exeunt* Nymphs.]
Thou sacred goddess
And queen of nuptials, daughter to great Saturn,
Sister and wife to Jove, imperial Juno,
Pity this passionate conflict in my breast,
This tedious war 'twixt two affections;
Crown one with victory, and my heart's at peace.

Enter HIPPOLITO *and* GUARDIANO, *like shepherds.*

HIPPOLITO: Make me that happy man, thou mighty goddess.

GUARDIANO: But I live most in hope, if truest love
Merit the greatest comfort.

ISABELLA: I love both
With such an even and fair affection,
I know not which to speak for, which to wish for,
Till thou, great arbitress 'twixt lovers' hearts,
By thy auspicious grace, design the man

69 *antemasque*: a prelude to the main masque often containing contrasting matter *belike*: in all likelihood 70 *entertain*: while away 75 *Ti'st*: tiest 77 *amaz'd*: bewildered 88 *tedious*: long 89 *one*: O reads 'me' 96 *design*: point out

Which pity I implore.
BOTH [HIPPOLITO *and* GUARDIANO.]: We all implore it.
LIVIA *descends like Juno* [*attended by* Cupids].
ISABELLA: And after sighs, contrition's truest odours,
I offer to thy powerful deity
This precious incense; may it ascend peacefully.
[*Aside.*] And if it keep true touch, my good aunt Juno
'Twill try your immortality ere't be long;
I fear you'll never get so nigh heaven again,
When you're once down.
LIVIA: Though you and your affections
Seem all as dark to our illustrious brightness
As night's inheritance, hell, we pity you,
And your requests are granted. You ask signs,
They shall be given you; we'll be gracious to you.
He of those twain which we determine for you
Love's arrows shall wound twice; the later wound
Betokens love in age; for so are all
Whose love continues firmly all their lifetime
Twice wounded at their marriage, else affection
Dies when youth ends. [*Aside.*] This savour overcomes me. –
Now for a sign of wealth and golden days,
Bright-ey'd Prosperity which all couples love,
Ay, and makes love, take that!
[*Throws flaming gold upon* ISABELLA, *who falls dead.*]
Our brother Jove
Never denies us of his burning treasure
T'express bounty.
DUKE: She falls down upon't;
What's the conceit of that?
FABRITIO: As overjoy'd, belike.
Too much prosperity overjoys us all,
And she has her lapful, it seems, my lord.
DUKE: This swerves a little from the Argument though:
Look you, my lords.
GUARDIANO [*Aside.*]: All's fast; now comes my part to toll him hither.
Then, with a stamp given, he's dispatch'd as cunningly.

s.d. *descends*: Livia is lowered from the 'heavens' by stage apparatus and suspended above the altar in the path of the poisoned fumes 101 *keep true touch*: prove trustworthy (the metaphor is derived from the 'touchstone' used to test gold) 105 *to*: in comparison to 114 *savour*: the poisoned incense. O reads 'favor' but in all probability a long 's' was misread as 'f' 120 *conceit*: meaning 122 *lapful*: alluding to Jove impregnating Danae in the form of a shower of gold 125 *fast*: gone to plan *toll*: decoy, entice

HIPPOLITO: Stark dead! O treachery! Cruelly made away!
[*Discovering* ISABELLA*'s body,* HIPPOLITO *angrily stamps the stage; the trap-door opens and* GUARDIANO *falls through it.*]
How's that?
FABRITIO: Look, there's one of the lovers dropp'd away, too.
DUKE: Why, sure, this plot's drawn false, here's no such thing.
LIVIA: O I am sick to th'death, let me down quickly;
This fume is deadly. O 't has poison'd me!
My subtlety is sped, her art has quitted me,
My own ambition pulls me down to ruin.
[*Dies.*]
HIPPOLITO: Nay, then I kiss thy cold lips, and applaud
This thy revenge in death.
[*Kisses the dead* ISABELLA.]
FABRITIO: Look, Juno's down too!
Cupids *shoot* [*and hit* HIPPOLITO].
What makes she there? Her pride should keep aloft.
She was wont to scorn the earth in other shows.
Methinks her peacocks' feathers are much pull'd.
HIPPOLITO: O death runs through my blood in a wild flame too!
Plague of those cupids! Some lay hold on 'em.
Let 'em not 'scape, they have spoil'd me; the shaft's deadly.
DUKE: I have lost myself in this quite.
HIPPOLITO: My great lords, we are all confounded.
DUKE: How?
HIPPOLITO: Dead; and I worse.
FABRITIO: Dead? My girl dead? I hope
My sister Juno has not serv'd me so.
HIPPOLITO: Lust and forgetfulness has been amongst us,
And we are brought to nothing. Some blest charity
Lend me the speeding pity of his sword
To quench this fire in blood. Leantio's death
Has brought all this upon us (now I taste it)
And made us lay plots to confound each other.
The event so proves it, and man's understanding
Is riper at his fall than all his lifetime.
She, in a madness for her lover's death,
Reveal'd a fearful lust in our near bloods,
For which I am punish'd dreadfully and unlook'd for;

130 *this plot*: i.e. the written outline or 'Argument' 133 *quitted*: either 'deserted' or 'requited' 137 *makes she*: is she doing 142 *spoil'd*: destroyed 145 *I worse*: I am damned (but 'I' could mean 'ay' = ever) 147 *forgetfulness*: i.e. wilful neglect of morality 156 *our near bloods*: i.e. an incestuous relationship

Prov'd her own ruin, too: Vengeance met Vengeance,
Like a set match, as if the plague of sin
Had been agreed to meet here altogether.
But how her fawning partner fell, I reach not,
Unless caught by some springe of his own setting –
For, on my pain, he never dream'd of dying,
The plot was all his own, and he had cunning
Enough to save himself. But 'tis the property
Of guilty deeds to draw your wise men downward.
Therefore the wonder ceases. – O this torment!

DUKE: Our guard below there!

Enter a Lord *with a* Guard.

LORD: My lord.

HIPPOLITO: Run and meet death then,
And cut off time and pain.

[*Runs on a* Guard's *halberd; dies.*]

LORD: Behold, my lord,
H'as run his breast upon a weapon's point.

DUKE: Upon the first night of our nuptial honours
Destruction play her triumph, and great mischiefs
Mask in expected pleasures! 'Tis prodigious!
They're things most fearfully ominous: I like 'em not.
[*To the* Guard.] Remove these ruin'd bodies from our eyes.

BIANCA [*Aside.*]: Not yet, no change? When falls he to the earth?

LORD: Please but your Excellence to peruse that paper,
Which is a brief confession from the heart
Of him that fell first, ere his soul departed;
And there the darkness of these deeds speaks plainly.
'Tis the full scope, the manner and intent;
His ward, that ignorantly let him down,
Fear put to present flight at the voice of him.

BIANCA [*Aside.*]: Nor yet?

DUKE: Read, read; for I am lost in sight and strength.

LORD CARDINAL: My noble brother!

BIANCA: O the curse of wretchedness!
My deadly hand is fall'n upon my lord.
Destruction take me to thee. Give me way;
The pains and plagues of a lost soul upon him
That hinders me a moment.

159 *a set match*: a conspiracy 161 *reach*: understand 162 *springe*: snare
166 *downward*: i.e. to hell, in Guardiano's case through the trap-door
173 *prodigious*: ill-omened 179 *him that fell first*: i.e. Guardiano 183 *present*: immediate 188 *way*: passage

DUKE: My heart swells bigger yet; help here, break't ope,
  My breast flies open next.
  [*Dies.*]
BIANCA: O with the poison
  That was prepar'd for thee, thee, Cardinal!
  'Twas meant for thee.
LORD CARDINAL: Poor prince!
BIANCA: Accursed error!
  Give me thy last breath, thou infected bosom,
  And wrap two spirits in one poison'd vapour.
  [*Kisses the dead* DUKE.]
  Thus, thus, reward thy murderer, and turn death
  Into a parting kiss! My soul stands ready at my lips,
  Ev'n vex'd to stay one minute after thee.
LORD CARDINAL: The greatest sorrow and astonishment
  That ever struck the general peace of Florence
  Dwells in this hour.
BIANCA: So, my desires are satisfied,
  I feel death's power within me.
  Thou hast prevail'd in something, cursed poison,
  Though thy chief force was spent in my lord's bosom.
  But my deformity in spirit's more foul:
  A blemish'd face best fits a leprous soul.
  What make I here? These are all strangers to me,
  Not known but by their malice, now th'art gone,
  Nor do I seek their pities.
  [*Drinks from the poisoned cup.*]
LORD CARDINAL: O restrain
  Her ignorant wilful hand!
BIANCA: Now do; 'tis done.
  Leantio, now I feel the breach of marriage
  At my heart-breaking! O the deadly snares
  That women set for women, without pity
  Either to soul or honour! Learn by me
  To know your foes. In this belief I die:
  Like our own sex, we have no enemy, no enemy!
LORD: See, my lord,
  What shift sh'as made to be her own destruction.
BIANCA: Pride, Greatness, Honour, Beauty, Youth, Ambition,
  You must all down together, there's no help for't.

207 *blemish'd*: probably the poison from the Duke's lips 'burns' her flesh
211 *ignorant*: reckless 213 *heart-breaking*: i.e. point of death 219 *shift*: expedient

Yet this my gladness is, that I remove,
Tasting the same death in a cup of love.
[*Dies.*]

LORD CARDINAL: Sin, what thou art these ruins show too piteously.
Two kings on one throne cannot sit together,
But one must needs down, for his title's wrong;
So where Lust reigns, that prince cannot reign long.
Exeunt.

FINIS

222 *remove*: die

The Changeling

by THOMAS MIDDLETON
and WILLIAM ROWLEY

The Changeling was entered in the Stationers' Register on 19 October 1652 to Humphrey Moseley and published in 1653. The copy-text for this edition is the 1653 Quarto (Q). In 1973 the Scolar Press published a facsimile of a copy in the British Museum.

DRAMATIS PERSONAE

VERMANDERO, *father to Beatrice*
TOMAZO DE PIRACQUO, *a noble lord*
ALONZO DE PIRACQUO, *his brother, suitor to Beatrice*
ALSEMERO, *a nobleman, afterwards married to Beatrice*
JASPERINO, *his friend*
ALIBIUS, *a jealous doctor*
LOLLIO, *his man*
PEDRO, *friend to Antonio*
ANTONIO, *the changeling*
FRANCISCUS, *the counterfeit madman*
DE FLORES, *servant to Vermandero*
Madmen [*and* Fools]
[Gentlemen *and* Gallants]
Servants
BEATRICE[-JOANNA], *daughter to Vermandero*
DIAPHANTA, *her waiting-woman*
ISABELLA, *wife to Alibius*
[Gentlewomen]

The Scene: Alligant.

changeling: idiot, but see Introduction   DE FLORES: from the Latin for 'deflowers'   *Alligant*: Alicante

ACT ONE

[SCENE I]

Enter ALSEMERO.

ALSEMERO: 'Twas in the temple where I first beheld her
And now again the same; what omen yet
Follows of that? None but imaginary;
Why should my hopes or fate be timorous?
The place is holy, so is my intent:
I love her beauties to the holy purpose,
And that, methinks, admits comparison
With man's first creation, the place blest,
And is his right home back, if he achieve it.
The church hath first begun our interview
And that's the place must join us into one,
So there's beginning and perfection too.

Enter JASPERINO.

JASPERINO: O sir, are you here? Come, the wind's fair with you,
Y'are like to have a swift and pleasant passage.

ALSEMERO: Sure y'are deceived, friend, 'tis contrary
In my best judgment.

JASPERINO: What, for Malta?
If you could buy a gale amongst the witches,
They could not serve you such a lucky pennyworth
As comes a' God's name.

ALSEMERO: Even now I observ'd
The temple's vane to turn full in my face,
I know 'tis against me.

JASPERINO: Against you?
Then you know not where you are.

ALSEMERO: Not well indeed.

JASPERINO: Are you not well, sir?

ALSEMERO: Yes, Jasperino.
Unless there be some hidden malady

6 *the holy purpose*: i.e. marriage 8 *the place blest*: Paradise 18 *lucky pennyworth*: bargain 19 *a' God's name*: free, gratis 20 *vane*: wind-vane

Within me, that I understand not.

JASPERINO: And that
I begin to doubt, sir; I never knew
Your inclinations to travels at a pause
With any cause to hinder it till now.
Ashore you were wont to call your servants up,
And help to trap your horses for the speed.
At sea I have seen you weigh the anchor with 'em,
Hoist sails for fear to lose the foremost breath,
Be in continual prayers for fair winds,
And have you chang'd your orisons?

ALSEMERO: No, friend,
I keep the same church, same devotion.

JASPERINO: Lover I'm sure y'are none, the stoic
Was found in you long ago; your mother
Nor best friends, who have set snares of beauty,
Ay, and choice ones too, could never trap you that way.
What might be the cause?

ALSEMERO: Lord, how violent
Thou art; I was but meditating of
Somewhat I heard within the temple.

JASPERINO: Is this violence? 'Tis but idleness
Compar'd with your haste yesterday.

ALSEMERO: I'm all this while a-going, man.

Enter Servants.

JASPERINO: Backwards, I think, sir. – Look, your servants.

SERVANT 1: The seamen call; shall we board your trunks?

ALSEMERO: No, not today.

JASPERINO: 'Tis the critical day, it seems, and the sign in Aquarius.

SERVANT 2 [*Aside.*]: We must not to sea today; this smoke will bring forth fire.

ALSEMERO: Keep all on shore; I do not know the end
(Which needs I must do) of an affair in hand
Ere I can go to sea.

SERVANT 1: Well, your pleasure.

SERVANT 2 [*Aside.*]: Let him e'en take his leisure too, we are safer on land.

Exeunt Servants.

Enter BEATRICE, DIAPHANTA, *and* Servants. [ALSEMERO *greets* BEATRICE *and kisses her.*]

26 *doubt*: fear or suspect 30 *for the speed*: to hasten matters 34 *orisons*: prayers 36 *stoic*: Stoics practised an austere code of ethics characterized by the suppression of all passions 49 *critical*: astrologically crucial *sign in Aquarius*: favourable for a sea-voyage since Aquarius is the 'Water-carrier'

JASPERINO [*Aside.*]: How now! The laws of the Medes are chang'd sure! Salute a woman? He kisses too: wonderful! Where learnt he this? And does it perfectly too; in my conscience he ne'er rehears'd it before. Nay, go on, this will be stranger and better news at Valencia than if he had ransom'd half Greece from the Turk.

BEATRICE: You are a scholar, sir?

ALSEMERO: A weak one, lady.

BEATRICE: Which of the sciences is this love you speak of?

ALSEMERO: From your tongue I take it to be music.

BEATRICE: You are skilful in't, can sing at first sight.

ALSEMERO: And I have show'd you all my skill at once.
I want more words to express me further
And must be forc'd to repetition:
I love you dearly.

BEATRICE: Be better advis'd, sir:
Our eyes are sentinels unto our judgments
And should give certain judgment what they see;
But they are rash sometimes, and tell us wonders
Of common things, which when our judgments find,
They can then check the eyes, and call them blind.

ALSEMERO: But I am further, lady; yesterday
Was mine eyes' employment, and hither now
They brought my judgment, where are both agreed.
Both Houses then consenting, 'tis agreed,
Only there wants the confirmation
By the hand royal, that's your part, lady.

BEATRICE: O there's one above me, sir. [*Aside.*] For five days past
To be recall'd! Sure, mine eyes were mistaken,
This was the man was meant me; that he should come
So near his time, and miss it!

JASPERINO [*Aside.*]: We might have come by the carriers from Valencia, I see, and sav'd all our sea-provision: we are at farthest sure. Methinks I should do something too; I meant to be a venturer in this voyage.

57 *laws of the Medes*: unalterable laws (Daniel 6. 8) 59 *in my conscience*: upon my word 60 *Valencia*: a port on the east coast of Spain, approximately 75 miles north of Alicante 65 *sing at first sight*: sight-read music/make avowals of love at a first meeting 79–80 once both Houses of Parliament ('eyes' and 'judgment') have passed a Bill, only the royal assent ('hand royal') is required for it to become law 81 *one above me*: her father and, above him, God 85 *carriers*: overland transport 86 *at farthest*: either 'the end-point of our journey', or 'wildly off-course' 87 *venturer*: a shareholder in the expenses and profits of a commercial voyage

Yonder's another vessel, I'll board her; if she be lawful prize, down goes her topsail.

[*Approaches* DIAPHANTA.]

Enter DE FLORES.

DE FLORES: Lady, your father –

BEATRICE: Is in health, I hope.

DE FLORES: Your eye shall instantly instruct you, lady.
He's coming hitherward.

BEATRICE: What needed then
Your duteous preface? I had rather
He had come unexpected; you must stall
A good presence with unnecessary blabbing:
And how welcome for your part you are,
I'm sure you know.

DE FLORES [*Aside.*]: Will't never mend this scorn
One side nor other? Must I be enjoin'd
To follow still whilst she flies from me? Well,
Fates do your worst, I'll please myself with sight
Of her, at all opportunities,
If but to spite her anger; I know she had
Rather see me dead than living, and yet
She knows no cause for't, but a peevish will.

ALSEMERO: You seem'd displeas'd, lady, on the sudden.

BEATRICE: Your pardon, sir, 'tis my infirmity,
Nor can I other reason render you,
Than his or hers, of some particular thing
They must abandon as a deadly poison,
Which to a thousand other tastes were wholesome;
Such to mine eyes is that same fellow there,
The same that report speaks of the basilisk.

ALSEMERO: This is a frequent frailty in our nature;
There's scarce a man amongst a thousand sound
But hath his imperfection: one distastes
The scent of roses, which to infinites
Most pleasing is, and odoriferous;
One oil, the enemy of poison;
Another wine, the cheerer of the heart
And lively refresher of the countenance.
Indeed this fault (if so it be) is general,

88 *lawful prize*: a ship which may be legitimately seized/an unmarried woman
88–9 *down goes her topsail*: a sign of surrender 94 *stall*: forestall/make stale
95 *good presence*: i.e. her father 112 *basilisk*: mythical creature that could kill by a glance 114 *sound*: healthy 116 *infinites*: infinite numbers of people

There's scarce a thing but is both lov'd and loath'd.
Myself (I must confess) have the same frailty.

BEATRICE: And what may be your poison, sir? I am bold with you.

ALSEMERO: What might be your desire, perhaps, a cherry.

BEATRICE: I am no enemy to any creature
My memory has, but yon gentleman.

ALSEMERO: He does ill to tempt your sight, if he knew it.

BEATRICE: He cannot be ignorant of that, sir,
I have not spar'd to tell him so; and I want
To help myself, since he's a gentleman
In good respect with my father, and follows him.

ALSEMERO: He's out of his place then now.
[*They talk apart.*]

JASPERINO: I am a mad wag, wench.

DIAPHANTA: So methinks; but for your comfort I can tell you, we have a doctor in the city that undertakes the cure of such.

JASPERINO: Tush, I know what physic is best for the state of mine own body.

DIAPHANTA: 'Tis scarce a well-govern'd state, I believe.

JASPERINO: I could show thee such a thing with an ingredient that we two would compound together, and if it did not tame the maddest blood i' th'town for two hours after, I'll ne'er profess physic again.

DIAPHANTA: A little poppy, sir, were good to cause you sleep.

JASPERINO: Poppy? I'll give thee a pop i'th'lips for that first, and begin there. [*Kisses her.*] Poppy is one simple indeed, and cuckoo (what you call't) another: I'll discover no more now, another time I'll show thee all.

BEATRICE: My father, sir.
Enter VERMANDERO *and* Servants.

VERMANDERO: O Joanna, I came to meet thee;
Your devotion's ended?

BEATRICE: For this time, sir.
[*Aside.*] I shall change my saint, I fear me, I find

125 Q reads 'And what might be your desire perhaps, a cherry.' Most editors emend this as it seems unlikely that Alsemero would answer one question with another. It is possible the initial 'And' was copied in error from the line above
130–1 *and I want To help myself*: I am powerless to do anything about it
136 *doctor in the city*: i.e. Alibius 140 *ingredient*: Q reads 'Ingredian'
142 *profess physic*: declare myself expert in medical matters 143 *poppy*: i.e. the narcotic extract of the poppy 145 *simple*: medicinal herb 145–6 *cuckoo (what you call't)*: cuckoo-pint plant or wild arum, with particular reference to its phallic appearance 146 *discover*: reveal 151 *change my saint*: i.e. from a heavenly to an earthly one

A giddy turning in me. – Sir, this while
I am beholding to this gentleman
Who left his own way to keep me company,
And in discourse I find him much desirous
To see your castle: he hath deserv'd it, sir,
If ye please to grant it.

VERMANDERO: With all my heart, sir.
Yet there's an article between, I must know
Your country; we use not to give survey
Of our chief strengths to strangers; our citadels
Are plac'd conspicuous to outward view
On promonts' tops; but within are secrets.

ALSEMERO: A Valencian, sir.

VERMANDERO: A Valencian?
That's native, sir; of what name, I beseech you?

ALSEMERO: Alsemero, sir.

VERMANDERO: Alsemero; not the son
Of John de Alsemero?

ALSEMERO: The same, sir.

VERMANDERO: My best love bids you welcome.

BEATRICE [*Aside.*]: He was wont
To call me so, and then he speaks a most
Unfeigned truth.

VERMANDERO: O sir, I knew your father.
We two were in acquaintance long ago,
Before our chins were worth Iulan down,
And so continued till the stamp of time
Had coin'd us into silver: well, he's gone;
A good soldier went with him.

ALSEMERO: You went together in that, sir.

VERMANDERO: No, by Saint Jacques, I came behind him.
Yet I have done somewhat too; an unhappy day
Swallowed him at last at Gibraltar

158 *article between*: a pre-condition 164 *native*: of the same nationality. The two towns had strong links, as Alicante had been one of the major provinces of the ancient kingdom of Valencia 167–9 Vermandero is accustomed to term his daughter 'My best love', and he is therefore certainly correct if he means that Beatrice bids Alsemero welcome 171 *Iulan down*: the first growth of a beard. The name of Iulus Ascanius in the *Aeneid* was thought by some commentators to have been derived from the Greek ἴουλος, the first growth of a beard 176 *Saint Jacques*: St James the Greater, patron saint of Spain 178 *Gibraltar*: the battle of Gibraltar, 1607, in which the Dutch fleet defeated the Spanish

In fight with those rebellious Hollanders,
Was it not so?
ALSEMERO: Whose death I had reveng'd
Or followed him in fate, had not the late league
Prevented me.
VERMANDERO: Ay, ay, 'twas time to breathe:
O Joanna, I should ha' told thee news,
I saw Piracquo lately.
BEATRICE [*Aside*.]: That's ill news.
VERMANDERO: He's hot preparing for his day of triumph,
Thou must be a bride within this sevennight.
ALSEMERO [*Aside*.]: Ha!
BEATRICE: Nay, good sir, be not so violent; with speed
I cannot render satisfaction
Unto the dear companion of my soul,
Virginity, whom I thus long have liv'd with,
And part with it so rude and suddenly;
Can such friends divide, never to meet again,
Without a solemn farewell?
VERMANDERO: Tush, tush, there's a toy.
ALSEMERO [*Aside*.]: I must now part, and never meet again
With any joy on earth. – Sir, your pardon,
My affairs call on me.
VERMANDERO: How, sir? By no means;
Not chang'd so soon, I hope? You must see my castle
And her best entertainment, ere we part;
I shall think myself unkindly us'd else.
Come, come, let's on; I had good hope your stay
Had been a while with us in Alligant;
I might have bid you to my daughter's wedding.
ALSEMERO [*Aside*.]: He means to feast me, and poisons me beforehand.
– I should be dearly glad to be there, sir,
Did my occasions suit as I could wish.
BEATRICE: I shall be sorry if you be not there
When it is done, sir, but not so suddenly.
VERMANDERO: I tell you, sir, the gentleman's complete,
A courtier and a gallant, enrich'd
With many fair and noble ornaments.
I would not change him for a son-in-law

181 *the late league*: the Treaty of the Hague, 1609, provided for a twelve-year truce between Spain and the Netherlands 185 *his*: Q reads 'this' 193 *toy*: a trifling or foolish speech

For any he in Spain, the proudest he,
And we have great ones, that you know.
ALSEMERO: He's much
Bound to you, sir.
VERMANDERO: He shall be bound to me,
As fast as this tie can hold him; I'll want
My will else.
BEATRICE [*Aside.*]: I shall want mine if you do it.
VERMANDERO: But come, by the way I'll tell you more of him.
ALSEMERO [*Aside.*]: How shall I dare to venture in his castle,
When he discharges murderers at the gate?
But I must on, for back I cannot go.
BEATRICE [*Aside.*]: Not this serpent gone yet?
[*Drops her glove.*]
VERMANDERO: Look, girl, thy glove's fall'n;
Stay, stay. – De Flores, help a little.
[*Exeunt* VERMANDERO, ALSEMERO, JASPERINO, *and* Servants.]
DE FLORES [*Offering glove.*]: Here, lady.
BEATRICE: Mischief on your officious forwardness!
Who bade you stoop? They touch my hand no more:
There, for tother's sake I part with this,
[*Takes off the other glove and throws it down.*]
Take 'em and draw thine own skin off with 'em.
Exeunt [*all but* DE FLORES].
DE FLORES: Here's a favour come, with a mischief! Now I know
She had rather wear my pelt tann'd in a pair
Of dancing pumps, than I should thrust my fingers
Into her sockets here; I know she hates me,
Yet cannot choose but love her:
No matter, if but to vex her, I'll haunt her still;
Though I get nothing else, I'll have my will.
Exit.

[SCENE 2]

Enter ALIBIUS *and* LOLLIO.
ALIBIUS: Lollio, I must trust thee with a secret,
But thou must keep it.

215 *want*: be deprived of 219 *murderers*: small cannons or mortars
227 *favour*: i.e. the glove, which was probably dropped as a 'favour' or love-token for Alsemero

LOLLIO: I was ever close to a secret, sir.
ALIBIUS: The diligence that I have found in thee,
The care and industry already past,
Assures me of thy good continuance.
Lollio, I have a wife.
LOLLIO: Fie, sir, 'tis too late to keep her secret, she's known to be married all the town and country over.
ALIBIUS: Thou goest too fast, my Lollio; that knowledge
I allow no man can be barr'd it;
But there is a knowledge which is nearer,
Deeper and sweeter, Lollio.
LOLLIO: Well, sir, let us handle that between you and I.
ALIBIUS: 'Tis that I go about, man; Lollio,
My wife is young.
LOLLIO: So much the worse to be kept secret, sir.
ALIBIUS: Why, now thou meet'st the substance of the point;
I am old, Lollio.
LOLLIO: No, sir, 'tis I am old Lollio.
ALIBIUS: Yet why may not this concord and sympathize?
Old trees and young plants often grow together,
Well enough agreeing.
LOLLIO: Ay, sir, but the old trees raise themselves higher and broader than the young plants.
ALIBIUS: Shrewd application! There's the fear, man;
I would wear my ring on my own finger;
Whilst it is borrowed it is none of mine,
But his that useth it.
LOLLIO: You must keep it on still then; if it but lie by, one or other will be thrusting into't.
ALIBIUS: Thou conceiv'st me, Lollio; here thy watchful eye
Must have employment, I cannot always be at home.
LOLLIO: I dare swear you cannot.
ALIBIUS: I must look out.
LOLLIO: I know't, you must look out, 'tis every man's case.
ALIBIUS: Here I do say must thy employment be:
To watch her treadings, and in my absence
Supply my place.
LOLLIO: I'll do my best, sir, yet surely I cannot see who you should have cause to be jealous of.

3 *ever close to a secret*: good at keeping/ferreting out secrets 24–5 i.e. old men are likely to acquire cuckold's horns 27 *ring*: wedding ring. The pun on the cunt is made clear by the subsequent reference to a finger/penis 'thrusting into't'
35 *look out*: go out/take care

ALIBIUS: Thy reason for that, Lollio? 'Tis a comfortable question.

LOLLIO: We have but two sorts of people in the house, and both under the whip, that's fools and madmen; the one has not wit enough to be knaves, and the other not knavery enough to be fools.

ALIBIUS: Ay, those are all my patients, Lollio.
I do profess the cure of either sort;
My trade, my living 'tis, I thrive by it;
But here's the care that mixes with my thrift:
The daily visitants, that come to see
My brainsick patients, I would not have
To see my wife: gallants I do observe
Of quick enticing eyes, rich in habits,
Of stature and proportion very comely:
These are most shrewd temptations, Lollio.

LOLLIO: They may be easily answered, sir; if they come to see the fools and madmen, you and I may serve the turn, and let my mistress alone, she's of neither sort.

ALIBIUS: 'Tis a good ward; indeed, come they to see
Our madmen or our fools, let 'em see no more
Than what they come for; by that consequent
They must not see her, I'm sure she's no fool.

LOLLIO: And I'm sure she's no madman.

ALIBIUS: Hold that buckler fast, Lollio; my trust
Is on thee, and I account it firm and strong.
What hour is't, Lollio?

LOLLIO: Towards belly-hour, sir.

ALIBIUS: Dinner time? Thou mean'st twelve o'clock.

LOLLIO: Yes, sir, for every part has his hour: we wake at six and look about us, that's eye-hour; at seven we should pray, that's knee-hour; at eight walk, that's leg-hour; at nine gather flowers and pluck a rose, that's nose-hour; at ten we drink, that's mouth-hour; at eleven lay about us for victuals, that's hand-hour; at twelve go to dinner, that's belly-hour.

ALIBIUS: Profoundly, Lollio! It will be long
Ere all thy scholars learn this lesson, and
I did look to have a new one entered. Stay,

42 *comfortable*: comforting 47 *of either sort*: fools were those born simple-minded. Madmen were the insane 50 *daily visitants*: Bethlehem Hospital (Bedlam) and other madhouses were popular resorts of entertainment 55 *shrewd*: strong or dangerous 59 *ward*: defensive guard in fencing 61 *consequent*: conclusion 64 *buckler*: a small shield (continuing the fencing metaphor) 71–2 *pluck a rose*: urinate 72–3 *lay about*: search 73 *victuals*: food and drink

I think my expectation is come home.
Enter PEDRO, *and* ANTONIO *like an idiot.*

PEDRO: Save you, sir; my business speaks itself,
This sight takes off the labour of my tongue.

ALIBIUS: Ay, ay, sir,
'Tis plain enough, you mean him for my patient.

PEDRO: And if your pains prove but commodious, to give but some little strength to his sick and weak part of nature in him, these [*Gives money.*] are but patterns to show you of the whole pieces that will follow to you, beside the charge of diet, washing, and other necessaries fully defrayed.

ALIBIUS: Believe it, sir, there shall no care be wanting.

LOLLIO: Sir, an officer in this place may deserve something; the trouble will pass through my hands.

PEDRO: 'Tis fit something should come to your hands then, sir.
[*Gives money.*]

LOLLIO: Yes, sir, 'tis I must keep him sweet, and read to him; what is his name?

PEDRO: His name is Antonio; marry, we use but half to him, only Tony.

LOLLIO: Tony, Tony, 'tis enough, and a very good name for a fool; what's your name, Tony?

ANTONIO: He, he, he! Well, I thank you, cousin; he, he, he!

LOLLIO: Good boy! Hold up your head: he can laugh, I perceive by that he is no beast.

PEDRO: Well, sir,
If you can raise him but to any height,
Any degree of wit, might he attain
(As I might say) to creep but on all four
Towards the chair of wit, or walk on crutches,
'Twould add an honour to your worthy pains,
And a great family might pray for you,
To which he should be heir, had he discretion
To claim and guide his own; assure you, sir,
He is a gentleman.

LOLLIO: Nay, there's nobody doubted that; at first sight I knew him for a gentleman, he looks no other yet.

PEDRO: Let him have good attendance and sweet lodging.

80 *takes off*: saves the necessity for 83 *commodious*: successful 85 *patterns*: samples 86 *charge*: cost 93 *Tony*: the name became a synonym for 'fool', probably as a result of the influence of *The Changeling* 97–8 According to Aristotle, laughter was one of the distinguishing features of humanity
110 *gentleman*: although now only a polite form of address, in the 17th century the term denoted considerable rank

LOLLIO: As good as my mistress lies in, sir; and as you allow us time and means, we can raise him to the higher degree of discretion.

PEDRO: Nay, there shall no cost want, sir.

LOLLIO: He will hardly be stretch'd up to the wit of a magnifico.

PEDRO: O no, that's not to be expected, far shorter will be enough.

LOLLIO: I'll warrant you [I'll] make him fit to bear office in five weeks; I'll undertake to wind him up to the wit of constable.

PEDRO: If it be lower than that it might serve turn.

LOLLIO: No, fie, to level him with a headborough, beadle, or watchman were but little better than he is; constable I'll able him: if he do come to be a Justice afterwards, let him thank the keeper. Or I'll go further with you; say I do bring him up to my own pitch, say I make him as wise as myself.

PEDRO: Why, there I would have it.

LOLLIO: Well, go to, either I'll be as errant a fool as he, or he shall be as wise as I, and then I think 'twill serve his turn.

PEDRO: Nay, I do like thy wit passing well.

LOLLIO: Yes, you may; yet if I had not been a fool, I had had more wit than I have too; remember what state you find me in.

PEDRO: I will, and so leave you: your best cares, I beseech you.

ALIBIUS: Take you none with you, leave 'em all with us.

Exit PEDRO.

ANTONIO: O my cousin's gone! Cousin, cousin! O!

LOLLIO: Peace, peace, Tony, you must not cry, child, you must be whipp'd if you do; your cousin is here still, I am your cousin, Tony.

ANTONIO: He, he! Then I'll not cry, if thou be'st my cousin, he, he, he!

LOLLIO: I were best try his wit a little, that I may know what form to place him in.

ALIBIUS: Ay, do, Lollio, do.

LOLLIO: I must ask him easy questions at first: Tony, how many true fingers has a tailor on his right hand?

ANTONIO: As many as on his left, cousin.

LOLLIO: Good; and how many on both?

ANTONIO: Two less than a deuce, cousin.

114 *want*: be wanting; i.e. all expenses will be paid 115 *magnifico*: title bestowed upon Venetian magnates and thus, by extension, upon any high-ranking official 118 *wit of constable*: constables were proverbially dull-witted 119 *serve turn*: be sufficient 120 *headborough*: a petty constable *beadle*: an under-officer of justice notorious for bumbling inefficiency 121 *I'll able him*: I'll make him fit for 122 *Justice*: Justices of the Peace were also renowned for stupidity 126 *errant*: arrant, unmitigated (possibly with a pun on 'errant' = wandering as in 'knight-errant') 130 *state*: status; i.e. keeper of fools 140 *true*: tailors were proverbially dishonest

LOLLIO: Very well answered; I come to you again, cousin Tony: how many fools goes to a wise man?

ANTONIO: Forty in a day sometimes, cousin.

LOLLIO: Forty in a day? How prove you that?

ANTONIO: All that fall out amongst themselves, and go to a lawyer to be made friends.

LOLLIO: A parlous fool! He must sit in the fourth form at least, I perceive that; I come again, Tony: how many knaves make an honest man?

ANTONIO: I know not that, cousin.

LOLLIO: No, the question is too hard for you: I'll tell you, cousin, there's three knaves may make an honest man, a sergeant, a jailer, and a beadle; the sergeant catches him, the jailer holds him, and the beadle lashes him; and if he be not honest then, the hangman must cure him.

ANTONIO: Ha, ha, ha, that's fine sport, cousin!

ALIBIUS: This was too deep a question for the fool, Lollio.

LOLLIO: Yes, this might have serv'd yourself, though I say't; once more, and you shall go play, Tony.

ANTONIO: Ay, play at push-pin, cousin, ha, he!

LOLLIO: So thou shalt; say how many fools are here.

ANTONIO: Two, cousin, thou and I.

LOLLIO: Nay, y'are too forward there, Tony; mark my question: how many fools and knaves are here? A fool before a knave, a fool behind a knave, between every two fools a knave; how many fools, how many knaves?

ANTONIO: I never learnt so far, cousin.

ALIBIUS: Thou put'st too hard questions to him, Lollio.

LOLLIO: I'll make him understand it easily; cousin, stand there.

ANTONIO: Ay, cousin.

LOLLIO: Master, stand you next the fool.

ALIBIUS: Well, Lollio?

LOLLIO: Here's my place: mark now, Tony, there a fool before a knave.

ANTONIO: That's I, cousin.

LOLLIO: Here's a fool behind a knave, that's I, and between us two fools there is a knave, that's my master; 'tis but we three, that's all.

ANTONIO: We three, we three, cousin!

Madmen *within*.

MADMAN 1: Put's head i'th'pillory, the bread's too little.

146 *goes to*: make up/visit 151 *parlous*: cunning 162 *push-pin*: the name of this children's game obviously suggests a bawdy quibble 180 *the bread's too little*: presumably complaining about a lack of food, but the exact sense of the madmen's outbursts is obviously unclear

MADMAN 2: Fly, fly, and he catches the swallow.

MADMAN 3: Give her more onion, or the Devil put the rope about her crag.

LOLLIO: You may hear what time of day it is, the chimes of Bedlam goes.

ALIBIUS: Peace, peace, or the wire comes!

MADMAN 3: Cat whore, cat whore, her permasant, her permasant!

ALIBIUS: Peace, I say; their hour's come, they must be fed, Lollio.

LOLLIO: There's no hope of recovery of that Welsh madman, was undone by a mouse, that spoil'd him a permasant; lost his wits for't.

ALIBIUS: Go to your charge, Lollio, I'll to mine.

LOLLIO: Go you to your madmen's ward, let me alone with your fools.

ALIBIUS: And remember my last charge, Lollio.

Exit.

LOLLIO: Of which your patients do you think I am? Come, Tony, you must amongst your school-fellows now; there's pretty scholars amongst 'em, I can tell you, there's some of 'em at *stultus, stulta, stultum.*

ANTONIO: I would see the madmen, cousin, if they would not bite me.

LOLLIO: No, they shall not bite thee, Tony.

ANTONIO: They bite when they are at dinner, do they not, cuz?

LOLLIO: They bite at dinner indeed, Tony. Well, I hope to get credit by thee, I like thee the best of all the scholars that ever I brought up, and thou shalt prove a wise man, or I'll prove a fool myself.

Exeunt.

181 *catches the swallow*: alluding to the proverb 'Fly and you will catch the swallow' 182 *crag*: neck. The rope is both the onion string and a hangman's halter 183 *the chimes of Bedlam*: the noise of the insane crying for food. 'Bedlam' referred specifically to Bethlehem Hospital for the insane, or more generally to any madhouse 184 *wire*: a wire whip 185 *Cat whore*: the Welshman is abusing his cat for failing to protect his cheese *her*: stage-Welsh for 'my' *permasant*: parmesan cheese 187 *Welsh madman*: the Welsh were proverbially fond of cheese 191 *last charge*: i.e. to keep Isabella under surveillance 194 *stultus, stulta, stultum*: i.e. they can decline the Latin for 'foolish'

ACT TWO

[SCENE I]

Enter BEATRICE *and* JASPERINO *severally.*

BEATRICE: O sir, I'm ready now for that fair service,
Which makes the name of friend sit glorious on you.
Good angels and this conduct be your guide,
[*Gives a paper.*]
Fitness of time and place is there set down, sir.

JASPERINO: The joy I shall return rewards my service.
Exit.

BEATRICE: How wise is Alsemero in his friend!
It is a sign he makes his choice with judgment.
Then I appear in nothing more approv'd
Than making choice of him;
For 'tis a principle, he that can choose
That bosom well, who of his thoughts partakes,
Proves most discreet in every choice he makes.
Methinks I love now with the eyes of judgment
And see the way to merit, clearly see it.
A true deserver like a diamond sparkles,
In darkness you may see him, that's in absence,
Which is the greatest darkness falls on love;
Yet is he best discern'd then
With intellectual eyesight; what's Piracquo
My father spends his breath for? And his blessing
Is only mine, as I regard his name,
Else it goes from me, and turns head against me,
Transform'd into a curse; some speedy way
Must be rememb'red; he's so forward too,
So urgent that way, scarce allows me breath

s.d. *severally*: separately 3 *conduct*: pass 12 *discreet*: judicious 21 *as I regard his name*: probably 'his' refers to her father, in which case the phrase appears to mean either, 'as long as I respect his authority' or 'as long as I maintain the family name by marrying well'. But it is possible that 'his' refers to Alonzo, with the sense 'as long as I think only of Alonzo' 22 *turns head*: opposes as an enemy 24 *he's*: probably Piracquo, but perhaps her father

To speak to my new comforts.
Enter DE FLORES.
DE FLORES [*Aside.*]: Yonder's she.
Whatever ails me? Now a-late especially,
I can as well be hang'd as refrain seeing her;
Some twenty times a day, nay, not so little,
Do I force errands, frame ways and excuses
To come into her sight, and I have small reason for't,
And less encouragement; for she baits me still
Every time worse than other, does profess herself
The cruellest enemy to my face in town,
At no hand can abide the sight of me,
As if danger or ill luck hung in my looks.
I must confess my face is bad enough,
But I know far worse has better fortune,
And not endur'd alone, but doted on;
And yet such pick-hair'd faces, chins like witches',
Here and there five hairs, whispering in a corner,
As if they grew in fear one of another,
Wrinkles like troughs, where swine-deformity swills
The tears of perjury that lie there like wash
Fallen from the slimy and dishonest eye;
Yet such a one pluck'd sweets without restraint
And has the grace of beauty to his sweet.
Though my hard fate has thrust me out to servitude
I tumbled into th'world a gentleman.
She turns her blessed eye upon me now
And I'll endure all storms before I part with't.
BEATRICE [*Aside.*]: Again!
This ominous ill-fac'd fellow more disturbs me
Than all my other passions.
DE FLORES [*Aside.*]: Now't begins again;
I'll stand this storm of hail though the stones pelt me.
BEATRICE: Thy business? What's thy business?
DE FLORES [*Aside.*]: Soft and fair,
I cannot part so soon now.
BEATRICE [*Aside.*]: The villain's fix'd. –
Thou standing toad-pool!

35 *At no hand*: on no account 40 *pick-hair'd*: probably indicates a thin, straggly beard 44 *wash*: discharge 47 *to his sweet*: as his sweetheart 58 *standing toad-pool*: toads were thought to breed in stagnant water. Presumably De Flores suffers from skin eruptions

DE FLORES [*Aside.*]: The shower falls amain now.
BEATRICE: Who sent thee? What's thy errand? Leave my sight.
DE FLORES: My lord your father charg'd me to deliver
A message to you.
BEATRICE: What, another since?
Do't and be hang'd then, let me be rid of thee.
DE FLORES: True service merits mercy.
BEATRICE: What's thy message?
DE FLORES: Let beauty settle but in patience,
You shall hear all.
BEATRICE: A dallying, trifling torment!
DE FLORES: Signor Alonzo de Piracquo, lady,
Sole brother to Tomazo de Piracquo –
BEATRICE: Slave, when wilt make an end?
DE FLORES [*Aside.*]: Too soon I shall.
BEATRICE: What all this while of him?
DE FLORES: The said Alonzo,
With the foresaid Tomazo –
BEATRICE: Yet again?
DE FLORES: Is new alighted.
BEATRICE [*Aside.*]: Vengeance strike the news! –
Thou thing most loath'd, what cause was there in this
To bring thee to my sight?
DE FLORES: My lord your father
Charg'd me to seek you out.
BEATRICE: Is there no other
To send his errand by?
DE FLORES: It seems 'tis my luck
To be i'th'way still.
BEATRICE: Get thee from me.
DE FLORES [*Aside.*]: So,
Why, am not I an ass to devise ways
Thus to be rail'd at? I must see her still!
I shall have a mad qualm within this hour again,
I know't, and like a common Garden-bull
I do but take breath to be lugg'd again.
What this may bode I know not; I'll despair the less
Because there's daily precedents of bad faces
Belov'd beyond all reason; these foul chops
May come into favour one day 'mongst his fellows:

58 *amain*: violently 61 *another since?*: yet again? 79 *qualm*: a sudden access of passion 80 *common Garden-bull*: bull-baiting at the Paris Garden in Southwark was a popular form of entertainment 81 *lugg'd*: baited 84 *chops*: cheeks

Wrangling has prov'd the mistress of good pastime;
As children cry themselves asleep, I ha' seen
Women have chid themselves abed to men.
Exit DE FLORES.

BEATRICE: I never see this fellow, but I think
Of some harm towards me, danger's in my mind still,
I scarce leave trembling of an hour after.
The next good mood I find my father in,
I'll get him quite discarded. O I was
Lost in this small disturbance, and forgot
Affliction's fiercer torrent that now comes
To bear down all my comforts.
Enter VERMANDERO, ALONZO, TOMAZO.

VERMANDERO: Y'are both welcome,
But an especial one belongs to you, sir,
To whose most noble name our love presents
The addition of a son, our son Alonzo.

ALONZO: The treasury of honour cannot bring forth
A title I should more rejoice in, sir.

VERMANDERO: You have improv'd it well; daughter, prepare,
The day will steal upon thee suddenly.

BEATRICE [*Aside*.]: Howe'er, I will be sure to keep the night,
If it should come so near me.
[BEATRICE *and* VERMANDERO *talk apart*.]

TOMAZO: Alonzo.

ALONZO: Brother?

TOMAZO: In troth I see small welcome in her eye.

ALONZO: Fie, you are too severe a censurer
Of love in all points, there's no bringing on you;
If lovers should mark everything a fault,
Affection would be like an ill-set book,
Whose faults might prove as big as half the volume.

BEATRICE: That's all I do entreat.

VERMANDERO: It is but reasonable;
I'll see what my son says to't: son Alonzo,
Here's a motion made but to reprieve
A maidenhead three days longer; the request
Is not far out of reason, for indeed
The former time is pinching.

91 *of*: i.e. for 99 *addition*: title 104 *keep the night*: refuse to consummate the marriage 108 *there's no bringing on you*: there's no convincing you. (However, Q has no punctuation to close the line, which may indicate that the phrase should be linked to what follows: 'I can't seem to make you understand that if . . .')

ALONZO: Though my joys
Be set back so much time as I could wish
They had been forward, yet since she desires it,
The time is set as pleasing as before,
I find no gladness wanting.
VERMANDERO: May I ever meet it in that point still:
Y'are nobly welcome, sirs.
Exeunt VERMANDERO *and* BEATRICE.
TOMAZO: So did you mark the dulness of her parting now?
ALONZO: What dullness? Thou art so exceptious still!
TOMAZO: Why, let it go then, I am but a fool
To mark your harms so heedfully.
ALONZO: Where's the oversight?
TOMAZO: Come, your faith's cozened in her, strongly cozened;
Unsettle your affection with all speed
Wisdom can bring it to, your peace is ruin'd else.
Think what a torment 'tis to marry one
Whose heart is leap'd into another's bosom:
If ever pleasure she receive from thee,
It comes not in thy name, or of thy gift;
She lies but with another in thine arms,
He the half-father unto all thy children
In the conception; if he get 'em not,
She helps to get 'em for him, in his passions;
And how dangerous
And shameful her restraint may go in time to,
It is not to be thought on without sufferings.
ALONZO: You speak as if she lov'd some other, then.
TOMAZO: Do you apprehend so slowly?
ALONZO: Nay, and that
Be your fear only, I am safe enough.
Preserve your friendship and your counsel, brother,
For times of more distress; I should depart
An enemy, a dangerous, deadly one
To any but thyself, that should but think
She knew the meaning of inconstancy,
Much less the use and practice; yet w'are friends.

125 *exceptious*: disposed to make objections 128 *cozened*: betrayed 138 *in his passions*: the phrase is obscure. Salgādo suggests: 'Though the lover cannot actually beget children, he shares in them, because the passions aroused in the woman during the act of procreation are due to her lover, not her husband' 139–41 i.e. the dangerous and shameful consequences of restraining her are painful to consider

Pray let no more be urg'd; I can endure
Much, till I meet an injury to her,
Then I am not myself. Farewell, sweet brother,
How much w'are bound to heaven to depart lovingly.
Exit.

TOMAZO: Why, here is love's tame madness; thus a man
Quickly steals into his vexation.
Exit.

[SCENE 2]

Enter DIAPHANTA *and* ALSEMERO.

DIAPHANTA: The place is my charge, you have kept your hour,
And the reward of a just meeting bless you.
I hear my lady coming; complete gentleman,
I dare not be too busy with my praises,
Th'are dangerous things to deal with.
Exit.

ALSEMERO: This goes well;
These women are the ladies' cabinets,
Things of most precious trust are lock'd into 'em.
Enter BEATRICE.

BEATRICE: I have within mine eye all my desires;
Requests that holy prayers ascend heaven for,
And brings 'em down to furnish our defects,
Come not more sweet to our necessities
Than thou unto my wishes.

ALSEMERO: W'are so like
In our expressions, lady, that unless I borrow
The same words, I shall never find their equals.
[*They embrace.*]

BEATRICE: How happy were this meeting, this embrace,
If it were free from envy! This poor kiss,
It has an enemy, a hateful one,
That wishes poison to't: how well were I now
If there were none such name known as Piracquo,

4–5 Diaphanta suspects Beatrice would be jealous if her praises of Alsemero are overheard 6 *cabinets*: cases for the safe custody of jewels, etc. 10 *And brings 'em down to furnish our defects*: ''em' refers to the heavenly gifts answering the 'requests' of the previous line. The sense of the phrase is therefore 'supply those things we lack'

Nor no such tie as the command of parents!
I should be but too much blessed.
ALSEMERO: One good service
Would strike off both your fears, and I'll go near it too,
Since you are so distress'd; remove the cause,
The command ceases, so there's two fears blown out
With one and the same blast.
BEATRICE: Pray let me find you, sir.
What might that service be so strangely happy?
ALSEMERO: The honourablest piece 'bout man, valour.
I'll send a challenge to Piracquo instantly.
BEATRICE: How? Call you that extinguishing of fear,
When 'tis the only way to keep it flaming?
Are not you ventured in the action,
That's all my joys and comforts? Pray, no more, sir.
Say you prevail'd, you're danger's and not mine then;
The law would claim you from me, or obscurity
Be made the grave to bury you alive.
I'm glad these thoughts come forth; o keep not one
Of this condition, sir; here was a course
Found to bring sorrow on her way to death:
The tears would ne'er 'a' dried, till dust had chok'd 'em.
Blood-guiltiness becomes a fouler visage.
[*Aside.*] And now I think on one. I was to blame,
I ha' marr'd so good a market with my scorn;
'T had been done questionless; the ugliest creature
Creation fram'd for some use, yet to see
I could not mark so much where it should be!
ALSEMERO: Lady –
BEATRICE [*Aside.*]: Why, men of art make much of poison,
Keep one to expel another; where was my art?
ALSEMERO: Lady, you hear not me.
BEATRICE: I do especially, sir;
The present times are not so sure of our side
As those hereafter may be; we must use 'em then
As thrifty folks their wealth, sparingly now,

22 *strike off*: in the sense that fetters are struck off 23–4 *remove the cause, The command ceases*: i.e. 'if I kill Piracquo in a duel your father can hardly force you to marry him'. Alsemero's formulation alludes to the scholastic commonplace 'remove the cause and the effect ceases' 25 *find*: understand 36 *one*: i.e. one thought 42 *marr'd so good a market*: i.e. ruined such a good opportunity 46 *art*: learning/cunning

Till the time opens.
ALSEMERO: You teach wisdom, lady.
BEATRICE: Within there – Diaphanta!
Enter DIAPHANTA.
DIAPHANTA: Do you call, madam?
BEATRICE: Perfect your service, and conduct this gentleman
The private way you brought him.
DIAPHANTA: I shall, madam.
ALSEMERO: My love's as firm as love e'er built upon.
Exeunt DIAPHANTA *and* ALSEMERO.
Enter DE FLORES.
DE FLORES [*Aside.*]: I have watch'd this meeting and do wonder much
What shall become of tother; I'm sure both
Cannot be serv'd unless she transgress, happily
Then I'll put in for one: for if a woman
Fly from one point, from him she makes a husband,
She spreads and mounts then like arithmetic,
One, ten, a hundred, a thousand, ten thousand,
Proves in time sutler to an army royal.
Now do I look to be most richly rail'd at,
Yet I must see her.
BEATRICE [*Aside.*]: Why, put case I loath'd him
As much as youth and beauty hates a sepulchre,
Must I needs show it? Cannot I keep that secret,
And serve my turn upon him? See, he's here. –
De Flores!
DE FLORES [*Aside.*]: Ha, I shall run mad with joy;
She call'd me fairly by my name De Flores,
And neither rogue nor rascal!
BEATRICE: What ha' you done
To your face a-late? Y'have met with some good physician;
Y'have prun'd yourself methinks, you were not wont
To look so amorously.
DE FLORES [*Aside.*]: Not I;
'Tis the same physnomy, to a hair and pimple,

52 *opens*: becomes more propitious 54 *Perfect*: complete 58 *tother*: i.e. Alonzo 59 *serv'd*: satisfied (with a sexual connotation) *happily*: either 'perhaps' or 'with any luck' 60 *put in for one*: apply for a share 61 *point*: penis/decimal point (the woman shifts away from 1.0, to 10.0 and then 100.0) 64 *sutler*: a seller of provisions to an army garrison 66 *put case*: suppose 69 *serve my turn upon him*: make use of him for my own ends 74 *prun'd*: preened 75 *amorously*: attractive 76 *physnomy*: physiognomy, face

Which she call'd scurvy scarce an hour ago:
How is this?
BEATRICE: Come hither; nearer, man!
DE FLORES [*Aside.*]: I'm up to the chin in heaven.
BEATRICE: Turn, let me see;
Faugh, 'tis but the heat of the liver, I perceiv't.
I thought it had been worse.
DE FLORES [*Aside.*]: Her fingers touch'd me!
She smells all amber.
BEATRICE: I'll make a water for you shall cleanse this
Within a fortnight.
DE FLORES: With your own hands, lady?
BEATRICE: Yes, mine own, sir; in a work of cure
I'll trust no other.
DE FLORES [*Aside.*]: 'Tis half an act of pleasure
To hear her talk thus to me.
BEATRICE: When w'are us'd
To a hard face, 'tis not so unpleasing;
It mends still in opinion, hourly mends,
I see it by experience.
DE FLORES [*Aside.*]: I was blest
To light upon this minute; I'll make use on't.
BEATRICE: Hardness becomes the visage of a man well,
It argues service, resolution, manhood,
If cause were of employment.
DE FLORES: 'Twould be soon seen,
If e'er your ladyship had cause to use it.
I would but wish the honour of a service
So happy as that mounts to.
BEATRICE: We shall try you –
O my De Flores!
DE FLORES [*Aside.*]: How's that?
She calls me hers already, 'my De Flores'! –
You were about to sigh out somewhat, madam.
BEATRICE: No, was I? I forgot – O!
DE FLORES: There 'tis again,
The very fellow on't.
BEATRICE: You are too quick, sir.

80 *heat of the liver*: Beatrice's diagnosis is in a sense ironic as the liver was thought at the time to be the seat of all passions 82 *amber*: i.e. of the perfume derived from ambergris 83 *water*: lotion 86 *act of pleasure*: sexual intercourse 94 *if cause were of employment*: if there were cause for employment 102 *quick*: perceptive

DE FLORES: There's no excuse for't now, I heard it twice, madam;
That sigh would fain have utterance, take pity on't,
And lend it a free word; 'las, how it labours
For liberty! I hear the murmur yet
Beat at your bosom.
BEATRICE: Would creation –
DE FLORES [*Aside.*]: Ay, well said, that's it.
BEATRICE: Had form'd me man!
DE FLORES [*Aside.*]: Nay, that's not it.
BEATRICE: O, 'tis the soul of freedom!
I should not then be forc'd to marry one
I hate beyond all depths, I should have power
Then to oppose my loathings, nay, remove 'em
Forever from my sight.
DE FLORES [*Aside.*]: O blest occasion! –
Without change to your sex, you have your wishes.
Claim so much man in me.
BEATRICE: In thee, De Flores?
There's small cause for that.
DE FLORES: Put it not from me,
It's a service that I kneel for to you.
[*Kneels.*]
BEATRICE: You are too violent to mean faithfully;
There's horror in my service, blood and danger;
Can those be things to sue for?
DE FLORES: If you knew
How sweet it were to me to be employed
In any act of yours, you would say then
I fail'd, and us'd not reverence enough
When I receive the charge on't.
BEATRICE [*Aside.*]: This is much, methinks;
Belike his wants are greedy, and to such
Gold tastes like angels' food. – Rise.
DE FLORES: I'll have the work first.
BEATRICE [*Aside.*]: Possible his need
Is strong upon him. [*Gives him money.*] – There's to encourage thee:
As thou art forward and thy service dangerous
Thy reward shall be precious.
DE FLORES: That I have thought on;
I have assur'd myself of that beforehand

113 *occasion*: opportunity 118 *mean faithfully*: intend faithful service
125 *Belike*: probably 126 *angels' food*: manna, the bread of heaven 129 *As thou art forward*: to the extent that you are keenly committed

And know it will be precious; the thought ravishes.
BEATRICE: Then take him to thy fury!
DE FLORES: I thirst for him.
BEATRICE: Alonzo de Piracquo!
DE FLORES: His end's upon him;
He shall be seen no more.
BEATRICE: How lovely now dost thou appear to me!
Never was man dearlier rewarded.
DE FLORES: I do think of that.
BEATRICE: Be wondrous careful in the execution.
DE FLORES: Why, are not both our lives upon the cast?
BEATRICE: Then I throw all my fears upon thy service.
DE FLORES: They ne'er shall rise to hurt you.
BEATRICE: When the deed's done,
I'll furnish thee with all things for thy flight;
Thou may'st live bravely in another country.
DE FLORES: Ay, ay, we'll talk of that hereafter.
BEATRICE [*Aside.*]: I shall rid myself
Of two inveterate loathings at one time,
Piracquo, and his dog-face.
Exit.
DE FLORES: O my blood!
Methinks I feel her in mine arms already,
Her wanton fingers combing out this beard,
And being pleased, praising this bad face.
Hunger and pleasure, they'll commend sometimes
Slovenly dishes, and feed heartily on 'em,
Nay, which is stranger, refuse daintier for 'em.
Some women are odd feeders. – I'm too loud.
Here comes the man goes supperless to bed,
Yet shall not rise tomorrow to his dinner.
Enter ALONZO.
ALONZO: De Flores.
DE FLORES: My kind, honourable lord.
ALONZO: I am glad I ha' met with thee.
DE FLORES: Sir.
ALONZO: Thou canst show me
The full strength of the castle?
DE FLORES: That I can, sir.
ALONZO: I much desire it.

132 *ravishes*: carries away with rapture; but the choice of verb also intimates De Flores's expectation of sexual reward 140 *cast*: throw of dice 144 *bravely*: gallantly 147 *his*: i.e. De Flores's *blood*: sensual desire

DE FLORES: And if the ways and straits
Of some of the passages be not too tedious for you,
I will assure you, worth your time and sight, my lord.
ALONZO: Puh! That shall be no hindrance.
DE FLORES: I'm your servant, then:
'Tis now near dinner time; 'gainst your lordship's rising
I'll have the keys about me.
ALONZO: Thanks, kind De Flores.
DE FLORES [*Aside.*]: He's safely thrust upon me beyond hopes.
Exeunt.

164 *'gainst your lordship's rising*: in readiness for the time when you rise from dining

ACT THREE

[SCENE 1]

Enter ALONZO *and* DE FLORES.
(*In the act-time* DE FLORES *hides a naked rapier.*)
DE FLORES: Yes, here are all the keys; I was afraid, my lord,
I'd wanted for the postern, this is it.
I've all, I've all, my lord: this for the sconce.
ALONZO: 'Tis a most spacious and impregnable fort.
DE FLORES: You'll tell me more, my lord: this descent
Is somewhat narrow, we shall never pass
Well with our weapons, they'll but trouble us.
ALONZO: Thou say'st true.
DE FLORES: Pray let me help your lordship.
ALONZO: 'Tis done. Thanks, kind De Flores.
DE FLORES: Here are hooks, my lord,
To hang such things on purpose.
[*Hangs up the swords.*]
ALONZO: Lead, I'll follow thee.
Exeunt at one door and enter at the other.

[SCENE 2]

DE FLORES: All this is nothing; you shall see anon
A place you little dream on.
ALONZO: I am glad
I have this leisure: all your master's house
Imagine I ha' taken a gondola.
DE FLORES: All but myself, sir, [*Aside.*] which makes up my safety. –
My lord, I'll place you at a casement here
Will show you the full strength of all the castle.
Look, spend your eye awhile upon that object.

s.d. *act-time*: the period between acts 2 *wanted*: lacked (the key) *postern*: back or side door 3 *sconce*: small fort or earthwork 2 *place you little dream on*: i.e. the grave 6 *casement*: window

ALONZO: Here's rich variety, De Flores.
DE FLORES: Yes, sir.
ALONZO: Goodly munition.
DE FLORES: Ay, there's ordnance, sir,
No bastard metal, will ring you a peal like bells
At great men's funerals; keep your eye straight, my lord,
Take special notice of that sconce before you,
There you may dwell awhile.
ALONZO: I am upon't.
DE FLORES: And so am I.
[*Stabs him with the hidden rapier.*]
ALONZO: De Flores! O De Flores,
Whose malice hast thou put on?
DE FLORES: Do you question
A work of secrecy? I must silence you.
[*Stabs him.*]
ALONZO: O, o, o.
DE FLORES: I must silence you.
[*Stabs him.*]
So, here's an undertaking well accomplish'd.
This vault serves to good use now. Ha! what's that
Threw sparkles in my eye? O 'tis a diamond
He wears upon his finger: it was well found,
This will approve the work. What, so fast on?
Not part in death? I'll take a speedy course then,
Finger and all shall off. [*Cuts off the finger.*] So, now I'll clear
The passages from all suspect or fear.
Exit with body.

[SCENE 3]

Enter ISABELLA *and* LOLLIO.
ISABELLA: Why, sirrah? Whence have you commission
To fetter the doors against me?
If you keep me in a cage, pray whistle to me,
Let me be doing something.

10 *munition*: defences *ordnance*: artillery 11 *bastard*: inferior 14 *dwell*: gaze; but De Flores will also conceal his body there 16 *Whose malice hast thou put on?*: whose hatred have you taken over? i.e. who put you up to this? 23 *approve the work*: confirm that the murder has been carried out 26 *suspect*: suspicion/suspicious evidence

LOLLIO: You shall be doing, if it please you; I'll whistle to you if you'll pipe after.

ISABELLA: Is it your master's pleasure, or your own,
To keep me in this pinfold?

LOLLIO: 'Tis for my master's pleasure, lest being taken in another man's corn, you might be pounded in another place.

ISABELLA: 'Tis very well, and he'll prove very wise.

LOLLIO: He says you have company enough in the house, if you please to be sociable, of all sorts of people.

ISABELLA: Of all sorts? Why, here's none but fools and madmen.

LOLLIO: Very well: and where will you find any other, if you should go abroad? There's my master and I to boot too.

ISABELLA: Of either sort one, a madman and a fool.

LOLLIO: I would ev'n participate of both then, if I were as you; I know y'are half mad already, be half foolish too.

ISABELLA: Y'are a brave saucy rascal! Come on, sir,
Afford me then the pleasure of your bedlam;
You were commending once today to me
Your last-come lunatic, what a proper
Body there was without brains to guide it,
And what a pitiful delight appear'd
In that defect, as if your wisdom had found
A mirth in madness; pray, sir, let me partake,
If there be such a pleasure.

LOLLIO: If I do not show you the handsomest, discreetest madman, one that I may call the understanding madman, then say I am a fool.

ISABELLA: Well, a match, I will say so.

LOLLIO: When you have a taste of the madman, you shall, if you please, see Fools' College, o'th'side; I seldom lock there, 'tis but shooting a bolt or two, and you are amongst 'em.

Exit.

Enter presently.

Come on, sir, let me see how handsomely you'll behave yourself now.

Enter FRANCISCUS.

FRANCISCUS: How sweetly she looks! O but there's a wrinkle in her brow as deep as philosophy; Anacreon, drink to my mistress's health, I'll

5–6 *I'll whistle to you if you'll pipe after*: 'I'll whistle if you'll sing in response', with a bawdy innuendo 8 *pinfold*: a pen where stray animals were pounded
9–10 Lollio elaborates on Isabella's metaphor and applies it in a bawdy sense
16 *abroad*: out of the house *to boot*: into the bargain 18 *participate of*: share in the nature of/take (sexual) advantage of 21 *Afford*: give 23 *proper*: handsome 33 *shooting a bolt*: i.e. unbolting the door, but alluding to the proverb 'A fool's bolt is soon shot' 37 *Anacreon*: the Greek poet was reputed to have died from choking on a grape-stone

pledge it: stay, stay, there's a spider in the cup! No, 'tis but a grape-stone, swallow it, fear nothing, poet; so, so, lift higher.

ISABELLA: Alack, alack, 'tis too full of pity
To be laugh'd at; how fell he mad? Canst thou tell?

LOLLIO: For love, mistress: he was a pretty poet too, and that set him forwards first; the Muses then forsook him, he ran mad for a chamber-maid, yet she was but a dwarf neither.

FRANCISCUS: Hail, bright Titania!
Why stand'st thou idle on these flow'ry banks?
Oberon is dancing with his Dryades;
I'll gather daisies, primrose, violets,
And bind them in a verse of poesy.

LOLLIO: Not too near; you see your danger.
[*Shows the whip.*]

FRANCISCUS: O hold thy hand, great Diomed,
Thou feed'st thy horses well, they shall obey thee;
Get up, Bucephalus kneels.
[*Kneels.*]

LOLLIO: You see how I awe my flock; a shepherd has not his dog at more obedience.

ISABELLA: His conscience is unquiet, sure that was
The cause of this. A proper gentleman.

FRANCISCUS: Come hither, Esculapius; hide the poison.
[LOLLIO *hides his whip.*]

LOLLIO: Well, 'tis hid.

FRANCISCUS: Didst thou never hear of one Tiresias, a famous poet?

LOLLIO: Yes, that kept tame wild-geese.

FRANCISCUS: That's he; I am the man.

LOLLIO: No!

FRANCISCUS: Yes, but make no words on't, I was a man seven years ago.

LOLLIO: A stripling I think you might.

FRANCISCUS: Now I'm a woman, all feminine.

LOLLIO: I would I might see that.

FRANCISCUS: Juno struck me blind.

38 *a spider in the cup*: spiders were believed to be poisonous 43 *forwards*: i.e. on the road to madness 45 *Titania*: queen of the fairies in *A Midsummer Night's Dream* 47 *Oberon*: king of the fairies *Dryades*: wood-nymphs 51 *Diomed*: Thracian king who fed his horses on human flesh 53 *Bucephalus*: Alexander the Great's horse which only he could ride 58 *Esculapius*: Greek god of medicine 60 *Tiresias*: in Greek mythology, a soothsayer (not poet) who changed from a man into a woman and then back again seven years later. He was blinded by Juno for revealing that women derived more pleasure from sexual intercourse than men 61 *tame wild-geese*: probably a cant term for prostitutes

LOLLIO: I'll ne'er believe that; for a woman, they say, has an eye more than a man.

FRANCISCUS: I say she struck me blind.

LOLLIO: And Luna made you mad; you have two trades to beg with.

FRANCISCUS: Luna is now big-bellied, and there's room
For both of us to ride with Hecate;
I'll drag thee up into her silver sphere,
And there we'll kick the dog, and beat the bush,
That barks against the witches of the night:
The swift lycanthropi that walks the round,
We'll tear their wolvish skins and save the sheep.
[*Tries to seize* LOLLIO.]

LOLLIO: Is't come to this? Nay, then my poison comes forth again. [*Flourishes whip.*] Mad slave, indeed, abuse your keeper!

ISABELLA: I prithee hence with him, now he grows dangerous.

FRANCISCUS (*Sings.*):

Sweet love, pity me,
Give me leave to lie with thee.

LOLLIO: No, I'll see you wiser first: to your own kennel.

FRANCISCUS: No noise, she sleeps, draw all the curtains round;
Let no soft sound molest the pretty soul
But love, and love creeps in at a mouse-hole.

LOLLIO: I would you would get into your hole.

Exit FRANCISCUS.

Now, mistress, I will bring you another sort, you shall be fool'd another while; Tony, come hither, Tony; look who's yonder, Tony.

Enter ANTONIO.

ANTONIO: Cousin, is it not my aunt?

LOLLIO: Yes, 'tis one of 'em, Tony.

ANTONIO: He, he! How do you, uncle?

LOLLIO: Fear him not, mistress, 'tis a gentle nigget; you may play with him, as safely with him as with his bauble.

ISABELLA: How long hast thou been a fool?

ANTONIO: Ever since I came hither, cousin.

ISABELLA: Cousin? I'm none of thy cousins, fool.

69 *eye*: perception/cunt 72 *Luna*: the moon *two trades*: i.e. madness and blindness 73 *big-bellied*: i.e. full 74 *Hecate*: Greek goddess of witchcraft, associated with the moon 76 *kick the dog, and beat the bush*: i.e. those belonging to the man in the moon 78 *lycanthropi*: victims of lycanthropia or wolf-madness, induced by the full moon 88 *mouse-hole*: cunt 92 *aunt*: slang for 'prostitute' 95 *nigget*: fool 96 *bauble*: the baton of a court fool/penis 99 *Cousin?*: Isabella rejects the term since it was also a cant term for 'trollop'

LOLLIO: O mistress, fools have always so much wit as to claim their kindred.

MADMAN (*Within.*): Bounce, bounce, he falls, he falls!

ISABELLA: Hark you, your scholars in the upper room are out of order.

LOLLIO [*Shouts.*]: Must I come amongst you there? – Keep you the fool, mistress; I'll go up and play left-handed Orlando amongst the madmen. *Exit.*

ISABELLA: Well, sir.

ANTONIO: 'Tis opportuneful now, sweet lady! Nay,
Cast no amazing eye upon this change.

ISABELLA: Ha!

ANTONIO: This shape of folly shrouds your dearest love,
The truest servant to your powerful beauties,
Whose magic had this force thus to transform me.

ISABELLA: You are a fine fool indeed.

ANTONIO: O 'tis not strange:
Love has an intellect that runs through all
The scrutinous sciences, and like
A cunning poet, catches a quantity
Of every knowledge, yet brings all home
Into one mystery, into one secret
That he proceeds in.

ISABELLA: Y'are a parlous fool.

ANTONIO: No danger in me: I bring nought but love
And his soft-wounding shafts to strike you with:
Try but one arrow; if it hurt you,
I'll stand you twenty back in recompense.

ISABELLA: A forward fool too!

ANTONIO: This was love's teaching:
A thousand ways he fashion'd out my way,
And this I found the safest and nearest
To tread the Galaxia to my star.

ISABELLA: Profound, withal! Certain, you dream'd of this;
Love never taught it waking.

ANTONIO: Take no acquaintance

105 *left-handed Orlando*: i.e. he will imitate the violent behaviour of the hero of Ariosto's *Orlando Furioso*, presumably in a cack-handed manner
107 *opportuneful*: appropriate 108 *amazing*: amazed 115 *scrutinous*: searching 119 *parlous*: cunning/perilous 125 *he*: Q reads 'she', which contradicts the masculine personification of love as Cupid in the lines above *fashion'd out my way*: prompted me 127 *Galaxia*: the Milky Way 128 *withal*: as well

Of these outward follies; there is within
A gentleman that loves you.

ISABELLA: When I see him
I'll speak with him; so in the meantime keep
Your habit, it becomes you well enough.
As you are a gentleman, I'll not discover you;
That's all the favour that you must expect:
When you are weary, you may leave the school,
For all this while you have but play'd the fool.

Enter LOLLIO.

ANTONIO [*Aside.*]: And must again. – He, he! I thank you, cousin;
I'll be your valentine tomorrow morning.

LOLLIO: How do you like the fool, mistress?

ISABELLA: Passing well, sir.

LOLLIO: Is he not witty, pretty well for a fool?

ISABELLA: If he hold on as he begins, he is like to come to something.

LOLLIO: Ay, thank a good tutor: you may put him to't; he begins to answer pretty hard questions. Tony, how many is five times six?

ANTONIO: Five times six, is six times five.

LOLLIO: What arithmetician could have answer'd better? How many is one hundred and seven?

ANTONIO: One hundred and seven, is seven hundred and one, cousin.

LOLLIO: This is no wit to speak on; will you be rid of the fool now?

ISABELLA: By no means, let him stay a little.

MADMAN (*Within.*): Catch there, catch the last couple in hell!

LOLLIO [*Shouts.*]: Again? Must I come amongst you? – Would my master were come home! I am not able to govern both these wards together.
Exit.

ANTONIO: Why should a minute of love's hour be lost?

ISABELLA: Fie, out again! I had rather you kept
Your other posture: you become not your tongue
When you speak from your clothes.

ANTONIO: How can he freeze,
Lives near so sweet a warmth? Shall I alone
Walk through the orchard of the Hesperides
And cowardly not dare to pull an apple?

133 *habit*: clothes 134 *discover*: reveal, disclose 152 *catch the last couple in hell*: alluding to the children's game of 'barley-brake', a form of tag in which two players are nominated to 'catch' other participants as they run through a central playing area known as 'hell'; but see Introduction 154 *wards*: i.e. the fools' and the madmen's 158 *when you speak from your clothes*: i.e. when your speech is inappropriate to the fool's costume you are wearing 160 *orchard of the Hesperides*: a fabulous garden in the 'Fortunate Isles' in which grew golden apples

This with the red cheeks I must venture for.
[*Tries to kiss her.*]
Enter LOLLIO *above.*

ISABELLA: Take heed, there's giants keep 'em.

LOLLIO [*Aside.*]: How now, fool, are you good at that? Have you read Lipsius? He's past *Ars Amandi*; I believe I must put harder questions to him, I perceive that.

ISABELLA: You are bold without fear too.

ANTONIO: What should I fear,
Having all joys about me? Do you smile,
And love shall play the wanton on your lip,
Meet and retire, retire and meet again:
Look you but cheerfully, and in your eyes
I shall behold mine own deformity
And dress myself up fairer; I know this shape
Becomes me not, but in those bright mirrors
I shall array me handsomely.

LOLLIO [*Aside.*]: Cuckoo, cuckoo!
Exit.
[*Enter*] Madmen *above, some as birds, others as beasts.*

ANTONIO: What are these?

ISABELLA: Of fear enough to part us;
Yet are they but our schools of lunatics,
That act their fantasies in any shapes
Suiting their present thoughts; if sad, they cry;
If mirth be their conceit, they laugh again.
Sometimes they imitate the beasts and birds,
Singing, or howling, braying, barking; all
As their wild fancies prompt 'em.
[*Exeunt* Madmen.]
Enter LOLLIO.

ANTONIO: These are no fears.

ISABELLA: But here's a large one, my man.

ANTONIO: Ha, he! That's fine sport indeed, cousin.

LOLLIO: I would my master were come home, 'tis too much for one

163 *giants*: the golden apples were guarded by a dragon, Ladon, which had been fathered by a giant 165 *Lipsius*: the scholar, Justus Lipsius (1547–1606), with a pun on 'lips' *Ars Amandi*: Ovid's *Art of Love* 168 *Do you smile*: an imperative, i.e. 'Smile and . . .' 169 *play the wanton*: dally 170 *Meet and retire*: kiss 173 *shape*: i.e. dressed as a fool 175 *Cuckoo, cuckoo*: implying that Alibius is about to be cuckolded 176 *Of fear enough*: sufficiently fearful in appearance/dangerous to our secret 177 *schools*: groups, classes 180 *conceit*: fancy

shepherd to govern two of these flocks; nor can I believe that one churchman can instruct two benefices at once; there will be some incurable mad of the one side, and very fools on the other. Come, Tony.

ANTONIO: Prithee, cousin, let me stay here still.

LOLLIO: No, you must to your book now you have play'd sufficiently.

ISABELLA: Your fool is grown wondrous witty.

LOLLIO: Well, I'll say nothing; but I do not think but he will put you down one of these days.

Exeunt LOLLIO *and* ANTONIO.

ISABELLA: Here the restrained current might make breach,
Spite of the watchful bankers; would a woman stray,
She need not gad abroad to seek her sin,
It would be brought home one ways or other:
The needle's point will to the fixed north,
Such drawing arctics women's beauties are.

Enter LOLLIO.

LOLLIO: How dost thou, sweet rogue?

ISABELLA: How now?

LOLLIO: Come, there are degrees, one fool may be better than another.

ISABELLA: What's the matter?

LOLLIO: Nay, if thou giv'st thy mind to fool's-flesh, have at thee!
[*Tries to kiss her.*]

ISABELLA: You bold slave, you!

LOLLIO: I could follow now as tother fool did:
'What should I fear,
Having all joys about me? Do you but smile,
And love shall play the wanton on your lip,
Meet and retire, retire and meet again:
Look you but cheerfully, and in your eyes
I shall behold my own deformity,
And dress myself up fairer; I know this shape
Becomes me not –'

and so as it follows; but is not this the more foolish way? Come, sweet rogue; kiss me, my little Lacedemonian. Let me feel how thy pulses beat; thou hast a thing about thee would do a man pleasure, I'll lay my hand on't.

188 *instruct two benefices*: alluding to the common practice whereby clergymen supplemented their income by holding more than one office 193 *put you down*: defeat in argument/fuck 196 *bankers*: repairers of the banks of rivers and dykes 199–200 i.e. beautiful women attract men from a distance just as the magnetic pole attracts a compass needle 203 *degrees*: degrees of rank 217 *Lacedemonian*: Spartan, referring either to their reputation for terse speech or to the career of Helen of Sparta/Troy

ISABELLA: Sirrah, no more! I see you have discovered
This love's knight-errant, who hath made adventure
For purchase of my love; be silent, mute,
Mute as a statue, or his injunction
For me enjoying, shall be to cut thy throat:
I'll do it, though for no other purpose,
And be sure he'll not refuse it.

LOLLIO: My share, that's all; I'll have my fool's part with you.

ISABELLA: No more! Your master.

Enter ALIBIUS.

ALIBIUS: Sweet, how dost thou?

ISABELLA: Your bounden servant, sir.

ALIBIUS: Fie, fie, sweetheart,
No more of that.

ISABELLA: You were best lock me up.

ALIBIUS: In my arms and bosom, my sweet Isabella,
I'll lock thee up most nearly. Lollio,
We have employment, we have task in hand;
At noble Vermandero's, our castle-captain,
There is a nuptial to be solemniz'd –
Beatrice-Joanna, his fair daughter, bride –
For which the gentleman hath bespoke our pains:
A mixture of our madmen and our fools
To finish, as it were, and make the fag
Of all the revels, the third night from the first;
Only an unexpected passage over,
To make a frightful pleasure, that is all,
But not the all I aim at; could we so act it,
To teach it in a wild distracted measure,
Though out of form and figure, breaking time's head,
It were no matter, 'twould be heal'd again
In one age or other, if not in this.
This, this, Lollio, there's a good reward begun,
And will beget a bounty, be it known.

LOLLIO: This is easy, sir, I'll warrant you: you have about you fools and madmen that can dance very well; and 'tis no wonder, your best dancers are not the wisest men; the reason is, with often jumping they jolt their

229 *bounden*: indebted/imprisoned 232 *nearly*: closely/intimately
237 *bespoke*: commissioned 239 *fag*: end, conclusion 241 *Only an unexpected passage over*: i.e. merely a brief surprise appearance 243–7 the point of this obscure passage appears to be that the 'wild distracted' performance of the madmen should highlight, as if by contrast, the order and ceremony of the marriage celebrations

brains down into their feet, that their wits lie more in their heels than in their heads.

ALIBIUS: Honest Lollio, thou giv'st me a good reason,
And a comfort in it.

ISABELLA: Y'have a fine trade on't,
Madmen and fools are a staple commodity.

ALIBIUS: O wife, we must eat, wear clothes, and live;
Just at the lawyer's haven we arrive,
By madmen and by fools we both do thrive.

Exeunt.

[SCENE 4]

Enter VERMANDERO, ALSEMERO, JASPERINO, *and* BEATRICE.

VERMANDERO: Valencia speaks so nobly of you, sir,
I wish I had a daughter now for you.

ALSEMERO: The fellow of this creature were a partner
For a king's love.

VERMANDERO: I had her fellow once, sir,
But heaven has married her to joys eternal;
'Twere sin to wish her in this vale again.
Come, sir, your friend and you shall see the pleasures
Which my health chiefly joys in.

ALSEMERO: I hear the beauty of this seat largely.

VERMANDERO: It falls much short of that.

Exeunt. Manet BEATRICE.

BEATRICE: So, here's one step
Into my father's favour; time will fix him.
I have got him now the liberty of the house:
So wisdom by degrees works out her freedom;
And if that eye be dark'ned that offends me
(I wait but that eclipse) this gentleman
Shall soon shine glorious in my father's liking,
Through the refulgent virtue of my love.

Enter DE FLORES.

257 *staple*: basic/common 259 *lawyer's haven*: i.e. wealth. Lawyers made their fortunes from those 'mad' enough to go to law 6 *vale*: i.e. vale of tears 9 *seat*: residence *largely*: expressed by many/expressed enthusiastically 14 *that eye*: i.e. Alonzo, alluding to the scriptural 'And if thine eye offend thee, pluck it out' (Matthew 18. 9) 17 *refulgent*: resplendent/reflecting

DE FLORES [*Aside.*]: My thoughts are at a banquet for the deed,
I feel no weight in't, 'tis but light and cheap
For the sweet recompense that I set down for't.
BEATRICE: De Flores.
DE FLORES: Lady.
BEATRICE: Thy looks promise cheerfully.
DE FLORES: All things are answerable, time, circumstance,
Your wishes, and my service.
BEATRICE: Is it done then?
DE FLORES: Piracquo is no more.
BEATRICE: My joys start at mine eyes; our sweet'st delights
Are evermore born weeping.
DE FLORES: I've a token for you.
BEATRICE: For me?
DE FLORES: But it was sent somewhat unwillingly,
I could not get the ring without the finger.
[*Shows the severed finger.*]
BEATRICE: Bless me! What hast thou done?
DE FLORES: Why, is that more
Than killing the whole man? I cut his heart-strings.
A greedy hand thrust in a dish at court
In a mistake hath had as much as this.
BEATRICE: 'Tis the first token my father made me send him.
DE FLORES: And I made him send it back again
For his last token; I was loath to leave it,
And I'm sure dead men have no use of jewels.
He was as loath to part with't, for it stuck
As if the flesh and it were both one substance.
BEATRICE: At the stag's fall the keeper has his fees:
'Tis soon applied, all dead men's fees are yours, sir;
I pray, bury the finger, but the stone
You may make use on shortly; the true value,
Take't of my truth, is near three hundred ducats.
DE FLORES: 'Twill hardly buy a capcase for one's conscience, though,
To keep it from the worm, as fine as 'tis.
Well, being my fees I'll take it;

18 *at a banquet for the deed*: ecstatic over this murder (because of the prospect of sexual reward) 22 *answerable*: in agreement 26 *token*: proof (of the murder)/keepsake, love-token (initiating a sequence of double meanings which Beatrice is slow to recognize) 31–2 i.e. there's many a greedy man has lost a finger accidentally when put in the way of the carving knife 39 after a deer had been taken, the game-warden had the right to certain portions of its corpse 44 *capcase*: wallet or small bag 45 *worm*: i.e. remorse

Great men have taught me that, or else my merit
Would scorn the way on't.

BEATRICE: It might justly, sir:
Why, thou mistak'st, De Flores, 'tis not given
In state of recompense.

DE FLORES: No, I hope so, lady,
You should soon witness my contempt to't then!

BEATRICE: Prithee, thou look'st as if thou wert offended.

DE FLORES: That were strange, lady; 'tis not possible
My service should draw such a cause from you.
Offended? Could you think so? That were much
For one of my performance, and so warm
Yet in my service.

BEATRICE: 'Twere misery in me to give you cause, sir.

DE FLORES: I know so much, it were so, misery
In her most sharp condition.

BEATRICE: 'Tis resolv'd then;
Look you, sir, here's three thousand golden florins:
I have not meanly thought upon thy merit.

DE FLORES: What, salary? Now you move me.

BEATRICE: How, De Flores?

DE FLORES: Do you place me in the rank of verminous fellows,
To destroy things for wages? Offer gold?
The life blood of man! Is anything
Valued too precious for my recompense?

BEATRICE: I understand thee not.

DE FLORES: I could ha' hir'd
A journeyman in murder at this rate,
And mine own conscience might have slept at ease
And have had the work brought home.

BEATRICE [*Aside.*]: I'm in a labyrinth;
What will content him? I would fain be rid of him. –
I'll double the sum, sir.

DE FLORES: You take a course
To double my vexation, that's the good you do.

BEATRICE [*Aside.*]: Bless me! I am now in worse plight than I was;
I know not what will please him. – For my fear's sake,

56 ***warm***: hot (from the exertion of the murder)/zealous 66 ***The life blood of man!***: i.e. for a man's death! 69 ***journeyman***: a hireling; in this case, a professional assassin 70 ***slept at ease***: not found in Q, but almost all editors accept that this line is incomplete and follow Dilke's addition

I prithee make away with all speed possible.
And if thou be'st so modest not to name
The sum that will content thee, paper blushes not;
Send thy demand in writing, it shall follow thee,
But prithee take thy flight.
DE FLORES: You must fly too then.
BEATRICE: I?
DE FLORES: I'll not stir a foot else.
BEATRICE: What's your meaning?
DE FLORES: Why, are not you as guilty, in, I'm sure,
As deep as I? And we should stick together.
Come, your fears counsel you but ill, my absence
Would draw suspect upon you instantly;
There were no rescue for you.
BEATRICE [*Aside.*]: He speaks home.
DE FLORES: Nor is it fit we two, engag'd so jointly,
Should part and live asunder.
[*Tries to kiss her.*]
BEATRICE: How now, sir?
This shows not well.
DE FLORES: What makes your lip so strange?
This must not be betwixt us.
BEATRICE [*Aside.*]: The man talks wildly.
DE FLORES: Come, kiss me with a zeal now.
BEATRICE [*Aside.*]: Heaven, I doubt him!
DE FLORES: I will not stand so long to beg 'em shortly.
BEATRICE: Take heed, De Flores, of forgetfulness,
'Twill soon betray us.
DE FLORES: Take you heed first;
Faith, y'are grown much forgetful, y'are to blame in't.
BEATRICE [*Aside.*]: He's bold, and I am blam'd for't!
DE FLORES: I have eas'd you
Of your trouble, think on't, I'm in pain,
And must be eas'd of you; 'tis a charity,
Justice invites your blood to understand me.
BEATRICE: I dare not.
DE FLORES: Quickly!
BEATRICE: O I never shall!
Speak it yet further off that I may lose
What has been spoken, and no sound remain on't.

90 *strange*: unfriendly 92 *doubt*: fear

I would not hear so much offence again
For such another deed.
DE FLORES: Soft, lady, soft;
The last is not yet paid for. O this act
Has put me into spirit; I was as greedy on't
As the parch'd earth of moisture, when the clouds weep.
Did you not mark, I wrought myself into't,
Nay, sued and kneel'd for't: why was all that pains took?
You see I have thrown contempt upon your gold,
Not that I want it [not], for I do piteously:
In order I will come unto't, and make use on't,
But 'twas not held so precious to begin with;
For I place wealth after the heels of pleasure,
And were I not resolv'd in my belief
That thy virginity were perfect in thee,
I should but take my recompense with grudging,
As if I had but half my hopes I agreed for.
BEATRICE: Why, 'tis impossible thou canst be so wicked,
Or shelter such a cunning cruelty,
To make his death the murderer of my honour!
Thy language is so bold and vicious,
I cannot see which way I can forgive it
With any modesty.
DE FLORES: Push, you forget yourself!
A woman dipp'd in blood, and talk of modesty?
BEATRICE: O misery of sin! Would I had been bound
Perpetually unto my living hate
In that Piracquo, than to hear these words.
Think but upon the distance that creation
Set 'twixt thy blood and mine, and keep thee there.
DE FLORES: Look but into your conscience, read me there,
'Tis a true book, you'll find me there your equal.
Push! Fly not to your birth, but settle you
In what the act has made you, y'are no more now;
You must forget your parentage to me:
Y'are the deed's creature; by that name
You lost your first condition, and I challenge you,

107 *put me into spirit*: i.e. animated both by the act of murder and by the prospect of sexual reward 109 *wrought myself into't*: worked to be given the task 112 *want*: need 113 *In order*: in due course 130 *distance*: i.e. difference in social rank 136 *parentage*: social superiority *to*: in your relationship with/in favour of 138 *first condition*: original innocence *challenge*: claim

As peace and innocency has turn'd you out,
And made you one with me.
BEATRICE: With thee, foul villain?
DE FLORES: Yes, my fair murd'ress; do you urge me?
Though thou writ'st maid, thou whore in thy affection!
'Twas chang'd from thy first love, and that's a kind
Of whoredom in thy heart; and he's chang'd now,
To bring thy second on, thy Alsemero,
Whom, by all sweets that ever darkness tasted,
If I enjoy thee not, thou ne'er enjoy'st;
I'll blast the hopes and joys of marriage,
I'll confess all; my life I rate at nothing.
BEATRICE: De Flores!
DE FLORES: I shall rest from all lovers' plagues then;
I live in pain now: that shooting eye
Will burn my heart to cinders.
BEATRICE: O sir, hear me.
DE FLORES: She that in life and love refuses me,
In death and shame my partner she shall be.
BEATRICE: Stay, hear me once for all; [*Kneels.*] I make thee master
Of all the wealth I have in gold and jewels:
Let me go poor unto my bed with honour
And I am rich in all things.
DE FLORES: Let this silence thee:
The wealth of all Valencia shall not buy
My pleasure from me;
Can you weep Fate from its determin'd purpose?
So soon may you weep me.
BEATRICE: Vengeance begins;
Murder I see is followed by more sins.
Was my creation in the womb so curs'd,
It must engender with a viper first?
DE FLORES: Come, rise, and shroud your blushes in my bosom;
[*Raises her.*]
Silence is one of pleasure's best receipts:
Thy peace is wrought for ever in this yielding.
'Las, how the turtle pants! Thou'lt love anon
What thou so fear'st and faint'st to venture on.
Exeunt.

141 *urge*: provoke 144 *chang'd*: i.e. into a corpse 163 *you*: not in Q
168 *receipts*: recipes/means to attain some end 170 *turtle*: turtle-dove

ACT FOUR

[SCENE I]

[*Dumb show.*]

Enter Gentlemen, VERMANDERO *meeting them with action of wonderment at the flight of* PIRACQUO. *Enter* ALSEMERO, *with* JASPERINO, *and* Gallants; VERMANDERO *points to him, the* Gentlemen *seeming to applaud the choice. [Exeunt in procession* VERMANDERO] ALSEMERO, JASPERINO, *and* Gentlemen; BEATRICE *the bride following in great state, accompanied with* DIAPHANTA, ISABELLA *and other* Gentlewomen; DE FLORES *after all, smiling at the accident;* ALONZO*'s ghost appears to* DE FLORES *in the midst of his smile, startles him, showing him the hand whose finger he had cut off. They pass over in great solemnity.*

Enter BEATRICE.

BEATRICE: This fellow has undone me endlessly,
Never was bride so fearfully distress'd;
The more I think upon th'ensuing night
And whom I am to cope with in embraces,
One that's ennobled both in blood and mind,
So clear in understanding (that's my plague now)
Before whose judgment will my fault appear
Like malefactors' crimes before tribunals;
There is no hiding on't, the more I dive
Into my own distress; how a wise man
Stands for a great calamity! There's no venturing
Into his bed, what course soe'er I light upon,
Without my shame, which may grow up to danger;
He cannot but in justice strangle me
As I lie by him, as a cheater use me;
'Tis a precious craft to play with a false die
Before a cunning gamester. Here's his closet,
The key left in't, and he abroad i'th'park:
Sure 'twas forgot; I'll be so bold as look in't.

s.d. *accident*: event 1 *undone me endlessly*: ravished me again and again/ruined me eternally 4 *cope*: meet/contend 5 *that's*: Q reads 'both' 9–10 i.e. the more I examine the situation, the more I realize there can be no possibility of hiding the truth 11 *Stands for*: represents; i.e. to the guilty, an encounter with a wise man is a calamity 16 *precious craft*: delicate art 17 *closet*: cabinet

[*Opens closet.*]
Bless me! A right physician's closet 'tis,
Set round with vials, every one her mark too.
Sure he does practise physic for his own use,
Which may be safely call'd your great man's wisdom.
What manuscript lies here? 'The Book of Experiment,
Call'd *Secrets in Nature*'; so 'tis, 'tis so;
'How to know whether a woman be with child or no'.
I hope I am not yet; if he should try though!
Let me see, folio forty-five. Here 'tis;
The leaf tuck'd down upon't, the place suspicious.
'If you would know whether a woman be with child or not, give her two spoonfuls of the white water in glass C . . .'
Where's that glass C? O yonder, I see't now:
'. . . and if she be with child, she sleeps full twelve hours after, if not, not.'
None of that water comes into my belly.
I'll know you from a hundred; I could break you now,
Or turn you into milk, and so beguile
The master of the mystery, but I'll look to you.
Ha! That which is next is ten times worse.
'How to know whether a woman be a maid or not';
If that should be applied, what would become of me?
Belike he has a strong faith of my purity,
That never yet made proof; but this he calls
'A merry sleight, but true experiment, the author Antonius Mizaldus. Give the party you suspect the quantity of a spoonful of the water in the glass M, which upon her that is a maid makes three several effects: 'twill make her incontinently gape, then fall into a sudden sneezing, last into a violent laughing; else dull, heavy, and lumpish.'
Where had I been?
I fear it, yet 'tis seven hours to bedtime.
Enter DIAPHANTA.
DIAPHANTA: Cuds, madam, are you here?

21 *vials*: phials *every one her mark*: each one labelled 25 *Secrets in Nature*: *De Arcanis Naturae*, by Antonius Mizaldus (1520–78). The tests Beatrice mentions are nowhere described in this work, but similar tests appear in his other writings 28 *folio*: page 38 *look to you*: watch out for you 42 *Belike*: probably 43 *That never yet made proof*: as he has never yet put it to the test 44 *sleight*: Q reads 'slight', an obsolete form of 'sleight'. However, 'slight' in the sense of 'trifle' could be correct 46 *several*: distinctive 47 *incontinently*: immediately, uncontrollably 48 *else*: thereafter 49 *Where had I been?*: i.e. what would have become of me (if I had not discovered this secret)? 51 *Cuds*: a mild oath, derived from 'God's'

BEATRICE [*Aside.*]: Seeing that wench now,
A trick comes in my mind; 'tis a nice piece
Gold cannot purchase. – I come hither, wench,
To look my lord.
DIAPHANTA [*Aside.*]: Would I had such a cause to look him too! –
Why, he's i'th'park, madam.
BEATRICE: There let him be.
DIAPHANTA: Ay, madam, let him compass
Whole parks and forests, as great rangers do;
At roosting time a little lodge can hold 'em.
Earth-conquering Alexander, that thought the world
Too narrow for him, in the end had but his pit-hole.
BEATRICE: I fear thou art not modest, Diaphanta.
DIAPHANTA: Your thoughts are so unwilling to be known, madam;
'Tis ever the bride's fashion towards bedtime
To set light by her joys, as if she ow'd 'em not.
BEATRICE: Her joys? Her fears, thou would'st say.
DIAPHANTA: Fear of what?
BEATRICE: Art thou a maid, and talk'st so to a maid?
You leave a blushing business behind,
Beshrew your heart for't!
DIAPHANTA: Do you mean good sooth, madam?
BEATRICE: Well, if I'd thought upon the fear at first,
Man should have been unknown.
DIAPHANTA: Is't possible?
BEATRICE: I will give a thousand ducats to that woman
Would try what my fear were, and tell me true
Tomorrow, when she gets from't; as she likes
I might perhaps be drawn to't.
DIAPHANTA: Are you in earnest?
BEATRICE: Do you get the woman, then challenge me,
And see if I'll fly from't; but I must tell you
This by the way, she must be a true maid,
Else there's no trial, my fears are not hers else.
DIAPHANTA: Nay, she that I would put into your hands, madam,
Shall be a maid.
BEATRICE: You know I should be sham'd else,
Because she lies for me.

52 *nice piece*: scrupulous girl 61 *pit-hole*: grave/cunt 62 *modest*: chaste
65 *ow'd*: owned 67 *maid*: virgin 68 *leave a blushing business behind*: i.e. you've had sex in the past 69 *Do you mean good sooth*: are you speaking in earnest?
76 *Do you get*: an imperative; i.e. 'Get . . .' 82 *lies for me*: sleeps with my husband/deceives on my behalf

DIAPHANTA: 'Tis a strange humour;
But are you serious still? Would you resign
Your first night's pleasure, and give money too?
BEATRICE: As willingly as live. [*Aside.*] Alas, the gold
Is but a by-bet to wedge in the honour.
DIAPHANTA: I do not know how the world goes abroad
For faith or honesty, there's both requir'd in this.
Madam, what say you to me, and stray no further?
I've a good mind, in troth, to earn your money.
BEATRICE: Y'are too quick, I fear, to be a maid.
DIAPHANTA: How? Not a maid? Nay, then you urge me, madam;
Your honourable self is not a truer
With all your fears upon you –
BEATRICE [*Aside.*]: Bad enough then.
DIAPHANTA: Than I with all my lightsome joys about me.
BEATRICE: I'm glad to hear't then; you dare put your honesty
Upon an easy trial?
DIAPHANTA: Easy? Anything.
BEATRICE: I'll come to you straight.
[*Goes to closet.*]
DIAPHANTA [*Aside.*]: She will not search me, will she,
Like the forewoman of a female jury?
BEATRICE [*Aside.*]: Glass M: ay, this is it. – Look, Diaphanta,
You take no worse than I do.
[*Drinks.*]
DIAPHANTA: And in so doing,
I will not question what 'tis, but take it.
[*Drinks.*]
BEATRICE [*Aside.*]: Now if the experiment be true, 'twill praise itself,
And give me noble ease: begins already;
[DIAPHANTA *gapes.*]
There's the first symptom; and what haste it makes
To fall into the second, there by this time!
[DIAPHANTA *sneezes.*]
Most admirable secret! On the contrary,

82 *humour*: fancy 86 *by-bet*: either 'the money is only a subsidiary point, a side bet' or 'an added inducement for her to sacrifice her honour' 87 *how the world goes abroad*: the common run of behaviour 91 *quick*: eager, with a pun on 'quick' = pregnant 92 *urge*: provoke 96 *honesty*: chastity 98–9 perhaps a reference to the fact that during her divorce proceedings in 1613 the Countess of Essex had been internally examined by a group of matrons and noblewomen to test her claim that the marriage had not been consummated

It stirs not me a whit, which most concerns it.
DIAPHANTA: Ha, ha, ha!
BEATRICE [*Aside.*]: Just in all things and in order
As if 'twere circumscrib'd; one accident
Gives way unto another.
DIAPHANTA: Ha, ha, ha!
BEATRICE: How now, wench?
DIAPHANTA: Ha, ha, ha! I am so, so light at heart – ha, ha, ha! – so pleasurable!
But one swig more, sweet madam.
BEATRICE: Ay, tomorrow;
We shall have time to sit by't.
DIAPHANTA: Now I'm sad again.
BEATRICE [*Aside.*]: It lays itself so gently, too! – Come, wench,
Most honest Diaphanta I dare call thee now.
DIAPHANTA: Pray tell me, madam, what trick call you this?
BEATRICE: I'll tell thee all hereafter; we must study
The carriage of this business.
DIAPHANTA: I shall carry't well,
Because I love the burthen.
BEATRICE: About midnight
You must not fail to steal forth gently,
That I may use the place.
DIAPHANTA: O fear not, madam,
I shall be cool by that time. [*Aside.*] The bride's place,
And with a thousand ducats! I'm for a Justice now,
I bring a portion with me; I scorn small fools.
Exeunt.

[SCENE 2]

Enter VERMANDERO *and* Servant.
VERMANDERO: I tell thee, knave, mine honour is in question,
A thing till now free from suspicion,

108 *which most concerns it*: either 'and I am the person to whom this test is most important' or 'the test is designed to detect such loss of virginity'
110 *As if 'twere circumscrib'd*: either 'as laid down' or 'as if she were following the instructions' *accident*: symptom 115 *lays itself*: dies down 116 *honest*: chaste/truthful 119 *carry't*: carry out/support Alsemero during sex
124–5 i.e. with her dowry she will be able to marry a JP, a 'big fool'

Nor ever was there cause. Who of my gentlemen
Are absent? Tell me and truly how many and who.

SERVANT: Antonio, sir, and Franciscus.

VERMANDERO: When did they leave the castle?

SERVANT: Some ten days since, sir, the one intending to Briamata, th'other for Valencia.

VERMANDERO: The time accuses 'em; a charge of murder
Is brought within my castle gate, Piracquo's murder;
I dare not answer faithfully their absence.
A strict command of apprehension
Shall pursue 'em suddenly, and either wipe
The stain off clear, or openly discover it.
Provide me winged warrants for the purpose.
See, I am set on again.

Exit Servant.

Enter TOMAZO.

TOMAZO: I claim a brother of you.

VERMANDERO: Y'are too hot,
Seek him not here.

TOMAZO: Yes, 'mongst your dearest bloods,
If my peace find no fairer satisfaction;
This is the place must yield account for him,
For here I left him, and the hasty tie
Of this snatch'd marriage, gives strong testimony
Of his most certain ruin.

VERMANDERO: Certain falsehood!
This is the place indeed; his breach of faith
Has too much marr'd both my abused love,
The honourable love I reserv'd for him,
And mock'd my daughter's joy; the prepar'd morning
Blush'd at his infidelity; he left
Contempt and scorn to throw upon those friends
Whose belief hurt 'em. O 'twas most ignoble
To take his flight so unexpectedly
And throw such public wrongs on those that lov'd him.

TOMAZO: Then this is all your answer?

VERMANDERO: 'Tis too fair
For one of his alliance; and I warn you

7 *Briamata*: in the source for the play (*The Triumphs of Gods Revenge against The Crying and Execrable Sinne of Wilfull and Premeditated Murther* by John Reynolds [1621]) this was the location of Vermandero's mansion 11 *answer faithfully*: explain with confidence 16 *set on*: harassed 18–19 i.e. I will revenge myself on you and yours if I can get no better explanation 34 *his alliance*: i.e. Alonzo's family

That this place no more see you.
Exit.
Enter DE FLORES.
TOMAZO: The best is,
There is more ground to meet a man's revenge on. –
Honest De Flores!
DE FLORES: That's my name indeed.
Saw you the bride? Good sweet sir, which way took she?
TOMAZO: I have blest mine eyes from seeing such a false one.
DE FLORES [*Aside.*]: I'd fain get off, this man's not for my company,
I smell his brother's blood when I come near him.
TOMAZO: Come hither, kind and true one; I remember
My brother lov'd thee well.
DE FLORES: O purely, dear sir!
[*Aside.*] Methinks I am now again a-killing on him,
He brings it so fresh to me.
TOMAZO: Thou canst guess, sirrah
(One honest friend has an instinct of jealousy),
At some foul guilty person?
DE FLORES: 'Las, sir, I am so charitable, I think none
Worse than myself. You did not see the bride then?
TOMAZO: I prithee name her not. Is she not wicked?
DE FLORES: No, no, a pretty, easy, round-pack'd sinner,
As your most ladies are, else you might think
I flatter'd her; but, sir, at no hand wicked,
Till th'are so old their sins and vices meet
And they salute witches. I am call'd, I think, sir.
[*Aside.*] His company ev'n o'erlays my conscience.
Exit.
TOMAZO: That De Flores has a wondrous honest heart;
He'll bring it out in time, I'm assur'd on't.
O here's the glorious master of the day's joy.
'Twill not be long till he and I do reckon.
Enter ALSEMERO.
Sir!
ALSEMERO: You are most welcome.

36 i.e. there are other places where I can seek out revenge 46 *jealousy*: suspicion 51 *round-pack'd sinner*: the phrase is obscure, but probably means Beatrice; although 'well-fleshed' for sexual temptation, and therefore capable of leading men into sin, she is not herself criminal in intent 54 *sins and vices meet*: the meaning is again obscure and some editors emend to 'chins and noses' 56 *o'erlays*: oppresses 60 *'Twill*: Q reads 'I will'

TOMAZO: You may call that word back;
I do not think I am, nor wish to be.
ALSEMERO: 'Tis strange you found the way to this house then.
TOMAZO: Would I'd ne'er known the cause! I'm none of those, sir,
That come to give you joy, and swill your wine;
'Tis a more precious liquor that must lay
The fiery thirst I bring.
ALSEMERO: Your words and you
Appear to me great strangers.
TOMAZO: Time and our swords
May make us more acquainted. This the business:
I should have a brother in your place;
How treachery and malice have dispos'd of him,
I'm bound to inquire of him which holds his right,
Which never could come fairly.
ALSEMERO: You must look
To answer for that word, sir.
TOMAZO: Fear you not,
I'll have it ready drawn at our next meeting.
Keep your day solemn. Farewell, I disturb it not;
I'll bear the smart with patience for a time.
Exit.
ALSEMERO: 'Tis somewhat ominous this, a quarrel enter'd
Upon this day. My innocence relieves me,
I should be wondrous sad else.
Enter JASPERINO.
Jasperino,
I have news to tell thee, strange news.
JASPERINO: I ha' some too,
I think as strange as yours; would I might keep
Mine, so my faith and friendship might be kept in't!
Faith, sir, dispense a little with my zeal
And let it cool in this.
ALSEMERO: This puts me on
And blames thee for thy slowness.
JASPERINO: All may prove nothing;
Only a friendly fear that leapt from me, sir.
ALSEMERO: No question it may prove nothing; let's partake it, though.
JASPERINO: 'Twas Diaphanta's chance (for to that wench
I pretend honest love, and she deserves it)

66 *lay*: allay 72 *holds his right*: i.e. by marrying Beatrice 75 *it*: i.e. his sword 76 *your day*: i.e. your wedding day 84–5 i.e. relieve me from the obligation of having to tell you bad news 85 *puts me on*: provokes my curiosity

To leave me in a back part of the house,
A place we chose for private conference;
She was no sooner gone, but instantly
I heard your bride's voice in the next room to me,
And lending more attention, found De Flores
Louder than she.
ALSEMERO: De Flores? Thou art out now.
JASPERINO: You'll tell me more anon.
ALSEMERO: Still I'll prevent thee:
The very sight of him is poison to her.
JASPERINO: That made me stagger too, but Diaphanta
At her return confirm'd it.
ALSEMERO: Diaphanta!
JASPERINO: Then fell we both to listen, and words pass'd
Like those that challenge interest in a woman.
ALSEMERO: Peace, quench thy zeal; 'tis dangerous to thy bosom.
JASPERINO: Then truth is full of peril.
ALSEMERO: Such truths are. –
O were she the sole glory of the earth,
Had eyes that could shoot fire into kings' breasts,
And touch'd, she sleeps not here! Yet I have time,
Though night be near, to be resolv'd hereof;
And prithee do not weigh me by my passions.
JASPERINO: I never weigh'd friend so.
ALSEMERO: Done charitably.
[*Gives key.*]
That key will lead thee to a pretty secret,
By a Chaldean taught me, and I've made
My study upon some. Bring from my closet
A glass inscrib'd there with the letter M,
And question not my purpose.
JASPERINO: It shall be done, sir.
Exit.
ALSEMERO: How can this hang together? Not an hour since,
Her woman came pleading her lady's fears,
Deliver'd her for the most timorous virgin
That ever shrunk at man's name, and so modest,
She charg'd her weep out her request to me,
That she might come obscurely to my bosom.

97 *prevent*: forestall 102 *challenge interest*: claim a right 107 *touch'd*: tainted/unchaste 112 *Chaldean*: one skilled in the occult, the term deriving from biblical references to Chaldean magical practices 121 *obscurely*: in darkness

Enter BEATRICE.

BEATRICE [*Aside.*]: All things go well. My woman's preparing yonder
For her sweet voyage, which grieves me to lose;
Necessity compels it, I lose all else.

ALSEMERO [*Aside.*]: Push, modesty's shrine is set in yonder forehead.
I cannot be too sure though. – My Joanna!

BEATRICE: Sir, I was bold to weep a message to you;
Pardon my modest fears.

ALSEMERO [*Aside.*]: The dove's not meeker;
She's abus'd, questionless. –

Enter JASPERINO [*with glass*].

O are you come, sir?

BEATRICE [*Aside.*]: The glass, upon my life! I see the letter.

JASPERINO: Sir, this is M.

ALSEMERO: 'Tis it.

BEATRICE [*Aside.*]: I am suspected.

ALSEMERO: How fitly our bride comes to partake with us!

BEATRICE: What is't, my lord?

ALSEMERO: No hurt.

BEATRICE: Sir, pardon me,
I seldom taste of any composition.

ALSEMERO: But this, upon my warrant, you shall venture on.

BEATRICE: I fear 'twill make me ill.

ALSEMERO: Heaven forbid that.

BEATRICE [*Aside.*]: I'm put now to my cunning; th'effects I know,
If I can now but feign 'em handsomely.
[*Drinks.*]

ALSEMERO [*To* JASPERINO.]: It has that secret virtue, it ne'er miss'd, sir,
Upon a virgin.

JASPERINO: Treble qualitied?

[BEATRICE *gapes, then sneezes.*]

ALSEMERO: By all that's virtuous, it takes there, proceeds!

JASPERINO: This is the strangest trick to know a maid by.

BEATRICE: Ha, ha, ha!
You have given me joy of heart to drink, my lord.

ALSEMERO: No, thou hast given me such joy of heart,
That never can be blasted.

BEATRICE: What's the matter, sir?

ALSEMERO [*To* JASPERINO.]: See, now 'tis settled in a melancholy.
Keep both the time and method, my Joanna!

134 *composition*: medicine, preparation of mixed ingredients 139 *virtue*: power, property

Chaste as the breath of heaven, or morning's womb,
That brings the day forth, thus my love encloses thee.
[*Embraces her.*] *Exeunt.*

[SCENE 3]

Enter ISABELLA *and* LOLLIO.

ISABELLA: O heaven! Is this the waiting moon?
Does love turn fool, run mad, and all [at] once?
Sirrah, here's a madman, akin to the fool too,
A lunatic lover.

LOLLIO: No, no, not he I brought the letter from?

ISABELLA: Compare his inside with his out, and tell me.
[*Gives him letter.*]

LOLLIO: The out's mad, I'm sure of that; I had a taste on't. [*Reads.*] 'To the bright Andromeda, chief chambermaid to the Knight of the Sun, at the sign of Scorpio, in the middle region, sent by the bellows mender of Aeolus. Pay the post.' This is stark madness.

ISABELLA: Now mark the inside. [*Takes letter and reads.*] 'Sweet lady, having now cast off this counterfeit cover of a madman, I appear to your best judgment a true and faithful lover of your beauty.'

LOLLIO: He is mad still.

ISABELLA: 'If any fault you find, chide those perfections in you, which have made me imperfect; 'tis the same sun that causeth to grow and enforceth to wither . . .'

LOLLIO: O rogue!

ISABELLA: '. . . Shapes and trans-shapes, destroys and builds again; I come in winter to you dismantled of my proper ornaments; by the sweet splendour of your cheerful smiles, I spring and live a lover.'

LOLLIO: Mad rascal still!

ISABELLA: 'Tread him not under foot, that shall appear an honour to

1 *waiting*: 'malign influence of the' (OED 'wait *v.*[1] I.1.b. intr. to keep hostile watch; to lie in wait') 6 *his inside with his out*: the contents of the letter with the cover/the inner man with his appearance 7–10 there may be glimmerings of sense behind this 'stark madness'. If Isabella is 'Andromeda', perhaps Franciscus imagines himself as Perseus, the hero of Greek legend who rescued her from the 'dragon', Alibius. Chambermaids were proverbially lascivious, while the Knight of the Sun was a hero of popular romance who was regularly mocked on the Jacobean stage. Scorpio is the astrological sign governing the 'middle region' or genitals, and Aeolus was the god of winds 20 *dismantled*: stripped

your bounties. I remain – mad till I speak with you, from whom I expect my cure. Yours all, or one beside himself, *Franciscus*.'

LOLLIO: You are like to have a fine time on't; my master and I may give over our professions: I do not think but you can cure fools and madmen faster than we, with little pains too.

ISABELLA: Very likely.

LOLLIO: One thing I must tell you, mistress: you perceive that I am privy to your skill; if I find you minister once and set up the trade, I put in for my thirds, I shall be mad or fool else.

ISABELLA: The first place is thine, believe it, Lollio,
If I do fall –

LOLLIO: I fall upon you.

ISABELLA: So.

LOLLIO: Well, I stand to my venture.

ISABELLA: But thy counsel now, how shall I deal with 'em?

LOLLIO: Why, do you mean to deal with 'em?

ISABELLA: Nay, the fair understanding, how to use 'em.

LOLLIO: Abuse 'em! That's the way to mad the fool, and make a fool of the madman, and then you use 'em kindly.

ISABELLA: 'Tis easy, I'll practise; do thou observe it;
The key of thy wardrobe.

LOLLIO: There; fit yourself for 'em, and I'll fit 'em both for you.
[*Gives her key.*]

ISABELLA: Take thou no further notice than the outside.
Exit.

LOLLIO: Not an inch; I'll put you to the inside.
Enter ALIBIUS.

ALIBIUS: Lollio, art there? Will all be perfect, think'st thou?
Tomorrow night, as if to close up the solemnity,
Vermandero expects us.

LOLLIO: I mistrust the madmen most; the fools will do well enough; I have taken pains with them.

ALIBIUS: Tush, they cannot miss; the more absurdity
The more commends it, so no rough behaviours
Affright the ladies; they are nice things, thou know'st.

31 *minister once and set up the trade*: fornicate once and become a whore 32 *thirds*: presumably Alibius and her lover would each receive a third as well 35 *stand to*: stand by *venture*: see note I.i.87 37 *Why*: Q's 'We' is an obvious error *deal*: cope. Lollio introduces the bawdy meaning of the term 38 *the fair understanding*: i.e. don't put an indecent construction on my words 40 *kindly*: gently/in accordance with their natures 41 *practise*: scheme 43 *fit*: dress yourself/prepare yourself 45 *I'll put you to the inside*: 'put to' was a slang term for having sex 53 *nice*: fastidious

LOLLIO: You need not fear, sir; so long as we are there with our commanding pizzles, they'll be as tame as the ladies themselves.

ALIBIUS: I will see them once more rehearse before they go.

LOLLIO: I was about it, sir; look you to the madmen's morris, and let me alone with the other; there is one or two that I mistrust their fooling; I'll instruct them, and then they shall rehearse the whole measure.

ALIBIUS: Do so; I'll see the music prepar'd. But Lollio,
By the way, how does my wife brook her restraint?
Does she not grudge at it?

LOLLIO: So, so; she takes some pleasure in the house, she would abroad else; you must allow her a little more length, she's kept too short.

ALIBIUS: She shall along to Vermandero's with us;
That will serve her for a month's liberty.

LOLLIO: What's that on your face, sir?

ALIBIUS: Where, Lollio? I see nothing.

LOLLIO: Cry you mercy, sir, 'tis your nose; it show'd like the trunk of a young elephant.

ALIBIUS: Away, rascal! I'll prepare the music, Lollio.

Exit ALIBIUS.

LOLLIO: Do, sir, and I'll dance the whilst. Tony, where art thou, Tony?

Enter ANTONIO.

ANTONIO: Here, cousin; where art thou?

LOLLIO: Come, Tony, the footmanship I taught you.

ANTONIO: I had rather ride, cousin.

LOLLIO: Ay, a whip take you; but I'll keep you out. Vault in; look you, Tony: fa, la la, la la.

[*Dances.*]

ANTONIO: Fa, la la, la la.

[*Dances.*]

LOLLIO: There, an honour.

ANTONIO: Is this an honour, cuz?

[*Bows.*]

LOLLIO: Yes, and it please your worship.

ANTONIO: Does honour bend in the hams, cuz?

LOLLIO: Marry does it; as low as worship, squireship, nay, yeomanry itself sometimes, from whence it first stiffened; there rise, a caper.

55 *pizzles*: whips made from bulls' penises 59 *measure*: dance 63 *she takes some pleasure in the house*: a veiled allusion to Antonio and Franciscus
69–70 probably intimating that Alibius has been 'led by the nose' 75 *ride*: quibbles on 'ride' = fuck were common 79 *honour*: a bow 82 *Does honour bend in the hams*: Antonio's query concerning the way of executing a bow is also a punning question: 'Do nobles bow to commoners'. Lollio's answer picks up on this, as well as the bawdy implication that 'bend in the hams' = copulate
84 *caper*: leap

ANTONIO: Caper after an honour, cuz?

LOLLIO: Very proper; for honour is but a caper, rises as fast and high, has a knee or two, and falls to th'ground again. You can remember your figure, Tony?

Exit.

ANTONIO: Yes, cousin; when I see thy figure, I can remember mine.

Enter ISABELLA [*disguised as a madwoman*].

ISABELLA: Hey, how he treads the air! Shough, shough, tother way!
He burns his wings else; here's wax enough below, Icarus, more than
will be cancelled these eighteen moons;
He's down, he's down, what a terrible fall he had!
Stand up, thou son of Cretan Dedalus,
And let us tread the lower labyrinth;
I'll bring thee to the clue.

ANTONIO: Prithee, cuz, let me alone.

ISABELLA: Art thou not drown'd?
About thy head I saw a heap of clouds,
Wrapp'd like a Turkish turban; on thy back
A crook'd chameleon-colour'd rainbow hung
Like a tiara down unto thy hams.
Let me suck out those billows in thy belly;
Hark how they roar and rumble in the straits!
Bless thee from the pirates.

ANTONIO: Pox upon you, let me alone!

ISABELLA: Why shouldst thou mount so high as Mercury,
Unless thou hadst reversion of his place?
Stay in the moon with me, Endymion,
And we will rule these wild rebellious waves
That would have drown'd my love.

ANTONIO: I'll kick thee if again thou touch me,

86 *rises*: Q gives 'rise' 88 *figure*: steps of a dance/appearance 90 *he*: Q reads 'she' 91 *Icarus*: in Greek myth Icarus's father, Daedalus, built them both wings made from wax and feathers with which they attempted to escape from Crete. Icarus flew too near to the sun and plunged into the sea when the wax melted
92 *cancelled*: destroyed (in legal terminology documents are cancelled)
95 *labyrinth*: a reference to the labyrinth which Daedalus constructed to hold the Minotaur 96 *clue*: alluding to the thread which Ariadne left to guide Theseus out of the labyrinth 102 *tiara*: a turban with a long tailpiece 103 *suck out those billows in thy belly*: perhaps a mock offer of fellatio 104 *straits*: Q reads 'streets'. However, Isabella still seems to be thinking of the Icarian sea between Greece and Crete 107 *Mercury*: messenger of the gods 108 *reversion of his place*: the right to succeed to his position 109 *Endymion*: in Greek mythology, the beautiful youth beloved of Luna, the moon

Thou wild unshapen antic; I am no fool,
You bedlam!

ISABELLA: But you are, as sure as I am, mad.
Have I put on this habit of a frantic,
With love as full of fury, to beguile
The nimble eye of watchful jealousy,
And am I thus rewarded?
[*Reveals herself.*]

ANTONIO: Ha! Dearest beauty!

ISABELLA: No, I have no beauty now,
Nor never had, but what was in my garments.
You a quick-sighted lover? Come not near me!
Keep your caparisons, y'are aptly clad;
I came a feigner to return stark mad.
Exit.

Enter LOLLIO.

ANTONIO: Stay, or I shall change condition,
And become as you are.

LOLLIO: Why, Tony, whither now? Why, fool?

ANTONIO: Whose fool, usher of idiots? You coxcomb!
I have fool'd too much.

LOLLIO: You were best be mad another while then.

ANTONIO: So I am, stark mad, I have cause enough;
And I could throw the full effects on thee
And beat thee like a fury!

LOLLIO: Do not, do not; I shall not forbear the gentleman under the fool, if you do; alas, I saw through your fox-skin before now. Come, I can give you comfort; my mistress loves you, and there is as arrant a madman i' th'house as you are a fool, your rival, whom she loves not; if after the masque we can rid her of him, you earn her love, she says, and the fool shall ride her.

ANTONIO: May I believe thee?

LOLLIO: Yes, or you may choose whether you will or no.

ANTONIO: She's eas'd of him; I have a good quarrel on't.

LOLLIO: Well, keep your old station yet, and be quiet.

ANTONIO: Tell her I will deserve her love.
[*Exit.*]

LOLLIO: And you are like to have your desire.

Enter FRANCISCUS.

113 *antic*: clown, grotesque figure 115 *frantic*: lunatic 122 *caparisons*: clothes 127 *usher*: under-master 133 *forbear*: show forbearance towards 134 *fox-skin*: disguise

FRANCISCUS (*Sings.*): '*Down, down, down a-down a-down*',
And then with a horse-trick,
To kick Latona's forehead, and break her bowstring.

LOLLIO [*Aside.*]: This is tother counterfeit; I'll put him out of his humour. [*Takes out letter and reads.*] 'Sweet lady, having now cast this counterfeit cover of a madman, I appear to your best judgment a true and faithful lover of your beauty.' This is pretty well for a madman.

FRANCISCUS: Ha! What's that?

LOLLIO: 'Chide those perfections in you, which [have] made me imperfect.'

FRANCISCUS: I am discover'd to the fool.

LOLLIO: I hope to discover the fool in you, ere I have done with you. 'Yours all, or one beside himself, *Franciscus*.' This madman will mend sure.

FRANCISCUS: What? Do you read, sirrah?

LOLLIO: Your destiny, sir; you'll be hang'd for this trick, and another that I know.

FRANCISCUS: Art thou of counsel with thy mistress?

LOLLIO: Next her apron strings.

FRANCISCUS: Give me thy hand.

LOLLIO: Stay, let me put yours in my pocket first. [*Puts away letter.*] Your hand is true, is it not? It will not pick? I partly fear it, because I think it does lie.

FRANCISCUS: Not in a syllable.

LOLLIO: So; if you love my mistress so well as you have handled the matter here, you are like to be cur'd of your madness.

FRANCISCUS: And none but she can cure it.

LOLLIO: Well, I'll give you over then, and she shall cast your water next.

FRANCISCUS: Take for thy pains past.
[*Gives him money.*]

LOLLIO: I shall deserve more, sir, I hope; my mistress loves you, but must have some proof of your love to her.

FRANCISCUS: There I meet my wishes.

LOLLIO: That will not serve, you must meet her enemy and yours.

FRANCISCUS: He's dead already!

LOLLIO: Will you tell me that, and I parted but now with him?

FRANCISCUS: Show me the man.

147 *Latona*: Latin form of Leto, the mother of Diana the huntress. The reference to the 'bow-string' may indicate that Franciscus has confused the two goddesses 160 *this trick, and another*: i.e. fraud and adultery 162 *of counsel*: i.e. in her confidence 164 *hand*: introduces a pun on hand and handwriting 165 *yours*: i.e. your handwriting/letter 172 *cast your water*: effect a diagnosis by examining your urine 177 *There I meet my wishes*: 'that would be my wish as well'. Lollio chooses to misinterpret him

LOLLIO: Ay, that's a right course now, see him before you kill him in any case, and yet it needs not go so far neither; 'tis but a fool that haunts the house and my mistress in the shape of an idiot; bang but his fool's coat well-favouredly, and 'tis well.

FRANCISCUS: Soundly, soundly!

LOLLIO: Only reserve him till the masque be past, and if you find him not now in the dance yourself, I'll show you. In, in! My master!

FRANCISCUS: He handles him like a feather. Hey!

[*Exit dancing.*]

Enter ALIBIUS.

ALIBIUS: Well said; in a readiness, Lollio?

LOLLIO: Yes, sir.

ALIBIUS: Away then, and guide them in, Lollio;
Entreat your mistress to see this sight.
Hark, is there not one incurable fool
That might be begg'd? I have friends.

LOLLIO [*Within.*]: I have him for you, one that shall deserve it too.

[*Exit* LOLLIO.]

ALIBIUS: Good boy, Lollio.

[*Enter* ISABELLA, *then* LOLLIO *with* Madmen *and* Fools.]

The Madmen *and* Fools *dance.*

'Tis perfect; well, fit but once these strains,
We shall have coin and credit for our pains.

Exeunt.

185 *well-favouredly*: soundly 192 *Well said*: stock phrase meaning 'Well done'
197 *begg'd*: i.e. obtained as a ward (so that Alibius could control his estate)
203 *fit but once these strains*: only prepare the music

ACT FIVE

[SCENE I]

Enter BEATRICE. *A clock strikes one.*
BEATRICE: One struck, and yet she lies by't – o my fears!
This strumpet serves her own ends, 'tis apparent now,
Devours the pleasure with a greedy appetite,
And never minds my honour or my peace,
Makes havoc of my right; but she pays dearly for't:
No trusting of her life with such a secret,
That cannot rule her blood to keep her promise.
Beside, I have some suspicion of her faith to me
Because I was suspected of my lord,
And it must come from her. – Hark! By my horrors,
Another clock strikes two.
Strikes two.
Enter DE FLORES.
DE FLORES: Pist, where are you?
BEATRICE: De Flores?
DE FLORES: Ay. Is she not come from him yet?
BEATRICE: As I am a living soul, not.
DE FLORES: Sure the Devil
Hath sow'd his itch within her; who'd trust
A waiting-woman?
BEATRICE: I must trust somebody.
DE FLORES: Push, they are termagants,
Especially when they fall upon their masters
And have their ladies' first-fruits; th'are mad whelps,
You cannot stave 'em off from game royal; then
You are so harsh and hardy, ask no counsel,

1 *lies by't*: locked away (with Alsemero in his chamber) (OED lie *v.* B. 1. 3)
7 *blood*: sexual appetite 16 *termagants*: fierce, shrewish women. The term is derived from the name of a savage god the Muslims were believed to worship
17 *fall upon*: take up with 19 *stave 'em off*: beat them away ('stave off', a technical term meaning to 'beat off dogs in bear- or bull-baiting', continues the imagery of 'mad whelps' from the line above) *game royal*: royal game (commoners were not allowed to hunt in royal preserves) 20 *harsh and hardy*: independent; some editors emend to 'harsh and rash'

And I could have help'd you to an apothecary's daughter
Would have fall'n off before eleven, and thank you too.

BEATRICE: O me, not yet? This whore forgets herself.

DE FLORES: The rascal fares so well; look, y'are undone,
The day-star, by this hand! See Phosphorus plain yonder.

BEATRICE: Advise me now to fall upon some ruin,
There is no counsel safe else.

DE FLORES: Peace, I ha't now;
For we must force a rising, there's no remedy.

BEATRICE: How? Take heed of that.

DE FLORES: Tush, be you quiet,
Or else give over all.

BEATRICE: Prithee, I ha' done then.

DE FLORES: This is my reach: I'll set some part a-fire
Of Diaphanta's chamber.

BEATRICE: How? Fire, sir?
That may endanger the whole house.

DE FLORES: You talk of danger when your fame's on fire?

BEATRICE: That's true; do what thou wilt now.

DE FLORES: Push, I aim
At a most rich success, strikes all dead sure;
The chimney being a-fire, and some light parcels
Of the least danger in her chamber only,
If Diaphanta should be met by chance then,
Far from her lodging, which is now suspicious,
It would be thought her fears and affrights then
Drove her to seek for succour; if not seen
Or met at all, as that's the likeliest,
For her own shame she'll hasten towards her lodging;
I will be ready with a piece high-charg'd,
As 'twere to cleanse the chimney: there 'tis proper now,
But she shall be the mark.

BEATRICE: I'm forc'd to love thee now,
'Cause thou provid'st so carefully for my honour.

DE FLORES: 'Slid, it concerns the safety of us both,
Our pleasure and continuance.

25 *Phosphorus*: the Day- or Morning-star. Q's 'Bosphorus' is an obvious error
26 *fall upon some ruin*: devise some desperate remedy 28 *force a rising*: wake the household 31 *reach*: plan 37 *light parcels*: small items 45 *piece*: fowling-piece, gun 46 *proper now*: fully formed 49 *'Slid*: an oath, contracted from 'God's (eye-)lid' 50 *continuance*: i.e. both of their adulterous pleasure and their lives

BEATRICE: One word now, prithee;
How for the servants?
DE FLORES: I'll dispatch them
Some one way, some another in the hurry,
For buckets, hooks, ladders. Fear not you;
The deed shall find its time – and I've thought since
Upon a safe conveyance for the body too.
How this fire purifies wit! Watch you your minute.
BEATRICE: Fear keeps my soul upon't, I cannot stray from't.
Enter ALONZO'S GHOST.
DE FLORES: Ha! What art thou that tak'st away the light
'Twixt that star and me? I dread thee not;
'Twas but a mist of conscience – all's clear again.
Exit.
BEATRICE: Who's that, De Flores? Bless me! It slides by;
[*Exit* GHOST.]
Some ill thing haunts the house; 't has left behind it
A shivering sweat upon me; I'm afraid now,
This night hath been so tedious. O this strumpet!
Had she a thousand lives, he should not leave her
Till he had destroy'd the last. – List, o my terrors!
Struck three o'clock.
Three struck by Saint Sebastian's!
[VOICE] (*within.*): Fire, fire, fire!
BEATRICE: Already? How rare is that man's speed!
How heartily he serves me! His face loathes one,
But look upon his care, who would not love him?
The east is not more beauteous than his service.
[VOICE] (*within.*): Fire, fire, fire!
Enter DE FLORES; Servants *pass over, ring a bell.*
DE FLORES: Away, dispatch!
Hooks, buckets, ladders! That's well said;
The fire-bell rings, the chimney works; my charge;
The piece is ready.
Exit.
BEATRICE: Here's a man worth loving –
Enter DIAPHANTA.
O y'are a jewel!

56 *Watch you your minute*: look out for the moment to act 66 *List*: listen
69 *loathes*: disgusts 74 *charge*: gunpowder

DIAPHANTA: Pardon frailty, madam;
In troth I was so well, I ev'n forgot myself.
BEATRICE: Y'have made trim work.
DIAPHANTA: What?
BEATRICE: Hie quickly to your chamber;
Your reward follows you.
DIAPHANTA: I never made
So sweet a bargain.
Exit.
Enter ALSEMERO.
ALSEMERO: O my dear Joanna;
Alas, art thou risen too? I was coming,
My absolute treasure.
BEATRICE: When I miss'd you,
I could not choose but follow.
ALSEMERO: Th'art all sweetness!
The fire is not so dangerous.
BEATRICE: Think you so, sir?
ALSEMERO: I prithee tremble not: believe me, 'tis not.
Enter VERMANDERO, JASPERINO.
VERMANDERO: O bless my house and me!
ALSEMERO: My lord your father.
Enter DE FLORES *with a piece.*
VERMANDERO: Knave, whither goes that piece?
DE FLORES: To scour the chimney.
Exit.
VERMANDERO: O well said, well said;
That fellow's good on all occasions.
BEATRICE: A wondrous necessary man, my lord.
VERMANDERO: He hath a ready wit, he's worth 'em all, sir;
Dog at a house of fire; I ha' seen him sing'd ere now:
The piece goes off.
Ha, there he goes.
BEATRICE: 'Tis done.
ALSEMERO: Come, sweet, to bed now;
Alas, thou wilt get cold.
BEATRICE: Alas, the fear keeps that out;
My heart will find no quiet till I hear
How Diaphanta, my poor woman, fares;
It is her chamber, sir, her lodging chamber.
VERMANDERO: How should the fire come there?

78 *trim*: vague term of approval, here used ironically *Hie*: hasten 92 *Dog at*: experienced with

BEATRICE: As good a soul as ever lady countenanc'd,
But in her chamber negligent and heavy;
She 'scap'd a mine twice.
VERMANDERO: Twice?
BEATRICE: Strangely twice, sir.
VERMANDERO: Those sleepy sluts are dangerous in a house
And they be ne'er so good.
Enter DE FLORES.
DE FLORES: O poor virginity!
Thou hast paid dearly for't.
VERMANDERO: Bless us! What's that?
DE FLORES: A thing you all knew once – Diaphanta's burnt.
BEATRICE: My woman, o, my woman!
DE FLORES: Now the flames
Are greedy for her; burnt, burnt, burnt to death, sir!
BEATRICE: O my presaging soul!
ALSEMERO: Not a tear more;
I charge you by the last embrace I gave you
In bed before this rais'd us.
BEATRICE: Now you tie me;
Were it my sister, now she gets no more.
Enter Servant.
VERMANDERO: How now?
SERVANT: All danger's past, you may now take your rests, my lords; the fire is throughly quench'd; ah, poor gentlewoman, how soon was she stifled!
BEATRICE: Dc Flores, what is left of her inter,
And we as mourners all will follow her:
I will entreat that honour to my servant,
Ev'n of my lord himself.
ALSEMERO: Command it, sweetness.
BEATRICE: Which of you spied the fire first?
DE FLORES: 'Twas I, madam.
BEATRICE: And took such pains in't too? A double goodness!
'Twere well he were rewarded.
VERMANDERO: He shall be;
De Flores, call upon me.
ALSEMERO: And upon me, sir.

99 *countenanc'd*: employed 100 *heavy*: sluggish (Beatrice may be alluding to Diaphanta's lingering in bed with Alsemero, and thus Beatrice's anger is possibly one of the 'mines' (i.e. conflagrations) referred to in the following line)
101 *Strangely*: miraculously 103 *And*: even if 108 *presaging*: prophetic

Exeunt [*all but* DE FLORES].

DE FLORES: Rewarded? Precious, here's a trick beyond me!
I see in all bouts, both of sport and wit,
Always a woman strives for the last hit.
Exit.

[SCENE 2]

Enter TOMAZO.

TOMAZO: I cannot taste the benefits of life
With the same relish I was wont to do.
Man I grow weary of, and hold his fellowship
A treacherous bloody friendship; and because
I am ignorant in whom my wrath should settle,
I must think all men villains, and the next
I meet, whoe'er he be, the murderer
Of my most worthy brother. – Ha! What's he?
Enter DE FLORES, *passes over the stage.*
O the fellow that some call honest De Flores;
But methinks honesty was hard bested
To come there for a lodging, as if a queen
Should make her palace of a pest-house.
I find a contrariety in nature
Betwixt that face and me: the least occasion
Would give me game upon him; yet he's so foul,
One would scarce touch [him] with a sword he loved
And made account of; so most deadly venomous,
He would go near to poison any weapon
That should draw blood on him; one must resolve
Never to use that sword again in fight,
In way of honest manhood, that strikes him;
Some river must devour't, 'twere not fit
That any man should find it. – What, again?
Enter DE FLORES.
He walks a' purpose by, sure, to choke me up,
To infect my blood.

DE FLORES: My worthy noble lord!

10 *bested*: beset, put to it 12 *pest-house*: hospital for infectious diseases, particularly plague and leprosy 15 *give me game upon him*: obscure phrase, probably meaning 'set me quarrelling with him' 17 *made account of*: valued

TOMAZO: Dost offer to come near and breathe upon me?
[*Strikes him.*]
DE FLORES: A blow!
[*Draws sword.*]
TOMAZO: Yea, are you so prepar'd?
I'll rather like a soldier die by th'sword
Than like a politician by thy poison.
[*Draws.*]
DE FLORES: Hold, my lord, as you are honourable.
TOMAZO: All slaves that kill by poison are still cowards.
DE FLORES [*Aside.*]: I cannot strike; I see his brother's wounds
Fresh bleeding in his eye, as in a crystal. –
I will not question this, I know y'are noble;
I take my injury with thanks given, sir,
Like a wise lawyer; and as a favour,
Will wear it for the worthy hand that gave it.
[*Aside.*] Why this from him, that yesterday appear'd
So strangely loving to me?
O but instinct is of a subtler strain,
Guilt must not walk so near his lodge again;
He came near me now.
Exit.
TOMAZO: All league with mankind I renounce for ever
Till I find this murderer; not so much
As common courtesy but I'll lock up:
For in the state of ignorance I live in
A brother may salute his brother's murderer
And wish good speed to th'villain in a greeting.
Enter VERMANDERO, ALIBIUS *and* ISABELLA.
VERMANDERO: Noble Piracquo!
TOMAZO: Pray keep on your way, sir,
I've nothing to say to you.
VERMANDERO: Comforts bless you, sir.
TOMAZO: I have forsworn compliment; in troth I have, sir;
As you are merely man, I have not left
A good wish for you, nor any here.
VERMANDERO: Unless you be so far in love with grief
You will not part from't upon any terms,
We bring that news will make a welcome for us.
TOMAZO: What news can that be?
VERMANDERO: Throw no scornful smile

33 *crystal*: crystal ball

Upon the zeal I bring you, 'tis worth more, sir.
Two of the chiefest men I kept about me
I hide not from the law, or your just vengeance.

TOMAZO: Ha!

VERMANDERO: To give your peace more ample satisfaction,
Thank these discoverers.

TOMAZO: If you bring that calm,
Name but the manner I shall ask forgiveness in
For that contemptuous smile upon you:
I'll perfect it with reverence that belongs
Unto a sacred altar.
[*Kneels.*]

VERMANDERO: Good sir, rise;
Why, now you overdo as much a'this hand,
As you fell short a' tother. – Speak, Alibius.

ALIBIUS: 'Twas my wife's fortune, as she is most lucky
At a discovery, to find out lately
Within our hospital of fools and madmen
Two counterfeits slipp'd into these disguises:
Their names, Franciscus and Antonio.

VERMANDERO: Both mine, sir, and I ask no favour for 'em.

ALIBIUS: Now that which draws suspicion to their habits,
The time of their disguisings agrees justly
With the day of the murder.

TOMAZO: O blest revelation!

VERMANDERO: Nay more, nay more, sir, I'll not spare mine own
In way of justice: they both feign'd a journey
To Briamata, and so wrought out their leaves;
My love was so abus'd in't.

TOMAZO: Time's too precious
To run in waste now; you have brought a peace
The riches of five kingdoms could not purchase.
Be my most happy conduct; I thirst for 'em:
Like subtle lightning will I wind about 'em,
And melt their marrow in 'em.
Exeunt.

76 *habits*: clothes 81 *wrought out*: obtained 85 *conduct*: guide 86–7: it was believed that lightning could kill by melting the marrow in the bones without leaving any external marks on the body

[SCENE 3]

Enter ALSEMERO *and* JASPERINO.

JASPERINO: Your confidence, I'm sure, is now of proof.
The prospect from the garden has show'd
Enough for deep suspicion.
ALSEMERO: The black mask
That so continually was worn upon't
Condemns the face for ugly ere't be seen:
Her despite to him, and so seeming bottomless.
JASPERINO: Touch it home then; 'tis not a shallow probe
Can search this ulcer soundly; I fear you'll find it
Full of corruption. 'Tis fit I leave you;
She meets you opportunely from that walk:
She took the back door at his parting with her.
Exit JASPERINO.
ALSEMERO: Did my fate wait for this unhappy stroke
At my first sight of woman? – She's here.
Enter BEATRICE.
BEATRICE: Alsemero!
ALSEMERO: How do you?
BEATRICE: How do I?
Alas! How do you? You look not well.
ALSEMERO: You read me well enough, I am not well.
BEATRICE: Not well, sir? Is't in my power to better you?
ALSEMERO: Yes.
BEATRICE: Nay, then y'are cur'd again.
ALSEMERO: Pray resolve me one question, lady.
BEATRICE: If I can.
ALSEMERO: None can so sure. Are you honest?
BEATRICE: Ha, ha, ha! That's a broad question, my lord.
ALSEMERO: But that's not a modest answer, my lady.
Do you laugh? My doubts are strong upon me.
BEATRICE: 'Tis innocence that smiles, and no rough brow
Can take away the dimple in her cheek.
Say I should strain a tear to fill the vault,
Which would you give the better faith to?

1 *confidence*: i.e. in Jasperino's allegations concerning Beatrice *of proof*: strong 3 *black mask*: i.e. Beatrice's hypocrisy. The pretence that she hates De Flores must mask a more terrible secret 7 *Touch it home*: get to the bottom of the mystery 21 *broad*: wide/bawdy 26 *vault*: heavens

ALSEMERO: 'Twere but hypocrisy of a sadder colour,
But the same stuff; neither your smiles nor tears
Shall move or flatter me from my belief:
You are a whore!

BEATRICE: What a horrid sound it hath!
It blasts a beauty to deformity;
Upon what face soever that breath falls,
It strikes it ugly. O you have ruin'd
What you can ne'er repair again.

ALSEMERO: I'll all demolish, and seek out truth within you,
If there be any left; let your sweet tongue
Prevent your heart's rifling; there I'll ransack
And tear out my suspicion.

BEATRICE: You may, sir,
'Tis an easy passage; yet, if you please,
Show me the ground whereon you lost your love;
My spotless virtue may but tread on that
Before I perish.

ALSEMERO: Unanswerable!
A ground you cannot stand on: you fall down
Beneath all grace and goodness, when you set
Your ticklish heel on't; there was a visor
O'er that cunning face, and that became you;
Now impudence in triumph rides upon't.
How comes this tender reconcilement else
'Twixt you and your despite, your rancorous loathing,
De Flores? He that your eye was sore at sight of,
He's now become your arm's supporter, your lip's saint!

BEATRICE: Is there the cause?

ALSEMERO: Worse: your lust's devil,
Your adultery!

BEATRICE: Would any but yourself say that,
'Twould turn him to a villain.

ALSEMERO: 'Twas witness'd
By the counsel of your bosom, Diaphanta.

BEATRICE: Is your witness dead then?

ALSEMERO: 'Tis to be fear'd
It was the wages of her knowledge, poor soul,
She liv'd not long after the discovery.

BEATRICE: Then hear a story of not much less horror
Than this your false suspicion is beguil'd with;

28 *sadder*: darker 38 *Prevent*: anticipate 41 *ground*: evidence, reason
46 *ticklish*: lascivious 48 *impudence*: immodesty

To your bed's scandal I stand up innocence,
Which even the guilt of one black other deed
Will stand for proof of: your love has made me
A cruel murd'ress.

ALSEMERO: Ha!

BEATRICE: A bloody one;
I have kiss'd poison for't, strok'd a serpent:
That thing of hate, worthy in my esteem
Of no better employment, and him most worthy
To be so employ'd, I caus'd to murder
That innocent Piracquo, having no
Better means than that worst, to assure
Yourself to me.

ALSEMERO: O the place itself e'er since
Has crying been for vengeance, the temple
Where blood and beauty first unlawfully
Fir'd their devotion, and quench'd the right one;
'Twas in my fears at first, 'twill have it now:
O thou art all deform'd!

BEATRICE: Forget not, sir,
It for your sake was done; shall greater dangers
Make the less welcome?

ALSEMERO: O thou shouldst have gone
A thousand leagues about to have avoided
This dangerous bridge of blood; here we are lost.

BEATRICE: Remember I am true unto your bed.

ALSEMERO: The bed itself's a charnel, the sheets shrouds
For murdered carcasses; it must ask pause
What I must do in this; meantime you shall
Be my prisoner only: enter my closet;
Exit BEATRICE.
I'll be your keeper yet. O in what part
Of this sad story shall I first begin? – Ha!
Enter DE FLORES.
This same fellow has put me in. – De Flores!

DE FLORES: Noble Alsemero?

ALSEMERO: I can tell you
News, sir; my wife has her commended to you.

62 *I stand up innocence*: I put forward innocence as my defence to the charge
74 *blood*: desire 75 *right one*: i.e. devotion to God 80 *about*: around
83 *charnel*: charnel house, a vault for the remains of the dead 84 *it must ask pause*: i.e. a situation of this seriousness demands time for thought before proceeding 86 *closet*: private room 89 *put me in*: provided my cue

DE FLORES: That's news indeed, my lord; I think she would
Commend me to the gallows if she could,
She ever lov'd me so well; I thank her.
ALSEMERO: What's this blood upon your band, De Flores?
DE FLORES: Blood? No, sure, 'twas wash'd since.
ALSEMERO: Since when, man?
DE FLORES: Since tother day I got a knock
In a sword and dagger school; I think 'tis out.
ALSEMERO: Yes, 'tis almost out, but 'tis perceiv'd though.
I had forgot my message; this it is:
What price goes murder?
DE FLORES: How, sir?
ALSEMERO: I ask you, sir;
My wife's behindhand with you, she tells me,
For a brave bloody blow you gave for her sake
Upon Piracquo.
DE FLORES: Upon? 'Twas quite through him, sure;
Has she confess'd it?
ALSEMERO: As sure as death to both of you,
And much more than that.
DE FLORES: It could not be much more;
'Twas but one thing, and that – she's a whore.
ALSEMERO: It could not choose but follow. O cunning devils!
How should blind men know you from fair-fac'd saints?
BEATRICE (*Within.*): He lies, the villain does belie me!
DE FLORES: Let me go to her, sir.
ALSEMERO: Nay, you shall to her.
Peace, crying crocodile, your sounds are heard!
Take your prey to you, get you in to her, sir.
Exit DE FLORES.
I'll be your pander now; rehearse again
Your scene of lust, that you may be perfect
When you shall come to act it to the black audience
Where howls and gnashings shall be music to you.
Clip your adult'ress freely, 'tis the pilot
Will guide you to the Mare Mortuum,
Where you shall sink to fadoms bottomless.

95 *band*: collar 102 *behindhand with*: indebted to 110 *belie*: slander
112 *crying crocodile*: crocodiles were believed to weep hypocritically as they devoured their victims 116 *black audience*: i.e. of devils 118 *Clip*: embrace *pilot*: Beatrice will supply the place of Charon, who ferried the dead over the Styx to Hades 119 *Mare Mortuum*: the Dead Sea, which was believed to be bottomless

Enter VERMANDERO, ALIBIUS, ISABELLA, TOMAZO, FRANCISCUS, *and* ANTONIO.

VERMANDERO: O Alsemero, I have a wonder for you.
ALSEMERO: No, sir, 'tis I, I have a wonder for you.
VERMANDERO: I have suspicion near as proof itself
For Piracquo's murder.
ALSEMERO: Sir, I have proof
Beyond suspicion for Piracquo's murder.
VERMANDERO: Beseech you hear me; these two have been disguis'd
E'er since the deed was done.
ALSEMERO: I have two other
That were more close disguis'd than your two could be,
E'er since the deed was done.
VERMANDERO: You'll hear me! These mine own servants –
ALSEMERO: Hear me! Those nearer than your servants,
That shall acquit them and prove them guiltless.
FRANCISCUS: That may be done with easy truth, sir.
TOMAZO: How is my cause bandied through your delays!
'Tis urgent in blood and calls for haste;
Give me a brother alive or dead;
Alive, a wife with him; if dead, for both
A recompense, for murder and adultery.
BEATRICE (*Within.*): O! O! O!
ALSEMERO: Hark, 'tis coming to you.
DE FLORES (*Within.*): Nay, I'll along for company.
BEATRICE (*Within.*): O! O!
VERMANDERO: What horrid sounds are these?
ALSEMERO: Come forth, you twins of mischief!

Enter DE FLORES *bringing in* BEATRICE [*wounded*].

DE FLORES: Here we are; if you have any more
To say to us, speak quickly, I shall not
Give you the hearing else; I am so stout yet,
And so, I think, that broken rib of mankind.
VERMANDERO: An host of enemies enter'd my citadel
Could not amaze like this: Joanna! Beatrice-Joanna!

134 *bandied*: tossed about 138 *adultery*: Tomazo's view that a binding pre-contract existed between Beatrice and Alonzo would have been accepted by many of the contemporary audience 139 *'tis*: i.e. the 'recompense' of the previous line 145 *so stout*: i.e. strong enough to hear you, provided you speak quickly 146 *broken rib of mankind*: i.e. Beatrice, alluding to the biblical doctrine that Eve was created from Adam's rib

BEATRICE: O come not near me, sir, I shall defile you:
I am that of your blood was taken from you
For your better health; look no more upon't,
But cast it to the ground regardlessly,
Let the common sewer take it from distinction.
Beneath the stars, upon yon meteor
Ever hung my fate, 'mongst things corruptible;
I ne'er could pluck it from him: my loathing
Was prophet to the rest, but ne'er believ'd;
Mine honour fell with him, and now my life.
Alsemero, I am a stranger to your bed,
Your bed was cozen'd on the nuptial night,
For which your false bride died.
ALSEMERO: Diaphanta!
DE FLORES: Yes, and the while I coupled with your mate
At barley-brake; now we are left in hell.
VERMANDERO: We are all there, it circumscribes here.
DE FLORES: I lov'd this woman in spite of her heart;
Her love I earn'd out of Piracquo's murder.
TOMAZO: Ha! My brother's murderer!
DE FLORES: Yes, and her honour's prize
Was my reward; I thank life for nothing
But that pleasure; it was so sweet to me
That I have drunk up all, left none behind
For any man to pledge me.
VERMANDERO: Horrid villain!
Keep life in him for further tortures.
DE FLORES: No!
I can prevent you; here's my penknife still.
It is but one thread more, [*Stabs himself.*] and now 'tis cut.
Make haste, Joanna, by that token to thee:
Canst not forget, so lately put in mind,

150–1: i.e. that infected part of your blood which has now been cleansed by blood-letting. (However, line 150 taken on its own could mean 'I am one of your own blood that was taken from you', i.e. that Beatrice is regarding herself as a 'changeling', a child stolen from its parents by fairies, i.e. De Flores or the Devil) 153 *distinction*: sight/individual existence 154 *Beneath the stars*: traditional cosmology held that the sphere of the fixed stars was not subject to change or corruption, unlike this sublunary world *meteor*: i.e. De Flores. Meteors, unlike the stars, were transient and impure, and often associated with disasters 156 *it:* i.e. my fate 163 *barley-brake*: Vermandero's comment points up the metaphorical significance of the game's terminology 167 *honour's prize*: virginity 175 *that token*: i.e. his self-inflicted wound (although possibly he is referring to the wound he gave her)

I would not go to leave thee far behind.
Dies.

BEATRICE: Forgive me, Alsemero, all forgive;
'Tis time to die, when 'tis a shame to live.
Dies.

VERMANDERO: O my name is enter'd now in that record
Where till this fatal hour 'twas never read.

ALSEMERO: Let it be blotted out, let your heart lose it,
And it can never look you in the face,
Nor tell a tale behind the back of life
To your dishonour; justice hath so right
The guilty hit, that innocence is quit
By proclamation, and may joy again.
Sir, you are sensible of what truth hath done;
'Tis the best comfort that your grief can find.

TOMAZO: Sir, I am satisfied, my injuries
Lie dead before me; I can exact no more,
Unless my soul were loose, and could o'ertake
Those black fugitives that are fled from thence,
To take a second vengeance; but there are wraths
Deeper than mine, 'tis to be fear'd, about'em.

ALSEMERO: What an opacous body had that moon
That last chang'd on us! Here's beauty chang'd
To ugly whoredom; here, servant obedience
To a master sin, imperious murder;
I, a suppos'd husband, chang'd embraces
With wantonness, but that was paid before;
Your change is come too, from an ignorant wrath
To knowing friendship. Are there any more on's?

ANTONIO: Yes, sir; I was chang'd too, from a little ass as I was to a great fool as I am, and had like to ha' been chang'd to the gallows, but that you know my innocence always excuses me.

FRANCISCUS: I was chang'd from a little wit to be stark mad,
Almost for the same purpose.

ISABELLA [*To* ALIBIUS.]: Your change is still behind,
But deserve best your transformation:
You are a jealous coxcomb, keep schools of folly,
And teach your scholars how to break your own head.

180 *record*: i.e. heavenly record of the wicked 182 *Let it be blotted out*: i.e. the entry on the record 186–7 *quit By proclamation*: acquitted by public proclamation 188 *sensible*: aware 193 *black fugitives*: i.e. the souls of Beatrice and De Flores 196 *opacous*: opaque, shadowed, and therefore ominous 201 *but that was paid before*: i.e. by Diaphanta's death 202 *Your*: i.e. Tomazo's 208 *still behind*: yet to come

ALIBIUS: I see all apparent, wife, and will change now
Into a better husband, and never keep
Scholars that shall be wiser than myself.
ALSEMERO: Sir, you have yet a son's duty living,
Please you accept it; let that your sorrow,
As it goes from your eye, go from your heart;
Man and his sorrow at the grave must part.

EPILOGUE

ALSEMERO: All we can do to comfort one another,
To stay a brother's sorrow for a brother,
To dry a child from the kind father's eyes,
Is to no purpose, it rather multiplies:
Your only smiles have power to cause relive
The dead again, or in their rooms to give
Brother a new brother, father a child;
If these appear, all griefs are reconcil'd.
Exeunt omnes.

FINIS

220 *stay*: allay

READ MORE IN PENGUIN

In every corner of the world, on every subject under the sun, Penguin represents quality and variety – the very best in publishing today.

For complete information about books available from Penguin – including Puffins, Penguin Classics and Arkana – and how to order them, write to us at the appropriate address below. Please note that for copyright reasons the selection of books varies from country to country.

In the United Kingdom: Please write to *Dept. EP, Penguin Books Ltd, Bath Road, Harmondsworth, West Drayton, Middlesex UB7 ODA*

In the United States: Please write to *Consumer Sales, Penguin Putnam Inc., P.O. Box 12289 Dept. B, Newark, New Jersey 07101-5289.* VISA and MasterCard holders call 1-800-788-6262 to order Penguin titles

In Canada: Please write to *Penguin Books Canada Ltd, 10 Alcorn Avenue, Suite 300, Toronto, Ontario M4V 3B2*

In Australia: Please write to *Penguin Books Australia Ltd, P.O. Box 257, Ringwood, Victoria 3134*

In New Zealand: Please write to *Penguin Books (NZ) Ltd, Private Bag 102902, North Shore Mail Centre, Auckland 10*

In India: Please write to *Penguin Books India Pvt Ltd, 11 Community Centre, Panchsheel Park, New Delhi 110017*

In the Netherlands: Please write to *Penguin Books Netherlands bv, Postbus 3507, NL-1001 AH Amsterdam*

In Germany: Please write to *Penguin Books Deutschland GmbH, Metzlerstrasse 26, 60594 Frankfurt am Main*

In Spain: Please write to *Penguin Books S. A., Bravo Murillo 19, 1° B, 28015 Madrid*

In Italy: Please write to *Penguin Italia s.r.l., Via Benedetto Croce 2, 20094 Corsico, Milano*

In France: Please write to *Penguin France, Le Carré Wilson, 62 rue Benjamin Baillaud, 31500 Toulouse*

In Japan: Please write to *Penguin Books Japan Ltd, Kaneko Building, 2-3-25 Koraku, Bunkyo-Ku, Tokyo 112*

In South Africa: Please write to *Penguin Books South Africa (Pty) Ltd, Private Bag X14, Parkview, 2122 Johannesburg*

PENGUIN AUDIOBOOKS

A Quality of Writing That Speaks for Itself

Penguin Books has always led the field in quality publishing. Now you can listen at leisure to your favourite books, read to you by familiar voices from radio, stage and screen. Penguin Audiobooks are produced to an excellent standard, and abridgements are always faithful to the original texts. From thrillers to classic literature, biography to humour, with a wealth of titles in between, Penguin Audiobooks offer you quality, entertainment and the chance to rediscover the pleasure of listening.

You can order Penguin Audiobooks through Penguin Direct by telephoning (0181) 899 4036. The lines are open 24 hours every day. Ask for Penguin Direct, quoting your credit card details.

A selection of Penguin Audiobooks, published or forthcoming:

Emma by Jane Austen, read by Fiona Shaw

Pride and Prejudice by Jane Austen, read by Joanna David

Beowulf translated by Michael Alexander, read by David Rintoul

Agnes Grey by Anne Brontë, read by Juliet Stevenson

Jane Eyre by Charlotte Brontë, read by Juliet Stevenson

Wuthering Heights by Emily Brontë, read by Juliet Stevenson

The Pilgrim's Progress by John Bunyan, read by David Suchet

The Moonstone by Wilkie Collins, read by Michael Pennington, Terrence Hardiman and Carole Boyd

Nostromo by Joseph Conrad, read by Michael Pennington

Tales from the Thousand and One Nights, read by Souad Faress and Raad Rawi

Robinson Crusoe by Daniel Defoe, read by Tom Baker

David Copperfield by Charles Dickens, read by Nathaniel Parker

Little Dorrit by Charles Dickens, read by Anton Lesser

Barnaby Rudge by Charles Dickens, read by Richard Pasco

The Adventures of Sherlock Holmes volumes 1–3 by Sir Arthur Conan Doyle, read by Douglas Wilmer

PENGUIN AUDIOBOOKS

READ MORE IN PENGUIN

A CHOICE OF CLASSICS

Adomnan of Iona	**Life of St Columba**
St Anselm	**The Prayers and Meditations**
Thomas Aquinas	**Selected Writings**
St Augustine	**Confessions**
	The City of God
Bede	**Ecclesiastical History of the English People**
Geoffrey Chaucer	**The Canterbury Tales**
	Love Visions
	Troilus and Criseyde
Marie de France	**The Lais of Marie de France**
Jean Froissart	**The Chronicles**
Geoffrey of Monmouth	**The History of the Kings of Britain**
Gerald of Wales	**History and Topography of Ireland**
	The Journey through Wales and The Description of Wales
Gregory of Tours	**The History of the Franks**
Robert Henryson	**The Testament of Cresseid and Other Poems**
Robert Henryson/ William Dunbar	**Selected Poems**
Walter Hilton	**The Ladder of Perfection**
St Ignatius	**Personal Writings**
Julian of Norwich	**Revelations of Divine Love**
Thomas à Kempis	**The Imitation of Christ**
William Langland	**Piers the Ploughman**
Sir Thomas Malory	**Le Morte d'Arthur** (in two volumes)
Sir John Mandeville	**The Travels of Sir John Mandeville**
Marguerite de Navarre	**The Heptameron**
Christine de Pisan	**The Treasure of the City of Ladies**
Chrétien de Troyes	**Arthurian Romances**
Marco Polo	**The Travels**
Richard Rolle	**The Fire of Love**
François Villon	**Selected Poems**
Jacobus de Voragine	**The Golden Legend**

READ MORE IN PENGUIN

A CHOICE OF CLASSICS

Oliver Goldsmith	**The Vicar of Wakefield**
Gray/Churchill/Cowper	**Selected Poems**
William Hazlitt	**Selected Writings**
George Herbert	**The Complete English Poems**
Thomas Hobbes	**Leviathan**
Samuel Johnson	**Gabriel's Ladder**
	History of Rasselas, Prince of Abissinia
	Selected Writings
Samuel Johnson/ James Boswell	**A Journey to the Western Islands of Scotland and The Journal of a Tour of the Hebrides**
Matthew Lewis	**The Monk**
John Locke	**An Essay Concerning Human Understanding**
Andrew Marvell	**Complete Poems**
Thomas Middleton	**Five Plays**
John Milton	**Complete Poems**
	Paradise Lost
Samuel Richardson	**Clarissa**
	Pamela
Earl of Rochester	**Complete Works**
Richard Brinsley Sheridan	**The School for Scandal and Other Plays**
Sir Philip Sidney	**Arcadia**
Christopher Smart	**Selected Poems**
Adam Smith	**The Wealth of Nations (Books I–III)**
Tobias Smollett	**Humphrey Clinker**
	Roderick Random
Edmund Spenser	**The Faerie Queene**
Laurence Sterne	**The Life and Opinions of Tristram Shandy**
	A Sentimental Journey Through France and Italy
Jonathan Swift	**Complete Poems**
	Gulliver's Travels
Thomas Traherne	**Selected Poems and Prose**
Henry Vaughan	**Complete Poems**